Scholes & Wolfson's

Taxes and Business Strategy

Sixth Edition

MERLE M. ERICKSON
University of Chicago

MICHELLE HANLON
Massachusetts Institute of Technology

EDWARD L. MAYDEW
University of North Carolina

TERRY SHEVLIN
University of California-Irvine

Cambridge
BUSINESS PUBLISHERS

SCHOLES AND WOLFSON'S TAXES AND BUSINESS STRATEGY, Sixth Edition, by Merle M. Erickson, Michelle L. Hanlon, Edward L. Maydew, and Terry Shevlin.

ISBN 978-1-61853-321-0

Bookstores & Faculty: to order this book, contact the company via email **customerservice@cambridgepub.com** or call 800-619-6473.

Students & Retail Customers: to order this book, please visit the book's Website and order directly online.

Printed in the United States of America.
10 9 8 7 6 5 4 3 2

ABOUT THE AUTHORS

MERLE M. ERICKSON is a Professor of Accounting at the Booth School of Business at the University of Chicago where he has taught "Taxes and Business Strategy" in the Booth MBA program for more than twenty years. Erickson earned a bachelor's degree in accounting from Rockhurst College in 1987, an MBA in 1989 from Arizona State University, and a PhD in accounting from the University of Arizona in 1996. He joined the Chicago Booth faculty in 1996.

He has published numerous articles in a variety of top academic journals (e.g., *Journal of Accounting Research, The Accounting Review, Journal of Accounting and Economics*). He has been given several awards from the American Taxation Association for his research and teaching. He has received the Outstanding Manuscript Award (twice) as well as an award for teaching innovation. He also has been named one of BusinessWeek's Outstanding Faculty at the University of Chicago. He is the author/editor of the casebook, Cases in Tax Strategy. In addition to teaching graduate students at Chicago Booth, Professor Erickson has taught courses to Morgan Stanley, Merrill Lynch, General Electric Capital Corporation, Baker McKenzie, Andersen Consulting, Accenture, CareerBuilder, and the IMCA (Investment Management Consultants Association) among others. From 2005–2011, he served as a co-editor of the *Journal of Accounting Research.*

Over the course of his career, Professor Erickson has consulted on complex GAAP and tax accounting issues (e.g., debt versus equity, FIN 48 and ASC 740 related issues, intercompany accounting and consolidation, employee stock option accounting) in a variety of contexts (e.g., bankruptcy, mergers and acquisitions, inversions, structured finance, investment planning, cross border and intercompany financing, tax sharing agreements, and various types of tax advantaged transactions). His clients have included, among others, the U.S. Department of Justice, the Internal Revenue Service, Fortune 500 companies in various industries, international financial institutions including investment banks, law firms, accounting firms, and individual taxpayers.

In addition to his scholarly activities, Professor Erickson is an avid fisherman. He received the Angler Award from the Billfish Foundation in 2003 for releasing the most striped marlin worldwide that year.

MICHELLE HANLON is the Howard W. Johnson Professor at the MIT Sloan School of Management. She earned her doctorate degree at the University of Washington. Prior to joining MIT, she was a faculty member at the University of Michigan. Professor Hanlon has taught undergraduates, MBA students, Executive MBA students, and Masters of Finance students. She is the winner of the 2013 Jamieson Prize for Excellence in Teaching at MIT Sloan. Professor Hanlon's research focuses primarily on the intersection of financial accounting and taxation. She has published research studies in the *Journal of Accounting and Economics*, the *Journal of Accounting Research*, *The Accounting Review*, the *Review of Accounting Studies*, the *Journal of Finance*, the *Journal of Financial Economics*, the *Journal of Public Economics*, and others. She has won many awards for her research and has presented her work at numerous universities and conferences. Professor Hanlon has served on several editorial boards and an editor at the *Journal of Accounting and Economics* (since 2009). Professor Hanlon is a co-author on two other textbooks: *Financial Accounting*, entering its sixth edition, and *Intermediate Accounting*, entering its second edition. She has testified in front of the U.S. Senate Committee on Finance and twice to the U.S. House of Representatives Committee on Ways and Means about tax and accounting issues. She served as a U.S. delegate to the American-Swiss Young Leaders Conference in 2010 and worked as an Academic Fellow at the U.S. House Ways and Means Committee in 2015. She serves on the academic advisory board to the International Tax Policy Forum, Washington, DC.

EDWARD L. MAYDEW is the David E. Hoffman Distinguished Professor of Accounting at the University of North Carolina at Chapel Hill. His teaching and research interests include taxation and accounting and their roles in economic decisions. He is director of the UNC Tax Center.

He has served as an editor of *The Accounting Review*, an associate editor of *Journal of Accounting and Economics*, and editorial board member of *Journal of Accounting Research* and *Review of Accounting Studies*.

His research is published in the leading academic journals in his field, including *Journal of Finance*, *Journal of Financial Economics*, *The Accounting Review*, *Journal of Accounting and Economics*, *Journal of Accounting Research*, *Review of Accounting Studies*, *Contemporary Accounting Research*, *Management Science*, *Journal of Public Economics*, *National Tax Journal*, *Auditing: A Journal of Practice and Theory,* and *Journal of the American Taxation Association*.

He has received awards for excellence in teaching and research, including the Weatherspoon Award for Excellence in Research and four Weatherspoon Awards for Excellence in Teaching.

Professor Maydew consults with prominent law firms and corporations on a variety of complex accounting and tax matters. He was employed by a predecessor of PwC in its Chicago office before he earned his PhD.

Prior to joining UNC Kenan-Flagler, he was on the faculty of the University of Chicago. He has been a visiting professor at Cornell University.

He received his PhD from the University of Iowa and BBA from Iowa State University.

TERRY SHEVLIN is President of the American Accounting Association 2019–2020. Terry served as AAA President-Elect 2018–1019, AAA Vice President-Research and Publications 2015–2018, and chaired the AAA Publications Committee 2013–2016. He has served as editor on 3 AAA journals: *Journal of the American Taxation Association* (1996-1999), senior editor of *The Accounting Review* (2002–2005), and co-editor of *Accounting Horizons* (2009–2012), as well as serving on numerous editorial boards (including the top 4 accounting journals). He has published over 40 articles in the very top accounting and finance journals.

Professor Shevlin earned his PhD from Stanford University in 1986 and joined the faculty at the University of Washington where he worked for 26 years until joining the University of California-Irvine in the summer of 2012. He holds a Paul Merage Chair in Business and he is Associate Dean for Research and Doctoral Programs at the Merage School of Business at UCI. He held the Paul Pigott/Paccar Professor of Business Administration from 2004–2012. While at Washington, he held various administrative positions, including faculty director of the PhD Program 1998–2006 and Accounting Department Chair from 2006–2012.

He has received a number of awards for his research and mentoring of PhDs, the most recent being named the American Accounting Association Outstanding Educator for 2012. He was also named the American Taxation Association 2005 Ray M. Sommerfeld Outstanding Tax Educator. He has won the American Taxation Association Tax Manuscript Award 3 times (in 2004, 1995, and 1992) and twice won the AAA Competitive Manuscript for young scholars (1990 and 1987). He has been awarded the UW Business School Dean's Faculty Research Award 4 times.

His research interests are broad and include the effect of taxes on business decisions and asset prices, capital markets-based accounting research, earnings management, research design and statistical significance testing issues.

His teaching interests are financial accounting, taxes and business decisions, and empirical research methodology. He has spoken at numerous doctoral consortiums.

PREFACE

> "The text to use if you are teaching Taxes and Business Strategy."
>
> **–Jeffrey Hoopes, *University of North Carolina at Chapel Hill***

Welcome to the sixth edition of *Taxes and Business Strategy*. The book's focus comes from integrating the tax law with the fundamentals of corporate finance and microeconomics. Through integration with traditional business school topics, the book provides a framework for understanding how taxes affect decision making, asset prices, equilibrium returns, and the financial and operational structure of firms. Relative to legal-based tax books, this text focuses more on the economic consequences of alternative contracting arrangements than on the myriad details and exceptions of the tax laws governing the arrangements. It is not meant to imply that the details of the tax laws are unimportant; they certainly are important. In fact, students new to tax law will find that this text provides them with significant tax legal knowledge in certain key areas where taxes play a big role in decision making and areas that business school graduates are likely to encounter in their careers (e.g., mergers and acquisitions, employee compensation, international tax).

In addition, the book integrates tax with financial accounting by emphasizing differences and tradeoffs between the taxation and the financial accounting of a transaction. Finally, the book presents many general rules about tax law, tax accounting, and financial accounting. The discussion herein is purposefully general to increase user accessibility and readability. However, readers should note that there are exceptions to many of the rules and concepts in this text, and those exceptions can be and often are important.

> "The book combines financial accounting, tax, economics and finance into one decision-making framework."
>
> **—Steve Matsunaga, *University of Oregon***

TARGET AUDIENCE

This book is written for anyone with an interest in learning about tax strategy. We initially wrote the book for MBA students, but it is also appropriate for undergraduate students, masters of accounting or finance students, and doctoral students. More specifically, this book is appropriate for those embarking on (or already in) careers in investment banking, corporate finance, strategy consulting, money management, or venture capital. The book is valuable to accountants and attorneys who want a rigorous framework for thinking about tax strategy and how tax strategy interacts with other aspects of the firm. In addition, those starting their own businesses and even just managing their own finances will find many aspects of this book valuable.

> "A good, robust, academically challenging book."
>
> **—Glenn Huels, *University of Rochester Simon Business School***

COMPETITIVE ADVANTAGE

We recognize that executives, entrepreneurs, and finance professionals are typically not aiming to become tax specialists. However, for each of these paths there is a competitive advantage that comes from a solid understanding of (1) the decision contexts that give rise to tax-planning opportunities, (2) how to integrate tax strategy intc the bigger picture of corporate decision making, and (3) the dramatic impact that changes in transaction structure can have on after-tax cash flows.

Every top business school program teaches its students the fundamentals of corporate finance, financial statement analysis, valuation, and investments. Every business school graduate knows how to perform a discounted cash flow analysis and apply the net present value (NPV) criterion—these are valuable skills, but not something that differentiates oneself. Business school programs historically have been deficient, however, at teaching their students about the pervasive role taxes play in decision making. Each of the authors has taught taxes and business strategy at the MBA level and often to students in other business school programs as well. Their courses have been, and are, uniformly popular at their respective institutions. Former students have reported back that they possess a competitive advantage over their peers who know little or nothing about tax strategy. The material in this book draws from and builds on the authors' classroom and business experiences, as well as the experiences of colleagues around the country, and is not duplicated in any other text.

This book provides a general framework for thinking about tax strategy. Readers should consult professional advisors for advice specific to their fact pattern. Tax laws contain many exceptions and grey areas, and are subject to change. The application of tax law to specific fact patterns can vary widely.

> "For the objectives of this course, this is the only book I would consider using."
>
> —**Bradford Hepfer, *Texas A&M University***

KEY FEATURES

Outstanding Author Team

Building on the expertise of Mark Wolfson and Myron Scholes, who received the Nobel Prize for Economics, Merle Erickson, Michelle Hanlon, Ed Maydew, and Terry Shevlin actively teach the tax and business strategy course and provide relevant examples from both classroom and real-world consulting experience.

In-depth Analysis

Analysis and explanatory material help the reader understand, think about, and retain information. A wealth of in-chapter examples, figures, and tables is provided to further illustrate the concepts.

Pedagogy to Reinforce Learning

Summary of Key Points: Each chapter concludes with a summary of the relevant takeaways discussed in the chapter.

Key terms are included in blue font throughout the text, and an end-of-book glossary defines terms for easy reference.

End of Chapter content includes a variety of questions, exercises, and tax planning problems.

CHANGES IN THE SIXTH EDITION

Our objectives for the revision include:

- Updating the text to 2-color format for enhanced visual appeal and to aid pedagogical understanding

- Updating the text to reflect major changes in the Tax Cuts and Jobs Act of 2017:
    - Organizational form chapter updated to incorporate the Qualified Business Income Deduction for pass-through entities.
    - International tax chapter updated to incorporate a broad discussion of available options for taxing multinational activity and the methods chosen in the TCJA, including the GILTI, the BEAT, and the FDII.
    - Tax rates and other rules updated throughout the book
- Adding examples relevant to today's economy
- Adding a new Savings Vehicle in Chapter 3
- Combining prior Chapters 5 and 7 to streamline the book
- Combining prior Chapters 10 and 11 to streamline international tax coverage

All chapters have been updated for tax law and financial accounting rule changes since the last edition.

TEACHING SUPPLEMENTS

- Solutions Manual: Created by the authors, the solutions manual contains complete solutions to all assignments.
- PowerPoint: Created by the authors, the PowerPoint slides outline key elements of each chapter.
- Website: All instructor materials are accessible via the book's website (password-protected), along with marketing information: **www.cambridgepub.com**

ACKNOWLEDGEMENTS

We would like to thank the following people for their feedback on various editions of the text:

Mark Bagnoli, *Purdue University*
Jennifer Blouin, *University of Pennsylvania*
Jennifer Brown, *Arizona State University*
Debra S. Callihan, *Virginia Polytechnic Institute and State University*
Ernest Carraway, *North Carolina State University*
Xia Chen, *Singapore Management University*
Anthony P. Curatola, *Drexel University*
Dan S. Dhaliwal, *University of Arizona*
John R. Dorocak, *California State University–San Bernadino*
Courtney Edwards, *University of North Carolina*
Alexander Gelardi, *University of St. Thomas*
Dan Gode, *New York University*
John Graham, *Duke University*
Paul A. Griffin, *University of California–Davis*
Bradford Hepfer, *Texas A&M University*
Jeffrey Hoopes, *University of North Carolina at Chapel Hill*
Steven J. Huddart, *Pennsylvania State University*
Glenn Huels, *University of Rochester*
Stacie Kelley LaPlante, *University of Wisconsin*
Kimberly G. Key, *Auburn University*
Mike R. Kinney, *Texas A&M University*
Taylor Klett, *Sam Houston State University*
Michael Knoll, *University of Pennsylvania*
Lynn Krausse, *Bakersfield College*
Gil B. Manzon, Jr., *Boston College*
Kevin Markle, *University of Iowa*
Barry Marks, *University of Houston–Clear Lake*
Robert Martin, *Kennesaw State University*
Brian S. Masterson, *Georgetown University Law Center*
Steve Matsunaga, *University of Oregon*
Gary L. Maydew, *Iowa State University, retired*
Jeffrey Maydew, *Baker & McKenzie*
Robert McDonald, *Northwestern University*
Lil Mills, *University of Texas–Austin*
Mary Margaret Myers, *University of Virginia*
Kaye J. Newberry, *University of Houston*
Patricia Nodoushani, *University of Hartford*
Thomas C. Omer, *University of Nebraska*
Mitchell Petersen, *Northwestern University*
Sonja Rego, *Indiana University*
John R. Robinson, *Texas A&M University*
Richard C. Sansing, *Dartmouth College*
Jim A. Seida, *University of Notre Dame*
Douglas A. Shackelford, *University of North Carolina*
Keith Smith, *George Washington University*

William D. Terando, *Butler University*
Ralph B. Tower, *Wake Forest University*
Shiing-wu Wang, *University of Southern California*
Ira Weiss, *University of Chicago*
Craig White, *University of New Mexico*
Jeffrey Wong, *University of Nevada at Reno*
Ronald Worsham, Jr., *Brigham Young University*
Robert W. Wyndelts, *Arizona State University, retired*
Robert J. Yetman, *University of California–Davis*
Frank Zhang, *Yale School of Management*

We are especially grateful to Myron Scholes and Mark Wolfson for their ground breaking work in developing the first edition of this book. Without their work, this book would not exist. We thank George Werthman, Katie Jones-Aiello, Debbie McQuade, Terry McQuade, and the entire team at Cambridge Business Publishers for their encouragement, enthusiasm, and guidance. Feedback is always welcome. Please feel free to contact us with your suggestions or questions.

Merle Michelle Ed Terry

January 2019

BRIEF CONTENTS

CONTENTS

Chapter Five

Choosing the Optimal Organizational Form 5-1

Chapter Six

Corporations: Formation, Operation, Capital Structure, and Liquidation 6-1

Chapter Seven

Nontax Costs of Tax Planning 7-1

Chapter Fifteen
Tax Planning for Divestitures **15-1**

Chapter Sixteen
Estate and Gift Tax Planning **16-1**

1

Introduction to Tax Strategy

After completing this chapter, you should be able to

1. List and briefly explain the three key themes underlying our approach to effective tax planning.
2. Explain the difference between effective tax planning and tax minimization.
3. Briefly explain the concept of implicit taxes.
4. Briefly explain the concept of tax clienteles.
5. Understand that explicit taxes affect pretax rates of return.
6. Understand that tax planning is a tax-favored activity.

Our broadest objective in this book is to provide you with a framework that is useful for thinking about how taxes affect decisions—both at the individual level and within organizations. This framework is intended to be applicable across time as tax rules change and across jurisdictions (as long as that jurisdiction applies an income tax). The recent tax reform act in the United States known as the Tax Cuts and Jobs Act (TCJA) (Public Law 115-97) provides a good example. We will discuss the TCJA and the effects of its changes using our framework throughout the book.

The framework we develop is highly integrative. For example, **investment strategies** and **financing policies** within businesses are linked through taxes. That is, the investments that a business undertakes depend on how they are financed. In addition, financing decisions depend on the investments that the business undertakes. By investments, we mean not only the actively managed assets the business uses to run its business but also passive assets, such as bonds, stocks, and direct investments in other entities.

Although we discuss start-up entities and choice of organizational form to some extent, much of our focus is on the evolving strategies applicable to existing businesses. These businesses make incremental investment and financing decisions that depend, in part, on past investment and financing decisions. New strategies depend on past strategies because it is costly to adjust investment and financing decisions once they have been made. From this brief introduction, it is obvious that we take a rather broad look at how taxes affect decisions and strategies.

1.1 THEMES OF THE BOOK

We adopt a planning approach to taxes and business strategy. More precisely, we adopt a global planning approach. The three key themes of this book's global planning framework are

1. Effective tax planning requires the planner to consider the tax implications of a proposed transaction for *all parties* to the transaction. This is a global or multilateral, rather than a unilateral, approach.

2. Effective tax planning requires the planner to consider *all taxes*. For example, in making investment and financing decisions, we consider not only **explicit taxes** (tax dollars paid directly to taxing authorities) but also **implicit taxes** (taxes that are paid indirectly in the form of lower before-tax rates of return on tax-favored investments). We are interested in a global, or total, measure of taxes, not simply explicit taxes.
3. Effective tax planning requires the planner to recognize that taxes represent only one among many business and transaction costs and that *all costs* must be considered in the planning process. For example, to be implemented, some proposed tax plans may require exceedingly costly restructuring of the business.

It is important to recognize that effective tax planning and tax minimization are very different things. **Effective tax planning** involves considering the role of taxes when implementing the decision rule of maximizing after-tax returns. In a world of costly contracting, implementation of **tax-minimization** strategies can introduce significant costs along nontax dimensions. For example, suppose an employer's tax rate is expected to increase while the employee's tax rate is expected to remain constant in the next period. Deferring payment of compensation to the employee until a later period saves taxes but subjects the employee to the risk of nonpayment if the business goes bankrupt. The employee may require an additional payment (a risk premium) to compensate him or her for the increased risk. Therefore, the tax-minimization strategy may be undesirable. A particularly easy way to *minimize* taxes is to avoid investing in profitable ventures, but this does not *maximize* after-tax returns. Our framework emphasizes the various elements a tax planner needs to take into account in maximizing the after-tax return on any transaction being considered.

We view efficient tax planning as part of the larger problem of the efficient design of organizations. In developing this organizational design theme, we adopt a **contractual perspective**. Contracts specify the rights of various parties to make decisions and to receive cash flows in differing circumstances. We focus on how the tax-related cash flows specified by contracts affect the prices at which assets are traded. We further stress how these cash flows affect the ways in which production is organized by business units.

Taxing Authority as Investment Partner

All of the interesting problems in tax planning arise because, from the standpoint of taxpaying entities, the taxing authority is an uninvited party to all contracts. The taxing authority brings to each of its "forced" ventures with taxpayers a set of contractual terms (tax rules). Unlike other contracting parties, the taxing authority generally does not negotiate these terms separately for each venture. Such a policy would simply be too expensive. Instead, it announces a standard set of terms taxpayers must accept. In addition, although the taxing authority claims an interest in taxpayer profits, it exercises no voting rights. Moreover, being a partner in all businesses enables the taxing authority to determine when taxpayers are reporting results far out of line with what other taxpayers are reporting in similar situations (information that is used to select returns for audit).

The specific contractual rules (the U.S. Internal Revenue Code (IRC)) that the taxing authority imposes on its joint venturers result from a variety of socioeconomic forces. Among other things, taxes are designed (1) to finance public projects (e.g., national defense and a legal system that enforces property rights), (2) to redistribute wealth (high-income individuals pay income tax at higher rates than do low-income individuals), and (3) to encourage a variety of economic activities deemed by Congress to be in the public interest (such as research and development and oil and gas exploration).

From a social policy standpoint, tax rules are most controversial when they are designed to discriminate among different economic activities. Success is achieved when the tax rules subsidize activities that benefit society as a whole more than they benefit the individuals engaging directly in the activities. For example, Congress subsidizes research and development (R&D) through a tax credit based on R&D spending by the business. Society benefits to the extent that the tax credit stimulates additional R&D relative to what R&D would have taken place without the credit. But this desirable outcome is by no means guaranteed if instead Congressional subsidies are based on special requests and favors rather than societal benefits.

For better or for worse, **tax-favored treatment** is granted to a variety of activities by taxing authorities around the world. Common examples include the favorable treatment accorded charitable organizations and educational institutions, energy-related investments, R&D activities, agricultural production, investments in productive equipment, foreign export activities, retirement-oriented savings vehicles, and entrepreneurial risk-taking activities. A more common occurrence in recent years is tax incentives (breaks) provided to companies to locate within a jurisdiction. For example, the 2018 competition to be home to Amazon's HQ2 involved tax incentives (and, at times, exemptions) in the states and cities where Amazon considered building its second headquarters.[1]

Noble as the objectives listed earlier might be (finance public projects, redistribute wealth, and encourage economic activities), any tax system designed to achieve a variety of social goals inevitably provides considerable private incentives to engage in tax planning. Any tax system that seeks both to redistribute wealth as well as to subsidize certain economic activities gives rise to explicit marginal tax rates that may vary widely from one contracting party to the next, for a given contracting party over time, and for a given contracting party over different economic activities.

Most taxpayers around the world pay no more tax than they believe they must, and they spend nontrivial resources to arrange their affairs to keep the tax bite as painless as possible. It is precisely this behavior that provides tax policy with so much potential as a means of achieving a variety of social goals.

To illustrate, consider the case of low-income housing that U.S. citizens, through their elected representatives, have chosen to subsidize for many years through various tax benefits. If taxpayers were not responsive to these tax incentives (and refused to build low-income housing to garner the tax benefits), subsidizing low-income housing through tax policy would be ineffective. Instead, the government would have to enter on the expenditure side, engaging directly in the construction and management of the low-income housing itself. Both tax subsidies and direct government expenditures to increase the supply of low-income housing generate deadweight costs. This suggests that we must be careful in criticizing tax subsidies if we desire to achieve our social objectives. The direct government expenditure alternative might be far more costly than a tax system that favors private construction of the properties.

Another example is renewable energy credits, which are offered by states and the federal government. Many of these credits are allowed to be "sold" to other taxpaying entities that can use the credits, leading to tax-equity investment structures. One form of this structure is where high-rate taxpayers finance projects in exchange for partial ownership and access to the energy credits from low-tax-rate energy developers, thus providing financing to the renewable-energy venture. Such tax-credit transfers have led to a new line of work as well—"tax-credit brokers" to match buyers and sellers (e.g., Tax Credits International and Clocktower Tax Credits, LLC). One alternative would be for the government to give grants directly to the low-tax-rate energy developer instead of the tax credits that then need to be sold. Indeed, the American Recovery and Reinvestment Act of 2009 allowed taxpayers eligible for the Federal Renewable Electricity Production Tax Credit (PTC) to take the Federal Business Energy Investment Tax Credit or to receive a grant from the U.S. Treasury Department instead of taking the PTC for new installations. The grant was only available to systems where construction began prior to December 31, 2011.

Although the deadweight costs associated with time spent in tax planning may seem socially wasteful, the relevant question is how much waste would exist using alternative means to achieve the same social goals? In other words, how does the net benefit of the altered economic activity brought about by the tax system compare with the net benefits of the next best alternative? Obviously, if we could implement social policy through a mechanism that would result in zero waste, we would do so, but this is not always a realistic goal.

Tax planning (or tax avoidance, as it is sometimes more pejoratively labeled) has long earned the blessing of the U.S. courts. For example, in a famous 1947 court opinion, Judge Learned Hand wrote (and similar statements appear in official documents of other countries as well):

> Over and over again courts have said that there is nothing sinister in so arranging one's affairs as to keep taxes as low as possible. Everybody does so, rich or poor, and all do right, for nobody owes any

[1] Leanna Garfield, "Cities Are Throwing Hundreds of Millions at Amazon to Land HQ2—Here's How They Stack Up." *Business Insider*, April 4, 2018, http://www.businessinsider.com/amazon-hq2-cities-developers-economic-tax-incentives-2017-10

public duty to pay more than the law demands: taxes are enforced exactions, not voluntary contributions. To demand more in the name of morals is mere cant.

(*Commissioner v. Newman*, 159 F.2d 848 [CA-2, 1947])

The Importance of a Contractual Perspective

Let us now return to the first of the three key themes that run throughout the book, namely, that to organize production to maximize after-tax return requires that the tax positions of all parties to the contract be considered, both at the time of contracting and in the future. To avoid operating at a competitive disadvantage, managers must understand how changes in tax rules influence the behavior of their customers, their employees, their suppliers, and their competitors. Among other things, this observation exposes the naiveté of distinguishing between business tax planning and personal tax planning, or of tax planning for one type of business in isolation from tax planning for all other types of business.

For example, as we will see in later chapters, it is costly to prescribe an effective compensation policy for a business without simultaneously conducting some personal tax-planning analysis for each of its employees. Similarly, it is costly to prescribe an effective capital structure policy for a business (i.e., determining whether operations should be financed with debt, preferred stock, common stock, or other financial instruments) without simultaneously considering how the returns to prospective lenders and shareholders of that business will be taxed.

To be more concrete, consider the decision of whether business equipment should be bought or leased. In the United States, as in most countries around the world, the government encourages capital investment by permitting rapid depreciation on buildings, equipment, and machinery. That is, the business can deduct the cost of the investment from its taxable income using a schedule in which the write-off rate for tax purposes exceeds the rate of economic depreciation of the investment. Indeed, in the TCJA, qualified property is depreciable in full in the first year the asset is placed in service—thus, it is an immediate write-off. Alternatively, if a business entity rented plant and equipment over its economic life, the rental payments could be deducted only as they were made. The present value of rental deductions is often far less than the present value of depreciation deductions.

We cannot conclude, however, that owning assets minimizes the taxes of all businesses using machinery and equipment. Once we analyze the tax positions of both low-tax-bracket and high-tax-bracket taxpayers, we might find low-tax-bracket taxpayers are better off passing up tax savings and renting. The reason is that low-tax-bracket and high-tax-bracket businesses will find it desirable to enter into a contract that arranges property rights so that the low-tax-bracket businesses effectively sell their tax benefits to high-tax-bracket businesses. This is accomplished by reducing the rental rate to the low-tax-bracket taxpayer in exchange for the right to take rapid depreciation, for tax purposes, on the equipment.

1.2 WHY DO TAX RULES INFLUENCE BEFORE-TAX RATES OF RETURN AND INVESTMENT DECISIONS?

Tax rates and rules affect the **before-tax rates of return** on assets. By before-tax rate of return, we mean the rate of return earned from investing in an asset before any explicit taxes are paid to domestic and foreign federal, state, and local taxing authorities. To illustrate our point, let $r = R(1 - t)$ where R is the before-tax rate of return, t is the tax rate, and r is the after-tax rate of return. A superficial analysis of this relation suggests that if we increase the tax rate, that is, increase t, then the after-tax rate is lowered (and vice versa). However, this analysis ignores the possibility that the tax rules affect the before-tax rate of return. If we expand the analysis to include multiple taxpayers facing different tax rates and multiple assets with their returns being taxed differently, then this simple result is no longer valid. Consider two bonds, a tax-exempt municipal bond where the interest on the bond is tax exempt at the federal level and a fully taxable corporate bond where the interest is fully taxed at the federal level. Further assume there are taxpayers facing a low tax rate and others facing a high tax rate. Taxpayers facing a high tax rate are expected to bid up the price of the tax-exempt municipal bond because this bond or cash flow stream is tax favored to them. Bidding up the price for a given promised cash flow stream will lower the before-tax rate of return, *R*. Thus, the tax rules affect before-tax rates of return.

This simple example explains why some taxpayers select investments with high before-tax rates of return whereas others select assets with low before-tax rates of return even when both types of investments are available to all taxpayers. On the assets side of the economic balance sheet, we emphasize that before-tax rates of return differ because (1) the returns on different types of assets are taxed differently, (2) the returns on similar assets are taxed differently if they are located in different tax jurisdictions, (3) the returns on similar assets located in the same tax jurisdiction are taxed differently if they are held through different legal organizational forms (e.g., a corporation versus a sole proprietorship), and (4) the returns on similar assets located in the same tax jurisdiction and held through the same legal organizational form are taxed differently depending on such factors as the operating history of the organization, the returns to other assets held by the organization, and the particular characteristics of the individual owners of the organization.

Tax rules also influence the financing decisions of businesses through their effect on the cost of financing business activities. A business is said to make a "capital structure decision" when it decides how it will finance its activities. The capital structure of a business is composed of various types of ownership claims, some called debt and others called equity. The cost of issuing a capital structure instrument depends, at a high level, on whether the instrument is debt or equity. Generally, the interest paid on debt securities is deductible (subject to some limitations) and dividends paid on equity securities is not deductible. This difference in tax treatment affects capital structure decisions taxpayers make.

Implicit Taxes and Tax Clienteles

The earlier leasing example and the municipal bond example both illustrate two very important concepts we will encounter time and time again throughout the text:

1. Implicit taxes
2. Tax clienteles

Implicit taxes arise because the before-tax investment returns available on tax-favored assets are less than those available on tax-disfavored assets. In the rent-or-buy example, a reduction in the rental rate is required to induce renters to forego the tax benefits of ownership, and this decreases the pretax investment return garnered by property lessors. Another example of implicit taxes is our example of the reduced yield available on tax-exempt municipal bonds in the United States relative to taxable corporate bonds of equal risk. Here, the reduced yield represents an implicit tax paid to the issuing municipalities rather than to the federal government.

As an example of the common misunderstanding of implicit taxes, consider the following from a *Wall Street Journal* article published when John Kerry was running for president and his wife, Teresa Heinz Kerry, released her tax returns:

> The news is that $2.78 million of that income came in the form of tax-exempt interest from what the Kerry campaign's press release attributed to investments in "state, municipal and public entity bonds." . . . On her remaining "taxable" income of $2.29 million, Mrs. Kerry paid $627,150 in taxes, for an overall average federal tax rate of only 12.4% on her $5.07 million in total income. . . . This puts Mrs. Kerry's tax rate at well below that of other filers in her super-rich neighborhood. But it also means she is paying a lower average rate than nearly all middle-class taxpayers paid in 2001, the last year for which the IRS has published the data.[2]

What the author of the article is incorrectly ignoring is the implicit taxes that Mrs. Kerry is paying by accepting a lower pretax rate of return on the municipal bond investment. Once the implicit tax (lower pretax return) is taken into account, her total tax rate is much higher than the 12.4% computed in the article.

[2] "Teresa's Fair Share," *Wall Street Journal*, October 18, 2004.

The **tax clienteles** and implicit tax concepts are closely related. Tax clienteles arise because of cross-sectional differences in tax rates. Certain taxpayers are more likely than others to own various kinds of assets or to organize production in particular ways. Examples of tax clienteles are high-tax-bracket taxpayers who are more likely to hold tax-exempt municipal bonds rather than taxable corporate bonds and who are more likely to be lessors and owners of depreciable equipment rather than lessees. In our previous example, Teresa Heinz Kerry is more likely to own a municipal bond because she is a high-explicit-rate taxpayer, and the after-tax return on the municipal bond is likely higher than the after-tax rate of return on fully taxed bonds and assets. Mrs. Kerry, as someone in the highest income tax bracket, bears implicit taxes on municipal bonds at a rate slightly lower than the explicit tax rate she would otherwise be subject to on fully taxable income. With every topic we cover throughout the book, we will encounter implicit taxes, tax clienteles, or both concepts.

Tax Planning as a Tax-Favored Activity

One reason governments use tax policy to encourage (or discourage) a variety of economic activities is that tax planning itself is a tax-favored activity. Specifically, money spent on tax planning by businesses is tax deductible, whereas any tax savings arising from the tax planning are effectively tax exempt because they reduce taxes payable.

Suppose a business taxpayer (who can deduct tax planning costs) could invest $10,000 in fully taxable corporate bonds for 1 year that yield 10% per annum before taxes. If the taxpayer faces a marginal tax rate of 28%, the after-tax rate of return is 7.2% (calculated as .10 × [1 – .28]). Alternatively, suppose the same business taxpayer could invest in tax-planning services for $10,000 to save $11,000 in taxes in the current year. The pretax rate of return is 10%. However, the after-tax rate of return is 52.78%, calculated as the tax savings net of the after-tax cost of the tax planning, $11,000 – $10,000 × (1 – .28), divided by the after-tax cost of the tax-planning services, $10,000 × (1 – .28), or $3,800/$7,200. Note that the tax-favored treatment of tax planning results here in an after-tax rate of return higher than the pretax rate of return. In this case, tax planning is more tax favored than is **tax exemption** (a situation in which an asset escapes explicit taxation such that the after-tax rate of return equals the pretax rate of return). Note also that the after-tax rate of return to tax planning depends on the taxpayer's marginal tax rate. For a business taxpayer facing a marginal tax rate of 15%, the after-tax cost of the tax planning services is $8,500, resulting in an after-tax rate of return of ($11,000 – $8,500)/$8,500 = 29.41%. For a business taxpayer facing a 35% marginal tax rate, the after-tax rate of return is ($11,000 – $6,500)/$6,500 = 69.23%. As long as the tax planning costs are deductible, the after-tax rates of return to tax planning are largest for high-tax-rate investors, so these taxpayers tend to be most responsive to tax-rule changes and to spend the most on the services of tax accountants and tax lawyers.

Why Study Tax Planning?

We answer this question with the following simple example. Suppose there were two skills that you could acquire: tax-planning and investing expertise. Further suppose you could only learn one. You are faced with the following fact pattern. You are endowed with $5,000 of after-tax cash, have a 20-year investment horizon, and face a current marginal tax rate of 35%, which also is the rate you expect to face over the next 20 years. You expect that investing passively in an index fund will generate a 10% pretax return each year for the next 20 years.

You choose to learn tax-planning skills and invest passively. You invest in a pension plan (such as a 401[k] plan, discussed in more detail in Chapter 3) such that the after-tax cost of the investment is $5,000. The investment is tax deductible, and tax on the returns in this plan is deferred until the end of the investment horizon. The after-tax accumulation from this investment is[3]

$$\frac{\$5{,}000}{(1-.35)}(1+.10)^{20}(1-.35)=\$33{,}650$$

[3] The formula used to calculate the accumulations is developed and discussed in more detail in Chapter 3. Our purpose here is simply to show the after-tax accumulations under the various alternatives and the advantages of (or returns to) tax-planning skills.

Suppose instead you choose investing expertise and behave as a day trader, actively moving in and out of stocks. You hold stock no longer than 1 month and, thus, there is no deferral of taxes on your annual returns. How much would you have to earn pretax to match the returns to the basic tax-planning example just presented? Because the basic tax-planning example earns 10% after-tax per year (as long as tax rates are constant), you would need to earn 15.38% pretax per year on your actively managed portfolio to earn 10% after-tax per year [15.38%(1 – .35) = 10%].

But what if, more realistically for most taxpayers, you just *thought* you could beat the market but really could not, and your active portfolio management yielded a 10% pretax return per year? In this case, you would accumulate after-tax wealth after 20 years of

$$\$5{,}000[1 + .10(1 - .35)]^{20} = \$17{,}618$$

This is substantially less than the return to basic tax planning.

But, of course, tax planning and investing expertise are not mutually exclusive. Consider now what happens if you can beat the market *and* be a good tax planner. That is, you invest in a pension plan such as a 401(k) plan *and* actively manage the investment in the plan, earning a 14% annual pretax rate of return for the next 20 years. Because the investment is in a 401(k) plan, the tax on the annual returns is deferred until the funds are withdrawn in 20 years. The after-tax accumulation at the end of 20 years is now

$$\frac{\$5{,}000}{(1-.35)}(1+.14)^{20}(1-.35) = \$68{,}717$$

Businesses spend billions of dollars on tax-planning activities and on tax compliance, which refers to record-keeping and return-preparation activities. For example, Slemrod and Blumenthal (1993) report that the 1,329 active corporations in the Internal Revenue Service's Coordinated Examination Program spent approximately \$1.4 billion on federal-tax-related activities in 1991.[4] These corporations paid \$51 billion in taxes, or over 50% of the total corporate tax revenues, in 1991. Mills, Erickson, and Maydew (1998) estimate that large corporations save, on average, \$4 for every \$1 spent on tax-planning activities. Thus, not only is tax planning a big business, but the returns on investments in tax planning can be very large.

1.3 INTENDED AUDIENCES FOR THIS BOOK

This book is appropriate for two categories of people:

1. Tax planners: Those who wish to avoid being beaten by other tax planners and by social planners. We use the term *tax planners* broadly. All individuals earning an income by working either for themselves or for another taxpayer can be viewed as tax planners, as they will find themselves encountering transactions and decisions with tax implications. This is especially true for MBA students, graduate tax students, undergraduate business and law students, and entrepreneurs from a variety of fields—the intended target audiences for this book.
2. Social planners: Those who wish to participate in the design of effective social policies while at the same time avoid being beaten by other social planners and by tax planners.

We believe that a course built around the ideas developed in this book differs fundamentally from traditional courses offered in business schools, law schools, and economics programs. These other courses tend to focus on (1) tax policy, with the objective of exploring the macro-economic effects of existing or proposed tax systems, or (2) tax law, concerned with principles of tax laws and judicial doctrines or with the details of the tax rules themselves and the ways to minimize taxes for a given set of transactions. Our book falls into neither of these camps. We develop neither a macro-tax-policy

[4] Corporations are included in the Coordinated Examination Program based on their size and complexity of return: the larger and more complex the return, the greater the likelihood of inclusion in the program. The tax returns of most of these corporations are audited by the Internal Revenue Service each year.

approach nor a transactional-tax-law approach. Instead, we adopt a *micro*economic perspective. Our interest is in the implications of tax rules for individual and corporate behavior.

Similarly, our primary goal is neither to evaluate the welfare effects of various tax rules nor to provide narrow training to exploit "tax loopholes." It is true that we will occasionally appear to take much pleasure in describing clever tax-planning techniques. And although our objective is certainly *not* to teach you how to "beat" the tax system, we will provide you with the tools necessary to successfully tax plan. This means that we are providing you with the tools to evaluate whether the tax system is meeting its various legislative objectives without giving rise to excessive distortions in economic activity. And perhaps most important, we hope that you will come away from reading this book recognizing that our framework applies to far broader issues than simply how taxes factor into business decisions. The framework can be applied to many nontax policies and regulations or many nontax costs as well.

As we stated at the outset, our intent is that this framework can be applied with respect to tax planning in many jurisdictions and over time. For example, global tax systems are constantly evolving to deal with changing revenue needs and changing economic forces. Thus, the tax rules vary across jurisdictions (countries and jurisdictions within countries) and the rules in almost all jurisdictions change over time. For example, the UK passed substantial tax reform starting in the late 2000s, including several corporate tax rate reductions and significant changes in how they taxed foreign earnings. Japan went through somewhat similar changes around the same time. As also mentioned at the beginning of the chapter, in December 2017, the United States passed large-scale tax reform in which the United States lowered its corporate tax rate from 35% to 21% (and making it a flat rate), enacted full-expensing of qualified investments, placed limitations on business interest deductions, fundamentally changed the way foreign earnings are taxed, lowered individual tax rates, and instituted many other changes. Prior to the TCJA, the last major restructuring of the IRC was the Tax Reform Act of 1986. However, Congress passed bills that changed the IRC in some smaller manner in 20 of the 25 years preceding the 1986 restructuring and in nearly every year since 1986 and before 2017. Absent a framework to determine the implications of the rules for business decisions, the knowledge gained in a rules-oriented course represents little more than accumulated trivia. This is precisely what led to the development of this book. We think that the basic toolkit we provide you is appropriate to deal with virtually any tax regime we are likely to experience in the future. Moreover, we believe you can use these tools just as appropriately to study non-U.S. taxes as to study U.S. taxes. Our intent is to make you leaders rather than followers in understanding how business activities inevitably become reorganized as the rules of the game evolve.

Table 1.1 presents the top income tax rates faced by individuals and corporations over the last 30 years. This table illustrates the incentives faced by individual taxpayers to have income taxed at more favorable capital gains tax rates, to shift income across periods, and to organize their investment activities in corporate form. The table also illustrates how these incentives change over time as both the level and relative tax rates change.

Although this is not a rules-oriented book, you will still learn a good deal about current income tax rules. This is necessary for three reasons: (1) to breathe life into the basic framework through illustrations, (2) to test the basic framework's ability to explain economic activities that are going on around us, and (3) to help you to apply the basic framework to specific decision contexts that many of you now face or will be facing in short order. For readers with little background in taxes, we present a simple introduction to the calculation of both individual taxpayers' and corporate taxpayers' tax liability in the appendix to this chapter. We also define some common tax terms in this appendix.

In each chapter, we cite some relevant research on the topics we cover. The intent is to provide those keen on learning more about how taxes affect decision making the sources with which to do so.

Table 1.1 Historical Top Statutory U.S. Income Tax Rates*

	Individual			C Corporation	
Time Period	Ordinary Income*	Capital Gains	Dividends**	Ordinary Income	Capital Gains
Pre–1981	.70	.28	.70	.46	.28
1982–1986	.50	.20	.50	.46	.28
1987	.39	.28	.39	.40	.28
1988–1990	.28	.28	.28	.34	.34
1991–1992	.31	.28	.31	.34	.34
1993–1996	.396	.28	.396	.35	.35
1997–2000	.396	.20	.396	.35	.35
2001–2002	.386	.20	.386	.35	.35
2003–2012	.35	.15	.15	.35	.35
2013–2017	.396	.20	.20	.35	.35
2018–	.37	.20	.20	.21 (flat)	.21 (flat)

* Our rates are income tax rates only and do not include payroll tax rates, which are additional taxes assessed on wage income up to certain limits. Starting in 2013, there is also an additional 3.8% tax on investment income for individuals with modified adjusted gross income greater than $250,000 (joint filers). These additional taxes (along with an additional 0.9% payroll tax for the same filers) were put in place to finance the national health care plan enacted by President Obama—the Patient Protection and Affordable Care Act.

** Starting in 2003, long-term capital gains rates apply to "qualified" dividends. To be qualified, the dividends must be paid from a domestic corporation (or certain foreign corporations), the shares must not be hedged, and the shares must be held for at least a specified minimum holding period.

Summary of Key Points

1. Tax rules are pervasive in their effect on the investment and financing decisions of businesses.
2. Because recontracting is costly (e.g., selling assets and retiring or repurchasing bonds), investment and financing decisions that have been made in the past influence current and future investment and financing decisions.
3. Tax rules influence investment and financing decisions because they affect the before-tax rates of return on investment and financing alternatives. More highly explicitly taxed investments require higher before-tax rates of return compared with alternatives that bear low explicit taxes. Investment and financing alternatives that face low explicit taxes (due to favored treatment under the tax law) bear high implicit taxes.
4. Taxpayers with low marginal tax rates are encouraged by the tax system to contract with taxpayers facing high marginal tax rates.
5. All tax-planning actions are tempered by the nontax costs of achieving tax savings.
6. Effective tax planning means considering (a) the tax implications of a proposed transaction to all parties of the contract; (b) explicit taxes, implicit taxes, and tax clienteles; and (c) the costs of implementing various tax-planning strategies.
7. Tax planning is a tax-favored activity in that the investment is tax deductible and the payoffs (reductions in tax payable) are tax exempt. The higher the taxpayer's marginal tax rate, the higher the returns to tax planning.

Appendix 1.1
Overview of Calculation of U.S. Income Tax Liability

Exhibit 1.1 presents the basic tax formula for determining federal income tax liability for domestic-only corporations (we discuss the international tax rules that apply to multinational corporations later in the text) and individual taxpayers. We start our description with economic income, which is defined as income from whatever source (wages and salaries, dividend and interest income, sales revenue, appreciation in assets owned, etc.). Economic income includes both realized and unrealized increases in the taxpayer's wealth. Unrealized income is (generally) excluded from taxation until realized via the sale of the underlying asset. Taxation is deferred until realization because, at that point, the taxpayer presumably has the cash from the sale to pay the taxes due. This leaves realized income, but not all realized income is taxable. The tax code specifically excludes from taxation some types of income. Major items of income excluded are gifts and inheritances, life insurance proceeds, social welfare payments, certain payments for injury and sickness, certain employer-provided fringe benefits, interest on state and local government (municipal) bonds, and gain from the sale of a personal residence (subject to certain restrictions). After these exclusions, we are left with gross income.

EXHIBIT 1.1 Basic Tax Formula

C Corporation	Individuals
Economic income	Economic income
– Unrealized income	– Unrealized income
= Realized income (§61)	= Realized income (§61)
– Exclusions	– Exclusions
= Gross income	= Gross income
– Deductions	– Deductions for Adjusted gross income (AGI)
	= AGI
	– Deductions from AGI: Max (itemized deductions or the standard deduction)
= Taxable income	= Taxable income
× Tax rate	× Tax rates[1]
= Gross tax	= Gross tax
– Credits and prepayments	– Credits and prepayments
= Regular tax	= Regular tax
	+ Excess (if any) of tentative minimum tax over the regular tax[2]
= Federal income tax liability	= Federal income tax liability

[1] Different tax schedules apply depending on filing status (single, married filing jointly, married filing separately, head of household)

[2] The tax code refers to this as the alternative minimum tax.

Taxpayers then deduct allowable items to arrive at taxable income. Note that all income is included in gross income unless specifically identified in the tax code as an allowable exclusion. In contrast, expenditures are not deductible unless specifically identified in the tax code. For corporations, all costs incurred in carrying on a trade or business are allowed as deductions. Examples include wages and salary paid to employees, cost of goods sold, depreciation on plant and equipment, interest on borrowings (subject to certain limitations), and state and local taxes. A percentage of dividends received on investments in other companies is also allowed to be deducted (the so-called corporate-dividends-received deduction discussed in further detail in later chapters). Note that whereas interest on borrowings is deductible (subject to certain limitations), dividends paid to the corporations' shareholders are not tax deductible to the paying corporation.

The calculation of taxable income for individual taxpayers is slightly more complex because deductions are partitioned into two categories: deductions *for* adjusted gross income (AGI) and deductions *from* AGI. Deductions for AGI are generally expenses associated with the individual taxpayer carrying on a trade or business. For example, the qualified business income deduction for pass-through income is a deduction for AGI, as is the deduction teachers can take for purchasing classroom supplies. Deductions from AGI are personal expenses that Congress has chosen to allow as deductions. The major deductions from AGI, also known as itemized deductions, are home mortgage interest expense, charitable contributions, medical expenses (with limits), and a maximum of $10,000 in state and local income (or sales) and property taxes. In an effort to simplify taxpayers' tax return preparation and record keeping, Congress allows a standard deduction for each taxpayer, with the amount varying with the taxpayer's filing status and age. Taxpayers itemize only if the claimed deductions exceed the standard deduction. We note that the standard deduction was substantially increased in the TCJA, so many more taxpayers will likely use the standard deduction and not itemize starting in the tax year 2018. Adjusted gross income is used in numerous tax calculations related to limitations on the amount allowed as a deduction from AGI (e.g., setting a minimum below which medical expenses are not deductible or a maximum above which the expenditure is not deductible, such as charitable contributions).

Given taxable income, the taxpayer then calculates the gross tax that is due by applying the tax-rate schedule applicable to that taxpayer's filing status. The taxpayer then deducts from the gross tax due any allowable tax credits and any tax prepayments to arrive at the regular tax due or tax refund. Tax credits can be classified as refundable tax credits and nonrefundable tax credits. Refundable tax credits can give rise to a tax refund (e,g, the child tax credit). Tax prepayments (such as withholding taxes on wages paid by the taxpayer to the government during the tax year or estimated tax payments made during the year) are refundable if overpaid or overwithheld. It should be obvious that tax credits, which reduce the gross tax dollar for dollar, are more valuable than deductions, which reduce taxable income dollar for dollar but reduce the gross tax liability by the taxpayer's tax rate.

Finally, the taxpayer performs an alternative calculation (known as the alternative minimum tax [AMT] calculation) and compares the alternative tax due to the regular tax due and pays the larger of the two. We do not discuss the AMT calculation but note that it is intended to make sure taxpayers with a large economic income pay some taxes (thus, the AMT includes some extra income items and disallows some deductions—the specifics are beyond our discussion here). We note that the TCJA changed the regular tax system and the AMT system such that many fewer individuals will be subject to the AMT starting in the tax year 2018. Indeed, the Tax Policy Center estimates that in 2018, the number of AMT payers will fall from 5.2 million to roughly 200,000 as a result of the TCJA. The TCJA eliminated the corporate AMT.[5]

[5] Tax Policy Center, 2018. *Table T18-0009*. Washington, DC: Urban-Brookings Tax Policy Center.

Questions

Q1-1. Why is tax minimization different from efficient tax planning?

Q1-2. Under what circumstances should social planners encourage taxpayers to engage in costly tax planning?

Q1-3. List five examples of tax-favored investments.

- *a.* Do these investments bear high implicit taxes?
- *b.* Who should undertake these investments? Do they?
- *c.* Who receives the implicit taxes?

Q1-4. Which of the following statements accurately describes an efficient tax plan?

- *a.* High-tax-bracket investors should invest in municipal bonds.
- *b.* Paying explicit taxes is rarely a good strategy.
- *c.* Renting durable business assets is more tax efficient than owning for low-tax-rate investors.
- *d.* Employees prefer to defer receipt of their compensation (assuming this succeeds in postponing the recognition of taxable income) whenever they expect their tax rates to fall in the future.

Q1-5. Refer to Exhibit 1.1. For an individual, prepare a list of the following:

- *a.* Income items that are taxed (specifically, items included in realized income)
- *b.* Items excluded from realized income
- *c.* Deductions
- *d.* Credits

Q1-6. Refer to Exhibit 1.1. For a C corporation, prepare a list of the following:

- *a.* Income items that are taxed (specifically, items included in realized income)
- *b.* Items excluded from realized income
- *c.* Deductions
- *d.* Credits

Q1-7. Why is it important for the tax planner to know the tax consequences of a particular transaction not only to the entity employing the tax planner but also to the other party (or parties) to the transaction? Provide a real-world example to illustrate your answer.

Q1-8. We generally think that taxes lower returns, which means that after-tax returns are lower than pretax returns. Is this always true, or can you provide counterexamples?

Q1-9. Explain the difference between tax avoidance and tax evasion. Provide an example of each activity.

Exercises

E1-10. Taxpayer A purchased $100,000 of corporate bonds yielding 12.5% per annum. The interest income from these bonds is taxed at a rate of 28%. Taxpayer B purchased $100,000 of municipal bonds yielding 9% per annum. The interest from these bonds is tax exempt. The bonds have similar maturities and risk. What is the after-tax rate of return earned by each taxpayer? Is taxpayer B paying taxes in any sense here?

a. Who are the taxes being paid to?

b. What is the implied tax rate?

E1-12. A taxpayer is considering buying a fully taxable corporate bond. The bond has a remaining maturity of 5 years, promises to pay 6% interest annually (assume the coupon interest is payable annually), and has a face value of $1,000. The taxpayer faces a 31% tax rate on the interest income and requires a pretax rate of return of 6% to invest. What price is the taxpayer willing to pay for this bond? The same taxpayer is also considering buying a tax-exempt municipal bond. The municipal bond has a remaining maturity of 5 years, also promises to pay 6% interest annually (again, the coupon interest is payable annually), and has a face value of $1,000. Assume the corporate and municipal bonds are equally risky. At what price is the taxpayer indifferent between the corporate and municipal bonds? (Alternatively stated, what price is the taxpayer willing to pay for the municipal bond assuming he or she requires a pretax rate of return of 6% and faces a marginal tax rate of 31%?) How does this example relate to the discussion of implicit taxes in the text? (This exercise assumes the reader is familiar with present-value techniques and the pricing of bonds.)

E1-13. A business taxpayer is considering two mutually exclusive alternatives. Alternative A is to hire a tax accountant at a cost of $20,000 to research the tax law on a tax-avoidance plan. If successful, the plan would save the taxpayer $21,000 in taxes. The probability of success is estimated to be 75%. Alternative B is to hire a marketing firm at a cost of $18,000, whose task would be to develop a marketing plan for the taxpayer's product. If successful, the plan would reduce other advertising costs by $25,000 without affecting sales revenue. The probability of success is estimated at 80%. Which alternative should the taxpayer choose if he or she faces a tax rate of 15%? Of 35%? Comment on your results. Is tax planning a tax-favored activity? Is so, for whom?

E1-14. A taxpayer works at a corporation nearing the end of its fiscal year. The company has had a very successful (profitable) year and has decided to award the employee a cash bonus of 20% of annual salary (a bonus of $30,000). The company has announced that the employee can take the cash bonus this year or defer it until next year. The taxpayer faces a current tax rate of 37%, but because she plans to work only a part-time schedule next year, she expects to face a tax rate of 24%. Assuming she can earn 5% after tax on her personal investments, should she accept the bonus this year or next year? Suppose she can earn 25% after tax on her personal investments. Would you change your recommendation?

Tax-Planning Problems

TP1-15. A large corporation hires you as a consultant. The corporation has accumulated tax losses, and it expects to be in this position for a number of years. The corporation needs a new distribution facility on the West Coast to service its West Coast customers more efficiently. The facility has an estimated cost of $10 million. The corporation is considering three alternative plans. Under plan A, the corporation can borrow the $10 million and purchase the facility. Under plan B, the corporation can issue common stock to raise the $10 million and purchase the facility. Under plan C, the corporation can lease the facility from the current owners. The corporation asks you to prepare a brief report outlining the tax consequences of each plan. Your report should also contain your recommendation as to the most tax-efficient plan. Assume the corporation is not limited with respect to its interest deductions.

TP1-16. The compensation committee of a large public corporation engages you to help design a tax-efficient compensation plan for the current chief executive officer (CEO). In a preliminary interview with the compensation committee, you ask for the opportunity to meet with the CEO to discuss her personal financial and tax situation. A member of the compensation committee questions why you would want to meet with the CEO. Prepare a response to this question.

TP1-17. Refering to the previous problem, what nontax considerations might you consider in designing a tax-efficient compensation contract for the CEO?

TP1-18. The ABC Corporation is a large multinational company that has facilities (both manufacturing and distribution) located in many U.S. states and in overseas countries. The corporation's long-serving chief financial officer (CFO) just retired, and his replacement is reviewing the corporation's economic balance sheet. She discovers that the corporation leases many of its distribution facilities and relies heavily on long-term debt for financing. She vaguely recalls having heard about implicit taxes and tax clienteles and would like these concepts explained and then applied to her observations to determine if the corporation is bearing implicit taxes and whether the corporation is in the right clientele.

References and Related Works

Commissioner v. Newman, 159 F.2d 848 (CA-2, 1947).

Gale, W., H. Gelfond, A. Krupkin, M. J. Mazur, E. Toder, 2018. "The Effects of the Tax Cuts and Jobs Acts: A Preliminary Analysis." Tax Policy Center.

Graham, J., M. Hanlon, T. Shevlin, and N. Shroff, 2014. "Incentives for Tax Planning and Avoidance: Evidence from the Field," *The Accounting Review*, vol. 89, p. 991–1024.

Hulse, D., 1996. "The Timing of the Stock Market Reaction to Rifle-Shot Transition Rules," *Journal of the American Taxa-tion Association* (Fall), pp. 57–73.

Mills, L., M. Erickson, and E. Maydew, 1998. "Investments in Tax Planning," *Journal of the American Taxation Association* (Spring), pp. 1–20.

Slemrod, J., and M. Blumenthal, 1993. *The Compliance Costs of Big Business*. Washington, DC: The Tax Foundation.

Tax Policy Center, 2018. *Table T18-0009*. Washington, DC: Urban-Brookings Tax Policy Center.

"Teresa's Fair Share," *Wall Street Journal*, October 18, 2004.

2

Tax-Planning Fundamentals

After completing this chapter, you should be able to

1. Describe how tax rules are designed to achieve socially desirable outcomes.
2. List and provide examples of the three broad types of tax planning.
3. Explain why there are broad legal restrictions on taxpayer behavior.
4. Outline the legislative process in the United States that leads to tax-rule changes.
5. Explain the role of revenue rulings, court cases, and secondary authorities in tax planning.
6. Explain how tax law ambiguity might affect tax planning.

In the introductory chapter, we discussed how the tax system seeks to achieve a variety of social goals and how this naturally gives rise to

- tax rates varying across different economic activities,
- tax rates varying across different individual taxpaying units, and
- tax rates varying for a given taxpaying unit over time.

These differential tax rates, in turn, provide strong incentives for taxpayers to engage in tax planning. These incentives are the key ingredients that allow the tax system to be used to implement desired social policy.[1]

A problem with this approach, however, is that tax rules adopted for the purpose of achieving certain social goals are generally too broad, which encourages some taxpayers to exploit their ambiguity and, as a result, leads to some **socially undesirable economic activity**. Socially undesirable economic activities are those undertaken with the major (or sole) purpose of reducing the taxpayer's tax bill without any real nontax benefits to society; often, these are unintended and unanticipated by lawmakers. The response is often to fine-tune the tax system. In particular, when taxpayers have gone "too far" in their efforts to avoid taxes, the Congress or the Treasury (or both) fight back by establishing legislative restrictions (tax bills), judicial restrictions (court cases), or administrative guidelines on what taxpayers can do. Of course, legislative changes are designed to do much more than simply plug tax loopholes. As noted in Chapter 1, Congress also uses them in attempts to change the distribution of wealth in the economy, to raise

[1] This view of the tax system is admittedly rather rosy. We adopt this perspective at this stage more for pedagogical convenience than for descriptive validity. We acknowledge that private parties have incentives to seek legislation that is beneficial to them, even if it leads to reduced social welfare. We do not mean to deny the existence of legislative "capture" on the part of certain groups of taxpayers, even when the public debate takes on a "public interest" melody. The interested reader might wish to browse two interesting and entertaining articles discussing proposed tax cuts by Dan Morgan in the *Washington Post* titled "Whale of a Tax Break for Eskimos" (July 22, 1999, p. A21) and "Business Gets Big Breaks in Tax Bills: Surpluses Allow Lobbyists to Win Billions in Relief from Capitol Hill GOP" (July 24, 1999, p. A01). The second article contains the following by a Democratic lobbyist. "If you're a business lobbyist and couldn't get into this legislation, you better turn in your six-shooter. There was that much money around." See the Example 2.1 discussion and articles regarding the debate over carried interest in the Tax Cut and Jobs Act for a more recent example.

revenue, and/or to change the degree to which certain economic activities are subsidized in light of changes in the economy.

To combat socially undesirable tax planning, Congress imposes two classes of restrictions. These include (1) very broad restrictions that apply to a great variety of transactions and (2) very specific restrictions that respond to particular abuses of the tax system. Of course, Congress must be careful not to impose *too* many restrictions or to make enforcement of the rules *too* uncertain. Tax rule and enforcement uncertainty may discourage precisely the transactions that Congress wishes to encourage. In other words, restrictions can be too broad as well.

Moreover, the costs associated with imposing many specific restrictions can be quite high. These include (1) legislative costs, such as the cost of elected representatives and their research and administrative staffs, and the cost of lobbyists; (2) the cost to the general public of becoming informed so that they can participate in the legislative process; and (3) compliance costs, which increase with the complexity of the tax system and the number of restrictions.

Life would be simple, indeed, if tax rules were unambiguous. But tax rules, like all other areas of the law, are far from clear. **Tax-law ambiguity** implies that even if you could claim to have committed to memory the entire Internal Revenue Code (IRC), you would be able to resolve only a small degree of ambiguity in how a tax return should be prepared. As technically detailed as the U.S. tax code may seem to be, it still contains rules that are far too general to indicate clearly how particular transactions are to be taxed.

The inherent ambiguity in the tax law gives rise to numerous disputes between taxpayers and the taxing authority, as these parties have opposing interests regarding the assessment of tax liabilities. In turn, the judicial branch of government (the court system) must resolve disputes. And as disputes are resolved by the courts, the tax rules take on greater and greater detail—that is, the courts help to interpret the rules.

We can make the tax system simpler if we abandon using it as a means of achieving desired social policies. In fact, the Tax Reform Act of 1986 (TRA 86) was a clear move in this direction. Many tax-rule changes brought about by this major piece of legislation were designed to "level the playing field," so to speak—that is, the changes removed or reduced tax subsidies for many economic activities. It is not obvious that governments should or should not use tax policy to influence behavior; there are mixed views on the topic. One question to consider is what alternative means the government would use to promote or discourage certain behaviors and whether such alternatives would be better or worse (in terms of efficiency, effectiveness, fairness, etc.). In addition, we know that in the years following TRA 86, Congress reintroduced substantial complexity into the tax code; thus, any simplicity achieved by TRA 86 was, for the most part, short-lived. The Tax Cuts and Jobs Act (TCJA) passed in 2017 simplified the tax code in some aspects. For example, the standard deduction for individuals was increased significantly, which serves to "level the playing field" in the sense that those with fewer itemized deductions (e.g., smaller home mortgages, fewer charitable donations) are able to claim greater deductions from adjusted gross income as described in Chapter 1. In addition, the home mortgage deduction was limited to a greater degree, as was the state and local tax itemized deductions.[2] However, the TCJA also increased complexity in some areas and continues to promote some social goals (some would say "pick winners and losers"). For example, green energy tax credits (mentioned in Chapter 1) remained in the code, a new Opportunity Zone tax benefit was added to the code, the child tax credit was expanded and made refundable to a greater degree (though personal exemptions were eliminated), and college savings accounts were expanded such that private school K-12 tuition can be paid for out of tax advantaged Section 529 plans (discussed in Chapter 3).

In this chapter, we consider some of the difficulties associated with using the tax system to achieve social goals. In particular, we identify a few classes of tax-planning games that aggressive taxpayers might naturally be inclined to play, and we provide examples of the broad restrictions that are imposed when such tax-planning games lead to socially undesirable outcomes.

In later chapters, we elaborate on the importance of more specific tax-rule restrictions. We also consider how transaction and information costs affect taxpayers' abilities to engage in socially unacceptable tax planning, and we will see that Congress need not impose as many tax-rule restrictions where transaction costs are high.

---

[2] Indeed, H&R Block has announced that it intends to close 400 offices as it expects fewer taxpayers to need help filing their returns due to these changes. See Michael Cohn, "H&R Block Plans to Close 400 Tax Prep Offices," *Accounting Today*, June 14, 2018.

2.1 TYPES OF INCOME TAX PLANNING

Over the years, taxpayers have displayed considerable ingenuity in their attempts to have their income (1) converted from one *type* to another, (2) shifted from one *pocket* to another, and (3) shifted from one *time period* to another. Briefly, we consider each of these types of tax-planning activities.

Converting Income from One Type to Another

"Capital gains" are typically realized on the sale of capital assets, such as common stock. Wages, interest on bonds, and royalties are items that are typically considered "ordinary income." In most countries, capital gains are taxed favorably relative to ordinary income for individual taxpayers. **Table 1.1** presented the top U.S. statutory tax rates for each income type from 1980 onward. The attempt to convert ordinary income into capital gains is a common tax-planning strategy, at times abused, among individual taxpayers.

Besides the capital gains/ordinary income distinction, tax liabilities are often affected by whether income is classified as

- Passive income or operating income,
- Earned domestically or abroad,
- Derived from a profit-seeking business or from an activity engaged in as a hobby.

For example, whether income is classified as interest or operating income may determine the amount of deductible interest expense. Whether income is deemed to be U.S. sourced or foreign sourced may affect not only the tax rate that applies to the income but also the foreign taxes paid that the United States will permit as a credit against U.S. income tax liability. Whether income is judged to come from an actively managed business or a passive investment may affect whether losses from such activities are currently tax deductible. Whether income is considered to come from an activity engaged in for profit or an activity that is a hobby may affect whether losses from such activities will ever be deductible. These examples are by no means exhaustive (and some of these are discussed in more detail in later chapters). Many other labeling distinctions are important to taxpayers, particularly in the international tax area.

EXAMPLE 2.1

The character of the compensation/returns to private equity managers is a good illustration of the effects of the type of income a taxpayer receives. By way of background, a private equity fund is a fund that invests in other companies or businesses with the objective of obtaining a controlling interest so that the fund can then restructure the businesses. Restructuring can occur via leverage buyouts, venture capital, angel investing, mezzanine debt, and other ways. After a successful restructuring, the fund often cashes out via an initial public offering (IPO), a sale or merger of the business, or a recapitalization. Most private equity funds are organized as limited partnerships with the investors holding limited partner interests. Thus, investors are taxed on the annual income from the partnership. The general partner is often an affiliate of the manager of the fund. Typically, the general partner is compensated with a fee based on the gross assets under management (e.g., 2% of the gross assets) and a profits interest of generally 20% of the fund's return. This latter profits interest is referred to as "carried interest." If the fund is successful, because carried interest is taxed as capital gains, most of the return to the general partner (the fund organizer) is not taxed as compensation for services but as a return on investment taxed at favorable capital gains tax rates.[3]

The taxation of carried interest has been the subject of much debate and controversy. The private equity industry argues that taxation at capital gains rates is necessary for managers to take risks and engage in private equity funding activities that they argue create jobs in the economy. Essentially everyone else argues that the profits interest portion that is earned without an underlying investment by the manager is compensation for services and should be taxed as such.

continued

[3] In addition, some structures waive the 2% fee for alternative profit-share arrangements, thus converting all income into capital gains.

continued from previous page

A proposed change to this tax policy has been included in several bills over time, in various presidential budgets, and in campaign platforms. The Tax Policy Center in its analysis of the 2013 budget noted,

> Under the president's budget proposal, a partner's share of income from an "investment services partnership interest" (ISPI) would be taxed as ordinary income, regardless of the character of the income at the partnership level. Partners would be required to pay self-employment taxes on income from an ISPI. If a partner sells an ISPI, the gain would be taxed as ordinary income, not as a capital gain. Income that a partner earns from capital invested in the partnership and gain on the sale of an ISPI would not be recharacterized, provided that the partnership reasonably allocates income across invested capital and carried interests. A partnership would be considered an investment partnership if substantially all of its assets are investment-type assets (securities, real estate, etc.). The administration estimates that the provision would raise $13.5 billion through 2022.[4]

The TCJA ultimately did not eliminate the carried interest provision, even though President Trump strongly vowed to kill the carried interest provision on his campaign trail, calling it a break where "paper pushers" are "getting away with murder." This is a good illustration of the lobbying efforts discussed at the opening of the chapter. The new law instead extends the holding period required to obtain long-term capital gains treatment to 3 years (rather than 1 year). In 2016, the Joint Committee on Taxation estimated that taxing the carried interest received as compensation for performing management services as ordinary income, making it subject to the self-employment tax (while not changing how returns to investing their own capital is taxed), would raise an estimated $20 billion in revenues from 2017 to 2026. In addition, as part of the scoring of the TCJA, the committee estimated that the 3-year holding period would raise $1.1 billion over the same window.[5]

Shifting Income from One Pocket to Another

All other things being equal, and barring any restrictions or limitations on such shifting, high-tax-bracket taxpayers would prefer to (1) have their income earned through a tax-exempt pension fund rather than on personal account, where it is fully taxable and/or (2) have their income earned by their low-tax-bracket children or by their low-tax-bracket business (perhaps one located in a low-tax, foreign jurisdiction) rather than earned by themselves.

EXAMPLE 2.2

One strategy that shifts income to a different pocket is the use of an individual retirement account, or IRA, to invest in a start-up or a business. If the business is a success, the returns are not taxed annually but are tax deferred until withdrawal during retirement. Potential nontax benefits are the focus on long-run performance and increased retirement savings (the goal of IRAs). The strategy is available, but it must be done with care (i.e., see a good attorney and IRA specialist before doing this). For example, the IRA needs to be what is called a self-directed IRA. Many nontax costs to this investment potentially exist (e.g., you cannot withdraw the earnings until you retire or you are subject to a penalty), the withdrawals (if from a non-Roth account, discussed further in Chapter 3) are taxed at ordinary income rates, and there are many restrictions in place from the Internal Revenue Service (IRS) to prevent abuse.

One example of this type of strategy is Mitt Romney's holdings of some of his Bain Capital investments via IRA accounts. The IRA accounts received a lot of attention during his presidential

continued

[4] Sapirie, M. "Carrying on with Carried Interest," *Tax Notes*, June, 19, 2018. Congressional Budget Office, "Tax Carried Interest as Ordinary Income," December 8, 2016.

[5] See Rappeport (2017), "Trump Promised to Kill Carried Interest. Lobbyists Kept It Alive," *New York Times* and Kapur, Jacobs, and Mohsin (2017), "How the Carried Interest Break Survived the Tax Bill," *Bloomberg*.

continued from previous page

bid because many were offshore accounts. However, the accounts being offshore did not save any "normal" income tax per se; the fact that the investments are in an IRA is enough to defer the income tax. In Romney's case, the accounts are offshore likely to avoid what is called the unrelated business income tax (UBIT). The UBIT is beyond the scope of this discussion, but the avoidance of UBIT by funds using offshore accounts is not uncommon or illegal. Indeed, it is likely why so many funds are located offshore.

Shifting Income from One Time Period to Another

If tax rates are constant or declining over time, taxpayers prefer to delay recognizing income until it can be taxed at as low of a rate as possible. It is also desirable to defer paying taxes as long as interest is not being charged on the tax liability. If tax rates are increasing over time, it pays to accelerate recognizing income unless interest rates are very high.

For example, if tax rates are 28% today and expected to be 33% in 1 year, it makes sense to accelerate paying the tax unless the taxpayer can invest 28 cents today to return more than 33 cents after tax in 1 year. Such an investment would have to yield nearly 18% *after tax* in 1 year to warrant postponing paying the tax.[6] Of course, nontax factors (e.g., financing current consumption) might also figure importantly in the taxpayer's decision of whether or not to defer income recognition.

The U.S. income tax system, as in most income tax systems around the world, taxes income based on a **realization principle**. That is, income is not typically taxed until certain types of exchanges take place. For example, income from the appreciation of most assets is not taxed until the assets are sold and, even then, the income *might* not be taxed until cash is received from the sale (e.g., the seller may accept a note receivable or promissory note from the buyer delaying the receipt of cash to the seller—an installment sale). This relief feature of the tax law (deferral of taxation until gains/losses are realized) is motivated by a desire by Congress to avoid forcing taxpayers to liquidate assets or borrow money to pay their accrued tax liabilities (i.e., to make sure taxpayers have the wherewithal to pay the tax). Such relief would be unnecessary if it were costless to liquidate assets or to borrow money—that is, if there were no market frictions. But in many circumstances, such frictions are very important, and without the relief provisions, taxpayers would be forced to engage in economically wasteful transactions to meet their tax liabilities. Alternatively, they might choose to forego socially desirable activities (e.g., the sale of an asset with a note to a buyer that can better utilize the asset) in anticipation of possible problems with making tax payments. Conversely, the granting of tax relief of this sort has drawbacks as well. Such relief offers tremendous potential for abuse, especially when the cost to liquidate certain assets is low. Although it may be socially inefficient for them to do so, taxpayers can and do incur real costs in timing their asset sales to shift income from one period to another.

EXAMPLE 2.3

A simple example of shifting income over time (there are many to choose from) is the recent corporate payout behavior accompanying the increase in the individual-level tax on dividends on January 1, 2013. The top dividend rate was 15% before the tax-law change and could have increased to 39.6% (the top ordinary income rate) plus the additional 3.8% for the Medicare surtax on investment income for joint filers with incomes greater than $250,000 put in place by the Patient Protection and Affordable Care Act of 2010—thus, a potential increase in the range of 3.8 percentage points to 28.4 percentage points ([39.6 – 15] + 3.8). When examining dividend

continued

[6] The 18% return can be, in this case, simply calculated as (.33/.28) – 1. But more formally, the after-tax return is calculated by solving first for R, the pretax rate of return, in the following equation: $\$1(1 - .28)[1 + R(1 - .33)] = \$1(1 + R)(1 - .33)$ and then recognizing that the after-tax rate of return $r = R(1 - t)$. The left-hand side represents the taxpayer paying the tax today and investing the after-tax amount of 72 cents for 1 year at R, the pretax rate of return, and paying tax on R at 33% in period 2. The right-hand side represents the taxpayer waiting 1 year to receive the $1 so that tax in the second period is on the entire amount $(1 + R)$. The equality represents the taxpayer being indifferent between the two choices. Solving for R gives .2665 and thus, $r = R(1 - .33) = .178$, or 18%.

continued from previous page

payments at the end of 2012 (for publicly traded firms with available data), there is a marked increase in "special" dividends at the end of 2012. Indeed, the number of firms that paid a special dividend in the last 2 months of 2012 was roughly 9 times the number of firms that paid a special dividend in 2011. There was also a shifting of regularly paid dividends from January into December. The increase in special dividends and shift of regular payouts were concentrated in companies with high insider ownership—where those controlling the dividend payments gain the most from timing the payments to lower taxes. Some companies disclosed their actions. For example, Walmart shifted its regularly scheduled January dividend to December of 2012; its announcement was as follows:

> There are complex fiscal and federal tax rate issues that may not be resolved in the next few weeks, despite the ongoing good faith negotiations between the administration and Congress to resolve details related to the fiscal cliff. In light of this uncertainty, the board determined that moving our dividend payment up by a few days to 2012 was in the best interests of our shareholders.[7]

With certainty, researchers will study the extent to which the shifting of corporate income occurred around the TCJA as the corporate tax rate fell from 35% to 21%.

To summarize, these illustrations provide examples of taxpayers reducing taxes by having their income (1) converted or relabeled from one *type* to another, (2) shifted from one *pocket* to another, and (3) shifted from one *time period* to another.[8]

2.2 RESTRICTIONS ON TAXPAYER BEHAVIOR

The tax authority has the ability to impose *broad legal restrictions* on taxpayer behavior, essentially giving the taxing authority the right to ask whether transactions "pass the smell test." Let us take a closer look at some of the broad restrictions that are involved.

Economic Substance, Business Purpose, and Substance over Form

Among the most powerful tools at the IRS's disposal to discipline aggressive tax planners are the closely related doctrines of economic substance, business purpose, and substance over form.[9] These doctrines were generally judicially developed and are not entirely separable, and their application by the courts has not always been consistent. Generally, the economic-substance doctrine is applied where a taxpayer attempts to claim tax benefits unintended by Congress via transactions that the taxing authorities claim have no economic purpose other than tax savings. On March 30, 2010, the Health Care and Educational Reconciliation Act of 2010 was signed into law. The act added section 7701(o) to the U.S. tax code, which codifies the economic-substance doctrine in the sense that it provides a definition of economic substance; whether economic substance is a relevant doctrine for a transaction is determined the same as before the act.[10] The section provides that the tax benefits of a transaction are "not allowable if the transaction does not have economic substance or lacks a

---

[7] See Hanlon and Hoopes (2013) for large-sample evidence and http://money.cnn.com/2012/11/27/investing/dividend-stocks/index.html for a press article about Walmart.

[8] The reader interested in more complex examples of aggressive tax-avoidance strategies is referred to Appendix A of the report by the Department of the Treasury (1999) and Wilson (2009). These transactions include the fast-pay or step-down preferred transaction, liquidating real estate investment trusts, and lease-in, lease-out (LILO) schemes.

[9] The discussion of these concepts herein is very general in nature and omits many important issues that can be significant to the adjudication of these concepts for a particular transaction.

[10] For more discussion of the history and application over time of the economic-substance doctrine, see the article by Battle (1997). The U.S. Department of the Treasury report (1999) also discussed the application of existing doctrines to corporate tax shelters and the difficulties of arriving at broad new rules to curb these shelters.

business purpose" (subpart 5). Further, the act imposes significant penalties for engaging in transactions that fail the economic-substance doctrine and for underreporting of facts related to such transactions.

The **business-purpose doctrine** disallows tax benefits in transactions where there is not a substantial motivation or purpose for the transaction other than saving taxes (tax avoidance).[11] Whether or not a tax-advantaged transaction has a valid business purpose is often the focus of the dispute between a taxpayer and the IRS. If a taxpayer engages in a set of transactions deemed by a court to have no valid business purpose other than tax avoidance, the tax benefits sought in the transactions are disallowed (and penalties may be levied). And if there *is* some business purpose to the transactions, the taxing authority may assert that the business purpose is insufficient. The courts play an important role in interpreting these concepts and in allowing their definition to evolve over time as the socioeconomic environment changes. The **substance-over-form doctrine** allows the IRS to look through the legal form of transactions to their economic substance.

The landmark case of *Gregory* (a taxpayer) *v. Helvering* (an IRS commissioner) illustrates these doctrines, particularly the business-purpose doctrine. In that case, the taxpayer tried to transform a dividend into a capital gain as follows: Gregory (1) split the corporation in two in a tax-free reorganization and (2) liquidated one of the two new corporations.

Prior to the 1986 Tax Act, the complete liquidation of a U.S. corporation (whose balance sheet included no inventories or depreciable assets) was a nontaxable event at the corporate level. The liquidation gave rise to a capital gain to shareholders, taxed at well below ordinary income tax rates, and much of the sale proceeds was received by shareholders as a nontaxable return of capital. The court viewed the economic substance of Gregory's two transactions as equivalent to a dividend, which at the time were taxed at much higher rates than long-term capital gains. Moreover, because it saw no business purpose for the two transactions other than tax avoidance, it ruled that the less favorable dividend treatment be applied for tax purposes.[12]

Of course, there are ways to transfer property out of a corporation and into the hands of shareholders at capital gains rates, or as a nontaxable return of capital, without liquidating. The simplest way is to repurchase shares of stock in the open market. If share repurchases are proportional to shareholder interests, however, the share repurchases will be considered to be an ordinary dividend. This is an example of the substance-over-form doctrine. If the repurchase is proportional, it is effectively a dividend and can be recharacterized as a dividend even if the transaction is technically accomplished as a repurchase of shares.

The IRS has also tried (often unsuccessfully) to use the substance-over-form argument when taxpayers essentially manufacture riskless assets from portfolios of risky assets. Whereas the returns on risky assets are generally taxable at capital gains rates, the returns on riskless assets are taxable (or tax deductible) at ordinary income tax rates. Consider the possibilities when capital gains tax rates are below ordinary tax rates. Suppose that taxpayers could borrow at the riskless interest rate, take an ordinary tax deduction for the interest, and then use the proceeds to purchase a portfolio of risky assets that, together, are not risky. If the portfolio of risky assets earns the riskless interest rate before tax but is taxed at favorable capital gains tax rates, such taxpayers could wipe out their tax bills. We revisit this tax arbitrage notion in Chapter 4.

The substance-over-form and business-purpose doctrines have also been codified in several parts of the IRC. By codified, we mean that Congress has passed tax bills transforming the judicial support for these doctrines into statutes or laws. IRC Section 482 has been used most extensively by the IRS in cases involving international transfer pricing (e.g., interest rates on loans and sales prices on transfers of goods or services between parent and subsidiary corporations operating in different countries). The motivation for playing games with transfer prices is that the parent and subsidiary may face very

---

[11] The Canada Revenue Agency (formerly known as Revenue Canada), the Canadian counterpart of the IRS in the United States, has access to a similar weapon, the general anti-avoidance rule (GAAR) introduced in 1988. As indicated by Ernst and Whinney (*Tax News International*, December 1988), "Revenue Canada can apply (the general anti-avoidance rule) to eliminate any form of tax advantage resulting from one transaction or a series of transactions, where any step in the series is undertaken primarily to obtain a tax benefit . . . and it represents a misuse of any one provision of the Income Tax Act, or an abuse of the Act overall" (p. 5).

[12] Similarly in the United Kingdom, "the case of *Furniss v. Dawson* . . . established that a pre-ordered series of transactions should be regarded as a single composite transaction for U.K. tax purposes where one or more steps were introduced with no business purpose other than U.K. tax avoidance" (Price Waterhouse, *International Tax Review*, January/February 1989, p. 11).

different tax rates. Section 482 has also been applied to a variety of transactions among related individuals who are taxed at different rates within the same tax jurisdiction (e.g., parents and children).[13]

Congress's motivation for allowing the IRS to invoke Section 482 and to recharacterize transactions is to prevent taxpayers from taking unreasonable advantage of situations where their left pocket and right pocket are taxed differently. A listing of the most relevant IRC sections that give the IRS broad powers is as follows:

Section 269	Grants authority to disallow certain acquired losses.
Section 446(b)	Allows the IRS to adjust a taxpayer's accounting method when the method chosen by the taxpayer "does not clearly reflect income."
Section 7701(l)	Grants authority to prescribe regulations recharacterizing any multiple-party financing transaction as a transaction directly among any two or more parties where it is determined that such recharacterization is appropriate to prevent avoidance of tax.
Section 7701(o)	Clarification of the economic-substance doctrine.

In its 2000 budget, the administration included several proposals designed to limit the growth of corporate tax shelters (such as those discussed in Appendix A of the Department of Treasury [1999] report). The American Jobs Creation Act of 2004 put many requirements for new disclosures into place, and subsequent tax acts have added to the required disclosures and rules that the U.S. Congress and IRS employ to restrict corporate tax-shelter activity. The following is a list of some of the central items (although this is not an exhaustive list):

1. Disclosure of corporate tax-shelter activities—"reportable transactions" (e.g., listed transactions [the IRS publishes a list of known transactions], transactions of interest, confidential transactions, transactions with contractual protection, loss transactions, and transactions with brief holding periods) all must be disclosed with the taxpayer's tax return,
2. Increased penalties relating to substantial understatement of income tax,
3. Additional provisions that disallow the use of tax benefits generated by a corporate tax shelter,
4. Consequences (i.e., penalties, etc.) to all the parties to the transaction (promoters, advisers, and tax-indifferent accommodating parties), primarily via expanded use of Code Section 6700 "Promoting Abusive Tax Shelters, Etc." and Sections 6701–6703,
5. Requirement of a new Schedule M-3 that provides more detailed disclosure of book-tax differences, and
6. Requirement of a new Schedule UTP in 2010 for large corporations that discloses and ranks the taxpayer's largest uncertain tax positions (but not with a dollar value).

Constructive-Receipt Doctrine

The IRS has the authority to adjust a taxpayer's tax accounting method to ensure that it "clearly reflects income." Most accounting-method abuses involve postponing taxable income. A related consideration comes under the **constructive-receipt** label. This doctrine basically prevents taxpayers from turning their backs on income they have already earned and could collect easily. Examples include (1) interest credited on bank accounts where funds are available for withdrawal at any time and (2) year-end paychecks that can be picked up at the payroll department.

[13] For readers wanting more discussion (history and application over time) of the economic-substance doctrine and its potential application to current corporate tax-avoidance schemes, see the article by Battle (1997). The Department of the Treasury report (1999) also discusses the application of existing doctrines to corporate tax shelters and the difficulties of arriving at broad new rules to curb these shelters.

Related-Party versus Arms-Length Contracts

It is worth noting that the IRS worries much more about substance-over-form problems in contracts between related parties than in contracts between unrelated parties. Why? Unrelated parties cannot always trust the other party enough to write a contract in which the legal form differs much from the economic substance. If one party fails to perform as promised under the contract, the courts may not enforce the other party's property rights in the desired way.

For example, suppose a manufacturer buys steel from several suppliers to use in his manufacturing operations. For tax purposes, he determines that it would be very advantageous for him to reduce his taxable income this period and increase it next period. He could arrange for a supplier to ship some steel at a very high price this year with the understanding that the price will be correspondingly lower next year.

The problem with such an arrangement is that once the supplier has received above-market payment for this year's shipments, there is little incentive for her to keep the manufacturer happy for the next year's shipment. Or the supplier might claim that the agreement was to deliver materials of inferior quality in the next period. If the contract is very explicit, so as to deter contractual breach by the supplier (because the breach of an explicit contract may be remedied by bringing legal action), the tax plan will fail if audited by the IRS. So it is not surprising that the IRS worries about related-party contracts more so than arms-length contracts.

Assignment-of-Income Doctrine

The courts have enabled the IRS to invoke another related doctrine, **assignment of income**. Here, the taxpayer instructs one party to pay income on the taxpayer's behalf to a third party, transferring the tax liability to the third party as well (the third party is presumably in a lower tax bracket). As an example, a taxpayer may wish to give a child an interest in partnership income (the fruit of the tree) but not an interest in partnership capital (the tree itself).[14] By the assignment-of-income doctrine, the taxpayer must give away the representative portion of the tree itself to be successful in shifting taxable income. Because taxpayers have devised numerous ways to skirt this doctrine, the U.S. tax code contains some restrictions to attack these income-shifting plans between parents and children. In particular, in what is known as the "kiddie tax." It has taken various forms over the years, but after the TCJA, *unearned* (passive) income earned by children under 18 years of age (or under 19 when they do not provide for more than half of their support with earned income or under 24, a full-time student, and do not provide for more than half their support with earned income) is taxed at the capital gain and ordinary income rates that apply to trusts and estates. Trusts and estates reach the highest tax bracket of 37% after only $12,500 of income, significantly faster than an individual, thus mitigating incentives to shift income from parents to children. A child's *earned* income is taxed at their own individual brackets and rates under the TCJA.

The landmark case in the assignment-of-income area is *Lucas v. Earl*. In this case, a husband and wife entered into a contract providing the wife with a claim to 50% of the husband's income. The taxpayer resided in a noncommunity-property state. (In a community-property state, the wife automatically is deemed to earn 50% of the husband's income.) The couple then filed separate tax returns and, given the progressive income tax schedule (tax rates increase with the level of taxable income), the total tax bill was less than it would have been had they filed a joint tax return. When the court agreed with the IRS commissioner that this was unacceptable, the assignment-of-income doctrine was born.

Interestingly enough, several Tax Court cases involving baseball players have clarified the assignment-of-income doctrine. One involves Randy Hundley, a Chicago Cubs catcher (48 TC 339 [1967]). His father trained him as a youth, and Hundley agreed as a teen to give his father half of any bonus he might receive later. The Tax Court blessed this arrangement, claiming that Hundley's father had earned his share of the bonus.

By contrast, consider the case of Philadelphia Phillies ballplayer Richie Allen (50 TC 466 [1969]). Although Allen arranged for his employer to pay his mother half of his bonus, the Tax Court

[14] This is similar to the situation that arose in the court case *Helvering v. Horst*, where a father sought to make a gift of detachable bond coupons to his son and have the son be taxed on the interest income. The Supreme Court ruled that it was the father who was taxable on the interest income.

ruled this to be an assignment of income and taxed the full bonus to Allen. In reaching its conclusion, the Tax Court emphasized that Allen's mother knew nothing about baseball.

2.3 THE LEGISLATIVE PROCESS AND SOURCES OF TAX INFORMATION

Despite the many broad restrictions that exist, numerous opportunities for abuse remain. Moreover, they will exist as long as the tax system encourages particular economic activities. Such restrictions also clearly make tax planning more difficult. As we mentioned in the introductory chapter, effective tax planning requires that the tax and nontax implications of proposed transactions be considered for all parties to the transaction. But, as we just discussed, simply determining the tax implications of proposed transactions is not a trivial undertaking: It requires knowledge of tax rules that are inherently ambiguous.

A crucial step in minimizing the ambiguities of the tax implications of proposed transactions is seeking the proper authority for applying a particular tax rule. The remainder of this chapter reviews how one does just this for U.S. tax rules. This should provide some idea of how the tax professionals you may hire spend their time. It will also help make it feasible for you to research your own tax problems, and it should give you a better idea of how the tax system is laid out.

Primary and Secondary Authorities

We can distinguish between primary and secondary types of authority for determining the appropriate tax treatment for a transaction. The most important **primary authority** is the IRC. The IRC provides statutory authority. Gathering authoritative support for the proper tax treatment of a particular transaction should always begin here. Other primary authorities include treasury regulations, judicial decisions, administrative pronouncements (e.g., by the IRS), and Congressional Committee Reports. Secondary authorities consist primarily of tax professionals (e.g., accountants and lawyers), commercial tax services, and tax journals. We now discuss each of these authorities.

To develop an understanding of how the primary authoritative sources can help clarify the way a transaction should be treated for tax purposes, we must understand the legislative process, the means by which tax bills are enacted. The passage of such legislation gives rise to the most dramatic changes in tax rules.

The Legislative Process

Figure 2.1 traces a tax bill's route from origin to final enactment. With minor exceptions, all tax bills originate in the House of Representatives and then are forwarded to the House Ways and Means Committee (arrow 1 in **Figure 2.1**). If the bill is a major one, the Ways and Means Committee will hold public hearings. Then, the Ways and Means Committee prepares a report that it sends back to the floor of the House (arrow 2). This committee report, which may provide important authoritative support by indicating the legislative intent of the bill, is often considered in court cases to help resolve taxpayer and IRS disputes.

The bill is then debated on the floor of the House, typically under closed rule, where debate is limited and no amendments are permitted (see Graetz, 1972). If the House bill is passed, it is sent to the Senate (arrow 3), where it is forwarded to the Senate Finance Committee (arrow 4). After public hearings, the Senate Finance Committee sends its report, along with proposed amendments to the House bill, back to the floor of the Senate (arrow 5). There, it is debated under open rule, with unlimited debate and amendment and under intensified lobbying pressure. If passed, both House and Senate Committee Reports are forwarded to a conference committee (arrow 6).

The conference committee is composed of members of both the House and the Senate. Its task is to iron out House and Senate disagreements. The conference committee's report contains recommendations for resolving differences between the House and Senate versions of the bill. In effect, the conference committee creates a compromise bill.[15] The report is sent back to the House and then

[15] The conference report for the TCJA is "Joint Explanatory Statement of the Committee of Conference" and can be found at https://docs.house.gov/billsthisweek/20171218/Joint%20Explanatory%20Statement.pdf.

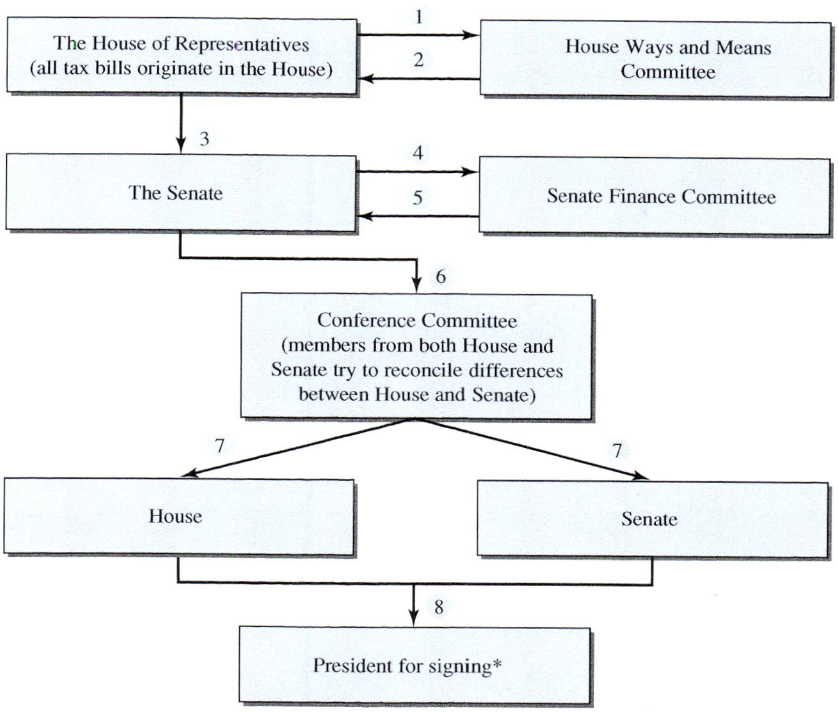

FIGURE 2.1 The Legislative Process

* If the president the vetoes, bill goes back to the House and Senate; 66% vote overrides a presidential veto.

the Senate for a vote (arrow 7). If both houses approve, the bill is sent to the president for signature or veto (arrow 8). If the president vetoes the bill, the veto can be overridden by a two-thirds override vote of the House and Senate members. Interestingly, the TCJA did not follow this process exactly but was passed via a legislative process known as reconciliation. This is where debate in the Senate is limited to 20 hours and involves many other detailed rules.

Regulations and Revenue Rulings that Result from the Passage of a Tax Act

Once a bill is passed, the Treasury is generally the first to interpret it. It issues **Treasury Regulations**, which provide general interpretations. Interested parties (e.g., tax lawyers, tax accountants, and other affected taxpayers) can request hearings on proposed regulations. A change following the TCJA is that the Treasury and the Office of Management and Budget (OMB) have jointly agreed that OMB will review the tax regulations issued by the Treasury and subject the regulations to cost-benefit analyses. (Previously, tax rules had been exempt from this kind of OMB oversight.) However, as part of the agreement, the OMB has agreed to act quickly, conducting their review within 10 days for rules implementing the TCJA if such urgency is demanded by the Treasury. The Treasury Department also issues **revenue rulings**, which are specific interpretations of existing or new laws. These result from a request for rules clarification from a taxpayer with a particular set of actual or proposed transactions. For example, a rulings request might be made when two corporations planning a tax-free reorganization wish to obtain IRS assurance that their merger will not be taxable to the target company's shareholders; that is, the IRS will bless the merger, in advance of the transaction, as being a tax-free reorganization.

Revenue Rulings represent official IRS policy. The Treasury will publish a rulings request from a taxpayer as a Revenue Ruling if it is of sufficient general interest. Otherwise, it issues a **private letter ruling**. Private rulings are available to the public under the Freedom of Information Act, but they cannot be cited as precedent in a court of law. Still, they may be valuable as an indicator of IRS policy. Another form of letter rulings is **technical advice memoranda**. When auditing a technical tax matter, the IRS district or appeals office may refer the matter to the IRS national office in Washington, D.C., for technical advice concerning the appropriate tax treatment. The answer is made available to the public as a letter ruling known as a technical advice memorandum.

Revenue Rulings are published in the weekly *Internal Revenue Bulletin*. They are also published in the "Current Matters" section of the Commerce Clearing House (CCH) and by Research Institute of America (RIA) tax services (described more fully later in this chapter). Because Revenue Rulings may be revoked or amended, their current status must be determined before relying upon them. Merten's *Law of Federal Income Taxation* contains a convenient current status table, as do the CCH and RIA tax services.

International Rules Applicable to U.S. Companies

We cover the U.S. rules governing multinational enterprises later in the book. However, it should be noted that U.S. multinationals are subject to the tax laws of the foreign jurisdictions in which they operate, to the extent the tax laws of the foreign country apply. In addition, the Organization for Economic Cooperation and Development (OECD) recently issued guidance with respect to the tax planning activities of global enterprises. Countries have "signed on" as agreeing to abide by those rules. Thus, this guidance by the OECD is another source of tax rules to which companies must abide (as long as their home country has agreed, as the United States has). For example, one of the requirements of the OECD is that certain multinational enterprises file country-by-country reports that detail their economic activity by country. U.S. companies are required to comply.[16]

The Role of Judicial Decisions

Judicial decisions also play an extremely important role in interpreting the tax rules. The two court levels are courts of original jurisdiction and courts of appeal. Courts of original jurisdiction include the U.S. Tax Court, U.S. district courts, and the U.S. Court of Federal Claims. Only U.S. district courts offer jury trials. The U.S. Tax Court hears only tax cases, and the presiding judge is more familiar with the tax law than is the typical judge presiding in other courts.

Courts of appeal include the 13 circuit courts (numbered 1 through 11 plus the District of Columbia plus the Federal Circuit Court) and the U.S. Supreme Court. Legal precedent is circuit specific—that is, different circuits can hand down different decisions based on identical facts. When this happens, the Supreme Court is often called upon to provide a final, overarching answer.

Decisions of the U.S. Tax Court for the more important cases are published in the *Tax Court Reporter*. Memorandum decisions of the U.S. Tax Court (dealing primarily with questions of fact with only one judge writing the decision) are published in CCH's *Tax Court Memorandum Decisions* and in RIA's *TC Memorandum Decisions*. All tax-related cases from all of the other courts (district courts, Federal Claims Court, circuit courts of appeal, and the Supreme Court) are published in CCH's *U.S. Tax Cases* and RIA's *American Federal Tax Reports*, among other places.

Secondary Authorities

To this point, we have discussed almost exclusively sources of *primary* authority: statutory (IRC), administrative (Treasury regulations, Treasury rulings), and judicial (cases from the U.S. Tax Court, district courts, Federal Claims Court, circuit courts, and Supreme Court). For the nonexpert, **secondary authorities** are probably more useful, particularly the commercial tax services. The two most popular tax services are CCH's *Standard Federal Tax Reporter* and RIA's *United States Federal Tax Reporter*. Each section of these services begins with a layperson's discussion of an area of the tax code, introducing the subject in general terms. This is followed in turn by (1) the text of the IRC section (the statutes established by the passage of tax legislation), (2) the text of Treasury Regulations (the Treasury's interpretation of the IRC), (3) editorial explanations (sometimes including tax-planning tips), and, finally, (4) synopses of court decisions, revenue rulings, and other Treasury pronouncements that pertain to the IRC section, along with citations to complete documents.

Another extremely useful reference is the Bureau of National Affairs's *Tax Management Portfolios*, of which there are several hundred. Each portfolio, 50–200 pages long, deals with a specific

[16] See Hanlon (2018) for a discussion of country-by-country reporting.

tax topic (e.g., sale-and-leaseback transactions or corporate acquisitions planning). The material proceeds from the general to the specific and offers excellent bibliographies. Also useful are the frequent excerpts from the congressional record that pertain to the enactment of relevant legislation. Note, too, the helpful sample contracts or wordings to be included in the corporate minutes. These are likely to pass muster with the taxing authority to secure the desired tax treatment.

Another useful reference is CCH's *Tax Articles,* which lists articles and their abstracts by IRC section number, by topic, and by author. In addition, the RIA tax service offers its "Index to Tax Articles," organized by IRC section number. Finally, the *Master Tax Guide* published by CCH is also a valuable resource of tax information for those wanting a summary (and references to the primary authorities).

Summary of Key Points

1. Tax rules designed to motivate socially desirable activities sometimes (unintentionally) motivate transactions that reduce taxpayers' tax liabilities but serve no social purpose. This gives rise to tax-rule restrictions that serve to limit exceedingly aggressive tax-planning behavior.
2. Ambiguity in the tax law is pervasive. As a result, numerous disputes arise between taxpayers and the taxing authority, two groups with opposing interests regarding the assessment of tax liabilities. The courts may be used to resolve these disputes.
3. Several common classes of tax-planning strategies include attempts to convert tax-disfavored types of income into more favorably taxed types, to shift income from a highly taxed pocket to a lower-taxed pocket, and to shift income from a time period of high tax rates into one of lower tax rates.
4. The economic-substance doctrine, business-purpose doctrine, and the substance-over-form doctrine are broad restrictions on taxpayer behavior. The taxing authority often has the right to recharacterize transactions in a way that affects the tax outcome if the transactions can be shown to have had no other purpose than tax avoidance and a simpler set of transactions could have been undertaken. The taxing authority can also look through a transaction's legal form to its economic substance. As a result, the taxing authority can deny tax benefits or recharacterize a transaction in a way that is less favorable to the taxpayer.
5. The economic-substance, business-purpose, and the substance-over-form doctrines have been to some extent codified in the U.S. tax code. That is, judicial support for these doctrines has been transformed into statutes or laws. For example, Section 482 allows the IRS to recharacterize transactions from their legal form into their economic substance. This section is used heavily in cases involving transfer-pricing transactions among related parties. The economic-substance doctrine has also been codified, as least as far as definition; whether the doctrine is relevant for a transaction is still a common-law doctrine.
6. Assignment of income is another important doctrine. The taxing authority uses this doctrine to prevent high-tax-bracket taxpayers from assigning their income to related low-tax-bracket taxpayers for the sole purpose of reducing their joint tax bill.
7. Tax laws are ambiguous. Ambiguity can frustrate legitimate tax planning, and taxpayers must be aware of primary and secondary authorities for determining appropriate tax treatment for a transaction. Understanding the legislative intent of Congress provides additional guidance in interpreting the tax rules. The intent of Congress may play an important role in the court's interpretation of the tax rules.
8. Various sources of information can provide guidance to taxpayers in predicting how transactions will be treated for tax purposes. Some of these sources appear in this chapter. Others are listed in the appendix to this chapter.

Appendix 2.1

Sources of Information on Tax Legislation

Several excellent publications follow the evolution of proposed tax legislation and document the dates on which certain legislative events take place. These include

- Bureau of National Affairs' (BNA) *Daily Tax Report*
- BNA's *Weekly Tax Report*
- *Tax Notes Today:* a daily electronic newsletter and also available in print from the publisher Tax Analysts
- *Tax Notes:* a weekly tax service from Tax Analysts. There is a print edition and the articles can be accessed online. Each issue contains:
    - a summary of bills introduced
    - a description of change in the status of bills, by day
    - a description of public hearings on proposed legislation
    - a calendar of future congressional hearings
    - a summary of lobbying letters sent to the Treasury, organized by IRC section number
    - a complete report of developments, all organized by IRC section number, relating to
        - Treasury regulations
        - judicial decisions
        - administrative pronouncements
- a list of recently published tax articles by IRC section number

Tax Analysts also offers other services, research tools, and publications; see its website in the next section.

Copies of Committee Reports (House Ways and Means, Senate Finance, or Conference) can be found in

- The government documents section of most law libraries
- *Weekly Internal Revenue Bulletin*, which is bound into Cumulative Bulletins every 6 months
- *U.S. Code Congressional and Administrative News*
- Parts of the major acts appear in the Research Institute of America (RIA) and Commerce Clearing House (CCH) tax services under the titles *United States Federal Tax Reporter* and *Standard Federal Tax Reporter*, respectively.
- The websites of the Ways and Means Committee, the Senate Finance Committee, and other parts of the government

Sometimes, it is important to know the date on which a particular rule that now appears in the IRC first became effective. Two good sources for laws passed prior to 1954 are

- *Federal Tax Laws Correlated* (Barton and Browning, 1936; Warren, Gorham, and Lamont, 1969)
- Seidman's *Legislative History of Federal Income Tax and Excess Profits Tax Law, 1939–1953* and Seidman's *Legislative History of Federal Income Tax Laws, 1861–1938*

Two additional sources that are useful for tracking down legislative histories of more recent changes in the U.S. tax code are

- RIA's *Federal Taxes Cumulative Changes*
- BNA's *Primary Sources*

Website Addresses

There are many websites for tax information searches. (These website addresses were valid at the time of writing—but website addresses can change.)

IRS home page
http://www.irs.gov

Senate Finance Committee
http://www.finance.senate.gov

House Ways and Means Committee
http://waysandmeans.house.gov

Commerce Clearing House (CCH) home page
http://www.cch.com

Research Institute of America (RIA) home page
http://www.riahome.com

Bureau of National Affairs (BNA) home page
http://www.bna.com

Tax Analysts, publisher of *Tax Notes*
http://www.tax.org

A site with extensive links is maintained by Professor Dennis Schmidt
http://www.taxsites.com

OECD BEPS Actions
http://www.oecd.org/ctp/beps-actions.htm

Big 4 accounting firms' home pages:

Deloitte & Touche
http://www.us.deloitte.com

Ernst & Young
http://www.ey.com

KPMG
http://www.kpmg.com

PriceWaterhouseCoopers
http://www.pwcglobal.com

Appendix 2.2

More Detailed Examples of Tax Planning

Here we present more examples of tax planning that exploited the tax rules in existence as of that time. These plans are no longer implementable because, not surprisingly, once identified, the U.S. Congress and Treasury moved quickly to restrict their use. However, as one tax plan gets shut down, other creative plans emerge.

EXAMPLE A2.1: Reclassifying corporate income to obtain more favorable tax treatment

Corporations are entitled to a dividends received deduction (DRD) on their holdings of stock in other corporations. The purpose of the DRD is to avoid triple (or more) taxation on the original corporation's earnings (once at the original corporation when earned, again at the second corporation when dividends are received, and third at the shareholder level when the second corporation distributes dividends to its shareholders). The DRD allows the firm to exempt a fraction of the dividends received from other corporations. The DRD gives corporate stockholders an incentive to attempt to classify proceeds from the sale of stock that would be taxed as capital gains (for corporations, this rate equals the tax rate on ordinary income) as a dividend to get the DRD. However, to obtain dividend treatment on redeeming (selling back) stock to the issuing company requires that the redemption not be "substantially disproportionate." Hence, *failing* the substantially disproportionate test is necessary for dividend treatment. Thus, if the shareholder simply sells back its shareholdings, this will be treated as disproportionate (because no other shareholder sold stock) and thus trigger sale treatment with no DRD. However, if the shareholder after the "sale" still holds approximately the same percentage of equity instruments in the issuing company, then the "sale" is not disproportionate and dividend treatment is allowed. One way to "sell" and keep the same approximate ownership interest is to receive warrants to buy the issuing corporation's stock as part of the proceeds of the "sale." These warrants count as equity instruments, thus maintaining the ownership percentage. Seagram did this in 1995, saving $1.7 billion in taxes in its redemption of its stockholdings in DuPont. For its part in the transaction, DuPont received about $700 million of the tax savings. This transaction is analyzed in Erickson and Wang (1999). As one might expect, Congress quickly reacted to this transaction. Sale treatment is now required when a corporate shareholder takes part in a redemption that is not pro rata as to all shareholders or is a partial liquidation.

EXAMPLE A2.2: Shifting income from one pocket to another

This example saves taxes at the state level (the "loophole" has been shut down at the federal level). Many retail firms lease or rent their stores. Some firms rent stores from their own majority-owned real estate investment trusts (REITs). The rent payment to the REIT is tax deductible as a business expense at the state level. As discussed in Chapter 5, if the REIT pays out its profits as dividends, the profits are not taxable to the REIT. And the dividends escape taxation to the recipient in this case because the REIT is close to 100% owned by a wholly-owned subsidiary of the parent retail store and dividends between a parent and subsidiary (or between a subsidiary and another wholly-owned business entity) are not taxed (so as to avoid triple or more levels of taxation as per Example A1). Thus the retail firm obtains a tax deduction at the state level for rent paid to itself. For another example, see our discussion of tax planning surrounding the qualified business income deduction for pass-through business income enacted in the TCJA in Chapter 5.

EXAMPLE A2.3: Shifting income from one time period to another

Many firms in the mid-1990s shifted income through corporate-owned life insurance (COLI). In this transaction, a corporation purchases a number of cash-value life insurance policies on lives of employees and either uses borrowed funds to pay the premium or borrows the premium directly back from the insurance company. The life insurance policy builds up in value over the term of the policy and when cashed out is subject to tax. Basically, this strategy exploits the fact that interest on the borrowings is deductible each period as it accrues (even if not paid), whereas the "inside buildup" on the insurance policy (the investment returns credited to the policy each year) is not taxable each year. Because the inside buildup is approximately equal to the accrued interest, there is little nontax benefit to the corporation from the policy.

These policies have been around for a long time, and Congress limited a corporation's interest deduction on the debt that was incurred to purchase or carry these policies in 1986, but the interest was only limited on borrowings that exceed $50,000 per insured life. Corporations responded by reducing the amount of insurance per employee but increased the number of employees covered (some firms insured all employees). The corporations made up in volume what they lost in size per contract.

In 1996, Congress limited a corporation's interest deductions on all debt that was directly traceable to COLI investments to interest on $50,000 of borrowing for up to 20 policies. Corporations were not yet beat. Some firms planned to have COLI contracts on the lives of their customers and to use general business borrowings rather than traceable indebtedness to finance these investments. Congress responded by disallowing interest deductions to the extent that the policies did not insure the lives of the corporations' employees.

EXAMPLE A2.4: Shifting income from one time period to another

The TCJA substantially lowered the top U.S. statutory corporate tax rate from 35% to 21%. As a result, we should expect to see shifting of revenue to years after passing of the TCJA and the shifting of deductions to years prior to the TCJA. Evidence consistent with this prediction was found by researchers

continued

continued from previous page

around the Tax Reform Act of 1986. Suppose a corporation has an unfunded defined benefit pension obligation. If they fund the obligation when the tax rate is 35%, they can deduct the amount then and reduce income that is taxed at 35%. If they wait until the tax rate is 21%, the value of the deduction is much lower. An early paper looking at pension contributions found that firms increased average pension contributions by 24% in 2017 relative to earlier years.[17] We expect other studies to document similar outcomes for other revenues and expenses in order to take advantage of the changing tax rates.

[17] Gaertner, F. B., D. Lynch, and D. Vernon, 2018.

Questions

Q2-1. Provide an example of a tax rule designed to motivate a socially desirable activity that may not achieve its purpose or may achieve its purpose while having unintended consequences.

Q2-2. Discuss. What policy options do governments have available as alternatives to the U.S. tax code to provide incentives and disincentives for certain behaviors?

Q2-3. Why might Congress and the Treasury avoid drafting tax rules that are very specific? What costs would such rules impose on the IRS? What benefits might they bestow on certain taxpayers?

Q2-4. Outline the path of a tax bill through Congress from proposal to passage. Why might a final tax bill differ from the original proposal?

Q2-5. What are the sources and causes of complexity in our tax system? Which, if any, of these causes are correctable?

Q2-6. How do such judicial doctrines as the economic-substance, substance-over-form, and business-purpose doctrines affect taxpayer behavior? Is it socially beneficial to have such doctrines?

Q2-7. What incentives exist for taxpayers to shift income from one party to another? Are there costs associated with such income shifting? Give examples of such costs in a family-planning situation. How would the elimination of the assignment-of-income doctrine affect the costs of shifting income? What could taxpayers do to ease these costs?

Q2-8. Why do the tax laws sometimes discriminate against related-party contracts? Is this always in society's best interest?

Q2-9. Should the taxing authority always agree to provide a private revenue ruling requested by a taxpayer to clarify the tax treatment of a proposed transaction? Should taxpayers requesting rulings be assessed a fee to cover the taxing authority's cost of responding?

Q2-10. Suppose the United States were to convert its tax system from an income tax to a national sales tax on sales of goods and services. Certain necessities, like food, would be exempted from taxation, and low-income households would be granted tax refunds. Would such a tax system eliminate incentives to shift activities (a) from one period to the next, (b) from one type to another, and (c) from one pocket to another?

Q2-11. Suppose the United States were to convert its tax system from an income tax to a flat tax. For individuals, there would be no itemized deductions allowed, a high standard deduction (thus, low-income taxpayers would not have to file returns), and tax exemptions for dividend and interest income. Businesses could deduct all expenditures on salaries and immediately expense asset acquisition costs. Would such a tax system eliminate incentives to shift activities (a) from one period to the next, (b) from one type to another, and (c) from one pocket to another? Do you believe a flat tax with no itemized deductions is politically feasible in the United States?

Q2-12. Assume you are an individual taxpayer. If you expected your marginal tax rate to decline in the next period, what tax planning might you undertake in the current period?

Exercises

E2-13. Suppose the taxpayer can time when he is to receive $100,000 of income that is fully taxable. Current interest rates are 10% on fully taxable securities, and the taxpayer faces a current tax rate of 32%. If the taxpayer delays receipt, the amount will grow to $110,000 at the end of year 2. The taxpayer must decide whether to receive the money today at the end of year 1 or at the end of year 2.

a. When should the taxpayer elect to receive the income?

b. Is there an interest rate at which the taxpayer is indifferent between the two options?

c. The taxpayer expects tax rates to increase to 35% in year 2. Now when should he elect to receive the income?

d. At what tax rate in period 2 is the taxpayer indifferent between the two options?

E2-14. Suppose a taxpayer invests $100,000 in a partnership. Also assume that as was the case in the 1970s, the taxpayer faces a personal tax rate of 70% and a tax rate on capital gains of 28%. In the first year, the partnership spends the entire $100,000 on research, which the taxpayer can claim as a deduction against her other income. In the second year, the partnership sells the developed technology, and the taxpayer's share of the sale price is $50,000, which is taxed as a capital gain. (Ignore the time value of money in your answer.)

a. What is the pretax rate of return to the taxpayer?

b. What is the after-tax rate of return to the taxpayer?

E2-15. The taxpayer is the sole owner-employee of a small C corporation that prepares tax returns. Before paying himself any salary or dividends or taking fringe benefits, the corporation has taxable income of $100,000. Summarize the tax consequences to both parties (the corporation and the taxpayer) of

a. paying a salary of $50,000.

b. paying no salary but dividends of $50,000.

E2-16. A taxpayer owns two separate companies. Company A is fully taxable at 21%, and company B has substantial tax loss carryforwards. Company A sells all its output to B at cost, and B sells to outsiders at a markup of 50%. Company A's revenues total $2 million, whereas company B's revenues total $3 million. What are the tax implications of this arrangement? How will the IRS react?

E2-17. A taxpayer owns and operates an art gallery with a large inventory of paintings held for sale to customers. She took one of the paintings home and hung it in her dining room. A week later, a dinner guest liked the painting so much that he purchased it at a large profit to the taxpayer. The taxpayer believed that because the painting was displayed at home, it was a personal investment and therefore a capital asset with the profit treated as a capital gain. The painting cost the taxpayer $50,000 and was listed for sale while at the gallery for $90,000. The dinner guest paid $80,000 for the painting. As an IRS agent, how might you react? What tax do you think the IRS agent will assess the taxpayer (assuming the taxpayer faces the top U.S. statutory tax rates)?

E2-18. Suppose a corporation (the investor company) owns 164 million shares in another corporation (the investee company). The investor company wishes to liquidate the majority of its holdings. The average basis per share of the investor company's holdings is $17.62, and the investee company is currently trading at $61 per share.[18] (Note that, in this problem, we keep tax rates and DRD rules at historical values that were applicable when the example transaction actually occurred.)

a. Assume that the investor company's tax rate is 35%. What are the tax consequences of an open-market sale of 95% of its holdings in the investee company (i.e., a sale of 156 million shares)?

b. Note that the after-tax gain to the investor is the same if, instead of an open-market sale, the investor sold the stock back to the investee company directly. Now, instead of selling the stock back to the investee company, suppose the transaction could be structured such that the "sale proceeds" would be taxed as a dividend to the investor company. Further suppose the investor company could exclude from taxable income 80% of the dividend received (because the investor company owned approximately 25% of the investee company prior to this transaction). What are the tax consequences of dividend treatment of the "sales proceeds?"

c. Which tax treatment is better for the investor company? What are the tax effects, if any, for the investee company? Are there any nontax costs to the dividend treatment?

Tax-Planning Problems

TP2-19. A taxpayer suffered a $20,000 capital loss early this year (from selling some securities) and is considering two alternatives for generating extra income. The first alternative is to find part-time

[18] This problem is based on a real-world transaction. For an excellent analysis of the transaction, see Erickson and Wang (1999). Erickson and Wang discuss the rules that control dividend treatment for this transaction and how the two parties structured the transaction to satisfy the rules. Erickson and Wang also provide estimates of how the tax savings arising from dividend treatment were shared between the two parties. The interested reader is also referred to the *Forbes* article "The High Cost of Hollywood" (*Forbes*, April 1997, pp. 44–45), which discusses the use to which Seagrams put the proceeds from liquidating its position in DuPont.

employment at the local university teaching courses on taxes. The second alternative is to purchase a fixer-upper bungalow and spend his evenings and weekends cleaning, repairing, installing shiplap, and painting it, then sell the fixed up property. The taxpayer estimates that his income before taxes would be about $45,000 from either alternative. Evaluate the taxpayer's options.

TP2-20. Taxpayer A earned $50,000 working as a carpenter during the year. Taxpayer B, also a carpenter by trade, worked the entire year renovating her house. Comment on the after-tax position of both carpenters. Does it matter if taxpayer B plans to live in her house for 1 more year versus 10 more years?

TP2-21. A taxpayer is forming a new C corporation and has $500,000 to invest in her company. Following the advice of her tax consultant, the taxpayer designated $300,000 for the purchase of corporate stock and $200,000 as a loan to the corporation. Comment on this tax plan.

TP2-22. A taxpayer uses borrowed funds to acquire non-dividend-paying corporate stock. Note that interest on borrowed funds may be deducted in the period paid, up to the amount of net investment income from other stocks or investments (i.e., interest and dividend income if taxable at ordinary income tax rates). Comment on the tax consequences of this plan.

TP2-23. Prior to the TCJA, firms that incurred a tax loss were allowed to carry back the tax loss to obtain a refund of taxes previously paid. To the extent the losses could not be carried back 2 years to obtain a refund (because past taxable income was less than the current tax loss), the losses could be carried forward to be deducted against future taxable income. The Taxpayer Relief Act of 1997 reduced the carryback period to 2 years from 3 years and extended the carryforward period to 20 years from 15 years beginning in 1998. Thus, a firm with tax losses in 1997 could elect to carry back the losses to obtain a refund of 1994 taxes paid, then of 1995 taxes paid, and then of 1996 taxes paid (up to the point that the losses are fully offset). The TCJA of 2017 eliminated the carryback period and only allows tax losses to be carried forward, indefinitely. However, losses carried forward can be used only to the extent of 80% of taxable income in the future year. In addition, the corporate tax rate was reduced from 35% to 21% in the TCJA.

a. In general, what effect will the shortening (lengthening) of the carryback (carryforward) period have on firms that incur a tax loss?

b. Assume a corporation in November 1997 expected to report a tax loss of $250,000 for the tax year 1997. The CFO argued that the firm should defer recognition of $50,000 of income until 1998, thus increasing the tax loss to be carried back to $300,000. The corporation reported an annual taxable income of $100,000 in each of the past 5 years. The firm expected to earn $500,000 in 1998 (before any shifting of income). The firm uses an after-tax discount rate of 6% to discount cash flows. The statutory tax rate was expected to remain unchanged at 35%. Evaluate the CFO's plan. How much in taxes would the company have saved if the CFO's plan had been implemented?

c. How much in taxes would the corporation save if the statutory tax rate in the carryback period were 45% rather than 35%?

d. Now consider the year 2017. If a C corporation were expecting a loss in 2017 but was profitable in 2016 and expected to be profitable in 2018, what would you recommend given a similar fact pattern as in part b?

e. Under what conditions would you advise a firm to carry forward a tax loss rather than carry back the tax loss to obtain an immediate tax refund?

TP2-24. The CEO of ABC Corporation is a dog lover. He and his spouse like cocker spaniels and have a purebred male cocker spaniel. Because of their love for dogs, they decide to breed and sell cocker spaniel pups. In the first year, they spend $25,000 building some kennels, $5,000 on veterinarian fees, $5,000 buying breeding females, and $1,000 on food and sundry supplies. By the end of the first year, they have successfully produced their first litters but have not yet sold any puppies. They would like to deduct their losses (which they calculate by simply summing all their expenditures, a total of $36,000), but they have heard something about hobby-activity loss rules. Under the IRC, for activities classified as hobbies, only losses up to any income generated by the activity can be deducted. If, however, the activity is classified as a trade or business, and the taxpayer is actively engaged in the business, the losses are deductible against the taxpayer's other income.

a. Why might Congress distinguish between hobby activities and trade or business activities?

b. If you were writing the tax code, what rules (or tests) would you write to distinguish an activity as a hobby versus a trade or business? Explain the purpose of each rule (or test).

c. Would the CEO's dog-breeding activity be classified as a hobby or business under your rules?

d. Refer to one of the sources listed in Appendix 2.1 to ascertain the IRC rules for classification. Would the CEO's dog-breeding activity be classified as a hobby or business under IRC rules?

e. If the dog-breeding activity were classified as a business, how much would the CEO be allowed to deduct against his other income?

References and Additional Readings

Anderson, K. E., T. R. Pope, and J. L. Kramer (editors), 2007. *Federal Taxation 2001 Corporations, Partnerships, Estates and Trusts*. Upper Saddle River, NJ: Prentice Hall.

Battle, F., Jr., 1997. "Corporate Tax Shelters, Financial Engineering, and the *Colgate* Case," *Taxes* (December), pp. 692–705.

Enis, C., and L. Christ, 1999. "Implications of Phase-Outs on Individual Marginal Tax Rates," *Journal of the American Taxation Association* (Spring), pp. 45–72.

Erickson, M., and S. Wang, 1999. "Exploiting and Sharing Tax Benefits: Seagrams and Dupont," *Journal of the American Taxation Association* (Fall), pp. 35–54.

Erickson, M., S. Heitzman, and F. Zhang, 2013. "Tax-Motivated Loss Shifting," *The Accounting Review* (88): 1657–1682.

Gaertner, F. B., D. Lynch, and D. Vernon. 2018. "The Effects of the Tax Cuts and Jobs Act of 2017 on Defined Benefit Pension Contributions." Working paper, University of Wisconsin–Madison.

Graetz, M., 1972. "Reflections on the Tax Legislative Process: Prelude to Reform," *Virginia Law Review* (November), pp. 1389–1450.

Guenther, D., 1994. "Earnings Management in Response to Corporate Tax Rate Changes: Evidence from the 1986 Tax Reform Act," *The Accounting Review* (1), pp. 230–243.

Hanlon, M., 2018. "Country-by-Country Reporting and the International Allocation of Taxing Rights," *Bulletin for International Taxation*, vol. 72 (number 4/5), pp. 218–219.

Hanlon, M., and J. Hoopes, 2014. "What Do Firms Do When Dividend Tax Rates Change? An Examination of Alternative Payout Responses to Dividend Tax Rate Changes," *Journal of Financial Economics* (114), pp. 105–124.

Kapur, S., J. Jacobs, and S. Mohsin, 2017. "How the Carried Interest Break Survived the Tax Bill," *Bloomberg News*, December 22.

Klassen, K., M. Lang, and M. Wolfson, 1993. "Geographic Income Shifting by Multinational Corporations in Response to Tax Rate Changes," *Journal of Accounting Research* (Supplement), pp. 141–173.

Klassen, K., and D. Shackelford, 1998. "State and Provincial Corporate Tax Planning: Income Shifting and Sales Apportionment Factor Management," *Journal of Accounting and Economics* (3), pp. 385–406.

Lightner, T., 1999. "The Effect of the Formulatory Apportionment System on State-Level Economic Development and Multijurisdictional Tax Planning," *Journal of the American Taxation Association* (Supplement), pp. 42–57.

Lopez, T., P. Regier, and T. Lee, 1998. "Identifying Tax-Induced Earnings Management around TRA 86 as a Function of Prior Tax-Aggressive Behavior," *Journal of the American Taxation Association* (2), pp. 37–56.

Maydew, E., 1997. "Tax-Induced Earnings Management by Firms with Net Operating Losses," *Journal of Accounting Research* (1), pp. 83–96.

Murray, A., and J. Birnbaum, 1987. *Showdown at Gucci Gulch* (New York: Random House).

Rappeport, A., 2017. "Trump Promised to Kill Carried Interest. Lobbyists Kept It Alive" *New York Times*. December 22.

Scholes, M., P. Wilson, and M. Wolfson, 1992. "Firms' Responses to Anticipated Reductions in Tax Rates: The Tax Reform Act of 1986," *Journal of Accounting Research* (Supplement), pp. 161–191.

U.S. Department of Treasury, 1999. *The Problem of Corporate Tax Shelters: Discussion, Analysis and Legislative Proposals* (July).

Wilson, R., 2009. "An Examination of Corporate Tax Shelter Participants," *The Accounting Review* (84[3]), pp. 969–999.

3

Returns on Alternative Savings Vehicles

After completing this chapter, you should be able to

1. List seven alternative savings vehicles and describe their differing tax treatments.
2. Calculate the after-tax accumulations and after-tax rates of return for the seven savings vehicles.
3. Explain and illustrate the advantage of an investment's tax deductibility.
4. Explain and illustrate the advantage of deferring taxation.
5. Explain and illustrate the effect of tax rate changes over time on the various savings vehicles.
6. Compare investment in a deductible (individual retirement account) IRA with a Roth IRA pension account.
7. Evaluate the conversion decision from a deductible IRA to a Roth IRA.

In this chapter, we begin by discussing different legal forms through which individuals save for the future. To facilitate comparisons, the same underlying investment will be held in each of the savings vehicles. As a result, the before-tax rate of return will be identical in each case. The investment returns will be taxed quite differently across the alternatives, however, so the after-tax rate of return will differ widely. Examples of forms used as savings vehicles include money market mutual funds and pension fund accounts. In Chapter 5, we discuss alternative organizational forms, including corporations and partnerships, through which goods and services are produced. Later in the text, we cover other topics such as compensation plans. Our major objective is to introduce some basic algebra that we will exploit throughout subsequent chapters. Algebra offers a powerful tool to capture and present the differences in after-tax returns arising from the differences in taxation across different savings vehicles, investments, compensation plans, organizational forms, and so on.

In the absence of transaction and information costs (or frictions) and/or explicit restrictions imposed by the taxing authority, different after-tax returns across the savings vehicles would allow investors to eliminate their taxes by employing tax arbitrage strategies. By **tax arbitrage**, we mean earning a relatively high after-tax rate of return by investing through a tax-favored form, financed at a relatively low after-tax cost by borrowing through a different form. We defer a discussion of the nature of existing restrictions and frictions that keep the system in check until we cover some preliminaries. At this stage, our objective is simply to demonstrate the sensitivity of investment performance to differences in the tax treatment across alternative savings arrangements. This objective is why we assume that the before-tax rates of return are identical across the alternatives. It allows us to turn only one dial at a time. With differing underlying investments, after-tax returns would differ because of both risk and tax differences, and, as a result, it would be difficult to separate the effects of the different tax treatments on after-tax returns.

We begin in Section 3.1 by comparing the relative attractiveness of seven differently taxed savings vehicles when tax rates are constant year to year. In Section 3.2, we demonstrate how changes in tax rates over time can affect the relative attractiveness of the seven savings arrangements. Finally, in Section 3.3, we apply the concepts to an analysis of deductible IRAs and Roth IRA pension accounts. Throughout our analysis, we assume transaction costs and fees are zero (or at least not different across the savings vehicles).

3.1 INTERTEMPORALLY CONSTANT TAX RATES

We assume in this section that tax rates are constant over time. We also assume that our investor cannot affect the before-tax rates of return on the investment by buying more or less of it. In other words, the market for investment is perfectly competitive. We begin by considering some relatively straightforward ways to save for future consumption. In particular, suppose that the only investment that can be held in each savings form is an interest-bearing security, such as a fully secured (virtually riskless) corporate bond.

Table 3.1 lists seven categories of savings vehicles (SV) that are distinguished by their tax attributes. Tax treatments across the seven savings vehicles differ along three dimensions:

1. Whether deposits into the savings accounts give rise to an immediate tax deduction (Vehicle VI and VII do).
2. The frequency with which investment earnings are taxed (annually, as in Vehicles I and III; only when the investment is liquidated, as in II, IV, and VI; or never, as in V and VII).
3. The rate at which the investment earnings are taxed (ordinary rates, as in Vehicles I, II, and VI; capital gains rates, as in III and IV; or complete tax exemption, as in V and VII).

Each of these forms has existed in the United States as well as in many foreign tax jurisdictions. The labels "Saving Vehicle I–VII" are not used in practice in any country. Rather, they are a framework we have developed to evaluate after-tax accumulation from investing in different investment forms. This framework should be able to be used across countries and across time, albeit with some modifications at times. Our main point is that how and when income is taxed can make a very large difference in the after-tax return to the investor. We will provide some examples to go along with the vehicles, but you may think of different examples, and new types of investments may develop in the future or exist in other jurisdictions that fit within these seven vehicle descriptions as well. Examples

Table 3.1 Seven Legal Forms (Savings Vehicles) through Which Investors Can Hold Riskless Bonds

Savings Vehicle (Example)	Is the Investment Tax Deductible?	Frequency with Which Earnings Are Taxed	Rate at Which Earnings Are Taxed	After-Tax Accumulation per After-Tax Dollar ($I) Invested
I (Money market fund)	No	Annually	Ordinary	$\$I[1+R(1-t)]^n$
II (Single-premium deferred annuity)	No	Deferred	Ordinary	$\$I(1+R)^n(1-t)+t\$I$
III (Mutual fund)	No	Annually	Capital gains	$\$I[1+R(1-t_{cg})]^n$
IV (Foreign corporation)	No	Deferred	Capital gains	$\$I(1+R)^n(1-t_{cg})+t_{cg}\$I$
V (Roth retirement account)	No	Deferred	Exempt	$\$I(1+R)^n$
VI (Pension)	Yes	Deferred	Ordinary	$\left(\frac{\$I}{1-t}\right)(1+R)^n(1-t)$ or $\$I(1+R)^n$
VII (Health savings account)*	Yes	Deferred	Exempt	$\left(\frac{\$I}{1-t}\right)(1+R)^n$
VII (Heath savings account)**	Yes	Deferred	Taxable	$\left(\frac{\$I}{1-t}\right)(1+R)^n(1-t)$ or $\$I(1+R)^n$

*Assuming withdrawals are used for qualified medical expenses

** Assuming withdrawals are NOT used for qualified medical expenses

of Savings Vehicle I include corporate bonds and money market accounts offered by mutual funds, banks, and savings and loan associations. Common examples of Savings Vehicle II in the United States are the single-premium deferred annuity contract (SPDA) (offered by insurance companies) and a one-time contribution to a nondeductible IRA. Vehicle III includes certain mutual funds, and IV includes shares in certain corporations located in tax jurisdictions where the interest on investment is tax exempt. Whereas Savings Vehicle III and IV are relatively rare, V and VI are used heavily. Examples of V include 529 college savings plans (named after the U.S. tax code section), Roth IRAs, education savings accounts, and the savings portion of certain life insurance policies in the United States. An example of VI is a defined contribution type pension account, including the traditional, or classic, IRA, and a one-time contribution to a traditional 401(k) plan. An example of Savings Vehicle VII is a Health Savings account which can be used to fund out-of-pocket medical costs or used for retirement savings under certain conditions.

Note again, however, that the example used for each savings vehicle is for convenience only. It is the tax characteristics (i.e., deduction upon investment, rate of tax, and frequency of tax) of the vehicles and the effects on the after-tax rates of return we wish to stress.[1] Thus, instead of thinking in terms of savings vehicles, the reader could think in terms of what happens to the after-tax rate of return as we vary the taxation of the investment, holding constant the pretax rate of return on the investment. For example, consider an investment in a simple, nondividend-paying common stock. This investment meets the tax characteristics of Savings Vehicle IV—no deduction when the investment is made, income is deferred until the sale of the stock, and the rate applied is the long-term capital gains rate as long as the investor holds the stock for more than 1 year. If the company that issued the stock started paying dividends, the investment return computation would change because there would now be income taxed annually at the tax rate applicable to dividends as well as a capital gains tax upon the sale on any gain realized.

In the following discussion, we elaborate on the examples presented in the parentheses in **Table 3.1**, but we avoid technical nuances that apply to each of them. Discussing these nuances would simply cloud the general points and obscure the taxonomy we are developing in this chapter. Throughout the text, we will use the following definitions:

I = after-tax dollar amount of initial investment
R = before-tax rate of return
n = number of time periods
r = after-tax rate of return
t = tax rate applicable to ordinary income
t_{cg} = tax rate applicable to capital gains income

In **Table 3.1**, we show the after-tax accumulations per after-tax dollar of initial investment ($\$I$) of seven legal forms through which investors can hold our riskless asset. The after-tax accumulations are a function of their respective tax treatments, the before-tax rate of return on the investment, the number of periods the investment is held, and the tax rates on ordinary income and capital gains. Examples of ordinary income include wages earned from employment and interest earned on bonds. Examples of capital gains income include the realized gain on the sale of a capital asset, such as common stock or other investments.

Review of Compound Interest

An understanding of the algebraic expressions in **Table 3.1** requires an understanding of the simple principle of compound interest. If $\$I$ is invested at an after-tax rate r per period, and the principal plus interest is reinvested for n periods, the accumulation after n periods is

$$\$I[(1 + r)(1 + r) \ldots (1 + r)], \text{ or } \$I(1 + r)^n$$

[1] For example, Savings Vehicle III is labeled a mutual fund, but this mutual fund should not be confused with a common stock mutual fund. Investors in a common stock mutual fund will be taxed annually on any dividends received on stock held by the mutual fund even though such dividends are not distributed to the mutual fund investors. Similarly, the mutual fund investors will be taxed annually on any capital gains realized by the mutual fund as it trades stock in its portfolio. See Bergstresser and Poterba (2002) for a discussion of taxation of mutual funds and how this affects investors' choice of which funds to invest in.

For example, if the after-tax rate of return on investment is 12% per year, the after-tax accumulation per dollar invested for 10 years is $(1 + .12)^{10} = \$3.11$. We denote this accumulation as F (for future value of the investment). If we wish to know the annualized rate of return, r, we start by noting that $F = \$I(1 + r)^n$. Solving for r, we get $r = (F/\$I)^{1/n} - 1$. For example, if we know that a \$1 investment today accumulates to \$3.11 in 10 years, we compute the annualized rate of return of 12% per year $(\$3.11/\$1)^{(1/10)} - 1 = .12$, or 12%.

In the case of Savings Vehicle I, tax at rate t must be paid each period on the interest earned at the before-tax rate R. The after-tax interest rate earned each period r, then, is $R - tR$, or $R(1 - t)$. Substituting $R(1 - t)$ for r in the above equation yields

$$\$I[1 + R(1 - t)]^n \qquad (3.1)$$

which is the expression given in **Table 3.1**.

Investments in Savings Vehicles I and II

Savings Vehicle I Deposits into a money market savings account are not tax deductible. Earnings on the investment are typically taxed fully each year at ordinary tax rates. Savings Vehicle I is the least tax advantageous of our savings vehicles in the sense that it produces the lowest after-tax accumulation when individual tax rates are assumed to be constant over time.

Savings Vehicle II Deposits into a **single-premium deferred annuity** (SPDA) contract through an insurance company in the United States are not tax deductible. Although slightly oversimplified, the mechanics of an SPDA investment are as follows: The investor turns over cash to an insurance company, which in turn invests in interest-bearing securities. The insurance company pays no taxes on the interest it accumulates from holding the securities. The taxes on the investment earnings to the investor are deferred and taxed at ordinary income tax rates only when the investor takes money out of the contract. This annuity contract is established with a single lump-sum payment by the owner. There is no investment limit regarding how much one can invest in an SPDA.

Another example of Savings Vehicle II that might be more familiar is the nondeductible IRA. Contributions are not tax deductible (i.e., contributions are made with after-tax dollars, usually because the investor is part of a retirement plan at work and/or earns too much income to be able to deduct the contributions), and earnings are not taxed until withdrawn in retirement, at which time they are taxed as ordinary income.

The value of deferral (and, hence, the attractiveness of Vehicle II over Vehicle I) can be considerable. In Savings Vehicle II, the investment earnings compound at the before-tax rate of return, R, rather than at the after-tax rate of return, $R(1 - t)$, as in Vehicle I. Just prior to liquidation of the investment, then, each dollar invested in Vehicle II grows to $(1 + R)^n$. Tax at rate t is paid only on the earnings at the end of time period n when the account is liquidated, $(1 + R)^n - 1$. This leaves the investor with

$$\$I(1 + R)^n - t[\$I(1 + R)^n - \$I]$$

where the first term is the pretax accumulation and the second term is the tax due on the earnings. This equation can be simplified to

$$\$I(1 + R)^n - t\$I(1 + R)^n + t\$I = \$I(1 + R)^n(1 - t) + t\$I \qquad (3.2)$$

which is the expression given for Savings Vehicle II in **Table 3.1**. Another way to understand this result is to note that the first term, $\$I(1 + R)^n (1 - t)$, calculates the tax due on the entire accumulation at the end of n, including tax on the initial investment. The last term, $t\$I$, adds this tax back to arrive at the correct after-tax accumulation, where only the cumulative earnings on the initial investment are taxed. In other words, the original investment is not taxed again when withdrawn because there was not a deduction up front with this vehicle.

In **Table 3.2**, we illustrate the after-tax accumulation and the after-tax annualized rate of return achieved by investing in Savings Vehicles I and II for different holding periods, assuming that $R =$ 7% and $t = 30\%$. The after-tax accumulations are plotted in **Figure 3.1**. The after-tax rate of return on

Table 3.2 After-Tax Accumulation per Dollar Invested and Rates of Return for Different Holding Periods for Savings Vehicles I and II When $R = 7\%$ and $t = 30\%$, Assuming Constant Tax Rates

Holding Period (*n* years):	1	5	10	20	40	100
After-Tax Accumulation ($)						
Savings Vehicle						
I	1.05	1.27	1.61	2.60	6.78	119.55
II	1.05	1.28	1.68	3.01	10.78	607.70
After-Tax Rates of Return per Period (%)						
Savings Vehicle						
I	4.90	4.90	4.90	4.90	4.90	4.90
II	4.90	5.09	5.31	5.66	6.12	6.62

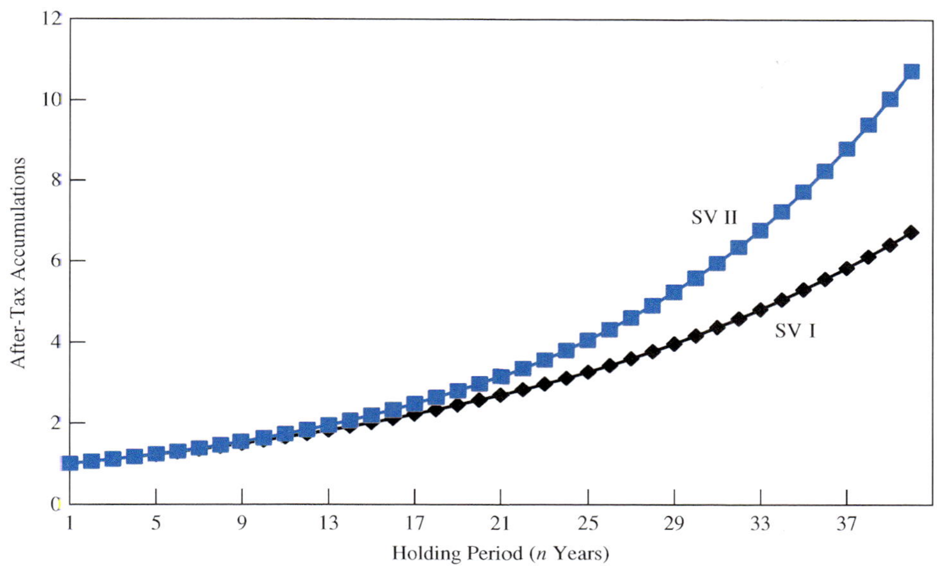

FIGURE 3.1 After-Tax Accumulations for Savings Vehicles I and II: $R = 7\%$, $t = 30\%$

Savings Vehicle I, a money market account, would be 7% × (1 – .30) = 4.9% per year after tax. This is true no matter how long the investment horizon is. In contrast, the after-tax rate of return on Savings Vehicle II, an SPDA, changes with its holding period. To calculate the after-tax rate of return per year on Savings Vehicle II, we must first find the after-tax accumulation for a given holding period. Let us suppose that an investor deposits $1 in Savings Vehicle II for 5 years. This $1 accumulates to $1.28 after tax (as shown in **Table 3.2**, with a holding period of 5 years). To show how $1.28 was derived, note that an investment of $1 for 5 years at 7% grows to $\$1(1.07)^5$, or $1.40 before tax. At the end of 5 years, on withdrawing the accumulated sum from the account, tax is owed on the amount withdrawn in excess of the initial investment. In this example, the excess is equal to $.40, and the tax on the excess is .30 × $.40, or $.12, leaving $1.28 after tax, of $1.40 – $.12.

Alternatively, using Equation 3.2 , we can derive the same after-tax dollar amount directly:

$$\$1(1.07)^5(1 - .30) + \$.30 = (\$1.40 \times .70) + \$.30 = \$1.28$$

Notice that, except for investment horizons of only one period (when an SPDA becomes equivalent to a money market account), the after-tax accumulation in an SPDA (Vehicle II) always exceeds that in a money market account (Vehicle I). Remember, we are assuming here that the taxpayer faces constant across-time tax rates. Moreover, the longer the holding period, the greater the difference in the accumulation. After 40 years, for example, $1 accumulates to $10.78 after tax in an SPDA, or 59% more than the $6.78 in a money market account.

The after-tax annual rates of return are shown in the bottom panel of **Table 3.2**. For example, after 5 years, an investment of $1 in Vehicle I grows to $1.27, which translates to an annual rate of return of $(1.27)^{(1/5)} - 1$, or 4.9%. All the after-tax annualized rates of return are 4.9% in a money market savings account, but these rates increase in an SPDA with the number of holding periods. In fact, as the number of periods becomes large, the after-tax rate of return per period approaches the before-tax rate of 7%.

Although 7% is equal to the before-tax rate of return, we must be careful not to conclude that a long-term investment in an SPDA is *equivalent* to achieving tax exemption on investment returns. Consider that as n grows very large, the accumulation from investing in an SPDA *approaches* $(1 - t)$ (or 70% in our example) of the accumulation from investing tax-free at rate R per period. The reason is that as the investment horizon becomes very large, nearly all the value in the SPDA is interest (the original dollar deposited becomes relatively unimportant over long investment periods), and when the SPDA is cashed out, the earnings (which represent almost the entire contract when n is very large) will be taxed fully at ordinary rates.[2] To illustrate, suppose $n = 40$ years and you invest at 7% tax-free per year ($R = .07$). The investment will accumulate to $(1 + .07)^{40}$ = $14.97. Compare this to the accumulation of $10.78 reported in **Table 3.2** for an SPDA invested for 40 years with $R = .07$ and $t =$ 30%. Note that $10.78 is 72% of $14.97 or close to $(1 - t)$, where $t = 30\%$, of $14.97 (it is not equal to because of the +.30 added back in the SPDA calculation in **Table 3.2**).

Hybrid Savings Vehicles

Although not listed in **Table 3.1**, certain savings vehicles permit tax deferral on only a part of the earnings until the investment is liquidated. Previously untaxed earnings are then taxed at ordinary rates. This savings vehicle is taxed as a hybrid of Vehicles I and II. For example, consider an investment in a dividend-paying common stock. There would be income taxed annually at the tax rate applicable to dividends as well as a capital gains tax upon the sale on any gain realized. The after-tax return available through this hybrid vehicle will always be between that available in Vehicle I (no deferral) and Vehicle II (100% deferral). Certain trusts can also give rise to this hybrid tax treatment.[3] Still another example is a contingent interest bond, where part of the interest is paid at maturity as a function of some performance index.

Differences in After-Tax Accumulations in Savings Vehicles I and II as a Function of Pretax Rates of Return

The advantage of an SPDA over a money market account increases with the level of pretax rates of return. For example, if R were 12% rather than 7%, Vehicle I would accumulate to $5.02 in 20 years, and Vehicle II would accumulate to $7.05 for each dollar invested. Vehicle II returns just over 40% more than Vehicle I when $R = 12\%$, whereas **Table 3.2** indicates that Vehicle II beats Vehicle I by less than 16% ($3.01 versus $2.60) when $R = 7\%$.

Investments in Savings Vehicle III

Deposits into Vehicle III are nondeductible, as were deposits into Vehicles I and II discussed above. Unlike Vehicles I and II, however, in Savings Vehicle III, investment earnings are taxed periodically at capital gains tax rates using the following equation:

$$\$I[1 + R(1 - t_{cg})]^n \qquad (3.3)$$

There is generally a distinction between the rates at which capital gains income and ordinary income are taxed. Most countries tax capital gains at lower tax rates. Capital gains and losses arise from the

---

[2] SPDAs are available to individual taxpayers. An additional excise tax of 10% is levied if the SPDA is surrendered, in part or in whole, prior to age 59.5, unless withdrawals take the form of a life annuity. We are assuming no difference in fees and setup costs for each savings vehicle, but in reality, these fees may be very different across the different types of investments.

[3] A trust is a legal entity through which property is managed by one party for the benefit of another. For U.S. income tax purposes, the undistributed earnings of a trust are often taxed to the trust rather than to the beneficiary. The hybrid tax treatment discussed in the text can be achieved in certain cases when the tax rate of the trust is below that of the beneficiary.

sale or exchange of capital assets, including such passive investments as common stocks, bonds, and real estate. Refer to **Table 1.1** to see the history of the relative tax rates from 1981 to the present in the United States.

At this point, you need not understand the specific sources of difference between ordinary income rates and capital gains rates. You should simply be aware that, in many circumstances, the distinction is important. You should also be aware that the difference between ordinary income, and capital gains tax rates is likely to change numerous times in the future, the implications of which we address in Section 3.2.

The Vehicle III category includes arrangements where capital gain is recognized annually through mark-to-market rules or annual sale. Mark-to-market means the asset is marked up to its market value at year end and the increase or decrease in value is included in taxable income. Mark-to-market rules apply to futures contracts in the United States, where they are classified as capital assets, and where assets still held at year end are taxed *as if* they were sold at that time. The annual sale treatment would apply to certain mutual funds that invest exclusively in our fully taxable bonds and that distribute annual income by repurchasing mutual fund shares from fundholders. The share repurchase triggers capital gains treatment equal to the income on the underlying bonds held in the fund.[4]

Comparison of Savings Vehicles II and III

Savings Vehicle III may be more or less attractive than Savings Vehicle II depending on n, the length of time the investment is held, and t_{cg}, the tax rate on capital gains. For example, if $t_{cg} = 0$, Vehicle III always dominates Vehicle II, even for $n = 1$. In this case, the returns on the investment are tax exempt. For $0 < t_{cg} < t$, Vehicle III dominates Vehicle II for short investment horizons, but Vehicle II dominates Vehicle III for long investment horizons.

Assume, for example, that $t_{cg} = .5t$; that is, the capital gains rate is half the ordinary rate. At the end of year 1, then, \$1 grows to $[1 + R(1 - .5t)]$. When $R = 7\%$ and $t = 30\%$ (implying $t_{cg} = 15\%$), the after-tax return is 5.95% (or $7\%[1 - .5 \times 30\%]$) per year. This return exceeds the money market savings account return by 1.05% per year (or $5.95\% - 7\%[1 - 30\%]$). The 15% tax rate reduction on capital gains (relative to ordinary income) multiplied by the 7% pretax return yields the 1.05% after-tax return difference. In this example, earning 5.95% per year after tax in Savings Vehicle III dominates the after-tax return from investing in SPDAs (Savings Vehicle II) for holding periods of up to 31 years. Beyond 31 years, SPDAs provide the superior after-tax investment returns. Specifically, for $n = 31$ years, the SPDA earns 5.95% per year, which equals the annual after-tax return on the mutual fund, and for $n = 32$ years, the SPDA earns 5.97%.

Investments in Savings Vehicle IV

In Savings Vehicle IV, as with the preceding vehicles, deposits are not tax deductible. However, the tax on the earnings is deferred and taxed at capital gains rates when the investment is liquidated. An example of this type of vehicle that can invest in a bond in the United States is not obvious at this point in time. Such vehicles have existed in the past and do exist in other countries. For example, investments in the common stock of an investment company located in a tax-haven country (i.e., one in which the tax rate is near 0%)[5] and bond investments held by corporations in tax-haven countries.[6] The equation to determine earnings for the vehicle is

$$\$I(1+R)^n(1-t_{cg}) + t_{cg}\$I \tag{3.4}$$

[4] See Toder and Viard (2016) for a proposal to replace the corporate income tax with mark to market at the shareholder level.

[5] This opportunity is no longer available for U.S. investors in companies that invest only in passive investments, such as stocks and bonds. These companies are classified as "passive foreign investment companies" and income is *de facto* taxed as earned at ordinary tax rates (as Savings Vehicle I). This opportunity still exists, however, for investors residing in a number of other countries.

[6] The corporation holding bonds in tax-haven countries must be engaged in real economic activities, rather than just holding passive investments, if the U.S. shareholder is to qualify for Vehicle IV tax treatment. For the qualifying corporation, interest income is tax free to the tax-haven corporation. For U.S. shareholders, income is subject to capital gains taxation when shares are sold or when the corporation is liquidated, as long as the corporation is not a so-called "controlled foreign corporation"—that is, it does not have five U.S. shareholders that together own more than 50% of the common stock.

Note from this equation that the accumulation in Vehicle IV is similar to that in Vehicle II except that income from Vehicle IV is taxed at the more favorable capital gains rate t_{cg} rather than at the ordinary rate t. Vehicle IV is superior to Vehicles II and III except for special cases: $t_{cg} = 0$ (capital gains are tax exempt, as they have been for many taxpayers in a number of countries) and $t_{cg} = t$ (capital gains are taxed at ordinary rates as in the United States 1988–1990). When $t_{cg} = 0$, Vehicles III and IV both yield after-tax returns equal to before-tax rates of return (7% in our example). When $t_{cg} = t$, Vehicle IV becomes equivalent to an SPDA (i.e., Vehicle II). **Table 3.3** illustrates the superiority of Vehicle IV over Vehicles I and II when capital gains are taxed at half the ordinary rates. The after-tax accumulations are plotted in **Figure 3.2**.

Table 3.3 After-Tax Accumulation per Dollar Invested and Rates of Return for Different Holding Periods for Savings Vehicles I, II, and IV When $R = 7\%$, $t_{cg} = .5t$, and $t = 30\%$, Assuming Constant Tax Rates

Holding Period (n Years):	5	10	20	40	100
After-Tax Accumulation ($)					
Savings Vehicle					
I	1.27	1.61	2.60	6.78	119.55
II	1.28	1.68	3.01	10.78	607.70
IV	1.34	1.82	3.44	12.88	737.71
After-Tax Rates of Return per Period (%)					
Savings Vehicle					
I	4.90	4.90	4.90	4.90	4.90
II	5.09	5.31	5.66	6.12	6.62
IV	6.06	6.18	6.37	6.60	6.83

FIGURE 3.2 After-Tax Accumulations for Savings Vehicles I, II, and IV, $R = 7\%$, $t = 30\%$, $t_{cg} = 15\%$

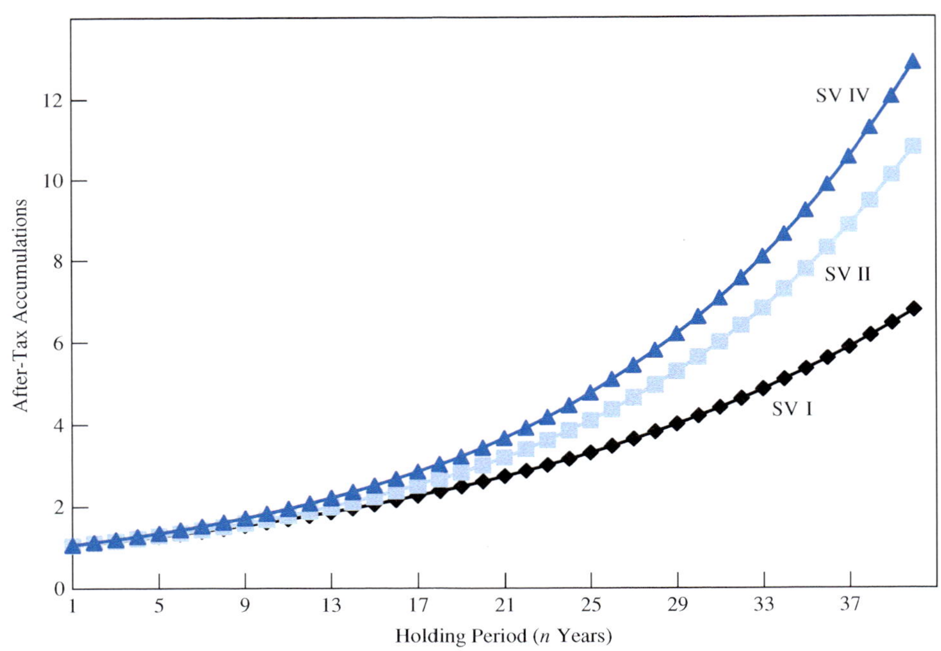

Investments in Savings Vehicle V

Deposits into Savings Vehicle V accounts are not tax deductible, but the earnings on the investment are entirely tax exempt. Equation 3.5 shows how to calculate the after-tax accumulation for this vehicle:

$$\$I(1+R)^n \tag{3.5}$$

An example of this investment vehicle is the 529 college savings plan. After-tax dollars are contributed and for tax years after December 31, 2001, distributions are tax free provided they are used for qualified college-related education expenses, including college tuition, room and board, fees, books, and certain costs of computers. The Tax Cuts and Jobs Act of 2017 (TCJA) added an additional allowable expense—up to $10,000 in tuition at private K-12 schools.

A second example is the Coverdell Education Savings Account, where distributions to fund education-related (not just college) expenses are tax free. Contributions, however, are limited to $2,000 per beneficiary per year.[7] A third example is Roth retirement accounts, such as Roth IRAs and Roth 401(k)s, both discussed below. A final example is the savings portion of a whole life (or universal life) insurance contract. A whole life policy consists of term (or pure) insurance plus a savings account. Earnings on bonds held in the savings account are tax exempt, so the pretax return is also equal to the after-tax return. Insurance companies typically invest the savings portion of the portfolio in ordinary interest-bearing securities.[8]

Note that the after-tax accumulation for Savings Vehicle V dominates that for Savings Vehicles I through IV as long as the capital gains tax rate is not 0%. In the special case of tax exemption for capital gains income, Vehicles III and IV generate exactly the same after-tax accumulations as Vehicle V.

Investments in Savings Vehicle VI

In Savings Vehicle VI, the investment is tax deductible, and investment earnings are tax deferred. Equation 3.6 determines the after-tax accumulation in this vehicle:

$$\left[\frac{\$I}{(1-t)}\right](1+R)^n(1-t) \quad \text{or } \$I(1+R)^n \tag{3.6}$$

An example is a defined contribution pension plan. Although contributions to the plan are tax deductible and earnings on investments in the plan are not taxed, distributions from the plan are fully taxable to the pensioner and at ordinary income tax rates.[9]

Each dollar deposited into the pension fund grows to $(1 + R)^n$ dollars in n periods before the pension assets are distributed to the taxpayer and to $(1 + R)^n(1 - t)$ dollars after tax if the entire accumulation is taxed at rate t at time n when it is withdrawn. Note that earnings in a pension account are taxed as ordinary income when withdrawn, even if the investment in the account generated capital gains or were tax exempt if the pension invested in tax-exempt municipal bonds. This taxation raises the question as to what types of assets taxpayers should put in their pension accounts. We defer this question to Chapter 9, where we discuss pensions in greater detail. We are also assuming here for simplicity that the earnings in the pension account are taken as a lump-sum payment and not spread out as an annuity. An additional complicating issue for the pension account is that there are contribution limits, such that one can only contribute up to a certain amount and get a deduction. These limits become important when comparing alternative investments.

Because each dollar invested in the pension fund costs only $(1 - t)$ dollars after tax, the after-tax accumulation per after-tax dollar invested can be shown as follows when tax rates are constant over time:

$$\frac{\$1}{(1-t)}(1+R)^n(1-t) = (1+R)^n$$

[7] And the modified adjusted gross income of the contributor to the account must be less than $220,000 if filing a joint return. For additional discussion of education savings accounts, see http://www.savingforcollege.com/intro_to_esas/ and https://www.irs.gov/publications/p970.

[8] If the insurance policy is surrendered prior to death, a portion of the interest may be taxable as ordinary income. In particular, if withdrawals from the policy exceed the premiums paid into the policy, including both the savings and the insurance components of the premiums, the excess is taxed as ordinary income. In this case, the insurance policy becomes an example of Savings Vehicle II. Why? Because only a portion of the interest income is taxable (i.e., only that portion of the interest that exceeds the term insurance premiums), and even this is taxable only when the policy is surrendered for cash.

[9] We initially ignore here the penalties for early withdrawal from pension plans (i.e., a 10% nondeductible excise tax penalty on withdrawal before age 59.5).

When tax rates are constant over time, Vehicles V and VI are equivalent; that is, pension savings are equivalent to tax exemption. Think of the pension fund as a tax-free partnership with the government. For every $(1 - t)$ dollars you invest in the partnership, your partner (the government) invests t dollars. Collectively, the partnership has $1 invested. This dollar grows at rate R each period for n periods. Before liquidating, the partnership has accumulated $(1 + R)^n$ dollars. You are entitled to a fraction $1 - t$ of the partnership assets, and your partner takes the remaining fraction, t. So, you take home $(1 - t)(1 + R)^n$ dollars on an initial investment of $(1 - t)$ dollars. Your return per dollar invested is simply $(1 + R)^n$.

Savings Vehicle VII

With Savings Vehicle VII, the investment is tax deductible and investment earnings are tax exempt if used for qualified medical expenses. Equation 3.7 shows the calculation for this vehicle:

$$\left[\frac{\$I}{(1-t)}\right](1+R)^n \tag{3.7}$$

An example is a health savings account (HSA). HSAs are tax-advantaged savings accounts intended to help individuals pay out-of-pocket medical expenses. To contribute to an HSA, the taxpayer must have a high-deductible health plan (HDHP), have no other health insurance that is not a HDHP, cannot be enrolled in any part of Medicare, and cannot be claimed as a dependent on someone else's tax return.[10] The taxpayer also cannot contribute to a flexible spending account in the same year they contribute to an HSA.[11] HSA contributions limits vary depending on the taxpayer's situation. For example, in 2018, the contribution limit is $3,450 for a single taxpayer and $6,950 for a family. If the taxpayer is 55 years old or older, the limits are increased by $1,000. The funds can be withdrawn tax free as long as they are used to pay for qualified medical expenses.[12] HSAs can be carried over from year-to-year—they are not required to be forfeited if not used. However, if HSA funds are used for expenses other than qualified medical expenses when withdrawn prior to age 65, a 20% penalty is applied.

HSAs have been available since 2004. A report from the Employee Benefit Research Institute (EBRI) in 2017 found that in 2016, there were an estimated 20.2–22.6 million policyholders and their dependents enrolled in a high-deductible, HSA-eligible plan. The report also states, that there were an estimated 20 million HSAs at the end of 2016. Paul Fronstin (2018) reported that between 2011 and 2017, average total contributions (individual and employer) increased from $2,348 to $2,843. Overall, 66% of account holders withdrew funds—the average amount distributed was $1,725 in 2017, implying an average rollover of $1,119. In 2017, 5% of the accounts had investments other than cash.[13]

HSA plans could be used as investment vehicles to a greater degree. HSAs offer several advantages for taxpayers with the right circumstances. For taxpayers with enough other funds to cover their medical expenses prior to retirement, the funds in the HSA can be left in the HSA, invested in a portfolio of investments, and withdrawn during retirement. As is the case prior to retirement, if the funds are used for qualified medical expenses during retirement, the withdrawals are tax free. Using HSA funds to pay for medical expenses in retirement is a very tax efficient way to fund these costs, especially given the tax deduction upon contribution.

If the funds are used for expenses other than qualified medical expenses during retirement, the taxpayer will be taxed on the withdrawals. But if the taxpayer is over age 65, he or she will avoid the

[10] Additional rules when the taxpayer is 65 years of age or older are beyond the scope of this book.

[11] A flexible spending account (FSA) is an account where taxpayers can set aside funds on a pre-tax basis to cover medical expenses. The contribution limit on FSAs in 2018 is $2,650. Funds in these accounts must be used for medical expenses or the funds will be forfeit. Generally, the taxpayer must use the funds by the end of the plan year – the "use it or lose it" rule. However there are small exceptions, for example a carryover option (to carryover $500 to the next year) and a grace period (of two and one-half months after the end of the plan year to use funds).

[12] Qualified medical costs include a variety of costs such as co-payments, dental expenses, vision care, prescription medicines, a portion of premiums for long-term care insurance, hearing aids, and other costs. In addition, qualified medical costs include in-home nursing care, retirement community fees for lifetime care, long-term care services, nursing home fees, and some other related costs.

[13] Fronstin, Paul. Employee Benefit Research Institute (EBRI) Issue Brief, "Trends in Health Savings Account Balances, Contributions, Distributions, and Investments, 2011–2017: Estimates from the EBRI HSA Database" October 29, 2018.

20% penalty. In this case, the HSA becomes a Savings Vehicle VI and like a 401(k) account. However, one benefit of the HSA relative to the 401(k) account is that HSAs do not have rules for required minimum distributions (RMDs) starting at age 70.5.

To summarize, we compare all SVs under the stated assumptions, including constant tax rates, in **Table 3.4**.

Table 3.4 After-Tax Accumulation per Dollar Invested and Rates of Return for Different Holding Periods for Savings Vehicles I–VII When $R = 7\%$, $t_{cg} = .5t$, and $t = 30\%$, Assuming Tax Rates Are Constant and Ignoring Contribution Limits

Holding Period (n Years):	5	10	20	40	100
After-Tax Accumulation ($)					
Savings Vehicle					
I	1.27	1.61	2.60	6.78	119.55
II	1.28	1.68	3.01	10.78	607.70
III	1.34	1.78	3.18	10.09	323.67
IV	1.34	1.82	3.44	12.88	737.71
V	1.40	1.97	3.87	14.97	867.72
VI	1.40	1.97	3.87	14.97	867.72
VII*	2.00	2.81	5.53	21.39	1,239.59
After-Tax Rates of Return per Period (%)					
Savings Vehicle					
I	4.90	4.90	4.90	4.90	4.90
II	5.09	5.31	5.66	6.12	6.62
III	5.95	5.95	5.95	5.95	5.95
IV	6.06	6.18	6.37	6.60	6.83
V	7.00	7.00	7.00	7.00	7.00
VI	7.00	7.00	7.00	7.00	7.00
VII*	14.91	10.89	8.93	7.96	7.38

* Assuming these funds are used for qualified medical expenses

Dominance Relations and Summary Comments

Table 3.4 presents after-tax accumulation and after-tax returns for the seven savings vehicles under the assumptions we have stated above. One result we have not discussed may be surprising to many: The annual after-tax rate of return for SV VII declines the longer the holding period. Indeed, as the holding period increases, the annual after tax rate of return converges to that of SVs V and VI. The reason is that when the holding period is short (e.g., $n = 5$ in **Table 3.4**), the initial deduction value is a larger proportion of the ending value (i.e., the return). Thus the after-tax rate of return is larger (in our example, greater than 7%). As time goes on, this initial deduction value becomes less important relative to the rest of the investment such that the rate of return converges to 7% in our example. Note that if the tax rate is larger when the contribution is made, then it takes longer for the after-tax rate of return to converge to that of Savings Vehicles V and VI, and if the tax rate is smaller, then convergence happens more quickly. Indeed, if the tax rate is zero when the contribution is made, the after-tax rate of return is equal to that of Savings Vehicles V and VI in every year.

Up to this point, we have demonstrated that investors realize different after-tax rates of return on identical assets held through different legal forms (i.e., savings vehicles). We have shown several strict dominance relations among the savings vehicles—that is, investors would always prefer to avoid some of the savings vehicles. In the absence of frictions and restrictions, we would never observe such tax-disfavored savings vehicles as ordinary money market savings. And yet, in the real world, money market savings command a larger share of our savings than most tax-favored forms of savings. The reasons, as we suggested earlier, stem largely from frictions and restrictions. For example, money market funds offer investors access to their funds at any time (i.e., liquidity) as opposed to retirement accounts, which often lock up the savings until retirement.

3.2 CHANGES IN TAX RATES OVER TIME

In this section, we relax the assumption of constant tax rates through time. Note, however, that for pedagogical reasons, we assume here that future tax rates are known. We relax this assumption in later chapters. Even without frictions and restrictions, the dominance relations derived in Section 3.1 disappear when we introduce intertemporal changes in tax rates. In such a setting, Vehicles V and VI are no longer equivalent; tax-exempt saving through a Roth account is no longer equivalent to saving through a pension account of the SV VI type. In particular, when tax rates are rising over time, SV VI (i.e., non-Roth) pensions (and single-premium deferred annuities) become less attractive, and when tax rates are falling over time, they become more attractive.

Vehicle V returns $(1 + R)^n$ irrespective of tax rates, but Vehicle VI returns

$$\left(\frac{\$I}{1 - t_0}\right)(1 + R)^n(1 - t_n) \tag{3.8}$$

where the subscript on each tax rate refers to the time at which taxes are saved or paid. A subscript of 0 indicates the tax rate in the period when the contribution is made, assumed here to be the current period, and the subscript n indicates the tax rate in the future period n when withdrawals are made. When $t_n > t_0$ (i.e., tax rates in retirement at time n are relatively high), Vehicle V is superior. Conversely, if $t_n < t_0$ (i.e., tax rates today are relatively high), Vehicle VI is superior. When retirement planning, there are generally two ways in which tax rates can change. First, the tax law can change making rates higher or lower. Second, the rate for the taxpayer can change, even if the law is constant. For example, many people are in a higher tax bracket in their prime earning years than in their retirement years, when their income is often lower.

As mentioned previously, we can view a pension plan as a tax-exempt partnership with the government in which the taxpayer puts up a fraction $(1 - t_0)$ of the capital in exchange for a fraction $(1 - t_n)$ of the liquidation proceeds from the partnership. The taxpayer does better than tax exemption when t_n is lower than t_0 and worse than tax exemption when t_n is higher. For example, consider a situation faced by many high-income taxpayers following the passage of the Tax Reform Act of 1986. Suppose the marginal tax rate in 1986 was 50%, but the rate was expected to fall to 28% in retirement. With this configuration of tax rates, a pension provides an after-tax accumulation of 44% more than complete tax exemption! Using Equation 3.8 for a \$1 investment (i.e., I = \$1), we get the following:

$$\frac{1}{(1 - t_0)}(1 + R)^n(1 - t_n) = \frac{1}{(1 - .50)}(1 + R)^n(1 - .28) = 1.44(1 + R)^n$$

Conversely, in 2012, with the impending expiration of the so-called Bush tax cuts (and increasing national deficits), many high-income taxpayers, facing tax rates of 35%, expected tax rates to increase and stay high into retirement. If they expected rates to increase to 45% at the time of retirement, then pensions would accumulate as follows:

$$\frac{1}{(1 - .35)}(1 + R)^n(1 - .45) = .85(1 + R)^n$$

This is 15% *less* after tax than complete tax exemption. In this case, investing in the pension plan is exactly the same as investing in a tax-exempt insurance policy that imposes a back-end termination fee of 15% on all distributions. Note that the TCJA also reduced the top statutory tax rate, but only by

2.6 percentage points, so not as drastic as in 1986. In addition, because of the high levels of national debt as mentioned, many economists do not expect these lower rates to persist.

In fact, when tax rates are increasing, the pension plan is even worse than investing in a money market savings account over short investment horizons. If current tax rates are 35% and will increase to 45% in 5 years (i.e., $n = 5$) and $R = 7\%$, a pension investment accumulates at a rate of only 3.5% per year after tax, or 0.9 percentage points less per year than ordinary money market savings.[14]

Conversely, for $n = 10$, the after-tax return from investing in a pension plan is 5.2% per year, which is better than investing in money market savings. The best after-tax return among all the alternatives when tax rates are expected to rise in the future is the 7% available through investing in Savings Vehicle V, such as Roth IRAs or universal life insurance policies.

The best alternative among the savings vehicles depends not only on how a particular form is taxed but also on how tax rates in the future are expected to differ from current rates. Although one particular form may dominate another when tax rates remain constant, the ranking could change if tax rates increase or decrease. When we add frictions and restrictions, the rankings change further and in ways that differ across taxpayers, even when they face the same set of statutory tax rates over time.

3.3 MORE ON PENSION PLANS[14]

In this section, we provide some institutional detail on pension plans and apply the savings vehicles concepts to a comparison of deductible IRAs with Roth IRAs. Taxpayers have a variety of pension plans to use in saving for retirement. We provide the 2018 contribution limits in our discussion, but note that these limits are often increased year to year.

Employers often set up retirement plans for their employees. An example is a **401(k)** plan where the employee elects to contribute, pretax, a portion of his or her current salary to the plan, where it is invested (at the direction of the employee) and grows tax free until withdrawal. The contribution limits for such accounts (and for 403[b] plans available to public education organizations and certain nonprofits) was $18,500 ($24,500 if age 50 or higher).[16] The employer often matches the employee's pretax contributions (at a rate chosen by the employer). If the employer matches dollar for dollar, this means for every pretax dollar the employee contributes, the employer also contributes a dollar. Employees can start withdrawing from the account without penalty at 59.5 years of age and must start withdrawing at 70.5 years of age or penalties will be assessed.

Firms can also offer employees a **Roth 401(k)** plan where the employee contributes *after-tax* dollars and the earnings are exempt from future taxation. The contribution limits and withdrawal age rules are the same as those for a 401(k).[17] Employers can match the employee contributions to a Roth account, but the matching funds cannot receive Roth treatment—meaning matching contributions must be made on a pre-tax basis and the matched funds are placed in a separate, traditional 401(k) account (and distributions of matched funds are taxable when withdrawn in retirement).

For small employers, or employers wishing to avoid the complexities of the plans just discussed, there are the alternative **simplified employee pension plan (SEP)** and **savings incentive match plan for employees (SIMPLE)**. A SEP is a program in which the employer opens and contributes to IRAs for its employees up to 25 employees. For 2018, up to the maximum of the lesser of $55,000 a year or 25% of the employee's income could be contributed by the employer. A SIMPLE plan can be adopted by firms with as many as 100 employees and can be set up as an IRA for each employee. Employees are allowed to make elective contributions of up to $12,500 pretax

---

[14] After tax, the individual invests $1/(1 – .35) at a 7% rate of return for 5 years and then pays tax on the accumulated amount at a 45% rate. At the end of 5 years, the after-tax accumulation is $\$1/(1 - 35) \times (1.07)^5 \times (1 - .45) = \$1.1868$. The annualized rate of return is $(1.1868)^{(1/5)} - 1 = .0348$, or 3.5%. The 4.4% after-tax rate of return on the money market savings account is calculated as $[1 + .07(1 - .35)]^4[1 + .07(1 - .45)] = \$1.2408$, implying $r = (1.2408)^{(1/5)} - 1 = .0441$ or 4.4%.

[15] The United States is currently considering changes to retirement accounts such as offering more types of accounts, offering or requiring more annuities, and changing the age and income limitations, among other changes. At the time of this writing, the reform process is just starting.

[16] For most retirement plans, what are known as catch-up contribution limits—higher allowed contributions—apply for taxpayers over age 50.

[17] Employee contributions to both types of plans combined, 401(k) and Roth 401(k), cannot exceed the stated limits.

per year (2018 limits), which the employer matches up to a maximum of 3% of the employee's salary.[18]

Traditional Deductible IRAs

As of 2018, an eligible taxpayer may contribute up to $5,500 (or 100% of compensation if less than $5,500) per year to a **traditional deductible IRA**. If age 50 or older, the maximum annual contribution limit is $6,500. Contributions are tax deductible, and earnings in the pension account are tax deferred until the taxpayer makes withdrawals in retirement. Thus, the deductible IRA belongs to the Savings Vehicle VI category. Nonworking spouses may also contribute (up to the same limits). For taxpayers participating in a pension plan offered by their employer, the tax deductibility of the IRA contribution is phased out depending on the taxpayer's income and filing status. For example, for 2018, the phase-out range for joint filers is between $101,000 and $121,000. That is, if the tax payer earns more than $121,000, none of the contribution is tax deductible.[19]

Nondeductible IRAs

If the taxpayer does not or cannot make a deductible contribution to a traditional IRA account because of the income limitations, the taxpayer may make nondeductible contributions of up to $5,500 per year (2018). The earnings in the account are tax deferred until the taxpayer makes withdrawals in retirement. Thus, the **nondeductible IRA** belongs to the Savings Vehicle II category.

Roth IRAs

As of 1998, taxpayers can contribute to a **Roth IRA**. Contributions are not tax deductible, but withdrawals are tax free if taken after age 59.5. That is, earnings in a Roth IRA are not tax deferred but tax exempt (provided the withdrawals meet certain conditions). Note that there is no requirement that investors start withdrawing funds from a Roth IRA at age 70.5 as there is with many other retirement accounts. The Roth IRA fits in the Savings Vehicle V category. Taxpayers can contribute up to $5,500 ($6,500 if age 50 or older, 2018 limits), with the contribution limit phased out depending on the taxpayer's income and filing status. For example, in 2018, the limit is phased out for joint filers with income between $189,000 and $199,000. That is, joint filers with income above $199,000 cannot contribute to a Roth IRA. The $5,500 limit is reduced by the amount, if any, the taxpayer contributes to a deductible IRA.

Although high-income taxpayers cannot directly contribute to a Roth IRA, they can make what are known as "backdoor" Roth IRA contributions in which the taxpayer contributes to a non-deductible traditional IRA and then immediately converts the account to a Roth IRA. As of 2010, there are no income limits on Roth IRA conversions. If there is a gain in the account between the time of the traditional IRA contribution and the conversion, that gain is taxable. But if the conversion is done nearly simultaneously, the gain is zero, and the taxpayer has just made a Roth IRA contribution via the back door![20]

Comparison of the Deductible and Roth IRAs—New Contributions

As indicated in **Table 3.1**, the Roth IRA (Savings Vehicle V) will accumulate over n years to $\$I(1 + R)^n$, and the deductible IRA (Savings Vehicle VI) will accumulate as follows:

$$\frac{\$I}{(1 - t_0)}(1 + R)^n(1 - t_n) = \$I^* \times (1 + R)^n(1 - t_n)$$

[18] For additional detail on various retirement plan options, please see https://www.irs.gov/retirement-plans/choosing-a-retirement-plan-retirement-plan-options. Note that there are additional types of plans available for the self-employed. For additional information on these plans, see http://www.irs.gov/Retirement-Plans/Retirement-Plans-for-Self-Employed-People and IRS Publication 560. Note that retirement plans for self-employed people were formerly referred to as "Keogh plans" after the law that first allowed unincorporated businesses to sponsor retirement plans. Because the law no longer distinguishes between corporate and other plan sponsors, the term is seldom used.

[19] For additional information on IRAs, see http://www.irs.gov/publications/p590/index.html.

[20] There are certain requirements for a backdoor Roth IRA contribution. See IRS Publication 590 and https://www.rothira.com/what-is-a-backdoor-roth-ira.

$\$I^*$ denotes pretax dollars invested (Note: In this example, we are not at the contribution limit, we discuss the case where one is at the limit below). Suppose the taxpayer wishes to contribute $1,000 of after-tax dollars to an IRA and expects no change in the current tax rate of 30% between now and retirement in 30 years, when the taxpayer plans to withdraw the funds. Assume the individual can earn 8% per year pretax in either type IRA account. The Roth IRA will accumulate to $\$1{,}000(1 + .08)^{30} = \$10{,}063$.

The deductible IRA will accumulate to $\frac{\$1{,}000}{(1-.30)}(1 + .08)^{30}(1 - .30) = \$10{,}063$. The accumulations are the same because the tax rate is expected to be unchanged between the contribution date and the withdrawal date. The government is contributing t percent of the pretax investment to the deductible IRA but then taking t percent of the accumulation. If the taxpayer expects the tax rate to increase to 35% at retirement, the deductible IRA will accumulate to $\frac{\$1{,}000}{(1-.30)}(1 + .08)^{30}(1 - .35) = \$9{,}344$. Thus, the Roth IRA is favored (disfavored) if the taxpayer expects the tax rate to be higher (lower) in retirement than the tax rate during the contribution period.

We compared alternative vehicles V and VI earlier by using the after-tax accumulation and by converting the after-tax accumulation F to an annualized rate r, or $r = (F/\$I)^{1/n} - 1$. A third way of comparing alternatives is to find the difference in the algebraic expressions and simplify, as follows:

$$\begin{aligned}
&\textbf{Roth IRA accumulation} - \textbf{IRA accumulation}\\
&= \$1{,}000(1 + R)^n - \frac{\$1{,}000}{(1 - t_0)}(1 + R)^n(1 - t_n)\\
&= \$1{,}000(1 + R)^n - \$1{,}000(1 + R)^n\left(\frac{1 - t_n}{1 - t_0}\right)\\
&= \$1{,}000(1 + R)^n\left(1 - \frac{1 - t_n}{1 - t_0}\right)
\end{aligned} \tag{3.9}$$

If the expression in Equation 3.9 is positive, the Roth IRA is preferred. We can analyze which investment alternative is preferred simply by analyzing the last term in parentheses (because the sign of the expression in Equation 3.9 depends only on the sign of the last term). Thus, as the above calculation illustrates, if $t_0 = t_n$, then the accumulations are the same (the difference in the accumulations is zero as per Equation 3.9). If $t_0 < t_n$, Equation 3.9 is positive, and the Roth IRA is preferred. For example, if $t_0 = .30$ and $t_n = .40$, the Roth IRA accumulates to $[1 - \frac{(1-.40)}{(1-.30)}] = .1428$, or 14.3% more than the deductible IRA. Finally, if $t_0 > t_n$, Equation 3.9 is negative, and the deductible IRA is preferred (because the future tax rate is lower, the government is extracting a smaller percentage than it contributed).

Next, let us compare investments when the taxpayer is contributing an amount close to or at the contribution limit for the savings vehicle. Note that a taxpayer can contribute $5,500 after tax to a Roth IRA account and only $5,500 maximum pretax to a deductible IRA account. The equivalent maximum after-tax amount depends on the taxpayer's tax rate. If the rate is 30%, the maximum $5,500 pretax contribution is equivalent to a maximum $3,850 after-tax contribution. Thus, we must be careful when comparing investments in deductible IRAs with Roth IRAs. For a valid comparison, we must have equal after-tax amounts invested in each alternative. In the previous example, this was not a problem because the taxpayer was contributing less than the maximum allowed. For the taxpayer with a tax rate of 30% wishing to contribute the maximum amount possible to either IRA, it is important to recognize the taxpayer has an additional $1,650 after tax to invest in a different vehicle if choosing the deductible IRA. In other words, contributing $5,500 to a deductible IRA provides a deduction on the taxpayer's tax return that will save $1,650 in taxes if the taxpayer's rate of tax is 30%. The taxpayer will then have this additional $1,650 to invest, but investing it in an IRA is not allowed because the taxpayer is at the contribution limit for IRAs. For comparison purposes, we will assume this excess is invested in an SPDA. (The reader can conduct the comparison assuming the excess is invested in one of the other savings vehicles listed in **Table 3.1**.) Thus, the accumulation in a deductible IRA with the excess (i.e., the tax savings) invested in an SPDA is the sum of the accumulation in each account (the sum of Savings Vehicles V and II):

Deductible IRA + SPDA accumulation

$$\frac{\$5{,}500(1 - t_0)}{(1 - t_0)}(1 + R)^n(1 - t_n) + \$5{,}500t_0[(1 + R)^n(1 - t_n) + t_n] \tag{3.10}$$

The numerator in the first term—$5,500(1 − t_0)—equals the after-tax investment amount, and the denominator grosses the amount up to the pretax quantity because the contribution is deductible. Alternatively stated, because the two (1 − t_0) terms cancel out, the $5,500 is in pretax dollars.

Again, to compare an investment in a Roth IRA with the deductible IRA + SPDA alternative, we can find the difference in the accumulations and simplify as follows:

Roth IRA accumulation − Deductible IRA + SPDA accumulation

$$= \$5{,}500(1 + R)^n - \{\$5{,}500(1 + R)^n(1 - t_n) + \$5{,}500t_0[(1 + R)^n(1 - t_n) + t_n]\} \tag{3.11}$$
$$= \$5{,}500(1 + R)^n t_n - \$5{,}500t_0[(1 + R)^n(1 - t_n) + t_n]$$

The Roth IRA is preferred if Equation 3.11 is positive. If the taxpayer's tax rate is expected to remain constant throughout retirement, then Equation 3.11 simplifies to $\$5{,}500t^2[(1 + R)^n - 1]$, which is greater than zero, so the Roth IRA is favored. The math shows that the Roth IRA earns R% on the entire $5,500. However, in the deductible IRA + SPDA alternative, only the after-tax equivalent of the deductible IRA component, $5,500(1 − .30) = $3,850, earns R%, whereas the SPDA component, $5,500(.30) = $1,650, earns less than R%.

If $t_0 < t_n$, then Equation 3.11 > 0 and the Roth IRA is favored. If $t_0 > t_n$, then Equation 3.11 is positive or negative depending on the relative magnitude of the two tax rates.

The algebra in this example can be easily adapted to compare the employee's choice between a traditional 401(k) and the new Roth 401(k) plan where the maximum investment of $5,500 is replaced with $18,500 (for 2018). If the employer's matching contribution is the same in both cases and is made to a pretax account, then the employer's contribution total can be ignored in this comparison because it is the same across the two alternatives. **Table 3.5** presents the after-tax accumulations and after-tax rates of return assuming the maximum contribution of $18,500 to each 401(k), with the excess amount under the traditional 401(k) invested in an SPDA (Savings Vehicle II account). Panel A sets the holding period to 35 years and examines the effect on accumulations and returns, varying the tax rate the employee will face in retirement. Because the holding period is constant, the Roth accumulation is constant across the tax rates. As the tax rate in retirement declines, the accumulations and after-tax rates of return increase for the traditional 401(k) such that when the tax rate in retirement, t_n, is 25%, the after-tax accumulation in the traditional 401(k) exceeds the Roth accumulation. Panel B sets the tax rate in retirement to 35% (the same as the tax rate in the contribution period) and varies the holding period. Because the tax rates are the same in the contribution and retirement periods, the analysis in Equation 3.11 shows that the Roth dominates regardless of the holding period.

Comparison of the Deductible and Roth IRAs—the Conversion Decision

Taxpayers with balances in traditional IRAs (deductible or nondeductible) can convert the IRA to a Roth IRA. The amount converted, less any basis, is included in the taxpayer's taxable income in the year of the conversion. To analyze the decision to convert, we assume that any taxes due on the conversion are paid by non-IRA funds, the taxpayer has a zero basis in the IRA (the IRA is a deductible traditional IRA), and the tax payment avoided by not converting is invested in an SPDA. If the taxpayer does not convert to a Roth IRA, the deductible IRA will accumulate to

$$\textbf{Deductible IRA accumulation} = V(1 + R)^n(1 - t_n) \tag{3.12}$$

where V is the market value of the accumulation in the deductible IRA at the decision date.

Table 3.5 After-Tax Accumulations of Maximum Allowed Contribution to Roth 401(k) and Traditional 401(k): Contribution $18,500, $R = 8\%$, and $t_0 = 35\%$. Tax Savings from the Traditional 401(k) Account Are Invested in Savings Vehicle II (SPDA).

Panel A: Holding period $n = 35$ years, allowing t_n to vary.

Tax Rate in Period n	0.45	0.40	0.35	0.30	0.25	0.20	0.15
After-Tax Accumulation ($)							
Roth 401(k)	$273,528.87	$273,528.87	$273,528.87	$273,528.87	$273,528.87	$273,528.87	$273,528.87
Traditional 401(k)	$206,008.94	$224,148.38	$242,287.83	$260,427.28	$278,566.73	$296,706.18	$314,845.63
Difference	$ 67,519.93	$ 49,380.49	$ 31,241.04	$ 13,101.59	$ (5,037.86)	$(23,177.31)	$(41,316.76)
After-Tax Rates of Return per Period (%)							
Roth 401(k)	8.00%	8.00%	8.00%	8.00%	8.00%	8.00%	8.00%
Traditional 401(k)	7.13%	7.39%	7.63%	7.85%	8.06%	8.25%	8.43%

Panel B: $t_n = 35\%$, allowing holding period to vary

Holding Period (n):	10	20	25	30	35	40	50
After-Tax Accumulation ($)							
Roth 401(k)	$ 39,940.11	$ 86,227.71	$126,696.79	$186,159.15	$273,528.87	$401,903.65	$867,679.83
Traditional 401(k)	$ 37,313.70	$ 77,931.06	$113,442.68	$165,620.91	$242,287.83	$354,936.70	$763,355.30
Difference	$ 2,626.41	$ 8,296.64	$ 13,254.11	$ 20,538.25	$ 31,241.04	$ 46,966.95	$104,024.53
After-Tax Rates of Return per Period (%)							
Roth 401(k)	8.00%	8.00%	8.00%	8.00%	8.00%	8.00%	8.00%
Traditional 401(k)	7.27%	7.46%	7.52%	7.58%	7.63%	7.66%	7.72%

With a conversion, the after-tax accumulation in a Roth IRA will be

$$\textbf{Converted Roth IRA accumulation} = V(1+R)^n - Vt_0[(1+R)^n(1-t_n)+t_n] \quad (3.13)$$

The first term in Equation 3.13 is the accumulation in the Roth IRA (the entire amount V is invested in the Roth IRA because we assume taxes are paid from non IRA-converted funds). The second term in Equation 3.13 is the tax due on the conversion plus the lost SPDA earnings on the tax paid. To determine whether the taxpayer should convert, we subtract the deductible IRA accumulation from the Roth accumulation:[21]

$$\text{Roth IRA} - \text{deductible IRA} = V(1+R)^n - Vt_0[(1+R)^n(1-t_n)+t_n] - V(1+R)^n(1-t_n)$$

[21] It is evident from the math that it does not matter whether the second term in Equation 3.13—representing the taxes due and the earnings lost on the taxes—is subtracted from the Roth accumulation or added to the deductible IRA accumulation alternative.

This equation simplifies to:[22]

$$V(1 + R)^n - Vt_0[(1 + R)^n(1 - t_n) + t_n] - V(1 + R)^n + V(1 + R)^n t_n = V(1 + R)^n t_n - Vt_0[(1 + R)^n(1 - t_n) + t_n] \quad (3.14)$$

If $t_0 = t_n = t$, then Equation 3.14 simplifies to $Vt^2\,[(1 + R)^n - 1]$, which is greater than zero, and so the conversion is tax preferred. If $t_0 < t_n$, then Equation 3.14 > 0 and, again, the conversion is preferred. Finally, if $t_0 > t_n$, then Equation 3.14 is positive, zero, or negative, depending on R, n, and the relative change between t_0 and t_n. Specific cases can be easily analyzed using Equation 3.14, or the sensitivity of the decision can be assessed via spreadsheet analysis. As mentioned at the start of the comparisons, Equations 3.10 and 3.13—and the equations derived from them—can be easily modified to incorporate alternative investment vehicles, such as a money market account or mutual fund.

Summary of Key Points

1. Numerous legal forms are available for savings. We considered a number of alternative savings vehicles that were distinguished by the tax treatment of investment returns. Although investments made in most savings vehicles do not give rise to immediate tax deductions, investments in many types of retirement accounts do. And although the earnings on some investments are taxed annually, the earnings on others are partially or fully tax deferred or may be tax exempt altogether. Earnings in some vehicles are taxed at ordinary rates, whereas earnings in other vehicles attract tax at capital gains rates. Because of these differing tax treatments, the after-tax accumulation and rate of return from holding a fully taxable bond in each of these savings vehicles varies dramatically across the alternatives.
2. With constant tax rates, pension accounts (defined contribution savings accounts) and Roth-style retirement accounts, Section 529 college savings accounts, and the tax-exempt portion of savings in insurance contracts dominate money market plans and such other savings vehicles as single-premium deferred annuities.
3. Without nontax factors (e.g., liquidity), frictions, and restrictions, the dominant returns available from some forms would result in tax arbitrage opportunities. Investors would save only through the dominant forms.
4. If tax brackets change through time, the dominance relations can change. For example, when tax rates are increasing over time, money market accounts (the least tax-advantageous form when tax rates are constant) can provide higher after-tax rates of return than pension accounts (one of the most tax-advantageous forms when tax rates are constant).
5. The introduction of frictions and restrictions further alters the rankings of the alternatives. Empirically, we find that investors use all the forms we analyze.
6. There are a variety of retirement savings vehicles available to taxpayers. In addition to corporate sponsored pension plans, individuals can contribute to individual retirement accounts (IRAs) and other retirement savings accounts, subject to income limits. With many of these retirement plans, contributions are tax deductible and plan asset earnings are tax deferred until withdrawn during retirement. Exceptions are the Roth IRA, the Roth 401(k), and the nondeductible IRA: contributions to these accounts are not tax deductible, and earnings are not taxed during the life of the plan. Withdrawals from the Roth accounts are tax free, but withdrawals from the nondeductible IRA are taxed.
7. Depending on the configuration of current and future tax rates, the Roth IRA often dominates the deductible IRA even though contributions are not tax deductible. Taxpayers are allowed to convert the balances in their traditional IRAs into Roth IRAs. The conversion requires taxpayers

[22] The observant reader should notice the similarity between Equations 3.11, used when evaluating a new contribution, and Equation 3.14, used when evaluating the conversion decision. The only difference is the substitution of V, the value of the funds to be rolled over, for I, the after-tax new contribution amount.

to pay income tax on the amount converted less any basis in the IRA. Provided the tax is paid from non-IRA funds, conversion will generally be preferred if tax rates are expected to rise, but if tax rates are expected to fall in retirement, the deductible IRA will likely be preferred.

Questions

Q3-1. Identify three tax characteristics that differ among alternative savings vehicles.

Q3-2. The interest income on bonds issued by tax-exempt organizations is often exempt from federal taxation in the United States. When comparing savings vehicles, why is it inappropriate to view these bonds as perfect substitutes for such savings accounts as tax-exempt life insurance contracts?

Q3-3. With constant tax rates over time, why does a single-premium deferred annuity contract (SPDA) provide greater after-tax rates of return than a money market account? How is the difference in after-tax accumulations in these two vehicles affected by the level of interest rates? Why does the length of the holding period affect the after-tax rates of return per period for SPDAs and not money market accounts?

Q3-4. Under what circumstances is an investment that is taxed each period at capital gains rates preferred to an SPDA contract taxed at ordinary rates on investment income but only at the point of liquidation? When is Savings Vehicle IV (income deferred and taxed at capital gains rates at the point of liquidation) preferred to an SPDA?

Q3-5. Why do a Savings Vehicle VI-type pension account and a Savings Vehicle V-type retirement account provide the same after-tax rates of return if tax rates are constant over time? When comparing these two savings vehicles, is it appropriate to have the same number of dollars invested in both alternatives?

Q3-6. If tax rates are constant over time, why might a taxpayer prefer to save through a money market account rather than a pension account, a Roth IRA, or a tax-exempt insurance policy?

Q3-7. If tax rates are changing over time, do pension accounts dominate tax-exempt savings accounts?

Q3-8. Why do rising tax rates make SPDAs and pension accounts less attractive relative to ordinary money market accounts than when tax rates are falling?

Q3-9. When analyzing whether to contribute to a deductible IRA or a Roth IRA in Equation 3.11, we assumed a single lump-sum contribution ($\$I$). How would the choice change if the taxpayer were considering contributing $\$I$ every year from the current period to the last year before retirement?

Q3-10. When analyzing the conversion decision in Equation 3.14, we assumed that any tax due on the conversion would be paid in the year of the conversion. For 1998 only, the taxpayer could elect to spread the tax (more specifically, include equal portions of the conversion amount in taxable income) over 4 years. Under what conditions does this election *not* make sense?

Exercises

E3-11. A taxpayer can invest $1,000 in a money market fund that yields an annual pretax rate of return of 8% or buy an acre of land for $1,000 that appreciates at a 7% annual rate. The taxpayer plans to sell the land after 20 years and faces a 25% tax rate each year. (For purposes of this problem, ignore any risk differences between the investments.)

a. What is the after-tax accumulation at the end of 20 years from each investment?

b. What is the annualized after-tax rate of return from each investment?

(Exercise adapted from a problem written by Richard Sansing, Dartmouth College.)

E3-12. A taxpayer can invest $5,000 in a common stock that pays no dividends but appreciates at a rate of 8%. The taxpayer's tax rate is 30%. He plans to sell the stock after 30 years.

a. Find the after-tax accumulation and the annualized after-tax rate of return for this investment.

b. What would have been the annualized after-tax rate of return on the stock if there were a special tax rate of 20% on capital gains?

(Exercise adapted from a problem written by Richard Sansing, Dartmouth College.)

E3-13. A corporation can invest $10,000 in preferred stock that pays a 6% dividend and does not appreciate in price. The corporation faces a 21% tax rate. Dividends from the stock are eligible for the 50% corporate dividends received deduction. That is, the corporation has to include only 50% of the dividend in its taxable income. This results in an effective tax rate on the dividend of 10.5% (i.e., .50 x .21). Assume dividend income is reinvested in more 6% preferred stock.

a. Find the after-tax accumulation for this investment after 10 years.

b. Find the annualized after-tax rate of return on this investment after 10 years.

(Exercise adapted from a problem written by Richard Sansing, Dartmouth College.)

E3-14. Suppose a taxpayer, when 25 years old, made one tax-deductible $2,000 contribution of her after-tax salary to a deductible IRA. Her investment (taxable corporate bonds) earned a 12% annual return, and she liquidates the investment 10 years, later when she retires. Her tax rate is 35%, but she must pay an additional 10% excise tax because she liquidates the IRA before reaching age 59.5.

a. After taxes, how much cash does she have when she liquidates the IRA?

b. Was it a mistake for the taxpayer to have set up an IRA? What would she have earned had she invested her after-tax salary in the taxable corporate bonds directly instead of through an IRA?

E3-15. A taxpayer is about to receive a $1,000 bonus from his employer. He would like to put this bonus into a retirement account. He has come to you for advice as to whether he should put the $1,000 into a traditional deductible IRA or a Roth IRA. You learn that he faces a current marginal tax rate of 28% and expects to face the same rate in 40 years, when he plans to withdraw the funds at age 70. He expects to earn a pretax rate of return of 10% in either retirement account by investing the funds in corporate bonds. Advise the taxpayer as to what he should do.

E3-16. Assume the same facts presented in E3-15 with the exception that the taxpayer expects his tax rate to be 20% when he retires in 40 years. What should the taxpayer do now?

E3-17. A taxpayer wants to invest the maximum allowed in his retirement account. He has come to you for advice as to whether he should contribute to a traditional deductible IRA or a Roth IRA. You learn he faces a current marginal tax rate of 24% and expects to face the same rate in 40 years, when he plans to withdraw the funds at age 70. He expects to earn a pretax rate of return of 10% in either retirement account by investing the funds in corporate bonds. Advise the taxpayer as to what he should do. Be explicit about any assumptions you need to make when comparing the two alternative retirement accounts.

E3-18. Assume the same facts presented in E3-17 with the exception that now the taxpayer expects his tax rate to increase from its current 24% level to 35% when he retires in 40 years. Again, be explicit about any assumptions you need to make when comparing the two alternative retirement accounts.

E3-19. A taxpayer currently has $20,000 in a traditional deductible IRA. She comes to you for advice about whether to convert the $20,000 into a Roth IRA. The taxpayer faces a current tax rate of 24%, and she expects to face the same rate when she retires in 40 years. She is currently earning 12% per year pretax in the deductible IRA, and she expects to continue to earn this pretax rate of return regardless of whether she is investing in a deductible IRA or a Roth IRA. Should the taxpayer convert to a Roth IRA? Assume any taxes due on the conversion are paid from non-IRA funds. Be explicit about any assumptions you make in advising the taxpayer.

E3-20. Assume the same facts presented in E3-19 with the exception that the taxpayer elects to pay the taxes on the conversion from the IRA funds. Should the taxpayer convert to a Roth IRA?

E3-21. Assume the same facts presented in E3-19 with the exception that the taxpayer expects her tax rate to decline from the current 24% to 10% when she retires in 40 years. Should the taxpayer convert to a Roth IRA?

E3-22. Many taxpayers who elected to convert the funds in their traditional deductible IRAs to Roth IRAs in the summer of 1998 converted back to traditional IRAs in September 1998 after the stock market fell (the Dow Jones Industrial Average fell from approximately 9,300 to 7,500). Many of these taxpayers, after converting back to the traditional IRA, then converted to the Roth IRA at the lower stock market levels.[23] Note that Treasury regulations at the time allowed taxpayers to undo a conversion and to reconvert at a later date. Also note that the TCJA eliminated the rules that allowed for this type of transaction and, thus, now once a conversion to a Roth IRA is completed, it cannot be undone.

a. Explain the rationale for reversing the original conversion and then making the reconversion at the lower stock market level. In your explanation, assume that a taxpayer facing a marginal tax rate of 39.6% at the time converted $100,000 from a traditional IRA into a Roth IRA at the start of the summer of 1998. After the conversion, the stock market declined 20% (i.e., the value of the assets in the pension account declined in value by 20% since the taxpayer had invested the plan assets in

[23] See the *Wall Street Journal* (May 4, 1999), p. B9, Your Money Matters column titled "IRA Holders Do Flip-Flops over Accounts" for financial press discussion of Roth IRA conversions.

the stock market). Assume also that the taxpayer had a 20-year investment horizon and faced a tax rate of 39.6% currently and in retirement.

b. Does your answer to part (a) depend on the future performance of the stock market (i.e., on *R*)?

Tax-Planning Problems

TP3-23. Assume that fully taxable bonds yield 10% per year before tax, tax-exempt bonds yield 6.5%, and the pretax return on SPDAs is 9.5%.

a. What are the after-tax rates of return per period for holding periods of 3, 5, 10, and 20 years for an investment in tax-exempt bonds, taxable bonds, SPDAs cashed out after age 59.5 (no excise tax), and SPDAs cashed out *before* age 59.5, requiring a 10% nondeductible excise tax (in addition to the normal tax) on the accumulated interest, for an investor facing a 40% ordinary tax rate each period and a 30% ordinary tax rate each period?

Holding Period	Tax-Exempt Bonds	Taxable Bonds	SPDAs (with no penalty)	SPDAs (with penalty)
3 years				
30% taxpayer				
40% taxpayer				
5 years				
30% taxpayer				
40% taxpayer				
10 years				
30% taxpayer				
40% taxpayer				
20 years				
30% taxpayer				
40% taxpayer				

b. How do optimal investment strategies change as a function of tax rates, lengths of investment horizon, and age?

c. At age 34.5, you deposited $50,000 into an SPDA yielding 9.5% pretax. Ten years later, to finance the purchase of a second home, you require a mortgage exceeding the net of tax cash-out value of your SPDA. As an alternative to liquidating your SPDA, you can borrow funds at an annual interest rate of 11%, tax deductible, for 15 years. Assume the interest and principal are all paid at the end of the loan period. Your current tax rate is 30%, and you expect it to remain at that level. How much better or worse off, after tax, will you be at age 59.5 if you invade your SPDA today (and incur the 10% excise tax) to reduce the size of the required mortgage?

d. How does your answer to part (c) change if the interest expense incurred on the debt used to finance the expenditure is not tax deductible (e.g., you purchased a flashy, expensive automobile)?

TP3-24. Equation 3.11 analyzes the choice between a deductible IRA and a Roth IRA for new contributions when the taxpayer wishes to contribute the maximum allowed. Equation 3.11 indicates that if the taxpayer expects her future tax rate to decline, the contribution choice depends on the relative magnitude of the taxpayer's current and future tax rates (t_0 and t_n), the holding period (n), and the pretax rate of return expected (R) to be earned on plan assets. (Note also that Equation 3.11 assumes that any excess funds under the deductible IRA are invested in an SPDA.) Assume the taxpayer's current tax rate is 40% (i.e., t_0 is .40). Complete the following spreadsheet, first assuming that $R = 10\%$. Then repeat the spreadsheet for $R = 5\%$ and $R = 15\%$.

Holding Period (n)	$t_n = .40$	$t_n = .35$	$t_n = .30$	$t_n = .25$
5 years				
10 years				
20 years				
30 years				

Interpret the results of your analysis. How does the contribution decision vary as a function of the pretax rate of return, holding period, and relative magnitudes of tax rates?

TP3-25. Equation 3.14 indicates that the choice as to whether to convert from a deductible IRA to a Roth IRA when the taxpayer expects her future tax rate to decline depends on the relative magnitude of the taxpayer's current and future tax rates (t_0 and t_n), the holding period (n), and the pretax rate of return expected (R) to be earned on plan assets. (Note also that Equation 3.14 assumes that any taxes due on conversion are paid in the conversion year from nonconverted funds that would otherwise be invested in an SPDA.) Assume V = \$50,000 and $t_0 = .40$. Complete the following spreadsheet, first assuming that $R = 10\%$, then repeat the spreadsheet for $R = 5\%$ and $R = 15\%$.

Holding Period n	$t_n = .40$	$t_n = .35$	$t_n = .30$	$t_n = .25$
5 years				
10 years				
20 years				
30 years				

Interpret the results of your analysis. How does the conversion decision vary as a function of the pretax rate of return, holding period, and relative magnitudes of tax rates?

TP3-26. When comparing the deductible IRA with the Roth IRA, we assumed that any excess funds left after investing the maximum pretax dollars in a deductible IRA were invested in an SPDA. How would the comparison change if the excess funds were invested instead in Savings Vehicle III (a special type of mutual fund)?

TP3-27. When analyzing the conversion decision in Equations 3.13 and 3.14, we assumed that any taxes due would be paid from nonconverted funds that would otherwise be invested in an SPDA. How would these equations and, thus, the relevant comparisons in the conversion decision change if

a. any taxes due were paid from the converted funds (ignore the 10% excise tax penalty due on early withdrawals)?

b. instead of paying the taxes from funds invested in an SPDA, the taxes were paid from funds invested in Savings Vehicle III (a special type of mutual fund)?

References and Additional Readings

Bergstresser, D., and J. Poterba, 2002. "Do After-Tax Returns Affect Mutual Fund Inflows?" *Journal of Financial Economics*, pp. 381–414.

Fronstin, P. "Trends in Health Savings Account Balances, Contributions, Distributions, and Investments, 2011–2017: Estimates from the EBRI HSA Database," *EBRI Issue Brief*, October 29, 2018.

Hrung, W., 2007. "Determinants of the Choice Between Roth and Deductible IRAs," *Journal of the American Taxation Association* (Spring), pp. 27–42.

Hulse, D., 2003. "Embedded Options and Tax Decisions: A Reconsideration of the Traditional vs. Roth IRA Decision," *Journal of the American Taxation Association* (Spring), pp. 39–52.

Luna, L. and R. Alexander, 2005. "State Sponsored Section 529 Plans: The Influence of Tax and Non-Tax Factors on Investors' Choice" *Journal of the American Taxation Association*, Supplement, pp. 29–50.

Sieda, J., and J. Stern, 1998. "Extending Scholes/Wolfson for Post-1997 Pension Investments: Application to the Roth IRA Contribution and Rollover Decisions," *Journal of the American Taxation Association* (Fall), pp. 100–110.

Toder, E., and A. D. Viard, 2016. "Replacing Corporate Tax Revenues with a Mark to Market Tax on Shareholder Income." *Tax Policy Center*.

4

Implicit Taxes and Clienteles, Marginal Tax Rates, and Arbitrage

After completing this chapter, you should be able to

1. Explain the concept of and calculate the implicit tax rate on a variety of assets.
2. List assets that are tax favored and therefore bear implicit taxes.
3. Explain and illustrate the concept of tax clienteles.
4. Define and distinguish among the concepts of marginal tax rate, average tax rate, and effective tax rate.
5. Explain and illustrate the difficulties of estimating corporate marginal tax rates.
6. Explain the concept of tax arbitrage and why it is important.
7. Discuss the importance and provide examples of market frictions and tax-rule restrictions.
8. Define tax plan reversibility, adaptability, indemnity, and strategy dependence.

In Chapter 3, we discussed how different tax treatments of investment returns influence the after-tax rates of return to alternative savings vehicles. To facilitate comparisons, we held the same investment in each savings vehicle. In the first half of this chapter, we hold the organizational form constant and vary the tax treatments for different economic activities. We stress how taxing activities unequally influence the relative pricing and the *before-tax rates of return* on investments. The pretax rates of return change because the relative pricing of assets changes in the marketplace due to favorable or unfavorable tax treatment. For example, if we buy a building to rent space to others, we can deduct from rental income not only the costs of running the business but also part of the building purchase price each year (i.e., depreciation) before paying taxes on any remaining income. Conversely, an investment in equipment that generates the same pretax cash flows as the rental building might give rise to more liberal depreciation allowances and, as a result, higher after-tax cash flows than the real estate investment. Because the equipment's after-tax cash flows exceed those for the rental property, investors are willing to pay more for the equipment. More generally, when two assets give rise to identical pretax cash flows and the cash flows from one asset are taxed more favorably than those from the other asset, taxpayers will bid for the right to hold the tax-favored asset. As a result, the price of the tax-favored asset will increase relative to the price of the tax-disfavored asset. And because the before-tax cash flows for the two investments are identical, the pretax rate of return to the tax-favored asset will fall below that for the tax-disfavored asset. Stated another way, explicit taxes can affect pretax rates of return such that the after-tax rates of return will be the same to some investors (i.e., the marginal investors).

Given differences in tax treatment, if after-tax returns are to be equalized, then before-tax rates of return must differ across assets. More lightly taxed investments require lower before-tax rates of return than do more heavily taxed investments. As a result, investors pay taxes *explicitly* on heavily taxed investments and *implicitly* on lightly taxed investments through lower before-tax rates of return. Moreover, taxing investments differentially gives rise to **tax clienteles**—the proper investors (i.e., clientele) for lightly taxed assets will often be a different set of investors than for the more heavily taxed investments.

In order to determine after-tax rates of return and which assets to invest in, a taxpayer needs to know his or her marginal tax rate. However, several different tax rates are commonly used by academics, in practice, and by the press. In addition, it turns out the incorrect rate is sometimes used to make decisions at both the business and individual levels. Also, the definitions of these terms are not standard across academic disciplines, in practice, or by the press. We define the terms as follows: The **marginal tax rate** is the present value of the additional tax to be paid per dollar of additional (or marginal) taxable income. If a taxpayer earns an additional dollar of taxable income (or obtains an additional dollar of deductions), how much in tax will this cost (save) the taxpayer now and in the future? The marginal tax rate is taxpayer specific. A different rate entirely is the **average tax rate** computed broadly as some measure of taxes paid divided by some measure of income. Two examples of an average corporate tax rate are the generally accepted accounting principles (GAAP) effective tax rate (ETR) and the cash ETR. The **GAAP ETR** is computed as total tax expense divided by pretax income (i.e., income before taxes), both of which are on the firm's income statement. The **cash ETR** is cash taxes paid divided by pretax income. Importantly, an average rate will likely not be the rate that is paid on the taxpayer's next transaction (i.e., the marginal transaction) but instead is the average rate that is paid on all transactions combined. The GAAP and ETR and average tax rates are also taxpayer specific. We argue that GAAP ETR and cash ETRS are inappropriate for incorporating the tax effects in corporate decision making. There is also, of course, the **statutory tax rate**, which is the rate set by the tax statutes for a particular transaction or time period that applies to a wide set of taxpayers (married-filing-jointly taxpayers in certain income brackets have the same statutory tax rate). The same taxpayer can have different statutory, marginal, and average rates in the same time period.[1] We also illustrate complications in determining the corporate marginal tax rate for decision making.

Where differences in statutory tax rates exist across taxpayers, time, organizational forms, and economic activities, taxpayers have incentives to contract with one another in ways that may alter their specific marginal tax rates. In our discussion and analysis, we initially assume that **market frictions** (i.e., brokerage fees and other information-related costs required to buy or sell assets in imperfect markets) and **tax-rule restrictions** do not exist. Under these conditions, if one savings vehicle or organizational form dominated another savings vehicle or organizational form, taxpayers could eliminate all their taxes. They would accomplish this by holding negative quantities of wealth through the inferior vehicles (i.e., borrow or promise to pay the after-tax rate earned on the inferior vehicle) and positive amounts of wealth through the superior vehicles. This is a form of **tax arbitrage**. We cannot overemphasize that when examining our discussion and examples, the reader must keep in mind that we are initially assuming no tax-rule restrictions—such as interest on personal loans is not tax deductible by individual taxpayers. Although the arbitrage strategies are theoretically possible in many cases, market frictions often, for all practical purposes, prevent their implementation. And where market frictions are insufficient, tax-rule restrictions are often introduced to prevent most of these arbitrage opportunities.

Next, we move to a consideration of the forces that prevent tax arbitrage from effective implementation—namely, tax-rule restrictions and market frictions. In Chapter 2, we discussed some of the broad tax law restrictions that prevent taxpayers from engaging in socially undesirable tax planning, such as the economic-substance, business-purpose, and substance-over-form doctrines. In this chapter, we consider some of the more specific restrictions in the tax law that are designed to prevent taxpayers from being too successful in reducing their taxes through tax arbitrage. Both tax-rule restrictions and market frictions play a central role in preventing arbitrage, and, in some respects, they are substitutes. In fact, as the creation of new markets or transaction-enhancing technologies reduce or eliminate frictions, the imposition of new tax-rule restrictions may be required to prevent the forms of arbitrage we discuss in this chapter. As the cost for implementing tax-planning strategies increases, the number of restrictions required to prevent such strategies decreases.

---

[1] In economics and policy discussions, another rate, the marginal ETR, is often used. This rate is based on tax codes and measures the wedge between the pre- and post-tax return on the marginal investment project after taking into account the return on the investment, inflation, and the amount and timing of depreciation deductions and investment tax credit. This is very different from the ETR calculated in accounting and the marginal tax rate used in corporate finance.

We then consider strategies an entity might undertake to alter its marginal tax rate via tax arbitrage techniques. The tax planner's problem is to maximize after-tax returns net of nontax costs given the history of decisions and outcomes that brought the firm to where it is today. Most investment and financing decisions are undertaken in an uncertain environment. Once plans are implemented, events unfold. Given the outcomes of the process, entities must decide how to alter their investment and financing decisions. And given these outcomes, many entities would undertake clientele-based arbitrage strategies to change their marginal tax rates if doing so were costless. However, restrictions and frictions curtail such strategies. We consider the tax-planning strategies available to low-tax-bracket firms, such as those with net operating losses.

We follow this with a brief discussion centered on dynamic tax-planning strategies—that is, how to plan for future contingencies. Recall that efficient tax planning requires identifying appropriate taxpayer-specific investment and financing clienteles. Identification is relatively straightforward in a static environment. But when decisions have uncertain consequences over many tax years, such clienteles depend on the reorganization costs of altering investment and financing policies in response to changes in taxpayers' circumstances. In the presence of uncertainty regarding future pretax cash flows and the tax rules themselves, a premium is placed on contracts that offer flexibility in tax planning to respond to unexpected changes in tax status. But building flexibility into contracts does not come free. For example, it may require a degree of mutual trust among the contracting parties (as in discretionary employee bonus plans) that cannot be sustained. In addition, flexibility typically requires greater contracting costs.

Suppose a firm knows that because its tax rate is high in the current period, it should finance new projects with debt to take advantage of explicit tax deductions for interest payments. However, the firm is unsure of its future tax rate. It could issue equity instead of debt, but the implicit tax deduction provided by an equity issue is usually of less value than the explicit tax deduction of bond interest if the firm is fully taxable. A more flexible approach would be to borrow money for 1 year, and if the firm's tax rate in 1 year remains high, the firm can issue debt for an additional year. However, certain fixed costs associated with issuing debt make it more economical to issue longer-term debt. Efficient tax planning here requires trading off the transaction cost savings from issuing less flexible debt (i.e., long-term debt) against the restructuring cost or the cost of being in the wrong clientele if the taxpayer's situation changes.

Consider also the question of whether to buy or lease depreciable assets, such as office buildings or manufacturing equipment. As we have already discussed, depreciable assets are tax favored under the present tax system of generous depreciation allowances. As a result, the efficient owners from a tax standpoint are those with the highest marginal tax rates because they benefit most from the generous depreciation allowances. Firms with lower marginal tax rates are better off leasing. Suppose a firm's tax rate is currently very high, but the rate is likely to decline in the future, at which point it would no longer be tax efficient to own depreciable assets. Under what conditions should the firm purchase the depreciable assets? The answer depends on the probability that the firm's tax rate will decline as well as the resulting cost of being in the wrong clientele. If it leases the asset, the firm bears the cost of being in the wrong clientele now, when its rate is high. If the firm buys the asset, it may bear the cost of being in the wrong clientele later if its tax rates does, in fact, decrease. The cost of being in the wrong investment or financing clientele at some future date, if the firm's tax rate changes, depends on several factors. We explore three of them in this chapter:

1. The reversibility of the tax plan
2. The adaptability of the tax plan
3. The ability to insure against adverse changes in tax status

4.1 TAX-FAVORED STATUS AND IMPLICIT TAXES

As briefly discussed in Chapter 1, implicit taxes arise because the prices of investments that are tax favored are bid up in the marketplace (e.g., municipal bonds). As a result, the *before-tax* rates of return on tax-favored investments are lower than are those on tax-disfavored investments. Taxes are paid implicitly through lower before-tax rates of return on investment. To calculate implicit taxes requires a **benchmark asset** against which to compare pretax returns. Suppose our benchmark asset is an asset whose returns are taxed fully each year at ordinary rates. That is, tax is not deferred on any part of the economic gain that accrues from holding the asset. A fully taxable bond that is default free, with its interest rate set to market rates each period, is such an asset. Moreover, there are no changes in the economic value of the bond over time with which to contend. We would then refer to investments that are taxed more lightly than fully taxable bonds as *tax-favored* investments and those that are taxed more heavily as *tax-disfavored* investments.

Investments may enjoy one or more of several types of tax-favored status, including

- Full tax exemption (e.g., municipal bonds in the United States)
- Partial tax exemption or lower marginal tax rates (e.g., capital assets in most countries)
- Tax credits (e.g., investment tax credit, targeted jobs credit, alcohol fuel credit, research and experimental credit, low-income housing credit, energy investment credit, payroll tax credit, and rehabilitation investment credit)
- Tax deductions permitted at a rate faster than the decline in economic value of the asset (e.g., immediate expensing or accelerated depreciation on business property, immediate expensing of research and experimental costs, and advertising expenditures)
- Taxable income permitted to be recognized at a rate slower than the increase in the economic value of the asset's cash flows (e.g., most assets that appreciate in value)

Similarly, there are many sources of tax-disfavored treatment, including

- Special tax assessments (e.g., windfall profits tax on oil, import duties, and excise taxes)
- Taxable income recognition at a rate faster than income is earned (e.g., risky bonds where the high coupon rate received is fully taxable even though it includes a default premium that, economically, represents a return of capital rather than interest income)
- Tax deductions at a rate slower than the decline in economic value (e.g., non-amortizable trademarks that have finite economic lives)

The lower before-tax rates of return on municipal bonds, relative to fully taxable bonds of comparable risk, provide the most direct and vivid illustration of the concept of implicit taxes. State and local authorities issue municipal bonds, and the interest earned on most of these bonds is exempt from federal taxation in the United States.[2] For this reason, they are called tax-exempt bonds, and investors bid up the prices of these bonds such that their before-tax return is lower than the before-tax return on fully taxable bonds.

The residents of certain states are exempt from tax at the federal level and at the state level if they hold municipal revenue or general obligation bonds issued by authorities within that state. These instruments are called doubly tax exempt. If residents of a given state hold municipal bonds of out-of-state issuers, however, these residents pay state income taxes on the interest earned on these out-of-state bonds. State taxation also affects the prices of municipal bonds. Certain states (e.g., California and New York) tax their residents at high marginal tax rates and exempt their residents from paying tax on interest from state and local bonds issued within their own borders. Municipal bonds issued by such states are priced to yield a lower rate of return relative to municipal bonds issued by states with low marginal tax rates (e.g., Texas, which has no state individual income tax) or states that tax the interest on bonds issued by municipalities within their own borders.

Other types of bonds also receive some form of preferential tax treatment. For example, interest earned on obligations issued by the federal government (e.g., Treasury bills, bonds, and notes) and certain authorities (e.g., the Federal Farm Credit Bank System) is fully taxable at the federal level and exempt from all state income taxes. Puerto Rico also issues bonds that are tax exempt at the federal level and in all 50 states. Note that, in contrast, interest derived from an investment in corporate bonds is fully taxable at both the federal and state levels.

Thus, given nontrivial tax rates, even after controlling for differences in risk, the before-tax returns to Treasury securities tend to be lower than the returns to non-Treasury securities. For

[2] Bonds issued by local governments are not exempt from taxation at the national level in all countries. Provincial bonds in Canada, for example, are fully taxable at the federal level.

example, a California resident facing a 10% state and a 30% federal marginal tax rate would be indifferent between holding Treasury securities yielding 9% and equally risky non-Treasury securities yielding 10%. Both securities yield 6.3% after all relevant taxes.[3]

In many countries, taxpayers have been granted investment tax credits on the purchase of certain types of equipment equal to a fraction of the asset's purchase price. A tax credit is like a tax receipt. For example, if equipment costs $20,000 and a 10% tax credit is available, the tax credit would be $2,000. If the taxpayer owed $15,000 in taxes on other income, the $2,000 tax credit reduces the required tax payment from $15,000 to $13,000. Generally, a tax credit is more valuable than a deduction. Whereas tax credits reduce taxes dollar for dollar, deductions reduce taxes by a fraction equal to the tax rate. The 1986 Tax Reform Act eliminated investment tax credits in the United States.

Liberal depreciation allowances and tax credits on equipment affect the required before-tax rates of return on investment. The more liberal the depreciation allowances or investment tax credits, the lower the required before-tax rate of return on investment (and, as we will see later in the chapter, the higher the implicit tax). In the United States, Section 179 of the U.S. tax code allows the immediate expensing of a certain amount of investment costs. The Economic Stimulus Act of 2008 increased the Section 179 limits. In addition, the legislation enacted bonus depreciation to incentivize investment during recessionary and recovery economic periods. Specifically, the 2008 law increased the limit on the Section 179 deduction from $125,000 to $250,000 and the limit on the total amount of equipment purchased from $500,000 to $800,000. In addition, the act provided for 50% bonus depreciation that allowed businesses to recover the costs of capital expenditures faster than ordinary depreciation by permitting businesses to immediately write off 50% of the cost of depreciable property above the Section 179 deduction limits. The limits for both Section 179 and bonus depreciation have changed over time. Starting January 1, 2018, under the TCJA, the Section 179 deduction limit is $1,000,000 on capital purchases of no more than $2,500,000 and the bonus depreciation rate is set at 100%. Research and development investments and advertising expenditures are also accorded rapid write-off or credit treatment.

To illustrate the effects of liberal depreciation on the implicit tax rate, assume that the taxing authority allows immediate expensing of the cost of certain equipment. Also assume that all of the returns resulting from the investment are fully taxable. We denote the investor's marginal tax rate as t_o today and t_n in n years. For simplicity, suppose our project generates no cash flows until time n, at which time it generates $(1 + R)^n$ dollars (so the before-tax rate of return on investment per period is R). The after-tax return per dollar of after-tax investment can be expressed this way:

$$\frac{\textbf{After-Tax Return}}{\textbf{After-Tax Investment}} = \frac{\$1(1+R)^n(1-t_n)}{\$1(1-t_o)} \qquad \textbf{(4.1)}$$

Because the taxpayer deducts the investment cost, a $1 investment today has an after-tax cost of $\$1(1 - t_o)$. For example, if the investor's marginal tax rate were 40%, the after-tax investment cost would be $.60 per dollar invested. If the investment is held for n years and returns $(1 + R)^n$ before tax for every dollar invested, the taxpayer retains $\$1(1 + R)^n(1 - t_n)$ after tax because tax at rate t_n is paid on the entire dollar return. Thus, if the project returns 8% per year before tax for 5 years and the taxpayer's marginal tax rate remains 40%, the taxpayer retains $.882 after tax [($\$1.08)^5(1 - 40\%)$] per dollar invested. Because the taxpayer earned $.882 after tax on an after-tax investment of $.60, the 5-year return per dollar invested is $1.469, or $.882/.60. The return per year is 8%, or $1.469^{1/5} - 1$.[4]

In the special case of constant-across-time tax rates (i.e., $t_n = t_o$), the before-tax return and the after-tax return on investment are the same (i.e., 8% in the previous illustration). We can see this from Equation 4.1. With constant tax rates, Equation 4.1 simplifies to $(1 + R)^n$. This means the after-tax

[3] The after-tax returns are calculated as follows: For the Treasury security, .09(1 – .30) = .063, or 6.3%. Because state taxes are deductible at the federal level, the California resident here faces an effective state tax rate of .10(1 – .30) = .07, or 7%. The total tax rate faced by the California resident is 30% + 7% = 37%, implying an after-tax rate of return on non-Treasury securities of .10(1 – .37) = .063, or 6.3%.

[4] The reader can easily adjust this example to reflect the corporate statutory tax rate of 21% effective in 2018. Other marginal tax rates can also easily be inserted.

rate of return per period is R. But R is also the before-tax rate of return on investment, so the before and after-tax rates of return on investment coincide—the return is tax exempt.

If we assume that marginal tax rates are constant, the required before-tax rate of return, R, on this project must be equal to the after-tax bond rate, r_b. Note that this is exactly the required return on tax-exempt municipal bonds as well. If investors could earn rates of return higher than r_b, they could profit by borrowing at rate r_b after tax and investing at the higher rate. As a result, they would bid up the prices of the inputs necessary to undertake the tax-favored investment. In addition, with more investment, they might reduce the output prices of goods and services to consumers. This would continue until the expected after-tax rate of return on the last dollar of investment is equal to that on the next best alternative, the after-tax bond rate or the municipal bond rate.

Equation 4.1 is familiar to us because we used the same algebra when describing the returns to investing in pension funds in Chapter 3 (Savings Vehicle VI). In both the investment here and pension fund investing, we deduct the cost of the investment, and the returns are fully taxable. The major difference is that the pension fund can invest in fully taxable bonds to return the before-tax bond rate. However, with the investment example, competition causes the before-tax return on the tax-favored investment to be equal to the after-tax bond rate (assuming equal risk or, as discussed later in the chapter, on a risk-adjusted basis). The difference between the pretax rate of return on fully taxable bonds and that on the tax-favored investment represents an implicit tax paid to customers (by way of reduced prices) and/or factor suppliers (by way of increased prices for inputs).

In Equation 4.1, we allowed for the possibility that marginal tax rates change over time. If tax rates were expected to fall (i.e., $t_n < t_o$), the required before-tax rate of return on investment would be less than the after-tax bond rate, r_b. If tax rates were expected to increase (i.e., $t_n > t_o$), the converse would be true. To illustrate the power of tax-rate changes, consider the following example. Assume that $t_o = 35\%$, $t_n = 21\%$, $n = 5$ years, and $r_b = 7\%$. We know that, on a risk-adjusted basis, in equilibrium, the cumulative n-year after-tax return for this investment and a fully taxable bond must be the same:

$$\frac{(1+R)^n(1-t_n)}{(1-t_o)} = (1+r_b)^n \qquad (4.2)$$

Solving for the required risk-adjusted before-tax rate of return per period, R, we find that

$$R = \left[\frac{(1+r_b)^n(1-t_o)}{(1-t_n)}\right]^{1/n} - 1$$

Substituting the values for r_b, t_o, and t_n from our example, we find that

$$R = \left[\frac{(1+.07)^5(1-.35)}{(1-.21)}\right]^{1/5} - 1 = .0291, \text{or } 2.91\%$$

A before-tax required rate of return of 2.91% is well below the after-tax rate of return on bonds of 7%. Because the government puts up 35% of every dollar invested and requires only 21% of the resultant returns, investors bid up the investment price of the project (or reduce prices for goods and services) such that the before-tax rate of return falls below the tax-exempt bond rate. By construction, the pretax return of 2.91% per year for 5 years provides exactly the same after-tax return per dollar of after-tax investment as investing in fully taxable (or tax-exempt) bonds—that is, 7%.

Conversely, if tax rates are expected to increase, the required before-tax rates of return on the project would exceed the after-tax bond rate, and the project would bear some explicit tax. An analogous result occurs when tax rates remain constant over time and the depreciation and tax credit allowances are less than an immediate expensing of the cost of the investment. Explicit taxes will be paid on the project's returns, and the before-tax required rate of return on the project will exceed the municipal bond rate.

Favorable tax treatment (e.g., liberal depreciation allowances or investment tax credits) stimulates demand for investments. Increased investment exerts upward pressure on factor prices (e.g., labor costs and equipment costs) unless the supply of such factors is perfectly elastic. In other words, as prices increase, more of the product is supplied without limit. Increased investment also exerts downward pressure on consumer prices unless consumer demand is perfectly elastic.[5] For example, accelerating depreciation rates on buildings (referred to as real property in the tax code) encourages the production of more rental units. But the increase in supply of rental units puts downward pressure on rental rates (more rental suppliers are competing to get renters). This, in turn, encourages people to rent the units at the lower prices. Because of the anticipated increased supply of rental units and lower rental rates, the resale prices of existing rental units do not increase by the full value of the increase in present value of the depreciation-related tax savings.

If we had a capital stock that could be redeployed instantly to new uses (i.e., perfect markets with no tax-rule restrictions and no frictions), the capital stock and the prices of goods and services would adjust immediately to unanticipated changes in depreciation allowances and the prices of underlying assets would not change. With adjustment costs to change the capital stock, neither the supply of capital nor prices would adjust as quickly, and an unanticipated liberalization of tax allowances would generally create capital gains for the holders of capital assets. Conversely, the owners of the capital stock would experience capital losses on an unanticipated elimination of a tax shelter (e.g., less liberal depreciation allowances).

Computing the Implicit Tax

The **implicit tax** on the returns to any asset is defined as the difference between the before-tax return on a fully taxable bond (our benchmark security) and the risk-adjusted before-tax return on an alternative asset (e.g., a tax-favored municipal bond).[6] For example, assume that the pretax return on fully taxable bonds is 10% and the risk-adjusted pretax return on tax-exempt bonds is 7%. The implicit tax on tax-exempt bonds would then be 3 percentage points, simply 10% less 7%. The implicit tax on the fully taxable bond is zero.

The **implicit tax rate**, t_{Ia}, on a particular investment, a, is that tax rate that, if applied explicitly to fully taxable bonds, would leave a return equal to the *before-tax* rate of return on the alternative investment. If we define R_b as the risk-adjusted before-tax return on fully taxable bonds (the **b**enchmark asset) and R_a as the risk-adjusted before-tax return on the **a**lternative investment, the implicit tax rate is given by

$$R_b(1 - t_{Ia}) = R_a$$

or

$$t_{Ia} = (R_b - R_a)/R_b \qquad (4.3)$$

Substituting for $R_b = 10\%$ and $R_a = 7\%$, we find that the implicit tax rate on municipal bonds is 30%, or (10% − 7%)/10%.[7] Thus, paying tax at a rate of 30% on fully taxable bonds would result in a return of 7%, the same as the before-tax rate of return on tax-exempt bonds. Although investors do not pay any explicit tax on the interest earned from holding municipal bonds, they pay the tax implicitly at a tax rate of 30% through a lower before-tax rate of return.

To whom is the implicit tax paid? In our tax-exempt municipal bond example, it is paid to the issuers of the tax-exempt securities. The issuing municipalities receive an implicit subsidy by way of a lower cost of capital. In the example, the subsidy is at the rate of 30% of normal (i.e., fully taxable) borrowing costs. This taxing scheme, which uses implicit taxes to subsidize municipal spending programs, is similar to an alternative scheme in which all bonds, including municipal bonds, are fully

---

[5] Elasticity refers to the ratio of the proportionate change in quantity as price changes. A demand function with unit elasticity implies that as price changes, the quantity demanded changes such that total revenue is unchanged. An inelastic demand function implies no change in quantity demanded as price changes (thus, demand quantity is not a function of price). A perfectly elastic demand curve implies that a small price change leads to a large change in quantity demanded (the demand curve is relatively flat). A perfectly elastic supply curve implies that a small change in price leads to a large change in the quantity supplied.

[6] We use the term *risk adjusted* to indicate that we are comparing the returns on alternative investments after adjusting for risk differences. In practice, we require a model to adjust for differences in risk. Such models as the capital asset pricing model or the arbitrage pricing model, for example, could be used to compute before-tax risk premiums on common stock investments. We assume here that we know the required pretax risk premium.

[7] Although our discussion will concentrate on pretax return differences between fully taxable bonds and tax-favored assets, we could also calculate implicit taxes on assets whose returns are taxed less favorably than fully taxable bonds. These assets would yield a pretax premium. They would be priced to yield a *negative* implicit tax.

taxable at the federal level, and the federal government remits the tax collected on municipal bonds to each issuing authority. In this alternative setting, the before-tax returns on municipal and fully taxable bonds would be 10%. Whether the bond was labeled a municipal or a taxable bond would make no difference to investors.

4.2 CLIENTELES

Taxpayers bear a total tax burden equal to the sum of explicit and implicit taxes. Taxpayers in a 30% statutory tax bracket would be indifferent between investing in taxable bonds yielding 10% before tax and municipal bonds yielding 7% (as well as any other investment in the economy that returns 7% after tax on a risk-adjusted basis). Such taxpayers are indifferent between paying all implicit, all explicit, or any combination of explicit and implicit taxes that totals 30%. Taxpayers who are indifferent between purchasing two equally risky assets, the returns on which are taxed differently, are called **marginal investors**. Investors with tax rates different from those marginal investors face are *not* indifferent to the choice of differently taxed assets and are called **inframarginal investors**. We now turn to a consideration of investment strategies for these inframarginal investors.

Taxpayers in the same tax brackets are attracted to investments that are taxed similarly. Returning to our tax-exempt and taxable bond example, investors with high marginal tax rates prefer tax-exempt bonds, and investors with low marginal tax rates prefer fully taxable bonds. Taxpayers preferring one investment over another (i.e., inframarginal investors) are the tax clientele for the preferred investment. Unless investors correctly identify their proper tax clienteles, they will not maximize their after-tax rates of return.

For example, assume that the implicit tax rate on municipal bonds is 30% and taxable bonds yield 10% before tax. The clientele for fully taxable bonds are taxpayers with marginal tax rates below 30%. A taxpayer with a 20% marginal tax rate will earn 8% after tax by investing in fully taxable bonds, 1% greater than municipal bonds. The investor is better off paying explicit taxes of 20% by investing in taxable bonds than paying implicit taxes of 30% by investing in municipal bonds.

Analogously, an investor whose marginal tax rate is 40% is better off investing in municipal bonds. Paying an implicit tax rate of 30% is less expensive than an explicit tax rate of 40%. Whereas the implicit tax rate on a given asset is the same for all investors, explicit tax rates vary among investors. Taxpayers with high explicit tax rates are led to invest in assets that bear high implicit taxes. Only the marginal investors lack brand loyalty. In the absence of transaction costs, marginal investors would jump back and forth between taxable and municipal bonds as relative prices change.

Tax clienteles are pervasive, and they apply to organizations as well as individuals. For example, if a corporation faces a lower statutory tax rate than the implicit tax rate on tax-exempt assets, holding fully taxable bonds is a superior investment to holding municipal bonds. With different clienteles, market frictions or tax-rule restrictions are required to prevent arbitrage opportunities. We will develop this theme later in the chapter.

Evidence on the Existence of Implicit Taxes and Clienteles

We have predicted that tax-favored treatment leads to lower pretax rates of return on the tax-favored assets as taxpayers bid up the prices of the tax-favored assets. Tax-favored treatment results in lower explicit tax bills for the taxpayer and lower pretax returns. We label this as the implicit tax model. In the United States, if individual investors are the marginal holders of stock, we would expect stocks to bear implicit taxes relative to bonds and low-dividend-paying stocks to bear more implicit taxes than high-dividend-paying stocks. In other words, we would expect the before-tax risk-adjusted returns on stocks to be below those of bonds and the risk-adjusted returns of low-dividend-paying stocks to be below those for high-dividend-paying stocks. Research in the accounting literature suggests asset prices reflect explicit taxes.[8]

One stream of empirical research examines stock returns around unexpected announcements of tax-law changes affecting the taxation of corporate dividends or capital gains. Ayers, Cloyd, and Robinson (2002) examined stock returns around the increase in individual tax rates in 1993 and reported

[8] The effect of explicit taxation on asset prices has also been labeled as "tax capitalization." There is much empirical literature addressing this issue, far too voluminous to summarize here.

evidence that stock prices declined more for high-dividend-yield firms. However, the decline was mitigated by the level of institutional holdings in the firm. Dhaliwal, Li, and Trezevant (2003) found that stock returns are positively associated with a firm's dividend yield (consistent with investors demanding a higher pretax rate of return because of the higher level of shareholder taxation). However, this positive association between stock returns and dividend yields decreased with the level of institutional and corporate ownership, their proxy for whether the marginal investor is an individual facing a high dividend tax rate. In addition, several studies have derived an estimate of a firm's expected pretax rate of return (or cost of equity capital) using accounting-based valuation models. These models are based on the present value of future earnings, which can be inverted using the current stock price and analysts' forecasts of future earnings to solve for an implied cost of equity capital.[9] Dhaliwal, Li, and Moser (2005) documented a positive relationship between the implied cost of equity capital and dividend yield. Again, this positive relationship decreases in the proportion of the firm's stock held by institutional investors. Dhaliwal, Krull, and Li (2007) examined changes in the implied cost of equity capital around the 2003 reduction in dividend and capital gains taxes. They found a decline in the equity cost of capital that is smaller for firms with larger institutional holdings, consistent with individual investor shareholder-level taxes being reflected in stock returns.

Erickson and Maydew (1998) examined the stock price reaction to a proposed reduction in the corporate dividends received deduction (DRD). In a surprise announcement in December 1995, the Treasury proposed reducing the corporate DRD from 70% to 50%. Recall from Chapter 2 that the corporate DRD allows corporations to deduct or exclude from their taxable income a certain percentage depending on their level of holdings of any dividends they receive on stock they hold in other domestic corporations. If high-dividend-yield stocks bear an implicit tax because of this tax preference, then an unexpected proposal to lower the amount of the corporate DRD will lower the price of the stock (i.e., investors will not bid up the price as much). Erickson and Maydew found that the prices of preferred stock, which pay high dividends, declined and the prices of high-dividend-yield common stock did not. These results are consistent with preferred stock but not common stock bearing corporate DRD-related implicit taxes. Alternatively stated, the results are consistent with corporations being the marginal investors in preferred stock but not in common stock. Individuals and institutions such as mutual funds, index funds, pension funs, and so forth are likely the marginal investors in common stock, and these investors are not eligible for the corporate DRD. Erickson and Maydew also provided an excellent discussion of the problems facing researchers in testing for implicit taxes in equity securities, including common stocks.

Several studies have documented that prices paid by acquiring firms incorporate the tax effects of the acquisition to the selling firm and selling firm's shareholders—that is, the higher the tax costs to the selling parties, the higher the purchase price in order to compensate the seller for the higher taxes.[10] Also, any tax benefits to the acquiring firm (e.g., a step-up in basis of the acquired assets or the tax deductibility of goodwill after 1993) are also associated with higher purchase prices.[11] That is, buyers bid up the price to reflect the tax-favored treatment of the assets acquired.

One approach that has been somewhat successful in documenting the existence of implicit taxes is to examine price changes of assets affected by tax-rule changes. Guenther (1994) examined the change in prices (more specifically, the yields) of Treasury bills around the time of statutory tax rate reductions. Treasury bills have a zero coupon rate and are therefore sold at a discount. The interest income from the discount is not taxable to a cash-basis taxpayer until the bill matures. Thus, the interest from two different Treasury bills maturing across a year end that coincides with a change in tax rates is taxed at different rates depending on whether the bill matures in December or January. If the decrease in tax rates results in a decrease in the pretax return required from debt securities by investors, the implicit tax model predicts yields will decrease from December of the high-tax year to January of the low-tax year. Guenther found such a difference when examining yields after the tax rate reductions in 1981 and 1986, providing evidence consistent with the existence of implicit taxes.

Another interesting example of the effect of changed tax treatment of an asset on that asset's price is provided by Key (2008), who examined the effect of special bonus depreciation rules for thoroughbred horses. Yearlings (young horses) purchased between 2002 and 2004 were eligible for

---

[9] See Ohlson (1995) for an accounting-based valuation model and Gebhardt, Lee, and Swaminathan (2001) and Gode and Mohanram (2003) for an application of the model to estimate an equity cost of capital.

[10] See, for example, Hayn (1989), Erickson (1998), and Erickson and Wang (1999).

[11] See, for example, Henning, Shaw, and Stock (2000); Ayers, Lefanowicz, and Robinson (2000); and Weaver (2000).

bonus depreciation. Key found that the price of yearlings (controlling for other characteristics that determine yearling prices at auction) was bid up during this time.

In a non-U.S. setting, Edwards and Shevlin (2011) examined changes in stock prices surrounding the unexpected announcement in 2006 of a change in the taxation of Canadian income trusts. Edwards and Shevlin reported a 13% price drop in the 3 days surrounding the tax-rule change. That is, prior to the proposed tax-law change, investors bid up the price of the income trusts and were willing to accept lower pretax rates of returns. However, with the removal of the tax-favored treatment, investors required a higher pretax return, resulting in the large price decline. This study provides compelling evidence that the tax-favored treatment accorded to income trusts prior to the proposed tax-rule change was factored into pretax rates of return.

Finally, because detailed data on ownership of securities are difficult to obtain, most researchers elect to test for the existence of implicit taxes rather than clienteles because data on prices, returns, and yields are easier to obtain. However, several studies examine changes in investor mix around tax-rule changes. For example, Dhaliwal, Erickson, and Trezevant (1999) found that when non-dividend-paying stocks initiate dividend payments, the shareholder base of the firm shifts from individuals to institutions. This shift is consistent with individual investors selling their shares to investors who pay lower rates of tax on dividends, such as tax-exempt entities like pension funds. Such a result is consistent with the existence of dividend tax clienteles.[12]

4.3 IMPLICIT TAXES AND CORPORATE TAX BURDENS

Over the years, some corporations have not paid explicit taxes. The primary reasons for this include the availability of generous depreciation deductions, tax credits, immediate write-offs of certain investments (e.g., advertising, research and development [R&D], and certain personnel costs), and interest expense deductions, along with myriad opportunities to postpone the recognition of taxable income. Some industries enjoy special tax rules. The oil industry receives very rapid write-offs of the cost of drilling wells, timber companies may treat much of their profits as capital gains, and pharmaceutical companies enjoy the R&D tax credit. Wilkie (1992) documented a consistent (across years) and statistically significant negative relationship between tax subsidies and pretax accounting rates of return, evidence consistent with implicit taxes. Wilkie used a tax subsidy measure we can think of as the reduction in explicit taxes due to investments in tax-favored assets: It is the difference between what explicit taxes would be if the firm's income were taxed at the top statutory tax rate and actual taxes. However, the negative relation is weaker than predicted for a perfectly competitive and frictionless economy, suggesting the presence of nontrivial market frictions.

Not paying explicit taxes can have political and reputation costs. For example, Citizens for Tax Justice published a study in 1985 titled "Corporate Taxpayers and Corporate Freeloaders." The study highlighted corporations that paid little or no explicit taxes. This group's mission is to make public that certain corporations use loopholes to avoid paying taxes. During the period of the 1985 study, the federal corporate tax rate was 46% on pretax profits. The study claimed that "129 of the companies—or almost half—managed to pay absolutely nothing in federal income taxes, or to receive outright tax rebates, in at least one of the 4 years from 1981 to 1984. . . . The 129 companies earned $66.5 billion in pretax domestic profits in the years they did not pay federal income taxes." Nine companies paid no federal taxes in each of the 4 years: Boeing, ITT, General Dynamics, Transamerica, First Executive, Mitchell Energy and Development, Greyhound, Grumman, and Lockheed.[13] The study lauded

[12] See Seida (2001) and Lightner, Morrow, Ricketts, and Riley (2008) for other examples of papers documenting clientele shifts around major tax-rule changes.

[13] Consider the case of General Dynamics. By using the completed contract method of accounting, General Dynamics was able to postpone the payment of all explicit federal taxes for many years. To the extent that General Dynamics must bid competitively against other firms for the right to supply goods to the Defense Department, however, it may pay substantial sums of implicit taxes. If the defense contract market were perfectly competitive, General Dynamics would pay a full implicit tax. The recipient of the implicit tax in this case would be the Defense Department. Because of this accounting method, the Defense Department is charged lower prices for goods and services through the competitive bidding process. However, some people might argue that the defense market is not very competitive. As a result, General Dynamics might have been able to capture a large fraction of the explicit tax savings for itself, and the study by Wilkie (1992) provides evidence consistent with firms in less competitive industries capturing some of the benefits of the tax-favored treatment of investments. Note that the completed contract method of accounting for tax purposes was eliminated in the Tax Reform Act of 1986.

those corporations that paid explicit taxes, claiming it is inherently unfair that some corporations avoid paying their share. Many in Congress believe that because of tax loopholes, corporations avoid paying taxes and, as a result, fail to pay their fair share of the tax. For this reason, Congress passed an alternative minimum tax (AMT) provision to replace a weaker add-on corporate tax as part of the Tax Reform Act of 1986. The AMT has as its goal that every corporation should pay some explicit taxes. The TCJA removed the corporate AMT.

The debate continues today. Data indicate explicit corporate tax receipts are falling as a percent of reported book income. There was much concern over the use of corporate tax shelters in the late 1990s and early 2000s.[14] Treasury and Congress put various rules in place to limit the use of corporate tax shelters (e.g., increased disclosure; penalties for all parties to the shelter, including the promoter; and increased taxes). Evaluating the effects of implicit taxes, if any, in tax shelters and those resulting from special provisions in the tax code is often a difficult task. However, much like the *Wall Street Journal* article mentioned in Chapter 1 that did not properly consider implicit taxes and thus criticized Theresa Kerry for not paying enough taxes, an evaluation of corporate tax burdens will only be complete if implicit taxes are computed and taken into account.

4.4 MARGINAL TAX RATES

To engage in any tax-planning activity, it is important that the taxpayer know his or her marginal tax rate. Thus, we turn to a discussion of marginal tax rates. For an individual taxpayer earning wages or a salary, the marginal tax rate is usually the statutory tax rate on the last dollar of taxable income and is given by the Internal Revenue Service (IRS) tax rate schedules for individuals. An issue for individuals is the effect of the AMT on their marginal tax rate. Because the AMT is essentially a flat tax with a maximum rate of 28%, when taxpayers are in the AMT range, the effect of this rate on their marginal decisions should be considered. However, the TCJA decreased the number of taxpayers likely subject to the AMT by increasing the exemption amount, limiting the state and local tax deduction, and removing personal exemptions.

For businesses, the marginal tax rate is much more complex because of the tax loss carryback and carryforward rules. We define the marginal tax rate as the present value of current plus future income taxes to be paid per dollar of additional (or marginal) taxable income earned in the current period. Notice here that we extend the definition of marginal tax rate to include the effect of a current dollar of taxable income on future-period tax liabilities.

To explain and illustrate the concept of the marginal tax rate for a business taxpayer, it is useful to consider four scenarios derived from two variables—whether taxable income in the current period is positive or negative (TI_t) and whether the business has a net operating loss (NOL) carryforward at the beginning of the period (NOL_{t-1}):

	$TI_t < 0$	$TI_t > 0$
$NOL_{t-1} = 0$	1	3
$NOL_{t-1} > 0$	2	4

We will work through these four scenarios, and a few caveats should be kept in mind. The marginal tax rate basically combines the effects of the statutory tax rate the firm is subject to with the effects of the time value of money from having to carry tax losses back and forward rather than using them immediately. We spend a lot of time here explaining the effects of tax losses. What is equally important is a consideration of what statutory tax rate the taxpayer is actually subject to. This sounds simple, but it is not. For example, businesses operating in foreign countries face different statutory tax rate schedules on the taxable income earned in each country. Thus, for example, multinational companies need to calculate a jurisdictional-specific marginal tax rate. Businesses would also consider any state or local taxes in considering the tax effects of any decisions, an issue we model later in the chapter.

[14] See U.S. Congressional Research Service (2000), *Average Effective Tax Rates*; U.S. Department of the Treasury (1999), *The Problem of Corporate Tax Shelters*; Manzon and Plesko (2002); and Desai (2002).

In the following analysis, we use the U.S. statutory tax rate for C corporations, but we are cognizant that internal decisions would be made with more detailed information.

Also note that the TCJA removed the ability of U.S. C corporations to carry back their domestic losses. Corporations must now carry them forward. However, we first present all four scenarios, which include loss carrybacks because many countries allow carrybacks (and it is possible that the United States will reintroduce the carryback of losses in the future).

Scenario 1: $TI_t < 0$, $NOL_{t-1} = 0$

Suppose a corporate taxpayer calculates its current period taxable income as a loss of $10 million. The firm has been profitable in the recent past, with a taxable income of $6 million in each of the past 5 years. The firm paid taxes at the top statutory tax rate of 35% in each of these years and, because of its recent profitability, has no NOL carryforward at the beginning of the year. What is the company's marginal tax rate in the current period given the tax loss? Does earning another dollar of income escape taxation, implying a zero marginal tax rate? No. The firm can carry back the tax loss (currently up to 2 years)—the carryback is first applied to claim a refund of taxes paid in year −2 of $2.1 million, or $6 million × .35, using up the first $6 million of the loss, leaving $4 million to be carried back to year −1 to claim a refund of $1.4 million, or $4 million × .35. If the firm had earned an extra dollar of income in the current period, the tax loss would have been $1 less, or $9,999,999, implying $1 less carryback and 35 cents less refund. Thus, earning an additional dollar of income in the current period results in a refund that is 35 cents less, implying a marginal tax rate of 35%. More formally, if the entire amount of the loss can be carried back, then the marginal tax rate in the current period, $t = 0$, is

$$\mathbf{mtr}_t = \mathbf{str}_{t-v} \tag{4.4}$$

where str is the statutory tax rate in the period $t - v$, where v is the period in which the carryback loss is exhausted (prior to the TCJA, the limit in the United States was 2 years for carryback, $v = 1$ or 2).

If the firm has insufficient positive taxable income in the carryback period to exhaust the tax loss, the remaining tax loss must be carried forward, meaning the firm has an NOL carryforward at the end of the current period. We discuss this case in the following scenario.

Scenario 2: $TI_t < 0$, $NOL_{t-1} > 0$

Suppose a corporate taxpayer calculates its current period taxable income as a loss of $10 million. The firm has been unprofitable in the recent past such that it has a $5 million NOL carryforward at the beginning of the current period. Thus, at the end of the current period, it has a $15 million NOL carryforward that it can deduct against future income.

With $15 million of NOLs, the firm faces no immediate tax liability on an extra dollar of income. Does this mean its marginal tax rate is 0%? Far from it. Suppose the firm expects to earn $6 million per year starting in year +1. The prospect of earning $6 million per year of taxable income means the firm will begin to pay taxes in 3 years. So, an extra dollar of taxable income today would reduce the NOL carryback by $1, which would trigger a tax payment of 35 cents in 3 years. The present value of this tax, assuming the firm's after-tax discount rate is 7%, is $\$.35/1.07^3 = 28.57$ cents, so the corporate marginal tax rate in this case is 28.57%. More generally, for a firm with an NOL carryforward at the end of period t, the current period marginal tax rate is calculated as

$$\mathbf{mtr}_t = \frac{\$1 \times \mathbf{str}_s}{(1+\mathbf{r})^s} \tag{4.5}$$

where str_s denotes the expected statutory tax rate in period s, the future period in which the firm is eventually taxed on the extra dollar of income earned in the current period, and r is the firm's after-tax discount rate.

If the current statutory rate of 35% is scheduled to change in 1 year to 25%, then the current marginal tax rate of our NOL firm would be 20.41% or $.25/1.07^3$, although the rate for a firm without

NOLs would remain 35%. Analogously, if the statutory rate is scheduled to increase to 50% in 1 year, the current marginal tax rate of our NOL firm would be 40.81% or $.50/1.07^3$. This illustrates that, in the face of tax rate changes over time, the marginal tax rate of NOL firms can exceed that of firms paying taxes at the full statutory rate currently in effect!

Scenario 3: $TI_t > 0$, $NOL_{t-1} = 0$

Suppose a corporate taxpayer calculates its current-period taxable income as $10 million. The firm has been profitable for many years such that it has no NOL carryforward at the beginning of the year and is expected to be profitable for many years to come. In this scenario, an extra dollar of income would trigger an immediate tax of 35 cents, assuming that the top statutory corporate tax rate is 35%, so the marginal tax rate is 35%.

Suppose instead of forecasting positive taxable income into the foreseeable future, the firm forecasts a temporary drop in demand for its products and expects to report zero taxable income in year +1 and a tax loss of $15 million in year +2, returning to positive profits thereafter. The tax loss in year +2 can be carried back to the current period to claim a refund of all taxes paid in the current period, leaving the firm with a $5 million NOL carryforward at the end of year +2. If the firm had earned an extra dollar of income in the current period such that its taxable income would be $10,000,001, then the tax refund in period 2 would be 35 cents higher, leaving a $4,999,999 carryforward at the end of the period.[15] Even though this result might appear to be a wash, an opportunity cost arises due to the time value of money because the IRS does not pay interest on funds arising from an NOL carryback. Assuming an after-tax discount rate of 7%, the opportunity cost is $.35 - .35/1.07^2 = .0443$. However, by earning the additional dollar of income in the current period, the NOL carryforward at the end of year +2 is reduced by $1, resulting in an increase in taxes on an additional dollar of income in the future. Suppose the NOL would have been used up in period +3, where the statutory tax rate is also 35%. Thus, we have to add $.35/1.07^3 = .2857$ to the marginal tax rate calculation, meaning the firm's marginal tax rate is $.0443 + .2857 = .33$, or 33%, not 35%. More formally,

$$\mathbf{mtr}_t = \mathbf{str}_t - \mathbf{str}_n/(1+r)^n + \mathbf{str}_s/(1+r)^s \quad (4.6)$$

where n is the future period in which the refund is claimed assuming a 2-year carryback ($n = 1$ or 2) and s is the future period in which the NOL carryforward at the end of period n is eventually used up. In words, the marginal tax rate, mtr, is the difference between the current period statutory tax rate, str, and the present value of the refund in n years plus the additional taxes due in s years when the NOL is eventually used up. Thus, the marginal tax rate incorporates the time value of money benefits with NOL carryover provisions. Rather than a marginal tax rate of +.35 for every dollar of income and a marginal tax rate of −.35 for every dollar of loss if losses were immediately refundable, the marginal rate is affected a great deal by the time value of money due to the carryover provisions.

Finally, if the carryback period is limited to 2 years, and if a currently profitable firm does not expect to incur tax losses within the next 2 years, then it is safe to assume its marginal tax rate in the current period is the statutory tax rate it faces in the current period.

Scenario 4: $TI_t > 0$, $NOL_{t-1} > 0$

Suppose a corporate taxpayer calculates its current period taxable income as $10 million. The firm has experienced losses in recent years resulting in an NOL carryforward of $6 million at the beginning of the period. If the firm had earned an additional dollar of income in the current period, it would have no effect on the use of the NOL carryforward and would result in an additional 35 cents of taxes in the current period.

If the NOL carryforward at the beginning of the period had been $12 million, then the current period taxable income of $10 million would have escaped taxation, leaving a $2 million NOL carryforward

[15] If the tax loss in year +2 can be completely carried back to the current period, then earning an additional dollar of income in the current period does not affect the amount of the refund so mtr_t equals str_t.

at the end of the current period. Earning an additional dollar of income in the current period, the NOL carryforward at the end of the period would have been reduced by $1 to $1,999,999 and the marginal tax rate on this additional dollar of income is estimated as in Scenario 2, Equation 4.5.

Marginal Tax Rate Estimation under TCJA

The TCJA ended the allowance to C corporations to carry back losses—they must be carried forward. The carryforward period is now indefinite, replacing the prior 20 year limit. However, the NOL deduction is limited to 80% of taxable income before the NOL. With no carryback of tax losses allowed, firms in scenario 1 (tax loss in the current period, with no NOL balance at the start of the period) must now carryforward the loss, and the firm is effectively in Scenario 2. The marginal tax rate is estimated using Equation 4.5, $\frac{\$1 \times str_s}{(1+r)^s}$ and what needs to be determined is the future period, s, in which the current period tax loss likely to be used up.

Firms in Scenario 3 (positive taxable income in the current period, no NOL balance at the start of the period) no longer face the issue of a possible carryback from a future loss into the current period, simplifying the calculation for these firms. Their marginal tax rate in the current period is the statutory tax rate on the last dollar of income in the current period: $mtr_t = str_t$.

For firms in Scenario 4 (positive taxable income in the current period, a positive NOL balance at the start of the period), their marginal tax rate depends on the size of the current period positive taxable income relative to the positive balance in the NOL at the start of the period. If $TI_t > NOL_{t-1}$ then the NOL carried forward can be deducted against current period income, leaving a reduced positive taxable income, which puts the firm in Scenario 3, meaning $mtr_t = str_t$. If $TI_t < NOL_{t-1}$, then there still exists an NOL at the end of the current period, which puts the firm in Scenario 2, meaning $mtr_t = \frac{\$1 \times str_s}{(1+r)^s}$.

As noted above, under the TCJA, for any tax losses incurred after 2017, the annual NOL deduction in any carryforward period is limited to 80% of taxable income in that year. In estimating the marginal tax rate above, we ignored this limitation. However, the limitation can be easily incorporated into calculations. The effect of the 80% annual limitation is to likely extend the carryforward period, reducing the present value of the future taxes due as a result of earning another dollar of income today, lowering the marginal tax rate. Alternatively stated, the present value of the tax benefit of an NOL carryforward is reduced.

Evidence on NOLs for U.S. Corporations

Because losses are so important in the computation of the marginal tax rate, the question arises as to how pervasive tax losses and NOL carryforwards are in the U.S. corporate sector. Cooper and Knittel (2006) used confidential corporate tax return data to provide some descriptive evidence on this issue. They estimated that 51% of all C corporations filing a tax return in 2003 reported a tax loss (this number was in the mid-40s through the 1990s). Cooper and Knittel also reported the time in years before the loss was deducted in a future year. Because their sample covered 1993 to 2003, we report the over-time usage of tax losses for the 1993 year. The total tax loss across C corporations in 1993 was $71 billion, $9.2 billion (13%) of which was carried back to obtain a refund, $26.9 billion (38%) was carried forward and subsequently deducted in the following 10 years, $13.1 billion (18%) remained as an NOL carrryforward as of the end of 2003, and $21.7 billion (31%) was estimated to have been lost (not deducted because the firm likely has gone out of business).

Of the $26.9 billion deducted over the 10-year period, the plot in **Figure 4.1** shows the time pattern of NOL utilization. Approximately $6 billion and $5 billion were deducted in 1995 and 1997 (or 2 and 4 years after the initial tax loss), respectively, with a declining pattern thereafter. Unless these firms turned their operations around, much of the $13.1 billion NOL carryforward existing at the end of 2003 would have expire unused. Across all sample years, Cooper and Knittel concluded that approximately 10%–15% of losses generated in a given tax year are carried back for an immediate refund (thus having minimal effect on the firm's marginal tax rate, unless the statutory tax rate differs in the carryback period from the current period), 40%–50% of the losses are deducted in future years, approximately 25%–30% of the tax losses are lost (implying a marginal tax rate close to zero for these firms), and 10%–20% remain as NOL carryforwards at the end of the sample period. These data show that many firms experience tax losses, and these losses must be carried forward sometimes for many years, and sometimes until they expire, suggesting that many firms face a marginal tax rate below the top statutory tax rate.

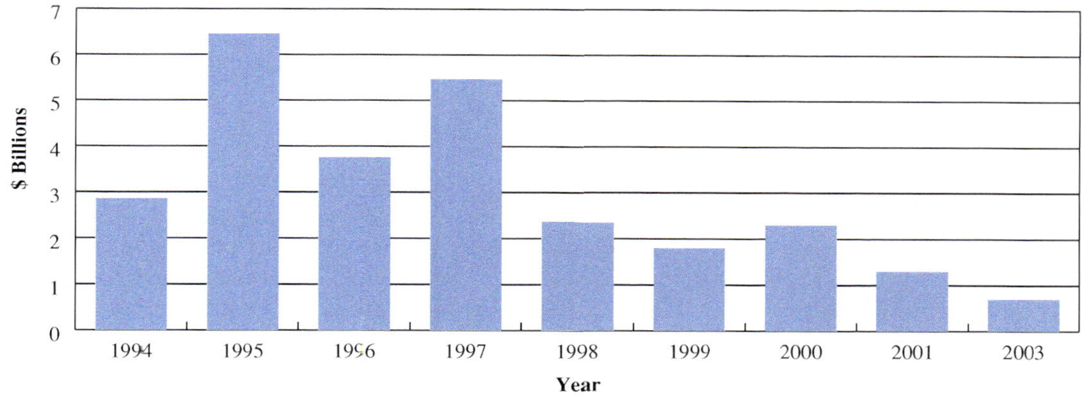

FIGURE 4.1 1993 NOL Carryforward Utilization

Estimating Corporate Marginal Tax Rates in Practice

The scenarios just discussed raise the question as to how one estimates a firm's marginal tax rate. The key factors one needs are forecasts of taxable income and the applicable statutory tax rates to apply. Whether or not the firm has operating losses (i.e., negative taxable income) is the most important issue because the carryovers of the losses affect the computation a great deal. For firms that have no NOL carryovers currently and forecast no future operating losses, the marginal tax rate is the statutory tax rate for the appropriate jurisdiction. However, for firms with NOL carryforwards, the tax planner needs to estimate the number of years before the NOL will be used up. In addition, if carrybacks are allowed, firms with forecasted future operating losses need to consider the carryback of these losses and then the carryforward of any excess. This means the tax planner needs forecasts of future-period taxable income for the length of time the NOLs can be carried forward.

For a tax planner internal to the firm, access to the firm's budgets and plans can help these forecasts. Once the forecasts of taxable income are in hand, the tax planner uses these forecasts along with the appropriate discount rate and knowledge of statutory tax rates to compute the present value of the tax effect of earning additional income (or taking additional deductions) in the current period. Again, the marginal tax rate incorporates the time value of money benefits and costs of having an asymmetric tax function with NOL carryover provisions.

The computation is more difficult for tax planners and parties external to the firm (e.g., accounting and economics researchers, policymakers, and parties dealing with the firm) because they do not have inside information with which to estimate taxable income and how soon tax losses might be expected to be utilized or whether losses will be incurred. However, estimates can be made in a variety of ways, some of which are discussed here.

Considerable literature addresses forecasting accounting earnings (as opposed to forecasting taxable income) using either the past history or patterns in earnings or a detailed analysis of the firms operations. The former is based on statistical analysis; the latter is based on fundamental or financial statement analysis. Discussion of this literature is outside the scope of this text, and the interested reader is referred to Easton, McAnally, Sommers, and Zhang (2018). Additionally, the outside tax planner could use analysts' forecasts of earnings for public firms. Analysts provide both short- and longer-term earnings forecasts. In Chapter 7, we discuss how an outside tax planner can estimate a corporation's taxable income from its financial statements.

Manzon (1994) suggested the following simple approach to estimating the number of periods, s, before a firm returns to tax-paying status after incurring a tax loss. He exploited a simple valuation model to derive an estimate of the expected future constant stream of taxable income:

$$V = \frac{E}{r} \tag{4.7}$$

where V is the market value of the firm's common equity, E is expected future earnings or taxable income, and r is the after-tax discount rate. Rearranging, we can estimate E:

$$E = V \times r \tag{4.8}$$

Given an estimate of future annual earnings (i.e., taxable income), we can now solve for s, the number of periods before we use up the NOL carryforward, by dividing the NOL amount by our estimate of E:

$$s = \frac{NOL_t}{E_t} \tag{4.9}$$

We then insert s into Equation 4.5 (or 4.6 if future losses are allowed to be carried back), depending on the firm's circumstances, and estimate the marginal tax rate. For example, suppose a firm has an NOL carryforward of $2 million, a market value of equity of $6.25 million, and $r = .07$. These data imply an expected annual future taxable income of $437,500 from Equation 4.8, further implying $s = 4.57$ years from Equation 4.9. Next, assuming the statutory tax rate is expected to remain at 21% over the foreseeable future and taxes are paid at the end of the year (implying $s = 5$), the marginal tax rate equals 15% (i.e., $.21/1.07^5$).[16]

A more complex procedure is to forecast future taxable income based on the firm's historical taxable income series. Shevlin (1990) and Graham (1996b) developed a simulation approach; an easy-to-read discussion of the procedure appears in Graham and Lemmon (1998). Shevlin incorporated the NOL carryback and carryforward rules, and Graham extended the approach to include tax credits and the corporate alternative minimum tax. Shevlin reported the following mean marginal-tax-rate estimates across 100 firms in each of the four scenarios discussed earlier for the sample year 1974 in which the top corporate statutory tax rate was 48%:

	$TI_t < 0$	$TI_t > 0$
$NOL_{t-1} = 0$	**1.** 27.66%	**3.** 42.56%
$NOL_{t-1} > 0$	**2.** 21.50%	**4.** 26.62%

Based on these results, which are consistent with what we expect, Shevlin suggested a trichotomous classification of firms: firms in scenario 3 are assumed to face the highest marginal tax rates, those in scenario 2 the lowest rates, and those in scenarios 1 and 4 intermediate rates. Therefore, this classification scheme requires only an estimate of the current-period taxable income and beginning-of-period NOL.

The simulation approach is somewhat complex and requires several assumptions to implement. The interested reader is referred to the original papers. However, Graham's estimates for a large sample of publicly listed firms are available online.[17]

How well does the simulation approach work? Plesko (2003) used 1 year of actual corporate tax return data to evaluate the accuracy of the simulation approach. He found the simulation approach is reasonably accurate in estimating marginal tax rates, noting that his analysis used only 1 year of taxable income data, thus ignoring the important effects of the carryback and carryforward rules. Graham and Mills (2008) extended the Plesko analysis by incorporating more years of tax-return data into the simulations. They showed that the simulation approach using taxable income estimated from the financial statements is highly correlated with the marginal-tax-rate estimate derived from the tax-return taxable income. This suggests that the use of book numbers does not introduce much measurement error into the marginal-tax-rate estimates.[18]

---

[16] Note that Manzon's approach cannot be implemented for private firms because they do not have publicly available market-value data.

[17] See http://www.duke.edu/~jgraham under the "tax rates" option. See also Blouin, Core, and Guay (2010) for estimates of the marginal tax rate using a different method of forecasting taxable income.

[18] Graham and Mills (2008) also provided a good discussion of when a domestic-versus-worldwide and a pre- versus post-financing marginal-tax-rate estimate might be required. What we mean here is that the tax input into a company's decision to, for example, borrow money should be based internally on the estimate of the marginal tax before the debt is issued. In other words, what is the company's marginal tax rate now, and then how will it change on the margin after issuing new debt? Graham and Mills also estimated regression coefficients based on a broad sample of U.S. firms that can be used to derive estimates of a firm's book-simulated marginal tax rate. Note, however, the equation presented by Graham and Mills is based on tax rules prior to the TCJA, which lowered the top corporate statutory tax rate and disallowed carryback of losses.

Additional Details on Local-Level Tax Rates and Individual-Level Marginal Rates

C corporations located in California and Massachusetts pay taxes at rates of 8.4% and 8%, respectively whereas corporations in Texas and Washington state pay zero state tax on income (they pay other taxes based on, for example, net worth or sales revenue). Some counties and cities also assess their own income taxes. To obtain a comprehensive or total marginal tax rate, the additional state and local taxes should be included along with federal taxes to determine the overall marginal tax rate. Note that state and local income taxes are deductible at the federal level.[19] As such, the state tax rate should not be simply added to the federal rate to obtain statutory tax rates when calculating marginal tax rates. Rather, the total statutory tax rate is calculated as

$$(t_{fed}) + (t_{state} + t_{local})(1 - t_{fed})$$

For example, assume the federal statutory tax rate is 21% and the sum of state and local taxes is 10%. The total statutory tax rate is .21 + (.10)(1 − .21) = .289, or 28.9%. Deductibility at the federal level reduces the state and local tax rate to .10(1 − .21) = .79, or 79%.

Individual taxpayers who conduct businesses requiring Schedule C on their tax returns also face the carryforward and carryback rules for Schedule C business losses. Individuals also face carryforward rules on capital losses and passive losses. Individual taxpayers must carryforward capital losses to the extent they exceed capital gains plus $3,000. Passive losses can offset only passive income, so passive losses must be carried forward to offset future passive income, or until the passive loss-generating assets are sold. For individuals, the marginal tax rate is also affected by the presence of rules that tie certain tax deductions to the level of adjusted gross income. For example, under U.S. law, medical deductions and the deductibility of certain losses on passive investment activity are tied to the level of adjusted gross income. In the case of medical deductions, higher income leads to a permanent loss of deductions, and in the case of passive loss deductions (e.g., on real estate activity), higher income may lead to a postponement of the deduction.

The TCJA also capped the itemized deduction for state and local taxes at $10,000 for individual taxpayers. In addition, as mentioned, individual taxpayers need to consider the effects of the alternative minimum tax as well. Given all the above, it is very difficult for taxpayers with more complex tax returns to estimate their marginal tax rate, which makes tax planning more difficult.

Average and Effective Tax Rates

Recall that there are several definitions (or variants) of average tax rates, but each is basically some measure of taxes over some measure of pretax income. For corporations there are two common measures of average tax rate also known as effective tax rate. The GAAP effective tax rate is defined as the total tax expense divided by income before tax (also referred to as pretax book income). The tax-expense figure is insensitive to the timing of tax payments. That is, a dollar of taxes paid currently is treated no differently than a dollar of taxes to be paid many years into the future. The cash effective tax rate is defined as cash taxes paid in the current period divided by pretax book income (sometimes, it is divided by cash flows from operations before subtracting cash taxes paid). The numerator excludes tax deferrals; that is, timing differences in calculating income for tax purposes and for financial reporting purposes (timing differences are discussed in more detail in Chapter 7) .

We argue that GAAP and cash effective tax rates have little economic meaning for decision making. In making economic choices such as investment or financing decisions, it is the marginal tax rate that is important. In a survey of U.S. corporate tax directors, Graham, Hanlon, Shevlin, and Shroff (2017) found that 20% of public companies and 34% of private companies use the top statutory tax rate for incorporating taxes into their decisions, 27% (20.5%) of public (private) use the GAAP effective tax rate, and 11% (12%) of public (private) firms use a marginal tax rate. **Figure 4.2** plots these numbers. This result is not as bad as it seems because many of the public firms for which we could estimate simulated marginal tax rates had estimated marginal tax rates close to the top statutory tax rate. However,

[19] Generally, federal income taxes are not deductible at the state level.

the estimate of GAAP effective tax rates is simply not appropriate for incorporating taxes into corporate decisions.

FIGURE 4.2 Tax Rates Used in Corporate Decision Making Reproduced from Graham et al. (Figure 1, 2017)

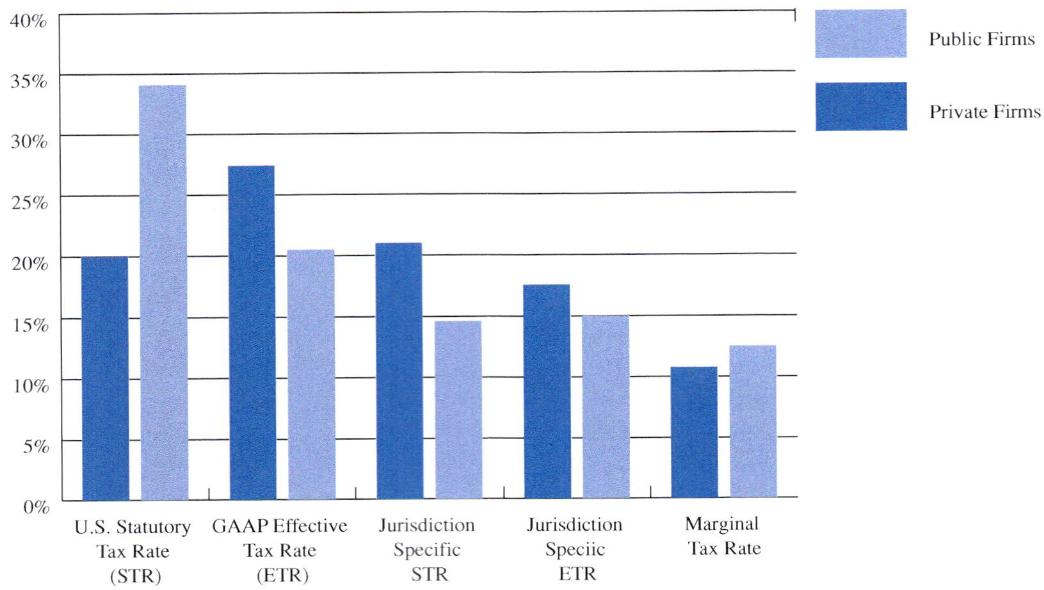

This figure presents the responses to the survey questions "What is the primary tax rate your company uses to incorporate taxes into each of the following forecasts or decision-making processes?" The survey respondent is allowed to choose from the following options (or, write in and answer if the options given are not sufficient): (1) US statutory tax rate, (2) GAAP effective tax rate, (3) jurisdiction-specific statutory tax rate, (4) jurisdiction-specific effective tax rate, (5) marginal tax rate, and (6) other. The question then listed a number of decisions and settings for the respondent to indicate the primary tax rate used in that decision: (1) mergers and acquisitions, (2) capital structure (debt versus equity), (3) investment decisions (property, equip., etc.), (4) decision to purchase versus lease (property, equip., etc.), (5) weighted average cost of capital, (6) where to locate new facilities, and (7) compensation decisions. The figure provides the percentage of firms using each tax rate averaged across all seven decision contexts. The results are separately shown for public and private firms.

4.5 TAX ARBITRAGE

We next demonstrate that in the absence of market frictions and tax-rule restrictions, if one savings vehicle or organizational form dominated another savings vehicle or organizational form—that is, provided higher after-tax rates of return—taxpayers could eliminate all their taxes through **tax arbitrage**. As with any type of arbitrage, tax arbitrage is the purchase of one asset (a "long" position) and the sale of another (a "short" position) to create a sure profit despite a zero level of net investment. We also consider the forces that prevent tax arbitrage from being implemented effectively—namely, tax-rule restrictions and market frictions.

We distinguish between two types of tax arbitrage: (1) organizational-form arbitrage and (2) clientele-based arbitrage. **Organizational-form arbitrage** is the taking of a long position in an asset or a productive activity through a *favorably* taxed organizational form and a short position in an asset or a productive activity through an *unfavorably* taxed organizational form. Although **clientele-based arbitrage** may also involve taking a long position in a tax-favored asset and a short position in a tax-disfavored asset, the nature of clientele-based arbitrage depends on whether the taxpayer starts out with a relatively high or a relatively low marginal tax rate. For the high-tax-rate taxpayer, clientele-based arbitrage is taking a long position in a relatively tax-favored asset (i.e., one that bears a relatively low explicit but likely high implicit tax) and a short position in a tax-disfavored asset (i.e., one that bears, relatively more explicit tax). For the low-tax-rate taxpayer, clientele-based arbitrage is taking a long position in a tax-disfavored asset and a short position in a tax-favored asset.

Organizational-Form Arbitrage[20]

Suppose that the same asset could be held in two differentially taxed organizational forms and the asset bears no implicit tax.[21] Further suppose that taxpayers' marginal tax rates are always positive—that is, when taxable income is negative, the government shares in the loss by sending a check to the taxpayer. In such circumstances, the taxpayer could create infinite wealth. For example, assume that a taxpayer invests in a single-premium deferred annuity (SPDA), which in turn invests in the riskless bond that appreciates in value at the rate of R per period before tax for 2 years. Tax on the appreciation is deferred until the end of year 2. Also suppose that the investment is financed by borrowing (via issuing bonds) at before-tax rate R. Interest payments are deductible at the end of each year, resulting in an annual after-tax cost of $R(1 - t)$. The taxpayer undertakes an additional loan at the end of the first period equal to the after-tax interest that accrues in the first period. For marginal tax rate t, each dollar employed in the strategy gives rise to an after-tax dollar return calculated as follows:

$$\begin{aligned}&\textbf{After-tax SPDA accumulation} - \textbf{After-tax loan repayment}\\&= [(1 + R)^2 (1 - t) + t] - [1 + R(1 - t)]^2\\&= R^2t(1 - t) > 0\end{aligned} \qquad (4.10)$$

Without restrictions or frictions, the taxpayer would continue to borrow to increase wealth without limit as long as t remains positive.

For example, if we assume $R = 10\%$ and $t = 40\%$, the taxpayer accumulates $1,000(.10^2).40(1 – .40) = $2.40 after tax on a zero-net-investment position per $1,000 borrowed and invested in a 2-year SPDA contract. That is, a $1,000 investment in the SPDA accumulates to $1,126 after tax, or $1,000(1.10^2 × .60 + .40), and is financed at an after-tax cost of $1,123.60, or $1,000 × 1.06^2 for a net benefit of $2.40. The government provides a rebate of tR on the interest expense in the first year and collects tax on the cumulative SPDA interest in year 2.

Note that this illustration of organizational-form arbitrage shows a long position in bonds invested through a favorably taxed organizational form (i.e., the SPDA or nondeductible IRA) and a short position in bonds invested through an unfavorably taxed organizational form (i.e., a loan that generates ordinary taxable income to the lender and a corresponding deduction for the borrower each period). This is not consistent with investor equilibrium.

Restrictions on Organizational-Form Arbitrage

Arbitrage of the type we just described could be prevented by placing limits on taxpayers' ability to deduct interest from their taxable income. For example, taxpayers could be permitted to deduct interest only to the extent of other taxable investment income earned (i.e., no net interest deduction). Such restrictions would prevent the taxpayer from making the after-tax cost of borrowing lower than the after-tax return available on the tax-favored savings vehicle. Section 163(d) of the Internal Revenue Code provides such a restriction.

An exception to the interest deduction limitation is provided for home mortgage interest in the United States. But taxpayers cannot really exploit this exception in a way that enables them to effect organizational-form tax arbitrage. After all, one must actually buy a house to qualify for a mortgage. Any arbitrage opportunity available through home ownership should affect the purchase

[20] Examples A2.2, A2.3, and A2.4 discussed in Chapter 2, Appendix 2.2 are examples of organizational-form arbitrage. Example A2 discusses retail firms leasing stores through captive REITs to save state income taxes, Example A3 discusses corporate-owned life insurance (COLI), and Example A4 discusses shorting against the box. Another example of organizational-form arbitrage is income shifting within commonly owned or closely related groups of firms. For example, Gramlich, Limpaphayom, and Rhee (2004) showed that Japanese keiretsu group member firms are subject to lower effective tax rates than non-keiretsu member firms. Group members exhibit lower effective tax rates as a result of income shifting between group members (who are compensated for such income shifting via increased dividends).

[21] Examples include riskless corporate bonds (our benchmark asset) and depreciable assets that give rise to income taxed at ordinary rates and depreciation deductions for tax purposes that are equal in present value to the path of economic depreciation.

price of the home, creating an implicit tax. Moreover, the U.S. tax code contains restrictions on the deductible amounts of home mortgage interest.

The Effects of Frictions on Organizational-Form Arbitrage

Let us now reconsider opportunities to engage in organizational-form arbitrage in the presence of market frictions but without tax-rule restrictions. Suppose that, because of special costs incurred to invest in a particular savings vehicle (e.g., transactions costs and fees), the taxpayer loses a fraction, f, of the before-tax rate of return, R, from the vehicle. That is, the taxpayer realizes only $R(1 - f)$ of the before-tax return in the savings vehicle. Alternatively, the frictions might relate to special costs, such as loan-processing costs and increased interest to reflect risk, incurred to borrow funds to finance other investments, in which, case the before-tax borrowing rate becomes $R(1 + f)$, even when the loan is riskless.

Returning to the strategy of investing in an SPDA funded by borrowing, assume $f = 2\%$: The pretax annual return in the SPDA is now 8%, and the pretax cost of borrowing is 12%. This results in a net benefit to the strategy of $\$1{,}000[(1 + .08)^2(1 - .40) + .40] - [1 + .12(1 - .40)]^2 = -\$49.30$ per $1,000. The strategy is no longer profitable.

Clientele-Based Arbitrage

Clientele-based arbitrage strategies mean reducing explicit tax liabilities at the expense of increasing implicit tax liabilities, or vice versa. Such strategies arise when (1) taxpayers can take both long and short positions in differentially taxed assets, at least one of which bears some implicit tax, and (2) taxpayers face different marginal tax rates. In most income tax regimes, statutory tax rates are progressive, with marginal tax rates rising with taxable income. However, the TCJA introduced a flat 21% tax rate for C corporations, but the tax rate schedule remains progressive for individuals. Progression in the tax rate schedule is an attempt to achieve an equitable distribution of tax burdens (or to redistribute income). At the same time, because Congress uses the tax system to encourage various economic activities, assets are taxed differentially. As we have discussed, the result of taxing assets differentially is the creation of a system of implicit taxes where the prices of tax-favored assets are bid up such that their before-tax rates of return fall below those of equally risky but less-tax-favored assets. Without frictions or restrictions, clientele-based arbitrage would result in all taxpayers facing the *same* marginal tax rates in equilibrium (which could very well be zero!). In addition, all assets would bear the same total (i.e., implicit plus explicit) tax rate. To preserve the ability to redistribute income through progressive marginal tax rates, the federal government has set up many tax rules to prevent clientele-based arbitrage.

The following is an example of clientele-based arbitrage in a world with no frictions or restrictions. We then discuss the restrictions that prevent it. A particularly simple example of clientele-based tax arbitrage is the purchasing of tax-exempt bonds with a loan that gives rise to tax-deductible interest. Although this strategy could succeed in eliminating explicit taxes, it also creates an implicit tax liability. Let us assume $100,000 of salary income is expected over the forthcoming year and the statutory tax rate is 40%. Taxable bonds yield 10% before tax, and taxpayers can borrow at this rate in unlimited quantities. Finally, suppose that municipal bonds yield 7% tax free. Note that municipal bonds bear an implicit tax of 30%, or (.10 − .07)/.10.

To eliminate income tax on $100,000 of salary income, assume we borrow $1,000,000, or $100,000/.10) and invest the proceeds in municipal bonds to earn $70,000, or $1,000,000 × .07, after tax and deduct the interest expense from our taxable income. Note that we have converted salary income taxed explicitly at 40% into municipal bond interest income taxed implicitly at 30%. As the example illustrates, clientele-based arbitrage left unchecked enables high-tax-bracket taxpayers to convert income that would be taxed at high explicit marginal rates into income that is taxed at lower implicit tax rates. If low-tax-bracket taxpayers can take short positions in tax-favored assets, they can profitably pursue the opposite strategy.

In our example, when taxpayers face tax rates below 30%, they would not want to borrow for the purpose of purchasing municipal bonds because that would actually increase their tax rate. For example, if taxpayers face tax rates of 25% on the first $50,000 of salary income and 40% on the next $50,000, the optimal strategy would be to borrow enough to reduce taxable income not from $100,000 to $0, but only to $50,000. This is achieved by borrowing $500,000 at a 10% rate of interest and investing the proceeds in municipal bonds at a 7% rate of interest to yield \$35,000 in tax-exempt interest. The net position after tax is

$$\$50{,}000(1 - 25\%) + \$35{,}000 = \$72{,}500$$

By contrast, a strategy of no borrowing would leave

$$\$50{,}000(1 - 25\%) + \$50{,}000(1 - 40\%) = \$37{,}500 + \$30{,}000 = \$67{,}500$$

And borrowing \$1 million to eliminate all explicit taxes would leave \$70,000, or \$1,000,000 × 7%.

In an attempt to preserve a more progressive tax-rate structure, Congress imposes restrictions on such clientele-based arbitrage. In addition to the interest deduction limitations discussed earlier, Internal Revenue Code Section 265 prevents the deduction of interest on loans used to purchase certain assets that yield tax-exempt income, such as municipal bonds.[22] Note that for taxpayers facing explicit tax rates less than the implicit tax rate on municipal bonds (the cutoff point is 30% in our illustration), this restriction has no effect. Moreover, the restriction may have no effect on more highly taxed taxpayers if there is a positive spread between the riskless interest rate and the rate at which taxpayers can borrow. For example, if taxpayers must pay interest at a rate of 12% to borrow when equally risky taxable bonds earn only 10%, the implicit tax rate becomes 41.67%, or (.12 − .07)/.12. Because this implicit tax rate exceeds the explicit tax rate of 40% on the last \$50,000 of salary income, market frictions are sufficient to prevent this clientele-based arbitrage strategy from being profitable.[23]

As indicated earlier, it is unprofitable for taxpayers with low marginal tax rates to borrow to purchase tax-favored assets. But the reverse strategy would be profitable if permitted. These taxpayers would prefer to issue municipal bonds, for example, and invest the proceeds in taxable bonds. If they could issue the bonds at a 7% before-tax rate of return and buy fully taxable bonds that return 10% before tax, their taxable income would increase until their marginal tax rate was equal to 30%. The clientele-based arbitrage opportunity disappears at that point.

Clientele-Based Arbitrage with Investments in Tax-Favored Assets Other than Tax-Exempt Bonds

Whereas restrictions exist on borrowing to finance the purchase of municipal bonds, no such restrictions exist on borrowing to buy such tax-favored investments as stocks, land, equipment that is eligible for accelerated depreciation, or a host of other tax-favored investments. If the marginal tax rate reflected in market prices for tax-favored investments is below a taxpayer's explicit tax rate on other fully taxed income, the taxpayer can borrow to purchase such assets to effect clientele-based arbitrage. Prior to the TCJA, because U.S. C corporations were not subject to limitations on interest deductions, such clientele-based arbitrage activities were especially advantageous for them. Even after the TCJA, where interest deductions are somewhat limited, C corporations can still engage in this arbitrage activity.

Note, however, that assets that are tax favored due to accelerated or immediate tax deductions are not as effective in bringing about clientele-based arbitrage as tax-exemption-type shelters such as municipal bonds. Arbitrage via accelerated deductions requires other taxable income against which to take the accelerated deductions. And because municipal bond investments do not require deductions against other taxable income to achieve tax exemption, taxpayers can shift much larger amounts of taxable income from explicit to implicit taxation. This helps to explain why special restrictions apply to the deductibility of expenses incurred to generate tax-exempt interest income that do not apply to these other types of tax-favored assets.

---

[22] A generous *de minimus* rule applies, however. Corporations may hold up to 2% of their total U.S. assets in tax-exempt securities or receivables without running afoul of Section 265. Still, this limit can be a problem for businesses that sell goods or services on credit to tax-exempt entities.

[23] For many years, banks and insurance companies were allowed to engage in clientele-based arbitrage; they could deduct interest on loans used to buy municipal bonds. As long as the implicit tax rate on municipal bonds was below their explicit tax rate on fully taxed income, these firms could profit by engaging in clientele-based arbitrage. Various tax acts during the 1980s restricted these activities. For further discussion of these tax-rule changes and their impact on banks' holdings of municipal bonds, see Scholes, Wilson, and Wolfson (1990).

4.6 TAX PLANNING FOR LOW-MARGINAL-TAX-RATE FIRMS

A low-marginal-tax-rate firm has a number of tax-planning options available. For simplicity, assume that the firm has an NOL carryforward of $20 million that will be used up in year 12 if no tax-planning actions are taken because the firm expects to generate more tax losses before it generates positive taxable income. Assuming a statutory tax rate of 21% for the foreseeable future and an after-tax discount rate of 10% gives a marginal tax rate of $.21/1.10^{12} = .067$, or 6.7%.

As discussed above, because the firm faces a low marginal tax rate, clientele-based arbitrage suggests the firm buy highly taxed securities such as corporate bonds (assuming the marginal investor in corporate bonds faces a higher marginal tax rate). This will give rise to income taxable at 6.7%, or an after-tax rate of return of $R_b(1 - \text{mtr})$. If the firm does not have cash available to invest, what type of securities, if any, should it issue? Issuing corporate bonds gains the firm nothing because the after-tax cost will equal $R_b(1 - \text{mtr})$ or worse, given that borrowing rates exceed lending rates because of financial intermediation and frictions. The firm could issue preferred stock to other corporations because it will then obtain an implicit tax deduction arising from the DRD available to corporate investors.[24] That is, the after-tax cost of issuing preferred stock will be lower than the after-tax cost of issuing corporate bonds because highly taxed corporations will bid up the price of the preferred stock to capture the DRD.

Issuing preferred stock to buy bonds is not necessarily the most effective way to exploit the firm's temporarily low tax rate. The firm also might consider a number of other strategies:

- Enter into deferred compensation contracts with employees.
- Sell some equipment to high-marginal-tax-rate taxpayers who can better use accelerated depreciation deductions and lease back the equipment at a bargain rental rate, thereby realizing an implicit tax subsidy. This type of transaction is referred to as a sale-leaseback arrangement, and these arrangements often result in a financial accounting gain on the sale as well.
- Form a research and development (R&D) partnership with high-marginal-tax-rate taxpayers to allow them to obtain the tax benefits from writing off R&D expenditures in exchange for current income.
- Retire any current outstanding debt and issue preferred stock or, if it bears high implicit taxes, issue common stock.
- Consider a merger with a company that faces a higher marginal tax rate. A highly taxed organization might be able to pay more for the right to use the firm's NOLs than they are worth internally to the firm. However, in a friction-filled world, it is not likely that NOL companies will be able to sell their losses for anywhere near $.21 on the dollar. One reason is that the cost to evaluate a prospective merger partner can be large, and buyers must charge for these costs. In addition, buyers must worry about hidden-information problems, as we discuss in Chapter 7. Another reason, as we discuss in the chapters on mergers and acquisitions, is the express limitations in the U.S. tax code on the ability of the acquirer to use the acquired firm's NOLs, foreign tax credits, R&D credits, and capital loss carryovers (called tax attributes of the target firm). These limitations, in Sections 382 and 383, reduce the value of these attributes to the acquiring firm.

  And note that if the firm's future tax rates are decreasing because of statutory decreases in rates and it cannot use up its NOLs internally before statutory tax rates decline, a merger with a high-tax-rate firm becomes more desirable than when tax rates are constant or increasing through time.

Of course, costs to implement a tax-motivated restructuring apply to all these alternatives. A sale-and-leaseback involves contracting costs, monitoring costs, and possibly explicit tax costs, such as depreciation recapture, which we discuss more fully in later chapters. R&D limited partnerships may be very expensive to organize and operate and may suffer from severe incentive

---

[24] Note, however, that although there is no restriction on borrowing and the deduction of interest to purchase stock, the DRD available to corporate investors can be reduced if the corporation borrows directly to purchase stock. Thus, corporations need to be careful in undertaking this arbitrage activity to not run afoul of this restriction (see §246).

problems, as we discuss in Chapter 7. Retiring debt is also not costless to the firm. As always, efficient tax planning requires careful consideration of these frictions.

4.7 ADAPTABILITY OF THE TAX PLAN

Most tax plans cannot be reversed without excessive cost. **Adaptive tax planning** is designed to offset the cost of being in the wrong clientele following unexpected changes in tax status where reversibility is impossible or impractical.[25]

If a business purchases depreciable assets and its tax rate declines, the costs of selling the assets may far outweigh the benefits. In addition to the costs to broker the deal, the transaction might give rise to ordinary taxable income (arising from depreciation recapture) as well as taxable capital gains. Moreover, for tax purposes, the new owner may not be able to use as generous a depreciation schedule as the old owner. For example, an office building purchased during the period 1987–1993 in the United States was depreciable over a 31.5-year period on an accelerated basis. If the building were sold after 1993, however, its new owners would be entitled only to straight-line depreciation over 39 years or 40 years for alternative minimum tax purposes.

However, if the business's objective in selling the property is to transfer the rights to depreciation deductions to a higher-bracket taxpayer, better alternatives might be available. In particular, restructuring other assets and equities of the business could cost less. For example, tax-favored assets, such as municipal bonds or common stocks, might be sold and replaced with ordinary income-producing assets, such as high-yield bonds, at reduced transaction costs. Or businesses might issue stock and purchase bonds with the proceeds. If the businesses can use these substitutes at sufficiently low cost, it would not be very costly for the business to be in the wrong investment clientele if tax rates decline unexpectedly.

Transaction Costs and Tax Clienteles

The joint presence of transaction costs and uncertainty with respect to future tax status can influence tax clienteles. Suppose you are choosing between two investments: fully taxable bonds yielding 10% pretax per year and tax-exempt bonds yielding 7% per year. Both investments have 3-year maturities. At the time of investment, you are unsure, because of the uncertain profitability of your other investments already in place, as to whether your tax rate will be 40% over the 3 years or 0%. You assess a 70% chance of the former. This makes your expected marginal tax rate 28%, or .7(40%) + .3(0%).

If you are risk neutral and must choose one investment or the other and hold it for the entire 3-year period, you would be better off choosing taxable bonds. At an expected tax rate of 28%, taxable bonds yield 7.2% after tax, whereas tax-exempt bonds yield 7%.

Adaptability in Investment and Financing Decisions

With tax-rate uncertainty and transaction costs, it can pay to purchase or issue short-term securities at less favorable yields relative to longer-term securities. Short-term securities introduce an element of flexibility that is valuable in such circumstances. For similar reasons, it might pay to issue callable securities or to purchase puttable securities, even if such options are costly. Or it might be desirable to issue (or purchase) securities that can be repurchased (resold) in the marketplace at low

[25] We also discuss this concept in Chapter 5 in the context of corporations that find the partnership form of organization to be tax advantageous following changes made by the 1986 Tax Reform Act. Many corporations would like to have reorganized as a partnership subsequent to the act. However, for most of them, the tax and nontax costs of the reorganization exceeded the tax benefits. If these firms knew when they first organized that the law would change in the future to favor partnerships, many of them might have organized as a partnership from the start. We also discuss ways in which corporations could undertake transactions that would move them closer to *de facto* partnership tax treatment without undergoing changes in legal organizational form. In particular, the corporate tax burden is mitigated when the corporation distributes pretax profits to owners, employees, and other factor suppliers in forms that are tax deductible at the corporate level. For example, owner-employees could tie their compensation more closely to their firm's profitability. Chapter 5 also discusses the problem that arises under the TCJA for flow-through entities that do not qualify for the business income deduction.

cost. This problem is related to the one of choosing the efficient duration of legal agreements where there is a tradeoff between the fixed costs of writing contracts and the deteriorating efficiency of the agreements over time as circumstances change. In our tax-planning problem, one source of the deteriorating efficiency of the agreements is the possibility of being in the wrong tax clientele due to unexpected changes in tax rates.[26]

4.8 REVERSIBILITY OF TAX PLANS

In some contracts, if tax rates or tax rules change in ways that make existing agreements inefficient, the contracts can be voided. If the contract can be voided when specified tax-related contingencies occur, then the contract allows for the **reversibility of tax plans**. Consider the following examples:

1. Closely held U.S. corporations run the risk that the IRS will view a salary payment to an owner-manager as a disguised dividend. In such a case, the corporation loses its tax deduction for the payment. The corporate minutes of many closely held organizations provide that if the IRS claims that owner-employees have received excessive compensation and treats these payments as disguised dividends, the recipients should return the payments to the corporation. In other words, the transaction is reversed due to the unfavorable tax treatment accorded the transaction, and the firm avoids the cost of being in the wrong clientele for paying a dividend.
2. Many municipal bonds used to fund private activities include standard clauses in the contract that provide for a refund to the investor in the event the IRS deems the bonds to be taxable because they are not issued for an exempt purpose.
3. An exception to the rule that dividend payments are nondeductible to the U.S. corporations that declare them deals with dividends paid on shares held by employee stock ownership plans (ESOPs). An ESOP is a type of pension plan that invests primarily in the stock of the employer on behalf of its employees.[27] The tax deductibility of such dividends has been controversial since it was introduced into law. To guard against adverse changes in the law, some shares issued to ESOPs (typically convertible preferred stock) contain provisions making the shares callable at the issuer's discretion in the event the dividend deduction is eliminated.[28]

4.9 INSURING AGAINST ADVERSE CHANGES IN TAX STATUS

Tax status can change unexpectedly for at least two reasons besides differences between projected and actual future profitability: how the taxing authority and the courts interpret the tax laws and future legislative changes in the tax laws.

In a number of countries, including the United States and Canada, one way a taxpayer can reduce tax treatment uncertainty is by requesting an advance ruling from the tax authority on how a proposed transaction will be treated for tax purposes. In the United States, such requests must include a comprehensive statement of facts describing the proposed transaction along with a documentation of the relevant points of judicial, statutory, and secondary authority. The legal costs of such requests are typically in the $50,000 range, but some requests can be considerably more costly, especially those involving complicated multinational corporate reorganizations. In addition, there is a fee due to the IRS, and it can take 6 to18 months to receive a ruling.

Of course, the risk in seeking such clarification of the rules is that the IRS may rule unfavorably and is likely to audit the return unless the return is filed in a manner consistent with the ruling. As a result, the taxpayer might be better off undertaking the transaction without a ruling request, taking the desired position on the tax return, and hoping the IRS either ignores the issue or the examining agent rules favorably.

[26] Another example for individual taxpayers is a traditional individual retirement account (IRA), which, as discussed in Chapter 3, offers the ability to be converted into a Roth IRA. Hulse (2003) analyzed the value of this option.

[27] We discuss ESOPs in more detail in Chapter 9.

[28] See, for example, Morgan Stanley's "Leveraged ESOP Presentation for Unocal Corporation" (February 15, 1989), pp. III–3.

A second way a taxpayer can secure insurance against unexpected tax treatment is to purchase professional legal opinions. Tax shelter limited partnerships and real estate investment trusts (REITs) are notorious for the many facets of the investment for which tax treatment uncertainty exists. In fact, the Securities and Exchange Commission (SEC) requires that all limited partnership prospectuses contain an extensive section on risk factors, including "income tax aspects" of the investment, that thoroughly discusses uncertainties regarding tax treatment. General comments and warnings such as the following are common:

> Qualifying as a real estate investment trust (a "REIT") under the Internal Revenue Code of 1986, as amended (the "Code") requires complying with highly technical and complex tax provisions that courts and administrative agencies have interpreted only to a limited degree. Due to the complexities of our ownership, structure, and operations, the Trust is more likely than are other REITs to face interpretive issues for which there are no clear answers. Also, facts and circumstances that we do not control may affect the Trust's ability to qualify as a REIT. The Trust believes that since the taxable year ended December 31, 1995, the Trust has qualified as a REIT. The Trust intends to continue to operate so as to qualify as a REIT. However, the Trust cannot assure you that the Trust will continue to qualify as a REIT. If the Trust failed to qualify as a REIT for any prior tax year, the Trust would be liable to pay a significant amount of taxes for those years. Similarly, if the Trust fails to qualify as a REIT in the future, our liability for taxes would increase. (Starwood Hotels and Resorts, Form S-3 Registration Statement, filed November 18, 1999, p. 12)

Firms merging with or acquiring another firm often obtain legal opinion as to the tax treatment of the planned transaction structure. For example, the Boeing Company in its 1998 10-K filing with the SEC discussed its proposed acquisition of part of the Rockwell International Corporation as follows:

> Consummation of the Transaction is conditioned on the receipt of opinions of counsel that (i) the Contribution and the Distribution qualify as transactions described in Sections 351 and 355 of the Code and/or as a "reorganization" under Section 368(a)1)(D) of the Code and (ii) the Merger qualifies as a "reorganization" under Section 368(a)(1)(B) of the Code. An opinion of counsel is not binding on the Internal Revenue Service ("IRS") or the courts.[29]

In its 1996 acquisition of McDonnell Douglas Corporation, the Boeing Company stated in the document "Exchanging McDonnell Douglas Stock to Boeing Stock,"

> According to opinions received from attorneys for Boeing and McDonnell Douglas, the receipt of Boeing stock in exchange for McDonnell Douglas stock will be tax-free for U.S. Federal income tax purposes, except that shareholders will recognize gain or loss with respect to cash received in lieu of fractional shares of Boeing stock.

Given a legal tax opinion, investors can and typically do sue the lawyers in the event that significant expected tax benefits, on which legal counsel has expressed a favorable opinion, are disallowed by the IRS.

The two forms of insurance we just discussed deal with uncertainty over existing tax rules. But some forms of insurance also exist regarding legislative changes. For example, in November 1984, the U.S. Treasury Department announced its proposal to overhaul the federal income tax system. Among many proposed changes was one to reduce maximum federal tax rates to 35% as of July 1, 1986. Because lower tax rates reduce the value of depreciation deductions, many limited partnerships that invested in real estate and other depreciable assets were having trouble raising funds in the face of this uncertainty. In response to investor concern, a number of partnership contracts provided that the limited partners' share of profits would be increased if the tax proposals were passed. An example is the Stanford Capital Realty Fund:

> The General Partner has agreed, in the event of reduction in the Maximum Tax Rate effective for any year prior to 1990, to reduce its interest in Net Sale or Refinancing Proceeds available for distribution

[29] These tax code sections are discussed in more detail in later chapters, and the reader does not need to understand the structure of the Boeing transaction here.

after the Capital Return Date (that is, after limited partners have already received distributions from the partnership equal to 100% of their initial investment), to attempt to mitigate any adverse impact upon Limited Partners of such a reduction in the Maximum Tax Rate.

The prospectus then gives the tax-rate-contingent formula for sharing profits and works through an example based on tax-loss projections given in the prospectus. If the maximum federal tax rate on July 1, 1986, were to decline to 35% in the example, "[t]he percentage of Net Sale or Refinancing Proceeds to which the Limited Partners would be entitled would increase from the current 83.33% to 95.17% (and the General Partner interest would decline from 16.67% to 4.83%)."

The is an example of a **tax indemnity**. The issuer of securities indemnifies the investor against less favorable tax treatment than that promised. Such indemnities may conserve costs in that investors need not research the tax rules as comprehensively, given the insurance. However, the contracting parties should also be sensitive to the allocation of risk if they are risk averse. Tax indemnities typically allocate all the tax risk to one party, which is not always efficient, but concentrating the risk in the hands of one party may provide efficient incentives for lobbying against unfavorable changes in tax rules. It may also induce the insuring party to effect adaptive tax planning—organizational restructuring—following changes in tax rules.

A final way to insure against unfavorable changes in tax laws is to purchase investments that will be affected favorably by the tax law changes or take short positions in securities that will decline in value if the tax laws are changed. For example, someone concerned about unexpected declines in federal tax rates might wish to avoid the purchase of municipal bonds, the prices of which are likely to fall if tax rates are reduced as they become less tax favored.

4.10 TAX PLANNING WHEN A TAXPAYER'S MARGINAL TAX RATE IS STRATEGY DEPENDENT

In many tax-planning situations, the firm's marginal tax rate is affected by the very decisions the firm undertakes to alter its investment and financing activities. For example, if the firm buys bonds with the proceeds of a preferred stock issue, the additional taxable cash flows generated from the bond interest income can affect the computation of the marginal tax rate. If clientele-based arbitrage activities do alter a firm's marginal tax rate, the firm cannot rely on its initial calculation to make an optimal decision. This is what we mean when we say the computation of the marginal tax rate is **strategy dependent**. Strategy dependence increases the complexity of tax planning.

We illustrated strategy dependence earlier in this chapter where we showed that a taxpayer subject to a progressive tax would wish to engage in certain clientele-based arbitrage transactions only in limited volume. The reason is that the attractiveness of further transactions decreases as the transactions alter the investor's marginal tax rate.

The strategy dependence of marginal tax rates also hampers researchers and others in their examination of the role of taxes in firms' investment and financing decisions. For example, theory predicts that high-tax firms will use debt to lower their tax bills or that high-tax firms should exhibit higher debt levels. By increasing debt, however, firms increase their interest deduction and lower their marginal tax rate. Thus, in equilibrium, all firms may appear to face similar marginal tax rates. If so, tests can fail to detect a relationship between ex-post debt levels and ex-post marginal tax rates when, in fact, high-tax firms increased their debt levels to garner the tax shield offered by debt. Two solutions address this problem. First, instead of examining debt levels, the researcher can examine the role of taxes in new debt issuances. Both Mackie-Mason (1990) and Graham (1996a) illustrated how a "debt changes" (rather than "debt levels") approach allows a more powerful test of the role of taxes in corporate capital structure decisions. Second, use marginal tax rates (and, where necessary, other variables) estimated on a "but for" approach (also referred to as "pre-if" or "as if" measures). An example of this approach is Graham, Lemmon, and Schallheim (1998), who showed that debt levels and the usual after-financing tax rates are negatively correlated and that debt levels and before-financing tax rates (i.e., but-for marginal tax rates) are positively associated as predicted by theory.

A second relevant problem plaguing the study of debt levels, as well as other firm choices, is that a firm's capital structure reflects past decisions based on expectations that may not have been fulfilled because of unexpected outcomes, such as a change in product markets, competition, the economy, or tax policy. Thus, even if decisions were tax motivated when undertaken, in subsequent periods, these decisions may appear contrary to predicted tax responses. Because it is costly to restructure capital, cross-sectional studies of debt levels may erroneously conclude that taxes do not affect capital-structure decisions. In other words, firms may not quickly restructure their economic balance sheets because of recontracting costs when their tax status changes unexpectedly. Thus, cross-sectional tests of debt levels can fail to find a tax effect when one exists.

Unanticipated changes in tax rules and tax status should be viewed as the rule rather than the exception for most taxpayers. It is important to factor such uncertainty into the tax-planning process and to be prepared to plan your way out of undesired clienteles as the uncertainty is resolved. Our objective is to provide you with the tools necessary to approach this task in a systematic and rational fashion.

Summary of Key Points

1. Different economic activities are taxed differently, even when undertaken in the same organizational form. The unequal taxation of returns affects the demand for investment and thereby affects pretax rates of return. Specifically, if two assets yield identical pretax cash flows and one is more heavily taxed than the other, then the price of the more lightly taxed asset will be bid up relative to the price of the more heavily taxed asset, leading to differences in pretax rates of return. For example, those investments that are tax favored relative to fully taxable bonds earn lower before-tax rates of return than fully taxable bonds. The difference in pretax rates of return between fully taxed bonds and the tax-favored asset is an implicit tax. Thus, differential tax treatment of asset returns gives rise to implicit taxes. That is, a tax is paid implicitly through the lower before-tax rates of return.
2. Investments that are tax disfavored relative to fully taxable bonds earn *higher* before-tax rates of return than fully taxable bonds, and, taking fully taxable bonds as the benchmark, the implicit tax on the relatively tax-disfavored asset is negative.
3. If, in addition to differentially taxed assets, we have differentially taxed investors, the proper clientele for investments depends on the mix of implicit and explicit taxes levied on the investments. The marginal investor setting prices in the market is the taxpayer who is indifferent between investing in the differentially taxed assets. The proper clientele for high-implicitly-taxed investments are investors whose statutory tax rates exceed that of the marginal investor setting prices in the market. And the proper clientele for high-explicitly taxed investments are investors whose statutory tax rates are less than that of the marginal investor.
4. Many policymakers appear to ignore implicit taxes in their public statements. If we measure the progressiveness of our tax structure by focusing exclusively on explicit taxes, the U.S. tax structure does not appear very progressive. That is, the explicit tax as a percentage of the total income is about the same for wealthy and poor taxpayers. If, conversely, implicit taxes and subsidies are incorporated into the tax-burden calculations, the tax schedule is much more progressive. The reason is that wealthy investors tend to own assets with high implicit taxes, such as municipal bonds, common stock, and real estate.
5. Taxpayers need to know their marginal tax rate to undertake effective tax planning. To calculate the marginal tax cost of a dollar of fully taxable C corporation income requires including the effect on the value of future-period tax liabilities. One must also include the effects of additional income on the availability of tax deductions and tax credits, especially for individual taxpayers.
6. When statutory tax rates are constant over time, C corporations that experience NOL carryforwards typically face lower marginal tax rates than those that do not. In the presence of NOL and other carryforwards, the current marginal tax rate is sensitive to future changes in statutory tax rates.

7. As marginal tax rates change over time, so do investment and financing clienteles. Because it is costly to change investment and financing clienteles as tax status changes, taxpayers place a premium on strategies that allow activities to be reorganized at low cost.
8. Effective tax rates are commonly used to determine the average rate of tax paid by taxpayers. Two popular definitions exist, a GAAP definition and a cash definition. Such tax rates provide little guidance for identifying tax clienteles or for tax planning.
9. In the absence of market frictions and tax-rule restrictions, if one savings vehicle or organizational form dominated another savings vehicle or organizational form, taxpayers could eliminate all their taxes through tax arbitrage. Tax arbitrage is the purchase of an asset (i.e., a long position) and the sale of another (i.e., a short position) to create a sure profit despite a zero level of net investment.
10. Organizational-form arbitrage arises when taxpayers take a long position in an asset through a tax-favored organizational form and a short position in the asset through an unfavorably taxed organizational form. Clientele-based arbitrage arises when taxpayers face different tax rates and when assets are taxed differentially, which gives rise to implicit taxes. Clientele-based arbitrage is a conversion of taxable income from an explicitly taxed to an implicitly taxed form, or vice versa.
11. Asset returns can be exempt from explicit taxation either through the nontaxability of future returns (e.g., with municipal bonds in the United States) or through immediate deductibility of investment followed by full taxation of returns. Were it not for tax-rule restrictions relating to interest deductions, tax-exempt bonds would be more effective in clientele-based arbitrage strategies than would assets that achieve tax exemption due to the deductibility of investment cost.
12. Market frictions impede taxpayers' ability to undertake tax arbitrage. Most market frictions arise because information is costly and not all taxpayers have the same information. This is a point we will consider more thoroughly in Chapter 7.
13. Many of the detailed provisions of the U.S. tax code represent restrictions on taxpayers' ability to effect tax arbitrage. As numerous as these restrictions might appear to be (and they are indeed numerous; we have mentioned only a few of the more important ones here), they are far fewer in number than if there were no market frictions (i.e., if implementation of tax arbitrage strategies were costless).
14. Contractual arrangements that can be voided when specified tax-related contingencies occur introduce an element of reversibility into tax plans.
15. Adaptive tax planning is designed to offset the cost of being in the wrong clientele following unexpected changes in tax status where reversibility is impossible or impractical.
16. In many contracts, one party explicitly indemnifies other parties against tax treatment that turns out to be less favorable than promised. Such provisions are designed to reduce the costs of contracting.
17. A taxpayer's marginal tax rate is often affected by the very investment and financing strategies implemented to take advantage of its initial tax status. This adds an element of recursion to tax planning. We refer to marginal tax rates in this case as being strategy dependent. Thus, calculating the marginal tax rate in realistic settings is rather challenging.

Questions

Q4-1. True or false? Discuss.

a. The implicit tax rate on an asset cannot be calculated without a benchmark asset against which to compare pretax returns.

b. The implicit tax rate is always positive.

c. The implicit tax rate is always less than the explicit tax rate.

d. Whereas explicit taxes are paid to taxing authorities, implicit taxes are subsidies paid to the issuers of securities, consumers of goods and services, and suppliers of factor inputs.

Q4-2. List five assets that bear positive implicit taxes. Carefully explain why each asset bears an implicit tax (i.e., how the asset is tax favored).

Q4-3. Provide an example of an asset that bears a negative implicit tax and explain why the asset bears a negative implicit tax.

Q4-4. Capital investment in many countries is tax favored. For example, in 1989, Singapore allowed a 100% tax depreciation write-off in the year of purchase for certain automated production equipment. Similar tax treatment was allowed on a variety of capital expenditures in the United Kingdom during the early 1980s. The United States often enacts bonus depreciation, and the TCJA allows certain capital expenditures to be immediately expensed. How do investment tax credits and liberal depreciation allowances affect the required before-tax rates of return on investment? Could the risk-adjusted before-tax rates of return on investment be lower than the tax-exempt riskless bond rate in equilibrium? Why or why not? Could the risk-adjusted before-tax rate of return on investment be higher than the before-tax riskless bond rate? Why or why not?

Q4-5. Why do countries encourage investment by offering tax incentives such as investment tax credits or liberal depreciation allowances? What alternative methods exist to achieve the same goals? How would you judge whether tax incentives are superior to the alternatives?

Q4-6. What is an investment tax clientele? If the market sets implicit tax rates, why are we interested in determining the proper clientele for various investments? Why should a corporate strategist be interested in clienteles?

Q4-7. True or false? Explain.

a. In undertaking tax-planning strategies, the effective tax rate has no meaning.

b. In calculating marginal tax rates for the purpose of determining investment and financing clienteles, ignoring future taxes is appropriate.

c. By borrowing, taxpayers can always reduce their personal tax rate on partnership income to the implicit tax rate on municipal bonds.

d. The marginal tax rate for firms with NOL carryforwards is below that of firms currently paying tax by a discount factor reflecting the delay in when the NOL firm is expected to begin paying taxes.

Q4-8. How is the marginal tax rate affected by the presence of rules that reduce current tax deductions by a fraction of incremental income? How is the marginal tax rate affected by the presence of rules that postpone current tax deductions or tax credits by a fraction of incremental income?

Q4-9. How difficult is it in reality to compute a C corporation's marginal tax rate? Why? What factors are really important? If we observe that a firm has NOLs, does this mean that the firm has not hired a smart tax-planning strategist?

Q4-10. What is organizational-form arbitrage? Give an example of organizational-form arbitrage that would create infinite wealth for a taxpayer. What conditions are necessary to prevent this from happening?

Q4-11. What is clientele-based arbitrage? Provide an example of such a strategy. Is clientele-based arbitrage restricted to high-tax-bracket taxpayers?

Q4-12. What alternative investment and financing instruments can firms use to alter their marginal tax rate? Why might a firm prefer to repackage its capital structure (i.e., the mix of financial instruments it issues to finance operations) instead of changing its operating decisions to effect clientele-based arbitrage?

Q4-13. What does it mean for a tax plan to be reversible? Give examples to illustrate this concept. What costs are associated with contractual provisions that make tax plans reversible?

Q4-14. What is the meaning of the term *adaptability of tax plans*? Give some examples to illustrate the concept. What are the costs of undertaking such plans?

Q4-15. Why might a firm offer insurance against adverse changes in tax status? Do you see a great deal of this form of insurance? Why or why not?

Q4-16. What is meant by the term *strategy dependence* as it relates to the computation of the marginal tax rate? How does strategy-dependence affect the computation of the marginal tax rate? How does it affect decision-making strategies?

Exercises

E4-17. *a.* A taxpayer is considering buying a fully taxable corporate bond. The bond has a remaining maturity of 5 years, promises to pay 6% interest annually (assume the coupon interest is payable annually), and has a face value of $1,000. The taxpayer faces a 30% tax rate on the interest income and requires a pretax rate of return of 6% to invest. What price is the taxpayer willing to pay for this bond?

b. The same taxpayer is also considering buying a tax-exempt municipal bond. The municipal bond has a remaining maturity of 5 years, also promises to pay 6% interest annually (again, the coupon interest is payable annually), and has a face value of $1,000. Assume the corporate and municipal bonds are equally risky. At what price is the taxpayer indifferent between the corporate and municipal bond? (Alternatively stated, what price is the taxpayer willing to pay for the municipal bond assuming he requires a pretax rate of return of 6% and faces a marginal tax rate of 30%?) How does this exercise tie to the discussion of implicit taxes in the text?

E4-18. If the before-tax rate of return on a riskless fully taxable bond is 7% and the before-tax rate of return on a riskless tax-favored asset is 5%, what is the implicit tax rate on the tax-favored asset? If a tax-exempt riskless asset earns a before-tax rate of return of 4%, what is the explicit tax rate for the marginal investor on the riskless tax-favored asset that returns 5%?

E4-19. Suppose a C corporation is equally likely to earn $2 million this year or lose $3 million. The firm faces a tax rate of 40% on each dollar of taxable income, and pays no taxes on losses. In this simple 1-period scenario, ignore the carryback and carryforward rules. The firm's expected taxable income is thus a loss of $500,000, calculated as .50(–$3) + .50($2). What is the firm's expected marginal tax rate?

Suppose a second C corporation is equally likely to earn $3 million this year or lose $2 million. This firm also faces a tax rate of 40% on each dollar of taxable income and pays no taxes on losses. Again, in this simple 1-period scenario, ignore the carryback and carryforward rules. The firm's expected taxable income is thus a profit of $500,000, calculated as .50($3) + .50(–$2). What is the firm's expected marginal tax rate?

Explain and discuss your results. Why is the first firm's marginal tax rate not 0%? Why is the second firm's marginal tax rate not 40%?

E4-20. Suppose a C corporation has a tax loss of $5 million in the current period. The firm's after-tax discount rate is 10%. Assume the firm is allowed to carry back losses. Over the preceding 5 years, the firm reported the following taxable income:

	Year					
	–5	–4	–3	–2	–1	Current
Taxable income ($ millions)	$1.0	$1.0	$1.5	$4.0	$3.0	–$5.0
Statutory tax rate	40%	40%	35%	35%	30%	30%

a. If the carryback period is 3 years, what is the firm's marginal tax rate in the current period?

b. If the carryback period is 2 years, what is the firm's marginal tax rate in the current period?

c. Suppose the firm is prohibited from carrying back losses, what is its marginal tax rate assuming it will earn $2 million in each of the next 5 years?

d. Suppose the carryback period is 2 years and taxable income in period –1 was only $1 million. What is the firm's marginal tax rate in the current period?

E4-21. Suppose a C corporation has a tax loss in the current period of $10 million, which when added to prior tax losses gives it an NOL carryforward of $15 million. The top statutory tax rate for the foreseeable future is 21%. Assume an after-tax discount rate of 10% and future taxable income per annum of $2 million.

a. What is the firm's marginal tax rate?

b. What is the firm's marginal tax rate if the top statutory tax rate is expected to increase to 40% within the next 2 years?

E4-22. Find the annual report for a publicly listed high-technology company that has losses. Refer to the tax footnote in the report to extract the NOL carryforward. Assume an after-tax discount rate of 10%. Calculate the firm's marginal tax rate using the Manzon (1994) market-value approach. Discuss and explain your result.

E4-23. Suppose that insurance policies were fully tax exempt and (a) policies pay less than the fully taxable bond return to cover the costs of the insurance company and (b) loans can be secured only at a higher rate than the fully taxable bond rate to cover the lender costs. Can we use an insurance policy strategy to eliminate the tax on $100,000 of taxable income? What is the implicit tax rate on this strategy? How does it arise, and where does it go? Would every taxpayer want to use this strategy? Explain.

Tax-Planning Problems

TP4-24. Assume you are a tax planner for a client with the following concerns:

a. Suppose there exist three riskless assets. The first yields a fully taxable return of 7% before tax, the second yields a pretax return of 6%, only half of which is taxable, and the third yields a 5% fully tax-exempt return. Over what range of tax rates does each asset yield the highest after-tax return? How does this relate to tax clienteles?

b. Suppose the tax-rate schedule is as follows: 20% on the first $5,000 of investment income, 30% on the next $5,000 of investment income, and 40% on investment income exceeding $10,000. If you had $150,000 to invest and had to invest in only one of the three assets, which one would maximize after-tax income?

c. Can you beat the investment strategy in (b) by investing in a portfolio of assets? What is the optimal investment (i.e., the one that maximizes after-tax income) over the range of investment from $0 to $500,000?

TP4-25. Suppose a firm has a tax loss in the current period of $10 million, which when added to prior tax losses gives it an NOL carryforward of $15 million. The current top statutory tax rate is 35% but is expected to increase to 45% in 2 years. Assume an after-tax discount rate of 10% and future taxable income per annum of $2 million. The firm has a large NOL carryforward. Should the firm undertake clientele-based arbitrage by issuing preferred stock and buying corporate bonds?

TP4-26. Your colleague picks up the 2016 annual report of Alphabet Inc. (parent company of Google) and finds that Alphabet reports an effective tax rate of 19.3% for fiscal year 2016 and 16.85% for fiscal year 2015. He argues that Alphabet faces a low tax rate. Your colleague argues that Alphabet should not have much long-term debt in its capital structure, it should have issued preferred stock and invested idle cash in taxable bonds, and it should be leasing assets. Evaluate your colleague's argument.

TP4-27. Following a substantial earthquake, a major West Coast university suffered $100 million in property damage. Suppose that this loss enabled the university to borrow an additional $100 million worth of tax-exempt bonds. The university issued 20-year zero-coupon bonds yielding 7% to maturity—that is, the university will pay bondholders $100 million × 1.0720, or $386.97 million, at maturity. Any gift money raised from friends of the university can be invested to earn 10% in riskless taxable bonds.

a. How much must the university raise in gifts to pay off its bond obligation at maturity?

b. How would your answer change if the bonds matured in 30 years rather than 20 years?

TP4-28. Suppose you are a high-tax-bracket taxpayer. How could you take advantage of a situation in which the implicit tax rate on a tax-exempt asset is different from the marginal tax rate on income from a fully taxable asset? How would a low-tax-bracket taxpayer take advantage of this situation? What impediments—frictions and restrictions—exist to limit your ability to take advantage of this arbitrage possibility?

TP4-29. Assume you work for a local municipality and there are no tax-rule restrictions preventing a municipality from buying taxable bonds financed by tax-exempt bonds yielding a lower before-tax rate of return. What arbitrage strategy should the municipality adopt? When does the opportunity disappear? Once the municipality no longer has arbitrage opportunities, what arbitrage opportunities must exist for taxable investors? When do these opportunities disappear? When will neither tax-exempt nor taxable investors face arbitrage opportunities simultaneously? What tax-rule restrictions are necessary to prevent this form of clientele-based arbitrage?

TP4-30. Assume you work for a local municipality. Under what conditions is it tax advantageous for municipalities to undertake profit-making ventures? Why don't we see more municipality-operated activities? Can you think of some taxable business ventures currently operated by municipalities? Would the same arguments apply to other tax-exempt entities, such as universities, hospitals, and charities?

TP4-31. The CFO of the ABC Corporation asks you to address three questions, keeping in mind ABC faces a top corporate marginal tax rate of 35% on both ordinary income and on capital gains:

a. The firm is considering investing in some equipment costing $500,000. A 10% investment tax credit is available on the equipment. The equipment is depreciable using straight-line depreciation over 3 years with a zero salvage value. The firm uses an after-tax discount rate of 10% for this type of investment. The CFO asks you to estimate the present value of the tax savings from this investment. Assume the tax credit and first-year depreciation are taken immediately. How do the present value of the tax deductions compare with immediate expensing of the total outlay (with no investment tax credit)?

b. The equipment above is expected (assumed here for simplicity) to generate a one-time pretax cash flow of approximately $805,255 at the end of year 5. The CFO asks you to estimate the expected annualized pretax and after-tax rates of return on this investment. Would you recommend undertaking this investment? Is this a tax-favored investment? Does it bear implicit taxes?

c. The firm has $5 million in short-term investments. The money is to be used to expand facilities. However, due to regulatory delays in obtaining environmental approval, the expansion has been delayed 5 years. The firm now wishes to invest the funds in longer-term higher-yielding securities. The firm is considering three options:

i. Invest in corporate bonds yielding 12% per annum pretax.
ii. Invest in non-dividend-paying corporate equities expected to earn 12% per annum pretax.
iii. Invest in preferred stock of other corporations paying a 10% dividend per year. The corporation is eligible for a 70% DRD.

Which option would you recommend, and why? State any assumptions you need to make.

d. The CFO asks you to prepare a proposal outlining any tax-arbitrage strategies that the firm might be able to undertake to reduce its taxes. In preparing your proposal, make sure the strategies do not run afoul of the tax-rule restrictions listed in this chapter. Provide a numerical example of each strategy to illustrate how it would work and how much in taxes it would save.

TP4-32. A currently profitable brick-and-mortar retail firm is under attack from several internet start-ups. The top management has decided to open an online store. Strong competition and price-cutting by the upstart internet firms makes the future profitability of the firm uncertain. Given this doubt, the firm's CFO is concerned about the firm being in the wrong investment and financing clientele. She has asked you to prepare a memo outlining possible actions, together with your recommendations, the firm might take to reduce the expected costs of finding itself in the wrong clientele. She has asked that any assumptions you make be made explicit.

TP4-33. Suppose you operate a very profitable sole proprietorship. Your current-year marginal tax rate is 40%, but you expect it to increase to 50% next year due to legislative changes. Your business includes exclusive rights to distribute microcomputer software packages in specified geographical areas. Your typical gross margin on software sales for the programs distributed is an impressive 50%.

The end of the year is approaching, and you wonder whether a special price reduction to promote sales in the current tax year would be desirable. You assess that a 10% across-the-board price reduction for the remainder of the year will generate $400,000 of new sales, but $800,000 of normal sales for the rest of the year will be made at a 10% discount.

Moreover, $1 million of next year's sales will be cannibalized. That is, a 10% price cut will result in $1 million of next year's product line being sold this year for $900,000, and $800,000 of normal sales for the rest of this year will yield $720,000 in revenues, but you will also pick up $400,000 in new sales this year.

a. How much better or worse off would you be *before and after tax* if you employ the year-end sales strategy and it goes according to plan?

Your customers fall roughly into three categories: corporations whose tax rates typically will not change from this year to next year, individuals who are not entitled to tax deductions for the purchase of your software, and small businesses, many of which face tax-rate increases similar to yours. Assume such businesses take tax deductions for the purchase of software in the year the software is acquired.

b. How are your customers likely to respond differently to the temporary price cut?

TP4-34. When evaluating new projects and investments, ABC Corporation calculates after-tax cash flows and earnings assuming the firm's marginal tax rate equals the top federal statutory tax rate of 21%. The firm is a large multinational with operations in many countries as well as many U.S. states.

a. Under what future profitability conditions is it advisable for ABC Corporation to use the statutory tax rate in its project evaluations?

b. What problems might arise by ignoring foreign, state, and local taxes in these project evaluations?

c. The firm's financial accountant calculates that the company's effective tax rate is 15% and argues that the firm should be using this rate in its project evaluations. Do you agree?

Suppose the ABC Corporation, due to the Asian economic crash and internet-based competition, faces some uncertainty about its future profitability.

d. What effect might this uncertainty have on the firm's marginal tax rate?

e. Given this uncertainty, the firm's CFO, who is concerned about the firm being in the wrong investment and financing clientele, asks you to prepare a memo outlining possible actions, together with your recommendations, the firm might take to reduce the expected costs of finding itself being in the wrong clientele. She asks that any assumptions you make be made explicit.

References and Additional Readings

Atwood, T. J., 2003. "Implicit Taxes: Evidence from Taxable, AMT, and Tax-Exempt State and Local Government Bond Yields," *Journal of the American Taxation Association* (Spring), pp. 1–20.

Auerbach, A. J., and K. A. Hassett, 2006. "The 2003 Dividend Tax Cuts and the Value of the Firm: An Event Study," in *Taxing Corporate Income in the 21st Century*, edited by A. Auerbach and J. Slemrod. (Cambridge: Cambridge University Press).

Ayers, B., B. Cloyd, and J. Robinson, 2002. "The Effect of Shareholder-Level Taxes on Stock Prices: Evidence from the Revenue Reconciliation Act of 1993," *The Accounting Review*, pp. 933–947.

Ayers, B., C. Lefanowicz, and J. Robinson, 2000. "The Effects of Goodwill Tax Deductions on the Market for Corporate Acquisitions," *Journal of the American Taxation Association* (Supplement), pp. 34–50.

Ayers, B., C. Lefanowicz, and J. Robinson, 2003, "Shareholder Taxes in Acquisition Premiums: The Effect of Capital Gains," *Journal of Finance* (58), pp. 2783–2801.

Ayers, B., C. Lefanowicz, and J. Robinson, 2004, "The Effect of Shareholder-Level Capital Gain Taxes on the Taxability and Method of Payment in Corporate Acquisitions," *The Accounting Review* (4), pp. 859–887.

Berger, P., 1993. "Explicit and Implicit Tax Effects of the R&D Tax Credit," *Journal of Accounting Research* (2), pp. 131–171.

Black, F., and M. Scholes, 1974. "The Effect of Dividend Yield and Dividend Policy on Common Stock Prices and Returns," *Journal of Financial Economics* (1), pp. 1–22.

Callihan, D., and R. White, 1999. "An Application of the Scholes and Wolfson Model to Examine the Relation between Implicit and Explicit Taxes and Firm Market Structure" *Journal of the American Taxation Association* (Spring), pp. 1–19.

Cannavan, D., F. Finn, and S. Gray, 2004. "The Value of Dividend Imputation Tax Credits in Australia," *Journal of Financial Economics* (73), pp. 167–197.

Chetty, R., J. Rosenberg, and E. Saez, 2006. "Market Responses to Dividend Announcements and Payments: Evidence from the 2003 Dividend Tax Cut and the Time Series," *Taxing Corporate Income in the 21st Century*, edited by A. Auerbach and J. Slemrod (Cambridge: Cambridge University Press).

Chetty, R., and E. Saez, 2005. "Dividend Taxes and Corporate Behavior: Evidence from the 2003 Dividend Tax Cut," *Quarterly Journal of Economics* (120), pp. 791–833.

Dai, Z., E. Maydew, D. Shackelford, and H. Zhang, 2008. "Capital Gains Taxes and Asset Prices: Capitalization or Lock-in?" *Journal of Finance*, pp. 709–742.

Desai, M., 2002. "The Corporate Profit Base, Tax Sheltering Activity, and the Changing Nature of Employee Compensation," Working Paper 8866, Cambridge, MA: National Bureau of Economic Research.

Dhaliwal, D., M. Erickson, M. M. Frank, and M. Banyi, 2003. "Are Shareholder Dividend Taxes on Corporate Retained Earnings Impounded in Equity Prices?" *Journal of Accounting and Economics*, pp. 179–200.

Dhaliwal, D., M. Erickson, and S. Heitzman, 2004. "The Effect of Seller Income Taxes on Acquisition Price: Evidence from Purchases of Taxable and Tax-Exempt Hospitals," *Journal of the American Taxation Association* (Fall), pp. 1–22.

Dhaliwal, D., M. Erickson, and L. Krull, 2007. "Incremental Financing Decisions and Time-Series Variation in Personal Taxes on Equity Income," *Journal of the American Taxation Association* (Spring), pp. 1–26.

Dhaliwal, D., M. Erickson, and R. Trezevant, 1999. "A Test of the Theory of Tax Clienteles for Dividend Policies," *National Tax Journal*, pp. 179–194.

Dhaliwal, D., L. Krull, and O. Z. Li, 2007. "Did the 2003 Tax Act Reduce the Cost of Equity Capital?" *Journal of Accounting and Economics* (March), pp. 121–150.

Dhaliwal, D., L. Krull, O. Z. Li, and W. Moser, 2005, "Dividend Taxes and Implied Cost of Equity Capital," *Journal of Accounting Research* (December), pp. 675–708.

Dhaliwal, D., O. Z. Li, and R. Trezevant, 2003. "Is a Dividend Tax Penalty Incorporated into the Return on a Firm's Common Stock?" *Journal of Accounting and Economics*, pp. 155–178.

Dyreng, S., M. Hanlon, and E. L. Maydew, 2008. "Long-Run Corporate Tax Avoidance," *The Accounting Review* (83), pp. 61–82.

Easton, P., M. McAnally, G. Sommers, and X-J. Zhang, 2018. *Financial Statement Analysis & Valuation,* 5th edition, Cambridge Business Publishers.

Edwards, A., and T. Shevlin, 2011. "The Value of a Flow-Through Entity in an Integrated Corporate

Tax System," *Journal of Financial Economics*, pp. 473–491.

Erickson, M., 1998. "The Effect of Taxes on the Structure of Corporate Acquisitions," *Journal of Accounting Research* (2), pp. 279–298.

Erickson, M., and E. Maydew, 1998. "Implicit Taxes in High Dividend Yield Stocks," *The Accounting Review* (October), pp. 435–458.

Erickson, M., and S. Wang, 1999. "The Effect of Transaction Structure on Price: Evidence from Subsidiary Sales," *Journal of Accounting and Economics* (April), pp. 149–176.

Fama, E., and K. French, 1998. "Taxes, Financing Decisions, and Firm Value," *Journal of Finance*, pp. 819–843.

Gebhardt, L., C. Lee, and B. Swaminathan, 2001. "Toward an Implied Cost of Capital," *Journal of Accounting Research* (39), pp. 135–176.

Gode, D., and P. Mohanram, 2003. "Inferring the Cost of Capital Using the Ohlson–Juettner Model," *Review of Accounting Studies* (8), pp. 399–431.

Graham, J., M. Hanlon, T. Shevlin, and N. Shroff, 2017. "Tax Rates and Corporate Decision-Making," *Review of Financial Studies* (30, 9) pp. 3128–3175.

Gramlich, J, P. Limpaphayom, and S. Ghon Rhee, 2004. "Taxes, Keiretsu Affiliation, and Income Shifting," *Journal of Accounting and Economics* (37), pp. 203–228.

Grinstein, Y., and R. Michaely, 2005. "Institutional Holdings and Payout Policy," *Journal of Finance* (60), pp. 1389–1426.

Guenther, D., 1994. "The Relation between Tax Rates and Pre-Tax Returns: Direct Evidence from the 1981 and 1986 Tax Rate Reductions," *Journal of Accounting and Economics* (November), pp. 379–393.

Hanlon, M. and S. Heitzman, 2010. "A Review of Tax Research," *Journal of Accounting and Economics*, pp. 127–178.

Hanlon, M., J. Myers, and T. Shevlin, 2003. "Dividend Taxes and Firm Valuation: A Re-Examination," *Journal of Accounting and Economics*, pp. 119–153.

Harris, T., and D. Kemsley, 1999. "Dividend Taxation in Firm Valuation: New Evidence," *Journal of Accounting Research*, pp. 275–291.

Hayn, C., 1989. "Tax Attributes as Determinants of Shareholder Gains in Corporate Acquisitions," *Journal of Financial Economics* (June), pp. 121–153.

Henning, S., and W. Shaw, 2000. "The Effect of the Tax Deductibility of Goodwill on Purchase Price Allocations," *Journal of the American Taxation Association* (Spring), pp. 18–37.

Henning, S., W. Shaw, and T. Stock, 2000. "The Effect of Taxes on Acquisition Prices and Transaction Structure," *Journal of the American Taxation Association* (Supplement), pp. 1–17.

Kern, B., and M. Morris, 1992. "Taxes and Firm Size: The Effect of Tax Legislation during the 1980s," *Journal of the American Taxation Association* (Spring), pp. 80–96.

Key, K. G., 2008, "Taxes and Assets Prices: The Case of Thoroughbreds," *Journal of the American Taxation Association* (Spring), pp. 29–48.

Lang, M., and D. Shackelford, 2000. "Capitalization of Capital Gains Taxes: Evidence from Stock Price Reactions to the 1997 Rate Reduction," *Journal of Public Economics*, pp. 69–85.

Liang, J. W., S. Matsunaga, and D. Morse, 2002, "The Effect of the Expected Holding Period on the Market Reaction to a Decline in the Capital Gains Tax Rate," *Journal of the American Taxation Association* (Supplement), pp. 49–64.

Lightner, T., M. Morrow, R. Ricketts, and M. Riley, 2008. "Investor Response to a Reduction in the Dividend Tax Rate: Evidence from the Jobs & Growth Tax Relief Reconciliation Act of 2003," *Journal of the American Taxation Association* (Fall), pp. 21–46.

Litzenberger, R., and K. Ramaswamy, 1979. "The Effect of Personal Taxes and Dividends on Capital Asset Prices," *Journal of Financial Economics* (7), pp. 163–195.

Litzenberger, R., and K. Ramaswamy, 1982. "The Effects of Dividends on Common Stock Prices: Tax Effects or Information Effects?" *Journal of Finance* (37), pp. 429–443.

Manzon, G., and G. Plesko, 2002. "The Relation between Financial and Tax Reporting Measures of Income," *Tax Law Review*, pp. 175–214.

Miller, M., and M. Scholes, 1982, "Dividends and Taxes: Some Empirical Evidence," *Journal of Political Economy* (90), pp. 1118–1141.

Naranjo, A., M. Nimalendran, and M. Ryngaert, 1998, "Stock Returns, Dividend Yields, and Taxes," *Journal of Finance* (53), pp. 2029–2057.

Novack, G., 2005. "Treasury Bill Yield Reactions to the 1997 Capital Gains Tax Rate Reduction," *Journal of the American Taxation Association* (Supplement), pp. 55–70.

Ohlson, J., 1995. "Earnings, Book Value, and Dividends in Security Valuation," *Contemporary Accounting Research* (11), pp. 661–687.

Scholes, M., P. Wilson, and M. Wolfson, 1990. "Tax Planning, Regulatory Capital Planning, and Financial Reporting Strategy for Commercial Banks," *Review of Financial Studies*, pp. 625–650.

Seida, J., 2001. "Evidence of Tax-Clientele-Related Trading Following Dividend Increase," *Journal of the American Taxation Association* (Supplement), pp. 1–21.

Shackelford, D., 1991. "The Market for Tax Benefits: Evidence from Leveraged ESOPs," *Journal of Accounting and Economics*, pp. 117–145.

Shackelford, D., 2000. "Stock Market Reaction to Capital Gains Tax Changes: Empirical Evidence from the 1997 and 1998 Tax Acts." in *Tax Policy and the Economy*, Vol. 14, edited by J. Poterba (Cambridge, MA: MIT Press).

Shackelford, D., and T. Shevlin, 2001. "Empirical Tax Research in Accounting," *Journal of Accounting and Economics* (September), pp. 321–387.

Shevlin, T., and S. Porter, 1992. "The Corporate Tax Comeback in 1987: Some Further Evidence," *Journal of the American Taxation Association* (Spring), pp. 59–79.

Weaver, C., 2000. "Divestiture Structure and Tax Attributes: Evidence from the Omnibus Budget Reconciliation Act of 1993," *Journal of the American Taxation Association* (Supplement), pp. 54–71.

Wilkie, P., 1992 "Empirical Evidence of Implicit Taxes in the Corporate Sector," *Journal of the American Taxation Association* (Spring), pp. 97–116.

Yin, G., 2003. "How Much Tax Do Large Public Corporations Pay? Estimating the Effective Tax Rates of the S&P 500," *Virginia Law Review* (December), pp. 1793–1856.

Zodrow, G., 1991. "On the 'Traditional' and 'New' Views of Dividend Taxation," *National Tax Journal*, pp. 497–509.

5

Choosing the Optimal Organizational Form[1]

After completing this chapter, you should be able to

1. Explain the characteristics of various organizational forms, including the tax and nontax costs and benefits of each form.
2. Explain and calculate the after-tax rate of return to investment via the partnership form.
3. Explain and calculate the after-tax rate of return to investment via the corporate form.
4. Explain and illustrate the importance of deferral of shareholder-level taxation in the corporate form.
5. Explain and illustrate the importance of capital gains treatment for shareholders.
6. Estimate the required corporate pretax return that results in equal after-tax returns to the corporate and partnership forms.
7. Discuss how the tax disadvantage of double taxation of the corporate form has changed as Congress has changed tax rates.

In this chapter, we focus on the taxation of the returns on businesses that produce goods and services. Examples of these types of businesses include sole proprietorships, partnerships, and corporations. As we will see, these differing legal organizational forms can generate significant differences in tax treatment even in cases when entities are undertaking identical investment projects that result in the same before-tax cash flows. Such tax treatment differences can have an important influence on the organizational form selected to conduct business.

To illustrate the nature of these tax differences, let us consider a few important tax rules affecting corporations and partnerships in the United States. C corporations must pay an **entity-level tax** on their taxable income. They file tax returns and pay tax on corporate taxable income in ways very similar to individuals. Shareholders pay additional tax (at their own statutory rates) on dividends that are paid out of corporate earnings and profits, and they pay tax on gains from the sale of their shares. This gives rise to the phrase that corporate profits are subject to **double taxation**. Corporate stockholders are effectively taxed twice on income, once at the corporate level and again when profits are distributed as a dividend or when shares are sold.

In some countries (e.g., Australia, Canada, and New Zealand), corporate and personal taxes are *integrated* in that shareholders are granted a tax credit for the corporate taxes they pay indirectly as owners. In fully integrated systems, this arrangement results in single taxation of income earned through corporations (i.e., no double taxation of the corporate entity). We present an example of integration in Appendix 1. Note that double taxation can also be avoided via

[1] We appreciate helpful comments from Ira Weiss on this chapter.

other tax policy choices, such as when distributions of corporate income (dividends and capital gains) are deductible at the corporate level or exempted from taxation to owner-recipients. This situation is approximated in countries where capital gains are exempted from taxation and dividend yields are low. The United States does not have C corporate integration, but it does have preferential (lower) tax rates at the individual level on both long-term capital gains and dividends. These lower rates, in effect, reduce the level of double taxation of corporate earnings. In addition, the Tax Cuts and Jobs Act of 2017 (TCJA) lowered the statutory tax rate on C corporations substantially.

In contrast to the corporation business form, partners and sole proprietors are subject to only one level of taxation, at their own personal rates. Rather than pay an entity-level tax, partnerships and proprietorships act as **conduits**, also known as **pass-through entities**, through which income passes to their owners. For example, partners record their share of partnership profits and losses on their own tax returns whether or not the profits are distributed.

The TCJA for the first time in U.S. tax history, applies different tax treatment to pass-through business income at the individual level as compared with, say, wage income at the individual level. This provision in the law is the qualified business income (QBI) deduction. At a general level, the rule allows a 20% deduction of domestic pass-through business income, so only 80% of such income is taxable. Effectively, this can be viewed as a taxpayer in the 37% tax bracket having a 29.6% tax rate on QBI (37% * 80%). The intent of creating this change was to bring the tax rate on business income from pass-throughs more in line with that of C corporations. The QBI deduction applies to tax years 2018–2025 (per the law as of the time of this writing).

In addition to this change in treatment, however, the TCJA placed more limitations on the use of losses of pass-through entities. Tax losses for years 2018–2025 from pass-through business income potentially cannot be fully deducted against other sources of income on the individual return. Specifically, excess business losses cannot be deducted in the current year and must be carried over. An excess business loss is the excess of aggregate business deductions for the tax year over the sum of 1) aggregate business income and gains for the tax year and 2) $250,000 ($500,000 filing jointly). The excess business loss is carried over and can be deducted under the rules for net operating losses (NOLs). As a result, effectively, the pass-through business losses cannot (in the year incurred) offset more than $250,000 of income (or more than $500,000 for joint filers) from sources such as salary, self-employment income, interest, dividends, and capital gains, and forces the taxpayer to spread the use of the loss over time (at least one year). These new rules apply at the owner level, and they apply after applying the passive activity loss rules.[2]

In this chapter, we begin by describing the various alternative organizational forms available in the United States. We discuss the tax treatment and the nontax costs and benefits of each form. We then analyze the effects of taxes on the returns from productive activities U.S. corporations and U.S. partnerships undertake. We employ a simplified model without transaction and information costs (frictions). The model's primary implication is that, when considering tax effects, an investor's choice between the corporate form of organization (i.e., two levels of taxation) and the partnership form (i.e., one level of taxation) depends on the length of the investment horizon as well as three tax parameters: (1) the investor's personal tax rates on ordinary income, (2) corporate-level tax rates, and (3) the shareholder-level tax rates on the returns to investing in corporate shares.

However, the model has limitations. The model does not explain, for example, how partnerships and corporations can compete successfully against each other in the marketplace. In fact, one implication of this model is that we would not expect to observe both partnerships and corporations producing the same goods and services if all investors faced exactly the same three tax parameters. In other words, everyone would choose the organizational form the model determines is preferred.

Moreover, in the absence of frictions and restrictions, even if investors initially faced differences in these three tax parameters—leading some investors to produce goods and services in partnership form and others to produce identical goods and services in corporate form—tax arbitrage opportunities would prevent these initial differences in taxes from being an equilibrium situation. As investors exploited the arbitrage possibilities, their tax positions would change, and this activity would continue until all investors faced the same three tax characteristics. As a result, once again, we would not expect to observe both partnerships and corporations producing the same goods and services.

[2] See Sonya Foster's 2018 article "The TCJA and Deducting Pass-Through Business Losses," available online at https://www.dalbycpa.com/the-tcja-and-deducting-pass-through-business-losses/, for more information.

In the real world, however, partnerships and corporations *do* compete head to head. This can occur quite naturally when market frictions and tax-rule restrictions are present. To maximize after-tax returns, investors must consider both tax and nontax factors (i.e., all costs). In this chapter, we consider special tax provisions for both partnerships and corporations that reduce the differences in after-tax rates of return the model otherwise predicts. Similarly, we touch on market frictions that might prevent one organizational form from dominating another. That is, although one organizational form may enjoy less favorable tax treatment than another, the tax-disfavored entity may still be able to compete effectively against its rival if nontax factors cause its *before*-tax profitability to be greater. For example, if tax rules favor partnerships over corporations, the corporate form may still be preferable because corporate owners enjoy limited liability, easy transferability of ownership, and a relatively active market for management control.

Next, we move on to a discussion of start-up businesses. What organizational form should start-ups choose based on all the tax and nontax considerations? We discuss what one might expect to observe in terms of the choice of organizational form based on the model just presented and consideration of other tax attributes. We then look at some recent data. What do we actually observe and why? We close with a brief look at organizational form choice over time in response to changing tax rates.

5.1 ORGANIZATIONAL FORMS FOR PRODUCING GOODS AND SERVICES

We begin with a brief overview of the taxation of several organizational forms used to produce goods and services. We include a discussion of more specialized organizational forms at the end of the chapter.

Sole proprietorship: The taxable income or loss from a sole proprietorship is filed along with the owner's personal tax return (Schedule C of Form 1040). The profits of the business are taxed only once at the personal level. In this regard, the sole proprietorship serves as a conduit through which the income of the business is passed through to the tax return of its owner. If the business incurs a loss, the loss can offset other income of the taxpayer subject to some restrictions, including the new restrictions in the TCJA. For example, the business has to be a legitimate business (e.g., with profit-making intent) and not a hobby of the taxpayer (the so-called "hobby loss rules" prevent taxpayers from deducting the costs of their hobbies on their tax returns).[3]

Partnership: The partnership is a legal organizational form that serves as a tax conduit between the business and its partners. The partnership files its own information tax return (Form 1065), including an income statement, a balance sheet, and a schedule of specific allocations to each partner (Schedule K-1). These allocations are broken down by type of income and expense (e.g., depreciation, interest, rent, and capital gains), and partners report their designated share of income and expense by type on their own tax returns (e.g., capital gains and losses retain the capital character on the partner's return). The partnership entity does not pay any entity-level income tax. Partnerships may have two classes of partners: **general partners** and **limited partners**. As with a sole proprietor, a general partner's personal liability is limited only by the individual's personal resources and the bankruptcy laws. A limited partner, on the other hand, has **limited liability**—the investor usually is at risk for only the amount he or she has invested in the business. A limited partner typically does not participate actively in the operations of the business. Indeed, active participation in the management of the business may void the limited liability protection of limited partners.

Losses incurred by the partnership flow through to the partners. But the extent to which the losses can be included on the partner's tax return and used to offset other income is potentially limited. First are what are known as **at-risk limitations**. The partner cannot deduct losses in excess of the amount at risk in the partnership. Second are the **passive activity** loss rules that limit the deductibility of losses for passive investors. Passive activities are trade or business activities in which the taxpayer does not materially participate during the year and rental activities, even if the taxpayer does materially participate in them (unless a real estate professional) (see Section 469 for

[3] Rental real estate losses are subject to restrictions, and the passive activity loss rules, discussed later in the chapter, also extend to Schedule C for taxpayers.

detailed rules). Passive activity losses are only deductible to the extent of passive income until the ownership interest is sold, at which time any suspended passive losses become deductible as ordinary losses. If the losses are not considered passive on the individual taxpayer's return, the operating losses can be used to offset other nonpassive (and passive) income. For tax years 2018–2025, however, the TCJA limits the amount of the other income to be offset to $250,000 ($500,000 for joint filers), as mentioned above. To the extent the taxpayer has excess business losses, so-called net operating losses (NOLs), these losses can be carried forward to future tax returns and used to offset up to 80% of the future year's taxable income. Capital losses can also be carried back and forward, but they are subject to shorter carryover periods. Finally, if and when partners sell their partnership interest, the gain or loss on the sale (computed as the difference between the sale price and the tax **basis** of the asset) is taxable as capital gains or losses.

Limited liability company (LLC): LLCs are hybrid entities that, under state law, are neither partnerships nor corporations. Under state law, this structure offers shareholders limited liability (i.e., protection from personal liability for entity debts). Under current federal tax law, these entities can elect to be taxed as a partnership. Prior to 1997, determining whether the LLC qualified for partnership tax treatment was very complex, but the 1997 check-the-box regulations simplified the entity-classification process.[4] The **check-the-box regulations** allow eligible entities that are not automatically treated as a corporation to elect (i.e., check the box) to be treated as a corporation for federal tax purposes.[5] Those not electing corporate tax treatment are treated as pass-through entities. We will treat LLCs as being taxed as partnerships.

If treated as a partnership for tax purposes, the LLC offers the advantages of single-level taxation with limited liability and an unlimited number of investors are allowed to be owners. The entity files an informational return as a partnership, with each LLC owner (partner) receiving a schedule (Schedule K-1) of specific allocations to be reported on the partner's individual tax return. Again, each allocation will retain its character—for example, capital losses retain their capital nature at the individual owner level. The rules governing losses, passive activity losses for the owners, and the sale of LLC interests are the same as those just discussed for partnerships.

Data on Partnerships and LLCs

The Statistics of Income (SOI) division of the Internal Revenue Service (IRS), found at SOI.gov, noted the following in its "Partnership Returns, 2014" report:

- Partnerships filed more than 3.6 million tax returns for 2014 (the last year compiled on SOI), a 4.4-percent increase over the number filed for 2013. These returns represented 27.7 million partners, up 0.8 percent from the previous year.
- Limited liability companies LLCs made up the majority (67.4 percent) of all partnerships, surpassing all other entity types for the 13th consecutive year.
- Limited partnerships represented only 11.5 percent of all partnerships but reported the most profits (32.2 percent), and the largest share of partners (44.2 percent).
- Real estate and rental and leasing accounted for about half (50.3 percent) of all partnerships and over a quarter (28.5 percent) of all partners. The finance and insurance sector reported the largest shares of total net income (loss) (41.4 percent), total assets (56.4 percent), and total receipts (Number of Partnerships by Type of Entity, Tax Years 2005–2014 Domestic limited liability companies.

In addition, the SOI provided the graph shown in **Figure 5.1**. The most striking aspect is the growth in LLC entities over the last decade.

[4] Prior to 1997, to be taxed as a partnership, the tax law required that a partnership differ in economically significant ways from a corporation. Any association (including a partnership) was taxed as a corporation unless it failed to exhibit at least two of the following characteristics: (a) continuity of life, (b) centralization of management, (c) easy transferability of ownership, (d) limited liability, and (e) an economic purpose to the organization.

[5] Basically, entities automatically treated as corporations for tax purposes include firms incorporated under federal or state law, joint-stock companies, insurance companies, and banks. The check-the-box election is also not available to trusts, real estate investment trusts, real estate mortgage investment conduits, or publicly traded partnerships. These organizations are discussed later in the chapter. Check-the-box elections are used often in international tax planning.

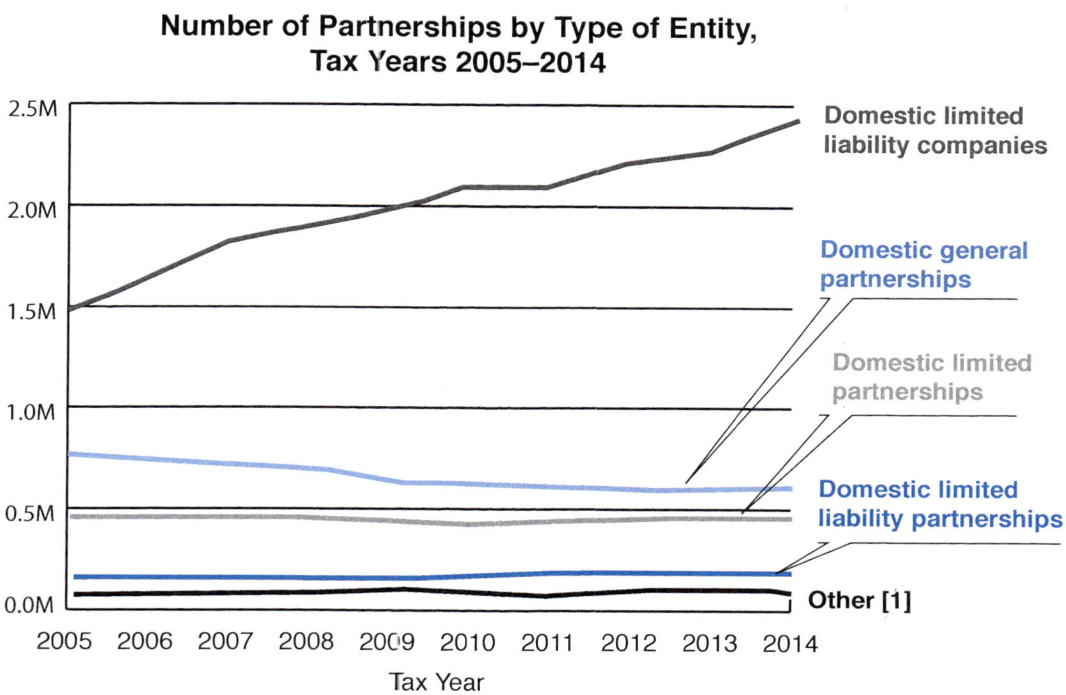

[1] Data for "other" partnerships include foreign partnerships, as well as partnerships which checked the "other" box, Form 1065, Schedule B, line 1, Type of Entity, or did not check a box.
Source: IRS, Statistics of Income Division, Partnerships, April 2016.

FIGURE 5.1 Number of Partnerships by Type of Entity, Tax Years 2005–2014

S Corporation: S corporations are LLCs that are taxed as pass-through entities.[6] In other words, legally, they are corporations with limited liability but taxed as pass-through entities. Stockholders annually report their pro rata share of income (loss) on their own income tax returns just as if they were taxed as partners. However, the allocation rules are generally less flexible for S corporations than for partnerships. The rules governing the flow through of losses, shareholder ability to use passive activity losses, and the sale of S corporation interests are the same as those for partnerships.

The number of shareholders allowed in an S corporation has always been limited. Initially set at 10 shareholders, the limit has been increased over time, with the American Jobs Creation Act of 2004 setting the current limit at 100. Other requirements could limit the ability of S corporations to raise large amounts of capital. For example, the type of shareholder is also restricted—corporate shareholders, partnership shareholders, and foreign shareholders are generally not allowed. However, some trusts (e.g., small business trusts) and some exempt organizations (e.g., qualified retirement plan trusts, as described in Internal Revenue Code [IRC] Sec 401[a], and some charitable organizations, as described in IRC Sec 501[c][3]) are allowed to be S corporation shareholders. Other limitations exist that are beyond the scope of this text.

An additional point of note about S corporations is warranted here to highlight our "all taxes" theme in this text. As is the case for any other corporation, the Federal Insurance Contribution Act tax, or payroll tax, is imposed only on employee wages and not on distributive shares of income to shareholders. Thus, relative to a partnership, for an LLC taxed as a partnership or sole proprietorship, employment tax savings are generally available via the S corporation form. It is important to recognize, though, that shareholder-employees need to be paid reasonable (i.e., market) wages for their work for the entity. It is not uncommon for the IRS and state tax authorities to recharacterize distributions paid to shareholder-employees as wages if shareholder-employees are not paid a reasonable wage for the services they perform in their positions within the company. In a recent study, Lee (2011) reported that based upon S corporation National Research Program samples, the Government

[6] The letters *C* and *S* are derived from the subchapters of the tax code defining the structure of each type of corporation. Most corporations listed on U.S. stock exchanges are organized as C corporations.

Accounting Office estimated that 887,000 S corporations in 2003 and 2004 misreported shareholder compensation in the aggregate amount of $23.6 billion, thus underreporting wage taxes. The Tax Gap Analysis Subgroup Report (2008) stated, "The self-employment aspect of S corporations is a very common planning issue, likely to be associated with noncompliance." The issue was highlighted during John Edwards's presidential campaign when it was revealed that he incorporated his partnership interest in a law firm and saved thousands of dollars of self-employment tax by taking his share of partnership income through an S corporation as distributions (and it was also discovered that Newt Gingrich operated similarly, which is why this is sometimes called the "Gingrich-Edwards" loophole). In response, when working on legislation for 2010, the U.S. House passed a bill (H.R. 4213) that included a provision imposing self-employment payroll taxes on S corporation pass-through income where an S corporation is engaged in a professional service business and its principal asset is the reputation and skill of three or fewer employees or where the S corporation is a partner in a professional service business. The S corporation proposal, however, was rejected by the Senate, and no such provision was included in the TCJA.[7]

C Corporation: C corporations are taxed directly, at the entity level, on their corporate taxable income. In addition to corporate-level taxes, stockholders are also taxed on dividend income and realized capital gains at their own personal rates. If corporate taxable income is $1 and the corporate tax rate is 21%, corporate after-tax profits are $0.79, or $1(1 – 0.21). If the corporation then pays a cash dividend of $0.79 (its entire after-tax profits), shareholders pay tax on this dividend at the rate that is applicable to dividend income when the dividend is received. Since the passage of the Jobs and Growth Tax Relief Reconciliation Act of 2003 (JGTRRA, signed in May 2003), qualified dividend income is subject to taxation at long-term capital gains rates.[8] For example, currently, the income tax rate applicable to qualified dividends is 20% (the 20% applies if the taxpayer is in the highest tax bracket, the qualified dividend rate is otherwise 15% or 0% depending on income level). Thus, in our example, with these rates, the shareholder would retain, after all income taxes, $0.63, or $0.79(1 – 0.20), of the initial $1 of corporate before-tax earnings. Combining the corporate and individual level taxes, the total rate of tax on the $1 earned is 37%. Shareholders also realize capital gains and losses on the sale of their stock, much like the sale of all the ownership interests we have discussed for the other organizational forms.

The treatment of losses for C corporations is different than the other organizational forms, however, because the C corporation entity itself is taxable. Net operating losses generated by C corporations do not flow through to the owners but are suspended at the corporate level. These losses can be carried forward.[9] Thus, corporations that incur a large loss can offset future taxable income, inducing variation into marginal tax rates observed across companies. For example, start-up companies often take several years to generate taxable profits, if they ever turn profitable at all. Because of the loss carryforward rules, a start-up company's marginal tax rate is often far less than the statutory corporate tax rate. We come back to how this affects the organizational form choice of start-up enterprises later in the chapter.

Although income earned by U.S. corporations is subjected to two levels of tax, the common reference to the corporation as a "double-tax system" can be misleading for several reasons. First, the after-tax income earned at the corporate level is not taxed instantly to shareholders unless the corporation immediately pays out all its after-tax earnings as a dividend or shareholders sell their shares each period. Second, shareholders are taxed only on the after-corporate tax profits earned by the corporation. The taxes paid by the corporation are effectively deducted in determining the income taxed at the shareholder level. Other sources of reduction in the two-level tax include the ability to distribute corporate profits in a tax-deductible way via interest, rent, royalty, compensation, and other payments rather than by way of nondeductible dividends to stockholders and reduced tax rates at the

---

[7] For a more extensive discussion, see Peter J. Reilly's article "S Corporation SE Avoidance Still a Solid Strategy," published on *Forbes* August 25, 2013, https://www.forbes.com/sites/peterjreilly/2013/08/25/s-corporation-se-avoidance-still-a-solid-strategy/#4eea8525161f.

[8] Note also that starting on January 1, 2013, dividend income is also subject to the Medicare surtax on investment income of 3.8% for taxpayers with modified adjusted gross incomes of greater than $250,000 for joint filers. This surtax was enacted as part of the Patient Protection and Affordable Care Act signed into law in 2010. We ignore this additional tax in our computations for simplicity.

[9] Prior to the TCJA, corporate NOLs could be carried back 2 years and forward 20 years.

shareholder level upon the sale of shares, including share repurchases (e.g., as discussed earlier, capital gains in most countries are taxed at lower rates than ordinary income such as dividends).

Data on Corporations

Data from the IRS's SOI division shows that for the tax year 2013 (the latest year of data available), 1.6 million C corporation returns were filed with total income subject to tax of roughly $1.2 trillion. There were 4,257,909 S corporation returns filed in 2013, and the number of shareholders for these entities totaled roughly 7.1 million. The total income (less deficits) reported on these returns was $446 billion ($516 billion excluding deficits). The S corporation is and has been the most prevalent type of corporation (out of the group of C corporations, real estate investment trusts, and all entities that file any type of corporate Form 1120) but is much smaller in terms of income and assets. For example, for tax year 2003, about 61.9% of all corporations filed a Form 1120S; by 2009, the percentage was close to 70%, and by 2013, the percentage was a little over 72%. In 2006, 60% of S corporations had a single shareholder, 89% had two or fewer shareholders, and 94% had three or fewer shareholders. This pattern is fairly consistent over time; in 2010 the average number of shareholders per S corporation return was 1.7 (and is the same in 2013, as can be computed using the numbers above for 2013).[10]

Figures 5.2 and **5.3** are from the Tax Foundation and provide a sense of the relative number and income in different types of organizational forms.[11] The growth of the pass-through business form

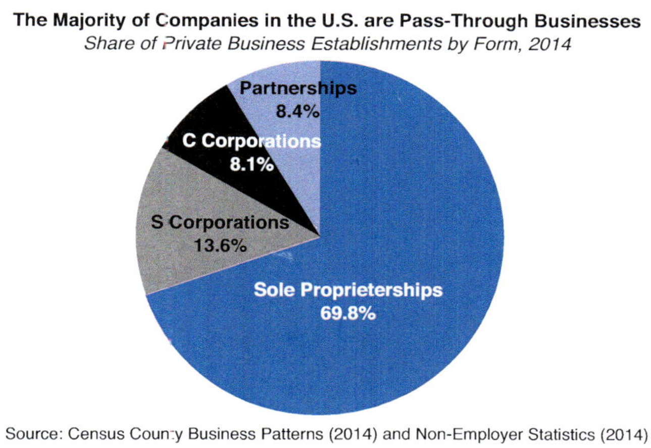

FIGURE 5.2 Percentage of Organizational Forms in U.S. 2014

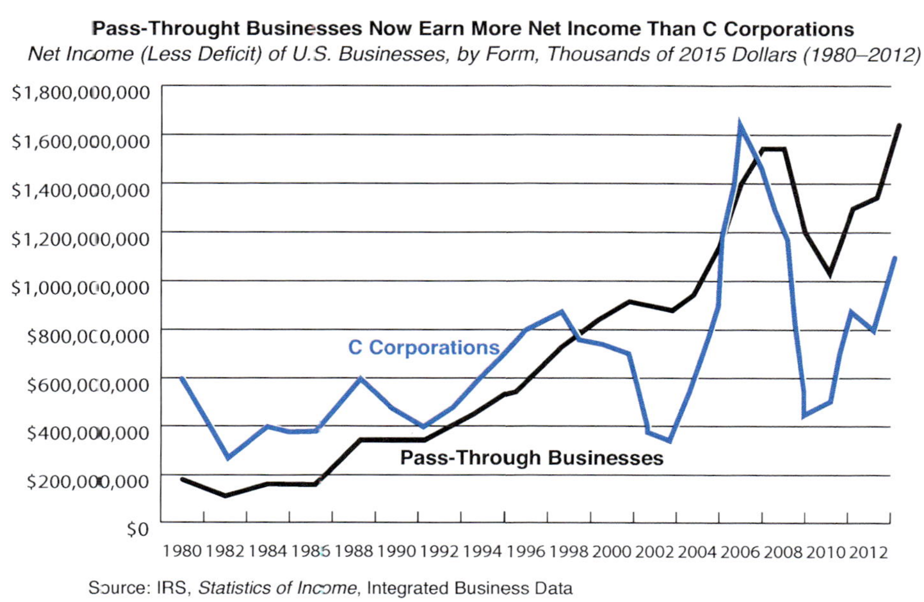

FIGURE 5.3 Aggregate Net Income Reported by C Corporations and Pass-Through Businesses

[10] The years for the different data type vary based on the latest data available on the SOI website.

[11] https://taxfoundation.org/pass-through-businesses-data-and-policy/

has been so great that the majority of businesses in the U.S. are pass-throughs and pass-through businesses account for more in terms of net income (but not revenues). Pass-through businesses also employ more than half of the private sector work force.

5.2 COMPUTATION OF AFTER-TAX RETURNS TO PASS-THROUGH AND NON-PASS-THROUGH FORMS OF ORGANIZATION

In this section, we develop a simple model to compare the after-tax returns from investing in a pass-through organizational form, such as a partnership or sole proprietorship, to those from investing in a non-pass-through form, such as a C corporation. We assume that the before-tax rate of return on a project is constant at a rate of R per year whether the project is undertaken in corporate or partnership form. Our algebra here requires an assumption that R is positive; if the entity is incurring tax losses, the algebra does not incorporate loss limitation rules. The project lasts for n years, at which point the organization is assumed to liquidate. All after-tax income generated in the interim that is not distributed is reinvested in the business at rate R per period before tax.

The QBI deduction enacted as part of the TCJA requires more discussion. As we mentioned above, taxpayers may deduct up to 20% of QBI from a pass-through entity. There are limitations for higher income taxpayers, and the deduction is disallowed for higher income taxpayers in certain service trades or businesses. We will briefly explain the various limitations here, but we assume for our exercises the deduction is either fully or not at all allowable for simplicity.

The first limitation to consider is the taxable income of the owner. If the taxable income (i.e., total taxable income, not just income from the pass-through) is equal to or less than $157,500 for single taxpayers ($315,000 for married filing jointly taxpayers), then the QBI is allowed without limitation—a deduction for up to 20% of the domestic QBI (excluding capital gains) from the pass-through. On the other hand, if the owner's taxable income is greater than the amounts just listed, then further limitations may apply. (The threshold amounts involved in determining the QBI deduction will be adjusted for inflation starting in 2019.)

The taxpayer must next consider whether his or her business is a specified service trade or business. In general, this kind of business relies on the reputation or skill of the owner and more specifically includes professionals such as lawyers, accountants, doctors, and professional athletes. It does not, however, include architects and engineers.[12] Taxable income of the owner must be considered for a special service business. If the taxable income is greater than $207,000 for single taxpayers ($415,000 if married filing jointly), then no QBI deduction is allowed. If taxable income is equal to or less than these amounts, a partial deduction is allowed. In other words, for example, the deduction is phased out between incomes of $315,000 and $415,000 for an accountant filing a joint return and is completely disallowed once taxable income reaches $415,000.01.

If the taxpayer is not in a specified service—for example, a plumber, the owner of a construction business, or an architect—then for incomes over the $157,500 ($315,000) limitations on the deduction may apply based on the W-2 wages of the business or on W-2 wages plus property. More specifically, the deduction is limited to the greater of 1) 50% of W-2 wages paid by the business or 2) the sum of 25% of the W-2 wages paid plus 2.5% of the unadjusted basis of certain property the business uses to produce QBI.

The limitations and determination of specified service businesses complicate the tax code a great deal. The new code section is Section 199A. For our purposes, we will assume that the owners of the pass-through businesses obtain a 20% deduction or do not obtain any QBI deduction (i.e., we ignore any phase-out range). For a taxpayer in the highest tax bracket, this is equivalent to a tax rate of 29.6%, or 37% × 80%. If no QBI is allowed (e.g., for accountants), then the tax rate is 37%. We denote the new (equivalent) tax rate as t_{qbi}. If we are assuming the taxpayer is not able to take the QBI or discussing the issue at a more conceptual level, we will use t_p just to denote whatever tax rate applies at the personal level.

---

[12] The definition of the businesses that do not qualify are generally taken from IRC Section 1202 regarding the deduction for qualified small business stock (although Section 1202 has no exception for engineers and architects). Thus, the same businesses that cannot issue qualified small business stock are also phased out in terms of the QBI deduction.

If the project is undertaken in partnership form, partners pay tax at their marginal personal tax rates, t_p, each year, as income is earned. Let's assume the partner obtains the QBI deduction in this example and apply the rate t_{qbi}. We assume distributions at rate $t_{qbi}R$ are made each period from the partnership to enable partners to pay their personal tax. A partner's after-tax accumulation for an initial $\$I$ investment is[13]

$$\$I[1 + R(1 - t_{qbi})]^n \tag{5.1}$$

Assume, for example, that $R = 10\%$, $n = 5$ years, and $t_{qbi} = 29.6\%$. A partner's after-tax accumulation for a \$1 investment is

$$\$1[1 + .10(1 - .296)]^5 = \$1.41.$$

This provides an annual after-tax rate of return of 7%, or $1.41^{1/5} - 1$ or, more simply, .10(1 – .296).

Now consider if the project is undertaken in corporate form. We assume initially the corporation pays no interim dividends. In this case, shareholders pay tax at their capital gains rate, t_{cg}, when the firm liquidates or when shareholders sell their shares. The corporation must pay taxes each year at rate t_c on the before-tax return, R. Combining the annual corporate-level tax and the end-of-investment shareholder-level tax, the after-tax accumulation to the owners in a corporation for an initial $\$I$ investment is

$$\$I\{[1 + R(1 - t_c)]^n - t_{cg}(\$I[1 + R(1 - t_c)]^n - I)\}$$

where the first term is the proceeds from the liquidation (or sale of shares) and the second term is the shareholder tax due on the liquidation.[14] This equation can be rearranged to

$$\$I[1 + R(1 - t_c)]^n (1 - t_{cg}) + t_{cg}\$I \tag{5.2}$$

More specifically, the accumulation in Equation 5.2 is exactly the same as that on a single-premium deferred annuity (i.e., savings vehicle II) for n periods in which the account grows at rate $R(1 - t_c)$ each period and all earnings are taxed at time n at rate t_{cg}.

Assuming that $t_c = 21\%$ and the shareholder faces a capital gains rate of 20%, the 5-year after-tax accumulation in corporate form for an initial \$1 investment is

$$\$1[1 + .10(1 - .21)]^5 (1 - .20) + .20\$1 = \$1.37$$

This provides an annualized after-tax rate of return of 6.5%, or $1.37^{1/5} - 1$, which is 0.5 percentage points less than the partnership.

Ignoring nontax considerations, a taxpayer will prefer to invest in a partnership or proprietorship rather than a corporation whenever the accumulation in Equation 5.1 exceeds that of Equation 5.2, or

$$\underbrace{\$I[1 + R(1 - t_p)]^n}_{\text{Partnerships (P)}} > \underbrace{\$I[1 + R(1 - t_c)]^n (1 - t_{cg}) + t_{cg}\$I}_{\text{Corporations (C)}} \tag{5.3}$$

For what values of t_c, t_p (or t_{qbi}, whichever is applicable), and t_{cg} in Equation 5.3 will investors prefer the partnership form to the corporate form? Before considering the question at this level of generality, let us consider the case of $n = 1$. When $n = 1$, Equation 5.3 simplifies to

$$(1 - t_p) > (1 - t_c)(1 - t_{cg}) \tag{5.4}$$

For example, for a 1-period investment, if $t_p = 40\%$, $t_c = 30\%$, and $t_{cg} = 10\%$, the corporate form is preferred to the partnership form because

$$(1 - .40) = .60 < (1 - .30)(1 - .10) = .63$$

[13] Note that this assumes there is no capital gain or loss on the liquidation of the partnership interest. At time n, partners receive a liquidating distribution of all after-tax partnership income generated over n periods plus their initial dollar invested.

[14] Note that in both the corporate and partnership forms in our examples, we assume that any incremental valuation gain beyond that already included as the entity's taxable earnings (R) is the same across both organizational forms and taxed the same, at capital gain rates. Thus, because this incremental valuation is the same across both types, we can ignore it for our comparative purposes.

Although there are two levels of taxation on corporate income, the product of one minus the corporate-level tax rate and one minus the shareholder-level tax rate happens to be higher than one minus the ordinary personal tax rate in this example. If the shareholder-level capital gains tax rate were 14% rather than 10%, investors facing a 40% marginal tax rate would be indifferent between investing in the partnership and corporate forms, as can be seen by substituting for t_{cg} = 14%, t_p = 40%, and t_c = 30% in Equation 5.4.

Once we leave the world of 1-period investments, whether the partnership is preferred to the corporation depends also on the value of deferring the payment of the shareholder capital gains tax. The value of the deferral is greater the higher the after-tax accumulation in the corporation, $R(1 - t_c)$, and the *longer* the deferral period, n. Because shareholders accumulate more after tax if they can defer the payment of shareholder-level taxes, the firm's dividend policy also affects the after-tax accumulation. Shareholders who receive dividends pay tax earlier than shareholders who do not receive dividends. Moreover, if t_{cg} is less than the tax rate on dividends, omitting dividends is a tax-advantaged policy. Thus, whether the partnership form provides greater after-tax rates of return than the corporate form depends on four factors (still ignoring nontax costs):

1. The individual ordinary tax rate, t_p, and whether the taxpayer qualifies for the QBI deduction to obtain a rate equivalent to t_{qbi}
2. The corporate tax rate, t_c
3. The taxes paid on capital gains and qualified dividends at the shareholder level, t_{cg}
4. The length of the investment horizon, n

Let us consider the following cases using Equation 5.3 for the analyses. Here, we ignore nontax costs, assume the business is profitable, assume the C corporation does not pay dividends, and assume that the partner/shareholder exits completely by redeeming his or her partnership interest or C corporation shares back to the business entity:

- The corporate tax rate, t_c, is equal to the ordinary tax rate, t_p (either after incorporating the QBI deduction, or if $t_p = t_c$, with no QBI deduction if the taxpayer does not qualify), and t_{cg} = 0. For a C corporation that does not pay dividends and all gains are realized via a sale of shares, investors are indifferent between producing in partnership or corporate form. Both provide investors the same after-tax rate of return. In effect, corporate income is taxed only once and at the same rate as if generated in partnership form.
- The corporate tax rate, t_c, is equal to the individual ordinary tax rate, t_p, but $t_{cg} > 0$. Even if the C corporation does not pay dividends, because shareholders pay additional tax on the same level of after-tax profits as is earned in partnership form, a partnership is preferred to a corporation. Specifically, as the income flows through to the partners, their basis in their partnership interest increases. The corporate shareholders, however, receive no similar increase in share basis because the shareholder has not been assigned any taxable income to increase basis (even though the corporation is paying the corporate-level tax). Thus, when their ownership interest is liquidated, the C corporation shareholder will have a gain to recognize, but the partner in the partnership will not (because the partner's basis has increased as income and has been allocated to him or her annually).

  To illustrate the advantage of the partnership form over the corporate form, assume that $t_c = t_p = .35$, $t_{cg} = .15$, and R = 10%. Partnership investments return 10% × (1 − .35) = 6.5% after tax, whereas corporate investments return 10% × (1 − .35) × (1 − .15) = 5.525% after tax for 1-year investments. If shareholders can defer but not eliminate the payment of shareholder-level taxes, the advantage of the partnership over the corporation is reduced.
- The corporate tax rate, t_c, is less than the personal tax rate, t_p, and $t_{cg} = 0$. In this case, investing through the corporation dominates investing through a partnership for any length of the investment horizon. For example, with a 10% before-tax rate of return on investment, a corporate tax rate, t_c, of 35%, and a personal tax rate, t_p, of 40%, investors earn a 6.5% after-tax rate of return on investment in the corporate form and 6% in the partnership form.
- The corporate tax rate, t_c, is less than the personal tax rate on partnership income, t_p, and $t_{cg} > 0$. With this configuration of corporate and personal tax rates, there is no clear-cut tax

preference for organizational form. Depending on shareholder-level taxes, either the corporate form or the partnership form could be preferred.

5.3 START-UP ENTERPRISES: DECISION FACTORS, EXPECTATIONS, AND OBSERVED DATA

When starting a business, what organizational form should be chosen for the business? It is important to consider both tax and nontax factors. Start-ups have nontax factors, which means the answer will not be the same across businesses and owners. Different types of owner groups may have different preferences and limitations (e.g., Are any of the owners foreign? Are any of the owners passive investors? What is the expected financing path of the start-up?). For a relatively simple new small business in which the investor is starting an operating business that will likely remain fairly small, the owner will continue to operate for the long run, and generally be profitable as the person's main career, the model established in the previous section is likely quite descriptive of the decision process. However, the degree of complexity in the business, the number of owners involved, and the likelihood and form of an eventual sale are all examples of factors that make nontax costs (and other tax costs) extremely important.

Let's start with the empirical observation that many new businesses lose money. Thus, rather than primarily focusing on tax rates on income across the organizational forms, we need to focus on the treatment of business losses across the forms. Another important consideration is the type of funding the business will need and the demands and preferences of those providing capital. Yet another important consideration is whether the owners intend to keep the business and operate it long term or plan to sell. If the latter, then what is the exit strategy? We discuss some issues that become important with respect to each of these items, then provide a brief discussion of some other nontax factors (e.g., administrative burden) as well as some observations from research studies. We consider this discussion an introduction to the issues; however, anyone considering a start-up venture should seek professional tax advice for his or her specific situation.

As discussed earlier, the treatment of losses varies across the organizational forms. With the pass-through entity types, losses are passed through to the owners and are potentially available to offset income from other sources for the owner (subject to the limitations discussed above). This would tend to favor a pass-through form over the corporate form because although C corporation losses can be carried forward (as can business losses at the individual level), they cannot be used to offset other income of the owners. The tax benefits of losses for pass-through entities are also superior to C corporations in certain exit strategies because NOL carryovers of C corporations can effectively be lost or at least diminished in value when the C corporation has a change in ownership. For now, all that is important to recognize is that much of the value of C corporation losses can sometimes be lost when the C corporation ownership is transferred.

Beyond losses, if the owners of the business plan on eventually selling the business (rather than going public via an IPO), a pass-through entity (e.g., the S corporation) is likely preferable because the pass-through form could result in a higher sales price. As shown in more detail in our chapter about taxable acquisitions of S corporations and in Erickson and Wang (1999b), the purchase of a pass-through entity, in contrast to a freestanding C corporation, is more likely to be structured for the buyer to obtain a step-up in basis, making the acquired business more valuable to the buyer and thus leading to a higher price for the pass-through entity in a competitive bidding setting.

These advantages for pass-through s might lead one to expect that many, if not all, start-ups would be organized as pass-through entities for tax purposes. However, there are situations where this is not the case—indeed, C corporation start-ups turn out to be surprisingly common. This is especially the case in start-ups where the founder obtains extensive outside funding and intends to exit the business rather than operate it over the long run. Why is this? One reason is that the losses that can be passed to the owners by the pass-through entity are sometimes not immediately usable by the owners. For example, if the owner is a passive investor, he or she can only deduct the passive losses against passive income until his or her interest is liquidated, at which time the passive losses are freed up and can be used without limit. In addition, if any of the owners are tax-exempt entities or foreign investors not subject to the U.S. tax system, the losses are not valuable to them. Thus, often times, the value of the losses may not be as great as it first appears because some investors cannot use the losses. The full set of costs and benefits need to be evaluated for the specific owner group.

Let's consider venture capital (VC) investors as one example where some of these issues can be illustrated (and one we have some research evidence about).[15] VCs raise funds from limited partnerships to invest in businesses. The limited partnerships are owned by individuals and entities that have contributed the capital. Each limited partnership might have many limited partners (i.e., investors) and might invest in many ventures. At first glance, one might expect the underlying start-ups to be organized as pass-through entities. In this case, the losses would flow through to the VC investors and be available to offset any pass-through profits from other underlying investments and/or other income (i.e., a netting of profits and losses from all underlying investments). However, it is common for VC-backed start-ups to be C corporations. Why is this and what does it imply?

Based on several studies of this issue, numerous reasons are likely behind what we observe. First, C corporations can issue convertible preferred stock, which is the most common structure for VCs to invest, and this familiarity allows for quick investments. Second, the laws for C corporations are more established and familiar, and transfer of ownership is relatively simple. Third, current tax rules have a federal tax benefit called qualified small business stock that can allow many VC investments to completely avoid capital gains taxes. The investment has to be in C corporation stock and held for at least 5 years to avoid recognition of capital gains.[16] Fourth, the investor base of limited partners in many VC funds includes a large proportion of tax-exempt entities and foreign investors (Fleischer, 2003). These tax-exempt and foreign investors do not always value the losses that would flow through from a pass-through entity. Other important considerations because of this investor type also exist when the entity is profitable or has some type of income allocations. For example, consistent with our "all taxes" theme, tax-exempt investors also like the C corporation form because it enables them to avoid having unrelated business taxable income, which is, income separate from their tax-exempt purposes that would otherwise be taxable under U.S. tax code. Foreign investors also prefer the C corporation form because pass-through entities could allocate them ordinary income, which is subject to the U.S. tax system, whereas an investment in a C corporation will not subject them to the U.S. tax system because the investment returns would be dividends or capital gains upon liquidation (i.e., they are not allocated annual income). One common approach to avoid these issues is to set up what are known as "blocker corporations," whereby a U.S. corporation is established between the foreign/tax-exempt investors and the investee entity that is generating the unrelated business income to block such investors from receiving income allocations. This increases the complexity of the structure but enables different treatments for different owners based on their preferences.

One agency issue that appears to be relevant is that the general partners of the VC funds (i.e., those making the decisions) would typically not participate in any of the pass-through losses. Rather, they would be paid only upon realization of the funds' profits generated from the sale of investments. Thus, the general partners do not have compensation incentives to maximize the value of the loss by pass-through entities (Allen and Raghavan, 2012).

A final reason VC-back start-ups become C corporations is the relative administrative burden of a C corporation compared to a pass-through entity. When an investor invests in a C corporation, the income tax is paid at the corporate level. With a pass-through entity, each investor receives a K-1 that contains his or her share of annual income items. Imagine an investor (a VC fund or otherwise) who invests in multiple entities—he or she receives a K-1 for each investment. Furthermore, this would include a federal K-1 and different state K-1s depending on where the underlying companies are required to file. Thus, the administrative burden and compliance cost are much higher for a pass-through than for a C corporation.

How much value do VCs leave on the table by organizing the underlying businesses as C corporations and not utilizing the flow through of losses? Allen, Allen, Raghavan, and Solomon (2018) examined a sample of 1,128 VC-backed firms that reached the initial public offering (IPO) stage between 1997 and 2014. They found that 97.8% of the firms that ultimately go IPO are structured as

---

[15] Bankman (1994); Fleischer (2003–2004); Johnson (2009); Allen and Raghavan (2012); Allen, Allen, Raghavan, and Solomon (2018); and Polksy (2018) are excellent studies on these issues. See also "Choice of Entity" at *Startup Law Blog*, http://www.startuplawblog.com/choice-of-entity.

[16] See IRC Section 1202. The rules and benefits of Section 1202 have changed over time.

a C Corporation. About 92% of the IPO firms examined reported an accumulated NOL. The authors estimated that only 21% of these firms with accumulated losses will ever become profitable enough to use the losses at the corporate level. Under what the authors called their baseline assumptions, they estimated that these firms lose almost 3% of the value of the amount invested ($2.86 billion) in taxes from not utilizing losses. Their estimate is even greater for a larger, non-IPO sample of VC-backed companies. For this set of firms, the estimated tax loss from organizing as a C corporation is roughly 5.2% of invested equity, or $41.5 billion. What do these lost tax savings represent? It is hard to imagine that the explanation is that VC funds are not sophisticated investors. The alternative hypothesis is that these tax savings are indicative of the value of the nontax costs one would have to incur to organize as an LLC.

An interesting thought experiment is to imagine what might happen if the underlying entities were all organized as pass-through entities with annual loss allocations available for investors. What might happen to the investor base of VC funds? Would a different clientele be attracted to this type of investment—perhaps profitable publicly traded domestic C corporations? Johnson (2009) argued that the availability of losses would bid up the price of the venture fund interests and drive tax-exempt institutions from the investor pool. Fleisher (2003–2004) observed, however, that there would be yet another trade-off to contend with—the investing C corporations would be allocated partnership losses for tax and for financial accounting purposes, thus causing the earnings reported to shareholders to be lower. This would increase the nontax costs of such an investment for those firms as well.

5.4 CHANGING PREFERENCES FOR ORGANIZATIONAL FORMS INDUCED BY TAX-RULE CHANGES

As one can see from an evaluation of the model in Section 5.2, as tax rates change over time, the preference for certain types of organizational forms also changes. The most descriptive and stunning example of this is regards the Tax Reform Act of 1986 (TRA 1986). The act decreased both corporate and individual tax rates, lowering the individual tax to a greater extent. The U.S. corporate tax rate declined from 46% to 34%, the U.S. individual ordinary income tax rate declined from 50% to 28%, and capital gains tax rates jumped from 20% to 28%. Thus, after TRA 1986, the income tax rate for income at the individual level at 28% was lower than the income tax rate for corporations, set at 34%. In response to these tax-rate changes, many more entities organized themselves as (or changed to be organized as) S corporations to take advantage of the lower individual rates. In 1985, there were approximately 75,000 S corporation elections. In the 5 weeks spanning the end of 1986 and the beginning of 1987, there were approximately 225,000 S corporation elections—three times as many occurred over this 5-week period than during all of calendar year 1985.[17] This suggests that the tax benefits of switching to S corporation status outweighed any potential nontax costs of operating as an S corporation.

The recent TCJA provides another setting where tax rates changed dramatically, especially for C corporations, as well as for some pass-through business income. The change in the rates and rules provides another setting where taxpayers will evaluate whether their organizational form should be changed and will influence how new organizations are formed going forward. In this section, we develop a more formal, generalizable structure to incorporate tax-rule changes that occur over time into the decision-making process.

The Required Before-Tax Rates of Return on Corporate and Partnership Activities

Although pass-throughs have become more important over time, to be a publicly traded entity with access to large amounts of equity capital, for the most part, the entity has to be a C corporation (some exceptions are discussed later). Thus, C corporations are extremely important to the economy. In this section, we determine how large the before-tax return of corporations must be to preserve indifference between the partnership and the fully taxable corporation.

[17] *Tax Notes*, February 1, 1988, p. 434, quoting Ronald Perlman. See also Plesko (1999) for evidence on S conversions after 1986.

Let us denote the before-tax rate of return in corporate form as R_c and in partnership form as R_p.[18] Previously, we assumed that the before-tax rate of return R, was the same in corporate and partnership forms. In this section, we allow for the possibility that, for nontax reasons, it might be less costly to produce identical goods and services in a corporation than in a partnership. For example, partners might not enjoy as well-defined property rights (due to relatively sparse case law) as corporate stockholders. In addition, partnerships might have poorer access to capital markets and might face higher administrative costs. And partners might have less monitoring ability over management than corporate shareholders.

After corporate-level taxes, *but before shareholder-level taxes,* the corporation realizes a return of r_c, where $r_c = R_c(1 - t_c)$. After personal taxes, the partnership realizes a return of r_p, where $r_p = R_p(1 - t_p)$. Let us assume that both R_c and R_p are constant across time, so we need not employ a second subscript to denote time.

What level of corporate after-tax return, r_c, will make a tax planner indifferent between corporate and partnership forms? We will denote this particular level of return as r_c^*. To find r_c^*, we continue to assume that the corporation pays no dividends and shareholders pay tax on realized capital gains at rates below the personal tax rate (i.e., $0 < t_{cg} < t_p$). Suppose the typical shareholder holds stock for n years. To be competitive, the after-tax rate of return on shares must be equal to the after-tax rate of return on undertaking the same investment in partnership form. By starting with Equation 5.3 and equating the after-tax returns from an initial investment of $\$I$ in both corporate and partnership forms, we can derive the following:

$$\$I[1 + R_p(1 - t_p)]^n = \$I[1 + R_c(1 - t_c)]^n(1 - t_{cg}) + t_{cg}\$I \tag{5.3}$$

$$\begin{aligned}(1 + r_p)^n &= (1 + r_c^*)^n(1 - t_{cg}) + t_{cg} \\ [(1 + r_c^*)^n(1 - t_{cg}) + t_{cg}]^{1/n} - 1 &= r_p\end{aligned} \tag{5.5}$$

Recall that t_p in these equations could be t_p or equivalent to t_{qbi}, the rate effectively applied if the taxpayer is allowed a full QBI deduction. The left side of Equation 5.5 has the following interpretation: A corporation earns after-corporate-level tax at a rate r_c^* per year for n years. At time n, the firm buys back all its shares and a shareholder-level tax is paid at rate t_{cg} on the entire value of the repurchased shares, except for the initial I dollars invested, which are returned tax free to the investor. The after-tax accumulation at time n is $(1+ r_c)^n (1 - t_{cg}) + t_{cg}$. As previously noted, accumulation in non-dividend-paying common stock is equivalent to a savings vehicle IV. The annual rate of return is determined by taking the nth root of the after-tax accumulation per dollar invested and then subtracting 1.

We can rearrange Equation 5.5 to solve directly for r_c^*, the after-corporate-level-tax—but before-shareholder-level-tax—rate of return that will make a tax planner indifferent between corporate and partnership forms:

$$\mathrm{r}_c^* = \{[(1 + r_p)^n - t_{cg}]/1 - t_{cg}\}^{1/n} - 1 \tag{5.6}$$

Even armed with Equation 5.6, the tax planner has a difficult task to determine r^*_c. The tax planner must know the holding period and the personal tax rate of the firm's shareholders. And the task is complicated further because shareholders face different tax rates and investment horizons and tax rates may change over time.

Still, Equation 5.6 holds the key to determining before-tax required rates of return. Consider current tax rules. Assume that the typical shareholder has a personal tax rate, after the QBI deduction of t_{qbi}, of 29.6%; has a capital gains rate, t_{cg}, of 20%; and holds shares for 5 years (i.e., $n = 5$). Assume further that projects undertaken in partnerships return 10% before tax (i.e., $R_p = 10\%$). Then after-tax partnership returns are 7.0%, or 10%(1 − .296). To be competitive, the corporate form must earn a rate exceeding 7.0%. The required return is given by solving for r_c^*. The corporate form must earn a rate of 7.5% per year (after corporate-level taxes but before shareholder-level taxes):

---

[18] Again, these represent the internal returns generated via taxable income. We ignore stock or partnership interest appreciation due to other factors, such as the value of intangibles, and market power. In other words, we assume that these are equal across the organizational forms.

$$r_c^* = \{[(1 + .070)^5 - .20]/(1 - .20)\}^{1/5} - 1 = .085$$

An 8.5% return results in a 7.0% after-tax rate of return to shareholders. That is, if shareholders pay tax on their realized capital gains at the end of 5 years, they realize exactly the same after-tax rate of return as if they had invested in a partnership that yields 10% pretax and 7.0% after tax. Each dollar invested in stock at a before-tax return of 8.5% per year grows to $1.50 in 5 years. After paying tax at a capital gains rate of 20% on the $0.50 of realized gain, shareholders retain $1.40. Accumulating $1.40 after tax in 5 years per dollar of initial investment is equivalent to an after-tax rate of return of 7.0% per year, or $1.40^{1/5} - 1 = .070$. **Table 5.1** gives the required annual before-tax rate of return on corporate shares, r_c^*—highlighted by boldface type—for various holding periods and marginal tax rates.

Note that for any level of the personal tax rate, t_p, the required before-shareholder-tax rate of return, r_c^*, falls as the holding period increases. As n increases without limit, r_c^* approaches the after-tax return on partnerships. The required return on shares before shareholder-level tax decreases as the investment horizon lengthens because holding onto the shares allows the capital gains tax to be deferred. Therefore, for any given rate of annual appreciation on shares, r_c^*, the after-tax return on shares increases with the length of the holding period, just as was true for a single-premium deferred annuity contract. We can view this as a reduction in the shareholder-level tax rate as the holding period on shares increases. As this tax rate decreases, so does the level of the before-tax return on shares required to achieve a target level of after-tax return. Also, because of the favorable capital gains tax rates, the required return to shares before shareholder-level tax is below the before-tax rate of return to partnerships (10% in **Table 5.1**) even for short holding periods. Investors require higher before-tax rates of return on investments that are taxed less favorably.

Table 5.1 Required Annualized After-Corporate-Tax—but Before-Shareholder-Level Tax—Return on Shares, r_c^*, for Different Investor Marginal Tax Rates, t_p and t_{cg}, and Holding Periods, n, with a Partnership Before-Tax Return, R_p, of 10%

Shareholder Tax Rates (%)			Before-Shareholder-Level-Tax Required Rates of Return at the Corporate Level (%), r_c^{*a}					After-Tax Return[b] %
t_p	t_{cg}	R_p	$n = 1$	5	10	20	50	
50	20	10	**6.25**	**6.11**	**5.97**	**5.76**	**5.43**	5.0
40	16	10	**7.14**	**7.00**	**6.86**	**6.65**	**6.35**	6.0
30	12	10	**7.95**	**7.82**	**7.70**	**7.52**	**7.27**	7.0

[a] r_c^* is calculated using Equation 5.6. The numbers in boldface are calculated based on the parameter values in normal typeface.
[b] This is the after-tax rate of return on both stocks and partnerships.

The Required Rate of Return on Stocks in the Presence of Dividends

In establishing the required rate of return at the corporate level in Equation 5.6, we assumed that all returns were taxed as capital gains. If, instead, shares pay a dividend at rate d and such dividends are taxed at rate t_{div}, the required return on shares over a *single* period, r_c^*, satisfies[19]

$$[(1 + r_c^* - d)(1 - t_{cg}) + t_{cg}] + d(1 - t_{div}) = 1 + r_p \tag{5.7}$$

That is, the after-tax capital gain on shares, the first term in Equation 5.7, plus the after-tax dividend return on the shares, $d(1 - t_{div})$, the second term in Equation 5.7, must be equal to the after-tax partnership return. Solving for r_c^*, we find that

$$r_c^* = [(1 + r_p) - d(1 - t_{div}) - t_{cg}]/(1 - t_{cg}) + d - 1$$

If dividends are taxed less favorably than capital gains to individual shareholders, as we initially assume here, the required return on shares is increasing in the dividend yield. For example, when total stock returns are taxed at capital gains rates, a taxpayer facing tax rates of $t_p = t_{div} = 40\%$ and $t_{cg} = 16\%$ requires a before-tax return on stocks of 7.14% over a 1-year horizon to yield the 6% after-tax

[19] Note that certain arbitrage strategies may allow dividends to be taxed more favorably than at rate t_{div}.

return available in partnerships. (See the 40% row of **Table 5.1**.) That is, 7.14% × (1 − .16) = 6%. But when the dividend yield is 3%, the required r_c^* is

$$r_c^* = [(1 + .06) - .03(1 - .40) - .16]/(1 - .16) + .03 - 1 = .08$$

The total required return before shareholder-level tax, then, is 8%, consisting of 5% in capital gains and 3% in dividends.

Table 5.2 reports the required before-tax rates of return for various investor tax rates and holding periods for a stock that pays a 3% dividend. In calculating the values in **Table 5.2**, we assume that dividends distributed to shareholders are taxed at the investor's marginal tax rate, $t_{div} = t_p$, and the after-tax dividends are reinvested in the partnership sector at rate r_p.[20]

Table 5.2 Required Annualized After-Corporate-Level-Tax—but Before Shareholder-Level Tax—Return on Shares, r_c^*, Paying a 3% Dividend Rate for Different Investor Marginal Tax Rates, t_p and t_{cg}, and Holding Periods, n, with a Partnership Before-Tax Return, R_p, of 10%

Shareholder Tax Rates (%)			Before-Shareholder-Level-Tax Required Rates of Return at the Corporate Level (%), r_c^{*a}					After-Tax Return[b] %
$t = t_{div}$	t_{cg}	R_p	$n = 1$	5	10	20	50	
50	20	10	**7.38**	**7.28**	**7.17**	**7.02**	**6.76**	5.0
40	16	10	**8.00**	**7.90**	**7.80**	**7.64**	**7.40**	6.0
30	12	10	**8.57**	**8.48**	**8.38**	**8.24**	**8.04**	7.0

[a] r_c^* is calculated using the equation in note 20. The numbers in boldface are calculated based on the parameter values in normal typeface.

[b] This is the after-tax rate of return on both stocks and partnerships.

Compare required returns in **Tables 5.1** and **5.2**. **Table 5.2** indicates that required returns before shareholder-level tax are higher when dividend yields are positive. In addition, the required returns fall off more slowly in **Table 5.2** as the length of the investment horizon increases. The reason, of course, is that when dividends are paid, a smaller fraction of the total return on shares comes from capital gains, and it is only the tax on capital gains that is reduced as the investment horizon increases.

The Effective Annualized Tax Rate on Shares: t_s

Tables 5.1 and **5.2** show the required rates of return on stocks before shareholder-level tax necessary for corporations to compete with partnerships. These returns depend on the length of the investment horizon. We find it convenient to define a variable that captures the hypothetical annual tax rate that shareholders could pay *each year* on their pretax stock returns that would be equivalent to paying the shareholder-level tax they actually pay when they sell their shares. Call this variable the **effective annualized tax rate on shares**, and denote it t_s. If shareholders paid tax at rate t_s each year on their total stock returns (dividends plus capital gains), they would end up with the same after-tax accumulation as they actually achieve. The effective annualized tax rate on shares is found from

$$r_c^*(1 - t_s) = r_p \tag{5.8}$$

Thus,

$$t_s = 1 - \frac{r_p}{r_c^*} \tag{5.9}$$

[20] The table values for r_c^* satisfy (solved by iteration):

$$(1+r_c^* - d)^n(1-t_{cg}) + t_{cg} + d(1-t_{div})\sum_{t=1}^{n}(1+r_c^* - d)^{t-1}(1+r_p)^{n-t} = (1+r_p)^n$$

For example, in **Table 5.1**, we find that for a personal tax rate of 50% and a 10-year holding period, the annual required before-shareholder-level-tax rate of return, r_c^*, is 5.97%. Thus, $t_s = 1 - (.05/.0597)$, or 16.2%. If investors paid tax at a rate of 16.2% on accrued gains each year, this would be equivalent to paying tax at a 20% capital gains rate on selling their shares in 10 years.

Required Before-Tax Rate of Return: Corporations versus Partnerships: R_c^*

Having defined r_c^*, we can now easily express the required before-tax return on projects undertaken by corporations, R_c^*:

$$R_c^*(1-t_c)=r_c^* \qquad (5.10)$$

Substituting r_c^* from Equation 5.10 to Equation 5.8 gives us

$$R_c^*(1-t_c)(1-t_s)=r_p$$

And noting that $r_p = R_p(1 - t_p)$, we can now determine the required before-tax return, R_c^*, on corporate projects relative to partnership projects:

$$R_c^*(1-t_c)(1-t_s)=R_p(1-t_p)$$

or

$$\frac{R_c^*}{R_p}=\frac{(1-t_p)}{(1-t_c)(1-t_s)} \qquad (5.11)$$

If the corporate tax rate is 21%, the personal tax rate is 37%, and the effective shareholder-level tax rate is 20%, the required pretax return on corporate projects is approximately equal to that on partnership projects. However, if the personal tax rate is 29.6% rather than 37%,

$$\frac{R_c^*}{R_p}=\frac{(1-.296)}{(1-.21)(1-.20)}=1.114$$

In other words, the pretax return on corporate projects must exceed that on partnership projects by 11.1%. If partnership projects yield 10% pretax, corporate projects must yield 11.1% , or $.10 \times 1.114$, to provide the same after-tax return.

Armed with these relations, we can now quickly determine how the relative attractiveness of the corporate form versus the partnership form has fluctuated as Congress has changed tax rates. We summarize the comparisons in **Table 5.3**. In generating this table, we assume investments in the partnership form yield a 10% pretax rate of return, the investor holds the investment for a 10-year period, that the corporation is profitable and pays taxes at the top corporate statutory tax rate, and pays no interim dividends. In this table, we assume the investor faces the top statutory rate, but we provide two alternatives for the time period 2018 and forward (recall that the current law allows the QBI deduction only through 2025, but for simplicity, we assume the deduction never expires). We calculate the required before-tax return the corporation will need to earn to be competitive, R_c^*, with the pass-through entity earning 10% pre-tax under both the top personal tax rate and the top personal tax rate if the taxpayer is allowed the full QBI deduction. **Table 5.3** shows that the corporation needs to earn 10.50% per annum if the pass-through entity's income is eligible for the 20% deduction but only 9.44% per annum if the pass-through entity's income is taxed at the top individual tax rate (i.e., in cases where the pass-through does not qualify for the 20% deduction).

As one can see, the period prior to the 1980s was when the personal tax rate was the highest, with a maximum personal tax rate, t_p, of 70%. This rate was far greater than the corporate tax rate, t_c, at 46%. However, capital gains were taxed at rates substantially less than ordinary income tax rates and less than the corporate tax rates with a t_{cg} of 28%. This rate structure favored the corporate form

Table 5.3 Required Annualized Corporate-Level-After-Tax—but Before-Shareholder-Level Tax—Return on Corporate Earnings, r_c^*, Effective Annualized Tax Rate on Corporate Earnings, t_s, and Required Pretax Corporate Return, R_c^*, for Corporation to the Earn Same After-Tax Return as Partnership Form[a] (Assumes Investor Holding Period, n, of 10 Years and Partnership Before-Tax Return, R_p, of 10%.)

Period	R_p	t_c	t_p	t_{cg}	r_c^*	t_s	R_c^*
Pre–1981	10.0	46	70	28	**3.98**	**24.7**	**7.37**
1982–1986	10.0	46	50	20	**5.97**	**16.3**	**11.06**
1987	10.0	40	39	28	**7.81**	**21.9**	**13.02**
1988–1990	10.0	34	28	28	**9.12**	**21.1**	**13.82**
1991–1992	10.0	34	31	28	**8.77**	**21.3**	**13.29**
1993–1996	10.0	35	39.6	28	**7.77**	**22.0**	**11.91**
1997–2000	10.0	35	39.6	20	**7.16**	**15.7**	**11.02**
2001–2002	10.0	35	38.6	18	**7.14**	**14.0**	**10.99**
2003–2012	10.0	35	35	15	**7.34**	**11.5**	**11.30**
2013[b]–2017	10.0	35	39.6	20	**7.16**	**15.7**	**11.02**
2018–	10.0	21	29.6	20	**8.29**	**15.1**	**10.50**
2018–	10.0	21	37	20	**7.46**	**15.5**	**9.44**

[a] r_c^* is calculated using Equation 5.6, t_s is calculated using Equation 5.9, and R_c^* is calculated using Equation 5.11. The numbers in boldface are calculated based on the parameter values in normal typeface. The 18% capital gains tax rate in 2001–2002 is applied to assets held longer than 5 years.

[b] We ignore the additional surtaxes under the Patient Protection and Affordable Care Act signed into law in 2010.

(unless for nontax reasons current corporate profits were distributed as dividends and shareholders were unable to convert dividends into capital gains by using arbitrage strategies).[21] For example, as reported in **Table 5.3**, the required corporate return, R_c (before all taxes, both corporate- and shareholder-level taxes), for an investor to be indifferent between the partnership form earning 10% pretax and the corporate form was 7.37%. Thus, even though the corporate form is subject to double taxation, the deferral of taxation, the lower capital gains tax rate at the shareholder level, and the lower corporate tax rate relative to the personal tax rate all combined to make the corporate form tax advantaged during this period. Recall that these results are for a non-dividend-paying stock and an investor holding period of 10 years. For a dividend-paying stock, the required pretax corporate return will be somewhat higher than 7.37%. Why? The shareholder-level tax will be higher because there is no deferral for the dividend portion, which is taxed at the higher ordinary income tax rate.

Post TRA 1986 (1987, 1988–1990)

In contrast to the previous time period, after TRA 1986, the top personal tax rate fell below the top corporate tax rate and for two years was only 28%, the lowest in the time series that we examine in **Table 5.3**. With personal tax rates below corporate tax rates, the after-tax rate of return in partnership form is greater than the after-tax rate of return in corporate form. As a result, partnerships became even more tax favored relative to corporations as a way to minimize taxes. The 1987 tax year was a transition year as the new lower statutory tax rates were phased in over 2 years. Nevertheless, even in 1987, it is evident that the corporate form became more tax disfavored relative to the partnership form. In the period 1988–1990, the required pretax corporate return of 13.82% indicates that the pretax return on corporate projects needed to exceed that on partnerships by at least 38% for the corporation to earn the same after-tax return. This is a large tax disadvantage and the reason behind the large number of S corporation elections discussed at the beginning of this section. However,

[21] Such arbitrage strategies are not discussed here.

note that publicly traded companies could not convert to a pass-through entity unless they also went private. Thus, the nontax benefits of the C corporation form are substantial. Other factors considered by large and small entities at that time were the passive loss rules if the entity were converted to a pass-through. Finally, mom-and-pop businesses likely considered the ability to separate income into two pockets (i.e., corporate and personal), taking advantage of the lower brackets for each pocket that would be lost with a pass-through entity. Thus, although the change in the tax rates led to many entities converting to a pass-through organizational form, we did not observe all C corporations becoming pass-through entities after 1986.

The previous table and discussion assume an investor holding period of 10 years. We vary the holding period in the comparison in **Table 5.4** and show the required corporate rate of return for various time periods based on changing tax rates over time.

The results in **Table 5.4** indicate, as expected, that as the holding period increases, the required corporate pretax rate of return declines. The longer holding period allows investors to defer the shareholder-level tax in a non-dividend-paying stock. For investors with relatively long holding periods, under the current configuration of top statutory tax rates, there is only a slight tax disadvantage to the corporate form. We again present two alternatives for the time period 2018 and forward—we calculate the required before-tax return the corporation will need to earn to be competitive, R_c^*, with the pass-through entity under both the top personal tax rate and the top personal tax rate if the taxpayer is allowed the full QBI deduction.

Table 5.4 Required Pretax Corporate Return, R_c^*, for Corporation to Earn Same After-Tax Return as Partnership for Different Holding Periods[a] (Assumes Partnership Before-Tax Return, R_p, of 10% and Corporate Dividends of 0)

Period	R_p	t_c	t_p	t_{cg}	Required R_c^*, for n-Year Holding Period %				
					$n = 1$	5	10	20	50
Pre-1981	10.0	46	70	28	**7.72**	**7.55**	**7.37**	**7.09**	**6.56**
1982–1986	10.0	46	50	20	**11.57**	**11.32**	**11.06**	**10.67**	**10.06**
1987	10.0	40	39	28	**14.12**	**13.56**	**13.02**	**12.29**	**11.28**
1988–1990	10.0	34	28	28	**15.15**	**14.46**	**13.82**	**13.00**	**11.95**
1991–1992	10.0	34	31	28	**14.52**	**13.88**	**13.29**	**12.51**	**11.49**
1993–1996	10.0	35	39.6	28	**12.91**	**12.40**	**11.91**	**11.24**	**10.32**
1997–2000	10.0	35	39.6	20	**11.62**	**11.31**	**11.02**	**10.60**	**9.99**
2001–2002	10.0	35	38.6	18	**11.52**	**11.25**	**10.99**	**10.61**	**10.06**
2003–2012	10.0	35	35	15	**11.76**	**11.53**	**11.30**	**10.98**	**10.51**
2013[b]–2017	10.0	35	39.6	20	**11.62**	**11.31**	**11.02**	**10.60**	**9.99**
2018–	10.0	21	29.6	20	**11.14**	**10.81**	**10.50**	**10.07**	**9.50**
2018–	10.0	21	37	20	**9.97**	**9.70**	**9.44**	**9.07**	**8.55**

[a] R_c^* is calculated using Equation 5.11. The numbers in boldface are calculated based on the parameter values in normal typeface. In 2001–2002, for simplicity, we assume the 18% top capital gains tax applies to all holding periods.

[b] We ignore the additional surtaxes under the Patient Protection and Affordable Care Act signed into law in 2010.

Further Analysis of the 2003 Tax Act

As previously noted, the JGTRRA reduced the top capital gains tax rate to 15% and the top individual tax rate to 35%. However, in a radical departure from prior policy, the act also reduced the top individual tax rate on corporate dividends to 15% and the changes effective for 2013 retain, the treatment of qualified dividends as taxable at the long-term capital gains rate (top rate of 20% starting in 2013) rather than at the ordinary income rate.[22] With the reduction in the tax rate on dividends and the equating of the tax rates on dividends and capital gains, dividends are now less tax disfavored relative to capital gains, although capital gains still offer the advantages of deferral. We illustrate this in **Table 5.5**. With 100% payout of all taxable earnings, the after-tax accumulation to shareholders is calculated as

$$\$I[1 + R_c(1 - t_c)(1 - t_{div})]^n \tag{5.12}$$

and the annualized after-tax rate of return is

$$r_c = \$I[1 + R_c(1 - t_c)(1 - t_{div})]^{n(1/n)} - \$I$$

Table 5.5 After-Tax Return to Shareholders Assuming Corporate Pretax Rate of Return of 10% and Dividends and Capital Gains Both Taxed at 15%[a]

After-Tax Return to Shareholders, r_c

					Required R_c^*, for n-Year Holding Period %				
Dividend Policy	R_c	t_c	t_{div}	t_{cg}	$n = 1$	5	10	20	50
100% payout	10.0	35	15	15	**5.53**	**5.53**	**5.53**	**5.53**	**5.53**
0% payout	10.0	35		15	**5.53**	**5.56**	**5.72**	**5.90**	**6.17**

[a] The numbers in boldface are calculated based on the parameter values in normal typeface.

which, because of no deferral, simplifies to

$$r_c = R_c(1 - t_c)(1 - t_{div}) \tag{5.13}$$

Thus, because of no deferral of shareholder taxation, the after-tax rate of return is constant regardless of the holding period. In contrast, with zero dividends, capital gains offer the advantage of deferral, so the after-tax rate of return to shareholders increases as the holding period increases. The 0% payout line is calculated using Equation 5.2.

An alternative way to present these comparisons is to calculate the pretax rate of return required to be earned by corporations, R_c^*, to give the same after-tax return as investing in a partnership. With *100%* payout, we calculate R_c^* by equating the accumulations to each organizational form—that is, equating Equations 5.1 and 5.12:

$$\begin{gathered} \$I[1 + R_p(1 \quad t_p)]^n = \$I[1 + R_c(1 \quad t_c)(1 \quad t_{div})]^n \\ (1 + r_p)^n = [1 + r_c^*(1 \quad t_{div})]^n \end{gathered} \tag{5.14}$$

Solving for r_c^*, we get

$$\begin{gathered} (1 + r_p)^{n(1/n)} = [1 + r_c^*(1 \quad t_{div})] \\ (1 + r_p) \quad 1 = r_c^*(1 \quad t_{div}) \\ r_c^* = r_p / (1 \quad t_{div}) \end{gathered} \tag{5.15}$$

And R_c^* then is given by $R_c^* = r_c^*/(1 - t_c)$. For the zero-dividend-paying corporation, the required pretax rates of return are given by Equations 5.6 and 5.10 and can also be found in the second-to-last line

[22] President Bush initially proposed a 0% tax rate on dividends and an indexing of the taxpayers' basis in their stock for purposes of calculating capital gains for stocks paying out less than 100% of their taxable earnings (which would have resulted in adding more complexity to the U.S. tax code). The reduced dividend tax rate applies only to dividends that are paid from corporate earnings on which taxes have already been paid. Also instead of a 0% tax rate on dividends, an alternative is to (1) allow firms to deduct dividends in calculating their taxable income or (2) include dividends in the taxpayers' taxable income while allowing a credit for the corporate taxes paid on their personal tax returns. The latter alternative is referred to as an integrated or dividend imputation system. We analyze such a system in Appendix 1.

of **Table 5.4**. The required corporate pretax rates of return are reported in **Table 5.6** for different holding periods. Because there is no deferral of any taxes with a 100% dividend payout, the required corporate pretax rate of return is constant regardless of the holding period, whereas capital gains continue to offer deferral. When dividends are taxed at a lower rate, the required corporate pretax rate of return is correspondingly lower.

Table 5.6 Required Pretax Corporate Return, R_c^*, for Corporation to Earn Same After-Tax Return as Partnership for Different Holding Periods[a] (Assumes Partnership Before-Tax Return, R_p, of 10%)

					Required R_c^*, for n-Year Holding Period %				
Dividend Policy	R_c	t_c	t_{div}	t_{cg}	$n = 1$	5	10	20	50
100% Payout	10.0	35	35		**15.38**	**15.38**	**15.38**	**15.38**	**15.38**
	10.0	35	15		**11.76**	**11.76**	**11.76**	**11.76**	**11.76**
0% Payout	10.0	35		20	**12.50**	**12.16**	**11.82**	**11.35**	**10.70**
	10.0	35		15	**11.76**	**11.53**	**11.30**	**10.98**	**10.51**

[a] Assumes t_p = 35%. The numbers in boldface are calculated based on the parameter values in normal typeface.

The required corporate pretax rate of return can be thought of as the cost of equity capital *assuming* the next-best alternative for investors is the 10% pretax partnership return. Thus, lowering the tax on dividends from 35% to 15% for a firm paying out 100% of earnings reduces the firm's cost of capital from 15.38% to 11.76%. Lowering the capital gains rate for a non-dividend-paying firm also lowers its cost of capital. Further, the cost of capital is still lower for non-dividend-paying firms even when $t_{div} = t_{cg}$ because of the effects of tax deferral on capital gains (for n = 20 years, 100% payout, the required pretax corporate return is 11.76% compared with 10.98% with 0% payout). When a firm pays out some dividends but less than 100% of its earnings, the required corporate pretax rates of return (or its cost of capital) lie between the 100% and 0% payout required returns.

In summary, **Tables 5.3** to **Table 5.6** indicate that before 1981, corporations, even though subject to double taxation, were generally tax favored over partnership forms. During the early 1970s, many professional organizations were incorporated. Although they faced a shareholder-level tax when they liquidated their corporations, many doctors, lawyers, and consultants incorporated to escape the high personal tax rate and to shelter income at the lower corporate tax rate of less than 50%.[23] After the Economic Recovery Tax Act was passed in 1981, many of these corporations converted back to partnerships (or alternative organizational forms in which profits are taxed directly to owners rather than taxed first at the entity level). This movement accelerated with TRA 1986 as the corporate tax rate was set above the personal tax rate. The tables indicate that TRA 1986 substantially increased what the nontax advantage of corporations over partnerships had to be for corporations to overcome partnerships' tax advantage. In the years succeeding TRA 1986 through 2000, Congress gradually increased the tax rate on ordinary income, thus decreasing the after-tax return to partnerships. More recently, Congress also lowered the top capital gains tax rate and both individual-income and dividend tax rates. For non-dividend-paying stocks, the lowering of the top ordinary income tax rate favored the partnership form relative to corporations, but for dividend-paying stocks, the relative tax disadvantage of corporations declined. However, strictly considering taxes, it is still beneficial for firms to defer dividends to obtain deferred capital gains tax treatment for shareholders.[24]

[23] Another important factor contributing to the decision to incorporate was the generous opportunities to postpone the payment of tax by making tax-deductible contributions to pension accounts on behalf of corporate owner-managers.

[24] Generally, we assume that investors are taxable investors. However, recent research suggests that retirement plans (tax exempts) and foreigners displaced taxable investors. Indeed, recent estimates are that the share of U.S. corporate stock held in taxable accounts was roughly 24% in 2015 (Rosenthal and Austin, 2015).

The TCJA, Changing Organizational Form, and Tax Planning

The most recent tax act, the TCJA, as we have discussed, reduced the statutory U.S. corporate tax rate significantly and provides for a deduction of 20% of QBI for pass-through entities (subject to limitations). This will undoubtedly change the relative relations in some cases. For example, we see in the last line of **Table 5.4** that the corporation, though facing double taxation, is tax favored relative to pass-through entities that do not qualify for the QBI deduction. This is because of the substantially lower statutory corporate tax rate, historically speaking, and because we assume here that these pass-through entities do not qualify for the 20% deduction. On the other hand, for holding periods up to 20 years, the second-to-last line of the table shows the pass-through entity eligible for the 20% deduction is still slightly tax favored relative to the C corporation. However, at longer holding periods, the C corporation form will dominate in terms of tax treatment at least when dividends are zero.

Taxpayers can change organizational form if they so choose. Changing from a partnership to a C corporation is quite straightforward and not costly in terms of taxes. However, changing from the C corporation form is much more difficult and costly. The issue is the double taxation of C corporations. To get assets out of a C corporation, in general, some tax will need to be paid, either as a distribution to the owners (potentially taxed as a dividend) or a sale of the assets.

The TCJA may cause more businesses to want to be C corporations. The new 21% domestic tax rate is quite attractive. The nontax cost is that getting the assets out of the C corporation in a tax-free manner once the assets are owned by the C corporation is difficult because there is still double taxation.

An alternative for taxpayers is to stay in a pass-through entity and implement some tax planning to obtain more of the QBI deduction. For example, doctors are not entitled to any QBI deduction once their taxable income on a joint return exceeds $415,000 due to the limitations on specified service businesses. However, one potential planning idea is to separate the business into two parts. If the practice owns any real estate, which qualifies for the QBI deduction regardless of income levels, the real estate could be placed in a separate pass-through entity. This entity could then rent the building to the medical practice. This places income in the real estate pass-through rather than the medical practice, allowing the owners (presumably the same people) to obtain the QBI deduction where they otherwise would not. It is plausible that this same type of planning may work with the medical equipment of a medical practice as well.

Progressive Personal Income Tax Rates, t_p and t_{cg}

Finally, not all individuals face the same marginal tax rates on ordinary income and capital gains. The tax rate schedules for individuals are progressive: The statutory tax rate increases as a function of the taxpayer's taxable income. The schedule depends on filing status (single, married filing jointly, married filing separately, and head of household). Not all individuals face the top statutory tax rate and, for example, dividends and partnership income could be taxed at rates lower than the top statutory rate assumed in our model. Also, for lower-income individuals, the tax rate on capital gains is 0 or 15% instead of 20%. Finally, some taxpayers are subject to the Alternative Minimum Tax (AMT), meaning they have a lower rate (28%) but fewer allowable deductions (a broader base). (Note that the TCJA substantially reduced the number of taxpayers projected to pay AMT.) Thus, whether or not the taxpayer will fall under the AMT system and then what rates are applicable to a marginal decision should also be considered.

These complications do not invalidate the basic points illustrated in our model but do require the tax planner to exercise caution when conducting tax planning for individual taxpayers (what rates do they face?) or when making statements about the tax costs of different organizational forms. The actual tax costs will differ depending on the profitability of the business (and, hence, on t_c), the identity of the investor (individual, tax-exempt organization, or another corporation), and the investor's own marginal tax rate.

5.5 OTHER ORGANIZATIONAL FORMS THROUGH WHICH TO ORGANIZE PRODUCTION ACTIVITIES

The following is a brief discussion of several alternative, specific organizational forms and treatments of organizational forms under certain conditions.

Small Business Corporation (Section 1244): Original stockholders who collectively contribute up to $1 million of equity in certain domestic C corporations are permitted to deduct realized capital losses against their other income without regard to the usual annual limitation that applies to the sale of regular stock (currently $3,000). The annual Section 1244 deduction limit is $50,000 per taxpayer ($100,000 for a joint return). To qualify, the corporation must be essentially an operating company rather than engaging primarily in passive investment.

Qualified Small Business Stock (Section 1202): Shareholders, excluding corporations, of a qualified small business can exclude 50% of the gain realized if the taxpayer holds the stock for more than 5 years prior to the sale. The amount of gain that may be excluded is limited on a per-issuer basis to the greater of $10 million or 10 times the taxpayer's basis in the stock. The stock must have been issued after August 10, 1993, and other limitations and requirements apply.

Closely Held Corporation: The closely held corporation is owned by just a few shareholders, which is common in family and small businesses. Relative to widely held firms, closely held corporations tend to have considerable trust among the owners and employees. In fact, closely held firms are typically managed by the owner. By paying themselves generous salaries and bonuses, owner-managers can avoid part of the corporate-level tax and often take advantage of the lower brackets in the corporate tax rate schedule. Unlike dividend payments and capital gains to owner-managers, compensation payments are a tax-deductible expense to the corporation. Many incorporated consulting firms pay out most of their before-tax profits as year-end bonuses to avoid the corporate-level tax. There are limits here, however. The taxing authority may seek to treat part of compensation as a disguised dividend.

A special category of close corporations is personal service corporations. The principal activity of such entities is personal services performed by owner-employees. For example, a business-school professor who provides consulting services might incorporate her consulting business, with her as the sole shareholder, as a personal service corporation.

Not-for-Profit Corporation: A tax-exempt entity can produce certain goods and services and avoid the corporate tax on the earnings. Prominent examples include not-for-profit hospitals, universities, and religious organizations. In addition, prior to the 1960s, most savings and loan associations were effectively exempt from the corporate tax. The "owners" of these tax-exempt enterprises are effectively taxed as a special type of partnership. For example, doctors in not-for-profit hospitals may draw larger salaries as hospital income increases, and such income is taxed only at the personal level. Moreover, although the same opportunity exists in for-profit corporations, deferred salary in tax-exempt entities may be invested at rates of return that are not reduced by entity-level taxation.[25]

Master Limited Partnership (MLP): The MLP is basically a partnership with two types of partners: limited and general. Provided the limited partners do not actively participate in the management of the partnership, their liability for partnership debts is limited to their invested capital. General partners manage the partnership and have unlimited liability for the partnership debts. To provide limited liability to the general partner, the general partners are often organized as corporations. MLPs were the backbone of the tax shelter industry in the 1970s and early 1980s. Wealthy individuals contributed capital as limited partners to fund, for example, research and development or oil and gas exploration, which gave rise to losses in the first few years of the business that the limited partners could deduct against their other income.[26] As previously noted, TRA 1986 curbed these activities by limiting the ability of investors to take such losses. Many financial press commentators argued that this change adversely affected the U.S. real estate market. The LLC form tends to be a better choice than the MLP form because investors in an LLC can have both pass-through taxation and limited liability without giving up an active voice in management activities.

Publicly Traded Partnership (PTP): Publicly traded partnerships that derive at least 90% of their income from qualifying sources can retain partnership (flow-through) treatment for tax purposes. All other partnerships that are publicly traded will be taxed as corporations, paying a corporate

[25] The likelihood is great that before-tax rates of return are lower in activities that are tax exempt than in activities that are taxed at the corporate level.

[26] Such activities are not discussed in detail here.

tax, with partnership distributions treated as taxable dividends. Qualifying sources of income include interest, dividends, real estate rents, gain from the sale of real property, income from commodities or commodities futures, and income from mineral or natural resources activities. Thus, most PTPs operate in the areas of energy, timber, and real estate. (PTPs are specifically excluded from being able to elect partnership treatment under the check-the-box election.)[27] Today, PTPs are also referred to as MLPs and vice versa. When LLC interests are traded on public exchanges, the LLC is subject to the PTP tax rules of the tax code and is in effect a PTP.

Limited Liability Partnership (LLP): The LLP is a modified general partnership designed specifically for professional service organizations, such as the Big 4 accounting firms, to operate as a partnership with some personal liability protection. The partners are not protected for breaches of professional responsibility. Many states recognize LLPs, which offer advantages similar to the LLC—namely, limited liability with a single level of taxation.

Real Estate Investment Trust (REIT): The REIT entity is organized as a trust or corporation that receives most of its earnings from real estate activities. If all the earnings are distributed each year to beneficiaries or shareholders, the REIT avoids an entity-level tax. To qualify for pass-through treatment, the REIT must satisfy such constraints as having a minimum of 100 shareholders, no significant concentration of ownership, and passing two income tests (known as the 95%/75%, but basically income must be generated from real estate-related activities) and an asset test (at least 75% of its assets must be invested in qualified real estate).

Real Estate Mortgage Investment Conduit (REMIC): The REMIC is another pass-through entity. Substantially all of the REMIC's assets must consist of qualified mortgages and mortgage-related assets. REMICs have two classes of owners: owners of regular interests and owners of residual interests. The former are like bondholders, and the latter are like stockholders (except that REMICs do not pay an entity-level tax).[28]

Summary of Key Points

1. Different organizational forms can produce the same goods and services. Due to differences in tax treatment, conducting identical activities in different organizational forms can result in different after-tax rates of return.
2. Regular corporations are subject to double taxation in many countries, once at the corporate level and again at the shareholder level. In contrast, partnerships and other pass-through entities are taxed only at the investor level.
3. With equal before-tax rates of return on investment, the partnership is tax favored over the corporate form if the corporate tax rate and the tax rate that applies to pass-through business income at the shareholder level are the same and there is a non-zero tax on corporate profits at the shareholder level, $t_c = t_p$ and $t_s > 0$.
4. With equal before-tax rates of return on investment, the corporate form is tax favored over the partnership form if the corporate tax rate is below the tax rate that applies to the pass-through income at the shareholder level, $t_c < t_p$, and the tax at the corporate shareholder level, t_s, can be kept sufficiently low.
5. More generally, the corporate form is tax favored over the partnership form if one minus the corporate tax rate, multiplied by a factor of one minus the effective annualized tax rate on income from holding shares of corporate stock, exceeds one minus the tax rate on partnership income:

$$(1 - t_c)(1 - t_s) > (1 - t_p)$$

6. If the partnership form is tax favored over the corporate form and both forms undertake similar investments, some combination of market frictions, tax-rule restrictions, and nontax benefits of operating in corporate form would be necessary to prevent arbitrage.

[27] The well-known Blackstone Group LP is a PTP.

[28] Note that REITs are often used by retail firms to lower their state income taxes.

7. Cross-sectional differences in ordinary, pass-through, and shareholder-level tax rates create opportunities for tax arbitrage in the presence of both corporate and partnership forms of organization. Without frictions or restrictions, if some investors were indifferent between producing in either organizational form, other investors with different tax rates would strictly prefer to invest through one organizational form and finance the investment by borrowing claims against the returns to the other organizational form.
8. When the tax rate applicable to pass-through income exceeds corporate rates, there exists a unique tax rate on shares, t_s, for a given holding period for stock investment that makes producing through partnerships and corporations equally attractive. Investors with longer investment horizons prefer corporate investments; investors with shorter horizons prefer partnerships.
9. Changes in relative tax rates over time alter which organizational form is preferred.
10. In recent years, several organizational forms, such as LLCs and LLPs, have emerged that combine the benefits of limited liability and single-level taxation. A relaxation of the rules for S corporations has also made these forms more attractive.
11. When tax advantages to the corporate form exist, unless nontax benefits or nontrivial costs to corporate liquidation also exist, the tax rules would lead corporations to dissolve or convert to some other form.
12. Nontax benefits of the corporate form over the partnership form include limited liability, better established corporate case law, a more effective market for corporate control than for partnership control, superior corporate access to capital markets, and the ease of transferability of corporate ownership interests that enhances investor liquidity.
13. The TCJA lowered the corporate tax rate such that starting in 2018, the C corporation arguably has a tax advantage over pass-throughs if the entity is profitable, the QBI deduction is not allowed on the pass-through income, and the owner is in the top tax bracket.

Appendix 5.1

Dividend Imputation in the Corporate Form

Some countries have a dividend imputation system that converts part of the corporate-level tax into a partnership-level tax, which is intended to mitigate or eliminate the double taxation of corporate dividends inherent in a classical tax system. For example, Australia, France, Italy, Germany, and Canada allow partial or full imputation. By imputation we mean that if the corporation pays a dividend to its stockholders resident in that country from its after-tax corporate income, stockholders (1) receive a credit (as compensation for the corporate taxes that are imputed to have been paid by them) equal to some fraction of the dividend they receive and (2) declare as dividend income (on which ordinary tax rates are levied) the dividend received plus the tax credit amount. For example, if the corporate tax rate were 40%, $100 of before-tax profits results in $60 of profits after corporate tax. In a full imputation system, if the corporation pays a $60 cash dividend, it issues to its stockholders $40 in tax receipts along with a form instructing them to declare $100 of dividend income on their personal tax returns. The shareholder in a 40% tax bracket records $100 of income on which $40 tax is due. This offsets exactly the dividend tax credit, resulting in zero additional tax. The shareholder in a 30% tax bracket records $100 of income and $30 tax is due. The $40 tax receipt leaves a net credit of $10 to be used to offset any tax due on other income. Dividends on which a credit is attached are referred to as franked dividends. With 100% dividend payout, the imputation system converts the corporate form to the partnership form of taxation for those investors with sufficient taxable income to use the tax credit. The corporate income attracts only one level of taxation, at personal tax rates. As a result of the imputation system, tax-exempt shareholders, such as pension funds, are forced to pay tax at high corporate marginal tax rates. For them, the $40 tax receipt has no value unless they generate unrelated business income that is otherwise taxable.

More formally, the shareholder is taxed as follows on a fully franked dividend:

$$\textbf{Div} - [t_p\textbf{Div}/(1 - t_c) - t_c\textbf{Div}/(1 - t_c)] \tag{5A.1}$$

where the middle term is the amount of personal tax due on the grossed-up dividend before credit for corporate taxes paid, which is calculated as per the final term. This equation can be rearranged as

$$\begin{aligned}&\textbf{Div}[1 - t_p/(1 - t_c) + t_c/(1 - t_c)]\\ &= \textbf{Div}(1 - t_p)[1 + t_c/(1 - t_c)].\end{aligned} \tag{5A.2}$$

To check, we insert our earlier example:

$$\$60(1 - .40)[1 + .40/(1 - .40)] = \$60(.60)[1 + .66667]$$
$$= \$60 \text{ after-tax dividend}^{29}$$

[29] The mechanics of the dividend tax imputation system, taxpayers receiving a credit for corporate taxes, is similar to the mechanics of the foreign tax credit for U.S. multinationals. Further, our description here closely resembles the Australian system introduced in 1987.

In some cases, shareholders can receive dividends that are not franked. Examples include, when the dividends are paid from profits that have not been taxed at the corporate level, profits earned and taxed overseas, and profits earned prior to the introduction of the imputation system. To illustrate, suppose a corporation pays a dividend of \$100 of which \$70 (i.e., 70%) consists of franked dividends. In this case, the shareholder faces the following:

The unfranked dividend of \$30 + The franked dividend of \$70

\$30(1 – .40) + \$70(1 – .40)[1 + .40/(1 – .40)]
= \$18 + \$70
= \$88 dividend after shareholder-level taxes

This solution can also be derived more simply as

$$= \text{Div}(1 - t_p)[1 + kt_c/(1 - t_c)] \qquad (5A.3)$$

where k is the percentage of the dividend that is franked. Substituting in our numerical example, we get

\$100(1 – .40)[1 + .70(.40)/(1 – .40)] = \$100(.60)(1 + .46667) = \$88

We can now adjust the equation used in **Table 5.2** for dividend imputation. If shares pay a dividend at rate d of which k percent is franked, and dividends are taxed at rate t_p, the required return on shares over a *single* period, r_c^*, satisfies

$$[(1+r_c^* - d)(1-t_{cg})+t_{cg}]+d(1-t_p)\{1+k[t_c/(1-t_c)]\}=1+r_p \qquad (5A.4)$$

which is Equation 5.7 adjusted for dividend imputation by including the term $\{1+k[t_c/(1-t_c)]\}$ which multiplies $d(1-t_p)$. Solving for r^*_c, we find that

$$r_c^* = [(1+r_p)-d(1-t_p)\{1+k[t_c/(1-t_c)]\}-t_{cg}]/(1-t_{cg})+d-1 \qquad (5A.5)$$

Assume d = .03, R_p = 10%, t_p = 40%, t_{cg} = 20%, t_c = 35%, and k (the percentage of dividends that is fully franked) = 100%:

$$r_c^* = [(1 + .06) - .03(1 - .40)(1 + 1.00(.35/(1 - .35))) - .20]/(1 - .20) + .03 - 1 = .0704$$

With k = 70%,

$$r_c^* = [(1 + .06) - .03(1 - .40)(1 + .70(.35/(1 - .35))) - .20]/(1 - .20) + .03 - 1 = .0740$$

Similarly, the multiperiod equation can be easily adapted:

$$(1+r_c^* - d)^n(1-t_{cg})+t_{cg}+d(1-t_p)\{1+k[t_c/(1-t_c)]\}\sum_{t=1}^{n}(1+r_c^* - d)^{t-1}(1+r_p)^{n-t}=(1+r_p)^n \qquad (5A.6)$$

We use this equation to generate the numbers in **Table 5A.1**.

The first line of the table is repeated from **Table 5.2** and indicates that required returns before shareholder-level tax are higher when dividend yields are positive compared with the zero-dividend case in **Table 5.1**. In addition, the required returns fall off more slowly in **Table 5.2** than in **Table 5.1** as the length of the investment horizon increases. The reason, of course, is that when dividends are paid, a smaller fraction of the total return on shares comes from capital gains, and it is only the tax on capital gains that is reduced as the investment horizon increases. With full dividend tax imputation (i.e., k = 100%), the required pretax corporate returns are lower. Further, because we model less than 100% dividend payout and $t_p > t_c$, there is still an advantage to deferral. With less than 100% franking on any dividends paid, the required pretax corporate return is between the required returns of the 100% and zero imputations.

Table 5A.1 The Effects of Dividend Imputation on the Required Annualized After-Corporate-Tax—but Before-Shareholder-Level Tax—Return on Shares, r_c^*, Paying a 3% Dividend Rate for Different Holding Periods n, with a Partnership Before-Tax Return, R_p, of 10%

Shareholder Tax Rates (%)			Before-Shareholder-Level Tax Required Rates of Return on Stocks (%), r_c^* (after corporate-level taxes but before shareholder-level taxes)[a]					After-Tax Return[b] %
t_p	t_{cg}	R_p	n =1	5	10	20	50	r
From Table 5.2—no dividend imputation								
40	20	10	**8.25**	**8.15**	**8.06**	**7.95**	**7.88**	**6.0**
With dividend imputation at *k* = 100%, *tc* = 35%								
40	20	10	**7.04**	**6.93**	**6.82**	**6.66**	**6.40**	**6.0**
With dividend imputation at *k* = 70%, *tc* = 35%								
40	20	10	**7.40**	**7.29**	**7.17**	**6.99**	**6.71**	**6.0**

[a] The numbers in boldface are calculated based on the parameter values in normal typeface.
[b] This is the after-tax rate of return on both stocks and partnerships.
[c] k = percentage of dividends that are fully franked.

Appendix 5.2

Various investment vehicles have evolved through which investors organize themselves or their investments. We briefly discuss them here.

Private Equity Fund: This fund invests in other companies or business with the objective of obtaining a controlling interest so the fund can restructure the business. Restructuring can occur via leveraged buyouts, venture capital, angel investing, mezzanine debt, and other ways. After a successful restructuring, the fund cashes out via an IPO, a sale or merger of the business, or a recapitalization. Most private equity funds are organized as limited partnerships with the investors holding limited partner interests. As a result, investors are taxed as limited partners (as discussed in the chapter). Most private equity funds are sold to institutional investors and wealthy individuals (e.g., individuals with greater than $1 million net worth and annual income above $200,000). These funds face substantially less regulation than ordinary mutual funds, which are open to all investors.

The general partner is generally an affiliate of the manager of the fund. Typically, the general partner is compensated with a fee based on the gross assets under management (e.g., 2% of the gross assets) and a profits interest of generally 20% of the fund's return. The latter is referred to as "carried interest." If the fund is successful, most of the return to the general partner (i.e., the fund organizer) is not taxed as compensation for services but as a return on investment taxed at favorable capital gains tax rates. For very successful funds, these profits can be substantial and have attracted the attention of Congress and the media with the charge that these fund managers are taking advantage of tax loopholes to receive what is effectively compensation for services (i.e., salary) without paying the 35% tax on ordinary income. Several bills have been introduced into the House and Senate requiring that carried interest be taxed as ordinary income, but as of the date of writing this text, none of these has passed.[30]

In mid-2007, the Blackstone Group, a large private equity fund, went public. Blackstone became a publicly traded partnership and argued that its income qualified as PTP income, meaning it should not be taxed as a corporation. Although the investments made by a private equity fund are actively managed, Blackstone argued that its investment activity met the exception (i.e., passive income of interest and dividends) needed to qualify as a PTP for tax purposes. With PTP treatment, the profits pass through to the limited general partners Blackstone's general partner's carried-interest profits qualify as capital gains. This case also motivated some in Congress to introduce bills, specifically S. 1624 by Senators Baucus and Grassley, that would tax PTPs performing asset-management activities as a corporation.[31]

Another private equity in the news is Cerberus Capital Management LP. Cerberus recently acquired 80.1% of the Chrysler Group from DaimlerChrysler AG. After the acquisition, Chrysler Group was reorganized as Chrysler LLC—a pass-through entity.

Hedge Fund: A hedge fund is a private investment fund open to wealthy investors and similar in many ways to private equity funds except that hedge funds generally invest in stocks, bonds, and other financial instruments undertaking arbitrage activities or risky positions. Unlike a private equity fund, the objective of a hedge fund is not to obtain a controlling interest to restructure the underlying business. Hedge-funds are generally registered offshore. Fifty-five percent of hedge funds, managing 65% of total hedge fund assets, were located in the Cayman Islands, British Virgin Islands, Bermuda, and the Bahamas) at the end of 2004. For hedge funds with a large U.S. taxpayer base, the funds are organized similarly to private equity funds, with investors purchasing limited partnership interests and the fund organizer acting as general partner. The United States accounted for 34% of funds, managing 24% of the assets. The general partner as manager charges a management fee (typically 1.5 to 4.0% of gross assets under management) and a performance fee (similar to the carried interest of an equity fund, normally around 20% of gross returns of the fund). Because most hedge funds invest in liquid assets, investors are generally permitted to enter or leave the fund on short notice, whereas the investments by private equity funds are often tied up for years (illiquid investments) such that the investors are locked in for long periods of time.

Hedge funds can be compared to mutual funds. Both are pass-through entities for tax purposes. However, mutual funds differ from hedge funds because the former accepts investments from the general investment population via public prospectuses and are regulated by the Securities and Exchange Commission (SEC). Hedge funds only accept investments from wealthy individuals, do not issue public prospectuses, and are only lightly regulated by the SEC. Mutual funds must price their fund price each day and be liquid on a daily basis.

Exchange Fund: This is a private placement limited partnership or LLC specifically designed for investors with large positions in a single, highly appreciated stock. The investor may want to diversify but does not want to liquidate and pay the substantial capital gains tax due upon sale. The individual can put his or her ownership into an exchange fund—such contribution is treated as a nontaxable partnership contribution (under Section 721). Investors are required to stay in the fund for a specified number of years and, upon leaving, are distributed a basket of different stocks. When the individual sells these stocks, the capital gains tax is triggered,

[30] See http://frwebgate.access.gpo.gov/cgi-bin/getdoc.cgi?dbname=110_cong_bills&docid=f:h2834ih.txt.pdf.

[31] See http://frwebgate.access.gpo.gov/cgi-bin/getdoc.cgi?dbname=110_cong_bills&docid=f:s1624is.txt.pdf.

equivalent to the difference between the basis of what was originally contributed (the person's shares in the undiversified position) and the fair market value of the portfolio of shares sold on the date of sale. This allows the investor to diversify while delaying stock both sales and gain recognition. The fund portfolio can consist of no more than 80% equities or other readily marketable securities. The remainder must be in illiquid assets, such as real estate.

Questions

Q5-1. Explain the phrase "corporations are subject to double taxation." Is this true for all corporate forms? Explain the phrase "taxed as a pass-through entity."

Q5-2. What role do corporate dividends play in comparing the relative tax positions of investors in corporations versus partnerships?

Q5-3. What are the major variables that affect the magnitude of the required after-corporate-level-tax-but-before-shareholder-level-tax rate of return, r_c^*? Give examples to illustrate the importance of each variable. Is it possible to rank the importance of each variable?

Q5-4. What are the major variables that affect the magnitude of the shareholder-level tax, t_s? Give examples to illustrate the importance of each variable. Is it possible to rank the importance of each variable?

Q5-5. What are the major variables that affect the magnitude of the pretax corporate rate of return, R_c? Give examples to illustrate the importance of each variable. Is it possible to rank the importance of each variable?

Q5-6. The data presented in **Table 5.3** suggest that the corporate form suffered a tax disadvantage relative to the partnership form from 1987 to 1992. List and explain the factors that caused this outcome. Why did more firms not convert from the corporate form to partnership form during this time?

Q5-7. What factors might lead to cross-sectional and time-series differences in corporate tax rates, personal tax rates, and shareholder-level tax rates? How do these differences affect tax planners? How do these differences affect tax policymakers?

Q5-8. Why might one group of investors prefer the corporate form and another group of investors prefer the partnership form?

Q5-9. If corporations face tax disadvantages relative to partnerships, why might we continue to observe the corporate form, especially for large public businesses? (Note that we examine whether they are in fact tax advantaged after the TCJA in question 5-16 below.)

Q5-10. Explain the check-the-box election. Prior to this election, how did the IRS determine whether a business was taxed at the entity level or as a pass-through entity?

Q5-11. Give five examples of organizational forms used to produce goods and services. What tax characteristics distinguish one from the other?

Q5-12. Compare and contrast the S corporation, the general partnership, and the limited liability company.

Q5-13. Explain how a dividend tax imputation system works.

Q5-14. What is the effect of dividend imputation on r_c^*, the required after-corporate-tax-but-before-shareholder-tax rate of return? What is the effect of dividend imputation on r_c^* as the percentage of dividends that are franked, k, declines toward zero?

Q5-15. Compare and contrast the following policies that provide relief from double taxation on C corporate profits:

a. Excluding dividends from taxation for individual taxpayers

b. Allowing firms a tax deduction for dividends paid

c. A dividend imputation system where taxpayers receive a tax credit for corporate taxes paid

d. Setting the corporate tax rate to zero

Q5-16. How did the TCJA alter the relative preferences in terms of organizational form? Illustrate this using a simple example where a business has pretax taxable income of $100 and operates:

a. A C corporation subject to a 21% tax rate, that pays out all after-tax earnings as dividends, and in which the shareholders are all taxable at 20% on qualified dividends and 37% on ordinary income

b. A pass-through that does not qualify for the QBI deduction

c. A pass-through that does qualify for the QBI deduction

Exercises

E5-17. Suppose that the tax rate on personal income, t_p, is equal to 37%; the corporate tax rate, t_c, is equal to 21%; and the capital gains tax rate, t_{cg}, is 20%. Also assume that the before-tax rate of return on investment to the corporate and partnership forms is 15% per year. These tax rates and investment returns are constant over time. On the basis of these facts, identify the following as true or false. (Support your answers with numerical examples.)

a. The annualized after-tax rate of return to investing in the corporate form increases with the length of the investor's holding period. Explain.

b. The annualized after-tax rate of return to investing in the partnership form increases with the length of the partner's holding period. Explain.

c. If a corporation paid out its entire after-tax profits as fully taxable dividends each year, shareholders would realize a lower before-tax rate of return than if the corporation retained the after-tax profits. Explain.

d. Because the corporate tax rate is below the personal tax rate, the corporate form is always preferred to the partnership form.

e. Because corporate income is subject to two levels of taxation, the partnership form is always preferred to the corporate form.

E5-18. Following TRA 1986, the corporate tax rate of 34% was set above the personal tax rate of 28% on ordinary income and 100% of realized capital gains became taxable at investors' ordinary rates. What were the required before-tax rates of return to corporations and to partnerships if investors required that the after-tax rate of return on investments of similar risk be equal to 15% per year and the typical shareholder holds shares for 8 years? Under what circumstances might we have seen both a corporation and a partnership producing the same goods and services in light of these required before-tax rates of return?

E5-19. A taxpayer capitalizes a wholly owned corporation with $100,000. The corporation invests in a project that earns an annual pretax rate of return of 15% and faces a 21% corporate tax rate. The taxpayer faces a personal tax rate on pass-through income of 29.6% and expects to liquidate the corporation after 20 years. The taxpayer has a capital gains tax rate of 20%.

a. What is the after-tax rate of return on this investment?

b. Do you recommend that the taxpayer make this investment via an S corporation to avoid double taxation? Assume the corporation distributes enough cash to the taxpayer each year to allow him to pay his taxes on the S corporation income.

(Exercise adapted from problem written by Richard Sansing, Dartmouth College.)

E5-20. Suppose Congress reduced the top capital gains tax rate, t_{cg}, to 10% from 20%. How would this affect the required pretax corporate return, R_c^*, calculated in the final line of **Table 5.4**? That is, recalculate the required pretax corporate return for the holding periods and other parameter values as listed for the last line in **Table 5.4**.

E5-21. Suppose Congress increased the top personal tax rate, t_p, to 45% from 37%. How would this affect the required pretax corporate return, R_c^*, calculated in the final line of **Table 5.4**? That is, recalculate the required pretax corporate return for the holding periods and other parameter values as listed for the last line in **Table 5.4**.

E5-22. Suppose Congress reduced the top corporate tax rate, t_c, to 15% from 21%. How would this affect the required pretax corporate return, R_c^*, calculated in the final line of **Table 5.4**? That is, recalculate the required pretax corporate return for the holding periods and other parameter values as listed for the last line in **Table 5.4**.

E5-23. What rate k, the percentage of dividends that are franked in a dividend imputation system, would equate to a tax rate of 25%? If necessary, assume the 2018 top tax rates.

Tax-Planning Problems

TP5-24. With TRA 1986, corporate tax rates fell from 46% in 1986 to 40% in 1987 and to 34% for income earned thereafter. Because the tax code allowed a 3-year carryback for NOLs during this period, would it be tax advantageous for those firms that were profitable during 1984–1986 to generate NOLs during 1987–1989 by (1) selling certain assets at a loss, (2) postponing the recognition of income, and (3) accelerating certain tax-deductible expenditures? If the after-tax discount rate is 7%, how tax advantageous are these strategy? What specific actions might a firm have undertaken to generate NOLs in 1987–1989?

TP5-25. Because U.S. corporations are allowed to exclude from taxable income 50% of the dividends they receive from other U.S. corporations in which they own up to 20%, tax planners sometimes suggest investing in dividend-paying common or preferred stock. Is it tax advantageous for a U.S. corporation to buy dividend-paying stock? Is it tax advantageous for a U.S. corporation to buy adjustable-rate preferred stock (i.e., short-term dividend-paying preferred stock with a dividend yield that floats in direct proportion to short-term treasury yields) instead of dividend-paying stock? Is it tax advantageous for a corporation to issue the preferred stock? Canadian firms can exclude 100% of the dividends they receive from other Canadian corporations. Is it tax advantageous for Canadian companies to buy common stock in other Canadian corporations?

TP5-26. An established corporation currently pays out 50% of earnings as dividends. The CFO asks you whether paying dividends to shareholders other than corporations is advantageous. How do you respond?

TP5-27. Let us assume, as was true of wealthy individuals in the United States in the 1960s, that the personal tax rate is 70% and realized capital gains are taxed at half the top personal tax rate—that is, t_{cg} = 35%. Assume that the top corporate rate is 48%. The before-tax rate of return on investments is 15%. You are asked to advise a doctor as to whether she should incorporate. What would be the tax-advantageous strategy for 5-, 10-, and 15-year investment horizons? Suppose that she did incorporate and that 5 years later , the personal tax rate unexpectedly falls to 50%. Should she liquidate her corporation and start a new partnership?

TP5-28. A wealthy taxpayer is planning to start an online business. The taxpayer expects to generate tax losses for at least the first 5 years of the business. The taxpayer also hopes to cash out of the business within 10 years by going public or selling to another business. Discuss the pros and cons of starting out as a regular C corporation versus a sole proprietorship (or some other pass-through entity). In your discussion, indicate whether the following matters.

a. The investor cashes out via going public or by selling to another business.

b. The investor is actively involved in the operations of the business.

How might your answers to parts (a) and (b) differ if the investor is not so wealthy?

TP5-29. Suppose you are advising a college basketball coach on whether to organize his summer basketball camps for high school students as a C corporation versus an S corporation. The taxpayer plans to operate the camps for 5 years, then wind up the corporation by simply paying any retained earnings as a dividend in the final year. The taxpayer faces a marginal tax rate of 32%, is eligible for the 80% QBI deduction because his taxable income is less than $315,000 (joint with his wife), and the corporate tax rate is a flat rate of 21%. In addition, the tax rate on dividends is equal to the long-term capital gains tax rate, 20%. The expected pretax rate of return on the camps is 12% per year (before any compensation or dividends to the taxpayer).

a. Assuming zero dividends are paid each year, which corporate form would you advise the taxpayer to select?

b. Assuming 50% of taxable income is distributed each year as dividends, which form would you advise the taxpayer to select? Explain your answer in words (no algebra is required here).

c. Assuming a zero dividend payout each year, what shareholder-level tax rate, t_s, in the C corporation form would equate the after-tax return to the taxpayer in both corporate forms?

TP5-30. ABC Corporation is considering a joint venture with another company to start an online business. Both companies are U.S., for profit, C corporations. The new business will tap into the expertise ABC has developed in writing the complex software algorithms the firm uses to schedule and manage its complex manufacturing and distribution processes. Each entity is required to initially contribute $20 million for a 50% share in the joint venture. As with most online businesses, the joint-venture partners do not expect to earn profits for the foreseeable future.

a. Discuss the pros and cons of the alternative organizational forms the joint venture might take. In your discussion, consider both the tax and nontax costs and benefits of the alternatives. Note that to file a consolidated tax return (i.e., to include another company on ABC's tax return), a corporation must own at least 80% of the voting shares of the other corporation (compared only 50% for financial accounting purposes). Which organizational form would you recommend the joint venture use?

b. In contributing the $20 million, ABC is considering two options:

i. Contribute the entire amount as equity.

ii. Treat $10 million as equity and $10 million as a note payable with an annual interest rate of 10%.

When the joint venture eventually becomes profitable in year 10, the business is expected to earn approximately 20% pretax per year. The joint venture is not expected to pay any dividends, and ABC expects to liquidate its position 20 years from today. ABC also expects to face the top corporate tax rate of 21% in each of the next 20 years. Finally, assume ABC's investment of $20 million in the joint venture was all equity.

c. If the joint venture is organized as a C corporation, what is the expected annual after-tax return to ABC?

d. If the joint venture is organized as an LLC, what is the expected annual after-tax return to ABC?

References and Additional Readings

Allen, E., and S. Raghavan, 2012. "The Impact of Non-Tax Costs on the Tax-Efficiency of Venture Capital Investments," Working Paper, University of Southern California.

Allen, E. J., J. C. Allen, S. Raghavan, and D. H. Solomon, 2018. "On the Tax Efficiency of Startup Firms," Working paper, University of Southern California.

Ayers, B., C. Cloyd, and J. Robinson, 1996. "Organizational Form and Taxes: An Empirical Analysis of Small Businesses," *Journal of the American Taxation Association* (Supplement), pp. 49–67.

Bankman, J., 1994. "The Structure of Silicon Valley Start-Ups," *UCLA Law Review*, Vol. 41, Issue 7 pp. 1737–1768.

Beatty, A., P. Berger, and J. Magliolo, 1995. "Motives for Forming Research & Development Financing Organizations," *Journal of Accounting and Economics* (2&3), pp. 411–442.

Carroll, R., and D. Joulfaian, 1997. "Taxes and Corporate Choice of Organizational Form," *U.S. Department of the Treasury, Office of Tax Analysts Working Paper 73*. Washington, DC: U.S. Department of Treasury.

Erickson, M., and S. Wang, 1999a. "Exploiting and Sharing Tax Benefits: Seagrams and Dupont," *Journal of the American Taxation Association* (Fall), pp. 35–54.

Erickson, M., and S. Wang, 1999b. "The Effect of Transaction Structure on Price: Evidence from Subsidiary Sales," *Journal of Accounting and Economics* (April), pp. 149–176.

Fleischer, V., 2004. "The Rational Exuberance of Structuring Venture Capital Start-Ups," *57 Tax L. Rev.*, pp. 137–186.

Gentry, W., 1994. "Taxes, Financial Decisions, and Organizational Form: Evidence from Publicly Traded Partnerships," *Journal of Public Economics* (February), pp. 223–244.

Goolsbee, A., 1998. "Taxes, Organizational Form, and the Dead Weight Cost of the Corporate Income Tax," *Journal of Public Economics* (July), pp. 143–152.

Goolsbee, A., and E. Maydew, 2002. "Taxes and Organizational Form: The Case of REIT Spin-Offs," *National Tax Journal* (September), pp. 441–456.

Gordon, R., and J. Mackie-Mason, 1994. "Tax Distortions to the Choice of Organizational Form," *Journal of Public Economics* (October), pp. 279–306.

Gordon, R., and J. Mackie-Mason, 1997. "How Much Do Taxes Discourage Incorporation?" *Journal of Finance* (June), pp. 477–505.

Guenther, D., 1992. "Taxes and Organizational Forms: A Comparison of Corporations and Master Limited Partnerships," *The Accounting Review* (January), pp. 17–45.

Hofmann, M. A., 2007. "Tax-Motivated Expense Shifting by Tax-Exempt Associations," *Journal of the American Taxation Association* (Spring), pp. 43–60.

IRS Advisory Council, 2008. "Tax Gap Analysis Subgroup Report," IRS.

IRS Statistics of Income Division, 2016. "Partnership Returns, 2014," *IRS*.

Johnson, C., 2009. "Why Do Venture Capital Funds Burn Research and Development Deductions?" *Virginia Tax Review* (29), pp. 31–32.

Lee, J. W., 2011. "Wage Taxes and Compensating S Corporation Officers and Members of LLCs and LLPs," Working Paper, William & Mary Law School.

Maydew, E., 1997. "Tax-Induced Earnings Management by Firms with Net Operating Losses," *Journal of Accounting Research* (Spring), pp. 83–96.

Omer, T., G. Plesko, and M. Shelley, 2000. "The Influence of Tax Costs on Organizational Choice in the Natural Resource Industry," *Journal of the American Taxation Association* (Spring), pp. 38–55.

Petroni, K., and D. Shackelford, 1995. "Taxation, Regulation, and the Organizational Structure of Property-Casualty Insurers," *Journal of Accounting and Economics* (3), pp. 229–253.

Plesko, G., 1999. "The Role of Taxes in Organizational Choice: S Conversions after the Tax Reform Act of 1986," Working Paper, Massachusetts Institute of Technology.

Polsky, G. I., 2018. "Explaining Choice-of-Entity Decisions by Silicon Valley Start-Ups," Working paper, University of Georgia Law School.

Rosenthal, S. M., and L. S. Austin, 2016. "The Dwindling Taxable Share of U.S. Corporate Stock," *Tax Notes*, May 16, pp. 923–934.

Scholes, M., and M. Wolfson, 1990. "The Effects of Changes in Tax Laws on Corporate Reorganization Activity," *Journal of Business* (January), pp. S141–164.

Shelley, M., T. Omer, and T. Atwood, 1998. "Capital Restructuring and Accounting Compliance Costs: The Case of Publicly Traded Partnerships," *Journal of Accounting Research* (2), pp. 365–378.

Shevlin, T., 1987. "Taxes and Off-Balance-Sheet Financing: Research and Development Limited Partnerships," *The Accounting Review* (3), pp. 480–509.

Terando, W., and T. Omer, 1993. "Corporate Characteristics Associated with Master Limited Partnership Formation," *Journal of the American Taxation Association* (Spring), pp. 23–45.

Willens, R., and H. Wright, 2002. "Tax-Free Real Estate Spin-Offs: Will They Catch On?" *Tax Notes* (February 4), pp. 619–627.

Wolfson, M., 1985. "Empirical Evidence of Incentive Problems and Their Mitigation in Oil and Gas Tax Shelter Programs," in *Principals and Agents: The Structure of Business,* edited by John W. Pratt and Richard J. Zeckhauser (Boston, MA: Harvard Business School Press), pp. 101–125, 221–224.

6

Corporations: Formation, Operation, Capital Structure, and Liquidation

After studying this chapter, you should be able to

1. Explain the tax consequences of forming a corporation.
2. Explain some of the special tax rules that apply to corporations.
3. Understand the possible tax benefits of leverage in firms' capital structures.
4. Describe the possible tax treatments of corporate distributions and share repurchases.
5. Understand how corporations and their shareholders are taxed in liquidation.

Partnerships and sole proprietorships are more numerous than corporations in the United States. However, corporations are the dominant form of U.S. business in terms of aggregate revenues. For example, most publicly traded firms in the United States are corporations.[1] A solid understanding of business tax strategy, therefore, must include some familiarity with the tax rules that are specific to corporations and the effects and incentives provided by such rules. This chapter provides the fundamentals of corporate taxation.

When we speak of corporations in this chapter, we are referring to corporations taxed under Subchapter C of the Internal Revenue Code (IRC), making them "C" corporations. Some corporations are taxed under Subchapter S and are known as "S" corporations, but they are taxed for the most part like partnerships.[2] In terms of size, C corporations are the dominant form of business in the United States. If you think of a large, publicly traded firm, you are probably thinking about a C corporation. There are also privately held C corporations. Again, unless we say otherwise, "corporation" means C corporation in this text.

The hallmark of corporate taxation is **double taxation** of corporate income. The first level of tax is at the corporate level, when the corporation pays corporate taxes on its income. The second level of tax is at the shareholder level, when the corporation distributes its income by paying dividends to its shareholders. Dividend payments are not tax deductible to the corporation but are income to the shareholder and taxed at the shareholder level (with exceptions). Most of the special tax rules for corporations, as well as the mergers and acquisitions rules, are designed to enforce double taxation of corporate income. As you read this chapter, keep in mind the tax authorities' overarching goal of double taxation, and the tax rules will make more sense to you. In many cases, simply remembering the concept of double taxation will allow you to predict how the tax law treats a given situation.

Despite its importance as an underlying concept, double taxation of corporate income is controversial and has been for as long as the practice has existed. As you saw in the previous chapter on organizational form, double taxation

[1] There are exceptions, of course.

[2] We do not mean to imply that S corporations are taxed *exactly* like partnerships. S corporations are subject to many tax rules that are different from those of partnerships. Partnerships are taxed under Subchapter K of the Internal Revenue Code.

can discourage corporate formation and distort economic behavior. In the United States, reducing this distortion became a priority for policymakers, and in 2003, Congress acted to reduce double taxation by lowering the tax on dividends and capital gains received by individuals. Although corporate tax rates were unchanged in 2003, reducing shareholder-level taxes reduced the double taxation of corporate profits. In 2017, Congress cut the corporate tax rate from 35% to 21% as part of the Tax Cuts and Jobs Act (TCJA), further reducing double taxation, as discussed in the prior chapter.

This chapter is organized to follow the life cycle of the corporation: corporate formation, operations, distributions, and liquidation. The chapter begins with a discussion of corporate formations under Section 351. Learning the taxation of corporate formations has a useful byproduct in that many of the concepts also apply to nontaxable acquisitions. In Section 6.2 we discuss some of the special tax rules governing corporate operations/specifically, rules that differ from generally accepted accounting principles (GAAP). Sections 6.3 and 6.4 examine taxes and capital structure, covering the classic finance theory on the tax benefits of leverage as well as empirical evidence, and a discussion of debt-equity hybrid securities, using trust preferred stock as an example. Next, Section 6.5 presents the tax rules applicable to getting cash out of the corporation and into the hands of shareholders by either declaring dividends or repurchasing shares. Section 6.6 discusses tax planning for distributions, including the nearly $1.5 billion in attempted tax savings by Seagram and DuPont in a single transaction. Finally, Section 6.7 concludes the chapter by completing the corporation life cycle with a brief discussion of corporate liquidations.

6.1 CORPORATE FORMATION

The beginning of the life cycle of a corporation is its formation. When a corporation is formed, one or more investors—individuals, other corporations, and so on—contribute property to the newly formed corporation in exchange for the newly issued stock of the corporation. Absent any special rules, such an exchange would be a taxable event and the investors would be taxed on the difference between their basis in the property contributed and its fair market value. However, if forming corporations were to trigger taxation that would inhibit entrepreneurial activity and investment. To better allow capital to flow to its highest and best use, the U.S. tax code has long allowed most corporate formations to be nontaxable or, more precisely, tax deferred. The idea is to leave the parties in approximately the same tax position as they were before the corporate formation.

Section 351 is the key IRC section for corporate formation. The section is important and will help you understand nontaxable acquisitions, which are covered in later chapters. Section 351 applies when three conditions are met: (1) the investors contribute property to the corporation, (2) the investors receive stock in the corporation, and (3) the investors collectively control 80% or more of the corporation after the transaction. Each of these requirements has additional nuances that are beyond the scope of this text (e.g., when does intellectual property count as property for the purposes of Section 351 and when does it count as services?).

Most corporate formations satisfy all three requirements. Some secondary offerings can also meet these requirements provided the investors taking part in the secondary offering collectively own 80% or more of the corporation after the offering.[3]

If Section 351 governs the transaction, then the investors are taxed on the lesser of their realized gain and the **boot** they receive in the transaction.[4] Think of boot as cash or other property received, including most anything except the firm's stock (e.g., T-bills). The corporation to which the property is contributed is not taxed.

[3] A secondary offering occurs when an existing corporation issues additional stock.

[4] Section 351 treatment is mandatory if its requirements are met. In the rare case that Section 351 would not apply to a corporate formation, the entire transaction would be taxable. Therefore, the shareholders contributing property to the corporation would recognize gain to the extent the fair market value of the stock they receive exceeded the basis of the property they contributed to the corporation. Shareholders contributing services in exchange for stock would recognize ordinary income to the extent of the fair market value of the stock received. The shareholders' basis in the corporation's stock would equal its fair market value, as would the corporation's basis in property received. An example of a corporate formation not covered by Section 351 would be if Smith and Dean formed DS Corporation, with Smith contributing property for half of the stock and Dean contributing services for the other half. Because the shareholder(s) contributing property (Smith) controlled less than 80% of the corporation, Section 351 would not apply.

For example, John, Friedrich, and Milton each contribute property to form JFM Corporation. John contributes oil wells with a fair market value of $470,000 and a tax basis of $100,000 and receives 47% of the stock of JFM. **Tax basis**, or simply "basis," is generally equal to the amount paid for an asset. Friedrich contributes $100,000 cash and networking equipment with a fair market value and basis of $370,000, also receiving 47% of the stock of JFM. Milton contributes a sports memorabilia collection with a fair market value of $150,000 and tax basis of $70,000 in exchange for the remaining 6% of the stock of JFM and $90,000 cash.

How will each party be treated for tax purposes? John will take a basis in his JFM stock equal to the basis of the property he contributed, $100,000, which is called a **substituted basis**. Presumably, the fair market value of the JFM stock is approximately equal to the $470,000 fair market value of the oil wells contributed, so if John later sells the stock, he will be taxed on his $370,000 unrealized gain. In that sense, Section 351 defers taxation but does not eliminate it. John's holding period in the JFM stock will include the time he held the contributed property. For example, if he had owned the oil wells for 14 months, then he is treated as though he had held the JFM stock for 14 months. JFM will take a $100,000 basis in the oil wells, which is called a **carryover basis**. If JFM sold the oil wells, it would recognize a $370,000 gain, so John's original $370,000 unrealized gain now exists at both his level and the corporation's level. JFM's holding period in the oil wells will include the 14 months John had owned them. So, even if JFM sold the oil wells immediately after receiving them in the corporate formation, the gain would be a long-term capital gain because the holding period exceeds the 12-month cutoff for determining whether a capital gain is long or short term. Under current law, however, corporations pay the same tax rate on capital gains as they do on ordinary income.

Friedrich will take a basis in his JFM stock equal to the basis of the property he contributed, which was $470,000, or $100,000 + $370,000. The holding period of 37/47ths of his JFM stock will include the holding period of his networking equipment contributed; 10/47ths of his JFM stock will start fresh because it was acquired through a cash contribution. JFM will take a $370,000 carryover basis in the networking equipment and obviously a $100,000 basis in the cash received (the basis of $1 cash is $1).

Milton's case is the tricky one. Because Milton received boot, he will be taxed on the transaction. Specifically, he will recognize a gain (but never a loss) equal to the lesser of the boot received or the realized gain. The boot received is $90,000. The realized gain is the difference between the fair market value and the basis of the property contributed, or $150,000 – $70,000 = $80,000. Thus, the taxable (or recognized) gain is equal to min($90,000, $80,000) = $80,000. Milton will take a basis in the JFM stock received equal to the basis of what he contributed plus any gain recognized less any boot received. In this case, $70,000 + $80,000 – $90,000 = $60,000.

Does the tax treatment for Milton make sense? The fair market value of the JFM stock Milton received is equal to the fair market value of what he gave, $150,000, less the $90,000 cash received, which equals $60,000. Because the fair market value and tax basis of the JFM stock are both $60,000, after the transaction, Milton has no unrealized gains. Before the transaction, Milton had an unrealized gain of $80,000. He recognized $80,000 of gain in the transaction, so he should not (and does not) have any more unrealized gain. JFM will take a basis in Milton's contributed assets equal to Milton's old basis plus any gain Milton recognized, or $70,000 + $80,000 = $150,000.

Here is an interesting side note: Was this transaction fair? John contributed property that essentially came with a hidden tax liability equal to the unrealized gain on his property ($370,000) times the corporate tax rate. John's GAAP financial statements will not necessarily reveal the deferred tax liability before the corporate formation because deferred tax liabilities arise from differences between GAAP book value and tax basis, not between fair market value and tax basis. If the fair market values we quoted do not reflect the hidden tax liability in John's contribution, then John got the best of Friedrich and Milton by transferring his unrecorded tax liability to the corporation they jointly own. Corporate formation can be a trap for the unwary.

6.2 TAXATION OF CORPORATE OPERATIONS

Once the corporation has been formed, it begins operations. This involves a wide variety of transactions, including selling goods or services to customers, paying suppliers, and compensating employees, to name a few. There is some good news in terms of your tax learning. Many of the tax rules applicable to corporations for their daily operations are the same tax rules applicable to individuals with business income. For example, the schedules used to calculate depreciation deductions usually are the same across taxpayers. More important, if you have a working knowledge of financial accounting, then you already know a good deal about how corporations are taxed. Many of the underlying concepts in the GAAP you are familiar with from financial accounting are present in corporate taxation, such as the concept of accrual method accounting. Corporations are subject to a number of special tax rules, however, even when the underlying concepts may be similar to accounting. This section provides a brief overview of the special tax rules applicable to corporations and how these rules differ from the GAAP firms follow in their financial reporting.

Book-Tax Differences: Taxable Income versus GAAP Income

Like all taxpayers, firms pay income taxes based on their taxable income. You can think of taxable income as similar to GAAP income in the sense that both represent some measure of revenues less some measure of expenses. However, differences between GAAP and the tax law arise because of differences in objectives. The objectives of GAAP are to provide information that is useful in making investment, credit, and other decisions; assessing the prospects for future cash flows; and in appraising the firm's resources, claims to those resources, and changes in them.[5] In contrast, Congress has many objectives when making the tax law, including raising revenue, stimulating the economy, and encouraging or discouraging certain behaviors. Providing information to investors is usually not one of the objectives. These differences in objectives lead to a number of differences between GAAP income and taxable income.

The differences that separate book income from tax income are collectively referred to as **book-tax differences**. These differences include items such as municipal bond interest, which is tax exempt at the federal level but counts as income for GAAP purposes. Different methods are also used for computing depreciation expense for GAAP and tax purposes.[6] For financial accounting (GAAP) purposes, there is some discretion over how to depreciate assets, but firms commonly use straight-line depreciation. For tax purposes, there is generally less discretion and the asset will be depreciated according to a schedule depending on the type of asset and when it was placed into service. Accelerated depreciation methods are common, where more of the depreciation deductions are available in the early years of the asset's life than in the later years. The public policy rational for accelerated depreciation is usually to encourage capital investment by increasing the present value of the tax benefits of the depreciation, thereby lowering the present value cost of the capital investment to the firm.

The good news is that despite these book-tax differences, if you have a basic knowledge of financial accounting, you already know a lot about corporate taxation. For example, as in their GAAP-based financial statements, corporations must use the accrual method when computing their taxable income.[7] That is, income is recognized as it is earned rather than when the cash is collected, and expenses are recognized as they are incurred rather than when they are paid. Further, when corporations prepare their income tax returns, they start with their GAAP numbers and make adjustments for differences between GAAP and the tax law. It is important to recognize that even when firms use the accrual method for tax purposes, differences between accruals for tax purposes and accruals for GAAP purposes can exist. However, unless there is a reason for an adjustment, the GAAP number winds up being the tax number by default.[8]

Net Operating Losses

When a firm has negative taxable income for the year, the firm has a **net operating loss (NOL)**. Under current laws, firms are allowed to carry forward their NOLs indefinitely to offset income in future years. The rules for NOLs have varied over time. Prior to 2018, firms were allowed to carry

[5] See "Conceptual Framework for Financial Accounting, Chapter 1, The Objective of General Purpose Financial Accounting," *Statement of Financial Accounting Concepts No. 8* (Stamford, CT: FASB, September, 2010).

[6] Book-tax differences and their impacts on financial accounting are discussed in the next chapter.

[7] Some small corporations can use the cash method.

[8] For a discussion of implicit pressure to conform tax and book income, see Hanlon, Maydew, and Shevlin (2008); Guenther, Nutter, and Maydew (1997); and Mills (1998).

back NOLs up to 2 years and carry them forward up to 20 years. Prior to 1997, the **carryback** period was 3 years and the carryforward period was 15 years. In addition, Congress has occasionally enacted temporary provisions to extend the NOL carryback period (e.g., to 5 years). Usually, those temporary provisions have been enacted as stimulus measures following economic downturns, as they have the effect of enabling firms to obtain refunds of taxes they had paid in past profitable years. The carryback and carryforward periods vary across countries and U.S. states.

Gains and Losses and Tax Basis

Tax gains and losses generally are computed in the same manner as in financial accounting. For example, consider a firm that purchased equipment for $100,000, depreciated it by $40,000 over some period for accounting purposes, and later sold it for $70,000. The firm would report a $10,000 accounting gain on the sale. The gain would be computed as the difference between the $70,000 proceeds and the $60,000 book value (i.e., $100,000 – $40,000 of accounting depreciation).

In tax, the basic idea is the same, except the amount the asset is purchased for is referred to as its *tax basis* and the tax basis less any accumulated depreciation is referred to as the asset's **adjusted tax basis**. Often, we will just use *basis* as shorthand for *adjusted basis*. Also recall that the accumulated depreciation for tax and GAAP purposes can be different, leading to differences between the gain or loss for tax and financial accounting. In the previous example, suppose that, although the accounting depreciation was $40,000, the tax depreciation was $55,000 due to accelerated depreciation for tax purposes. In that case, the tax gain upon the sale would be $25,000. The tax gain would be computed as the $70,000 proceeds less the $45,000 adjusted basis (i.e., $100,000 – $55,000 of tax depreciation).

Capital Gains and Losses

Most taxable income is so-called **ordinary income**. Examples include income from wages, services rendered, the sale of inventory, and interest. Gains and losses from the sale of **capital assets**, however, are capital gains and losses and treated somewhat differently. Most assets not used in a trade or business are considered capital assets, including stocks, bonds, puts, and calls. Inventory is not a capital asset. Contrary to conventional wisdom, equipment and buildings used in a trade or business are *not* capital assets. They are Section 1231 assets and discussed later. If a capital asset has been held for more than 1 year, the gain or loss from its sale is considered a long-term capital gain or loss.

Taxpayers are required to keep track of capital gains and losses separately from ordinary income. A complex netting procedure surrounds capital gains and losses, but we will not go into it here. If an individual has net long-term capital gains for the year, those gains are taxable at a maximum rate of 20% under current law. This rate compares favorably with the maximum individual tax rate of 37% under current law.[9] No special capital gains rate is granted for corporations. Rather, corporations pay the same rate on capital gains and ordinary income, generally 21%. Many people who are not tax savvy erroneously believe that corporations also have a special low long-term capital gains rate, but corporations have not had a special capital gains rate since the mid-1980s.

Net capital losses occur when the taxpayer has more capital losses than capital gains. Net capital losses cannot be used to offset ordinary income. Corporations are allowed to carry back net capital losses up to 3 years and carry them forward up to 5 years, and such carrybacks and carryforwards can be used to offset capital gains in those years. In contrast, individuals can use up to $3,000 of net capital losses per year to offset ordinary income. Individuals cannot carry back net capital losses, but they can carry them forward indefinitely.

Section 1231 Assets

Section 1231 assets are assets other than inventory used in a trade or business that have been held for more than 1 year. Examples include most buildings, machines, equipment, and land. If the taxpayer has net 1231 gains for the year, then such gains count as long-term capital gains. If the taxpayer has net 1231 losses for the year, then such losses count as ordinary losses and can hence offset ordinary

[9] For expositional ease, we are holding aside the additional 3.8% tax on net investment income and 0.9% Medicare surtax that apply to certain high-income taxpayers.

income. Thus, 1231 gains and losses represent the best of both worlds—gains taxable at potentially low long-term capital gains rates and losses deductible at high ordinary rates. Because, under current law, corporations pay tax on capital gains and ordinary income at the same rates, Section 1231 does not have as much importance as it once did. It is still useful, however, because net 1231 losses can be used to offset the corporation's ordinary income, whereas net capital losses cannot offset ordinary income. Also, to the extent individuals have 1231 gains from a sole proprietorship or flowing from a partnership, those gains can be taxed at the capital gains rate.

Dividends Received Deduction

Recall that the overarching principle of corporation taxation is the double taxation of corporate profits. Even though Congress apparently likes double taxation, it tries to avoid imposing more than two layers of taxation on corporate earnings. The **dividends received deduction (DRD)** is designed to prevent triple (or more) taxation when corporations receive dividends from other corporations. The amount of the DRD depends on how much the dividend-receiving corporation owns of the dividend-paying corporation. With less than 20% ownership, the DRD is 50%; from 20% to 79.9% ownership, it is 65%; and with 80% or more ownership comes a 100% DRD, or complete exclusion.

For example, if Google owned 10% of GE and received $100 million of dividends from GE, then Google would only be taxable on $50 million of those dividends. With a corporate tax rate of 21%, this deduction translates to a 10.5% tax rate on dividend income, assuming less than 20% ownership. How many layers of tax are eventually paid on the underlying earnings from GE? Three. One layer is paid by GE as it earns its profits, a partial layer is paid by Google when it receives a dividend from GE, and another layer is paid by Google's shareholders when Google pays a dividend or when they sell their Google stock and pay capital gains tax.

Consolidated Tax Returns

Most of what we think of as corporations are actually collections of corporations—the parent corporation, its subsidiaries and their subsidiaries, and so on. GAAP typically mandates consolidation of subsidiaries when the parent owns 50% or more of a subsidiary. The subsidiary being domestic or foreign does not matter. All that matters is control. Thus, when you examine Apple's financial statements, you are examining Apple's worldwide operations.

The tax rules for consolidations are somewhat different. First, only domestic subsidiaries can be part of the U.S. consolidated tax return. Foreign subsidiaries are not consolidated. Second, the ownership level for tax consolidation is 80%. Thus, a subsidiary that was 70% owned by the parent would be consolidated for GAAP purposes but not for tax.

Corporations are not forced to file consolidated returns but generally find it in their best interests to do so. The benefit of a consolidated return is that taxable income of one subsidiary can be offset by losses of another subsidiary. This benefit is important, especially to the extent that income in the various subsidiaries is not highly correlated. Without a consolidated return, the profitable subsidiaries would pay taxes and the unprofitable subsidiaries would have to rely on carrying back or forward their losses to offset their own income. Special rules inhibit the ability of a profitable company to purchase corporations with NOLs and use the purchased NOLs to offset the profitable company's income.

6.3 POSSIBLE TAX BENEFITS OF LEVERAGE IN FIRMS' CAPITAL STRUCTURES

One of the most critical issues in forming and operating a corporation is determining the proper mix of debt and equity in the firm's capital structure. Whether leverage can affect firm value is one of the oldest questions in corporate finance, dating back at least as far as Modigliani and Miller's (M&M) seminal work in 1958, which led to a Nobel Prize for Miller in 1990. You may already have a working knowledge of capital structure theory from your corporate finance classes, so we provide only a brief overview of the topic in this chapter.[10] We begin with the origins of modern thought on capital

[10] Most good corporate finance textbooks discuss the theory of the tax benefits of leverage; see R. Brealey, S. Myers, and F. Allen, *Principles of Corporate Finance*, 10th ed. (New York: McGraw-Hill, 2011).

structure (M&M, 1958) and work our way up to contemporary thinking and state-of-the-art empirical research on the subject. The discussion builds on the concepts of implicit taxes and tax clienteles, and the effects of nontax costs.

Theory of the Tax Benefits of Leverage

Like a physicist who explains the laws of nature by first considering movement in a frictionless world, M&M (1958) explained capital structure by first examining leverage in perfect capital markets. A **perfect capital market** has no transactions costs, no information asymmetries, no bankruptcy costs, and no taxes. M&M proved that with perfect capital markets, no gain comes from leverage. The intuition is straightforward. Imagine the value of the corporation's cash flows as represented by an extra-large pizza. The slices of pizza represent claims on the corporation's cash flows. Whether the slices are labeled equity or debt does not affect the size of the entire pizza. If the capital markets are perfect, no pizza is lost or gained by slicing it in different ways or by labeling the slices as debt or equity. M&M concluded that, absent some market imperfection, capital structure will not affect the value of the firm and is therefore irrelevant. M&M recognized, of course, that, in reality, markets are not perfect and that market imperfections may cause the value of the firm to depend on its capital structure. But M&M represented a major innovation in thinking by focusing the debate on the effects of the various market imperfections on optimal capital structure.

For the most part, we focus on the role of taxes in capital structure. M&M relaxed the assumption of perfect capital markets to include corporate taxation toward the end of their 1958 paper and then gave the matter of corporate taxes a fuller examination in their 1963 paper. They showed that if markets are perfect except for the existence of corporate taxes, the value of the firm is increasing in its leverage. Why? Because dividend payments on equity are not tax deductible to the corporation, whereas interest payments on debt are. Therefore, the label put on the pizza slices does matter with corporate taxation. The three types of pizza slices are debt, equity, and taxes (the government's claim on the firm's cash flows). Pizza slices labeled as debt reduce the size of the government's tax slice, whereas slices labeled as equity do not. The value of the levered firm, V_L, is equal to the value of an unlevered all-equity firm, V_U, plus the tax benefit of the leverage. M&M (1963) showed that the present value of the tax benefit to leverage is equal to τD, where τ is the corporate tax rate and D is the amount of debt:

$$V_L = V_U + \tau D \tag{6.1}$$

Because the value of the firm is increasing in the amount of leverage, in the M&M world, all firms would want to be at a "corner solution" in which they pay out all their cash flows in the form of interest on debt. Again, M&M realized that most firms are not so extremely levered, and their analysis was meant to further our understanding of the forces involved in the capital structure decision and the magnitude of those forces.

Quickly, the debate turned to what other market imperfections or nontax costs keep firms from being fully levered. Bankruptcy costs were an obvious candidate. As firms increase their leverage, they increase the chances that in some states of the world, they will not have sufficient cash flows to cover their interest payments. Bankruptcy or more general financial distress can be a cumbersome and costly process, and the increased likelihood of incurring financial distress costs may serve as a counterbalance to the tax benefits of leverage. However, with every dollar of debt increasing the value of the firm by τ (potentially 21 cents per dollar of debt at current tax rates), it was hard to imagine bankruptcy costs being much of a counterbalance. The tax gain from leverage is massive in the M&M 1963 world.

But the drama continued, albeit at the slow pace of academic research. In the 1970s, the pendulum swung back to no tax gains from leverage with Miller's (1977) paper. Miller, half of M&M, examined a world of perfect capital markets, except that he allowed for personal-level taxation as well as corporate-level taxation. Miller considered the case where the investor-level taxes on equity were less than the investor-level taxes on debt. For example, the return on a growth stock may be taxed at long-term capital gains rates, currently 20%, or may be taxed at a 0% tax rate if the stock is held until death.[11] Interest on debt, however, is taxed at ordinary tax rates, which are currently as high as 37% at the federal level.

[11] At death, the tax basis of a decedent's assets are stepped up to fair market value and the potential income taxation on the unrealized gains on the assets are exempt from income tax.

Miller reasoned that investors, who should be concerned with after-tax rates of return, will bid up the price of equity until its risk-adjusted after-tax return is the same as that on debt. In other words, equity will bear an implicit tax, or lower pretax rate of return, relative to debt because equity returns are tax favored at the investor level. Said another way, the pretax risk-adjusted cost of debt financing must be greater than that of equity financing to compensate investors for the higher tax rates they pay on interest income. Miller showed that, under certain conditions, the increased pretax return that must be paid on debt financing exactly offsets the tax benefits from the corporate-level interest deductions. Assuming all firms face the same marginal tax rate, any given corporation faces no net tax benefit from debt financing.[12] Miller's reasoning is extremely important because it shows that even in the absence of bankruptcy costs, costs to debt financing (high investor-level taxes) can offset the corporate-level tax advantage of interest deductibility.

Unfortunately, measuring implicit tax effects in debt and equity is difficult. The most direct way to measure the effects of taxes on pretax returns is to observe the pretax returns on a stock and a bond that had exactly the same risk. Unfortunately, such experiments are hard to find. Further, because equity is usually more risky than debt, the expected return on equity is typically larger than the return on debt. Without precise estimates of how risk affects expected returns, isolating the effects of taxes on returns is difficult.[13] How risk is priced remains a matter of some controversy in economics and finance. Thus, the pretax returns to assets are likely some function of their risk and their tax treatment, but disentangling the size of the two effects in practice is extremely challenging.

DeAngelo and Masulis (1980) extended Miller's analysis to allow for "nondebt tax shields," such as depreciation expense. Firms with a greater likelihood of NOLs have smaller expected marginal tax rates than other firms. The greater a firm's nondebt tax shields, the lower its expected tax benefit from interest tax deductions, giving rise to an optimal amount of leverage for each firm. DeAngelo and Masulis (1980) represent an important step in the theory of capital structure because for the first time, tax effects alone are shown to cause each firm to have an optimal amount of debt. No longer does theory predict extremes of no tax benefits to leverage (Miller, 1977) or massive tax benefits from leverage (M&M, 1963). DeAngelo and Masulis's work led to an important testable prediction. Firms with large amounts of nondebt tax shields should borrow less than firms with small amounts of nondebt tax shields, an example of a tax clientele effect.

Empirical Work on the Tax Benefits of Leverage[14]

Shevlin (1990) and Graham (1996) extended DeAngelo and Masulis's work by providing empirical estimates of firms' expected marginal tax rates, taking into account firms' current and past taxability, as well as the probability of future NOLs. Graham (1996) applied the marginal tax rate estimates to the role of taxes in capital structure and found that firms' leverage is increasing in their marginal tax rates. Graham recognized that as a firm borrows more, the increased interest deductions increase the firm's probability of future NOLs, reducing the marginal tax benefit of leverage. As the firm borrows more and more, eventually, the marginal benefit of leverage equals the marginal cost and the firm stops borrowing. Graham's results strongly suggest, but do not prove, that a tax gain from leverage exists.

Graham (2000) took this argument one step further, using his marginal tax rate estimates to produce firm-specific estimates of the actual tax benefits of leverage that firms obtain at their current debt levels, as well as the maximum tax benefits of leverage they could obtain if they were more fully levered. Van Binsbergen, Graham, and Yang (2010) examined the costs and benefits of debt and estimated that for the average firm in their sample, the net benefit of debt is equal to 3.5% of asset value. Other research used variation in corporate tax rates across countries and states, finding that corporations use more leverage when corporate tax rates are high, consistent with tax benefits

[12] Although no individual firm prefers debt over equity, an optimal amount of debt at the economy-wide level can be calculated in Miller's (1977) world. The reasoning is subtle, so you may want to refer to the source.

[13] There also are differences in pretax returns for securities that differ in terms of both tax treatment and risk that are not discussed here.

[14] See the references for additional research on taxes and capital structure.

of debt.[15] Blouin, Core, and Guay (2010) developed a new method of estimating marginal tax rates and argued that tax benefits are smaller than previously thought, such that most firms are at about the optimal level of leverage once the costs of financial distress are considered.

The big unresolved issue, however, is whether investor-level taxes affect the pretax cost of debt capital relative to equity. In a review of the literature, Graham (2003) summed this up, writing, "The truth is we know little about the identity or tax status of the marginal investor(s) between any two sets of securities and deducing this information is difficult. It would be useful if future research could quantify the relative importance of personal taxes on security prices, with an eye towards feedback into capital structure decisions." Some of the cross-country research mentioned earlier also examined variation in investor taxes and found that the amount of leverage corporations use is associated with investor-level tax rates.

6.4 DEBT-EQUITY HYBRIDS

Countries that allow interest to be deductible often have provisions in their tax codes to keep firms from having excessive amounts of debt relative to equity. These are sometimes referred to as "thin capitalization" or "earnings stripping" rules. Some countries set maximum ratios of debt to equity that firms can have in their capital structure for tax purposes. In the United States, for example, Section 163(j) limits the deductibility of interest to offset no more than 30% of income for most large firms.

More generally, there is also the question of what makes something debt in the first place. As we learned in the prior section, having interest on debt deductible and dividends paid on equity not deductible can give an incentive to favor debt financing over equity financing. What prevents corporations from just relabeling their equity as debt? In Section 385, Congress grants the Treasury authority to write regulations governing which securities will be treated as debt and which securities will be treated as equity for tax purposes. Despite the broad authority given to it by Congress decades ago, the Treasury has had a difficult time writing regulations. Questions about what debt and equity are have led to some interesting tax planning in the United States and other countries for some time.

Traditional Preferred Stock

Most tax and corporate finance books treat capital structure as a black-and-white choice between issuing common stock and issuing debt. In reality, firms have many hybrids between straight debt and common stock to choose from when raising capital. Traditional preferred stock has many characteristics of debt, such as fixed yields, no or limited voting rights, and preference over common stock in payment of dividends and in liquidation. A special type of preferred stock called trust preferred stock, or trust preferred securities, has many of the same nontax features as traditional preferred stock but has markedly different tax consequences. We first discuss the taxation of traditional preferred stock and then taxation of trust preferred stock. For each type of preferred stock, we compare the tax treatment with that of debt.

Traditional preferred stock is taxed as equity. At the issuer level, traditional preferred stock dividends are not tax deductible, whereas interest payments on debt are typically tax deductible. How dividends on preferred stock are taxed at the investor level depends on whether the investor is an individual or another corporation. If the investor is an individual, then in most circumstances, the dividends will be taxed at a maximum tax rate of 20%. If the investor is another corporation, then the dividend is only partially taxable due to the DRD described earlier in this chapter. Compared with debt, traditional preferred stock is tax disadvantaged at the issuer level but is tax advantaged to both individual investors and corporate investors. For example, a corporate investor choosing between investing in a bond that has a 8.5% yield and investing in a share of preferred stock that has an 8% yield typically chooses the preferred stock, assuming both options have the same risk. The reason is that the after-tax yield on the bond will be 6.72%, or 8.5%(1 − .21), to the corporate investor, whereas the after-tax yield on the preferred stock will be 7.16%, or 8%(1 − .21[1 − .5]). Because of the dividend received deduction, preferred stock has, in the past, been thought to be largely held by other corporations. With the tax rate

[15] See Faccio and Xu (2015) and Heider and Ljungqvist (2015).

on dividend income received by individuals at 20%, more individuals could wind up holding traditional preferred stock. Academia has not paid much attention to preferred stock, however, compared with common stock and debt. In one of the few studies of preferred stock, Erickson and Maydew (1998) documented that preferred stock does bear implicit taxes because of the DRD received by corporate holders of preferred stock.

Trust Preferred Stock[16]

There are many variations of debt-equity hybrids. Let us examine one type of debt-equity hybrid in detail to illustrate how hybrids can be structured and some of the different objectives that firms try to achieve with hybrids. Starting in the mid-1990s, traditional preferred stock began to fall from favor because of a new financial innovation: trust preferred stock. The basic idea behind trust preferred stock was to create a security that would be treated as debt for tax purposes but would not be treated as a liability for financial reporting and regulatory purposes.

The first trust preferred stock from a U.S. firm was a $350 million issue by Texaco on October 27, 1993. **Figure 6.1** illustrates the structure of the offering.[17]

FIGURE 6.1 How Trust Preferred Stock Is Structured

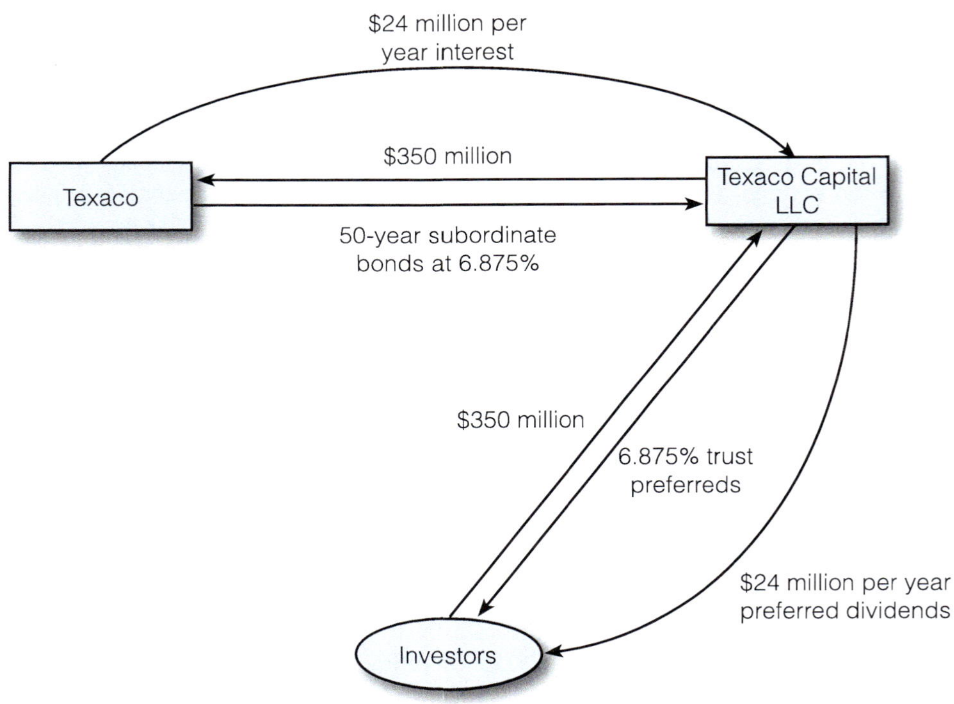

First, Texaco created Texaco Capital LLC, which was essentially a shell corporation that was wholly owned by Texaco. Next, Texaco Capital issued trust preferred stock to investors for $350 million in cash. Simultaneously, Texaco issued $350 million of subordinated debentures to Texaco Capital in exchange for the $350 million proceeds of the trust preferred stock. The Texaco debentures had terms and yield that were *identical* to those of the trust preferred stock, and the debentures provided the cash flow source of the recurring dividend payments to trust preferred holders. For example, Texaco Capital's trust preferred stock paid dividends at 6.875%, identical to

[16] This discussion is based on Engel, Erickson, and Maydew (1999).

[17] Actually, Texaco issued monthly income preferred securities, MIPS, which are essentially the same thing as trust preferred stock. Most investment banks offer their clients a similar product, but each generally gives the product a different name. Some acronyms include QUIPS for quarterly income preferred securities, TOPRS for trust originated preferred securities, and TRUPS for trust preferred stock.

the yield on the subordinated Texaco debt held by Texaco Capital. Subsequent to issuing the trust preferred stock, Texaco Capital simply acted as a conduit between Texaco and the trust preferred investors, with interest payments from Texaco on the debentures equaling the dividends paid to the trust preferred investors.

Contractually, trust preferred stock is quite similar to traditional preferred stock. Texaco's trust preferred stocks had maturities of 50 years, with a 50-year renewal option, so like traditional preferred stock, the trust preferred stock derived its market value almost entirely from the present value of its dividend payments. Most trust preferred stocks had maturities of between 20 and 50 years, with similar renewal options. Also like preferred stock, Texaco's trust preferred stocks generally were subordinated to all other debt. Texaco also had the right to defer payment of trust preferred dividends for up to 5 years at a time. However, as with traditional preferred stock, trust preferred stock issuers cannot pay dividends on their common stock while they are deferring trust preferred dividends. In the unlikely event of dividend deferral exceeding 5 years, trust preferred stock investors could appoint an outside trustee to Texaco Capital, and Texaco Capital could then sue Texaco for defaulting on its debt obligation to Texaco Capital.

Tax Treatment of Trust Preferred Stock The tax treatment of traditional preferred stock and trust preferred stock differs for both issuers and investors. Firms issuing traditional preferred stock receive no tax deductions for dividends paid on traditional preferred stock. Traditional preferred stock is, however, tax advantaged to both corporate and individual investors. Corporations receiving dividend income are eligible for the DRD. Individual investors are taxed on dividend income from traditional preferred stock at a maximum rate of 20%. In contrast, trust preferred stock is treated as debt for tax purposes, so its "dividends" are treated as interest and therefore are deductible by the issuer. However, corporate holders of trust preferred stock are not eligible for the DRD. Individual holders of trust preferred stock are taxed at ordinary tax rates to the extent they receive trust preferred dividends; there is no special 20% tax rate for trust preferred dividends.

Because trust preferred stock is not tax advantaged to investors relative to traditional preferred stock, issuers likely have to pay a higher pretax yield on trust preferred stock than they would on comparable traditional preferred stock. Whether a firm can reduce its cost of capital by replacing traditional preferred stock with trust preferred stock depends on the size of the additional yield that must be paid on trust preferred stock compared with traditional preferred stock as well as the level of the firm's marginal tax rates. For example, suppose the firm had a marginal tax rate of 21% and could issue traditional preferred stock at a 7.9% yield. If it could issue comparable trust preferred stock at anything less than a 10% yield, the firm would reduce its after-tax cost of capital by replacing the 7.9% traditional preferred stock with trust preferred stock.

Financial Reporting Treatment of Trust Preferred Stock Until 2003, trust preferred obligations were typically presented on the balance sheet as a separate line item between the liabilities and shareholders' equity sections, often described as "obligations under mandatorily redeemable preferred securities of affiliate" or "minority interest in subsidiary companies." By being classified outside of the liability section of the balance sheet, trust preferred stock had an advantage over otherwise similar subordinated debt. The favorable balance sheet treatment that trust preferred stock provided was likely instrumental to its popularity among many issuers. However, the favorable financial accounting treatment was short lived. The Financial Accounting Standards Board (FASB) issued a new standard in 2003 requiring most trust preferred stocks to be classified as liabilities on the issuer's balance sheet.

Regulatory Treatment of Trust Preferred Stock Many trust preferred issuers were regulated firms, such as commercial banks, insurance companies, and utilities. How trust preferred stock is treated for regulatory purposes adds another consideration beyond its tax and GAAP treatment. For example, commercial banks are required to maintain certain minimum levels of capital as a percentage of total assets and risk-weighted assets, which take into account the varying levels of risk of different assets (e.g., cash is less risky than mortgage receivables). When trust preferreds were first developed, it was unclear whether the Federal Reserve would approve them as regulatory capital. On October 21, 1996, the Federal Reserve ruled that trust preferred stocks may be included in equity capital for regulatory purposes. This regulatory treatment appears to have been a de facto prerequisite for commercial banks to issue trust preferred stock. No bank issued trust preferred stock before the Federal Reserve's announcement, but within a couple weeks of the announcement, banks issued billions of dollars of trust preferred stock. By the end of 2008, banks had issued more than $140 billion of trust preferreds according to an estimate from the Federal Reserve Bank of Philadelphia.[18] Use of trust preferreds by banks has been sharply curtailed in the post-crisis period. The Dodd-Frank Act, which became law in 2010, phases out the ability of large banks to include trust preferreds as part of Tier 1 capital. In 2013, the Federal Reserve Board approved new capital standards under what is called Basel III, which also phases out banks' ability to include trust preferreds as part of their regulatory capital.

The Lesson of Trust Preferred Stock We should not be surprised to see future innovation in the debt-equity hybrid area. Common stock and traditional debt are, after all, merely man-made creations. They exist because they are useful arrangements for many suppliers of capital and users of capital. But, as we have seen with trust preferred stock, different users of capital face different environments and thus have different objectives. For example, financial institutions face different regulatory requirements than manufacturing firms. Within financial institutions, banks have different regulatory requirements than insurance companies, and so forth. Similarly, different suppliers of capital face different environments and have different objectives. For example, individual investors are taxed differently than pension funds. Some investors have a short investment horizon, whereas others have a longer horizon. One way to think about debt-equity hybrids is as a market solution to the wide variation in objectives across suppliers and users of capital. As long as such variation exists, there will be a market for hybrid securities. As objectives change, there will be incentives to create new kinds of hybrids.

Zero-Coupon Bonds

We can also consider zero-coupon bonds to be a hybrid security. Zero-coupon bonds get their name from the fact that they pay no periodic interest. Rather, they are issued at a deep discount to their maturity value, and the discount represents the interest that essentially accrues to the investor over time. Zero-coupon bonds are senior to equity in cases of financial distress, like a conventional bond. Further, zero-coupon bonds generally have a fixed rate of return determined by the issue price, the maturity value, and the years to maturity. Like stockholders, however, holders of zero-coupon bonds generally have no right to cash flows from the corporation until sometime in the future: at maturity in the case of a zero-coupon bond and at liquidation in the case of common stock. Regardless of whether we consider them to be debt or a debt-equity hybrid, a great deal of misconception surrounds the taxation of zero-coupon bonds. The following discussion captures the essentials of how zero-coupon bonds are taxed. We then illustrate the taxation of zero-coupon bonds with a numerical example.

The taxation of zero-coupon bonds—and most bonds, really—closely mirrors their financial accounting treatment under historical cost accounting.[19] The main concern is what to do when the bond is issued at a price other than face value. When a bond is issued below face value, the difference between the face value and the issue price is called the **discount**. Conversely, when a bond is issued above face value, the difference between face value and issue price is called the **premium**. In financial accounting, discounts and premiums are amortized over the life of the bond using the constant-yield-to-maturity method. Because a discount represents deferred interest the firm will pay on the bond, as the interest is amortized, it increases the firm's interest expense. Amortization of premiums reduces the firm's interest expense.

In taxation, when a bond is issued for less than its face value, the difference is called **original issue discount (OID)**. Zero-coupon bonds are issued at a deep discount and nearly always have OID. Holders of bonds with OID must accrue interest income over the life of the bond using the constant-yield-to-maturity method, as they do under GAAP. Thus, an investor in a zero-coupon bond must recognize interest income and pay tax on that income each year as the income accrues, even though she has received no

[18] Federal Reserve Bank of Philadelphia, "SRC Insights," first quarter 2009.

[19] The comparison we are drawing here is to the financial accounting treatment under historical cost accounting. Accounting under fair value accounting is different and covered in financial accounting textbooks.

cash. Similarly, the corporation issuing a zero-coupon bond takes interest deductions for the amortized OID each year, even though it makes no cash payments until the bond matures.[20]

Another more subtle set of rules in taxation applies to market discounts. A **market discount** occurs if the price of the bond falls after issuance—that is, interest rates increased after issuance—and the bond is sold to a new investor. Like OID, market discounts are amortized over the remaining life of the bond. Unlike OID, holders of market discount bonds do not have to recognize amortized market discount as interest income. Rather, any capital gain realized on maturity or disposition of the bond is reduced by the amortized market discount.

Example of Taxation of Zero-Coupon Bonds Suppose a corporation issues a zero-coupon bond with a face value of $10,000 and a 10-year life when the market rate on such bonds is 10%. The bond will have an issue price of $3,855, which is simply the present value of $10,000 in 10 years at 10%.

The bond has $10,000 – $3,855.43 = $6,144.57 of OID.[21] The OID represents deferred interest. Over the life of the bond, the issuing corporation will report $6,144.57 of interest deductions using the constant-yield-to-maturity method.

The investor has an original basis in the bond of $3,855.43. The investor will recognize a corresponding $6,144.57 of interest income over the life of the bond, assuming the investor holds the bond until maturity, using the same yield-to-maturity method. Even a cash-basis investor must recognize interest income during the life of the bond. The investor's basis in the bond increases by the amount of interest income recognized. By the bond's maturity, the investor will have a $10,000 basis in the bond, so the maturity will produce no gain or loss.

The bond amortization schedule as shown in **Table 6.1** illustrates the taxation of zero-coupon bonds.

Table 6.1 Example of a Bond Amortization Table for a Zero-Coupon Bond

Year	Interest Expense/Revenue	Bond Carrying Value
Issue		**3,855.43**
1	385.54	4,240.97
2	424.10	4,665.07
3	466.51	5,131.58
4	513.16	5,644.74
5	564.47	6,209.21
6	620.92	6,830.13
7	683.01	7,513.14
8	751.31	8,264.46
9	826.45	9,090.90
10	909.09	10,000.00

The amortization table works this way: The interest expense is simply the bond's carrying value at end of the prior period multiplied by the effective yield of 10%, or $3,855.43(10%). The bond's carrying value at the end of the period is the carrying value from the end of the prior period plus the accrued interest expense from the current period; for example, $3,855.43 + $385.54 = $4,240.97.

[20] The U.S. tax code allows but does not require, investors to amortize bond premiums over the life of the bond. In most cases, investors would elect to amortize the premium because doing so will reduce their currently taxable income.

[21] OID can also occur in interest-bearing bonds if they are issued at less than face value. Some *de minimus* rules exclude small discounts from the OID rules.

6.5 TAXATION OF DISTRIBUTIONS AND SHARE REPURCHASES

We have discussed a great deal about how a corporation is taxed over its life cycle, starting with formation and continuing with its operations and capital structure decisions. When corporations are young, they often do not pay dividends to their shareholders, preferring instead to reinvest their earnings in the business. However, when corporations mature and have fewer growth prospects, it is common for them to begin paying dividends. Share repurchases are also common. Both dividends and share repurchases are methods of getting cash out of the corporation and into the hands of shareholders. In this section, we will describe the tax treatment of dividends and share repurchases.

Tax uses some different terminology than finance and accounting. In tax, a **distribution** refers to when a corporation pays cash or property to its shareholders without requiring something in return, which is a dividend in finance and accounting. A dividend in tax lingo refers to one possible treatment of a distribution. As we will see, a distribution may or may not be treated as a dividend for tax purposes. A **redemption** occurs when a corporation pays cash or property to its shareholders and gets some of its outstanding stock back in return, which is a share repurchase in finance and accounting. We begin by explaining the taxation of distributions. We will discuss redemptions later. For now, we simply note that most redemptions are taxed under sale or exchange treatment, which means the selling shareholders recognize a capital gain or loss on their sale of stock back to the corporation. However, some redemptions are treated as distributions for tax purposes, in which each shareholder sells a fixed proportion of his or her stock back to the corporation such that after the redemption, each shareholder owns the same proportion of the corporation as before the redemption.

Distributions can be taxed in three ways:

1. As a **dividend**: The distribution is taxable as income to the shareholder receiving it, often at a special 20% rate.
2. As a **return of capital**: The distribution is nontaxable but does reduce the shareholder's basis in the corporation's stock by the amount of the distribution.
3. As a **capital gain**: If the distribution is large enough to reduce the shareholder's basis in the stock to zero, any remaining distribution is taxed as a capital gain to the shareholder.

EXAMPLE 6.1 Distribution Taxed as a Dividend

Rachel receives a $10,000 distribution on the 5,000 shares of Berkeley Corporation she owns. Her basis in the Berkeley stock is $25,000. If the distribution is taxed as a dividend, Rachel will report $10,000 of income on her return and her basis in Berkeley is unchanged.

EXAMPLE 6.2 Distribution Taxed as a Return of Capital

Now assume that the distribution is not treated as a dividend. The distribution is treated as a nontaxable return of capital, and Rachel's basis in her Berkeley stock is reduced to $15,000.

EXAMPLE 6.3 Distribution Taxed as a Return of Capital and Capital Gain

With the same facts as Example 6.2, now assume that Rachel's basis in Berkeley was only $7,000 at the time of the distribution. In this case, the first $7,000 of the distribution is treated as a return of capital, bringing Rachel's basis in her Berkeley stock to zero. The remaining $3,000 of the distribution is treated as a capital gain.

Most distributions, but certainly not all, are taxed as dividends. Distributions to shareholders are not deductible by the corporation. Rather, interest paid to debt holders generally is deductible to the corporation.

The Concept of Earnings and Profits

Distributions are taxed as dividends when they are paid out of something called *earnings and profits,* or *E&P*. There are two types of E&P: current and accumulated. **Current earnings and profits** is the tax analogue to net income; **accumulated earnings and profits** is the tax analogue to retained earnings.

Although E&P and retained earnings are similar concepts, they are calculated somewhat differently. In particular, E&P is calculated using procedures specified in the tax law, whereas retained earnings is calculated using GAAP.

Current E&P is computed by starting with taxable income and making a series of adjustments. Most of the adjustments are intuitive if we recognize that the E&P concept tends to lie somewhere in the middle of taxable income and GAAP-based income. Some of the common additions to taxable income include the following:

1. Municipal bond interest: This is tax exempt but does increase the firm's E&P and GAAP income.
2. Federal income tax refunds: These refunds are not taxable but do increase the firm's E&P as they do the firm's GAAP income. An example is NOL carrybacks.
3. The DRD: This reduces the firm's taxable income but does not affect the firm's E&P or GAAP income.
4. A deduction from an NOL carryforward from a prior year: Such NOLs reduce the firm's taxable income but do not affect the firm's E&P or GAAP income.

Common subtractions from taxable income include the following:

1. Federal income taxes paid: These do not reduce taxable income but do reduce E&P as they do GAAP income.
2. Nondeductible fines and penalties: Although subtractions, these do not reduce taxable income. They do reduce E&P, just as they do GAAP income.

Finally, some adjustments can be either positive or negative. For example, the depreciation methods allowable for E&P purposes are less generous than those used to compute taxable income. Therefore, in the early years of an asset's life, firms will typically have to add back a portion of the depreciation they recognized for regular tax purposes when computing E&P. In the latter years of an asset's life, E&P depreciation will exceed regular tax depreciation, resulting in a negative adjustment to E&P.

Each year, the firm computes its current E&P as described. Accumulated E&P is the sum of all prior years' current E&P reduced by distributions from E&P.

Distributions are taxable as dividends if the corporation has sufficient accumulated or current E&P to cover the distribution. If the distributing corporation does not have sufficient E&P, then the distribution is treated as a return of capital and as a capital gain once the shareholder's basis in the stock is reduced to zero.

EXAMPLE 6.4 Positive Current and Accumulated E&P

Elizabeth Corp. pays a $50,000 distribution during 2019. Elizabeth Corp. began 2019 with $5 million of accumulated E&P and generated $200,000 of current E&P during 2019. The $50,000 is taxed as a dividend.

EXAMPLE 6.5 Positive Current and Negative Accumulated E&P

With the same facts as Example 6.4, assume Elizabeth Corp. began 2019 with a $1 million negative E&P. The $50,000 is still taxed as a dividend because Elizabeth Corp. has positive current E&P of sufficient size to cover the distribution.

EXAMPLE 6.6 Negative Current and Accumulated E&P

With the same facts as Example 6.5, now assume Elizabeth Corp. has negative current E&P of $1,000. In this case, the $50,000 distribution is treated as a return of capital, not a dividend, because Elizabeth Corp. had negative current and accumulated E&P.

Most distributions are taxed as dividends. Complicated rules govern the allocation of E&P to dividends made during a year that does not have sufficient E&P to have all the distributions taxable as dividends. Such rules are beyond the scope of this text.

As a practical matter, corporations are often lax about keeping the calculations of their E&P account up to date when they know they have positive E&P, in the same manner that individuals are often lax about balancing their checkbook when they know they have enough money in their account to cover their expenses. Sometimes, a corporation finds itself making a distribution that it suspects is not covered by E&P, such as distributions made after several years of losses. In such cases, corporations often hire an accounting firm to do an E&P study, reconstructing the corporation's E&P from the time the last E&P calculation was made, which may date back to the formation of the corporation to the present. Such studies, although profitable for the accounting firms, can be tedious because they require the accountants to learn tax laws that may have been repealed decades earlier but are still relevant for computing the E&P arising from those years.

Special Kinds of Distributions

Occasionally, firms pay distributions in the form of property instead of cash. Property distributions are taxed the same way as cash distributions, except that the corporation must recognize a gain but cannot recognize a loss on the property as it leaves the corporation. If property distributions were not taxed, it would be easy for corporations to avoid double taxation of their earnings. Losses on property distributions are not deductible because, if they were, problems could arise with corporations and their shareholders setting unreasonably low valuations on the property to generate tax losses at the corporate level. The gain is the difference between the property's fair market value and the property's basis, and the gain may be capital or ordinary depending on property. The shareholder takes a basis in the property received equal to the fair market value of the property.

EXAMPLE 6.7 Property Distribution

Zhang Corp. distributes property with a basis of $10,000 and a fair market value of $30,000 to a shareholder in lieu of a cash dividend. Zhang Corp. will recognize a $20,000 gain. The shareholder will recognize $30,000 of dividend income and will take a $30,000 basis in the property received.

Constructive dividends occur when shareholders receive some benefit without the firm declaring a formal dividend. Most common in closely held firms, constructive dividends include, among other things, unreasonably large compensation to a shareholder/employee, shareholder use of corporate property (e.g., a corporate jet), and below-market loans to shareholders. Constructive dividends are taxed the same as dividends if the firm has sufficient current or accumulated E&P.

EXAMPLE 6.8 Constructive Dividend

John owns all the stock of Golf Corp. During the year, Golf Corp. pays John a $150,000 salary for managerial duties. John reports $150,000 of wage income on his return and Golf Corp. reports $150,000 of deductions for wages paid on its corporate tax return. Following an IRS audit, it is determined that John's reasonable compensation would have been $40,000. John will be treated as having received $40,000 of wage income and $110,000 of dividend income. Golf Corp. will only be able to deduct $40,000 of wages paid because dividends are not deductible to corporations. Dividends are deductible from E&P, so Golf Corp. will reduce its E&P account by $150,000, or $40,000 + $110,000.

Stock dividends occur when the corporation distributes additional stock to its existing shareholders. For example, a shareholder with 10 shares will receive 1 additional share if the firm issues a 10% stock dividend.[22] Notice that the shareholder's proportionate interest in the firm is not affected by the stock dividend. The corporate "pie" simply is sliced into thinner pieces, but the corporation has no more or less cash or resources after the stock dividend than before the stock dividend. Realizing that a stock dividend is essentially a nonevent, the U.S. tax code treats most stock dividends as nonevents.[23] Returning to our example, assume the shareholder had a \$5.50 basis in each of his 10 shares of stock. Following the 10% stock dividend, he will allocate his \$55 of basis across 11 shares for \$5 of basis per share.

Taxation of Share Repurchases

A redemption occurs when the corporation repurchases some of its outstanding stock from its shareholders. In many cases, redemptions are accorded "sale or exchange" treatment for tax purposes. If so, the shareholders selling their stock have a capital gain or loss, calculated in the same manner as if they had sold their stock to a third party.

EXAMPLE 6.9 Redemption Treated as a Sale or an Exchange

Wolverine has 1 million shares of stock outstanding. Michelle owns 1,000 shares of Wolverine Inc., each share with a \$2 basis for a total basis of \$2,000. Wolverine repurchases 200 of Michelle's shares for \$500. Michelle recognizes a \$100 capital gain, or \$500 – \$400, which will be long term or short term depending on whether Michelle's holding period in the stock is greater or less than 12 months.

In some cases, however, redemptions are treated as dividends under the tax law.

EXAMPLE 6.10 Redemption Treated as a Dividend

Building on the previous example, if Michelle were the sole owner of Wolverine, then she would own 100% of Wolverine before and after the redemption. A redemption and a dividend would have essentially the same economic effect—\$500 of cash going from Michelle's corporation to Michelle, with Michelle controlling 100% of Wolverine the entire time. The U.S. tax code would treat such a redemption as a dividend. Accordingly, Michelle would recognize \$500 of dividend income, assuming Wolverine had sufficient E&P. Michelle's original \$2,000 basis would be spread across the remaining 800 Wolverine shares for a new basis of \$2.50 per share.

For a redemption to qualify for sale or exchange treatment, it must fall under one of the following categories (Sections 302 and 303):

1. Distributions not essentially equivalent to a dividend
2. Substantially disproportionate distributions
3. Distributions in termination of a shareholder's interest
4. Certain distributions in partial liquidation
5. Distributions to pay a shareholder's death taxes

Redemptions that do not qualify under one of these categories are treated as dividends, assuming sufficient E&P.

[22] Stock splits rely on essentially the same idea. For example, in a two-for-one stock split, a shareholder with 10 shares of stock will be given an additional 10 shares for a total of 20 shares.

[23] In rare cases, stock dividends are taxable to their recipients. Generally, this adverse treatment occurs if the stock dividend is designed to alter the shareholders' proportionate interests in the firm, such as having preferred shareholders receive common stock, or vice versa.

Perhaps the most common provision that gives rise to sale or exchange treatment is the disproportionate distribution provision in Section 302(b)(2). To be substantially disproportionate, the shareholder's ownership in the corporation after the redemption must be less than 80% of his interest before the redemption, and the shareholder must own less than 50% of the combined voting power in the corporation. Attribution rules apply, however, in determining the change in ownership and voting power. The specifics of such rules are beyond the scope of this text, but they generally require a shareholder's interest to include those of his spouse, children, grandchildren, parents, and, in certain cases, shares held by partnerships, corporations, and estates or trusts related to him.

EXAMPLE 6.11 Attribution Rules in Redemptions

Suppose a husband and wife each owned 50% of a corporation and half of the husband's shares were redeemed by the corporation. For the purposes of determining whether the redemption will get sale or exchange treatment, the husband would be treated as having owned 100% of the corporation before and after the redemption because all of his wife's shares are treated as his and vice versa.

When a redemption qualifies for sale or exchange treatment, the corporation generally reduces its E&P in proportion to the amount of stock redeemed. For example, if 10% of a corporation's stock is redeemed, generally, the corporation will reduce its E&P account by 10%.

6.6 TAX PLANNING USING THE TAX RULES FOR DISTRIBUTIONS AND SHARE REPURCHASES

Individual shareholders tend to prefer sale or exchange treatment to dividend treatment. There are two reasons for this. First, only the portion of the proceeds from the redemption in excess of the basis is taxed under sale or exchange treatment, whereas the entire proceeds are taxed under dividend treatment. Second, they have the opportunity to have their gain taxed at capital gains rates rather than rates applying to dividend income. Although these rates are currently the same at 20%, there have been periods when the capital gains rate has been less than the rate applicable to dividends.

Corporate shareholders, however, may prefer dividend treatment for a redemption. There are two reasons for this as well. First, corporations are only taxable on a portion of dividend income due to the DRD. Second, there is no special capital gains rate for corporations; they pay the same rate on capital gains as they do on ordinary income.

The rules governing the taxation of share repurchases are designed to make it difficult to get sale or exchange treatment to prevent abuse by disguising dividends as share repurchases for the benefit of individual shareholders. Consequently, corporations that want to divest ownership in another firm have engaged in strategies that involve purposely failing the preceding rules to have a redemption be taxed as a dividend. For example, Seagram did this on a massive scale, saving about $1.5 billion in taxes on the 1995 sale of its stake in DuPont. Congress and the IRS were not pleased. The $1.5 billion tax loss to the government from this *single* transaction represented about 1% of the total corporate taxes collected that year. The IRS later challenged Seagram's treatment of this transaction for tax purposes. In 2006, Vivendi, which had acquired Seagram in 2000, settled the dispute with the IRS for approximately $686 million. In the meantime, Congress also got involved by enacting a legislative "fix" so the Seagram-DuPont strategy will not work under current law, at least not using the same structure Seagram and DuPont used.[24]

6.7 TAXATION OF LIQUIDATIONS

The final stage in the life cycle of a corporation is liquidation. A corporation liquidates by paying off its liabilities and then distributing all of its assets to its shareholders in exchange for their stock. The

[24] For a detailed analysis of the Seagram-DuPont deal, see Erickson and Wang (1999) and Willens (1994, 1995). This transaction is also the subject of an exercise in Chapter 2.

corporation then goes out of existence. In keeping with the principle of double taxation of corporations, two layers of tax are levied. First, Section 336 provides that the corporation will recognize all unrealized gains and losses on property distributed in liquidation. For example, if the corporation distributed a piece of land to a shareholder in liquidation and the land had a basis and fair market value of $100 and $150, respectively, then the corporation would recognize a $50 gain. It is common in liquidation for the firm to sell its assets for cash and then distribute the after-tax proceeds to the shareholders. In that case, the corporate layer of taxation occurs naturally, as with any other sale of assets.

The second layer of taxation occurs at the shareholder level. The shareholders will recognize a capital gain or loss (long term if they held their stock more than 1 year) on the difference between the fair market value of the cash and property they get from the corporation and the basis of the stock in the corporation that they surrender, as based on Section 331. For example, if Joe received $20 cash and $90 of property from the corporation and gave up stock that had a basis of $70, then Joe would recognize a $20 + $90 – $70 = $40 gain. Joe would take a $90 basis in the property received. Note that the corporation's E&P does not affect the taxation of the liquidating distribution.

Parent-Subsidiary Liquidations

The U.S. tax code contains several provisions that treat parents and subsidiaries as a single economic entity. For example, the consolidated return rules generally allow a parent's losses to offset the income of its subsidiary, and vice versa. A similar set of provisions is found in Section 332, which allows parents to liquidate their subsidiaries without recognizing gain or loss.

To qualify under Section 332, the parent must own at least 80% of the total voting power of the subsidiary and at least 80% of the value of the subsidiary's stock. If the liquidation qualifies under Section 332, the rules are designed to put the parent into the shoes of the subsidiary. Specifically, the subsidiary recognizes no gain or loss upon liquidation under Section 332; the parent takes a carryover basis in the assets of the subsidiary it receives. Similarly, the subsidiary's NOL carryovers, capital loss carryovers, and E&P transfer to the parent.

Summary of Key Points

1. The hallmark of corporate taxation is double taxation of corporate profits. Earnings of a corporation are taxed once at the corporate level and again at the shareholder level when the corporation pays dividends.
2. Corporate formations are usually nontaxable events under Section 351.
3. Many similarities can be noted between GAAP and taxable income, but many book-tax differences also exist, such as depreciation and municipal bond income.
4. Corporations pay the same tax rate on capital gains as they do on ordinary income.
5. The dividends received deduction causes corporations to be only partially taxable on dividends they receive from other corporations.
6. Whether leverage provides a tax benefit—and, if so, how large a tax benefit—has been a topic of controversy in finance for decades. The most recent research is consistent with the existence of a tax gain from leverage.
7. Many capital structure alternatives are available in addition to common stock and debt. Traditional preferred stock is like debt in that it has a fixed payment. It is treated as equity for tax purposes, so the issuer cannot deduct dividends on straight preferred stock. Dividends on traditional preferred stock are taxed at low rates to both individual and corporate shareholders.
8. Trust preferred stock is an example of a debt-equity hybrid. It has generally been structured to be debt for tax purposes, such that payments on trust preferred stock are tax deductible to the issuer, as is interest expense, and taxable to the investor. For accounting purposes, trust preferred stock was presented between the liability and equity sections of the balance sheet until a rule change in 2003 forced liability treatment. For banks, trust preferred stock counted as Tier 1 equity capital for over a decade, leading to more than $140 billion of trust preferred issuances, but regulatory changes have largely curtailed this.

9. Zero-coupon bonds are treated much the same for tax purposes as they are under historical cost accounting. The difference between the issue price and the maturity value is called original issue discount (OID). OID represents the interest component that accrues over the life of the bond. Issuers deduct OID interest expense over the life of the bond under the constant-yield-to-maturity method; investors are taxable on OID interest income using the same method.
10. A distribution occurs when a corporation pays cash or property to its shareholders without requiring anything in return. Distributions can result in dividend, return of capital, or capital gains treatment; dividend treatment is the most common.
11. A redemption occurs when a corporation repurchases some of its outstanding stock from its shareholders. Most redemptions are taxed under sale or exchange treatment, meaning the selling shareholder reports a capital gain or loss for the difference between the selling price and the stock basis.
12. Liquidations occur when the corporation distributes all of its property to its shareholders in exchange for all of its outstanding stock. Liquidations are taxable to both the corporation and the shareholders. Liquidations of subsidiaries are an exception and generally nontaxable to both the parent and subsidiary.

Questions

Q6-1. From an economic policy perspective, do you think the provisions in Section 351 that allow nontaxable corporate formation are desirable? Why or why not?

Q6-2. What is the DRD? Why did Congress allow such a deduction?

Q6-3. Do parent corporations generally prefer to file consolidated tax returns with their subsidiaries as opposed to filing separate returns? Why or why not?

Q6-4. According to Miller's 1977 paper, leverage does not increase firm value even though interest expense on debt is tax deductible by corporations. Why?

Q6-5. Taking the perspective of a corporation that is raising capital, why would the pretax cost of equity and debt capital differ, other than because of differences in risk?

Q6-6. Why is it so difficult to measure the effects of taxes on the pretax returns of assets?

Q6-7. What is trust preferred stock? What advantages did it have over traditional preferred stock?

Q6-8. Many large banks issued billions of dollars of trust preferred stock until the financial crisis of 2008. Why did banks more so than, say, manufacturing firms, appear to like trust preferred stock as a source of capital?

Q6-9. When a corporation repurchases shares of its stock from investors, for tax purposes, do individual shareholders generally prefer the repurchase to be treated as a dividend or a sale? Why?

Q6-10. What are constructive dividends? Do you think constructive dividends are more likely to occur in large, publicly traded corporations or small, privately held corporations? Why?

Exercises

E6-11. Which of the following scenarios will qualify under Section 351 as a nontaxable corporate formation? For those that do not qualify, what requirement of Section 351 do they violate?

a. Ginger, Mary Ann, and Mrs. Howell form GMH Corp. Ginger contributes memorabilia in exchange for 40% of GMH's stock, Mary Ann contributes farmland in exchange for 30% of GMH, and Mrs. Howell contributes cash in exchange for the remaining 30%.

b. Clyde founded ABC Corp. in 2015 and owns all of ABC's 1,000 shares of outstanding stock. In 2019, ABC issues 300 shares of new stock to Bonnie in exchange for land that Bonnie owned. Will Bonnie's contribution qualify under Section 351?

c. With the same facts as part *b*, now ABC issues 4,500 shares of new stock to Bonnie in exchange for Bonnie's land.

d. Bert and Ernie form Duckie Corp. in late 2019. Bert contributes $10,000 cash in exchange for 60% of Duckie's stock. Ernie contributes services in exchange for the remaining 40% of Duckie.

E6-12. Conan and Andy decide to form a new corporation, LN Corp. Conan contributes property with a basis of $10,000 and a fair market value of $18,000 in exchange for five shares of LN stock and $13,000 in cash, which LN borrows from a bank to finance. Andy contributes property with a basis of $35,000 and a fair market value of $80,000 in exchange for 80 shares of LN stock.

a. How much taxable gain or loss will Conan recognize as a result of the transaction?

b. What basis will Conan take in the LN stock he receives?

E6-13. Tar Heel Inc. pays $100,000 of dividends in 2019, with $25,000 going to your client, Mr. Big. Tar Heel began 2019 with $120,000 in accumulated E&P and had $10,000 of current E&P in 2019. Mr. Big has a $40,000 basis in his Tar Heel stock.

a. How much dividend income will Mr. Big report from Tar Heel in 2019? What will Mr. Big's basis in Tar Heel be after the dividend?

b. Assume instead that Tar Heel began 2019 with a $2,000 deficit balance in its E&P account but did have $10,000 of current E&P for 2019. How much dividend income will Mr. Big report from Tar Heel in 2019?

E6-14. DMM Corporation is a diversified U.S. firm that has ownership stakes in two other U.S. corporations. Specifically, DMM Corporation owns 60% of the outstanding stock of Tax Shelter.com and 10% of the outstanding stock of Litigation.com. In 2019, DMM Corporation itself had $10 million of taxable income; TaxShelter.com and Litigation.com had $2 million and $3 million in NOLs, respectively. Neither TaxShelter.com nor Litigation.com has ever reported positive taxable income, and neither pays any dividends. How much taxable income will DMM Corporation report on its 2019 consolidated tax return?

E6-15. Which of the following were typical features of trust preferred stock, also known as monthly income preferred stock?

a. It was treated as debt on the issuer's GAAP balance sheet.

b. Corporate recipients of trust preferred dividends are eligible for the DRD.

c. Trust preferred stock is thought to have a greater pretax yield than traditional preferred stock of similar risk.

d. Trust preferred stock dividends are deductible to the issuer.

e. Trust preferred stock counts as Tier 1 capital for banks.

E6-16. Brad, Scott, and Jake each contribute property to form BSJ Corporation. Brad contributes a building with a fair market value of $450,000 and a basis of $100,000 and receives 45% of the stock of BSJ. Scott contributes $100,000 cash and equipment with a fair market value and tax basis of $350,000, receiving 45% of the stock of BSJ. Jake contributes a collection of vintage automobiles with a fair market value of $150,000 and tax basis of $130,000 in exchange for 10% of the stock of BSJ and $50,000 cash. What tax basis will each take in their respective BSJ stock?

References and Additional Readings

A sampling of research on book-tax differences:

Ayers, B., S. Laplante, and S. McGuire, 2010. "Credit Ratings and Taxes: The Effect of Book-Tax Differences on Ratings Changes," *Contemporary Accounting Review* (27), pp. 359–402.

Ayers, B., X. Jiang, and S. Laplante, 2009. "Taxable Income as a Performance Measure: The Effects of Tax Planning and Earnings Quality," *Contemporary Accounting Review* (26), pp. 15–54.

Graham, J., J. Raedy, and D. Shackelford, 2012a. "Accounting for Income Taxes: Primer, Extant Research, and Future Directions," *Foundations and Trends in Finance* (7), pp. 1–157.

Graham, J., J. Raedy, and D. Shackelford, 2012b. "Research in Accounting for Income Taxes," *Journal of Accounting and Economics* (53), pp. 412–434.

Guenther, D., S. Nutter, and E. Maydew, 1997. "Financial Reporting, Tax Costs, and Book-Tax Conformity," *Journal of Accounting and Economics* (23), pp. 225–248.

Hanlon, M., 2003. "What Can We Infer about a Firm's Taxable Income from Its Financial Statements?" *National Tax Journal* (56), pp. 831–864.

Hanlon, M. 2005. "The Persistence and Pricing of Earnings, Accruals, and Cash Flows When Firms Have Large Book-Tax Differences." *The Accounting Review* (80), pp. 137–166.

Hanlon, M., E. Maydew, and T. Shevlin, 2008. "An Unintended Consequence of Book-Tax Conformity: A Loss of Earnings Informativeness," *Journal of Accounting and Economics* (46), pp. 294–311.

Hanlon, M., S. Laplante, and T. Shevlin, 2005. "Evidence on the Possible Information Loss of

Conforming Book Income and Taxable Income." *Journal of Law and Economics* (48), pp. 407–442.

Lisowsky, P., 2010. "Seeking Shelter: Empirically Modeling Tax Shelters Using Financial Statement Information." *The Accounting Review* (85), pp. 1673–1720.

Mills, L., 1998. "Book-Tax Differences and Internal Revenue Service Adjustments," *Journal of Accounting Research* (36), pp. 343–356.

Mills, L., and G. Plesko, 2003. "Bridging the Reporting Gap: A Proposal for More Informative Reconciling of Book and Tax Income," *National Tax Journal* (56), pp. 865–893.

Shevlin, T., 2002. "Corporate Tax Shelters and Book-Tax Differences," *Tax Law Review* (55), pp. 427–443.

Research on the theory and evidence of the tax benefits of leverage:

Blouin, J., J. Core, and W. Guay, 2010. "Have the Tax Benefits of Debt Been Overestimated?" *Journal of Financial Economics* (98), pp. 195–213.

Brealey, R., S. Myers, and R. Allen, 2011. *Principles of Corporate Finance,* 10th ed. New York: McGraw-Hill.

DeAngelo, H., and R. Masulis, 1980. "Optimal Capital Structure under Corporate Taxation," *Journal of Financial Economics* (March), pp. 5–29.

Dhaliwal, D., R. Trezevant, and S. Wang, 1992. "Taxes, Investment-Related Tax Shields, and Capital Structure," *Journal of the American Taxation Association* (14), pp. 1–21.

Engel, E., M. Erickson, and E. Maydew, 1999. "Debt-Equity Hybrid Securities," *Journal of Accounting Research* (37), pp. 249–274.

Faccio, M., and J. Xu, 2015. "Taxes and Capital Structure," *Journal of Financial and Quantitative Analysis* 50(3), pp. 277–300.

Fama, E., and K. French, 1998. "Taxes, Financing Decisions, and Firm Value," *Journal of Finance* (53), pp. 819–843.

Graham, J., 1996. "Debt and the Marginal Tax Rate," *Journal of Financial Economics* (41), pp. 41–74.

Graham, J., 2000. "How Big Are the Tax Benefits of Debt?" *Journal of Finance* (55), pp. 1901–1941.

Graham, J., 2003. "Taxes and Corporate Finance: A Review," *Review of Financial Studies* (16), pp. 1074–1128.

Graham, J., M. Lang, and D. Shackelford, 2004. "Employee Stock Options, Corporate Taxes, and Debt Policy," *Journal of Finance* (59), pp. 1585–1618.

Heider, F., and A. Ljungqvist, 2015. "As Certain as Death and Taxes: Estimating the Tax Sensitivity of Leverage from State Tax Changes," *Journal of Financial Economics* (118), pp. 684–712.

Mackie-Mason, J., 1990. "Do Taxes Affect Corporate Financing Decisions?" *Journal of Finance* (December), pp. 1471–1493.

Miller, M., 1977. "Debt and Taxes," *Journal of Finance* (May), pp. 261–276.

Miller, M., and F. Modigliani, 1966. "Some Estimates of the Cost of Capital in the Electric Utility Industry, 1954–57," *American Economic Review* (June), pp. 333–391.

Modigliani, F., and M. Miller, 1958. "The Cost of Capital, Corporation Finance, and the Theory of Investment," *American Economic Review* (June), pp. 261–297.

Modigliani, F., and M. Miller, 1963. "Corporate Income Taxes and the Cost of Capital: A Correction," *American Economic Review* (June), pp. 433–443.

Myers, S., 1984. "The Capital Structure Puzzle," *Journal of Finance* (39), pp. 575–592.

Scholes, M., M. Wolfson, and P. Wilson, 1990. "Tax Planning, Regulatory Capital Planning, and Financial Reporting Strategy for Commercial Banks," *Review of Financial Studies* (3), pp. 625–650.

Shevlin, T., 1987. "Taxes and Off-Balance Sheet Financing: Research and Development Limited Partnerships," *The Accounting Review* (62), pp. 480–509.

Shevlin, T., 1990. "Estimating Corporate Marginal Tax Rates with Asymmetric Tax Treatment of Gains and Losses," *Journal of the American Taxation Association* (11), pp. 51–67. (This is not a capital structure paper, but it does provide the basis for Graham's marginal tax rate estimates.)

Van Binsbergen, J., J. Graham, and J. Yang. 2010. "The Cost of Debt," *Journal of Finance* (65), pp. 2089–2136.

A discussion of the Seagram-DuPont transaction:

Erickson, M., and S. Wang, 1999. "Exploiting and Sharing Tax Benefits: Seagram and DuPont," *Journal of the American Taxation Association* (21), pp. 35–54.

Willens, R., 1994. "Strategies for Divesting Equity Stakes in a Hostile Tax Environment," *Journal of Taxation* (August), pp. 88–93.

Willens, R., 1995. "DuPont/Seagram: Every Action Has an Equal and Opposite Overreaction," *Tax Notes* (June 5), pp. 1367–1371.

7

Nontax Costs of Tax Planning

After completing this chapter, you should be able to

1. Define a progressive tax-rate system and explain how it influences firms' risk-taking and hedging incentives.
2. Explain how a progressive tax-rate system influences firms' organizational form choices.
3. Describe how transaction costs and hidden-action problems affect tax planning.
4. Describe how hidden-information problems affect tax planning.
5. Explain why tax rules differ from accounting rules.
6. Define and give examples of temporary and permanent book-tax differences.
7. Interpret corporate disclosures relating to income taxes.
8. Describe how financial reporting issues influence tax planning.

Although the world would be easier to understand if economic exchanges could be undertaken free of all transaction costs, such costs are pervasive. While we have discussed many aspects of differing tax costs across organizational forms, recognizing that different ways of organizing economic activity give rise to differences in transaction costs as well is important. Hence, the efficient organizational choice is one that considers tax and nontax costs in computing returns.[1] We cannot emphasize too strongly the importance of nontax costs in forging efficient tax plans.

In the simplest case, one can think of the fees and costs to accomplish tax planning. As mentioned in Chapter 1, tax planning is a huge business. Billions of dollars are spent each year in the United States alone to secure professional assistance in reducing tax obligations and to maintain records to support taxpayers' claims concerning their tax obligations. In addition, billions of dollars are spent each year in legal and administrative fees to write and to enforce contractual agreements that are designed, in part, to reduce the joint tax burdens among contracting parties. Effective tax planning must be viewed relative to the costs of implementing these strategies. Although complex contracts may succeed in reducing more conflicts of interest among contracting parties, simple contracts are often observed in practice. Similarly, simple tax-planning strategies may be more efficient from an overall cost standpoint than more complicated strategies that would result in reduced tax payments.

Casual observation suggests that the effect of taxes pervades the way production and exchange are organized. It is equally indisputable that organizational arrangements arise because information is asymmetrically distributed among economic agents. Workers must often be monitored or offered incentives to induce them to perform in the owners'

[1] If these nontax cost differences are viewed as implicit taxes (after all, this is a tax-planning text), then the (deceptively) simple decision rule of seeking to minimize taxes is an efficient one. However, we will maintain the distinction between implicit taxes (as differences in pretax rates of return arising from differential explicit tax treatment) and other nontax costs.

best interests. Customers must often be offered warranties to induce them to buy products, and still a variety of consumer protection groups exist. Independent third parties are required to audit the financial statements of publicly owned corporations. And even absent any regulatory requirements, many firms voluntarily pay substantial sums to third parties to verify certain information disclosures designed to facilitate economic exchanges among parties that are not equally well informed.

In many contracting problems, a desire to achieve tax minimization encourages precisely the same organizational arrangements as do solutions to incentive problems among differentially informed and opportunistic agents. When this occurs, outside observers (e.g., researchers, consultants, corporate raiders, investment bankers, and regulators) face a so-called **identification problem** in sorting out which economic force is responsible for the observed contractual relations.

However, it is also true that tax considerations and information-related transaction cost considerations often have conflicting implications for efficient organizational design. Sometimes, tax considerations dominate in importance, and sometimes, information considerations dominate. But frequently, both factors are important and trade-offs must be made. Because of the need to make these trade-offs, efficient tax planning is often quite distinct from tax minimization. We develop this theme in this chapter and illustrate it in several later chapters.

So far, uncertainty has not been prominent in our discussion. We begin to remedy that here. In particular, we distinguish between two types of uncertainty:

- **Symmetric uncertainty**: All contracting parties are equally well informed but still uncertain about what the future cash flows from an investment might be.
- **Strategic uncertainty** (also known as information asymmetry): The contracting parties are not equally well informed about what the future investment cash flows might be.

We further distinguish between two types of information asymmetry regarding future cash flows:

- **Hidden action** or **moral hazard**: One contracting party has control over an action choice that affects future cash flows and that action choice is unobservable by other contracting parties.
- **Hidden information** or **adverse selection**: One contracting party has observed a characteristic of the production function he or she cannot control that affects future cash flows, and that characteristic is only imperfectly observable by the other contracting parties[2]

In this chapter, we illustrate how each form of uncertainty gives rise to efficient tax-planning strategies that sacrifice tax minimization. We discuss the effects of symmetric uncertainty in the context of progressive tax-rate schedules. Progressive tax-rate schedules can influence a firm's risk-taking incentives (even if the firm is risk-neutral) with respect to investment choices and hedging activities and can influence organizational choice (e.g., joint venturing with more profitable entities). Hidden-action problems can inhibit tax arbitrage through capital market activities by influencing borrowing and lending rates and can influence contracting in labor markets. Hidden-information problems can impede asset sales that might minimize taxes.

Income shifting and organizational forms that minimize taxes often give rise to costs along other dimensions, leading to a trade-off between taxes and nontax costs. For example, income shifting within an organization might require more centralized organizational structures, but information asymmetries might require more decentralized organizational structures. In addition, many tax-planning activities can result in unfavorable financial reporting effects, leading to a trade-off between tax benefits/savings and costs arising from reporting lower earnings or higher debt-to-equity (leverage) ratios. Finally, the use of complicated organizational structures, such as limited liability partnerships (LLPs), joint ventures, and special-purpose entities to achieve tax and/or financial accounting goals often creates serious conflicts of interest between parties, leading to forced trade-offs by tax planners. Therefore, efficient tax planning requires the tax planner to identify and weigh the nontax costs of any tax plan against the tax benefits.

[2] For further elaboration, see Arrow (1985).

7.1 SYMMETRIC UNCERTAINTY, PROGRESSIVE TAX RATES, AND RISK-TAKING

As we defined the term, symmetric uncertainty is where all contracting parties are equally well informed (i.e., there is no asymmetric information) but uncertain about what the future cash flows from an investment might be. Uncertainty about future cash flows means the investment is risky. When uncertainty about future cash flows (or profitability) is linked with a **progressive income tax system**, some taxpayers may be less inclined to take on risky investments than they might otherwise be. Assume a tax-rate schedule as follows:

- If income is positive, you pay a tax of 40%.
- If income is negative, the tax rate is 0%; that is, you get no tax refund.[3]

This tax-rate schedule is progressive. In **Figure 7.1**, tax payable is on the *y*-axis and taxable income is on the *x*-axis and the tax rate schedule is graphed as the blue line bent at the origin. When graphed, the tax-rate schedule appears as a convex function and therefore is also called a convex tax function.

Suppose you have $100,000 to invest in one of two projects. One project is riskless, yielding a certain profit of $20,000. The alternative project is risky, yielding a profit of $150,000 half the time and a loss of $100,000 half the time. Because each outcome for the risky project is equally likely, the expected pretax profit is $25,000 or .5($150,000) + .5(–$100,000). These pretax expected returns appear on the *x* axis in **Figure 7.1**. For the moment, assume that you are indifferent between a particular payoff with certainty and a risky payoff with equal expected value. In other words, you are risk neutral. Absent any taxes, in which project would you invest?

Given your indifference toward risk, you would choose the project providing the higher expected pretax profit. That project is the risky project, by $5,000, or $25,000 – $20,000. Alternatively stated, the expected pretax rate of return for the risky project is 25%, or 25,000/100,000, compared with 20% for the riskless project.

How does the a progressive tax-rate schedule affect project choice? Quite dramatically, as the following after-tax profit numbers show:

Riskless project:	$20,000(1 – .40) = $12,000 after tax Expected after-tax rate of return = 12%
Risky project:	.5 [$150,000(1 – .40)] + .5(–$100,000) = –$5,000 after tax Expected after-tax rate of return = -5%

The riskless project is now *preferred* over the risky one by $17,000 after tax, despite being the inferior choice (by $5,000) in the absence of taxes. (Note: For simplicity, we are assuming that the investment is not tax deductible.) Why is the riskless project now tax preferred? Because the tax-rate schedule is progressive, the expected tax is $22,000 higher for the risky project than for the riskless one ($30,000 compared with $8,000, as plotted in **Figure 7.1**). This example shows a general feature of a progressive (or convex) tax system: The average tax rate paid increases with the variability of

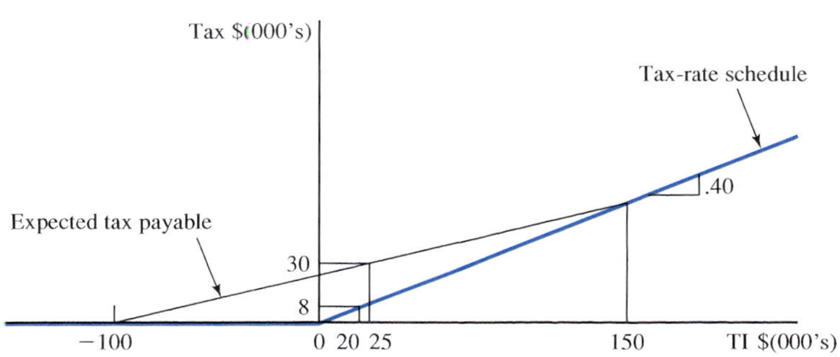

FIGURE 7.1 Progressive Tax-Rate Schedules and Risk-Taking Incentives

[3] Assume for the purposes of this example that tax losses can be carried neither back nor forward to offset income earned in other years. We discuss the effect of carrybacks and carryforwards later in the chapter.

taxable income levels.[4] So, even when taxpayers are risk neutral and face a progressive tax-rate schedule, they exhibit risk aversion toward assets with variable pretax returns.[5]

As discussed in Chapter 6, prior to 2017, corporations could carry back losses to obtain refunds of taxes paid in the last 2 years or carry forward the losses for 20 years to offset future taxes payable. Post the Tax Cut and Jobs Act of 2017 (TCJA), firms can no longer carry back losses, but they can carry them forward indefinitely; the tax rate schedule is under TCJA, if losses cannot be carried back and must be carried forward, the tax-rate schedule is still progressive (bent) around zero taxable income.[6] (Chapter 4 provides evidence on the extent of tax losses and their rate of usage by U.S. corporations.) Thus, start-ups with losses face progressive tax-rate schedules. In the extreme, if the risky investments do not prove successful, then the start-up effectively faces the tax-rate schedule in our example (i.e., tax losses obtain no tax benefit). In these situations, the progressive tax-rate schedule offers advantages to existing successful businesses (i.e., Microsoft Corporation, IBM, Intel, Merck) to undertake risky investments, because the losses can be immediately deducted against the businesses' other income, which reduces the after-tax cost of the investment. For start-ups with no income, however, there is a non-zero probability that the tax losses will not be used. Therefore, a progressive tax-rate schedule discriminates against start-ups organized as C corporations. For flow-through entities, the early losses flow through to the partners/investors and could be used to offset taxes on the partners'/investors' other income.

R&D and O&G Activities

Qualifying research and development (R&D) expenditures in the United States are immediately deductible as incurred under Section 174 of the Internal Revenue Code (IRC).[7] Moreover, the sale of successfully developed technology generally gives rise to capital gains. Similarly, oil and gas (O&G) investments receive favorable tax treatment because intangible drilling and development expenditures are immediately deductible (special limitations apply to integrated oil corporations). Further, O&G investments receive a percentage depletion allowance in which a percentage of revenues from the well is explicitly tax exempt and part of the income (sale of the well) may be subject to favorable capital gains treatment.[8] Recall that immediate deductibility of an investment, followed by full taxation of the returns at the same tax rate, is equivalent to tax exemption. With favorable taxation on the payoffs, the after-tax rates of return can exceed the pretax rates of return and can even turn a negative pretax return into a positive after-tax rate of return.

To illustrate the effects of tax code progressivity on firms' incentives to undertake R&D (and O&G), suppose a corporation makes an R&D investment of $1 (for realism, you can easily add 6 or 7 zeros). Suppose the firm's current-period marginal tax rate is 40%. Any income generated from the investment will be taxed in the future, when the firm's tax rate is expected to be 30%. Suppose further that an R&D tax credit of 10% of the investment expenditure is immediately available.[9] The research is very risky:

Probability	Payoff	Tax Rate
90%	$0 (worthless)	—
10%	$11 (successful)	30%

[4] Readers with a mathematical background might recognize this as an application of Jensen's Inequality, $E[f(X)] > f[E(X)]$, where $f(X)$ is the convex tax schedule.

[5] For further discussion, see Fellingham and Wolfson (1985).

[6] The TCJA also introduced a flat rate of 21%, whereas the previous marginal statutory tax rate increased with income, introducing some progressivity into the tax-rate schedule. However, the tax treatment of tax losses is the major cause of progressivity in the schedule.

[7] Beginning in 2022, R&D expenditures will no longer be immediately deductible and must be capitalized and amortized over 5 years if the R&D is conducted in the United States, 15 years if conducted overseas. Thus, R&D will not be as tax favored after 2022.

[8] The exact percentages and rules have varied over time, with the type of company (e.g., independent versus integrated oil and gas companies) and with the type of activity.

[9] The tax rate and R&D tax credit percentage are for illustration. The actual rates have varied over time. We are also assuming for simplicity that the dollar of R&D can be deducted as well as receive a tax credit. In reality, the deduction is reduced by the amount the taxpayer claims for the tax credit.

The expected pretax rate of return is 10%, computed as (.90 × \$0) + (.10 × \$11) = \$1.10 of expected cash return on a \$1 investment. But the expected after-tax rate of return is considerably higher, even if we assume that the \$11 return in the event of a successful outcome is fully taxed at 30%:

$$\frac{\$11(0.10)(1-.30)}{\$1.00-\$.40-\$.10}-1=\frac{\$.77}{\$.50}-1\text{, or }54\%$$

The denominator is the after-tax cost of the investment: \$1 cash investment less the \$.40 tax saved from the deduction and the \$.10 tax credit. If the research is undertaken by a firm with accumulated tax losses or by a start-up company with no income against which to offset the R&D deductions or the R&D tax credits, the after-tax returns decline dramatically. For example, suppose the R&D expenditures for a start-up that spreads the benefits of the deduction over time are effectively deductible at a rate of 20%. That is, the deduction has to be carried forward for 10 years, then deducted at a tax rate of 40%, and the present value at 7% per annum results in an effective tax rate of 20%: $.40/1.07^{10}$ In such a case, the present value of the R&D tax credit is only 5%, and any income is still taxed at 30%. Then, the after-tax expected rate of return declines from 54% to only 2.7%, or [\$.77/(\$1.00 – \$.20 – \$.05)] – 1.

One possible response to the unfavorable tax treatment that results in these situations is to undertake the investment anyway and suffer the tax cost. Another response is to abandon the investment. Either way, the tax rules discourage research expenditures by low-tax firms. However, low-tax firms can finance R&D in a way that sells the rights to favorable tax treatment to a party that is in a better position to take advantage of the tax write-offs.

The tax shelter industry in the 1970s and early 1980s was, in part, motivated by the progressiveness of the tax-rate schedule for start-up high-technology C corporations. Further, in the 1970s, the top individual statutory tax rate exceeded the top corporate statutory tax rate, so even profitable firms could benefit if they could place the tax deductions in the hands of higher-taxed taxpayers. Firms created limited partnerships (LPs)(see Chapter 5 for a discussion of these partnerships) in which limited partner interests were sold to outside parties (high-tax individuals) that could better use the immediate deductibility of the R&D and O&G (at tax rates up to 70%). Further, any payoffs were taxed as favorable capital gains to these parties. The company doing the research or exploration received a management fee and an interest in any revenue generated from licensing or selling the developed technology or oil. Shevlin (1987) provided empirical evidence consistent with the tax motivation for forming R&D LPs.[10] He found that firms sponsoring R&D LPs were younger and had more NOL carryforwards than firms conducting R&D in-house.

Both O&G and R&D activities are tax favored, and investors in LP investing in these activities likely bear implicit taxes by bidding up the prices of the LP interest (or by accepting a lower pretax rate of return). As a result, the R&D or O&G firm organizing the partnership is able to raise funds at a lower cost. Also, because the investment bears implicit taxes, high-tax-rate investors are the natural clientele for these investments (and, hence, these investments were marketed to high-income individuals).

As effective as these partnerships may be from a tax standpoint, they can create severe nontax costs. Such entities require considerable administrative costs to organize, including sales commissions and investment banking fees that can easily run to 10% or more of the total amount invested. Partnerships also may require disclosures to investors regarding the nature of the research that compromise the firm's competitive advantage. Further, as discussed in the next sections, these arrangements give rise to nontax costs arising from strategic uncertainty (both hidden-information and hidden-action problems). Therefore, tax planners must weigh the tax benefits and nontax costs of these organizational forms.

The Tax Reform Act of 1986 (TRA 86) effectively put an end to LPs as a way to sell the tax benefits to outside parties better able to use them by putting the **passive activity loss** rules into place. Essentially, these rules, which are still in force today, limit deductions for individuals with a passive interest in a business.[11] Passive activity losses are limited to the amount of passive income the investor reports on his or her tax return (active and passive are defined in Section 469 and the associated regulations). Such passive activity losses cannot be deducted against other types of income (i.e., nonpassive income)

[10] See also Beatty, Berger, and Magliolo (1995).

[11] Rental activities are also passive but subject to slightly different rules that are beyond the scope of this text.

until the underlying investments are sold. Losses from LP interests were classified in TRA 86 as passive activity losses for individual taxpayers. Since 1986, start-ups and low-tax firms are likely to form joint ventures with older, more profitable corporations that can use the tax benefits (i.e., these firms face a less progressive tax schedule). These joint ventures may suffer fewer agency (nontax) costs because both parties are likely more involved in the venture's activities. Further, joint ventures can also be motivated by nontax factors: outside parties may bring special research, marketing, or administrative expertise to the venture as well as risk-sharing benefits.

Progressive Tax Rates and Hedging

For corporations facing progressive tax schedules, **hedging** lowers expected tax liabilities. This decrease occurs through lowering the variance of the distribution of expected taxable income. Hedging can be undertaken via financial instruments such as options, swaps, and other derivatives. Thus, taxes can motivate firms to hedge their activities (in addition to hedging to reduce the expected costs of financial distress and to reduce agency costs between debt holders and shareholders).[12]

Graham and Smith (1999) provided some empirical estimates of firms' tax incentive to hedge. Graham and Smith analyze more than 80,000 firm-year observations for corporations on Standard & Poor's Compustat database. This database contains financial statement information for a majority of publicly traded U.S. firms. The researchers found that in approximately 50% of firm years, corporations faced convex (progressive) tax-rate schedules and therefore had a tax-based incentive to hedge. In 25% of firm years, corporations faced a linear tax-rate function and therefore had no tax incentive to hedge. In the remaining 25% of firm years, the corporations faced a concave (regressive) tax-rate function and therefore faced a tax-based disincentive to hedge.

For the 50% of firm years facing a convex tax-rate function, approximately 25% had potential tax savings from hedging that appear material. For the remaining 75% of the cases, the tax savings were small. Further, Graham and Smith's results suggest that corporations are most likely to face a convex tax-rate function when their expected taxable incomes are near the bend in the statutory tax schedule (i.e., taxable income is positive and near zero), their incomes are volatile, and they are likely to switch back and forth between profits and losses.[13]

7.2 TAX PLANNING IN THE PRESENCE OF RISK-SHARING AND HIDDEN-ACTION CONSIDERATIONS

In Chapter 4, we discussed in very general terms how market frictions drive a wedge between the buying and selling prices of assets, and this helps to prevent tax arbitrage opportunities from being used to eliminate income taxes. We illustrated the effect of a borrowing rate in excess of the lending rate on the desirability of organizational form and clientele-based arbitrage. We now examine this issue more closely.

Contracting in Capital Markets

Suppose there were no restrictions on the deductibility of interest on loans that are fully secured by single-premium deferred annuities (SPDAs). Would we expect the pretax rates of return on the annuity contract to be the same as the rate paid on the loan? No. The insurance company offering the deferred annuity contract must charge for its operating costs, as must the bank lending the funds.

What operating costs exist for the insurance company? The insurance company has a sales force that earns commissions for educating the public about deferred annuities. The company must also set up and maintain an information system to track its assets and policyholders, as well as invest in a system of internal controls to ensure that all funds received are invested and to assure all prospective policyholders that it is solvent. Moreover, the company must incur costs to create contracts that

[12] For further discussion of firms' incentives to hedge, see Nance, Smith, and Smithson (1993).

[13] For firms with expected continuing losses and existing NOL carryforwards, the firm has an incentive to increase the variance of taxable incomes so as to increase the probability of a large positive outcome against which it can offset the losses.

specify clearly its property rights and those of its policyholders in various contingencies. Annual expenses of companies offering deferred annuities often exceed 2% of funds invested.

What costs are there for the lender? The lender must also develop and maintain an information system and a system of internal controls and incur costs to write contracts. The lender must also pay brokers (e.g., loan officers) to identify appropriate borrowers. In addition, the lender must invest resources to investigate the insurance company whose deferred annuity secures the loan. The lender must be convinced that the insurance company assets backing the deferred annuity are adequate to pay market rates of return to annuity holders. Moreover, the lender must incur costs to ensure that the deferred annuity cannot be cashed out by the owner and put to alternative uses without the lender's knowledge. Otherwise, the loan would not really be secured. These costs add up. As a result, it is not unusual for the spread between the riskless borrowing rate and the secured lending rate to exceed 300 basis points, or 3%.

For example, one simple way to engage in secured borrowing is to borrow from a brokerage house or bank, pledging your stocks as collateral. Such loans have little risk for the lender because investors are initially permitted to borrow up to only 50% of the value of the stock. The broker can sell stocks if they decline in value to the point where they begin to jeopardize full repayment of the loan. Despite the apparent riskless nature of the loans, brokerage houses frequently charge interest rates well above the cost of borrowing (a 2% spread is common). In part, this spread pays for the costs brokers might incur if forced to sell customers' shares in big market drops and customers sue because they allege they did not receive fair treatment.

Of course, one would expect that extremely large investors, including groups of individual investors, can arrange for lower spreads, perhaps as low as .5%. These low transaction costs result from economics of scale, as most of the transaction costs we have mentioned are fixed in nature. If this is a correct characterization, such large investors would indeed have less difficulty borrowing to invest in some tax-favored savings vehicle, such as deferred annuities, which is the kind of tax arbitrage we discussed in Chapter 4. As a result, the tax system must impose restrictions on these activities. Perhaps the threat of these large, low-cost transactions has led to the specific restriction that secured borrowing to finance the purchase of SPDAs renders the interest expense nondeductible.

With secured borrowing to purchase deferred annuities ruled out by tax-rule restrictions, let's consider whether things look much different with *unsecured* borrowing. The rates on unsecured borrowing can be dramatically higher than the rates on secured borrowing. Moreover, unlike the case of secured borrowing, the borrowing rates for unsecured loans tend to increase with the level of borrowing for a given individual. The reason for this is fairly straightforward and relates to strategic uncertainty—hidden actions. Borrowers cannot always be trusted to act in ways they promise to act. That is, they may take actions that imperil the cash flows that stand behind the contracts (because they do not bear all of the costs of reduced cash flow), and lenders typically cannot observe such actions.

Suppose you invest your entire life savings of $100,000 in riskless bonds and have no liabilities. You go to the bank and apply for a $50,000 loan. You tell the bank the loan is to finance a vacation and an investment and you prefer not to invade your $100,000 savings account for these purposes. With $100,000 in riskless assets, we might suppose that the bank need not charge much of a default premium.

But suppose the vacation and investment you had in mind entail liquidating your savings account, going to Las Vegas, and betting $150,000 on the color red in a single spin of a fair roulette wheel. Would the bank be very happy? Not likely. If you win, you make a profit of $150,000 less a small fee for the use of the bank's $50,000 for the bet. If you lose, you lose only your $100,000 because you will default on the bank loan. Assuming that winning and losing are equally likely, your expected profit, ignoring the small fee for the "rent" on $50,000 for one day, is $25,000, calculated as .5 × $150,000 + .5 × (–$100,000). Your expected winnings of $25,000 are precisely equal to the bank's expected loss.

But you can do even better by taking on more risk. Suppose your strategy were to bet everything on 7 red with a 40-slot roulette wheel. Now, the payoffs are a 1/40th chance of $6,000,000 (or 40 × $150,000) less $50,000 to repay the loan, for a net return of $5,950,000, and a 39/40th chance of $0. For this bet, the expected terminal cash position is $148,750, $5,950,000 × 1/40, and the expected profit increases to $48,750, $148,750 – $100,000. The bank is repaid only 1 time in 40. As a result, its expected dollar payoff is only $1,250 on a $50,000 investment (before considering interest). Of course, your expected profit (and the bank's expected loss) could be made arbitrarily close to $50,000 by increasing the actuarially fair risk further; for example, if your number comes up after the first spin, reinvest everything on another spin.

The limited personal liability provided by the bankruptcy laws encourages unsecured debtors to engage in riskier investments because they do not bear fully the cost of such risks. An unfortunate aspect of this incentive problem is that an unsecured borrower who definitely intends not to buy risky assets may have no cost-effective way of convincing the lender that this is the case.

One way to lessen the problem is for the borrower to establish a reputation for not taking strategic advantage of the lender (e.g., by building up a good credit history with the lender). Tax shelter syndicators and investment advisors are very aware of the benefits of establishing a reputation, as we will discuss later in this chapter. But the moral here is that information costs resulting from strategic uncertainty (hidden action) drive deeper the wedge between borrowing and lending rates.

No wonder lenders often write extensive covenants into loan agreements that restrict borrowers' behavior. But such covenants are costly to write because there are so many possible future contingencies, some of which cannot even be foreseen at the time of contracting. These covenants are also costly to monitor. As a result, they cannot completely prevent opportunistic behavior on the part of borrowers. Further, restrictive covenants can prove costly to borrowers by hindering their activities in costly ways.

Contracting in Labor Markets

Let us now consider employee compensation contracting in simple settings. We begin with a single-period setting where there are no hidden-action (moral hazard) problems—that is, the employer need not worry about the employee taking actions on the job that are unobservable to the employer and that may improve the employee's welfare at some expense to the employer. This will enable us to expose easily the nature of the identification problem that we discussed earlier.

Suppose that the employee is subject to a constant tax rate independent of compensation received. The employer, though, is subject to a progressive-income-tax-rate function. If profits are high, so is the tax rate. Although it might seem unusual that employees face constant tax rates and employers face progressive tax rates, this is not really so. Assume, for example, that the employees are highly paid executives whose marginal tax rates are constant and that the employer is a start-up venture with expenses that currently generate NOLs, but profits are expected in the future. In such a setting, the tax-minimizing contract is one that loads up on compensation to the employee when profits are high (in the future) and the tax deduction to the employer for compensation paid is worth the most. Similarly, compensation should be minimized when profits and tax rates for the employer are low (which they are at the present time).

In this compensation plan, the employee forgoes current income for future compensation that is tied to the firm's profits. Note how this contract looks like an incentive-based arrangement despite the absence of any incentive problems. This arrangement could arise due to tax motives, incentive motives, or both. This collection of possibilities is what we mean by an identification problem. Such problems make it difficult to untangle the reasons we observe various contractual arrangements. Without a rich understanding of the situation, outside observers could easily misinterpret the economics of the contractual arrangements.

Suppose the firm assigns a manager to undertake a risky project. The project yields a pretax profit, before employee compensation expense, of $400,000 half the time and –$100,000 half the time. As in our earlier example, the tax rate is 40% when taxable income is positive and 0% otherwise. This tax schedule applies to both the firm and its employee. Assume that both the employee and the firm's owners are risk neutral. The employee has job alternatives that pay the equivalent of $75,000 in salary. This means the firm must offer a compensation contract that matches the after-tax salary of $45,000, or $75,000(1 – .40), available elsewhere.

What sort of compensation contract should the firm offer the employee? Note that a $75,000 salary contract would not be efficient from a tax-planning standpoint. Why? Because half the time (when a loss is generated) the employer would obtain no tax benefit from the salary payment. It would be better to pay nothing when profits are negative and a bonus of $150,000 when profits are positive. Because each situation occurs half the time, the *expected* pay is $75,000, and this satisfies the compensation requirements of the employee.

The expected after-tax cost of this arrangement to the firm is $45,000, or .5($0) + .5 [$150,000(1 – .40)]. This is $15,000 less than the expected after-tax cost of a $75,000 salary contract. The savings result from avoiding a compensation payment of $75,000 when the tax rate is 0% rather than paying it when the tax rate is 40% (a tax difference of $30,000), which occurs half the time.

Conflicts between Risk-Sharing and Tax Minimization

Let us now suppose that the employee is averse toward risk and the employer is indifferent toward risk. Because the employee is willing to pay to avoid risk and the employer does not mind bearing risk, from a risk-sharing standpoint, offering the employee a pure wage contract, independent of the firm's profitability, is desirable. This would result in the employer bearing all the risk of profit uncertainty.

But if the employee faces a constant tax rate and the employer an increasing tax rate, a pure wage contract results in an increase in joint tax payments relative to the tax-minimizing contract (a bonus contract that shifts all the risk to the *employee*). So, the two parties will find it desirable neither to minimize taxes nor to shield the risk-averse party from all risk. Instead, they will trade off the two forces.

Conflicts between Incentive Contracting and Tax Minimization

Now, let us expand our compensation contracting problem by introducing *hidden-action* concerns and contracts that extend over several time periods. Tax rates will be allowed to vary over time, and the employer will be concerned with aligning employee incentives with the employer's interests.

In particular, suppose the employer's tax rate today is greater than it will be in the future. Such a tax-rate configuration favors immediate salary over deferred compensation: It is preferable to take tax deductions when the employer's tax rate is highest, which it is presently.[14] Further suppose that the employee faces the opposite tax-rate configuration—rates are low today and will be high in the future. This further reinforces the desirability of accelerating compensation payments: The employee recognizes taxable income when tax rates are low. Finally, suppose that the employee can earn at least as much on marginal investments after tax, as can the employer. This also favors current compensation because deferred compensation effectively results in the employer investing on the employee's behalf. So, the tax-minimizing contract is clearly one that "loads up" on current compensation.

But now suppose that the employee works for a firm in which a durable good is manufactured and where employer and employee interests conflict. In particular, assume that the employee can take one of two actions. Action 1 is working hard and leads to the product lasting W periods. Alternatively, the employee can take action 2, which is shirking, in which case the product lasts S periods, where S is less than W. The employee prefers action 2 to action 1, but the market value of increased product durability is assumed to exceed this personal cost difference. In other words, if the employer could observe the employee's actions, the employer would be willing to pay a bonus for hard work that more than compensates for the personal cost to the employee of the additional effort.

We also assume that bankruptcy constraints and labor laws prevent the employer from exacting a large penalty from the employee in the event the product is observed to last only S periods, revealing that the employee has shirked. Finally, assume that the employee's objective is to maximize lifetime consumption, where consumption tomorrow is almost as good as consumption today. Consumption takes place as the employee receives compensation.

Then, ignoring tax considerations, the efficient incentive arrangement entails deferring compensation to the employee until after the manufactured product has been observed to last more than S periods, revealing that the employee performed the more costly (and more valuable) action. But this is in direct conflict with the tax-minimizing contract, which would accelerate compensation to take advantage of the tax rates changing over time. The production efficiency gains from deferring compensation may be insufficient to compensate for the resulting additional tax payments, and in general, the two considerations must be traded off.

---

[14] Chapter 8 discusses the tax effects of compensation alternatives in more detail.

In our example, employer and the employee tax rates were such that immediate salary reduced taxes relative to deferred compensation. Suppose that the tax rates over time were reversed and that, for tax reasons alone, deferred compensation is the desired contract. To defer compensation with a deferred compensation contract, the employee must be an unsecured creditor of the employer. When the employee is an unsecured creditor, he or she will want to ensure that the firm remains solvent. This may result in the employee passing up positive net-present-value projects if they also increase the risk of the firm defaulting on the deferred compensation contract. As with previous examples, tax minimization may have to be sacrificed to align incentives properly.

7.3 TAX PLANNING IN THE PRESENCE OF HIDDEN-INFORMATION CONSIDERATIONS

The examples considered so far have illustrated how the organizational arrangements encouraged by focusing narrowly on tax minimization may conflict with those encouraged by risk-sharing or hidden-action considerations. We turn next to an example in which tax minimization may not be achievable because of hidden-information problems. The classic setting in which this arises is in the sale of an asset such as in the used car market. The seller is assumed to be better informed than the buyer about the quality or value of the asset being sold.

Suppose that a firm has generated large tax losses in past years and currently has NOL carryforwards that are about to expire unused or will not be used before tax rates drop. Suppose further that it is widely understood that if a profitable firm merges with our NOL firm, some taxes can be saved. (Chapters 11 and 13 discuss the tax restrictions on NOLs in mergers and acquisitions.) As noted, sellers of assets are often better informed than prospective buyers about the value of the assets. If the owners of the NOL firm know the firm is worth more than the expected value assessed by prospective buyers given their limited information, a mutually agreeable price at which to sell the firm may not exist. Stated a bit more formally, if high-value firms are unable to distinguish themselves in the marketplace from low-value firms, high-value firms may be forced to withdraw from the market unless the tax gains are large enough to offset the bargain sales price (for high-value firms) that clears the market.

Of course, the sale of a business does not represent the only means by which the owners of the NOL firm could cash in the wasting asset that NOL carryforwards represent. But, all the substitutes (including issuing stock, repurchasing debt, and effecting a sale and leaseback of depreciable assets, among many other candidates) incur nontrivial transaction costs. And such costs may overwhelm the tax benefits of restructuring. So, in a friction-filled world, the common occurrence of NOL carryforwards, which clearly does not indicate a tax-minimizing state of affairs, need not imply inefficient tax planning.

A related situation in which the taxpayer may rationally forgo tax benefits is the sale of a depreciable business asset to recognize an immediate tax loss at ordinary rates. In this case, the asset has declined in value by more than the accumulated tax depreciation to date. The alternative to selling the asset is to recognize the loss in the future through depreciation deductions, but in a present-value sense, this is undesirable unless tax rates are expected to increase significantly in the future. Or it might be desirable to sell an asset that has appreciated in value if the gain is taxed at favorable rates and the new buyer is permitted to depreciate the asset at ordinary tax rates based on the stepped-up (to market value) tax basis. In both cases, buyers and sellers may agree that they could gain by trading the asset. However, they may fail to reach mutually agreeable contractual terms when the seller is better informed than the buyer about the value of the asset.

General corporate-level tax avoidance can also present hidden-information issues because it is not clear what management's intent is when engaging in tax avoidance. For example, Desai and Dharmapala (2006) provided several examples of firms using aggressive tax planning techniques that also give rise to favorable accounting treatment. The authors presented a case where it is not clear whether the firm entered into the transaction for tax or earnings-management purposes (an identification problem). More generally, they argued that aggressive tax planning and tax shelters are structured to obfuscate the underlying transaction to make identifying and fully unraveling the transaction difficult for the Internal Revenue Service (IRS). Such complex transaction structuring could also obfuscate management's actions and obscure underlying firm performance in the financial statements, thus facilitating opportunism or even rent extraction by the management (a hidden-action problem). As such, investors and other outsiders might interpret the firm's participation in a tax shelter or any evidence of aggressive tax planning in a negative light (even though in a world without hidden-information problems, most shareholders would prefer managers act aggressively in saving taxes). As a result, it is not clear whether investors will react positively to news that firms are engaged in aggressive tax reporting.

In a separate study, Hanlon and Slemrod (2009) found that, on average, a firm's stock price declines when the market first learns of a firm's participation in a corporate tax shelter, suggesting investors view such participation as negative. However, such an interpretation is confounded with investors anticipating the firm will now be subject to increased taxes and penalties from the IRS as a result of the shelter. And in a study of previously undisclosed information about tax-planning activities, Frischmann, Shevlin, and Wilson (2008) examined the stock market reaction to the new disclosures of unrecognized tax benefits under FIN 48, "Accounting for Uncertainty in Income Taxes" (see later discussion). Although these unrecognized tax benefits are classified as liabilities, as argued by Frischmann, Shevlin, and Wilson, they likely overstate the liability and include tax benefits that will be realized. Prior to these disclosures, investors had little information about firms' tax positions, and these disclosures represent new information to the market about the firm's tax-planning aggressiveness. The market reacted positively to the disclosures, suggesting that the market views tax aggressiveness in a positive manner and/or investors revised downward their estimates of the firm's tax burden from the reported tax expense numbers.

7.4 TAX PLANNING AND ORGANIZATIONAL DESIGN

When a complex organization is composed of distinct legal entities, its left pocket is often taxed differently than its right pocket. Sources of differences in taxation across legal entities include multijurisdictional taxation, industry-specific taxation, and special rules relating to NOLs and tax credits. In the NOL and tax-credit cases, as discussed in Chapter 11, tax rules often limit the availability of these attributes (NOLs and tax credits) in offsetting the tax liability of any other entity in the consolidated group following a merger. Shifting income from one pocket to another may require considerable coordination, and tax rules often induce a greater degree of centralization of management than would otherwise be optimal. **Centralized management** is defined as top management making most of the decisions for the organization. Conversely, because centralization for tax-planning purposes may undermine the efficiency of **decentralized management** for nontax reasons, sacrificing tax benefits to achieve these other goals is often desirable.[15] Tax rules are not unique in affecting organizational design. Similar issues arise with respect to myriad legal rules and regulatory policies, such as trade laws and antitrust laws.

Related considerations arise in choosing between local and foreign suppliers of goods used in production. Suppose that local supply is more cost effective, ignoring taxes, than foreign supply (e.g., because of lower monitoring costs, lower coordination costs, and lower transportation costs). But vertical integration with a foreign supplier may enable the corporation to recognize profits in a tax jurisdiction where the tax rate is lower, perhaps through judicious transfer pricing (subject to the scrutiny of the taxing authority, as we discuss in greater depth in the chapters on multinational tax planning). Conversely, judicious transfer pricing for tax-planning purposes may pollute the planning and control features of a transfer pricing system in a decentralized firm, where important information is widely dispersed within the organization.

As we discussed earlier, firms facing progressive tax schedules have tax-based incentives to form limited partnerships and joint ventures. When the outside investors do not play an active role in the management of the firm—a necessary condition for limited partners to obtain limited liability protection—hidden-action problems arise:[16]

[15] If lower-level (or on-site) managers have information superior to upper-level (or off-site) managers about conditions facing the lower level, then allowing the lower-level managers to make decisions based on their superior information likely leads to better decisions. Allowing lower-level managers to make decisions is defined as decentralized management. See Phillips (2003) for an empirical analysis of how firms compensate business unit managers to motivate them to consider taxes in their decisions.

[16] See Wolfson (1985) for further discussion.

1. The provision and pricing of goods and services by the R&D or O&G firm to the limited partnership (resource allocation issues).
2. The R&D or O&G firm learning information relevant to other projects from the limited partnership funded activity (proving up).
3. All revenues or income arising from the R&D or O&G program not being fully measurable (payoff allocation and measurement).
4. The R&D or O&G firm continuing the limited partnership activity when it is no longer economically justified from the viewpoint of the partnership's investors, because the limited partners are funding the activity (overinvestment).
5. The R&D or O&G firm not exercising its option to exploit commercially the developed technology or O&G reserves (undercompletion).

We illustrate the undercompletion problem. If a limited partnership venture (or joint venture) is formed in response to the progressive tax schedules, then a desire to maximize the tax benefits has the limited partners funding the upfront investment so they can claim the upfront deductions at their high tax rates. This is called a functional allocation drilling program in the O&G area. The sponsoring firm acts as the general partner and is responsible for the completion costs that come after drilling takes place. After drilling, the well is either completed or abandoned. Moreover, the general partner alone knows the status of the drilled hole. The general partner often bears 100% of completion costs but gets less than 100% of any resulting revenues, which creates the undercompletion problem. For example, suppose the general partner takes limited partnership dollars to drill a well. The general partner looks down the hole and sees $2 worth of oil. Suppose it costs $1 to complete the well. If the general partner were a sole proprietor, the well would be completed (regardless of the number of limited partnership dollars spent in drilling because they are a sunk cost: It is profitable to spend $1 to recover $2). But suppose the general partner in the partnership is entitled to receive only 40% of any revenue (a typical sharing percentage in these programs). The general partner will spend $1 and receive only $.80 if the well is completed, so it is not in the general partner's best interest to complete the well, and there is a $1 opportunity loss from abandonment.

This incentive problem can be minimized by drilling *exploratory* wells, which are wells having a low probability of being marginal. In an exploratory well, there is a high probability that no oil will be found at all and a low probability that a lot of oil will be found (in other words, the probability of a marginal well is relatively low). By contrast, developmental drilling results in a relatively high fraction of marginal wells.

Incentive problems may also be reduced when part of the return to the general partner comes from establishing a reputation as a skillful or honest general partner. Wolfson (1985) provided empirical evidence consistent with functional allocation programs drilling a higher percentage of exploratory wells than other types of programs (e.g., balanced programs [50/50 exploratory developmental wells] and developmental programs), noting that reputation effects are priced in the marketplace: A good track record enables sponsors to charge a higher price for the right to buy into subsequent partnerships.

7.5 ACCOUNTING FOR INCOME TAX BASICS AND THE IMPORTANCE OF FINANCIAL ACCOUNTING OUTCOMES IN TAX PLANS

Another set of nontax costs arises when the results of tax planning bring about lower reported earnings to shareholders and other stakeholders in the firm. Whereas the issues just discussed apply to many tax-planning settings, the financial accounting aspect is likely relevant to a smaller number but very economically important set of companies—namely, publicly traded businesses, businesses with other capital market or creditor pressure with respect to performance, and firms that base compensation-plan rewards on financial accounting metrics. For this subset of companies (fewer in number but larger in capital commanded), we cannot overstate the importance of financial accounting outcomes of tax planning.

Although corporate taxpayers typically wish to report low levels of taxable income to the taxing authority, they often wish to report high levels of income to investors. There are numerous reasons why managers might be concerned about the numbers in their financial statements:

1. Compensation contracts for top managers are often based on accounting earnings.
2. Bond covenants written by lenders to curb conflicts of interest between the lender and the borrower are often based on accounting numbers such as debt-to-equity ratios, restrictions on dividends as a percent of retained earnings, current assets to current liabilities, and interest coverage, earnings before interest, or interest.
3. Analysts and investors use accounting numbers to price securities (both debt and equity), and managers might be concerned that reporting lower income could lead to lower stock prices and higher interest costs.
4. Regulators often use accounting numbers to monitor and regulate firms.
5. Lobbyists and other interested parties use accounting numbers to push for increased taxes and other penalties.
6. Large differences between book income and taxable income can lead to greater scrutiny and audit adjustments by tax authorities, such as the IRS.

There are three important aspects when considering how tax planning interacts with financial accounting. First, tax planning—for example, a tax plan that results in an additional deductible amount—could result in a financial accounting expense item if accounted for in the same manner for financial accounting purposes as for tax purposes. Thus, income before taxes would be lowered by the transaction entered into to save taxes. This is the case where firms are faced with a trade-off of tax benefits and financial reporting costs. Second, certain types of tax planning can hold financial accounting earnings constant but lower income tax expense. Generally, this means that pretax accounting income is not reduced by the transaction, but income tax expense is reduced, thus increasing after-tax accounting earnings. In this case, there is a financial accounting benefit in that income tax expense is lower and earnings per share is higher. Third, certain types of actions reduce taxes but have no effect on after-tax reported financial accounting income. We provide several examples of each type in the following sections.

An example of a transaction that leads to a book-tax trade-off is when a firm owns assets for which the market value is below book value for tax purposes. Loss recognition is available if the assets are sold, but this move would also typically require recognizing a financial reporting loss (although we acknowledge that the amount of loss likely differs because the tax basis likely differs from the accounting book value because of differences in depreciation schedules for tax and book purposes). Even if buyers and sellers agree completely on asset values, sellers might be concerned that the sale of such assets at a loss would increase their cost of capital by an amount exceeding the tax savings. Alternatively, managers whose compensation is tied to reported profitability might rationally forgo tax savings due to an inherent conflict of interest. In this latter case, the sacrifice of tax savings is due to a hidden-action problem. Shareholders might prefer that the manager sell assets to reduce taxes in this circumstance, but as outsiders, they may lack the requisite information to discipline the manager who chooses not to do so.

We note that a trade-off is not always required when evaluating the impact of a transaction on pretax accounting income and taxable income. Sometimes, the tax incentives and financial accounting incentives are aligned. For example, in setting up R&D limited partnerships discussed earlier in this chapter, the sponsor firm avoids having to issue debt and having to expense the R&D; avoiding these two actions results in lower leverage ratios and higher reported earnings. Thus, the limited partnerships are tax motivated, but they also obtain favorable accounting consequences via the limited partnership choice.

An example of the type of tax plan that requires no financial accounting cost (no trade-off) is the decision of a multinational corporation to locate operations overseas. International tax planning is covered in more detail in Chapter 10 and later in this chapter in our coverage of the accounting for income taxes. One incentive to locate operations offshore for U.S. multinational corporations is to have income reported in countries with tax rates lower than the U.S. tax rate. Prior to 2018, as long as the corporation did not repatriate those foreign earnings back to the United States, the earnings were not taxable in the United States, so operating in a foreign jurisdiction saved taxes. In addition, as discussed later in this chapter, under the financial accounting rules, companies can designate those earnings as indefinitely reinvested and not record the deferred tax liability for the future U.S. taxes that would be due on any future repatriation. Because of this exception to deferred tax accounting (ASC 740-30), the company has financial accounting incentives to operate offshore as well—the lower tax-expense recorded for financial accounting purposes results in higher reported financial accounting earnings. Indeed, in a recent survey of corporate tax executives, the financial accounting incentives for locating operations offshore were ranked with just as important as the tax rates in foreign countries (Graham, Hanlon, and Shevlin, 2011). As of 2018, U.S. firms with foreign operations and income with certain exceptions (i.e., income subject to U.S. tax currently via the GILTI and the BEAT code provisions, discussed in Chapter 10) do not face any incremental U.S. taxation when they repatriate the earnings back to the United States as a dividend. So, while there is much uncertainty around the exceptions, firms may continue to have incentives for both tax and financial accounting to continue to locate operations and report earnings in low foreign tax jurisdictions. That is, little book-tax trade-off likely continues.

An example of a tax benefit that does not affect after-tax earnings for accounting purposes is the temporary difference arising from accelerated depreciation and bonus depreciation deduction incentives. For tax purposes, the company will take accelerated depreciation (or immediate expensing), and for book purposes, the company often uses straight-line depreciation. The tax benefit is the tax savings early in the asset's life (the time value of money). As we discuss further later in the chapter, this temporary difference, while reducing current taxes payable, increases the deferred tax expense (i.e., the difference between book and tax is only temporary, and financial accounting does not account for the time value of money), leaving the total tax expense and after-tax net income for financial accounting unchanged.

When evaluating the tax and book incentives and consequences, it is important to remember that tax rules often differ from financial reporting rules, resulting in differences between taxable income and reported accounting income. These differences must be kept in mind in determining whether there are any financial reporting implications of any tax plan. We next explain the differences between book and taxable incomes and how these differences are reported for financial accounting purposes. We use Alphabet Inc. to exemplify corporate disclosures discussing what we know from academic research and anecdotes about the importance of financial accounting and the extent to which firms trade tax dollars for accounting earnings.

Accounting for Corporate Income Taxes—Rules and Disclosure Example

Publicly traded corporations face two separate sets of rules for tax and financial reporting, each with different purposes. As explained in Chapter 1, the tax code is the outcome of multiple, sometimes conflicting, objectives: Raise revenue to fund government activities, redistribute wealth, encourage (or discourage) certain economic activities, and as a macroeconomic policy tool to stimulate the overall economy. In contrast, the financial accounting rules used by corporations to report the results of their activities to shareholders and other interested parties have a different objective: Provide financial information useful to investors, lenders, and creditors in making decisions about providing resources to the firm.[17] We will refer to the financial accounting rules as book or generally accepted accounting principles (GAAP) and/or International Financial Reporting Standards (IFRS) to differentiate from the tax rules. The standard-setting body for U.S. GAAP is the Financial Accounting Standards Board (FASB), and the standard-setting body for IFRS is the International Accounting Standards Board (IASB).

We discuss the accounting for corporate income taxes because a knowledgeable reader can sometimes learn a great deal from the corporate income tax disclosures about the company's tax situation. Tax returns are not publicly available, and investors, analysts, tax planners, governmental agencies, and academics can use financial statements to address a variety of issues. Did the firm pay cash taxes in the current year? If not, why not, especially if it is reporting large profits to shareholders in its publicly released financial statements? Does it have an NOL carryforward? Does it expect to realize the future tax benefits of the NOL carryforwards, and so on? We can sometimes also learn about

[17] See Concepts Statement No. 8 Conceptual Framework for Financial Reporting—Chapter 1, *The Objective of General Purpose Financial Reporting*, and Chapter 3, *Qualitative Characteristics of Useful Financial Information* (a replacement of FASB Concepts Statements No. 1 and No. 2). Issued 2009.

the firm's tax-planning activities. However, meaningful interpretation of these disclosures requires knowledge about how the tax and book numbers differ and how the accounting disclosures are prepared.[18] The difference between book and taxable income has attracted much political, academic, and financial press attention over the years because of the suspected causes: a perceived explosion in corporate tax shelters in the 1990s (reducing taxable income but not book income), employee stock-option treatment that varies widely between book and tax prior to 2005, and from financial accounting scandals (e.g. Enron) in the early 2000s.

There are three primary financial accounting statements: the income statement, statement of cash flows, and balance sheet. The income statement presents a summary of the results of operations of the corporation for the period using **accrual accounting**. The summary measure of performance is referred to as net income (or more generally book income or GAAP earnings). The statement of cash flows provides a summary of the cash inflows and outflows for the period and explains the change in the balance of the corporate cash account from the start to the end of the period. The operating section of the statement of cash flows calculates the cash flows from operations and can be thought of as a cash-based measure of the operating performance of the firm in contrast to net income, which uses the accrual basis. Under a cash basis method, sales revenue is recognized when the cash is received and expenses are recognized when paid, whereas under the accrual basis, sales revenue can be recognized before the cash is received (a credit sale) provided the firm is reasonably confident of collection and expenses can be recognized in periods different than when the cash is paid (e.g., facilities rent might be paid in advance for the period). Cash flow from operations generally starts with net income calculated under the accrual system, then makes adjustments to derive the cash flow from operations. The balance sheet lists the assets, liabilities, and shareholders' equity of the corporation at the end of the accounting period.

Given the different objectives of the tax code and GAAP (or IFRS), the same transaction is often accounted for differently in calculating taxable income versus financial accounting income. To achieve the objectives of the tax system, the tax rules generally allow less choice and are closer to a cash basis system of realization than those in the accrual-based income statement measurement of net income.[19] The difference can be substantial. **Table 7.1** reports the U.S. pretax book income and estimated U.S. taxable income (estimated as described in Equation 7.4 below) for all firms (other than financial firms) on Compustat with available data (Compustat is an electronic database compiled by Standard and Poor containing current and past years' financial statement data for most publicly traded U.S. corporations). The tabled numbers are graphed in **Figure 7.2**. Although these are estimates of taxable income and must be interpreted with caution, we note a few interesting observations. First, in the mid-1980s, book exceeded taxable income, with the difference reduced after the Tax Reform Act of 1986 broadened the corporate tax base such that taxable income exceeded book income in the early 1990s. The early 1990s also reflects a major change in the book accounting for postretirement benefits, which moved to an accrual basis from the prior cash basis.[20] In the late 1990s, book income again exceeded taxable income with a maximum difference of $65 billion in 1999. This large difference motivated the Treasury Department's concern with corporate tax shelters (U.S. Department of Treasury, 1999).

In 2001, book income fell below taxable income. One hypothesized reason is that the tech bubble burst around that time, causing many firms to incur large write-offs for financial reporting purposes. Remember that because financial accounting is accrual based and conservative (meaning losses are recognized early), companies wrote off expected losses (e.g., plant closing, severance, restructuring, etc.) but for tax purposes, these losses could not be recognized until actually paid. A similar

[18] For a more detailed and technical discussion of the accounting for income taxes, see Revsine, Collins, Johnson, and Mittelstaedt (2012) and Knott and Rosenfeld (2003). For further discussion of limitations that restrict what can be learned from financial statements, see Hanlon (2003).

[19] The Internal Revenue Code (Section 446[a]) states, "Taxable income shall be computed under the method of accounting on the basis of which the taxpayer regularly computes his income in keeping his books." The code (446b) further states taxable income must "clearly reflect income." Thus, it appears as though taxable income and book income should be very similar; however, this is not the case.

[20] See "Employers' Accounting for Postretirement Benefits Other Than Pensions," Statement of Financial Accounting Standards No. 106, 1990. For example, General Motors recorded a $20.8 billion one-time book charge on the adoption of SFAS 106 in its 1992 fiscal year.

Table 7.1 U.S. Pretax Book Income and Estimated U.S. Taxable Income by Year from Compustat

Year	N	U.S. Pretax Book Income	U.S. Estimated Taxable Income	Difference
1980	2,831	$ 169,853	$ 70,650	$ 99,203
1981	2,853	$ 167,554	$ 64,006	$ 103,549
1982	2,959	$ 150,263	$ 40,935	$ 109,327
1983	3,161	$ 174,441	$ 62,042	$ 112,399
1984	3,229	$ 146,318	$ 77,921	$ 68,397
1985	3,244	$ 136,627	$ 74,486	$ 62,141
1986	3,522	$ 118,616	$ 61,128	$ 57,488
1987	3,277	$ 123,964	$ 109,717	$ 14,248
1988	3,250	$ 137,008	$ 144,239	$ (7,231)
1989	3,190	$ 128,180	$ 143,813	$ (15,633)
1990	3,243	$ 120,673	$ 135,637	$ (14,964)
1991	3,280	$ 79,253	$ 116,564	$ (37,311)
1992	3,427	$ 114,734	$ 127,314	$ (12,579)
1993	3,743	$ 134,563	$ 165,671	$ (31,109)
1994	3,932	$ 209,660	$ 207,299	$ 2,360
1995	4,157	$ 217,990	$ 206,890	$ 11,100
1996	4,771	$ 256,356	$ 234,244	$ 22,112
1997	4,735	$ 270,957	$ 257,572	$ 13,385
1998	4,540	$ 261,732	$ 237,675	$ 24,058
1999	4,708	$ 304,519	$ 273,657	$ 30,862
2000	4,492	$ 275,258	$ 269,404	$ 5,853
2001	4,222	$ (40,817)	$ 184,613	$ (225,430)
2002	3,950	$ 124,435	$ 116,245	$ 8,190
2003	3,816	$ 295,105	$ 149,531	$ 145,574
2004	3,746	$ 298,267	$ 251,782	$ 46,485
2005	3,609	$ 365,188	$ 371,106	$ (5,919)
2006	3,523	$ 452,352	$ 391,074	$ 61,279
2007	3,349	$ 405,509	$ 416,624	$ (11,116)
2008	3,200	$ 115,118	$ 329,592	$ (214,474)
2009	3,112	$ 342,184	$ 154,360	$ 187,824
2010	3,030	$ 420,439	$ 213,641	$ 206,798
2011	3,019	$ 468,436	$ 153,607	$ 314,830
2012	3,073	$ 427,988	$ 337,920	$ 90,068
2013	3,280	$ 525,700	$ 295,807	$ 229,893
2014	3,293	$ 543,565	$ 454,624	$ 88,940
2015	3,128	$ 334,869	$ 225,855	$ 109,014
2016	2,988	$ 419,614	$ 290,170	$ 129,443
2017	1,983	$ 400,944	$ 481,264	$ (80,320)
Total		$9,597,415	$7,898,680	$1,698,734

U.S. pretax book income as reported.

Estimated U.S. taxable income = (current U.S. tax expense/top U.S. corporate statutory tax rate) less the change in the NOL carryforward. Prior to 2005, both estimated taxable income and pretax book income excluded the effects of the employee stock option (ESO) tax deduction and ESO compensation expense. Post 2005, estimated taxable income and pretax book income include the tax effect of the book ESO compensation expense.

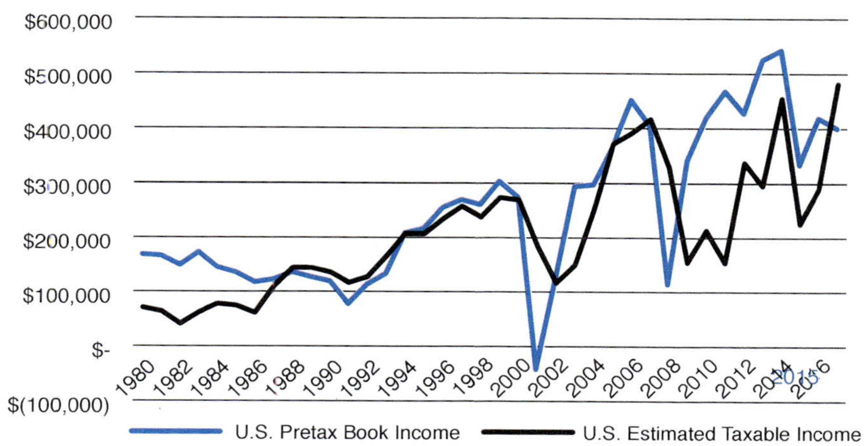

FIGURE 7.2 Plot of Total Pretax Book Income and Estimated Taxable Income

phenomenon can be observed with the financial crisis around the year 2008. Note that taxable income reveals similar declines as financial accounting but with a lag. This is likely for two reasons. First, expenses often cannot be deducted for tax purposes until paid; not accrued, as is true for accounting, as just discussed. So, some of the tax deductions occur later than the book expenses. Second, for tax purposes, firms can carry losses over, whereas for financial accounting, a loss in the current year is recorded and there is no carry over. Thus, for these two reasons, the tax losses are spread out over time, making the observed dips in the graph less severe for tax and occurring with a lag relative to financial accounting (although, again, we note that the taxable income is an estimate and may be overstated—e.g., due to stock options—or understated at times).

The differences between tax and book income can be partitioned into two major types:

- **Temporary differences**: The transaction is included in both sets of books (i.e., in calculating taxable and net income) but in different time periods (thus, these differences are sometimes also referred to as timing differences).
- **Permanent differences**: The transaction is included in one set of books (i.e., taxable or net income) but never the other.[21]

Examples of Temporary Differences

Some typical examples of temporary differences are summarized in **Table 7.2**. These examples assume we are dealing with a firm that uses the accrual method for accounting purposes and for tax purposes.[22] As we will see, however, there are some differences between the accrual method for tax and for accounting. Income is the difference between revenues and expenses. For book purposes, revenue is recognized (included in the calculation of book income) when the firm satisfies each performance obligation by transferring control of the promised goods or services to the customer. For tax purposes, revenue must be included in taxable income no later than when included in the firm's financial statements. However, in some cases, revenue is recognized earlier for tax purposes than for accounting purposes. For example, receiving cash in advance from customers will often trigger revenue recognition for tax purposes.

For book purposes, expenses are recognized in the period in which they can be matched to revenue (e.g., cost of goods sold and depreciation) or the period in which they are incurred (e.g., head office expenses and CEO salary), whereas, for tax purposes, an item cannot be deducted until it satisfies the "all events" test, which is all the events that determine the taxpayer's liability for the expense must have occurred, the amount must be determined with reasonable accuracy, and

[21] Current GAAP does not use the term *permanent difference*, but earlier statements did, and we continue to use the term as a convenient label for these types of differences.

[22] Whereas individuals are usually on the cash method for tax purposes, C corporations must use the accrual method for tax purposes if their average gross receipts exceed $25 million per year ($5 million pre-2017).

economic performance must have occurred—that is, the goods or services must have been provided to the taxpayer. Because of the all events test, expenses are often recognized in the books before they are deducted for tax purposes. For example, warranty expense, bad debt expense, loan losses, restructuring charges, and deferred compensation are generally expensed in book income on an accrual basis and deducted for tax purposes in a later period.

Another temporary difference is generated by NOL carryovers. Specifically, tax losses that cannot be carried back can be carried forward (currently, for 20 years). Recall that after 2017, tax losses must be carried forward with an indefinite carryforward period. These carryforwards will reduce taxable income in the future year when the loss is utilized. As a result, they create a future economic benefit (positive future cash flows from tax savings) and are classified in the period in which the loss is generated as a deferred tax asset for financial accounting purposes (the amount is equal to the loss carryforward times the expected tax rate in effect in the year the loss carryforward will be utilized). This is a temporary difference because taxable income will be lowered in the year the tax loss carryforward is used, but financial accounting income will not be lowered (there are no loss carryforwards for financial accounting purposes).

There are also significant differences between the accounting and tax treatments of certain acquisitions. We provide a terse discussion in **Table 7.2** and defer a more detailed discussion to Chapters 11–15.

Table 7.2 Typical Temporary Differences of Large Corporations

Item	Book Treatment	Tax Treatment
Depreciation	Method, useful life, and salvage value determined by management; generally, straight-line depreciation is used.	Property subject to Section 168 bonus depreciation can be fully expensed in the year of purchase.
Unearned revenue (cash received in advance)	Revenue deferred until firm satisfies the performance obligation by providing the good or service for which it has been paid	Deferral generally not allowed, thus, income recognized when cash received
Bad debts	Expense based on management's estimates of uncollectibles, recorded in same period as the credit sale giving rise to the accounts receivable	Deductible when specific receivable actually written off
Warranty expenses	Expense based on management's estimates of future warranty costs associated with current period's sales	Not deductible until meet all events test
Deferred compensation	Expensed when liability is incurred (when employee earns the deferred compensation) and based on actuarial assumptions	Deductible when counted as taxable income to the employee, usually when paid
Postretirement benefit obligations (other than pensions)	Expensed when liability is incurred (when employee earns the deferred compensation	Generally, not deductible until paid
Inventory valuation allowances	Application of lower of cost or market could result in write-downs	Reserves not allowed, generally loss recognized when inventory sold at lower price or written off
Prepaid expenses (rent, insurance)	Expensed when benefit received	Deductible when paid
Long-term construction contracts	Percentage of completion or completed contract allowed (income recognized at completion of contract)	Percentage of completion (income recognized during contract life); completed contract allowed in limited cases

continued

continued from previous page

<table>
<tr><th>Item</th><th>Book Treatment</th><th>Tax Treatment</th></tr>
<tr><td>Gain on installment sale (where customer promises to pay over a number of future periods)</td><td>Usually, gain recognized upon sale; installment method used (gain deferred until cash is received) when collection is highly uncertain</td><td>Installment method defers gain until cash received. Some types of sales cannot use installment treatment (e.g., sales of inventory)</td></tr>
<tr><td>Intangible assets—goodwill</td><td colspan="2">In an acquisition where the acquirer gets a step-up in the basis of the target's assets, goodwill, if it exists, is recorded for both book and tax purposes. In this case, goodwill is amortized over 15 years for tax purposes (Sec. 197) but is not amortized for book purposes and is instead subject to impairment testing (Accounting Standards Codification ASC 350). In this case, a deferred tax liability is created as the asset is amortized for tax purposes which will be reversed if the goodwill is ever impaired.

In an acquisition where the acquirer does not get a step-up in the basis of the target's assets, goodwill, if it exists, is recorded for financial accounting purposes but is not recorded for tax purposes. In this case, the goodwill for financial accounting purposes is subject to impairment testing, and if impaired, the impairment is a permanent book-tax difference.</td></tr>
<tr><td>Intangible assets—purchased in-process R&D (IPR&D)</td><td colspan="2">For accounting purposes, ASC 805 requires capitalization of IPR&D at its acquisition date fair value. It is accounted for initially as an indefinite-lived intangible asset (i.e., not subject to amortization).

Post-acquisition acquired IPR&D is subject to impairment testing until the completion or abandonment of the associated R&D efforts. If abandoned, the carrying value of the IPR&D asset is expensed. If the R&D efforts are completed, the carrying value of the acquired IPR&D is reclassified as a finite-lived asset and amortized over its useful life. (Prior to 2008, all acquired IPR&D was expensed at the time of the acquisition).

For tax purposes, the treatment depends on whether the transaction is one that receives a step-up in the basis of the target company assets or not (see Chapter 11) . If there is a tax basis step-up, then there is an asset for tax purposes and the amortization period is 15 years under Section 197 (a 15-year amortization period exists for all Section 197 intangibles). If the target asset bases are not stepped up, then for tax purposes, no purchased in-process R&D is recorded as an asset on the date of the acquisition.

Consider the case where the IPR&D project is completed and recorded as a finite-lived asset for financial accounting purposes. If the purchaser records a step-up in target asset bases for tax purposes, a temporary difference (deferred tax asset) is created and reversed as the asset is amortized over its life in the two sets of books (the book life is generally shorter than the tax life). If the deal is one where the purchaser does not record a step-up in basis for tax purposes, a deferred tax liability exists that is reversed as the asset is amortized for financial accounting purposes.</td></tr>
</table>

Examples of Permanent Differences

A permanent difference is an item that is recorded in one set of books but never recorded in the other set (i.e., there is no future reversal of the book-tax difference). The classic example of a permanent difference is the interest on tax-exempt municipal bonds. The interest is included in book income and excluded from taxable income. Another example is expenses for meals and entertainment. Such expenses are only partially or not deductible for tax purposes and fully expensed for financial accounting purposes. Another, more complicated, example is the dividends received deduction (DRD), discussed in Chapter 6. The DRD is a deduction for tax purposes that is part of tax policy in order to avoid multiple levels of taxation on dividends between domestic corporations. The DRD allows corporations to exclude from their taxable income a percentage of dividend income received on their holdings of stock in other corporations (this is discussed in more detail in Chapter 6). The DRD and the financial accounting rules both operate to include differing levels of dividends or income from investee companies based on the level of ownership the investing company owns. Let's take the simplest case, where the investor company owns less than 20% of the investee. In such a case, the investor will receive a DRD of 50% of the dividends received for tax purposes (so, 50% of the dividend is included in taxable income). However, for financial accounting purposes, the dividends received by the investor company are fully included in financial accounting income. Therefore, in this case, 50% of the dividends received is a permanent book-tax difference because the income is included in financial accounting earnings and never included in the taxable income of the investor company.[23] Another permanent difference is the domestic production activities deduction introduced in the Tax Act of 2004 effective for tax years 2005–2017. This deduction was introduced to encourage firms to produce goods and services in the United States, and income generated from these domestic activities were subjected to a lower tax rate (by allowing a maximum 9% deduction in taxable income arising from domestic activities, resulting in a reduced statutory tax rate of $.35 \times .91 = .3185$, or 31.85%, on this income). The full amount of the income is included in book earnings, but less than the full amount is included in tax income—thus, a permanent difference. The 2017 Tax Act removed this deduction.

Another item that decreases a firm's effective tax rate, and thus might be classified as a permanent difference, is excess tax benefits from stock compensation. As discussed more in Chapter 8, FASB changed the accounting for excess tax benefits of stock compensation—that is, when the tax deduction exceeds the compensation accrued in the accounting books. Firms do not change the recognized compensation expense in the accounting books but reduce their tax expense for the excess tax benefits (reducing their effective tax rates). Prior to this change, the excess tax benefits were directly credited to additional paid-in capital, bypassing the income statement.

Other permanent differences include some fines and penalties and excess nonperformance-based compensation (Section 162[m] discussed in Chapter 8). A final example is the treatment of life insurance premiums and proceeds. Life insurance premiums are not deductible for tax purposes but are expensed for book purposes. In addition, life insurance death benefits are included in book income but excluded from taxable income.

Interpreting Income Tax Expense Disclosures

The accounting for income taxes is set out in FASB's ASC 740 tax provisions. Here, we present a somewhat simplified discussion that takes an income statement approach, which for many readers and users of financial statements is more intuitive than the balance sheet approach in ASC 740. The income tax expense reported on the corporate income statement reflects the application of accrual accounting. For expositional purposes, we ignore some complexity here so as not to overburden the reader, and we can think of total tax expense as being equal to

$$\text{Total income tax expense} = (\text{Pretax book income} +/- \text{Permanent differences}) \times \text{Corporate statutory tax rate (STR)} \quad (7.1)$$

Total income tax expense is also referred to as the provision for income taxes. The total income tax expense is composed of two parts:

$$\text{Total tax expense} = \text{Current tax expense} + \text{Deferred tax expense} \quad (7.2)$$

where current tax expense is an estimate of the current taxes due on the firm's taxable income for the period (adjusted by some accounting accruals we discuss later) and deferred tax expense is the tax expense accrued due to temporary differences. In other words, the deferred tax expense is an estimate of the future tax effects arising from items included in the two sets of books at different time periods. Specifically,

[23] Ownership percentages greater than 20% lead to more complicated accounting. For example, ownership interests between 20% and 50% are accounted for using the equity method of accounting, where the proportional share of the investee company's income is included in the investing company's accounting income. For tax purposes, however, the incomes of the two entities are not combined. However, when the investee company pays a dividend to the investing company, the DRD is 65% for this ownership range. When ownership reaches 80% or greater, the DRD for tax purposes is 100%, but the two entities are allowed to be consolidated for tax purposes. For financial accounting, entities owned greater than 50% are consolidated with the investing company.

$$\textbf{Current tax expense} = \textbf{Taxable income} \times \textbf{STR (–Tax credits and +/– Accruals discussed later)} \quad (7.3)$$

To derive a very rough estimate of the firm's current period taxable income from publicly available reports we can rearrange Equation 7.3 to

$$\textbf{Estimated taxable income} = \textbf{Current tax expense/STR} \quad (7.4)$$

This calculation is only an estimate for multiple reasons. First, an important item that makes this equation incorrect, the accrual for contingent tax reserve for unrecognized tax benefits (discussed below), is difficult to adjust for.[24] Second, in our estimations, we use the U.S. statutory tax rate as the applicable tax rate, which ignores state and foreign taxes. Because companies are increasingly global and report substantial earnings from non-U.S. locations, and because foreign statutory corporate tax rates are generally lower than U.S. corporate tax rates (the U.S. rate was almost 10 percentage points higher than the average corporate tax rate in 2011 for countries in the Organization for Economic Cooperation and Development), severe missestimation can occur by using the U.S. rate. For example, assume that a company reports $10,000 of worldwide current tax expense. If we divide by .21, the U.S. statutory tax rate, we obtain an estimate of taxable income of $47,619. However, what if most of its income is earned in Ireland, where the corporate tax rate is 12.5%? The actual total would be $80,000, or $10,000/.125, a much higher number. The difficulty is that companies do not disclose exactly in which countries their earnings are earned and gathering statutory tax rates by country is not a trivial task (not to mention whether the company is actually subject to the statutory rate or instead granted a tax holiday). Thus, although we continue to use the U.S. statutory tax rate here, mostly because we do not have an easy place to refer readers for various rates across the world and cannot obtain company earnings by country, we caution the reader that if a company's earnings are earned to a large extent in foreign jurisdictions, be cautious in using (and possibly avoid using) such estimations.

Deferred tax expense or benefit can be calculated as the sum of temporary differences between pretax book income and taxable income times the statutory tax rate:[25]

$$\textbf{Deferred tax expense (benefit)} = \textbf{Temporary differences} \times \textbf{STR} \quad (7.5)$$

Example Illustrating Corporate Income Tax Disclosures

A simple numerical example illustrates the concepts just discussed. Suppose the following as facts:

Sales	$1,000
Cost of goods sold	–400
R&D	–200
Depreciation—book	–120
Interest expense	–100
Municipal bond interest income	+50
Pretax book income	230

Other information:

[24] Note also that the firm's tax liability (taxable income × str) is reduced by any tax credits (which are a dollar-for-dollar reduction in the tax liability). We ignore the effects of tax credits here.

[25] This presentation is for expositional purposes. Technically, the deferred tax expense for a period is based on a firm's tax and financial accounting balance sheets. Specifically, deferred tax expense is the change from the beginning to the end of period in the difference in the tax basis of the firms' net assets and their book basis (e.g., the difference in the accumulated depreciation of an asset for book versus tax purposes).

- The corporate statutory tax rate, STR, is 21%.
- Depreciation for tax purposes is $200.
- Municipal bond interest income is tax exempt.

In simple examples like this, total income tax expense can be computed as follows:

= (pretax book income − permanent differences) × corporate STR
= (230 − municipal bond interest which is tax exempt) × .21
= (230 − 50) × .21
= $37.80

More formally, total tax expense is the sum of current and deferred tax expense as per Equation 7.2. Current tax expense is calculated as taxable income × STR per Equation 7.3. Taxable income in this example is as follows:

Sales	$1000
Cost of goods sold	-400
R&D	-200
Depreciation—tax	-200
Interest expense	-100
Taxable income	100

Therefore, the current tax expense is $100 times .21, or $21.

Deferred tax expense (benefit) = temporary differences × STR as per Equation 7.5. The only temporary difference in this example is the differing amount of depreciation recognized for book versus tax in this period. Thus, deferred tax expense (benefit)

= (Tax depreciation less book depreciation) × STR
= (200 − 120) × .21
= 80 × .21
= $16.80

As noted in Equation 7.2, the sum of current and deferred tax expense equals total tax expense:

$21 + $16.80 = $37.80

An alternative way to estimate taxable income is

Pretax book income +/– Temporary differences +/– Permanent differences
= 230 – 80 – 50 = $100 (7.6)

ASC 740 requires firms to provide reasonably detailed disclosures about the income tax expense, and financial statement users with a reasonable understanding of the accounting for income taxes can sometimes learn much from the disclosures. Firms are required to explain (via a rate reconciliation) why the firm's effective tax rate, defined under GAAP as total tax expense/pretax book income, differs from the top U.S. corporate statutory tax rate (now 21%). Reference to Equation 7.1 shows that, generally, differences are due to the effects of permanent differences and not temporary differences:

Total income tax expense = (Pretax book income +/– Permanent differences) × STR **(Equation 7.1)**

Other items that can affect the rate reconciliation but that are not technically permanent differences include (1) income earned in lower-tax jurisdictions for which ASC 740-30 (formerly APB 23) is applied (discussed in Chapter 10) or income earned in higher-tax jurisdictions, (2) the effects of additional state taxes the company must pay over and above the U.S. federal tax rate, and (3) the effects of tax credits (e.g., R&D tax credit) that reduce the tax actually owed but do not affect book or taxable incomes.

In our simple example, the only permanent difference is the $50 of tax-exempt municipal bond interest. Firms present the reconciliation either in percentage terms or in tax-effect dollar terms. In our example, the $50 of tax-exempt municipal bond interest reduces the firm's effective tax rate by 4.6 percentage points, from 21% to 16.4%, or, if presented in dollar terms, reduced income taxes in the amount of $10.50.

	%	$
Top statutory tax rate	21	.21 × 230 = $48.30
Municipal bond interest	4.6	.21 × 50 = $10.50
Effective tax rate (37.80/230)	16.4	$37.80

Permanent differences that cause book income to exceed taxable income (e.g., tax-exempt municipal bond interest) result in an effective tax rate lower than the top U.S. statutory tax rate. Permanent differences that cause book income to be lower than taxable income (e.g., nondeductible fines, meals and entertainment expenses, or the impairment of financial accounting goodwill) result in an effective tax rate higher than the top statutory tax rate. The level of detail in financial statement disclosures varies across companies, limiting what we might learn. Not surprisingly, firms have incentives to mask their use of corporate tax shelters, and we might expect the ideal tax shelter (reduced taxable income with no effect on book income in the current or future periods—a permanent difference) to show up in the effective tax-rate reconciliation. An examination of the tax-rate reconciliation of firms named by the financial press and Treasury as having entered into tax shelters often fails to provide evidence of such tax-shelter activity.

Temporary differences give rise to either future tax liabilities or future tax deductions. Future tax deductions save future taxes and are referred to as deferred tax assets, whereas future tax liabilities are referred to as deferred tax liabilities because they represent future tax payments. (Note that because permanent differences do not give rise to either future liabilities or future tax deductions, they do not give rise to deferred tax liabilities or assets.) In our simple example, if this were the first year of operations, the deferred tax assets and liabilities at the start of the period would be zero, and at the end of the period would be the difference between the book and tax basis of the depreciable asset times the statutory tax rate. If we assume the firm paid $1,000 for the asset, the tax basis at the end of the period is $1,000 less accumulated tax depreciation of $200 = $800; the book basis is $1,000 less accumulated book depreciation of $120 = $880. The difference in the book and tax basis of the asset is $80 and represents future book depreciation, which has already been deducted for tax purposes—a temporary difference that will reverse in the future when book depreciation on the asset exceeds tax depreciation. Thus, in the current period, pretax book income exceeds taxable income but taxable income will be higher in some future periods, resulting in a higher tax liability. Therefore, the depreciation temporary difference gives rise to a future tax liability relative to future book income, which is shown as a deferred tax liability in the accounting books. The deferred tax liability is $80 × .21 = $16.80. In this example, the change in the deferred tax liability is $16.80 and we have no deferred tax assets, so the total change in the deferred tax assets and liabilities is $16.80, which equals the deferred tax expense calculated in Equation 7.5.[26]

Under ASC 740, firms are required to present a summary of their deferred tax assets and deferred tax liabilities (see Alphabet Inc. disclosure later in this chapter). However, the level of detail and hence the usefulness of the disclosures varies across companies. Furthermore, firm-specific data are not compiled anywhere in machine-readable form. Poterba, Rao, and Siedman (2011) hand collected these data for 73 firms over the period 1993 to 2004. The authors documented that the largest components of deferred tax assets were loss and credit carryforwards and employment and post-employment benefits (recall the expense is recognized in the books before the tax deduction sometime in the future). The largest components of deferred tax liabilities, not surprisingly, were property, plant, and

[26] Thus, in our simple example, total tax expense can also be written as = current taxes payable plus (increase in deferred tax liabilities and decrease in deferred tax assets) less (decrease in deferred tax liability and increase in deferred tax asset). Note also if the asset acquired for $1,000 was eligible for immediate expensing under the TCJA, the difference in the book and tax basis would be $880, or ($1,000 – $120) – $0), with a much larger deferred tax liability of $880 × .21 = $184.80.

equipment (arising from different depreciation schedules for book and tax, with more accelerated depreciation for tax), and leases. In 2004, for the 25 firms reporting net deferred tax assets, the aggregate net deferred tax asset was $61.9 billion; for the 48 firms reporting net deferred tax liabilities, the aggregate amount of liabilities was $223.8 billion. In 1993, approximately 50% of the firms reported net deferred tax assets, with this percentage declining to 34% in 2004.[27]

When a firm has deferred tax assets on its balance sheet, it is required to assess whether those assets are overvalued for the reporting period (similar to the accounting for many other assets— lower of cost or market for inventory, impairment tests for long-term tangible assets and goodwill, accounts receivable valued net of the bad debt reserve, etc.). For the deferred tax asset account, the company is required to assess whether future taxable income will be sufficient to realize the tax savings represented by the deferred tax asset—that is, whether the deferred tax asset will be utilized. If the firm believes it is more likely than not that some portion of the deferred tax asset will not be utilized, it must establish a valuation allowance reserve (accrual) against the deferred tax asset. For example, consider a company with deferred tax assets arising from past and current tax losses, where management does not expect the company will generate sufficient taxable income to be able to use the losses. In this case, a valuation allowance must be established to net against the deferred tax asset so the net asset is not overvalued on the balance sheet. Because the valuation allowance reduces the net book value of the deferred tax asset at the end of the period, the change in the net deferred tax asset is reduced, which affects the deferred tax expense component of the tax-expense number on the income statement. That is, the deferred tax benefit of the deferred tax asset is reduced, resulting in an otherwise higher tax expense and lower reported book income (because the tax benefits are not recognized this period).[28]

The previous discussion focuses on U.S. federal income taxes. U.S. corporations also pay state income taxes, which are deductible at the federal level. In addition, many large corporations also have foreign operations on which they pay taxes to foreign tax jurisdictions. Detailed discussion of the taxation of foreign operations is deferred until Chapter 10. Further, most large public corporations are organized as a parent corporation with divisions or segments of the business organized into wholly or partially owned subsidiaries. The tax and book rules differ on consolidation of subsidiaries—for tax purposes, firms can elect to consolidate U.S. subsidiaries if they own at least 80% of the stock of the subsidiary. U.S. firms do not consolidate their foreign subsidiaries for tax purposes even if wholly owned. For financial reporting purposes, U.S. firms consolidate domestic and foreign subsidiaries if they have control over the assets and operations of the subsidiaries. One criteria to assess control is the extent of ownership, and 50% ownership is often used as a cutoff to determine whether to consolidate a subsidiary for financial reporting purposes. Under ASC 740, firms are required to disclose, if material, both current and deferred tax expense partitioned into U.S., state, local, and foreign portions. Because of the differing consolidation rules, the reported tax expense and any resulting estimate of taxable income are only for the entities included in the consolidated financial reporting entity.[29]

---

[27] Gaertner, Laplante, and Lynch (2016) used aggregate-level IRS data to provide descriptive evidence on the major differences between taxable income and reported net income over the period 2004 to 2013. These data are from the M-3 schedule corporations file with the IRS as part of the tax return. The largest positive temporary components—items increasing book income relative to taxable income—not surprisingly are depreciation, gains from disposal of fixed assets, and other amortization or impairment write-offs. The largest negative temporary components—items reducing book income relative to taxable income—are bad debt expense and other amortization/impairment write-offs. With respect to permanent differences, the largest positive items are equity method earnings and dividends not eliminated in tax consolidation, and the largest negative items are gross foreign dividends not previously taxed (repatriations, see Chapter 10), and amortization/impairment of goodwill that arises from impairment of assets in the accounting books from prior nontaxable acquisitions (i.e., acquisitions in which there is no step-up in tax basis thus no goodwill for tax purposes).

[28] An increase in the valuation allowance decreases the deferred tax benefit, increasing total tax expense and thus reducing book income. By similar reasoning, a decrease in the valuation allowance increases book income. Because determining the valuation allowance is subjective, management has the ability to manage reported book income via the valuation allowance. However, Miller and Skinner (1998) found little evidence of firms managing reported book income via the valuation allowance. Consistent with these results, Dhaliwal, Kaplan, Laux, and Weisbrod (2013) and Edwards (2018) showed that the creation of the valuation allowance or reduction in existing valuation allowance is informative about future earnings and future creditworthiness of the firm. The reduction in a prior valuation allowance signals managers' expectation of an increase in reported earnings in future periods.

[29] There are several other points we should note. First, the total tax expense relates only to income from continuing operations. Items reported below this line item on the income statement are usually reported net of their specific tax effects (which tax effects are sometimes specifically disclosed). Second, because publicly traded corporations file their financial statements with the Securities and Exchange Commission before preparing and filing their tax returns with the IRS, the current tax expense is actually an estimate of the actual tax liability.

FIN 48 Accounting for Uncertain Tax Benefits

In July 2006, the FASB issued new rules on accounting for uncertain tax positions: "Accounting for Uncertainty in Income Taxes," FASB Interpretation No. 48, 2006 (FIN 48), now a part of ASC 740. Firms often take positions on their tax returns that might be challenged and overturned by taxing authorities. For example, is a tax-free spinoff or reorganization really tax free? Do all costs the firm included in the R&D tax credit calculation qualify? Are all claimed deductions allowed? Are all the transfer pricing arrangements used by the firm allowed by the tax authority? Is the decision not to file a tax return in some jurisdiction the right decision? These items are uncertain tax positions because the taxpayer is not certain he or she will get to retain the tax savings from the positions. How should we account in the firm's financial statements for tax benefits that are uncertain?

Prior to FIN 48, firms generally applied SFAS 5 Accounting for Contingencies (ASC 450), which governs the accounting for loss contingencies—losses are accrued (recognized) if the loss is probable and reasonably estimable. Different firms applied SFAS 5 differently, and very few firms disclosed the actual amount of the uncertain tax benefits. Thus, the FASB issued FIN 48 with the objective of bringing consistency and transparency to the accounting for uncertain tax benefits.

FIN 48 requires a two-step approach to the accounting for uncertain tax benefits. The first step, recognition, requires the firm to identify the uncertain tax position and then determine whether it is more likely than not the tax position will be sustained upon examination. (i.e., an audit). "More likely than not" is interpreted to mean a greater than 50% probability that the tax position will be upheld. The more-likely-than-not assessment is based solely on the technical merits of the position. The firm is to assume that the position will be examined by the appropriate taxing authority and the tax authority has full knowledge of all relevant information about the tax position. Previously, firms incorporated the probability of audit into their estimates of the expected tax benefits. If a tax position fails the more-likely-than-not test, the firm must establish a tax liability for 100% of the benefit. If a tax position passes the test, the company must measure the effect of the position. Thus, the second step of FIN 48 is measurement—how much of the tax benefit can be recognized in the financial statements (usually by a reduction in the income tax expense number on the income statement, increasing reported earnings). The amount of the tax benefit that is *not* recognized, the unrecognized tax benefit, is reported as a liability.

Under FIN 48, if a firm estimates that it has an unrecognized tax benefit, it credits a liability account and debits (increasing) the tax expense account, reducing reported earnings. If the liability is expected to be settled by payment of taxes within 1 year, it is classified as a current liability; otherwise, it is classified as a noncurrent liability, separate from the normal deferred tax liability, unless the unrecognized tax benefit arises from a taxable temporary difference (i.e., the IRS might dispute the period in which the revenue or deduction is taken).

FIN 48 is effective for all firms that follow U.S. GAAP. Zion and Varshney (2007) studied 361 firms when FIN 48 was adopted and found that the companies disclosed a total of $141 billion in unrecognized tax benefits. Based on data from 2007 to 2011, the average amount of the unrecognized tax liability was 1.1% of firm assets for a sample of almost 9,000 firm years (Hanlon, Maydew, and Saavedra, 2017). In addition to the unrecognized tax benefit (aka liability), the firm may have to accrue interest and penalties, if applicable, on its FIN 48 liability.

FIN 48 requires extensive disclosures (per paragraph 21) at the end of each annual reporting period:

> *a.* A tabular reconciliation of the total amounts of unrecognized tax benefits at the beginning and end of the period, which shall include at a minimum:
>
> 1. The gross amounts of the increases and decreases in unrecognized tax benefits as a result of tax positions taken during a prior period
> 2. The gross amounts of increases and decreases in unrecognized tax benefits as a result of tax positions taken during the current period
> 3. The amounts of decreases in the unrecognized tax benefits relating to settlements with taxing authorities

continued

continued from previous page

4. Reductions to unrecognized tax benefits as a result of a lapse of the applicable statute of limitations

b. The total amount of unrecognized tax benefits that, if recognized, would affect the effective tax rate

c. The total amounts of interest and penalties recognized in the statement of operations and the total amounts of interest and penalties recognized in the statement of financial position

d. For positions for which it is reasonably possible that the total amounts of unrecognized tax benefits will significantly increase or decrease within 12 months of the reporting date:

1. The nature of the uncertainty
2. The nature of the event that could occur in the next 12 months that would cause the change
3. An estimate of the range of the reasonably possible change or a statement that an estimate of the range cannot be made

e. A description of tax years that remain subject to examination by major tax jurisdictions

Item *b.* of the required disclosures is the total amount of unrecognized tax benefits (UTB) that, if recognized, would affect the effective tax rate (paragraph 21 item b). The UTB liability reflects two types of tax positions: uncertainty over whether the period in which an item is deductible or taxable, or timing difference, and uncertainty over whether a deduction is allowed or whether some income is taxable, or permanent differences. Audit adjustments for timing differences will affect the UTB but will have no effect on the total income tax expense (because the tax benefit amount is already reflected in income tax expense) or the effective tax rate. On the other hand, recognition of a UTB arising from the second type of tax position (uncertainty over whether a deduction is allowed or whether some income is taxable) will affect (decrease) the effective tax rate. For example, many pharmaceutical firms are heavy users of the R&D tax credit, which, if allowed, will reduce a firm's effective tax rate (because it is a credit).

When FIN 48 was enacted, many commentators thought these disclosures would provide a great deal of information to the tax authorities—a roadmap to tax positions that the tax authorities could challenge. However, evidence suggests otherwise, and in 2010, the IRS introduced a separate schedule for tax-filing purposes, Schedule UTP, for uncertain tax positions, which required firms to explain each of the major items comprising the UTB disclosed in the firm's financial statements.

In summary, the required corporate income tax disclosures include the current and deferred portions of the tax expense, broken down into the U.S., state, and foreign portions; a list of deferred tax assets and deferred tax liabilities; a reconciliation of the tax computed at the federal rate on pretax book income to the firm's GAAP effective tax rate; and detailed disclosures about the firm's unrecognized tax benefits (or its uncertain tax positions). Using these disclosures, the astute financial statement reader can do the following:

1. Estimate current taxable income from the disclosure of current tax expense.
2. Infer the firm's major temporary differences.
3. Infer the firm's major permanent differences.
4. Understand the potential liability the firm has related to unrecognized tax benefits.
5. Readily see how much of the firm's earnings are earned overseas.

Knowledge of the information in the tax note in the financial statements can help the external reader assess, to some extent, what major tax-favored activities the firm is entering into as reflected in the permanent and temporary differences because these differences often arise from tax-favored treatment under U.S. tax code. With the addition of the unrecognized tax-benefit disclosures, one can also assess how aggressive the firm is in its tax planning—larger reported UTBs generally suggest more aggressive tax planning. In addition, the information in the tax note provides some information about why a company's taxable income differs from its financial accounting income. Book-tax differences, especially the temporary differences, can also be used to infer how aggressive the firm might be in its accrual accounting choices in calculating net income.[30]

Example of Actual Corporate Disclosure

Pages 7-32 to 7-37 contain extracts from the *Alphabet Inc. 2017 Annual Report* for its fiscal year ending in December. Per GAAP, the 2017 income statement presents 3 years of results for comparison purposes. Alphabet reports pretax book income (labeled as "Income before income taxes") of $27,193 (all amounts are in millions) in 2017, up from $24,150 in 2016. The total tax expense (labeled "Provision for income taxes") is $14,531 for 2017 and $4,672 for 2016. These numbers imply a GAAP effective tax rate as follows:

	2015	2016	2017
Provision for income taxes	$ 3,303	$ 4,672	$14,531
Income before income taxes	$19,651	$24,150	$27,193
GAAP effective tax rate	16.8%	19.3%	53.4%

The income tax note disclosures (note 14 in the report) partitions the total tax expense in 2017 into a current tax expense of $14,354 and a deferred tax expense of $177, resulting in the total tax expense of $14,531 reported on the income statement.

The income tax note also discloses the U.S. and international components of "Income before taxes." In 2017, $10.7 billion is from domestic operations and $16.5 billion from foreign operations, which totals the $27.2 billion reported on the income statement: Nearly 61% of Alphabet's earnings are from foreign operations. The note also partitions current and deferred taxes into "Federal and State" and "Foreign." Thus, we can calculate a GAAP effective tax rate for domestic and foreign operations.

U.S. Domestic	2015	2016	2017
Total income taxes (current and deferred)	$ 2.597	$ 3.756	$12.828
Domestic income before income taxes	$ 8.3	$12.0	$10.7
GAAP effective tax rate	31.3%	31.3%	119.9%

Foreign	2015	2016	2017
Total income taxes (current and deferred)	$ 0.706	$ 0.913	$ 1.703
Foreign income before income taxes	$11.4	$12.1	$16.5
GAAP effective tax rate	6.2%	7.6%	10.3%

In 2015 and 2016, the U.S. domestic GAAP effective tax rate is close to the top statutory tax rate of 35%. However, in 2017, the US. domestic GAAP effective tax rate increases to 120%! The foreign effective tax rate is much lower, varying between 6% and 10%. This low rate indicates why many U.S. multinational companies locate some operations overseas in lower-tax-rate jurisdictions. This location choice is discussed in more detail in Chapter 10 and illustrates tax planning discussed in Chapter 2: shifting income from one pocket (the high-tax pocket in the United States) to another (the low-tax pocket overseas).

Alphabet presents an explanation of why the GAAP effective tax rate differs from the top U.S. statutory tax rate. Recall that the explanation takes the form of a tax-rate reconciliation and arises

[30] For example, see Phillips, Pincus, and Olhoft Rego (2003), who examined the ability to detect earnings management behavior by firms from deferred tax expense, and Hanlon (2005), who examined whether large temporary differences indicate less persistent net income arising from short-term earnings management.

from permanent differences and the other items discussed above that affect the GAAP effective tax rate. The schedule is reproduced below.

The reconciliation of federal statutory income tax rate to our effective income tax rate is as follows:

	Year Ended December 31,		
	2015	2016	2017
U.S. federal statutory tax rate	35.0%	35.0%	35.0%
Foreign income taxed at different rates	(13.4)%	(11.0)%	(14.2)%
Impact of the Tax Act			
One-time transition tax	0.0%	0.0%	37.6%
Deferred tax effects	0.0%	0.0%	(1.4)%
Federal research credit	(2.1)%	(2.0)%	(1.8)%
Stock-based compensation expense	0.3%	(3.4)%	(4.5)%
European Commission fine	0.0%	0.0%	3.5%
Other adjustments	(3.0)%	0.7%	(0.8)%
Effective tax rate	16.8%	19.3%	53.4%

*As calculated earlier and as reported by Alphabet

The firm's overall worldwide effective tax rate is lower than the statutory tax rate in 2015 and 2016 and jumps to 53.4% in 2017. The major reason for a decrease in the rates in 2015 and 2016 is "Foreign income taxed at different rates." As discussed earlier in this chapter, prior to the TCJA, U.S. firms with foreign operations (organized through U.S.-owned foreign subsidiaries) were subject to a worldwide tax system in the United States, meaning the company would pay U.S. income tax on the foreign earnings. However, there was a timing difference between book and taxable incomes because operating earnings of foreign subsidiaries were included in financial accounting income when earned but not included in taxable income until those earnings were repatriated back to the United States as dividends. When determining the accounting for income taxes for these earnings, management had to determine whether any of the foreign earnings were indefinitely (aka permanently) reinvested—meaning they did not intend to repatriate the earnings to the United States in the foreseeable future. If management designated these earnings as indefinitely reinvested for financial accounting purposes, the company did not have to accrue the future U.S. taxes that would be owed on a future repatriation. As discussed briefly, this was an exception to deferred tax accounting found in AC 740-30 (formerly APB 23). Note that Alphabet also records a deferred tax liability of $4,409 in 2016 for some of its foreign earnings in addition to the large rate reduction in the rate reconciliation. The company is indicating that some of its foreign earnings might be repatriated (those for which the deferred tax liability is recorded) but does not expect to bring some of these earnings back to the United States (those they designated as indefinitely reinvested). In its 2016 10-K, Alphabet stated,

"As of December 31, 2016, we have not recognized deferred U.S. income taxes and foreign withholding taxes on a cumulative total of $60.7 billion of undistributed earnings and other basis differences in our foreign subsidiaries. We intend to indefinitely reinvest those earnings and other basis differences in operations outside the U.S. If such earnings and other basis differences in our investment foreign subsidiaries were to be repatriated in the future, they would be subject to U.S. income taxes and applicable non-U.S. income and withholding taxes. Determining the unrecognized deferred tax liability related to such investments in foreign subsidiaries that are indefinitely reinvested is not practicable."

A major change in the TCJA that affects the income tax expense account is the movement to a modified territorial tax system from a worldwide tax system—see Chapter 10 for more discussion of these systems. As noted above, before the TCJA, the United States taxed U.S. multinationals on their worldwide income and allowed deferral of the U.S. tax until the profits were repatriated as dividend to the United States. Firms then received a tax credit for foreign taxes paid. As a result of these rules, many U.S. multinationals had accumulated foreign earnings in their foreign subsidiaries. Under a territorial system, foreign earnings are generally no longer subject to U.S. taxation (although the TCJA includes rules to make sure U.S. firms are paying some taxes on their foreign earnings).

Under the TCJA, there is a transition tax on the accumulated foreign earnings earned after 1986 and before the United States moved to a modified territorial tax system as part of the TCJA. The transition tax can be paid over an 8-year period.[31] If the profits are in the form of liquid assets (cash and marketable securities), the tax rate is 15.5%. If the profits are held in illiquid assets, the tax rate is 8%. The Treasury expects to receive $338 billion in taxes from this transition tax. Firms must accrue (i.e., recognize) this tax on their past unremitted foreign profits. This accrual requires a debit (increase) to income tax expense, increasing the reported income tax expense, and a credit (increase) to income taxes payable. When the taxes are paid in the future, the income taxes payable account is debited (reduced) and cash is credited (reduced). The FASB, in response to inquiries, has stated that there is no discounting to present value of this income tax payable.

U.S. GAAP requires deferred tax assets and deferred tax liabilities to be recorded at the statutory tax rates expected to be in effect when the temporary differences reverse. Recall that the TCJA reduced the corporate federal statutory tax to a flat 21% from a top rate of 35%. As such, firms were required to write down the value of both their deferred tax assets (DTA) and deferred tax liabilities, DTL in the reporting period in which the new tax rate was enacted. A write-down of the DTA requires a credit (reduction) to the asset account and a debit (increase) to the income tax expense account (specifically, deferred tax expense), increasing the reported income tax expense, and the GAAP effective tax rate, for the period. A write-down of the DTL requires a debit (reduction) to the liability account and a credit (decrease) to the income tax expense account, reducing the reported income tax expense for the period and the GAAP effective tax rate. Therefore, the effect on the income tax expense account (and GAAP effective tax rate) will depend on whether the firm has a net DTA or a net DTL. Alphabet has a net DTA, which leads us to expect an increase in the effective tax rate due to the write-down of the net NTA. However, Alphabet recognized a deferred tax benefit of $376 associated with the reduced statutory tax rate and other effects of the TCJA, which reduced its effective tax rate by 1.4%, as disclosed in its effective tax rate reconciliation schedule.

Alphabet explained the effects of these tax changes for 2017 in its 10-K as follows:

> The U.S. Tax Cuts and Jobs Act (Tax Act) was enacted on December 22, 2017 and introduces significant changes to U.S. income tax law. Effective in 2018, the Tax Act reduces the U.S. statutory tax rate from 35% to 21% and creates new taxes on certain foreign-sourced earnings and certain related-party payments, which are referred to as the global intangible low-taxed income tax and the base erosion tax, respectively. In addition, in 2017 we were subject to a one-time transition tax on accumulated foreign subsidiary earnings not previously subject to U.S. income tax.
>
> Due to the timing of the enactment and the complexity involved in applying the provisions of the Tax Act, we have made reasonable estimates of the effects and recorded provisional amounts in our financial statements as of December 31, 2017. As we collect and prepare necessary data, and interpret the Tax Act and any additional guidance issued by the U.S. Treasury Department, the IRS, and other standard-setting bodies, we may make adjustments to the provisional amounts. Those adjustments may materially impact our provision for income taxes and effective tax rate in the period in which the adjustments are made. The accounting for the tax effects of the Tax Act will be completed in 2018.
>
> Provisional amounts for the following income tax effects of the Tax Act have been recorded as of December 31, 2017 and are subject to change during 2018.
>
> *One-time transition tax*
>
> The Tax Act requires us to pay U.S. income taxes on accumulated foreign subsidiary earnings not previously subject to U.S. income tax at a rate of 15.5% to the extent of foreign cash and certain other net current assets and 8% on the remaining earnings. We recorded a provisional amount for our one-time transitional tax liability and income tax expense of $10.2 billion. We have recorded provisional amounts based on estimates of the effects of the Tax Act as the analysis requires significant data from our foreign subsidiaries that is not regularly collected or analyzed.

continued

[31] The transition tax can be paid in installments of 8% over the first 5 years, rising to 15%, 20%, and 25% in the final 3 years of the 8-year period.

continued from previous page

Deferred tax effects

The Tax Act reduces the U.S. statutory tax rate from 35% to 21% for years after 2017. Accordingly, we have remeasured our deferred taxes as of December 31, 2017 to reflect the reduced rate that will apply in future periods when these deferred taxes are settled or realized. We recognized a deferred tax benefit of $376 million to reflect the reduced U.S. tax rate and other effects of the Tax Act. Although the tax rate reduction is known, we have not collected the necessary data to complete our analysis of the effect of the Tax Act on the underlying deferred taxes and as such, the amounts recorded as of December 31, 2017 are provisional.

The net tax expense recognized in 2017 related to the Tax Act was $9.9 billion. As we complete our analysis of the Tax Act and incorporate additional guidance that may be issued by the U.S. Treasury Department, the IRS or other standard-setting bodies, we may identify additional effects not reflected as of December 31, 2017.

The largest effect for Alphabet is the transition tax on its accumulated unremitted foreign earnings. Alphabet directly discloses that it is recognizing $10.2 billion for the transition tax. This amount increases the firm's GAAP effective tax rate by 37.6% (as disclosed in the tax rate reconciliation schedule reproduced above). The firm's effective tax rate in 2017 is reported as 53.4% compared with 19.3% in 2016. The firm included the transition tax adjustment in the current portion of the income tax expense, which increased from $3.826 in 2016 to $12.608 in 2017. The firm also reports in the balance sheet an increase of $8.145 in income taxes payable—noncurrent ($12.812 – $4.677), reflecting the transition tax liability that will be paid over the next 8 years. Another interesting disclosure is that, in the schedule showing the reconciliation of the federal statutory income tax rate to the firm's effective tax rate, Alphabet starts with the 35% statutory tax rate and reduces it for the effects of foreign earnings taxed at lower rates before adjusting for the effects of the transition tax on accumulated foreign unremitted earnings. Note that the firm did not disclose the accumulated unremitted foreign earnings and it is difficult to "back out" because of the different tax rates that apply to the earnings (portion held in liquid assets and portion held in operating assets). However, if one looks at the 2016 10-K, Alphabet disclosed foreign earnings of $60.2 billion on which it had not provided incremental U.S. taxes due if the earnings were repatriated. Additionally, the firm disclosed it has a deferred tax liability of $4.409 billion in 2016, representing foreign earnings on which it has recognized (accrued) the expected U.S. taxes due on repatriation (this number is reduced to $68 million in 2017). Thus, Alphabet has large unremitted foreign earnings, which it can now access to be used in the United States because it is no longer subject to future taxes on repatriation. As an exercise, consider searching the media to see if Alphabet has announced plans for the use these funds.

Alphabet presents a description of its deferred tax assets and liabilities. Recall that deferred tax assets and liabilities arise from temporary differences—items that are recognized in both sets of books in different time periods. With respect to deferred income-tax assets, in 2017, the largest item, "Tax credits," is $1.187 billion. This vague description means that Alphabet recognized an expense for financial accounting for the item before it can take the tax deduction and which item will give rise to a tax credit at that time. The second largest item is "Basis difference in investment in Arris." This item indicates that the book value of the investment in Arris shares is less than the tax basis. The third largest item is "Prepaid cost sharing." This is a complex item that basically means the firm has expensed an item before it is included in the tax return.

The three items listed first are "Stock-based compensation expense," "Accrued employee benefits," and "Accruals and reserves not currently deductible." With respect to "Stock-based compensation expense," under the rules for the accounting for stock options and restricted stock granted to employees (the tax and accounting treatment of employee stock options and restricted stock are discussed in more detail in Chapter 8), Alphabet recognizes stock-option and restricted stock expense in its financial statements (lowering book income) over the vesting period of the options and restricted stock. The deduction for stock-option and restricted-stock compensation, however, is not allowed until the options are exercised or for restricted stock when vested. Therefore, earlier recognition of the expense for book than tax gives rise to a deferred tax asset in the amount of $251 ($574) in 2017 (2016). "Accrued employee benefits" refers to items expensed before the tax deduction, such as accruals for retiree health care benefits (discussed in Chapter 9). "Accruals and reserves not currently deductible" refers to items expensed in the books before the period in which they are deducted for tax purposes. Examples include bad debt expense and warranty expense. This item might also refer to deferred (unearned) revenue, which has been included in taxable income but not yet recognized as revenue in the accounting books. Finally, Alphabet also reported a deferred tax asset labeled "Net operating losses" in the amount of $320. The company describes the source of these losses in the paragraph below the listing of the deferred tax assets and liabilities.

Alphabet records a valuation allowance of $2.531 for 2017. Alphabet provides a discussion of the deferred tax assets that give rise to the valuation allowance: investment losses, California deferred tax assets, certain federal and foreign NOLs, and the book-tax difference in the basis of Arris shares. By recording a valuation allowance, Alphabet is disclosing that it does not think it will be able to fully utilize these losses (likely either due to limits on the use of the NOLs or an expectation of insufficient taxable income in the relevant taxing jurisdictions).

With respect to deferred income tax liabilities, Alphabet records a deferred tax liability related to "Depreciation and amortization" of $551 in 2017. This deferred tax liability represents the deferred tax amount on the difference between book depreciation and tax depreciation at the end of the current period. Recall, because tax depreciation is generally recorded in greater amounts early in the assets' lives relative to book depreciation, a deferred tax liability is generated. The line item "Identifiable intangibles" arises because Alphabet is likely amortizing identifiable intangibles (intangibles other than goodwill, such as acquired patents, trademarks, copyrights, customer lists) at a faster rate than for book. As discussed above, "Foreign earnings" in the deferred liability disclosure indicates that Alphabet has recognized U.S. incremental tax on some of its foreign earnings in 2016: that portion not designated as indefinitely reinvested. Alphabet records an amount labeled "Other" (as do most firms) that aggregates its deferred taxes for items that are too small to disclose separately.

Total net deferred assets are $250 (total deferred assets net of valuation allowance are $1.955 less the total deferred tax liabilities of $1.705). On its balance sheet in 2017, Alphabet discloses non-current deferred income tax assets of $680, and in the long-term liabilities section, deferred income taxes of $430, netting to $250 per the tax footnote disclosures. For many firms, the totals are not traceable to the balance sheet, usually because the netted amount is combined with other items in that section of the balance sheet under the rubric "Other" (e.g., "Other current assets" when a current deferred asset or "Other current liabilities" when a current deferred tax liability).

With respect to uncertain tax positions, Alphabet reports that as of the year ended December 31, 2017, the ending gross unrecognized tax benefits is $4.696 billion. Unrecognized means tax expense has not been reduced by this amount and this is the estimated liability associated with these uncertain tax positions. There was an $1.875 decrease in the UTB during the year due to settlements with the tax authorities, and an increase of $750 related to uncertain positions taken in the current year's tax return.

We also note that firms are required to disclose in a note in their statement of cash flows the amount of taxes paid during the year. This number is referred to as cash taxes paid and when divided by pre-tax income, we can estimate the cash effective tax rate (as discussed in Chapter 4). The estimates are as follows:

	2015	2016	2017
Cash paid for taxes, net of refunds	$ 3,651	$ 1,643	$ 6,191
Income before income taxes	$19,651	$24,150	$27,193
Cash effective tax rate	18.6%	6.8%	22.8%
GAAP effective tax rate	16.8%	19.3%	53.4%

In 2015, the cash and GAAP estimate tax rates are similar. However, in 2016 and 2017 they diverge. The difference in 2017 is largely due to the accrual (recognition) for the transition tax on accumulated foreign earnings which has not yet been paid by Alphabet. It is not clear what the specific explanations are for the large difference in 2016.

In conclusion, for firms with large unremitted foreign profits, large DTAs, or large DTLs, these changes from the TCJA and the subsequent accounting for the changes may make it difficult for financial-statement users to interpret the fiscal year-end 2017 financial statements and will likely disrupt financial-statement analysis, including analysis of effective tax rates.

Extracts from Alphabet Inc. 2017 Annual Report

Alphabet Inc.
CONSOLIDATED STATEMENTS OF INCOME
(In millions, except per share amounts)

	Year Ended December 31,		
	2015	2016	2017
Revenues	$74,989	$90,272	$110,855
Costs and expenses:			
Cost of revenues	28,164	35,138	45,583
Research and development	12,282	13,948	16,625
Sales and marketing	9,047	10,485	12,893
General and administrative	6,136	6,985	6,872
European Commission fine	0	0	2,736
Total costs and expenses	55,629	66,556	84,709
Income from operations	19,360	23,716	26,146
Other income (expense), net	291	434	1,047
Income before income taxes	19,651	24,150	27,193
Provision for income taxes	3,303	4,672	14,531
Net income	$16,348	$19,478	$ 12,662
Less: Adjustment payment to Class C capital stockholders	522	0	0
Net income available to all stockholders	$15,826	$19,478	$ 12,662
Basic net income per share of Class A and B common stock	$23.11	$28.32	$18.27
Basic net income per share of Class C capital stock	$24.63	$28.32	$18.27
Diluted net income per share of Class A and B common stock	$22.84	$27.85	$18.00
Diluted net income per share of Class C capital stock	$24.34	$27.85	$18.00

Alphabet Inc.
CONSOLIDATED BALANCE SHEETS
(In millions, except share and par value amounts which are reflected in thousands, and par value per share amounts)

	As of December 31, 2016	As of December 31, 2017
Assets		
Current assets:		
Cash and cash equivalents	$ 12,918	$ 10,715
Marketable securities	73,415	91,156
Total cash, cash equivalents, and marketable securities	86,333	101,871
Accounts receivable, net of allowance of $467 and $674	14,137	18,336
Income taxes receivable, net	95	369
Inventory	268	749
Other current assets	4,575	2,983
Total current assets	105,408	124,308

continued

continued from previous page

	As of December 31, 2016	As of December 31, 2017
Non-marketable investments	5,878	7,813
Deferred income taxes	383	680
Property and equipment, net	34,234	42,383
Intangible assets, net	3,307	2,692
Goodwill	16,468	16,747
Other non-current assets	1,819	2,672
Total assets	$167,497	$197,295
Liabilities and Stockholders' Equity		
Current liabilities:		
Accounts payable	$ 2,041	$ 3,137
Accrued compensation and benefits	3,976	4,581
Accrued expenses and other current liabilities	6,144	10,177
Accrued revenue share	2,942	3,975
Deferred revenue	1,099	1,432
Income taxes payable, net	554	881
Total current liabilities	16,756	24,183
Long-term debt	3,935	3,969
Deferred revenue, non-current	202	340
Income taxes payable, non-current	4,677	12,812
Deferred income taxes	226	430
Other long-term liabilities	2,665	3,059
Total liabilities	28,461	44,793
Commitments and contingencies (Note 10)		
Stockholders' equity:		
Convertible preferred stock, $0.001 par value per share, 100,000 shares authorized; no shares issued and outstanding	0	0
Class A and Class B common stock, and Class C capital stock and additional paid-in capital, $0.001 par value per share: 15,000,000 shares authorized (Class A 9,000,000, Class B 3,000,000, Class C 3,000,000); 691,293 (Class A 296,992, Class B 47,437, Class C 346,864) and 694,783 (Class A 298,470, Class B 46,972, Class C 349,341) shares issued and outstanding	36,307	40,247
Accumulated other comprehensive loss	(2,402)	(992)
Retained earnings	105,131	113,247
Total stockholders' equity	139,036	152,502
Total liabilities and stockholders' equity	$167,497	$197,295

Note 14. Income Taxes

Income from continuing operations before income taxes included income from domestic operations of $8.3 billion, $12.0 billion, and $10.7 billion for the years ended December 31, 2015, 2016, and 2017, and income from foreign operations of $11.4 billion, $12.1 billion, and $16.5 billion for the years ended December 31, 2015, 2016, and 2017.

continued

continued from previous page

The provision for income taxes consists of the following (in millions):

	Year Ended December 31,		
	2015	2016	2017
Current:			
Federal and state	$2,838	$3,826	$12,608
Foreign	723	966	1,746
Total	3,561	4,792	14,354
Deferred:			
Federal and state	(241)	(70)	220
Foreign	(17)	(50)	(43)
Total	(258)	(120)	177
Provision for income taxes	$3,303	$4,672	$14,531

The U.S. Tax Cuts and Jobs Act (Tax Act) was enacted on December 22, 2017 and introduces significant changes to U.S. income tax law. Effective in 2018, the Tax Act reduces the U.S. statutory tax rate from 35% to 21% and creates new taxes on certain foreign-sourced earnings and certain related-party payments, which are referred to as the global intangible low-taxed income tax and the base erosion tax, respectively. In addition, in 2017 we were subject to a one-time transition tax on accumulated foreign subsidiary earnings not previously subject to U.S. income tax.

Due to the timing of the enactment and the complexity involved in applying the provisions of the Tax Act, we have made reasonable estimates of the effects and recorded provisional amounts in our financial statements as of December 31, 2017. As we collect and prepare necessary data, and interpret the Tax Act and any additional guidance issued by the U.S. Treasury Department, the IRS, and other standard-setting bodies, we may make adjustments to the provisional amounts. Those adjustments may materially impact our provision for income taxes and effective tax rate in the period in which the adjustments are made. The accounting for the tax effects of the Tax Act will be completed in 2018.

Provisional amounts for the following income tax effects of the Tax Act have been recorded as of December 31, 2017 and are subject to change during 2018.

One-time transition tax

The Tax Act requires us to pay U.S. income taxes on accumulated foreign subsidiary earnings not previously subject to U.S. income tax at a rate of 15.5% to the extent of foreign cash and certain other net current assets and 8% on the remaining earnings. We recorded a provisional amount for our one-time transitional tax liability and income tax expense of $10.2 billion. We have recorded provisional amounts based on estimates of the effects of the Tax Act as the analysis requires significant data from our foreign subsidiaries that is not regularly collected or analyzed.

Deferred tax effects

The Tax Act reduces the U.S. statutory tax rate from 35% to 21% for years after 2017. Accordingly, we have remeasured our deferred taxes as of December 31, 2017 to reflect the reduced rate that will apply in future periods when these deferred taxes are settled or realized. We recognized a deferred tax benefit of $376 million to reflect the reduced U.S. tax rate and other effects of the Tax Act. Although the tax rate reduction is known, we have not collected the necessary data to complete our analysis of the effect of the Tax Act on the underlying deferred taxes and as such, the amounts recorded as of December 31, 2017 are provisional.

The net tax expense recognized in 2017 related to the Tax Act was $9.9 billion. As we complete our analysis of the Tax Act and incorporate additional guidance that may be issued by the U.S. Treasury Department, the IRS or other standard-setting bodies, we may identify additional effects not reflected as of December 31, 2017.

The reconciliation of federal statutory income tax rate to our effective income tax rate is as follows:

continued

continued from previous page

	Year Ended December 31,		
	2015	2016	2017
U.S. federal statutory tax rate	35.0%	35.0%	35.0%
Foreign income taxed at different rates	(13.4)%	(11.0)%	(14.2)%
Impact of the Tax Act			
One-time transition tax	0.0%	0.0%	37.6%
Deferred tax effects	0.0%	0.0%	(1.4)%
Federal research credit	(2.1)%	(2.0)%	(1.8)%
Stock-based compensation expense	0.3%	(3.4)%	(4.5)%
European Commission Fine	0.0%	0.0%	3.5%
Other adjustments	(3.0)%	0.7%	(0.8)%
Effective tax rate	16.8%	19.3%	53.4%

Our effective tax rate for each of the years presented was impacted by earnings realized in foreign jurisdictions with statutory tax rates lower than the federal statutory tax rate. Substantially all of the income from foreign operations was earned by an Irish subsidiary. Beginning in 2018, earnings realized in foreign jurisdictions will be subject to U.S. tax in accordance with the Tax Act.

Deferred Income Taxes

Deferred income taxes reflect the net effects of temporary differences between the carrying amounts of assets and liabilities for financial reporting purposes and the amounts used for income tax purposes. We recorded a provisional adjustment to our U.S. deferred income taxes as of December 31, 2017 to reflect the reduction in the U.S. statutory tax rate from 35% to 21% resulting from the Tax Act. Significant components of our deferred tax assets and liabilities are as follows (in millions):

	As of December 31,	
	2016	2017
Deferred tax assets:		
Stock-based compensation expense	$ 574	$ 251
Accrued employee benefits	939	285
Accruals and reserves not currently deductible	500	717
Tax credits	631	1,187
Basis difference in investment of Arris	1,327	849
Prepaid cost sharing	4,409	498
Net Operating Losses	305	320
Other	621	379
Total deferred tax assets	9,306	4,486
Valuation allowance	(2,076)	(2,531)
Total deferred tax assets net of valuation allowance	7,230	1,955
Deferred tax liabilities:		
Depreciation and amortization	(877)	(551)
Identified intangibles	(844)	(419)
Renewable energy investments	(788)	(531)
Foreign earnings	(4,409)	(68)
Other	(155)	(136)
Total deferred tax liabilities	(7,073)	(1,705)
Net deferred tax assets	$ 157	$ 250

continued

continued from previous page

As of December 31, 2017, our federal and state net operating loss carryforwards for income tax purposes were approximately $931 million and $785 million, respectively. If not utilized, the federal net operating loss carryforwards will begin to expire in 2021 and the state net operating loss carryforwards will begin to expire in 2018. It is more likely than not that certain federal net operating loss carryforwards and our state net operating loss carryforwards will not be realized; therefore, we have recorded a valuation allowance against them. The net operating loss carryforwards are subject to various annual limitations under the tax laws of the different jurisdictions. Our foreign net operating loss carryforwards for income tax purposes were $327 million that will begin to expire in 2021.

As of December 31, 2017, our California research and development credit carryforwards for income tax purposes were approximately $1.8 billion that can be carried over indefinitely. We believe the state tax credit is not likely to be realized.

As of December 31, 2017, we maintained a valuation allowance with respect to certain of our deferred tax assets relating primarily to investment losses that are capital in nature, California deferred tax assets, certain federal net operating losses, and certain foreign net operating losses that we believe are not likely to be realized. We established a deferred tax asset for the book-to-tax basis difference in our investments in Arris shares received from the sale of the Motorola Home business to Arris in 2013. Since any future losses to be recognized upon the sale of Arris shares will be capital losses, a valuation allowance has been recorded against this deferred tax asset to the extent such deferred tax asset is not likely to be covered by capital gains generated as of December 31, 2017. We reassess the valuation allowance quarterly and if future evidence allows for a partial or full release of the valuation allowance, a tax benefit will be recorded accordingly.

Uncertain Tax Positions

The following table summarizes the activity related to our gross unrecognized tax benefits from January 1, 2015 to December 31, 2017 (in millions):

	2015	2016	2017
Beginning gross unrecognized tax benefits	$3,294	$4,167	$5,393
Increases related to prior year tax positions	224	899	685
Decreases related to prior year tax positions	(176)	(157)	(257)
Decreases related to settlement with tax authorities	(27)	(196)	(1,875)
Increases related to current year tax positions	852	680	750
Ending gross unrecognized tax benefits	$4,167	$5,393	$4,696

The total amount of gross unrecognized tax benefits was $4.2 billion, $5.4 billion, and $4.7 billion as of December 31, 2015, 2016, and 2017, respectively, of which, $3.6 billion, $4.3 billion, and $3.0 billion if recognized, would affect our effective tax rate. The decrease in gross unrecognized tax benefits in 2017 was primarily as a result of the resolution of a multi-year U.S. audit.

As of December 31, 2016 and 2017, we had accrued $493 million and $362 million in interest and penalties in provision for income taxes, respectively.

We file income tax returns in the U.S. federal jurisdiction and in many state and foreign jurisdictions, our two major tax jurisdictions are the U.S. federal and Ireland. We are subject to the continuous examination of our income tax returns by the IRS and other tax authorities. The IRS completed its examination through our 2012 tax years; all issues have been concluded except for one which is currently under review in the U.S. Tax Court. The IRS is currently examining our 2013 through 2015 tax returns. We have also received tax assessments in multiple foreign jurisdictions asserting transfer pricing adjustments or permanent establishment. We continue to defend any and all such claims as presented.

Our 2016 tax year remains subject to examination by the IRS for U.S. federal tax purposes, and our 2011 through 2016 tax years remain subject to examination by the appropriate governmental agencies for Irish tax purposes. There are other ongoing audits in various other jurisdictions that are not material to our financial statements.

We regularly assess the likelihood of adverse outcomes resulting from these examinations to determine the adequacy of our provision for income taxes. We continue to monitor the progress of ongoing discussions with tax authorities and the impact, if any, of the expected expiration of the statute of limitations in various taxing jurisdictions.

continued

continued from previous page

> We believe that an adequate provision has been made for any adjustments that may result from tax examinations. However, the outcome of tax audits cannot be predicted with certainty. If any issues addressed in our tax audits are resolved in a manner not consistent with management's expectations, we could be required to adjust our provision for income taxes in the period such resolution occurs. Although the timing of resolution, settlement, closure of audits is not certain, it is reasonably possible that certain U.S. federal and non-U.S. tax audits may be concluded within the next 12 months, which could significantly increase or decrease the balance of our gross unrecognized tax benefits.
>
> We estimate that our unrecognized tax benefits as of December 31, 2017 could possibly decrease by approximately $500 million in the next 12 months. Positions that may be resolved include various U.S. and non-U.S. matters.

EVIDENCE ABOUT THE IMPORTANCE OF FINANCIAL ACCOUNTING INCOME

Book-Tax Trade-off: Income Shifting across Time

As discussed in Chapter 2, firms have incentives to defer (accelerate) taxable income if statutory tax rates are expected to decline (increase). The corporate tax-rate reductions in TRA 86 offered firms incentives to defer income to tax periods with lower tax rates. TRA 86 also gave researchers a relatively clean event to use to study firms' willingness to trade off tax savings with financial reporting costs. Although the trade-off of financial accounting costs and tax benefits was central to the studies of TRA 86, it is important to note that in considering the theme of "all costs," there are potentially a variety of other nontax costs associated with shifting income. For example, shifting income can change the timing of underlying economic activities, which may bring about large nontax costs, such as reduced operating efficiencies, deterioration in customer relations, and additional inventory holding costs (arising from delaying shipping). The planning and coordination of income-shifting activities also entails administrative and implementation costs, and managerial compensation plans might be affected by shifting income across periods. Another issue to keep in mind is our theme of "all parties," in that there could be tax costs to the other party to whom or from income is shifted (an example of multilateral tax planning).

Several academic studies specifically examined income shifting around TRA 86. The general findings are as follows. First, profitable companies appear to have shifted income to report more income when the tax rate was lower after TRA 86 (and more expenses before TRA 86). This shifting was significantly stronger for companies with lower relative financial accounting costs (e.g., companies that had less likelihood of violating a debt covenant). The fact that some companies had debt and the covenants relied on financial accounting numbers made the firms less likely to shift income in a manner that would save cash taxes because it would also have reduced accounting income. Thus, providing evidence that accounting earnings are valuable to companies and management. Similar in theme but looking at a different subset of firms, another finding in the literature is that firms that had NOLs typically shifted income in a manner opposite to profitable firms around TRA 86. Because tax rates declined after TRA 86, if a company had tax NOLs, the NOLs became less valuable after the tax rates declined. So, these firms had incentives to increase carryback losses to pre-TRA 86, when tax rates were *higher*. Again, the likelihood of a firm shifting income to save cash taxes was significantly lower for companies that had pressure to report high financial accounting earnings (e.g., firms with leverage and thus, covenants based on accounting earnings). These firms are less able to shift to save taxes because they have financial accounting incentives for reporting as well, creating the book-tax trade-off.[32] We expect similar shifting in response to the corporate tax-rate cuts in the TCJA.

Book-Tax Trade-off: LIFO/FIFO Studies

Another nice setting to test the book-tax trade-off is companies that have inventory and need to choose a method to account for their inventory. Last in, first out (LIFO) is an inventory accounting method that minimizes taxes (in those countries where it is an acceptable accounting method) when

[32] Interested readers should see Guenther (1994); Scholes, Wilson, and Wolfson (1992); and Maydew (1997).

prices are rising, inventory levels are nondecreasing, and tax rates are not increasing over time. If LIFO is used for tax purposes in the United States, it must also be used for financial reporting purposes (the LIFO conformity rule). Over time, LIFO firms have been allowed via footnote disclosures to report sufficient information for users to estimate earning that are first in, first out (FIFO) based. Thus, users have access to both LIFO and FIFO earnings numbers. However, because LIFO-based earnings are reported in the income statement, contracts (and even possibly capital market participants) that rely on audited reported numbers will likely use the lower LIFO-based earnings. As such, taxable income can be reduced only by reducing profits reported to shareholders, lenders, and other interested parties, and this may discourage the tax-minimizing strategy.

What is observed when looking at data on LIFO/FIFO decisions? Basically, the research shows that saving taxes is the primary determinant of choosing LIFO (the adoption decision). However, when financial reporting pressures are high, firms are more likely to liquidate LIFO layers—meaning shrink their inventory levels—leading to lower costs of goods sold being recorded for both book and tax and higher incomes under both systems as well. Thus, it seems that firms report higher taxable income and pay more in taxes in order to show higher accounting income. Finally, the evidence in the academic literature is also consistent with firms abandoning LIFO altogether at times, likely when the firm is more highly levered and closer to violating minimum working capital requirements. This evidence is also consistent with the conclusion that financial-statement effects influence the decision and even more so if it is cheaper for tax purposes (i.e., when the firm has a tax NOL that will eliminate the tax on the LIFO abandonment decision).[33]

Regulatory Costs

Financial reporting concerns extend to regulators as well as investors and creditors. For example, U.S. banks must maintain a minimum level of regulatory capital to preserve operating independence from bank regulators. Moreover, the quantity of federally insured demand deposits that banks are permitted to issue is tied to regulatory capital. To the extent transactions that reduce taxable income also reduce regulatory capital (and most do), banks may rationally sacrifice tax savings. This is particularly true of banks that face a relatively high probability of failure and low levels of regulatory capital. Such institutions find it particularly attractive to borrow money at the riskless rate by issuing insured demand deposits. In one of the early academic studies on the topic, Scholes, Wilson, and Wolfson (1990) documented that banks coordinate their tax planning with nontax considerations in managing their investment portfolios. That is, firms forgo tax savings (by not selling marketable securities with unrealized losses) and even incur tax costs (by selling securities that have appreciated) to boost regulatory capital. Beatty, Chamberlain, and Magliolo (1995) and Collins, Shackelford, and Wahlen (1995) extended the Scholes, Wilson, and Wolfson paper, examining the multiple ways, in addition to gains and losses from selling marketable securities, banks can manage their earnings, regulatory capital, and taxes and finding that regulatory capital and financial reporting concerns dominate tax concerns. Collins, Geisler, and Shackelford (1997) reported that taxes as well as regulatory concerns and financial-reporting effects are important in the insurance industry.

Another study that examined the trade-off of tax benefits and accounting costs focused on corporate decisions with respect to organizational form. A 1996 tax law change allowed commercial banks to convert from taxable C corporations to flow-through S corporations. Hodder, McAnally, and Weaver (2003) found that banks are more likely to convert if doing so saves taxes; specifically, when conversion saves dividend taxes, avoids the corporate alternative minimum tax, and minimizes state income taxes. Banks are less likely to convert when conversion restricts access to equity capital markets (e.g., for expansion), restricts use of the banks NOL carryforwards, and gives rise to potential penalty taxes on unrealized gains existing at the conversion date. Additionally, banks with large deferred tax assets are less likely to convert. The write-off of deferred taxes at conversion decreases regulatory capital and exposes the bank to potential costly regulatory oversight and intervention. As a result, tax savings are traded off against regulatory cost increases in this conversion decision.

---

[33] Interested readers should see Dopuch and Pincus (1988); Cushing and LeClere (1992); Johnson and Dhaliwal (1988); Dhaliwal, Frankel, and Trezevant (1994); and Hunt, Moyer, and Shevlin (1996).

Asset Divestitures

The book-tax trade-off has also been studied in the asset sale decision. As an example, Maydew, Schipper, and Vincent (1999) examined how firms trade off tax and nontax costs in the decision to divest assets via a taxable sale rather than a tax-free spin-off. With positive tax rates and zero nontax costs, assets with an unrealized taxable gain could be spun off tax free and assets with unrealized tax-deductible losses could be sold to provide tax benefits.

The authors found that for a sample of 270 asset divestitures during 1987 to 1995, at least 30% of the taxable asset sales and 33% of the nontaxable spin-offs were tax disadvantaged, suggesting either significant nontax costs or forgone tax benefits. They reported evidence consistent with firms incurring tax costs in order to achieve favorable financial reporting outcomes and to raise cash.

Dollar Estimates of Firms' Willingness to Forgo Tax Savings

The studies we just mentioned document that firm managers trade off tax savings with nontax costs—in particular, costs arising from financial-statement effects of any tax plans. This raises the question of how much firms are willing to "pay" (by forgone tax savings) for favorable financial-statement outcomes. Alternatively stated, an estimate of the forgone tax savings provides an estimate of the lower bound of financial statement costs. Several studies provide evidence on this issue.

Engel, Erickson, and Maydew (1999) examined trust preferred stock (TRUPS) to develop lower- and upper-bound estimates of what firms were willing to pay for favorable balance sheet treatment. Recall from Chapter 6 that TRUPS are treated like debt for tax purposes in that the preferred dividends are tax deductible, similar to interest. In contrast, for financial accounting purposes (during the period examined in the study), TRUPS were treated like traditional preferred stock (i.e., nondebt) on the balance sheet. Issuers of TRUPS used the proceeds to retire outstanding traditional preferred stock and outstanding debt and for general corporate uses. For TRUPS issuers that retired debt, tax deductibility was retained while the debt-to-asset ratio declined on average by 12.8%.[34] Engel, Erickson, and Maydew then estimated the lower and upper bounds of the costs to the firm of reducing the debt-to-asset ratio. The lower bound was derived as the average actual issuance costs of the TRUPS across issuers estimated to be $10 million. The upper bound was estimated using the TRUPS issuers that retired debt rather than outstanding traditional preferred stock. By not retiring the traditional preferred stock, the issuers chose to forgo tax benefits of, on average, $43 million. Therefore, firms were willing to pay between $10 million and $43 million to reduce their debt-to-asset ratio by 12.8%, improving the balance sheet.

Although most extant studies show firms are willing to forgo tax savings to avoid negative income or balance sheet consequences, evidence shows that some firms actually paid taxes on fraudulent book earnings. Erickson, Hanlon, and Maydew (2004) studied a sample of 27 firms that were required by the Securities and Exchange Commission (SEC) to restate their earnings as a result of SEC-alleged fraudulent behavior. In their restatements, these firms disclosed that they had paid approximately $320 million in taxes on overstated earnings of $336 billion (or an average of 11 cents per dollar of overstated earnings). Some of these firms even filed for a tax refund, which attracted media attention and some congressional action. These firms likely paid taxes hoping to avoid scrutiny by the IRS and shareholders (by reporting taxable income more in line with accounting income) and from others within their company (because the accounting and tax functions are separate departments in many companies). Obviously, these firms represent somewhat extreme behavior. Still, they show how far firms are willing to go (or how much they are willing to pay) to obtain an earnings outcome.

Survey Evidence and Anecdotes of Lobbying Activity

A survey by Graham, Hanlon, Shevlin, and Shroff (2014) of approximately 600 corporate tax executives provides more evidence on the book-tax trade-off. Their data show that 84% of publicly traded

[34] Engel, Erickson, and Maydew (1999) listed the potential benefits of reducing leverage (rating agency effects, relaxation of bond covenants, and possibly perceived reduction in the risk of the firm) but did not test whether these are significant explanatory variables explaining the choice.

firms responded that members of top management at their company cared at least as much about the GAAP effective tax rate as cash taxes paid, and 57% of public firms said that increasing earnings per share was an important outcome from a tax-planning strategy. These data show how important financial accounting earnings are to public companies—oftentimes, at least as (or more) important than actual cash flows. The survey data also reveal that private firms respond very differently than publicly traded firms. Of the private firms that responded, 48% of top management cared at least as much about the GAAP effective tax rate as cash taxes paid, and only 22% said that increasing earnings per share was an important outcome from a tax-planning strategy.

Consistent with the survey results, generally, we observe publicly traded companies being less willing to save taxes if there are financial accounting costs. Data on private firms are readily available for banks and insurance companies with regulatory filing requirements. For example, Beatty and Harris (1999) (examining banks) and Mikhail (1999) (examining insurance companies) reported results consistent with private firms being more aggressive tax planners, implying the nontax costs are lower for private firms. These results are what one would expect because private firms do not have to worry about stock market reactions to their reported earnings and also because private firms likely have fewer hidden-information problems because the managers are also owners.

Another way to evaluate the importance of financial accounting versus tax outcomes is in looking at corporate lobbying behavior. An interesting situation arose in the early 2000s when Congress was considering how to offer tax benefits to U.S. exporters after the prior tax benefit (exclusion from U.S. income of some extraterritorial income) was repealed. Congress considered a lower tax rate on manufacturing firms or an equivalent deduction for domestic manufacturing expenses. From a purely economics perspective, the tax savings are equivalent. However, under ASC 740, if a lower statutory tax rate were enacted, firms would have potentially had to use the lower statutory tax rate to recalculate their deferred tax assets and liabilities. Thus, firms with deferred tax assets would have likely had to reduce the recorded value of the deferred tax assets on the balance sheet (by using the new lower tax rate). This change in deferred tax asset value would have a corresponding increase in deferred tax expense that would lower reported book income. These firms lobbied heavily, and Congress chose the deduction alternative.[35]

Cash Effective Tax Rates

Cash effective tax rates are an important measure to firms and academics. Academics use cash effective tax rates to measure a firm's "tax avoidance" activities, as they reflect the outcome of a firm's tax planning activities. The measure captures tax planning that gives rise to permanent and temporary (deferral tax planning) differences, whereas GAAP effective tax rates reflect only the effects of tax planning that give rise to permanent differences and ignores deferral tax planning. Wilde and Wilson (2018) provided a detailed discussion of the empirical literature examining corporate tax avoidance. Here, we present an overview.

While some early studies have examined GAAP effective tax rates, cash effective tax rates came to the fore in Dyreng, Hanlon, and Maydew (2008). In this paper, the authors introduced the measure and calculated it on an annual basis and over 5- and 10-year periods. As **Figure 7.3**, reproduced from Dyreng, Hanlon, and Maydew shows, close to 25% of public companies have a long-run 10-year cash effective tax rate below 20%. That is, many firms are able to maintain low cash effective tax rates over long time periods. The sample average cash effective tax rate was 30% when the top statutory tax rate was 35%.

Not finished, Dyreng, Hanlon, Maydew, and Thornock (2017) examined the time trend in cash effective tax rates of U.S. corporations and also separately examined U.S. multinational corporations (U.S. firms with foreign operations or income) and purely U.S. domestic firms. **Figure 7.4** is reproduced from their paper. As is clearly evident from the plot, cash effective tax rates have been trending down for both US multinational and domestic-only firms. The two dips—2001–2003 and 2008–2011—reflect the internet crash and the financial crisis period, respectively. During both these periods, Congress also allowed for bonus depreciation on new asset purchases, which lowers cash taxes. A somewhat surprising result is that domestic firms' cash effective tax rates, while not only trending down, are also below

[35] See Poterba, Rao, and Seidman (2011) and Hanna (2012).

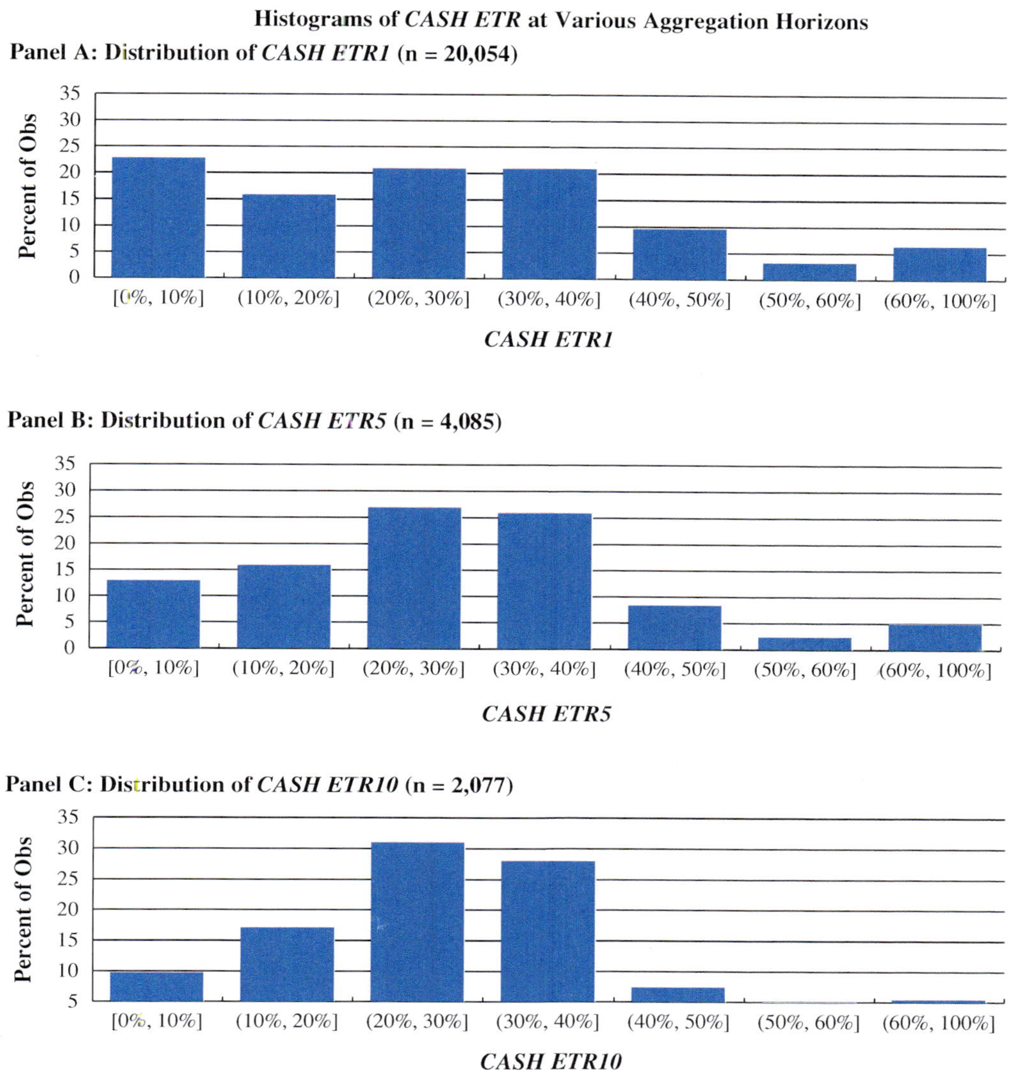

FIGURE 7.3 Plot of Cash Effective Tax Rates (ETR) for U.S. Firms Where Cash ETRs are Calculated over 1-, 5- and 10-Year Periods

CASH ETR1, *CASH ETR5*, *CASH ETR10* are calculated by summing cash tax paid (data317) over one, five, and ten years, respectively, and dividing by pretax income excluding special items (data170–data17) summed over one, five, and ten years, respectively. The number of observations in each panel reflects the total number of firm-observations with meaningful *CASH ETRs* for each aggregation horizon.

the annual means of multinational corporations. As the authors noted, this is a somewhat surprising result in the wake of all the media and political attention given to the apparent ability and alleged abuse of the tax system by U.S. multinational corporations. Dyreng, Hanlon, Maydew, and Thornock examined a standard list of determinants of tax avoidance—none of the examined firm variables explained the downward trend or the higher cash effective tax rates of the multinational corporations. A number of researchers are exploring this surprising result.

In addition to examining the determinants of (mostly) cross-firm variation in cash effective tax rates, research has also examined the consequences of firms having low cash effective tax rates. Recall, cash effective tax rates are used as a measure of the outcome from a firm's tax planning or tax avoidance, as it is labeled in this literature. Studies have shown that firms that avoid more taxes incur higher debt costs (lenders charge higher interest rates; Hasan, Hoi, Wu, and Zhang, 2014) but lower equity costs (Goh, Lee, Lim, and Shevlin, 2016), and are charged higher audit fees (Donohoe and Knechel, 2014), among other outcomes.

FIGURE 7.4
Mean Annual cash ETRs for U.S. Partitioned into MNCs and Domestic only

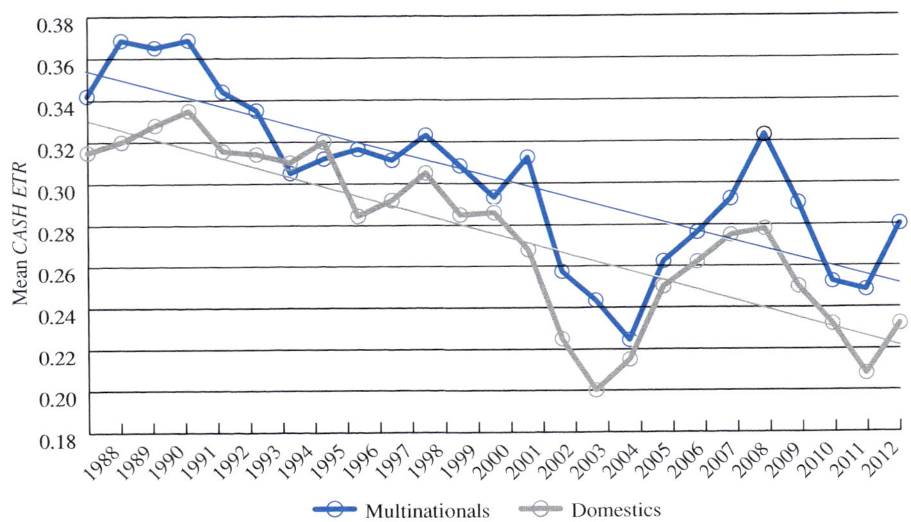

Fig. 4. Mean annual *CASH ETR* over the sample period separately for multinational and domestic firms. This figure plots annual mean *CASH ETR* over the sample period, 1988–2012. *CASH ETR* is the ratio of cash paid to pretax income. In this figure, a firm-year is considered multinational if the absolute value of pretax income is greater than zero or if the absolute value of foreign tax expense is greater than zero; otherwise it is considered domestic.

Implications of Large Book-Tax Differences

Remember, cash effective tax rates differ from the statutory tax rate due to both temporary and permanent book-tax differences. Thus, instead of examining cash effective tax rates, some studies have examined book-tax differences directly. As previously mentioned, Hanlon (2005) showed that firms with large positive temporary book-tax difference (i.e., deferred tax expense that results in pretax income being larger than taxable income) led to earnings that are less persistent. Hanlon argued that this result was due to managers managing pretax earnings upward using book accruals that have no contemporaneous effect on taxable income. Large temporary book-tax differences serve as a red flag of possible earnings management, and because accruals reverse, current earnings were less persistent. Philips, Pincus, and Rego (2003) examined the same research question and showed that increases in deferred tax expense were associated with firms more likely beating analysts' forecasts, avoiding an earnings decline, or a loss—all signals of upward earnings management.[36]

The reader will note that book-tax differences or cash effective tax rates have been used both to proxy for or identify earnings management and tax avoidance/planning. Given the divergence over time between pretax income and taxable income, equivalently, the growth in book-tax differences or decline in cash effective tax rates over time, some economists and lawyers have called for conforming the tax and book rules, with the common call being to conform the tax rules to the book rules. That is, tax firms directly on their book pretax income. These proponents argue that this would reduce the incentive for firms to manage their earnings upward, as this would increase their taxes while reducing the incentive to underreport taxable income, as this would mean reporting lower earnings to shareholders. Hanlon and Shevlin (2005) provided a discussion of the pros and cons of conforming. They pointed out the different objectives of financial accounting that produce book earnings versus the objective of the tax rules that produce taxable income. These differing rules are discussed in Chapter 1. Briefly, the financial accounting rules, U.S. GAAP and IFRS, are both intended to provide information useful to investors and other users of the financial statements, whereas the tax rules are intended to raise revenue for the government to fund its operations, encourage or discourage certain economic activities (e.g., R&D and investment in property, plant and equipment), redistribute income, and gain favor with voters. Hanlon and Shevlin argued that

[36] Philips, Pincus, and Rego (2003) state in their abstract, "Assuming greater discretion under GAAP than under tax rules, and assuming managers exploit such discretion to manage income upward primarily in ways that do not affect current taxable income, then such earnings management will generate book-tax differences that increase deferred tax expense." (p. 491).

if taxes were levied on book income, politicians would quickly become involved in setting the accounting rules. They further argued that there would be a loss of information to financial-statement users if book and tax were conformed.[37]

Summary of Key Points

1. A progressive tax-rate system encourages taxpayers to invest as though they were more risk averse than they really are (i.e., taxpayers will undertake less-risky projects). This is because average tax payments increase with the variability of taxable income with progressive taxes. This increases the after-tax cost of investment or, alternately stated, lowers the after-tax expected rate of return. Such a tax system increases the after-tax cost of risky investments for start-up firms because they likely face a progressive tax system (because of, for example, the tax-loss carryback and carryforward rules). These firms are likely to enter joint ventures to reduce the tax costs.
2. Although limited partnerships and joint ventures offer a tax-advantageous way to structure risky investments between parties facing different tax structures, such arrangements are not without costs. All joint investments create conflicts of interest. The party responsible for making decisions for the venture has an incentive to act in ways that are in its own best interest, which may not coincide with the actions the co-investors would prefer.
3. The presence of conflicts of interest creates demand for ways to reduce the costs of these conflicts. Monitoring, incentive contracts, performance bonds, warranties, reputation, and lawsuits are all responses to this demand.
4. A progressive tax-rate system encourages some firms to undertake hedging activities and diversification to reduce the volatility of cash flows (and taxable income) and increase the after-tax expected rate of return.
5. Market frictions cause the borrowing rate for funds to exceed the lending rate. These costs are high in part because borrowers cannot always be trusted to act as they promise. In particular, borrowers might have incentives to take actions that are unobservable to lenders and have unfavorable implications for their cash flows. This impairs borrowers' abilities to repay their debts.
6. In realistic market settings, where information differences among contracting parties are pervasive, efficient tax planning may deviate substantially from tax minimization.
7. Lenders seek to enhance the collectability of loans by writing extensive loan covenants that restrict borrowers' actions. But such covenants, which are costly to write and monitor, are imperfect in preventing opportunistic behavior by borrowers. Moreover, restrictive covenants may restrain borrowers from taking actions that would benefit both the borrower and the lender.
8. In organizational contracting problems, it is often difficult for outside observers (e.g., consultants, corporate raiders, investment bankers, regulators, or researchers) to determine whether contracts tied to profits are motivated by incentive considerations, tax considerations, or both. This identification problem makes it difficult to know what economic problem gave rise to the contractual microstructure.
9. When an employer is risk neutral and an employee is risk averse, a pure wage contract allocates risk-bearing between the parties in an efficient manner, ignoring taxes. If a profits-based compensation contract is preferred for tax purposes, however, tax considerations and risk-sharing considerations will be in conflict, and the two forces must be traded off.
10. Under conditions of moral hazard (hidden-action problems), a deferred compensation contract might have attractive incentive features. If, under such circumstances, an immediate salary is preferred for tax reasons, a conflict arises between the two forces, and they must be traded off.
11. Tax-savings strategies might naturally be sacrificed where there are hidden-information problems. The seller of an asset is generally better informed than prospective buyers about the quality or value of the asset being sold. Tax considerations might favor the sale of an asset to realize a loss that reduces taxable income. Prospective buyers, however, will have difficulty in distinguishing whether the motivation for selling the asset is to secure tax benefits or the asset is no longer as

[37] Hanlon, Laplante, and Shevlin (2005) and Hanlon, Maydew, and Shevlin (2008) provide evidence consistent with this argument.

productive as the seller asserts. As a result, the asset might not be sold because the buyer is rationally unwilling to pay full value for it, and tax benefits would be sacrificed.

12. Tax-planning considerations often conflict with nontax considerations in such organizational design issues as hierarchical structure (the degree of centralization and vertical integration) and whether to organize certain operations as branches or subsidiaries.

13. Many tax-planning strategies affect financial reporting to shareholders and other less direct stakeholders of the firm. Many tax-reducing strategies require transactions that reduce income reported to these other parties. To the extent financial accounting numbers are used in contracts (e.g. compensation, bond covenants, regulation) and by outside stakeholders (e.g., analysts and investors in valuing the firm's stocks and bonds), nontax costs of the business increase, and tax reduction may be discouraged.

14. Financial accounting for many transactions differs from how they are treated for tax purposes. These differences can be thought of as either temporary or permanent. Temporary differences are items that will be recognized or included in calculating both pretax book income and taxable income but will be recognized or included in different time periods. Depreciation is the classic example of a temporary difference. Permanent differences are items that are included in the calculation of one of the income numbers but not the other. Municipal bond interest is the classic example of a permanent difference (it is included in pretax book income but not taxable income).

15. There is a wealth of information in a firm's financial statement disclosures, especially the income tax footnote, about the differences between how a firm accounts for its transactions for book versus tax purposes. These detailed disclosures can be used by informed readers to derive an estimate of a firm's taxable income—both U.S. and, less accurately, worldwide taxable income—estimate effective tax rates separately for the U.S. and foreign earnings, and for a number of other reasons.

16. Effective tax planning must be viewed relative to the costs of implementing the requisite strategies. In addition to certain organizational inefficiencies such strategies may introduce, these costs include securing professional advice, keeping records, and writing and enforcing contracts. As such, effective tax planning must be distinguished from tax minimization.

Questions

Q7-1. True or false? Discuss.

a. In a progressive tax-rate system, risk-neutral investors prefer volatile assets over riskless assets because they can average their tax rates.

b. In a progressive tax-rate system, risk-neutral investors will demand portfolio diversification and hedging.

c. Hidden-information problems arise when symmetrically informed parties hide information from each other.

d. Hidden-action problems arise because it is costly for principals to monitor the actions of agents.

e. Symmetric uncertainty about future cash flows causes employees to prefer salary to deferred compensation contracts.

Q7-2. What role do hidden-action problems play in causing the borrowing rate for funds to be greater than the lending rate? Can we eliminate hidden-action problems? Why or why not? How does the difference in borrowing and lending rates affect the taxpayer's ability to undertake clientele-based arbitrage?

Q7-3. What is an identification problem? Illustrate conditions under which there might be an identification problem involving employee-employer compensation contracting, sale of an asset, and a merger. Why is it important for outsiders to recognize when an identification problem may be present?

Q7-4. If employers are risk neutral and employees are risk averse, why is a salary contract optimal, ignoring tax and asymmetric information considerations? Under what conditions in employee compensation contracting are tax- and risk-sharing considerations in conflict? As a result of these conflicts, do employees bear more risk than if the goal were simply to allocate risks efficiently?

Q7-5. In the presence of hidden-action problems, under what conditions will a deferred compensation contract both minimize taxes and provide desirable work incentives for employees?

Q7-6. How do hidden-information problems affect the costs of corporate restructuring? Might the tax benefits of such restructurings be sacrificed by corporations because of these problems?

Q7-7. What role do hidden-action problems play in limited partnerships and other joint ventures? How might the cost of these problems be reduced?

Q7-8. What is the undercompletion problem? Provide an example in an R&D drug research setting. How might the costs of this problem be reduced?

Q7-9. How might tax considerations conflict with financial reporting considerations? Provide an example from the banking industry.

Q7-10. How might bond covenants influence a firm's tax-planning activity? Provide an example for firms that use LIFO for inventory costing.

Q7-11. Managers are often concerned about the impact on reported profits of any actions recommended by the tax-planning department. Explain why.

Q7-12. If managers are compensated in part on the basis of a bonus based on accounting earnings, they are likely to object to any tax plans that reduce reported earnings. What actions could the firm take to mitigate this concern?

Q7-13. What are the tax benefits of deferring income recognition in advance of a decline in statutory tax rates? What, if any, are the nontax costs?

Q7-14. How might tax savings be sacrificed to achieve organizational design efficiencies or to mitigate political costs?

Q7-15. Below is an extract from Amazon's 2017 annual report. What is the firm's GAAP effective tax rate? Why does the rate differ from the top statutory tax rate? (To help answer this question, recast the rate reconciliation schedule in terms of tax rate percentage.) What are deferred taxes? What are the major deferred tax items for Amazon? What is the amount of unrecognized tax benefits Amazon has as of the year ended December 31, 2017?

	Year Ended December 31,		
	2015	2016	2017
Net product sales	$ 79,268	$ 94,665	$118,573
Net service sales	27,738	41,322	59,293
Total net sales	107,006	135,987	177,866
Operating expenses:			
Cost of sales	71,651	88,265	111,934
Fulfillment	13,410	17,619	25,249
Marketing	5,254	7,233	10,069
Technology and content	12,540	16,085	22,620
General and administrative	1,747	2,432	3,674
Other operating expense, net	171	167	214
Total operating expenses	104,773	131,801	173,760
Operating income	2,233	4,186	4,106
Interest income	50	100	202
Interest expense	(459)	(484)	(848)
Other income (expense), net	(256)	90	346
Total non-operating income (expense)	(665)	(294)	(300)
Income before income taxes	1,568	3,892	3,806
Provision for income taxes	(950)	(1,425)	(769)
Equity-method investment activity, net of tax	(22)	(96)	(4)
Net income	$ 596	$ 2,371	$ 3,033

Note 10—INCOME TAXES

In 2015, 2016, and 2017, we recorded net tax provisions of $950 million, $1.4 billion, and $769 million. We have tax benefits relating to excess stock-based compensation deductions and accelerated depreciation deductions that are being utilized to reduce our U.S. taxable income. Cash taxes paid, net of refunds, were $273 million, $412 million, and $957 million for 2015, 2016, and 2017.

The 2017 Tax Act was signed into law on December 22, 2017. The 2017 Tax Act significantly revises the U.S. corporate income tax by, among other things, lowering the statutory corporate tax rate from 35% to 21%, eliminating certain deductions, imposing a mandatory one-time tax on accumulated earnings of foreign subsidiaries, introducing new tax regimes, and changing how foreign earnings are subject to U.S. tax. The 2017 Tax Act also enhanced and extended through 2026 the option to claim accelerated depreciation deductions on qualified property. We have not completed our determination of the accounting implications of the 2017 Tax Act on our tax accruals. However, we have reasonably estimated the effects of the 2017 Tax Act and recorded provisional amounts in our financial statements as of December 31, 2017. We recorded a provisional tax benefit for the impact of the 2017 Tax Act of approximately $789 million. This amount is primarily comprised of the remeasurement of federal net deferred tax liabilities resulting from the permanent reduction in the U.S. statutory corporate tax rate to 21% from 35%, after taking into account the mandatory one-time tax on the accumulated earnings of our foreign subsidiaries. The amount of this one-time tax is not material. As we complete our analysis of the 2017 Tax Act, collect and prepare necessary data, and interpret any additional guidance issued by the U.S. Treasury Department, the IRS, and other standard-setting bodies, we may make adjustments to the provisional amounts. Those adjustments may materially impact our provision for income taxes in the period in which the adjustments are made.

The components of the provision for income taxes, net are as follows (in millions):

	Year Ended December 31,		
	2015	2016	2017
Current taxes:			
U.S. Federal	$ 215	$1,136	$(137)
U.S. State	237	208	211
International	417	327	724
Current taxes	869	1,671	798
Deferred taxes:			
U.S. Federal	473	116	(202)
U.S. State	(171)	(31)	(26)
International	(221)	(331)	199
Deferred taxes	81	(246)	(29)
Provision for income taxes, net	$ 950	$1,425	$ 769

U.S. and international components of income before income taxes are as follows (in millions):

	Year Ended December 31,		
	2015	2016	2017
U.S.	$2,186	$4,551	$5,630
International	(618)	(659)	(1,824)
Income (loss) before income taxes	$1,568	$3,892	$3,806

The items accounting for differences between income taxes computed at the federal statutory rate and the provision recorded for income taxes are as follows (in millions):

	Year Ended December 31,		
	2015	2016	2017
Income taxes computed at the federal statutory rate	$549	$1,362	$1,332
Effect of:			
Impact of foreign tax differential	350	(69)	1,178
State taxes, net of federal benefits	37	110	114
Tax credits	(99)	(119)	(220)
Stock-based compensation [1]	149	189	(917)
Domestic production activities deduction	(44)	(94)	—
Impact of 2017 Tax Act	—	—	(789)
Other, net	8	46	71
Total	$950	$1,425	$ 769

(1) Includes non-deductible stock-based compensation and beginning in 2017, excess tax benefits from stock-based compensation. For 2017, our tax provision includes $1.3 billion of excess tax benefits from stock-based compensation.

Our provision for income taxes in 2016 was higher than in 2015 primarily due to an increase in U.S. pre-tax income, partially offset by an increase in the proportion of foreign losses for which we may realize a tax benefit, an increase in tax amortization deductions, and a decline in the proportion of nondeductible expenses. We have recorded valuation allowances against the deferred tax assets associated with losses for which we may not realize a related tax benefit.

Our provision for income taxes in 2017 was lower than in 2016 primarily due to excess tax benefits from stock-based compensation and the provisional favorable effect of the 2017 Tax Act, partially offset by an increase in the proportion of foreign losses for which we may not realize a tax benefit and audit-related developments.

We regularly assess whether it is more likely than not that we will realize our deferred tax assets in each taxing jurisdiction in which we operate. In performing this assessment with respect to each jurisdiction, we review all available evidence, including recent cumulative loss experience and expectations of future earnings, capital gains, and investment in such jurisdiction, the carry-forward periods available to us for tax reporting purposes, and other relevant factors. In Q2 2017, we recognized an estimated charge to tax expense of $600 million to record a valuation allowance against the net deferred tax assets in Luxembourg.

The 2017 Tax Act includes a mandatory one-time tax on accumulated earnings of foreign subsidiaries, and as a result, all previously unremitted earnings for which no U.S. deferred tax liability had been accrued have now been subject to U.S. tax. Notwithstanding the U.S. taxation of these amounts, we intend to continue to invest most or all of these earnings, as well as our capital in these subsidiaries, indefinitely outside of the U.S. and do not expect to incur any significant, additional taxes related to such amounts.

Deferred income tax assets and liabilities are as follows (in millions):

	December 31,	
	2016	2017[6]
Deferred tax assets[1]:		
Loss carryforwards U.S. - Federal/States[2]	$ 198	$ 211
Loss carryforwards - Foreign[3]	1,062	2,149
Accrued liabilities, reserves, & other expenses	968	901
Stock-based compensation	1,073	1,026
Deferred revenue	330	349
Assets held for investment	66	35
Depreciation & amortization	179	279
Other items	171	167
Tax credits[4]	39	381

continued

continued from previous page

	December 31,	
	2016	2017[6]
Total gross deferred tax assets	4,086	5,498
Less valuation allowance[5]	(1,012)	(2,538)
Deferred tax assets, net of valuation allowance	3,074	2,960
Deferred tax liabilities:		
Depreciation & amortization	(2,332)	(2,568)
Acquisition related intangible assets	(226)	(531)
Other items	(62)	(58)
Net deferred tax assets (liabilities), net of valuation allowance	$ 454	$ (197)

(1) Deferred tax assets related to net operating losses and tax credits are presented net of tax contingencies.

(2) Excluding $18 million of deferred tax assets as of December 31, 2016, related to net operating losses that result from excess stock-based compensation. Beginning in 2017, losses resulting from excess stock-based compensation are now recognized immediately as a result of the adoption of new accounting guidance.

(3) Excluding $9 million of deferred tax assets as of December 31, 2016, related to net operating losses that result from excess stock-based compensation. Beginning in 2017, losses resulting from excess stock-based compensation are now recognized immediately as a result of the adoption of new accounting guidance.

(4) Excluding $659 million of deferred tax assets as of December 31, 2016, related to tax credits that result from excess stock-based compensation. Beginning in 2017, losses resulting from excess stock-based compensation are now recognized immediately as a result of the adoption of new accounting guidance.

(5) Relates primarily to deferred tax assets that would only be realizable upon the generation of net income in certain foreign taxing jurisdictions and future capital gains.

(6) We recorded a provisional adjustment to our federal deferred income tax assets and liabilities as of December 31, 2017 to reflect the reduction in the U.S. statutory federal corporate tax rate from 35% to 21% resulting from the 2017 Tax Act.

As of December 31, 2017, our federal, foreign, and state net operating loss carryforwards for income tax purposes were approximately $226 million, $8.0 billion, and $858 million. The federal, foreign, and state net operating loss carryforwards are subject to limitations under Section 382 of the Internal Revenue Code and applicable foreign and state tax law. If not utilized, a portion of the federal, foreign, and state net operating loss carryforwards will begin to expire in 2023, 2018, and 2019, respectively. As of December 31, 2017, our tax credit carryforwards for income tax purposes were approximately $1.1 billion. If not utilized, a portion of the tax credit carryforwards will begin to expire in 2021. As of December 31, 2017, our federal capital loss carryforwards for income tax purposes was approximately $359 million. If not utilized, a portion of the capital loss carryforwards will begin to expire in 2019.

Tax Contingencies

We are subject to income taxes in the U.S. (federal and state) and numerous foreign jurisdictions. Significant judgment is required in evaluating our tax positions and determining our provision for income taxes. During the ordinary course of business, there are many transactions and calculations for which the ultimate tax determination is uncertain. We establish reserves for tax-related uncertainties based on estimates of whether, and the extent to which, additional taxes will be due. These reserves are established when we believe that certain positions might be challenged despite our belief that our tax return positions are fully supportable. We adjust these reserves in light of changing facts and circumstances, such as the outcome of tax audits. The provision for income taxes includes the impact of reserve provisions and changes to reserves that are considered appropriate.

The reconciliation of our tax contingencies is as follows (in millions):

	December 31,		
	2015	2016	2017
Gross tax contingencies – January 1	$ 710	$1,181	$1,710
Gross increases to tax positions in prior periods	254	355	223
Gross decreases to tax positions in prior periods	(22)	(133)	(139)
Gross increases to current period tax positions	242	308	518
Lapse of statute of limitations	(3)	(1)	(3)
Gross tax contingencies – December 31[(1)]	$1,181	$1,710	$2,309

[(1)] As of December 31, 2017, we had $2.3 billion of accrued tax contingencies, of which $1.2 billion, if fully recognized, would decrease our effective tax rate.

As of December 31, 2016 and 2017, we had accrued interest and penalties, net of federal income tax benefit, related to tax contingencies of $67 million and $107 million. Interest and penalties, net of federal income tax benefit, recognized for the years ended December 31, 2015, 2016, and 2017 was $18 million, $9 million, and $40 million.

We are under examination, or may be subject to examination, by the Internal Revenue Service ("IRS") for the calendar year 2005 and thereafter. These examinations may lead to ordinary course adjustments or proposed adjustments to our taxes or our net operating losses with respect to years under examination as well as subsequent periods. As previously disclosed, we have received Notices of Proposed Adjustment ("NOPAs") from the IRS for transactions undertaken in the 2005 and 2006 calendar years relating to transfer pricing with our foreign subsidiaries. The IRS is seeking to increase our U.S. taxable income by an amount that would result in additional federal tax of approximately $1.5 billion, subject to interest. On March 23, 2017, the U.S. Tax Court issued its decision regarding the issues raised in the IRS NOPAs. The Tax Court rejected the approach from the IRS NOPAs in determining transfer pricing adjustments in 2005 and 2006 for the transactions undertaken with our foreign subsidiaries and adopted, with adjustments, our suggested approach. On September 29, 2017, the IRS filed a notice of appeal to the U.S. Court of Appeals for the Ninth Circuit. We will continue to defend ourselves vigorously in this matter. If the Tax Court decision were reversed on appeal or if the IRS were to successfully assert transfer pricing adjustments of a similar nature to the NOPAs for transactions in subsequent years, we could be subject to significant additional tax liabilities.

Certain of our subsidiaries were under examination or investigation by the French Tax Administration ("FTA") for calendar year 2006 and thereafter. In September 2012, we received proposed tax assessment notices for calendar years 2006 through 2010 relating to the allocation of income between foreign jurisdictions. In June 2015, we received final tax collection notices for these years assessing additional French taxes, interest, and penalties through September 2012. In December 2017, we settled this dispute with the FTA and included the impact thereof within our financial statements. In addition, in October 2014, the European Commission opened a formal investigation to examine whether decisions by the tax authorities in Luxembourg with regard to the corporate income tax paid by certain of our subsidiaries comply with European Union rules on state aid. On October 4, 2017, the European Commission announced its decision that determinations by the tax authorities in Luxembourg did not comply with European Union rules on state aid. This decision orders Luxembourg to calculate and recover additional taxes from us for the period May 2006 through June 2014. We believe this decision to be without merit and will consider our legal options, including an appeal. In December 2017, Luxembourg appealed the European Commission's decision. While the European Commission announced an estimated recovery amount of approximately 250 million, plus interest, the actual amount of additional taxes subject to recovery is to be calculated by the Luxembourg tax authorities in accordance with the European Commission's guidance. Once the recovery amount is computed by Luxembourg, we anticipate funding it, including interest, into escrow, where it will remain pending conclusion of all appeals. We may be required to fund into escrow an amount in excess of the estimated recovery amount announced by the European Commission. We are also subject to taxation in various states and other foreign jurisdictions including Canada, China, Germany, India, Japan, Luxembourg, and the United Kingdom. We are under, or may be subject to, audit or examination and additional assessments by the relevant authorities in respect of these particular jurisdictions primarily for 2008 and thereafter.

We expect the total amount of tax contingencies will grow in 2018. In addition, changes in state, federal, and foreign tax laws may increase our tax contingencies. The timing of the resolution of income tax examinations is highly uncertain, and the amounts ultimately paid, if any, upon resolution of the issues raised by the taxing authorities may differ from the amounts accrued. It is reasonably possible that within the next 12 months we will receive additional assessments by various tax authorities or possibly reach resolution of income tax examinations in one or more jurisdictions. These assessments or settlements could result in changes to our contingencies related to positions on tax filings in years through 2017. The actual amount of any change could vary significantly depending on the ultimate timing and nature of any settlements. We cannot currently provide an estimate of the range of possible outcomes.

Exercises

E7-16. Suppose the tax rate is 30% if taxable income is positive and 0% if taxable income is negative. Calculate the expected tax payable for the following four projects. The expected taxable income for each project is $50,000. For each project, also calculate the expected average tax rate (expected total taxes divided by expected taxable income). Explain and discuss your results.

a. Certain payoff $50,000

b. A 50% chance of $100,000 and a 50% chance of $0

c. A 50% chance of $200,000 and a 50% chance of a loss of $100,000

d. A 50% chance of $500,000 and a 50% chance of loss of $400,000

This problem can be solved by preparing a graph similar to **Figure 7.1**.

1. Draw the tax-rate schedule for taxable income in the range –$500,000 to +$500,000, with taxable income on the horizontal axis and tax payable on the vertical axis.
2. Mark the two endpoints on the tax schedule for each project. (For item b, the two endpoints are $0 and $50,000.) Draw a straight line between the two outcomes.
3. Draw a vertical line upward from the horizontal axis at taxable income equal to $50,000.
4. Finally, read off the expected tax payable for each project where the expected tax payable is the intersection point of the lines in (2) and (3).

E7-17. Suppose the tax rate is 30% if taxable income is positive and 0% if taxable income is negative. Consider the before-tax payoffs to the following three projects:

a. Riskless: 10% for sure

b. Moderately risky: 30% half the time, –10% half the time

c. Quite risky: 300% one time in 10, –20% nine times out of 10

1. Calculate the before- and after-tax expected rates of return for each project.
2. How does the variability of returns affect the expected tax rate? Why?
3. Does this tax structure encourage or discourage high-technology start-up ventures?

E7-18. Assume the firm's after-tax cost of capital is 6% per annum. What is the benefit of deferring $1 of income for 1 year, 2 years, and for 5 years assuming the firm's marginal tax rate is 21%? Suppose the firm expects the top statutory tax rate to increase to 25% next year. Does it still pay to defer income for 1 year, 2 years, or 5 years? Explain and discuss your results.

E7-19. Suppose Sonics Inc. just started business this period. The firm purchased 400 units of inventory during the period at various prices as follows:

Date	Units	Unit Cost	Total
January	100	$10	$1,000
March	100	$12	$1,200
June	100	$14	$1,400
October	100	$15	$1,500
Total	400		$5,100

The firm sold 250 units at $30 each on the following dates:

Date	Units	Unit Price	Total Sales
February	75	$30	$2,250
May	90	$30	$2,700
August	75	$30	$2,250
December	10	$30	$ 300
Total	250		$7,500

Assume the firm faces a marginal tax rate of 21%:

a. Calculate taxable income and taxes payable assuming the firm uses FIFO for inventory costing purposes.

b. Calculate taxable income and taxes payable assuming the firm uses LIFO for inventory costing purposes.

Discuss your results, including any nontax costs that might be associated with either inventory costing system.

E7-20. Assume Sonics Inc., from the prior exercise, uses LIFO with the periodic inventory system. Thus, the LIFO cost of ending inventory at year 1 of 150 units is $1,600 (100 @ $10 + 50 @ $12). Suppose in year 2, Sonics reports the following purchases and sales:

Date	Units	Unit Cost/Price	Total
Purchases			
June	100	$17	$1,700
Sales			
July	200	$30	$6,000

a. Calculate taxable income and taxes payable (again assuming Sonics faces a marginal tax rate of 21%) for year 2. How many more units did Sonics sell than purchase? What is the difference in the unit cost and latest purchase price for each of these units?

b. Instead of purchasing 100 units in June, Sonics purchased 110 units. Recalculate taxable income and taxes payable.

c. Instead of purchasing 100 units in June, Sonics purchased 90 units. Recalculate taxable income and taxes payable.

d. How many units should Sonics have purchased to avoid dipping into earlier layers of inventory?

e. Do you notice any opportunities for Sonics to smooth reported net income (by varying the amount purchased relative to sales)? Are there any costs associated with this strategy? Does FIFO offer the same opportunities?

f. Suppose the top managers of Sonics are compensated in part by a bonus linked to reported net income. What inventory costing method might you expect the managers to favor? What costs to the firm arise from this choice?

Tax-Planning Problems

TP7-21. A tax planner for a biotechnology start-up is advising her client about how to efficiently organize R&D activities. One suggestion the tax planner made is to form a joint venture with another biotechnology company. List and explain the tax benefits and nontax costs and benefits of such a plan. Does it matter if the other company is a start-up or an established, profitable company?

TP7-22. An owner-manager of a firm is contemplating selling it to any one of a number of prospective buyers. The firm has NOLs known to be worth $50 million more to the buyers than to the seller. The current owner knows the value of the firm, but the prospective buyers are uncertain whether the firm is worth $500 million (including the extra $50 million value in NOLs) or $700 million. The poorly informed buyers consider both possibilities to be equally likely.

a. How much should buyers offer to acquire the firm?

b. Will the seller always accept the highest rational offer made?

c. How does the analysis change if the uncertain values of the firm are $500 million and $540 million rather than $500 million and $700 million?

TP7-23. Suppose you work for a business that runs a fleet of cars the sales personnel use. The fleet consists of 30 Toyota Camry sedans. All the expenses (insurance, registration, fuel, maintenance, and repairs) are paid by the firm. You have determined that it is cost-effective (from a tax and operations cost viewpoint) to "roll the fleet over" every 3 years. You plan to auction the cars.

a. Are there any agency costs (incentive problems) with the arrangement that the firm pays all the costs of operating the cars?

b. Are there any agency costs with selling the cars?

c. How might you mitigate the problems in parts (a) and (b)? Outline any new problems your suggestions might create.

TP7-24. Suppose you are a high-tax-bracket taxpayer. How could you take advantage of a situation in which the implicit tax rate on a tax-exempt asset is different from the marginal tax rate on income from a fully taxable asset? What nontax costs exist to limit your ability to take advantage of this arbitrage possibility? Are there any ways to reduce these nontax costs?

TP7-25. You have been retained by a large internet-based firm to advise the compensation committee on how best to compensate the chief executive officer (CEO). The CEO is risk averse and his actions are not fully observable (hidden-action problems). The internet firm is currently generating tax losses, but if some investments prove successful, it will begin paying taxes in 3 years. What issues must the firm consider, and how might it structure a compensation contract that takes into account the manager's risk aversion and hidden actions and the tax positions of both the company and the CEO?

TP7-26. Suppose the top corporate statutory tax rate will decrease from 35% to 21% next year. The chief financial officer of ABC Corporation wants to defer as much income as possible and asks you to prepare a detailed list of actions to shift income (i.e., ways in which the firm can shift income). For each action, she wants you to outline any nontax costs associated with the action.

References and Additional Readings

Arrow, K., 1985. "The Economics of Agency" in *Principals and Agents: The Structure of Business,* edited by J. W. Pratt and R. J. Zeckhauser. Boston, MA: Harvard Business School Press, pp. 37–51.

Ayers, B., 1998. "Deferred Tax Accounting under SFAS No. 109: An Empirical Investigation of its Incremental Value-relevance relative to APB No. 11," *The Accounting Review* (73), pp. 195–212.

Ayers, B., C. Lefanowicz, and J. Robinson, 2002. "Do Firms Purchase the Pooling Method?" *Review of Accounting Studies* (March), pp. 5–32.

Ayers, B., S. Laplante, and S. McGuire, 2010. "Credit Ratings and Taxes: The Effect Book/Tax Differences on Ratings Changes," *Contemporary Accounting Research* 27 (2), pp. 359–402.

Bartov, E., 1993. "The Timing of Asset Sales and Earnings Manipulation," *The Accounting Review* (October), pp. 840–855.

Beatty, A., P. Berger, and J. Magliolo, 1995. "Motives for Forming Research & Development Financing Organizations," *Journal of Accounting and Economics* (March–May), pp. 411–442.

Beatty, A., S. Chamberlain, and J. Magliolo, 1995. "Managing Financial Reports of Commercial Banks: The Influence of Taxes," *Journal of Accounting Research* (2), pp. 231–261.

Beatty, A., and D. Harris, 1999. "The Effects of Taxes, Agency Costs and Information Asymmetry on Earnings Management: A Comparison of Public and Private Firms," *Review of Accounting Studies* (December), pp. 299–326.

Boynton, C., P. Dobbins, and G. Plesko, 1992. "Earnings Management and the Corporate Alternative Minimum Tax," *Journal of Accounting Research* (Supplement), pp. 131–153.

Blaylock, B., T. Shevlin, and R. Wilson, 2012. "Tax Avoidance, Large Positive Book-Tax Differences, and Earnings Persistence," *The Accounting Review* 87 (1), pp. 91–120.

Calegari, M., 2000. "The Effect of Tax Accounting Rules on Capital Structure and Discretionary Accruals," *Journal of Accounting and Economics*, pp. 1–31.

Choi, W., J. Gramlich, and J. Thomas, J., 2001. "Potential Errors in Detecting Earnings Management: Reexamining Studies Investigating the AMT of 1986," *Contemporary Accounting Research*, pp. 571–613.

Collins, J., G. Geisler, and D. Shackelford, 1997. "The Effects of Taxes, Regulation, Earnings, and Organizational Form on Life Insurers' Investment Portfolio Realizations," *Journal of Accounting and Economics* (1997), pp. 337–351.

Collins. J., D. Shackelford, and J. Wahlen, 1995. "Bank Differences in the Coordination of Regulatory Capital, Earnings, and Taxes," *Journal of Accounting Research* (2), pp. 263–291.

Cushing, B., and M. LeClere, 1992. "Evidence on the Determinants of Inventory Accounting Policy Choice," *The Accounting Review* (April), pp. 355–366.

Crabtree, A., and J. Maher, 2009. "The Influence of Differences in Taxable Income and Book Income on the Bond Credit Market. *The Journal of the American Taxation Association* 31 (1), pp. 75–99.

Desai, M., and D. Dharmapala, 2006. "Corporate Tax Avoidance and High-Powered Incentives," *Journal of Financial Economics* (January), pp. 145–179.

Dhaliwal, D., M. Frankel, and R. Trezevant, 1994. "The Taxable and Book Income Motivations for a LIFO Layer Liquidation," *Journal of Accounting Research* (Autumn), pp. 278–289.

Dhaliwal, D., and S. Wang, 1992. "The Effect of Book Income Adjustment in the 1986 Alternative Minimum Tax on Corporate Financial Reporting," *Journal of Accounting and Economics* (1), pp. 7–26.

Dhaliwal, D., S. Kaplan, R. Laux, and E. Weisbrod, 2013. "The Information Content of Tax Expense for Firms Reporting Losses," *Journal of Accounting Research* 51 (1), pp. 135–164.

Donohoe, M., and W. Knechel, 2014. Does Corporate Tax Aggressiveness Influence Audit Pricing? *Contemporary Accounting Research* 31 (1), pp. 284–308.

Dopuch, N., and M. Pincus, 1988. "Evidence on the Choice of Inventory Accounting Methods: LIFO Versus FIFO," *Journal of Accounting Research* (Spring), pp. 28–59.

Dyreng, S., M. Hanlon, and E. Maydew, 2008. "Long Run Corporate Tax Avoidance," *The Accounting Review* (83), pp. 61–82.

Dyreng, S., M. Hanlon, and E. Maydew, 2010. "The Effects of Managers on Corporate Tax Avoidance," *The Accounting Review* (85) pp. 1163–1189.

Dyreng, S., M. Hanlon, E. Maydew, and J. Thornock, 2017. "Changes in Corporate Effective Tax Rates over the Past Twenty-Five Years" *Journal of Financial Economics* (124), pp. 441–463

Edwards, E., 2018. "The Deferred Tax Asset Valuation Allowance and Firm Creditworthiness," *The Journal of the American Taxation Association* (Spring), pp. 57–80.

Engel, E., M. Erickson, and E. Maydew, 1999. "Debt-Equity Hybrid Securities," *Journal of Accounting Research* (Autumn), pp. 1–26.

Enis, C. R., and B. Ke, 2003. "The Impact of the 1986 Tax Reform Act on Income Shifting from Corporate to Shareholder Tax Bases: Evidence from the Motor Carrier-Industry," *Journal of Accounting Research* (41), pp. 65–88.

Erickson, M., M. Hanlon, and E. Maydew, 2004. "How Much Will Firms Pay for Earnings That Do Not Exist? Evidence of Taxes Paid on Fraudulent Earnings," *The Accounting Review* (2), pp. 387–408.

Fellingham, J., and M. Wolfson, 1985. "Taxes and Risk Sharing," *The Accounting Review* (January), pp. 10–17.

Frank, M. M., and S. O. Rego, 2006. "Do Managers Use the Valuation Allowance Account to Manage Earnings around Certain Earnings Targets?" *The Journal of the American Taxation Association* 28 (1), pp. 43–65.

Frischmann, P., T. Shevlin, and R. Wilson, 2008. "Economic Consequences of Increasing the Conformity in Accounting for Uncertain Tax Benefits," *Journal of Accounting and Economics* (December), pp. 294–311.

Goh, B. W., J. Lee, C. Y. Lim, and T. Shevlin, 2016. The Effect of Corporate Tax avoidance on the Cost of Equity," *The Accounting Review* 91 (6), pp. 1647–1670.

Gaertner, F., S. Laplante, and D. Lynch, 2016. "Trends in the Sources of Permanent and Temporary Book-Tax Differences During the Schedule M-3 Era," *National Tax Journal* 69 (4), pp. 785–808.

Graham, J., M. Hanlon, and T. Shevlin, 2011. "Real Effects of Accounting Rules: Evidence from Multinational Firms' Investment Location and Profit Repatriation Decisions," *Journal of Accounting Research* (Spring), pp. 137–185.

Graham, J., M. Hanlon, T. Shevlin, and N. Shroff, 2014. "Incentives for Tax Planning and Avoidance: Evidence from the Field," *The Accounting Review* 89 (3), pp. 991–1023.

Graham, J., J. Raedy, and D. Shackelford, 2012. "Research in Accounting for Income Taxes," *Journal of Accounting and Economics*, pp. 412–434.

Graham, J., and D. Rogers, 2001. "Do Firms Hedge in Response to Tax Incentives?" *Journal of Finance*, pp. 815–839.

Graham, J., and C. Smith, 1999. "Tax Incentives to Hedge," *Journal of Finance* (December), pp. 2241–2262.

Gramlich, J., 1991. "The Effect of the Alternative Minimum Tax Book Income Adjustment on Accrual Decisions," *Journal of the American Taxation Association* (Spring), pp. 36–56.

Guenther, D., 1994. "Earnings Management in Response to Corporate Tax Rate Changes: Evidence from the 1986 Tax Reform Act," *The Accounting Review* (January), pp. 230–243.

Guenther, D., E. Maydew, and S. Nutter, 1997. "Financial Reporting, Tax Costs, and Book-Tax Conformity," *Journal of Accounting and Economics* (3), pp. 225–248.

Hanlon, M., 2003. "What Can We Infer about a Firm's Taxable Income from Its Financial Statements?" *National Tax Journal* (16 December), pp. 831–864.

Hanlon, M., 2005. "The Persistence and Pricing of Earnings, Accruals, and Cash Flows When Firms Have Large Book-Tax Differences," *The Accounting Review* (80), pp. 137–167.

Hanlon, M., E. Maydew, and D. Saavedra, 2013. "The Taxman Cometh: A Tax-Based Explanation for Why Firms Hold So Much Cash" Working Paper, Cambridge, MA: Massachusetts Institute of Technology.

Hanlon, M., and J. Slemrod, 2009. "What Does Tax Aggressiveness Signal? Evidence from Stock Price Reactions to News about Tax Shelter Involvement," *Journal of Public Economics* (February), pp. 126–141

Hanlon, M. and T. Shevlin, 2005. "Book-Tax Conformity for Corporate Income: An Introduction to the Issues," in *Tax Policy and the Economy*, No. 19, edited by James M. Poterba. National Bureau of Economic Research, Cambridge, MA.

Hanlon, M, E. Maydew, and D. Saveedra, 2017. "The Taxman Cometh: Does Tax Uncertainty Affect Corporate Cash Holdings," *Review of Accounting Studies* 22, pp. 1198–1228.

Hanlon, M., E. Maydew, and T. Shevlin, 2008. "An Unintended Consequence of Book-Tax Conformity: A Loss of Earnings Informativeness," *Journal of Accounting and Economics* (46), pp. 294–311.

Hanlon, M, J. Graham, and T. Shevlin, 2010. "Barriers to Mobility: The Lockout Effect of U.S. Taxation of Worldwide Corporate Profits," *National Tax Journal* (63), pp. 1111–1144.

Hanlon, M., R. Lester and R. Verdi, 2015. "The Effect of Repatriation Tax Costs on U.S. Multinational Investment," *Journal of Financial Economics* (116), pp. 179–196

Hanlon, M., S. Laplante, and T. Shevlin, 2005. "Evidence on the Information Loss of Conforming Book Income and Taxable Income," *The Journal of Law and Economics* (48), pp. 407–442.

Hanna, C., 2012. "Corporate Tax Reform: Listening to Corporate America," *Journal of Corporation Law*, Forthcoming.

Hasan, I., C.-K. Hoi, Q. Wu, and H. Zhang, 2014. "Beauty in the Eye of the Beholder: The Effect of Corporate Tax Avoidance on the Cost of Bank Loans. *Journal of Financial Economics* 113 (1), pp. 109–130.

Hodder, L., M. L. McAnally, and C. Weaver, 2003. "The Influence of Tax and Nontax Factors on Banks' Choice of Organizational Form," *The Accounting Review* (78), pp. 297–325.

Hunt, A., S. Moyer, and T. Shevlin, 1996. "Managing Interacting Accounting Measures to Meet Multiple Objectives: A Study of LIFO Firms," *Journal of Accounting and Economics* (June), pp. 339–374.

Johnson, W., and D. Dhaliwal, 1988, "LIFO Abandonment," *Journal of Accounting Research* (Autumn), pp. 236–272.

Kinney, M., and W. Wempe, 2004. "JIT Adoption: The Effects of LIFO Reserves and Financial Reporting and Tax Incentives," *Contemporary Accounting Research* (Fall), pp. 603–638.

Klassen, K., 1997. "The Impact of Inside Ownership Concentration on the Trade-off between Financial and Tax Reporting," *The Accounting Review* (3), pp. 455–474.

Klassen, K., J. Pittman, and M. Reed, 2004. "A Cross-National Comparison of R&D Expenditure Decisions: Tax Incentives and Financial Constraints," *Contemporary Accounting Research* (Fall), pp. 639–681.

Knott, A., and J. Rosenfeld, 2003. "Book and Tax (Part One): A Selective Exploration of Two Parallel Universes," *Tax Notes* (May), pp. 865–897.

Lester, R., and D. Langenmayr, 2018. "Taxation and Corporation Risk-Taking," *The Accounting Review* 93, pp. 237–266

Lev, B., and D. Nissim, 2004. "Taxable Income, Future Earnings, and Equity Values," *The Accounting Review* 79 (4), pp. 1039–1074.

Ljungqvist, A., L. Zhang, and L. Zuo, 2017. "Sharing Risk with the Government: How Taxes Affect Corporate Risk Taking," *Journal of Accounting Research* 55 (3), pp. 669–707.

Manzon, G., 1992. "Earnings Management of Firms Subject to the Alternative Minimum Tax," *Journal of the American Taxation Association* (Fall), pp. 88–111.

Matsunaga, S., T. Shevlin, and D. Shores, 1992. "Disqualifying Dispositions of Incentive Stock Options: Tax Benefits versus Financial Reporting Costs," *Journal of Accounting Research* (Supplement), pp. 37–76.

Maydew, E., 1997. "Tax-Induced Earnings Management by Firms with Net Operating Losses," *Journal of Accounting Research* (Spring), pp. 83–96.

Maydew, E., K. Schipper, and L. Vincent, 1999. "The Impact of Taxes on the Choice of Divestiture Method," *Journal of Accounting and Economics* (December), pp. 117–150.

Mikhail, M., 1999. "Coordination of Earnings, Regulatory Capital, and Taxes in Private and Public Companies," Working Paper. Cambridge, MA: Massachusetts Institute of Technology.

Miller, G., and D. Skinner, 1998. "Determinants of the Valuation Allowance for Deferred Tax Assets Under SFAS No. 109," *The Accounting Review* (April), pp. 213–234.

Mills, L., 1998. "Book-Tax Differences and Internal Revenue Service Adjustments," *Journal of Accounting Research* (2), pp. 343–356.

Mills, L., M. Erickson, and E. Maydew, 1998. "Investments in Tax Planning," *Journal of the American Taxation Association* (Spring), pp. 1–20.

Mills, L., and K. Newberry, 2005. "Firms' Off-Balance Sheet and Hybrid Debt Financing: Evidence from Their Book-Tax Reporting Differences," *Journal of Accounting Research* (43), pp. 251–282.

Moyer, S., 1990. "Capital Adequacy Ratio Regulations and Accounting Choices in Commercial Banks," *Journal of Accounting and Economics* (July), pp. 123–154.

Nance, D., C. Smith, and C. Smithson, 1993. "On the Determinants of Corporate Hedging," *Journal of Finance* (March), pp. 267–284.

Nichols, N., C. Baril, and J. Briggs, 2007a. "Early Indications of the Impact of FIN 48," *Tax Notes* (July 9), pp. 119–125.

Nichols, N., C. Baril, and J. Briggs, 2007b. "And the Impact Is . . . First Quarter Results from Adopting FIN 48," *Tax Notes* (July 30), pp. 377–388.

Northcutt, W., and C. Vines, 1998. "Earnings Management in Response to Political Scrutiny of Effective Tax Rates," *Journal of the American Taxation Association* (Fall), pp. 22–36.

Petroni, K., and D. Shackelford, 1999. "Managing Annual Accounting Reports to Avoid State Taxes: An Analysis of Property-Casualty Insurers," *The Accounting Review* (3), pp. 371–393.

Phillips, J., 2003. "Corporate Tax Planning Effectiveness: The Role of Compensation-Based Incentives," *The Accounting Review* (July), pp. 847–874.

Phillips, J., M. Pincus, and S. Olhoft Rego, 2003. "Earnings Management: New Evidence Based on Deferred Tax Expense," *The Accounting Review* (78), pp. 491–521.

Phillips, J., M. Pincus and S. Rego, 2003. Earnings Management: New Evidence Based on Deferred Tax expense," *The Accounting Review* 78 (2), pp. 491–521.

Poterba, J. M., N. S. Rao, and J. K. Seidman, 2011. "Deferred Tax Positions and Incentives for Corporate Behavior around Corporate Tax Changes," *National Tax Journal* (64, 1, March), pp. 27–57.

Randolph, D., G. Salamon, and J. Seida, 2005. "Quantifying the Costs of Intertemporal Taxable Income Shifting: Theory and Evidence from the Property-Casualty Insurance Industry," *The Accounting Review* (80), pp. 315–349.

Revsine, L., D. W. Collins, W. B. Johnson, and F. Mittelstaedt, 2012. *Financial Reporting & Analysis,* 5th ed. Upper Saddle River, NJ: Prentice Hall.

Scholes, M., P. Wilson, and M. Wolfson, 1990. "Tax Planning, Regulatory Capital Planning, and Financial Reporting Strategy for Commercial Banks," *Review of Financial Studies*, pp. 625–650.

Scholes, M., P. Wilson, and M. Wolfson, 1992. "Firms' Responses to Anticipated Reductions in Tax Rates: The Tax Reform Act of 1986," *Journal of Accounting Research* 30, pp. 161–191.

Schrand, C. M., and M. H. F. Wong, 2003. "Earnings Management Using the Valuation Allowance for Deferred Tax Assets under SFAS No. 109," *Contemporary Accounting Research* 20 (3), pp. 579–611.

"Session 9. The Road Ahead: Tax Reform and U.S. Source Intangible Income," *Taxes, The Tax Magazine* (June 2013).

Shackelford, D., and T. Shevlin, 2001. "Empirical Tax Research in Accounting," *Journal of Accounting and Economics*, pp. 321–387.

Shevlin, T., 1987. "Taxes and Off-Balance Sheet-Financing: Research and Development Limited Partnerships," *The Accounting Review* (July), pp. 480–509.

Slemrod, J., 1997. *Measuring Taxpayer Burden and Attitudes for Large Corporations: 1996 and 1992 Survey Results.* Office of Tax Policy Research Working Paper No. 97–1. Ann Arbor, MI: University of Michigan Press.

Slemrod, J., and M. Blumenthal, 1993. *The Compliance Costs of Big Business.* Washington, DC: Tax Foundation.

Weber, R., and J. Wheeler, 1992. "Using Income Tax Disclosures to Explore Significant Economic Transactions," *Accounting Horizons* (September), pp. 14–29.

Weber, D., 2009. "Do Analysts and Investors Fully Appreciate the Implications of Book-Tax Differences for Future Earnings? *Contemporary Accounting Research* 26 (4), pp. 1175–1206.

Wheeler, J., and E. Outslay, 1986. "The Phantom Federal Income Taxes of General Dynamics Corporation," *The Accounting Review* (October), pp. 760–774.

Wilde, J., and R. Wilson, 2018. "Perspectives on Corporate Tax Avoidance: Observations from the Past Decade," *Journal of the American Taxation Association* pp. 63–81.

Wilson, R, 2009. "An Examination of Corporate Tax Shelter Participants," *The Accounting Review*, pp. 969–999.

Wolfson, M., 1985. "Empirical Evidence of Incentive Problems and Their Mitigation in Oil and Gas Tax Shelter Programs" in *Principals and Agents: The Structure of Business,* edited by J. W. Pratt and R. J. Zeckhauser. Boston, MA: Harvard Business School Press, pp. 101–125, 221–224.

Zion, D., and A. Varshney, 2007. "Peeking Behind the Tax Curtain," *Credit Suisse* (May 18).

8

Compensation Planning

After completing this chapter, you should be able to

1. Enumerate the factors relevant to determining whether current salary or deferred compensation is tax preferred.
2. Describe the taxation of restricted stock, performance share/units/cash awards, incentive stock options (ISOs), and nonqualified stock options (NQOs).
3. Determine when ISOs are tax preferred over NQOs.
4. Decide when restricted stock and employee stock options might be exercised early for tax reasons.
5. Discuss the implications of §162(m) for compensation design.

In this chapter, we discuss the tax-planning aspects of employee compensation planning. The two themes that we stress are (1) the importance of considering all parties to a contract and (2) the nontax features of the tax-planning alternatives. To begin, **Table 8.1** lists some categories of compensation, along with their tax treatment for both the employee and the employer.

Table 8.1 assumes that the employer can fully deduct the items listed as deductible to the employer. However, TCJA introduced a major change: for "qualified employees" the maximum deduction a public corporation can take for compensation to that employee is now $1 million per year. Previously, under **Section 162(m)**, the corporation was limited to a $1 million annual deduction only for nonperformance-based compensation. Generally, bonus and equity-related compensation were all viewed as performance-based and thus not subject to the limitation. However, under the TCJA, both nonperformance, for example, salary, and performance-based, for example, all equity-based compensation, is now subject to the limitation. Covered employees include the CEO, CFO, and the three highest paid employees.

If one assumes that covered employees earn a basic salary of $1 million or more, then all equity-based compensation is no longer deductible. Thus, all the analyses in this chapter that assume corporate tax deductibility of equity-based compensation no longer apply to covered employees. However, the analyses still apply to all other employees and to nonpublic corporations.

Many compensation experts (including those who contribute to the popular press and tax journals) have concluded that the compensation alternatives listed in **Table 8.1** are ordered in terms of decreasing desirability. In fact, however, once a global contracting perspective is adopted—one that takes account of both tax and nontax considerations of both the employer and employee—none of the compensation alternatives listed in **Table 8.1** can be ranked unambiguously. We illustrate the importance of the global contracting perspective by comparing some of the alternative compensation components listed in the table.

Table 8.1 Compensation Alternatives

Category	Employee Tax Effects	Employer Tax Effects
Nontaxable fringe benefits	Never taxed	Immediately deductible
Pensions	Deferred tax with tax exemption on investment returns	Immediately deductible
Incentive stock options (ISOs)	Deferred tax at capital gains rates	Never deductible
Deferred compensation	Deferred tax at ordinary rates	Deferred deduction
Restricted stock	Deferred tax at ordinary rates	Deferred deduction
Nonqualified stock options (NQOs)	Deferred tax at ordinary rates	Deferred deduction
Stock appreciation rights (SARs)	Deferred tax at ordinary rates	Deferred deduction
Performance shares/units/cash	Deferred tax at ordinary rates	Deferred deduction
Cash salary	Immediately taxed at ordinary rates	Immediately deductible
Cash bonus	Immediately taxed at ordinary rates	Immediately deductible

Notes: The deductibility of nontaxable fringe benefits were severely curtailed in TCJA 2017. The intrinsic value of the ISOs on the exercise date is included in AMT income. The TCJA limited the deduction for compensation to qualified employees, usually the CEO, CFO, and the three highest paid employees, to $1 million per year for public corporations. We assume full deductibility above.

8.1 SALARY VERSUS DEFERRED COMPENSATION

Let us start by considering a **deferred-compensation contract** between an employer and an employee. Different types of deferred compensation plans exist. There are two broad categories—qualified and nonqualified—and different types within each category. Qualified deferred compensation plans meet specific requirements in the tax code and are subject to the Employee Retirement and Security Act of 1974 (ERISA). Qualified plans are generally made available to all employees. Nonqualified deferred compensation plans are contracts in which an employee agrees to defer the receipt of current compensation until some future date, presumably saving the compensation for future consumption (e.g., during retirement). These deferred compensation plans are generally made available only to key, highly compensated (aka "top hat") employees. Nonqualified deferred compensation (NQDC) is often referred to as "inside debt" by economists because it represents fixed obligations for the company to make future payments to corporate insiders. Deferred compensation contracts are common. Roughly, 91% of *Fortune* 1000 companies and 92% of financial institutions offer NQDC plans. In addition, the amounts can be significant, sometimes exceeding $100 million for a CEO and occasionally amounting to a greater sum than a manager's equity investments in his or her firm's stock or stock options (Wei and Yermack, 2011).[1] The large extent of deferred compensation at financial institutions has come under recent scrutiny. For example, at Morgan Stanley, the proportion of bonus-eligible employee compensation that was deferred was 75% in 2011, up from 40% in 2009 (Lucchetti and Rapoport [WSJ], 2013).

In this chapter, we evaluate nonqualified deferred compensation plans. Whether compensation deferment is desirable purely from a tax standpoint, ignoring incentive considerations for now, depends on both the employee's and the employer's current and future tax rates as well as on the opportunities each has to invest idle funds in the marketplace. The specific question we wish to consider is whether to offer an employee salary paid today or an NQDC contract that promises to pay a stipulated amount at time period *n*. To see whether current salary or deferred compensation is preferred, we must avoid comparing apples and oranges. A convenient way to proceed is to determine the deferred compensation amount or bonus that leaves either the employer or the employee indifferent between the two plans and then see which of the plans is preferred by the other party to the contract. This will identify the mutually

[1] In their study of a sample of nonfinancial firms, Wei and Yermack (2011) state that seven CEOs on the ExecuComp database had inside debt balances exceeding $100 million at fiscal year-end 2006. More than two-thirds of the CEOs in the database had nonzero inside debt, with a mean value of $5.7 million. They find that inside debt compensation is more common among larger firms in slower-growth sectors of the economy such as manufacturing, utilities, and transportation.

preferred contract. Through negotiations, both parties can be made better off by sharing the gains from tax planning.

For example, how much can an employer afford to provide to an employee in n periods as a deferred compensation payment in exchange for not paying \$100 of salary to the employee today? If compensation is deferred, so is the timing of the tax deduction to the employer and the timing of taxable income to the employee. Note that by not paying \$100 of salary today, the employer saves only $\$100(1 - t_{co})$ dollars after tax, where t_{co} is the employer's marginal tax rate today.[2] In n years, the after-tax savings to the employer from salary deferral would accumulate to $\$100(1 - t_{co})(1 + r_{cn})^n$, where r_{cn} is the employer's annualized after-tax rate of investment return on marginal investments made for a period of n years. It is the rate of return that the employer can achieve with the after-tax cash saved from deferring the salary payment to the employee.

When the deferred compensation payment is made at time n (in the amount of D_n), the employer receives a tax deduction, so the after-tax cost of the payment becomes $D_n(1 - t_{cn})$, where t_{cn} is the employer's marginal tax rate in year n. To be indifferent between current salary and a deferred payment, the employer must be able to set aside $\$100(1 - t_{co})$ now to satisfy its future deferred compensation obligation: After-tax deferred compensation payment at time n is equal to what the $\$100(1 - t_{co})$ after-tax dollars saved by not paying current salary would accumulate to if invested for n periods. That is:

$$D_n(1 - t_{cn}) = \$100(1 - t_{co})(1 + r_{cn})^n$$

or

$$\mathbf{D_n = \$100(1 + r_{cn})^n \frac{(1 - t_{co})}{(1 - t_{cn})}} \tag{8.1}$$

If the employer's tax rate is constant over time ($t_{co} = t_{cn}$), the employer can afford to pay its own after-tax rate of return on the \$100 of salary as deferred compensation. If the tax rate is increasing, however, the employer can afford to pay an even larger amount of deferred compensation in the future because future deductions are more valuable. Conversely, if the tax rate is decreasing, the employer can afford to pay less than the after-tax rate of return on the savings.

Suppose that the after-tax corporate rate of return on investment is 6%, and tax rates are constant across time. The employer is contemplating a 5-year ($n = 5$) deferred compensation contract. That is, rather than paying \$1 of salary currently, the employer is considering a deferred compensation payment to be made in 5 years. If the employer's tax rate were constant, the employer could afford to offer a deferred payment of

$$(1 + .06)^5 = \$1.34.$$

How much more or less can the employer afford if its tax rate changes over time? The answer appears in **Table 8.2**. The differences can be significant. For example, if the employer's current tax rate is 46% and it will be 21% in 5 years, **Table 8.2** indicates that the employer can afford a deferred

Table 8.2 Deferred Compensation: Sensitivity to Changes in Tax Rates over Time

t_{co}	21%	35%	46%
t_{cn}			
21%	1.34	1.10	0.91
35%	1.63	1.34	1.11
46%	1.96	1.61	1.34

Assumes 5-year deferral period and an after-tax investment return, r_c, of 6% per year. t_{co}, t_{cn} = employer's current and future marginal tax rates, respectively.

Body of table reports deferred compensation amounts that have the same after-tax cost to the employer as a dollar of immediate salary. Calculated using Equation 8.1.

[2] Although t_{co} might be thought of as the current corporate tax rate, the employer need not be a corporation for the following analysis to apply.

compensation payment of only 91 cents in 5 years for each dollar of current salary deferred. However, if the employer's tax rate increases from a current rate of 21% to 46%, the employer can afford a deferred payment equal to $1.96 for each dollar of current salary postponed for 5 years.

Now that the employer is indifferent between a salary and a deferred compensation contract, let us turn to the employee. What contract does the employee prefer? The employee must compare salary today versus a deferred compensation payment n periods from today. That is,

$$\text{Salary} = \$100(1 - t_{po})(1 + r_{pn})^n$$

$$\text{Deferred compensation} = D_n(1 - t_{pn})$$

where r_p is the after-tax rate of return the employee could earn on his or her personal investments. Substituting for D_n from Equation 8.1:

$$= \$100(1+r_{cn})^n \frac{(1-t_{co})}{(1-t_{cn})}(1-t_{pn})$$

The employee will prefer whichever contract provides more after-tax dollars in n years. A little algebra shows that salary will be preferred to deferred compensation if and only if:

$$\frac{(1-t_{po})(1+r_{pn})^n}{(1-t_{pn})(1+r_{cn})^n} \quad \frac{(1-t_{co})}{(1-t_{cn})} \tag{8.2}$$

The left-hand side of the equation is the ratio of the after-tax accumulation to the employee of taking current salary to the after-tax accumulation to the employee of deferred compensation. The right-hand side is the ratio of the corporation's current and future tax rates.

In this relation, three key factors combine to determine precisely whether salary or deferred compensation is preferable:

1. The employee's tax rate today versus his or her tax rate n periods from today. If the employee's tax rate is declining, then deferred compensation tends to be preferable because the income is recognized when the employee's tax rate is low.
2. The employer's tax rate today versus its tax rate n periods from today. If the employer's tax rate is increasing, then deferred compensation tends to be preferable because the employer prefers to take the deduction when tax rates are high.
3. The after-tax rate of return on investment for the employer versus that of the employee. If the employer can earn a higher after-tax rate of return than can the employee, then deferred compensation tends to be preferable. In effect, a deferred compensation contract allows the employee to save at the employer's higher rate of return on investment.

Because deferred compensation is favored if the employee's tax rate is expected to *decrease* in the future, deferral may be especially appropriate for employees who expect to face a lower tax rate in retirement or for employees on temporary assignment in a high-tax-rate foreign country.[3] Deferred compensation arrangements may also be desirable when tax rates are expected to decrease due to statutory changes in tax rates voted by the legislature. Here, however, one must be careful not to adopt a unilateral tax-planning perspective. A decline in tax rates for the employee need not favor deferred compensation if tax rates also decline for the employer. We will take a closer look at this common phenomenon.

Because deferred compensation is favored if the employer's tax rate is expected to increase in the future, deferral may be especially appropriate when a firm in a net operating loss (NOL) carryforward position cannot effectively use current tax deductions. Deferring compensation increases current taxable income but reduces future taxable income. This smoothing of taxable income is tax-advantageous for firms experiencing NOL carryforwards.

[3] Some tax jurisdictions do not permit the deferral of taxable income through the adoption of deferred compensation arrangements. This is an example of a tax-rule restriction.

For the employer with an opportunity to earn at a greater after-tax rate of return than its employees, saving through the corporation by way of a deferred compensation contract is tax advantageous. To see this, assume that $r_{pn} = 6\%$ and $r_{cn} = 8\%$. Then, after tax, deferred compensation beats salary by a factor of

$$(1.08/1.06)^n - 1 = 1.9\% \text{ for } n = 1 \text{ year}$$
$$9.8\% \text{ for } n = 5 \text{ years}$$
$$20.1\% \text{ for } n = 10 \text{ years}$$

Employer and Employee Tax Rates Both Expected to Fall

We can use Equation 8.2 to examine the case when both the employer and employee expect their tax rates to fall in the future. Salary can be tax preferred to deferred compensation even when the employee's tax rate is decreasing over time. For example, the tax rate of many nonmanagement employees dropped from the 25% vicinity to 15% with the passage of the 1986 Tax Act. A deferral of compensation might seem quite desirable under such circumstances. After all, it enables employees to reduce tax payments by 40% per dollar of compensation received (from \$.25 to only \$.15). Yet in most businesses, salary was tax preferred in such circumstances. Why? Because the employer's preference for an immediate tax deduction was even stronger than the employee's preference for deferred taxation.

Consider a corporate employer facing a 46% tax rate in 1986 and a 34% tax rate in 1988. For each \$100 of salary deferred from 1986, the employer could afford to pay only D_n = \$82, or \$100(1 – .46)/(1 – .34), in compensation in 1988, plus after-tax earnings on investment for 2 years. Each compensation alternative had a present cost to the employer of \$54 after tax. To the employee taxed at a rate of 25%, the \$100 salary was worth \$75 after tax. Even at the 15% tax rate in 1988, however, the \$82 in deferred compensation, plus interest for 2 years, had a present value of only \$82(1 – .15) or \$70 to the employee. So, despite the employee's drop in tax rate, salary was tax preferred relative to deferred compensation. If the deferred compensation payment was set at the level that made the employer indifferent between salary and deferred compensation, salary would have provided the employee with 75/70, or in excess of 7%, more in after-tax compensation than would deferred compensation.

For more highly paid employees who faced a 50% marginal tax rate in 1986 and a 28% rate in 1988, deferred compensation was the superior arrangement from a tax standpoint: \$100 of salary in 1986 was worth \$50 after tax, and the \$82 in compensation, deferred until 1988, was worth \$59 after tax or \$82(1 – .28). This amount is 18% more than current salary.

2012 Tax Planning with Deferred Compensation Plans

Let us consider a more recent tax change, although much smaller in scale. At the end of 2012, the so-called Bush tax cuts were set to expire on December 31, and the imposition of the Patient Protection and Affordable Care Act of 2010 (aka ObamaCare) was to start on January 1. These changes led to an increase in the top tax rate on compensation from 35% to 40.5% (39.6% income tax rate and the 0.9% Medicare surtax). The U.S. corporate tax rate was unchanged. What incentives did this provide, assuming taxpayers placed a high expectation on the tax rates actually changing? It is likely that deferred compensation in the year 2012 became less preferred, as long as nontax factors remained the same. And with rising national deficits, increases in the top individual statutory tax rates continue to be likely in the future, while at the same time many think the top corporate statutory tax rate will be lowered, both working to reduce the attractiveness of deferred compensation plans.

2017 TCJA Tax Planning with Deferred Compensation Plans

Now consider the tax rate changes under TCJA. Is deferred compensation or salary preferred with the change in tax rates? Consider a corporate employer facing a 35% tax rate in 2017 and a 21% tax rate in 2018. For each \$100 of salary deferred from 2017, the employer could afford to pay only D_n = \$82.28, or \$100(1 – .35)/(1 – .21), in compensation in 2018, plus after-tax earnings on investment for 1 year. Each compensation alternative had a present cost to the employer of \$65 after tax. Further assume a mid-level employee's tax rate declined from 28% in 2017 to 24% in 2018. To the employee taxed at a rate of 28%, the $100 salary was worth $72 after tax. With a 24% tax rate in 2018, however, the $82 in deferred compensation, plus interest for 1 year, had a present value of only $82(1 – .24) or $62.32 to the employee. So, despite the employee's drop in tax rate, salary was tax preferred relative to deferred compensation. For more highly paid employees who faced a 40% marginal tax rate in 2017 and a 37% rate in 2018, salary was also the superior arrangement from a tax standpoint: $100 of salary in 2017 was worth $60 after tax, and the $82 in compensation, deferred until 2018, was worth $51.67 after tax or $82(1 – .37). Basically, the cut in the top corporate tax rate from 35% to 21% compared to the smaller cuts in the individual tax rates made the 2017 deduction for salary much more attractive than deferred compensation for the employer and thus the employee.

Summary of Deferred Compensation Plans

In this section we have emphasized the effects of changes in tax rates and differences in investment opportunities on the preferences of employers and employees for current or deferred compensation contracts. Whether deferred compensation contracts are desirable also depends on several nontax factors. First, what are the goals of the incentive contracts between employees and employers? Second, the employee becomes an unsecured creditor of the company. If the company enters into bankruptcy, there is no assurance the employee will be paid. Third, compliance costs can be significant, and potential penalties for violations with respect to deferred compensation can be large. **Section 409A** was added to the tax code as part of the American Jobs Creation Act of 2004 (partially in response to Enron executives accelerating payments before bankruptcy and because of general perceived abuses of the constructive receipt doctrine [Stumpff, 2007]). This code section places significant restrictions on the timing of distributions, restrictions on the acceleration of benefits, and restrictions of the timing of deferral elections. The penalties for violating the requirements in Section 409A are severe—all amounts deferred in the plan become immediately taxable plus a 20% penalty tax under some conditions (see Section 409A and regulations thereunder). Finally, not only are tax rates important, but uncertainty with respect to tax rates and income levels also makes the decision more complicated than what can be captured in the model.

8.2 SALARY VERSUS FRINGE BENEFITS

Now that we have illustrated the importance of considering the tax implications of compensation plans to all of the contracting parties, let us consider some of the other compensation alternatives. Let us begin with **fringe benefits** such as employer-provided term life insurance or employer-provided meals. Fringe benefits refer to items where the costs to the firm to provide the item are deductible while the benefits to the employee are excluded from their taxable income. Whether fringe benefits are preferred to salary depends on two factors:

1. Whether employees can deduct, on their own tax returns, the cost of fringes they pay for themselves, and
2. The extent to which employees place personal value on employer-provided fringes relative to their cost to the employer.

To illustrate the importance of these two factors, let us consider the following cases.

EXAMPLE 8.1 Salary versus Fringe Benefits

Suppose the employer contemplates paying $1,400 for group term life insurance and group health insurance in lieu of $1,400 in additional salary.

Because the employer receives a $1,400 tax deduction whether the expenditure is for salary or insurance, the employer is indifferent between the two alternatives. Suppose the employee is in a 32% tax bracket. Although $1,400 in salary gives rise to $952 in cash after tax, the fringe benefits are nontaxable, so the employee keeps $1,400 worth of benefits after tax. If, however, the

continued

continued from previous page

employee were to purchase the fringes directly and could not take a tax deduction for their cost, \$2,058 of salary would be required to buy the same benefits:[4]

$$\$2{,}058(1 - .32) = \$1{,}400$$

One problem here is that if these benefits are to qualify for tax-favored treatment, they must be offered on a nondiscriminatory basis to essentially all employees. Unlike cash salary, fringe benefits such as life and health insurance cannot be traded for other commodities easily. To some employees, the personal value of the benefits could be less than \$952, or \$1,400(1 – .32), the after-tax value of the salary alternative. For example, although costly to the employer, some employees with absolutely no bequest motive find life insurance to be a worthless benefit. For such employees, salary is a more efficient compensation component despite the tax-favored treatment accorded these benefits. A related problem arises when a wife and husband receive redundant benefits from their respective employers, such as health insurance that covers the entire family.[5]

Employer-Provided Meals

A tax issue regarding fringe benefits is the tax treatment of employer-provided meals. For example, Google, Facebook, Twitter, and Yahoo! all offer free meals onsite. Indeed, according to press coverage of the issue, Google has 120 cafés and serves around 50,000 meals a day (*Wall Street Journal*, April 7, 2013). At issue is whether these meals are taxable to the employees as part of their compensation. Generally, meals are tax exempt for employees when asked to work in remote locations or jobs that require them to remain onsite or where lunch breaks are not feasible. The high-tech firms claim that the cafeterias encourage collaboration and enable employees to work longer hours. Employers could deduct 50% of the cost of employer-provided meals or business-related meals and entertainment. Starting in 2026, the cost of employer-provided meals will no longer be deductible by the employer, but the benefit to employees will continue to be excluded from their taxable income.

The tax treatment of other fringe benefits has also been changed under the TCJA. Previously, qualified moving expenses of employees if paid by the employer were deductible to the employer while being excluded from taxable income of the employee. TCJA now requires moving expenses whether paid directly to the moving company or reimbursed to the employee to be included as compensation of the employee subjecting the amount to taxation. Employers can continue to deduct the payment. Some firms provide transportation-related benefits to employees such as transit passes, bussing, parking, etc. on a tax-free basis to employees. These costs were deductible by the firm. However, TCJA suspended the employer's ability to deduct these costs; they are still tax-free to employees.

8.3 CASH BONUS PLANS

Another compensation arrangement that may satisfy the demand for flexibility when tax rates change unexpectedly over time is a bonus plan, where the bonus is paid at year-end and the amount of bonus is at the discretion of the compensation committee of the board of directors rather than being set by

[4] Part or all of the health insurance premiums may be tax deductible for some employees. An itemized deduction for medical expenses, which includes insurance costs, is currently permitted in the United States to the extent they exceed 7.5% of adjusted gross income. In addition, part of the life insurance premium paid by the employer may be taxable to the employee.

Adjusted gross income is defined as follows: Total income less exempt income (for example, municipal bond interest income) equals gross income. Gross income less deductions for adjusted gross income (such as business expenses other than those incurred as an employee) equals adjusted gross income.

[5] For some employees, a "cafeteria plan," wherein employees can pick and choose among several fringe benefits, may help mitigate this problem.

a pre-specified formula. Such plans are extremely common in practice, but they are probably used more for incentive reasons than for tax-planning reasons. Although with mutual trust between the employer and the employee, the bonuses can be timed strategically to coincide with high tax rates for the firm and low tax rates for the employee.

As an example, Chrysler Corporation accelerated the timing of its 1990 incentive compensation payouts to managers. Such payments were typically made in January, but they were moved up a month because the 1990 Tax Act generated an increase in tax rates for most Chrysler executives, beginning January 1, 1991. The president of Chrysler indicated that the change in timing was made because "tax rates are higher next year" (*Wall Street Journal,* December 24, 1990).

General Motors Corporation, by contrast, considered but rejected a proposal to make executive incentive payments in December of 1990 rather than January of 1991. Although the switch "would have cut taxes for GM's top-ranking executives, [it would] have increased the tax bite for managers further down the ladder" (*Wall Street Journal,* February 8, 1991). We note that the Omnibus Budget Reconciliation Act of 1993 introduced an impediment to using discretionary bonuses to shift income for large corporations.

8.4 STOCK-BASED COMPENSATION COMPONENTS

Management compensation packages typically include one or more types of equity-based compensation components. The most common are employee stock options (ESOs), stock appreciation rights (SARs), restricted stock, and long-term performance awards.

Restricted Stock

Restricted stock grants are awards of stock to employees. Most grants restrict the employee from selling the stock until some future date, referred to here as the vesting date. Section 83 of the U.S. Tax Code details the tax treatment of restricted stock. Employees do not recognize taxable income until the vesting date, and hence we classify restricted stock as a form of deferred compensation. The amount of taxable income is the value of the stock on the vesting date.[6] The granting corporation receives a compensation tax deduction equal to the amount of income recognized by the employee.

However, under Section 83(b), recipients of restricted stock can elect to be taxed on the value of the grant at the grant date, hereafter referred to as a Section 83(b) election. Under a **Section 83(b)** election, the value of the restricted stock at grant date is taxed as ordinary income, and any subsequent price appreciation (or depreciation) is treated as capital gains (losses) qualifying for favorable long-term capital gains tax rates, provided the stock is held more than 12 months.

Figure 8.1 provides a plot and timeline to illustrate taxation of restricted stock with and without a Section 83(b) election. The left figure shows that the employee owes tax at the ordinary income tax rate on P_1, the value of the stock on its vesting date. The right figure illustrates a Section 83(b) election. With such an election, the value of the stock at the grant date, P_0, is taxed as ordinary income and all subsequent price appreciation (gains) are taxed as capital gains.

FIGURE 8.1 Section 83(b) Election to be Taxed at Grant Date of Restricted Stock

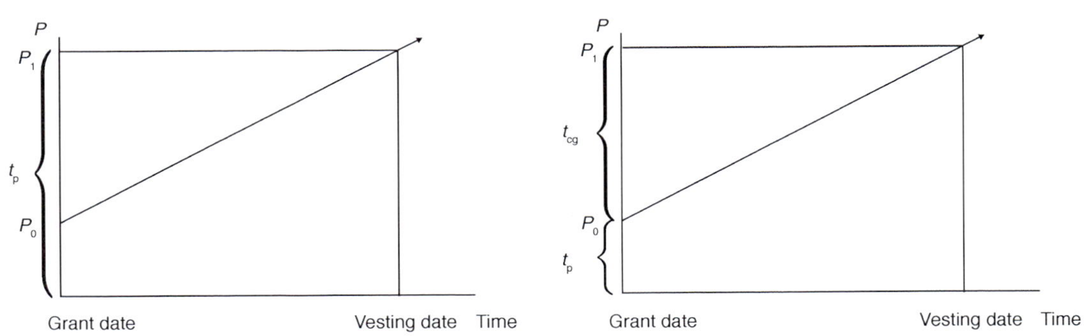

[6] In some instances, the employee pays some small amount for the stock. We assume this amount is zero in our discussion.

When might an employee elect Section 83(b) tax treatment? An intuitive answer might be when the employee expects the stock price to increase dramatically between the grant and vesting date and thus believes it is desirable to convert this future price appreciation from ordinary income to capital gains via the Section 83(b) election. However a Section 83(b) election is a risky strategy—if the stock price declines after the election is made, the employee has paid taxes on a phantom gain (although the subsequent stock price declines give rise to future capital loss deductions). But if the employee is very confident that the stock price will increase over the vesting period, an alternative strategy that does better than the Section 83(b) election is to purchase additional stock with the funds that would have been used to pay the taxes on the early election.[7] This strategy, however, is even riskier because the employee now owns even more stock. This additional risk compared to the do-nothing strategy is a nontax cost of the Section 83(b) election and its alternative of purchasing additional stock.

To show that a Section 83(b) election is dominated, from a purely tax viewpoint that ignores risk issues, by the alternative strategy of purchasing additional stock, we introduce the following notation:

P_0 is the stock price on the grant date,
P_1 is the stock price on the vesting date, when the stock is assumed to be sold,
t_p, as previously, is the employee's marginal tax rate on ordinary income,
t_{cg}, as previously, is the employee's marginal tax rate on capital gains income, and
r is the after-tax borrowing rate of the employee.

If the employee holds the restricted stock through the vesting period and then sells the stock, the after-tax accumulation per share of restricted stock is simply

$$P_1(1 - t_p) \tag{8.3}$$

If the employee makes a Section 83(b) election, the question arises as to what funds are used to pay the taxes at the grant date. A simple assumption is to assume the employee borrows the necessary amount to pay the taxes, $P_0 \times t_p$, at after-tax rate r.[8] The borrowing plus interest is repaid when the stock is sold at the subsequent vesting date. The after-tax accumulation from this strategy is

$$P_1 - (P_1 - P_0)t_{cg} - P_0t_p(1 + r)^n \tag{8.4}$$

where the first term is the gross proceeds from selling the stock, the second term is the capital gains taxes due on the gross proceeds, and the third term is the total amount of borrowing and interest to be repaid (at date 1, which is n periods from the grant date).

An alternative to the Section 83(b) election is to borrow the amount of taxes that would be due under the Section 83(b) election and buy additional stock in the corporation. The additional shares that can be purchased are simply $P_0t_p/P_0 = t_p$. That is, for each share of restricted stock that is granted, this strategy involves the employee purchasing t_p extra shares. If t_p is .37, the employee purchases .37 of one share per share of restricted stock granted. The after-tax accumulation from this strategy is then

$$P_1(1 - t_p) + t_pP_1 - t_p(P_1 - P_0)t_{cg} - P_0t_p(1 + r)^n \tag{8.5}$$

where the first term is the after-tax proceeds from the original grant of restricted stock, the second term is the gross proceeds from the extra shares purchased at the grant date, the third term is the capital gains taxes due on the extra shares purchased, and the fourth term is the repayment of the borrowing with interest when all the shares are sold at the vesting date.

[7] McDonald (2003) also arrives at this conclusion and shows the result more formally and provides a somewhat expanded analysis relative to that here. In certain unusual circumstances, such as the employee not being able to buy or sell stock on his or her personal account, a Section 83(b) election may be optimal. McDonald also shows that the election is even less desirable for dividend-paying stocks. We show below that a Section 83(b) election might be tax-favored if the employee expects to face a higher tax rate on ordinary income at the vesting date.

[8] The result is equivalent if we assume the employee purchases additional stock from liquidating other investments earning an after-tax rate of return r. That is, r simply represents the after-tax opportunity cost of funds to the employee.

A Section 83(b) election is not optimal when the after-tax accumulation from the alternative strategy exceeds the after-tax accumulation from the Section 83(b) election; that is, Equation 8.5 > Equation 8.4. Thus,

$$P_1(1 - t_p) + t_pP_1 - t_p(P_1 - P_0)t_{cg} - P_0t_p(1 + r)^n > P_1 - (P_1 - P_0)t_{cg} - P_0t_p(1 + r)^n$$

The $P_0t_p(1 + r)^n$ term cancels out, and expanding the first term gives

$$P_1 - P_1t_p + t_pP_1 - t_p(P_1 - P_0)t_{cg} > P_1 - (P_1 - P_0)\,t_{cg}$$

leaving

$$(P_1 - P_0)t_{cg} - t_p(P_1 - P_0)t_{cg} > 0$$

which simplifies to the condition

$$\mathbf{(P_1 - P_0)t_{cg}(1 - t_p) > 0} \qquad \textbf{(8.6)}$$

This expression is positive whenever $P_1 > P_0$, which is the condition that motivates the employee to consider a Section 83(b) election in the first place. Thus if the employee expects the stock price to increase over the period between the grant and vesting date, a Section 83(b) election is not optimal because it is dominated by the alternative strategy of borrowing the amount of taxes that would be payable under the Section 83(b) election and using these funds to buy additional stock. A simple numerical example illustrates the analysis.

EXAMPLE 8.2 Restricted Stock Section 83(b) Election

Suppose an employee is granted 1,000 shares of restricted stock with a current stock price of $25. The employee is restricted from selling the stock for 3 years until it vests. The employee faces a current tax rate of 37% on ordinary income and 20% on long-term capital gains. These rates are not expected to change over the vesting period. Finally, the employee faces a 10% after-tax borrowing rate. The employee expects the stock price to increase to $40 by the vesting date.

If the employee does nothing and simply waits until the vesting period and then sells the stock, the after-tax accumulation per share is given by Equation 8.3:

$$P_1(1 - t_p) = \$40(1 - .37) = \$25.20$$

A Section 83(b) election with borrowing to pay the taxes results in an after-tax accumulation given by Equation 8.4:

$$P_1 - (P_1 - P_0)t_{cg} - P_0t_p(1 + r)^n$$
$$= \$40 - (\$40 - \$25).20 - \$25(.37)(1 + .10)^3 = \$24.69$$

Instead of a Section 83(b) election, the employee can borrow the amount of the taxes due under the election and purchase additional stock. The after-tax accumulation with this strategy is given by Equation 8.5:

$$P_1(1 - t_p) + t_pP_1 - t_p(P_1 - P_0)t_{cg} - P_0t_p(1 + r)^n$$
$$= \$40(1 - .37) + .37(\$40) - .37(\$40 - \$25).20 - \$25(.37)(1 + .10)^3$$
$$= \$26.58$$

Thus, this strategy results in a greater after-tax accumulation of $26.58 – $24.69 = $1.89 per share or $1,890 over the 1,000 shares of restricted stock. Alternatively, we can use Equation 8.6 to directly determine whether a Section 83(b) election is preferable in this example:

$$(P_1 - P_0)t_{cg}(1 - t_p) = (\$40 - \$25).20(1 - .37) = \$1.89 > 0$$

Thus, the election is not optimal.

Table 8.3 summarizes the outcomes given a range of stock prices on the vesting date. The table illustrates that if the stock price is expected to increase, a Section 83(b) election is dominated by the alternative strategy of borrowing and buying additional stock. If the stock price is not expected to increase or is expected to increase by only a small amount, then doing nothing and simply selling the stock at the vesting date dominates.[9]

Table 8.3 Restricted Stock: Analysis of After-Tax Accumulations to Section 83(b) Election versus Borrowing and Purchasing Additional Stock.

	Do Nothing	Section 83(b) Election	Borrow and Buy Additional Stock	Difference Equation 8.5 – Equation 8.4
P_1	Equation 8.3	Equation 8.4	Equation 8.5	Equation 8.6
$20	$12.60	$ 8.69	$ 8.06	$(0.63)
25	15.75	12.69	12.69	—
30	18.90	16.69	17.32	0.63
35	22.05	20.69	21.95	1.26
40	25.20	24.69	26.58	1.89
45	28.35	28.69	31.21	2.52
50	31.50	32.69	35.84	3.15
55	34.65	36.69	40.47	3.78
60	37.80	40.69	45.10	4.41

Table values based on following: P_0 = $25, t_p = 37%, t_{cg} = 20%, n = 3 years, r = .10.

Employee Tax Rates Expected to Rise

Might it be optimal to make a Section 83(b) election if the employee expects to face a higher tax rate on ordinary income at the vesting date? Let t_0 (t_1) be the tax rate on ordinary income at the grant date (vesting date). We can modify Equations 8.4 and 8.5 as follows. The Section 83(b) election remains

$$P_1 - (P_1 - P_0)t_{cg} - P_0t_0(1 + r)^n \qquad (8.7)$$

And the alternative strategy of borrowing and buying additional stock becomes

$$P_1(1 - t_1) + t_0P_1 - t_0(P_1 - P_0)t_{cg} - P_0t_0(1 + r)^n \qquad (8.8)$$

where the second, third, and fourth terms all use the tax rate on ordinary income at the grant date because this reflects the amount of borrowing and additional shares purchased. The election is optimal if Equation 8.7 > Equation 8.8. The last term is common to both equations and drops out. We can expand the first term in Equation 8.8 such that P_1 drops out, leaving

$$\begin{aligned} &P_1t_1 - t_0P_1 + t_0(P_1 - P_0)t_{cg} - (P_1 - P_0)t_{cg} > 0 \\ &= P_1(t_1 - t_0) - (P_1 - P_0)t_{cg}(1 - t_0) > 0 \\ &= \frac{(t_1 - t_0)}{(1 - t_0)t_{cg}} \quad \frac{(P_1 - P_0)}{P_1} \end{aligned} \qquad (8.9)$$

Thus, whether the election is optimal depends on the increase in ordinary income tax rate relative to the expected increase in stock price.

[9] Specifically, if the stock price is expected to appreciate by less than $r/(1 - t_p)$, then the do-nothing strategy dominates.

EXAMPLE 8.3 Restricted Stock Section 83(b) Election with Employee's Tax Rate Expected to Increase in the Future

Assume the same facts as in the previous restricted stock example, except that the employee faces a current tax rate of 37% and expects to face a tax rate on ordinary income of 50% on the vesting date.

The do-nothing strategy results in $P_1(1 - t_1) = \$40(1 - .50) = \$20$. A Section 83(b) election results in an after-tax accumulation using Equation 8.7 of

$$P_1 - (P_1 - P_0)t_{cg} - P_0t_0(1 + r)^n$$

$$\$40 - (\$40 - \$25).20 - \$25(.37)(1 + .10)^3$$

$$= \$24.69$$

The alternative borrow-and-buy strategy results in an after-tax accumulation using Equation 8.8 of

$$P_1(1 - t_1) + t_0P_1 - t_0(P_1 - P_0)t_{cg} - P_0t_0(1 + r)^n$$

$$\$40(1 - .50) + .37(\$40) - .37(\$40 - \$25).20 - \$25(.37)(1 + .10)^3$$

$$= \$21.38$$

In this example, the election is optimal because the tax savings from being taxed at the lower rate exceed the earnings on the additional shares that can be purchased. Alternatively, we can directly use Equation 8.9:

$$= \frac{(t_1 - t_0)}{(1 - t_0)t_{cg}} > \frac{(P_1 - P_0)}{P_1}$$

$$\frac{(.50 - .37)}{(1 - .37).20} > \frac{(\$40 - \$25)}{\$40}$$

$$1.032 > .375$$

indicating that the election is optimal in this example.

Long-Term Performance Awards

Long-term performance awards are one of the fastest-growing types of compensation. In a recent survey of the long-term pay practices of the 250 largest companies in the United States, Fredrick W. Cook Inc., a compensation consulting firm, reports that 75% of these companies use long-term performance shares as a form of compensation, whereas only 67% use stock options. Long-term performance awards can take several forms: shares, units, or cash. Performance shares consist of actual shares or share units. The shares or units are earned based on performance over a predefined performance period. Performance units/cash are grants of cash or dollar-denominated "units," which are earned based on performance against predetermined objectives over a predefined period, most commonly over a 3-year period. Often the plans have a payout matrix under which performance shares are paid at differing levels (e.g., threshold, target, and maximum). At the end of the performance period, the company determines if the performance goals originally outlined at grant have been achieved. There may be an additional vesting period at the end of the performance period. Once the goals have been met, and the vesting requirements, if any, have been met, the contract is settled, the amounts are paid, and the employee owns the shares or cash outright.

In many ways, long-term performance awards are taxed similarly to restricted shares (indeed, restricted shares with a 1-year performance period and continued service-vesting are classified as performance shares). There are no tax consequences at the date of grant and generally no tax consequences in the period when the performance targets are met. Generally, the employee is taxed on the compensation when the contract is settled and payment is made (assuming payment is made when the employee vests).[10] If the employee receives shares and holds them, any gain or loss from

[10] Vesting can be different than payment date; a discussion of this situation is beyond the scope of the text.

the payment/vesting date until the sale date is capital in nature. One item of note that is important is that whereas restricted stock is a transfer of property and thus falls under Section 83 and an 83(b) election can be made to alter the timing of the taxable event, performance shares are a promise to deliver property at a future date and thus an 83(b) election is not available.[11] The employer can deduct the payments in the year the employee recognizes the ordinary income. The amounts must meet the requirements under Section 162(m) (discussed later in the chapter) to be deductible for the qualified executives.

Employee Stock Options and Stock Appreciation Rights

A stock option is a right to acquire stock at a specified price (exercise price) for a specified period of time (until the expiration date of the contract). **Employee stock options (ESOs)** are typically granted with an expiration date of 5 to 10 years and at an exercise price equal to the price of the underlying stock at the date of grant. Although the options may be quite valuable in that the expected return to the employee from owning the options may be substantial, the granting of options typically is a nontaxable event. Instead, taxation of the compensation is deferred until the option is exercised, unless the option is an "incentive stock option," as discussed later.

Stock appreciation rights (SARs) provide employees with cash payments equal to the change in market value of the firm's stock over some specified period of time. Taxation occurs when the employee exercises the right to receive the appreciation on the stock that has occurred since the date of grant. As with stock options, the employee does not make a payment to the firm in the event that the stock price declines below its value at the grant date. As a consequence, the expected return to the employee on a SAR can far exceed the expected appreciation on the stock.

To illustrate, suppose the current stock price is $20 per share, and this is the price at which the stock option or the SAR is granted. The future stock price is uncertain. Assume that its value on the expiration date of the option or the SAR is uniformly distributed between $10 and $40. That is, its future price is certain not to be below $10 or above $40, but every point in between is equally likely.[12] This uncertainty can be represented as in **Figure 8.2**.

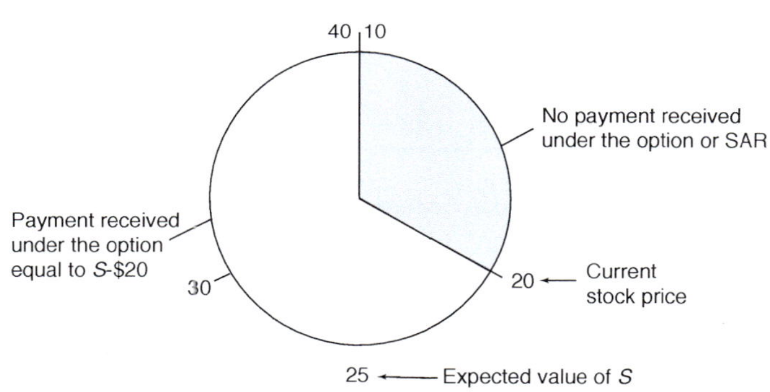

FIGURE 8.2 Distribution of Future Stock Price, S

The expected value of the future stock price is $25, or ($40 + $10)/2. If the future stock price turned out to be equal to the expected value of $25, the employee would receive $25 – $20 or $5 in cash from the SAR. Similarly, the employee would pay $20 to exercise the option to purchase stock worth $25, thereby realizing a "bargain" of $5. The $5 bargain could be converted into cash by selling the underlying stock in the market for $25, but the expected cash value of the SAR and option exceeds $5. Why? Because if the terminal stock price is less than $20, the employee receives $0 rather than a negative sum, whereas the employee keeps 100% of the terminal stock price in excess of $20. Because the stock price finishes "in-the-money" (that is, above $20) two-thirds of the time, and when it finishes in-the-money, its expected value is $30, or ($40 +$20)/2, the expected amount to be received under the option

[11] Long-term performance share/unit/cash plans can fall under the classification of nonqualified deferred compensation plans, however, and thus the rules of Section 409A must be considered.

[12] A uniform distribution for stock prices is not descriptively accurate for securities. The assumption is made here for pedagogical reasons.

or SAR is \$6.67, or 2/3 × (\$30 – \$20). The expected option or SAR value, then, relative to holding stock is \$1.67, or \$6.67 – \$5.00, to be paid at the expiration date of the option or SAR.

Suppose that the present value of the \$1.67 is \$1.25; then a year-end grant of 20,000 SARs or stock options would be equivalent, ignoring taxes and other considerations (such as risk-sharing and incentives), to a bonus of \$25,000. Unlike a bonus, however, the granting of a stock option or SAR does not give rise to immediate taxation. Instead, compensation deferral is achieved. Deferral may or may not be desirable from a tax-planning standpoint depending on the current and future tax rates of the employee and the employer. If compensation deferral is desirable, however, it may be a useful alternative to a deferred salary or deferred bonus arrangement. Such deferrals require an agreement prior to the services being rendered by the employee, whereas deferrals through SARs and options do not.

Tax Issues Relating to Incentive Stock Options and Nonqualified Stock Options

As we mentioned earlier, not all employee stock options are taxed the same. For U.S. tax purposes, the two types of options are **nonqualified stock options (NQOs)** and **incentive stock options (ISOs)**. The timeline in **Figure 8.3** should prove useful in comparing NQOs and ISOs.

FIGURE 8.3
Tax Treatment of NQOs and ISOs to Employee and Employer

Date	Option Granted	Option Exercised	Stock Sold
Stock price	X	P_e	P_s
Example	\$10	\$15	\$27
Tax consequences to the employee			
NQO	None	Ordinary income of $P_e - X = \$5$	Capital gain of $P_s - P_e = \$12$
ISO	None	None*	Capital gain of $P_s - X = \$17$
Tax consequences to the employer			
NQO**	None	Ordinary deduction of $P_e - X = \$5$	None
ISO	None	None	None

* The \$5 gain is included in the AMT calculation.

** The TCJA limited the deduction for compensation to qualified employees, usually the CEO, CFO, and the three highest paid employees, to \$1 million per year for public corporations. We assume deductibility above.

On exercising an NQO, the employee recognizes a gain of $(P_e - X)$, where P_e is the stock price on the exercise date and X is the exercise price determined at the grant date. This gain is taxed as ordinary income, t_p. With an ISO, the gain at the exercise date is deferred until the stock is sold and is taxed at capital gains rates, t_{cg}.[13] Although it might seem as though ISOs dominate NQOs, to draw such a conclusion is to commit the error of unilateral tax planning. It is also important to consider the tax consequences to the employer. The employer receives no tax deduction for the compensation paid to employees via ISOs. In contrast, NQOs give rise to an ordinary tax deduction for the employer at the same time and in the same amount as the ordinary income recognized by the employee.

Employee stock options are taxed differently around the world—as to if and when the employee is taxed and at what rate, and as to if and when the corporation receives a tax deduction. **Table 8.4** presents a summary—although all 26 countries listed in the table tax employees, some assess the tax at the grant date (6) and some at the stock sale date (8), whereas most countries (21) tax the employee on their gain at the exercise date (the numbers do not add to 26 because some countries, such as the United States, have both nonqualified and qualified ESOs). Fifteen of the 26 countries listed in the

[13] ISOs are defined in §422 and must satisfy several criteria. For example, stock obtained under an ISO cannot be disposed of within 2 years of the grant date nor within 12 months after exercise. Otherwise the ISO is "disqualified." ISOs cannot be granted with an exercise price below the stock price at grant date, and the aggregate stock value covered by the ISOs (number of options times grant date stock price) is limited to \$100,000 per year per employee.

table allow a corporate tax deduction at the exercise date, and 7 do not allow any deduction at all (the United States and three other countries allow deductibility on some options, but not on others—NQOs and qualified options, respectively).

Table 8.4 Taxation of Employee Stock Option—To Employees and Employing Corporations

	Taxation to Employee			Taxation to Employer	
Country	**Grant Date**	**Exercise Date**	**Stock Sale Date**	**Deductible**	**Not Deductible**
Australia	X	X			X
Austria		X			X
Belgium	X				X
Canada		X	X		X
Czech Republic	X			X	
Denmark		X	X	X	X
Finland		X		X	
Germany		X		X	
Greece		X		X	X
Hungary		X			X
Iceland		X	X	X	X
Ireland		X	X		X
Italy	X		X	X	
Japan		X		X	
Korea		X		X	
Mexico		X		X	
Netherlands	X	X		X	
New Zealand		X			X
Norway		X		X	
Poland		X		X	
Portugal		X		X	
Spain			X	X	
Sweden		X		X	
Turkey	X			X	
United Kingdom		X	X	X	
United States		X	X	X	X

NQOs versus ISOs

We can derive conditions under which one type of option is jointly preferred by the employee and employer over the other. In multilateral tax planning, to derive conditions under which one type of option is tax preferred over another, we must consider both parties. A simple way to consider multilateral interests is to hold one party indifferent and then determine what choice the other party favors. We will hold the employee indifferent between the two option types by having the firm reimburse the employee for any difference in tax costs between the two options. We assume the stock obtained from either option type is sold on the same future date at price P_s.

For simplicity, assume the option is granted with an exercise price (denoted X) equal to the stock price at grant date (denoted P_g), thus $X = P_g$. The employee prefers the ISO when the taxes due on the ISO are less than those due on the NQO:[14]

$$\textbf{ISO taxes} < \textbf{NQO taxes}$$
$$(P_s - X)t_{cg} < [(P_e - X)t_p + (P_s - P_e)t_{cg}]$$

The taxes due on the ISO can be partitioned into two parts: the tax due on the gain between the grant date and exercise date, even though the tax is not paid until the stock sale date, and the tax due on the gain between the exercise date and stock sale date:

$$[(P_e - X)t_{cg*} + (P_s - P_e)t_{cg}] < [(P_e - X)t_p + (P_s - P_e)t_{cg}]$$

which simplifies to

$$\begin{aligned} (P_e - X)t_{cg*} &< (P_e - X)t_p \\ (P_e - X)(t_{cg*} - t_p) &< 0 \\ (P_e - X)(t_p - t_{cg*}) &> 0 \end{aligned} \tag{8.10}$$

where t_{cg*} is the present value of the capital gains tax rate, also referred to as the effective capital gains tax rate, reflecting the deferral for n periods of the capital gains tax for the ISO—that is, $t_{cg*} = t_{cg}/(1 + r)^n$. Note that the deferral period is measured from the exercise date until the stock sale date. Because the employee would not exercise the option if it were not in-the-money ($P_e > X$), the ISO is preferred by the employee whenever the tax rate on ordinary income exceeds the present value of the tax rate on capital gains: $t_p > t_{cg*}$. Thus, even if ordinary income and capital gains are taxed at the same rate, the employee will prefer an ISO because the ISO defers the tax on the gain at exercise until the stock is sold.

Thus, to make the employee indifferent, the firm needs to reimburse the employee for the difference in taxes as in Equation 8.10, and because the reimbursement is taxable to the employee, the reimbursement amount is

$$\frac{(P_e - X)(t_p - t_{cg*})}{(1 - t_p)}$$

This payment is deductible to the employer.

The employer prefers the NQO when[15]

$$(P_e - X)t_c - \frac{(P_e - X)(t_p - t_{cg*})}{(1 - t_p)}(1 - t_c) \quad 0. \tag{8.11}$$

where $(P_e - X)t_c$ is the tax deduction to the employer of NQO treatment, the numerator in the second term is the incremental taxes to the employee of NQO treatment relative to ISO treatment which we assume the employer reimburses the employee, the $(1 - t_p)$ term grosses up the payment to the employee as the employee will pay taxes on the payment, and the $(1 - t_c)$ represents the after-tax payment to the employer as the payment is tax deductible to the employer.

This equation can be simplified as follows:

[14] We focus on taxes here as the pretax gain is the same regardless of option type.

[15] Note that the corporate tax rate here is the expected rate for the year in which the NQO is exercised.

$$\frac{(P_e - X)t_c(1-t_p) - (P_e - X)(t_p - t_{cg*})(1-t_c)}{(1-t_p)} \quad 0$$

$$\frac{(P_e - X)}{(1-t_p)}[t_c(1-t_p) - (t_p - t_{cg*})(1-t_c)] \quad 0$$

$$[t_c(1-t_p) - (t_p - t_{cg*})(1-t_c)] \quad 0 \qquad (8.12)$$

$$t_c - t_p + t_{cg*} - t_{cg*}t_c \quad 0$$

$$t_c(1-t_{cg*}) - t_p + t_{cg*} \quad 0$$

$$t_c \quad \frac{(t_p - t_{cg*})}{(1-t_{cg*})}$$

Equation 8.12 shows that NQOs are preferred if the corporation's marginal tax rate exceeds the difference in the employee's tax rate on ordinary income less the effective capital gains tax rate divided by one minus the employee's effective capital gains tax rate. Alternatively stated, the ISO is preferred if the incremental taxes to the employee of the NQO exceed the value of the deduction to the employer: $(t_p - t_{cg*})/(1 - t_{cg*}) > t_c$. In **Table 8.5**, we use Equation 8.12 to calculate the required corporate marginal tax rate, presented in boldface, above which NQOs will be tax preferred by both parties for various employee tax rates and holding periods.

Table 8.5 Values of Corporate Marginal Tax Rate, t_c, above Which NQOs Are Jointly Preferred by Employer and Employee (Table ignores the potential effects of the AMT on ISOs)

Time Period				Holding Period in Years after Exercise of ISO and Implied t_{cg*} for Holding Period				
				1	5	10	20	Death
	t_p		t_{cg}			t_{cg*}		
Pre-TRA 86	.50		.20	.187	.143	.102	.052	0
		t_c		**.385**	**.417**	**.443**	**.473**	**.50**
1988–1990	.28		.28	.261	.200	.142	.072	0
		t_c		**.025**	**.10**	**.161**	**.224**	**.28**
1991–1992	.31		.28	.262	.200	.142	.072	0
		t_c		**.065**	**.138**	**.195**	**.256**	**0**
1993–1997	.396		.28	.261	.200	.142	.072	0
		t_c		**.182**	**.245**	**.296**	**.349**	**.396**
1998–2002	.396		.20	.187	.143	.102	.052	0
		t_c		**.257**	**.296**	**.328**	**.363**	**.396**
2003–2012	.35		.15	.140	.107	.076	.039	0
		t_c		**.244**	**.272**	**.296**	**.324**	**.35**
2013–2017[a]	.396		.20	.187	.143	.102	.052	0
		t_c		**.257**	**.296**	**.328**	**.363**	**.396**
2018–	.37		.20	.187	.143	.102	.052	0
		t_c		**.225**	**.265**	**.299**	**.336**	**.396**

$t_{cg*} = t_{cg}/(1 + r)^n$, where n is the expected holding period in years. Employees' after-tax discount rate is assumed to be 7%. t_c is solved using Equation 8.12. NQO preferred if $t_c > (t_p - t_{cg*})/(1 - t_{cg*})$.

[a] Ignores the Medicare surtaxes of 3.8% and 0.9% from the Patient Protection and Affordable Care Act.

A few details are in order. First, to achieve long-term capital gain treatment on the stock price appreciation after exercise of an NQO, the stock must be held for at least 12 months. If the stock price declines after exercise but before sale, the employee has a capital loss (short-term or long-term depending on the holding period). In addition, note that although the gain at the exercise date of the ISO may be deferred until the sale date, it is not always so. This gain, although not included in the calculation of regular taxable income, is included as a preference item in calculating the individual alternative minimum tax (AMT), which could trigger tax at the exercise date. Because the ISO gain is a preference item in the AMT calculation, the individual can then receive credit for the taxes paid at the exercise date against the regular taxes due on the final stock sale date. That is, exercise of an ISO might trigger the alternative minimum tax, which has the effect of accelerating the taxes otherwise payable at the final sale date. In effect, the deferral advantages of an ISO are lost. We ignore the AMT here in our model.

As the employee's expected holding period of the stock obtained from exercising an ISO increases, the effective or present value of the capital gains rate declines. If the stock obtained from exercising an ISO is held until the employee's death, the gain at exercise escapes income taxation altogether and thus the effective capital gains tax rate is zero. As the effective capital gains tax rate declines, the required corporate tax rate above which NQOs are jointly preferred by both parties increases. Prior to TRA 86, NQOs were tax-preferred only if employees had short holding periods with high-tax corporate employers. For example, with a holding period of 5 years, corporations had to have tax rates above 41.7% before NQOs were jointly tax favored. But with an employee expected holding period of 20 years or higher, the required corporate tax rate cutoff was 47.3% or higher before NQOs were tax favored, and thus NQOs were not tax favored by any corporations because the top corporate tax rate was 46%. In the 1988–1991 period, when employees faced the same tax rate of 28% on ordinary income and capital gains, ISOs offered only deferral advantages and the required corporate tax rate cutoff declined, thus making NQOs more tax favored for more corporations. As the tax rate on ordinary income increased to 39.6% and capital gains rates either held at 28% (1993–1997) and then declined to 20% (1998–2002), ISOs again offered both capital gains and deferral advantages to employees facing the top 39.6% rate, and thus the required corporate tax rate increased. With the reduction in both the top ordinary income tax rate (favoring NQOs) and capital gains rate (favoring ISOs) in 2003, the effects offset somewhat but the required corporate marginal tax rate above which NQOs are tax favored declined slightly. In 2013, the individual top statutory tax rates returned to 1988–2002 levels, with a slight increase in the required corporate tax rate for NQOs to be tax favored over ISOs.

After 2017, the required corporate tax rate above which NQOs are jointly tax favored is 22.5% or above, depending on the holding period. However, TCJA reduced the corporate tax rate to a flat 21%. Thus for highly compensated individuals, those facing a 37% tax rate, ISOs are jointly tax favored. Additionally, recall TCJA also limited public corporations' compensation tax deduction to $1 million for "qualified" employees. Thus, NQOs issued to qualified employees are most likely no longer deductible as their salary and bonus likely exceeds this limit, making ISOs further tax favored. However, there is a $100,000 limit per year grant of ISOs to individual employees.

The TCJA provides new tax benefits to employees of private start-up entities in new Section 83(i). Recall when a restricted stock grant vests, the employee owes tax at ordinary income tax rates (on the value of the stock at the vesting date). For nonqualified stock options (as opposed to incentive stock options), ordinary income tax is normally due at the exercise date (on the value of the stock less the exercise price paid). However, for nonpublicly traded companies it was sometimes hard for employees to have the liquidity to pay the tax because the shares could not be sold on a readily available market. Under the TCJA, the employee now can defer ordinary income taxation until the earlier of 5 years or when the stock of the company becomes tradable on an established securities market, or the election is revoked. Further the gain subject to ordinary income taxation is calculated at the vesting date for restricted stock and exercise date for stock options. Any appreciation in value after that date is subject to reduced capital gains tax rates. Individual employees are eligible if at least 80% of the employees of the firm receive stock options (or restricted stock) with the same privileges.

If the election is made for restricted stock to defer taxation at vesting, the employee cannot also undertake a Section 83(b) election (to be taxed at the grant date on the value of the restricted stock). And if the election is made for incentive stock options, then the gain at exercise is included in calculating FICA taxes.

EXAMPLE 8.4 NQOs versus ISOs when $t_c = t_p$

If the employer and the employee always face the same tax rate on ordinary income ($t_p = t_c$), then NQOs are preferred to ISOs because the derivation of Equation 8.12 can be rearranged as follows:

$$t_c - t_p + t_{cg*} - t_{cg*}t_c > 0$$

with $t_p = t_c$

$$t_{cg*}(1 - t_c) > 0$$

which is satisfied if

$$t_{cg*} > 0.$$

In other words, with NQOs and $t_p = t_c$, no net tax is paid on the stock price appreciation between the grant date and the exercise date because the tax paid by the employee is equal to the tax reduction achieved by the employer. By contrast, tax *will* be paid with an ISO, although it will be delayed until the stock is sold and the tax will be at capital gains rates. Therefore, NQOs are preferred when $t_p = t_c$ due to the asymmetric tax treatment of the employer and the employee under ISOs.

EXAMPLE 8.5 NQOs versus ISOs when $t_c > t_p$

If the employer's tax rate exceeds the employee's, NQOs are even more preferred over ISOs because the net tax paid becomes negative with the NQO. However, if the employer's tax rate is below the employee's, the ISOs could be preferred. Specifically, as shown in **Table 8.5**, ISOs are preferred if $t_c < (t_p - t_{cg*})/(1 - t_{cg*})$. So for employees facing high tax rates, ISOs may have a place in the compensation programs of companies with low tax rates, such as start-up companies or other companies with net operating loss (NOL) or investment tax credit carryforwards.

Evidence on the Role of Taxes in the Choice of ISOs

On an aggregate level, the relative use of ISOs, also known as qualified options, and NQOs has changed over time consistent with changes in the tax laws favoring one or the other option type. For example, Hite and Long (1982) document that firms switched from ISOs to NQOs after the Tax Reform Act of 1969 lowered the top rates faced by individuals; t_p fell relative to t_c, making ISOs less tax favored. Similarly, TRA 86 reduced the attractiveness of ISOs considerably because the top individual rate was set below the top corporate rate and the capital gains rate was set equal to the tax rate on ordinary income. Balsam, Halperin, and Mozes (1997) report that after 1986 NQO usage increased relative to ISOs.[16] Jaquette, Knittel, and Russo (2003) estimate that in the late 1990s and early 2000s, 89% of options granted were NQOs. NQOs continue to dominate ISO usage today.

Disqualifying Dispositions of ISOs

One of the interesting tax-planning features of ISOs is that they allow the firm to receive NQO tax treatment if tax rates change such that NQO tax treatment is tax favored relative to ISO tax treatment. This feature is an example of the adaptability of a tax plan. Specifically, firms can receive NQO tax treatment by having the employee undertake a disqualifying disposition of the ISO. A **disqualifying disposition** of an ISO occurs when the option-holder disposes of the stock within 12 months of exercise. The disqualification means that the ISO is then taxed as an NQO. In a disqualifying disposition, the firm's gross tax benefit (GTB) is $(P_e - X)t_c$. However, the employee's tax costs are higher due

[16] However, Madeo and Omer (1994) report that firms that switched from ISOs to NQOs following the 1969 Tax Act tended to be firms with low tax rates, when the tax model here predicts that it would be the high-tax firms switching. Austin, Gaver, and Gaver (1998) report evidence that the firm's marginal tax rate appears to have played little role in the choice of option type during the 1981–1984 period, with the choice appearing to be driven by minimizing the executives' tax burden. Thus the evidence is somewhat mixed on taxes driving the choice between ISOs and NQOs. See also Balsam, Halperin, and Mozes (1997) for further evidence.

to the difference in tax treatment of NQOs and ISOs, which is given in Equation 8.10. A disqualifying disposition results in the employee facing an incremental tax cost because the gain on exercise $(P_e - X)$ is now taxed as ordinary income rather than at capital gains rates and the tax on the gain is no longer deferred until the stock sale date.

Whether a disqualifying disposition is tax favored can be analyzed similarly to the initial grant. Suppose we hold the employee indifferent by having the firm reimburse the option-holder for incremental tax costs. Of course the payment, denoted R for reimbursement, is taxable to the option-holder and therefore needs to be grossed up by $(1 - t_p)$. At the same time, this payment is tax deductible to the firm. Thus a disqualifying disposition is tax favored if the net tax benefits (NTBs) are positive:

$$\text{NTB} = \text{GTB} - \frac{R}{(1-t_p)}(1-t_c) > 0$$

Substituting $(P_e - X)t_c$ for GTB and R from Equation 8.10, we get[17]

$$\mathbf{NTB} = (P_e - X)t_c - \frac{(P_e - X)(t_p - t_{cg*})}{(1-t_p)}(1-t_c) \quad \mathbf{0} \tag{8.13}$$

EXAMPLE 8.6 Disqualifying Disposition of ISO

Suppose an employee holds 100 ISOs with an exercise price of \$10 and a current stock price of \$25. The employee faces a tax rate of 28% on both ordinary income and capital gains. The firm faces a tax rate of 34%. (These tax rates were in effect in the post–TRA 86 period). The employee plans to hold the options for another 5 years to maturity before exercising and has an after-tax discount rate of 10%. Should the firm and employee consider a disqualifying disposition of the ISOs?

We first need to calculate the present value of the capital gains tax rate $t_{cg*} = t_{cg}/(1 + r)^n = .28/(1.10)^5 = .174$. If the options are disqualified, the firm stands to gain gross tax benefits (GTBs) of \$15(.34) = \$5.10 per option. The employee faces an increase in tax costs of \$15 (.28 – .174) = \$1.59 per option from Equation 8.10. If we solve holding the employee indifferent between disqualifying and not disqualifying, then the employee requires a pretax payment of \$1.59/(1 – .28) = \$2.21 per option. The after-tax cost of this payment to the firm is \$2.21(1 – .34) = \$1.46. Thus, as shown in Equation 8.13, a disqualifying disposition would save the two parties \$5.10 – \$1.46 = \$3.64 per option, or \$364 in total.

Many firms that could have saved substantial sums in taxes by paying cash to employees to disqualify ISOs in the post–TRA 86 era failed to do so. Why? One possibility is that they were simply unaware of the advantages. At least one fly in the ointment is that the firm's payment to the option holder, $R/(1 - t_p)$, is recorded as an expense in calculating the firm's accounting earnings and thus reduces reported earnings. This reduction in accounting earnings represents a nontax cost of the transaction. Matsunaga, Shevlin, and Shores (1992) predict that firms with higher leverage (debt/total assets), lower interest coverage (earnings before interest/interest), and lower dividend coverage (earnings/dividends) face higher nontax costs and are thus less likely to undertake a disqualifying disposition of ISOs. They report results consistent with these predictions.[18]

[17] Equation 8.13 can be simplified to Equation 8.12, but it is convenient to use Equation 8.13 to analyze the disqualifying disposition.

[18] An alternative to a disqualifying disposition is the conversion or swapping of NQOs for ISOs. Matsunaga et al. (1992) find little evidence that many firms converted. Similar to a disqualifying disposition, with a conversion, accounting compensation expense to the firm may arise from reimbursing the employee. Also, if NQOs are issued in exchange for ISOs when the exercise price is *below* the current market price, accounting compensation expense must be recognized for the difference. Apparently this requirement discouraged many firms from converting. The interested reader is also referred to the Microsoft Corporation annual reports for 1988–1990, in which the firm reported gross tax benefits of \$11.5, \$14, and \$20 million from disqualifying dispositions and ISO conversions for the 1988, 1989, and 1990 fiscal years. Microsoft paid 50% of its gross tax benefits to employees to induce them to undertake the disqualification and/or conversion.

The Role of Taxes in the NQO Exercise Decision

Most options have a contract life or term to maturity from the grant date of 10 years. However, many employees exercise their options well before their maturity date.[19] Early exercise can stem from a need for liquidity, consumption, and/or diversification so as to reduce the amount of wealth at risk within the firm, and/or tax reasons.[20] Before turning to the tax reasons, early exercise motivated by consumption or the need for diversification requires the employee to exercise and shortly thereafter sell the stock. Because sale of stock within 12 months of exercise of an ISO leads to a disqualifying disposition and thus increased taxes, NQOs rather than ISOs are more likely to be exercised early for liquidity and/or diversification reasons.

Early exercise of an NQO for tax reasons might arise either from an incentive to start the "clock" rolling for capital gains treatment on any subsequent stock price appreciation or an expected future increase in tax rates on ordinary income. **Figure 8.4** illustrates that the earlier the exercise date relative to the stock sale date and the greater the price appreciation after the exercise date, the more the price appreciation is taxed at favorable capital gains tax rates.

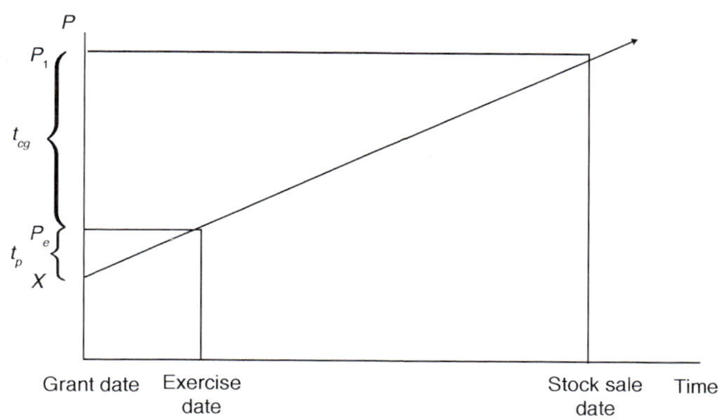

FIGURE 8.4 Early Exercise of NQO to Start the Clock Rolling for Favorable Capital Gains Treatment

The analysis of the early exercise decision to start the clock rolling for capital gains treatment on any subsequent stock price appreciation is similar to the analysis of the Section 83(b) election for restricted stock. Recall that a Section 83(b) election is not optimal unless we expect tax rates on ordinary income to increase (and stock price to increase). We show that this conclusion also applies to the early exercise of ESOs. To analyze the early exercise decision, we assume the employee borrows at an after-tax rate r, or equivalently liquidates other investments earning r, to pay the exercise price and taxes on the ESO, $X + (P_e - X)t_p$, where P_e is the stock price on the date at which we are considering early exercise. The borrowing and interest are repaid at the later stock sale date. The after-tax accumulation under this early exercise strategy is

$$P_s - (P_s - P_e)t_{cg} - [X + (P_e - X)t_p](1 + r)^n \quad (8.14)$$

where the first term is the gross proceeds from the subsequent sale of the stock, the second term is the capital gains due on the sale, and the third term is the amount of borrowing and interest to be repaid.

An alternative strategy is to borrow the amount that would be paid for early exercise (the exercise price and taxes) and buy additional stock. The employee can buy $N_s = [X + (P_e - X)t_p]/P_e$ of additional shares. The after-tax accumulation from this strategy is

[19] Huddart and Lang (1996) document the early exercise behavior of over 50,000 employees from eight different corporations. Hemmer, Matsunaga, and Shevlin (1996) examine the exercise behavior of the top managers from 65 firms. It is estimated that about 75% of NQO exercises are associated with immediate sale of the acquired stock, implying about 25% of exercises are exercise-and-hold transactions.

[20] Employees often have much of their wealth tied up in the value of the firm. This wealth includes the present value of their future earnings. Risk-averse employees would like to diversify their portfolio of wealth to reduce their risk. One method is to exercise their options and sell the stock with the proceeds invested in some other asset, reducing the overall risk of the employee's wealth. Huddart (1994) develops this intuition more formally.

$$(P_s - X)(\mathbf{1} - t_p) + N_sP_s - N_s(P_s - P_e)t_{cg} - N_sP_e(\mathbf{1} + r)^n \qquad \textbf{(8.15)}$$

where the first term is the after-tax proceeds from the ESO exercise and immediate sale of the stock, the second term is the gross proceeds from the additional stock purchased by the employee, the third term is the tax due on these additional shares, and the fourth term is the amount of borrowing and interest to be repaid. Borrow-and-buy additional shares is tax favored if the after-tax accumulation is greater than that of early exercise, Equation 8.15 > Equation 8.14. Note that $N_sP_e = [X + (P_e - X)t_p]$, the amount borrowed is the same under both alternatives, so that the last term is common to both alternatives and drops out of the comparison:

$$\begin{aligned}(P_s - X)(\mathbf{1} - t_p) + N_sP_s - N_s(P_s - P_e)t_{cg} - P_s + (P_s - P_e)t_{cg} > \mathbf{0}\\ P_s - X - (P_s - X)t_p + N_sP_s - N_s(P_s - P_e)t_{cg} - P_s + (P_s - P_e)t_{cg} > \mathbf{0}\\ N_sP_s - X - (P_s - X)t_p + (P_s - P_e)t_{cg}(\mathbf{1} - N_s) > \mathbf{0}\end{aligned} \qquad \textbf{(8.16)}$$

One can show that this expression is always positive and thus early exercise to start the clock rolling to obtain favorable capital gains treatment is not tax favored.[21] Note, however, that both are very risky strategies—if the stock price declines, the early-exercise-and-hold strategy results in paying taxes on phantom gains while the additional purchase strategy results in losses.[22] This additional risk compared with the do-nothing strategy is a nontax cost of the exercise early strategy and its alternative of purchasing additional stock.

EXAMPLE 8.7 Early Exercise of an NQO

Suppose an employee holds an NQO option with an exercise price of $10. The current stock price is $15, and the employee fully expects the stock price to increase to $35 at the option maturity date in 3 years. The tax rate on ordinary income is 35% and on capital gains is 15%. These rates are not expected to change. The employee can borrow at an after-tax rate of 10%. The employee is considering two alternative strategies: borrowing and exercising the option now and holding the stock 3 years before selling versus borrowing and buying additional shares and exercising and selling all shares after 3 years.

The after-tax accumulation from the early exercise strategy is given by Equation 8.14:

$$\begin{aligned}&P_s - (P_s - P_e)t_{cg} - [X + (P_e - X)t_p](1 + r)^n\\ &= \$35 - (\$35 - \$15).20 - [\$10 + (\$15 - \$10).37](1 + .10)^3\\ &= \$15.23\end{aligned}$$

The after-tax accumulation to the borrow-and-purchase additional stock strategy is given by Equation 8.15:

$$(P_s - X)(1 - t_p) + N_sP_s - N_s(P_s - P_e)t_{cg} - N_sP_e(1 + r)^n$$

where $N_s = [X + (P_e - X)t_p]/P_e = [\$10 + (\$15 - \$10).37]/15 = .79$ shares. Thus,

$$\begin{aligned}&(\$35 - \$10)(1 - .37) + .79(\$35) - .79(\$35 - \$15).20 - .79(\$15)(1 + .10)^3\\ &= \$24.47\end{aligned}$$

The after-tax accumulation of the borrow-and-buy additional stock strategy exceeds that of the early exercise strategy by $9.24 = $24.47 – $15.23. Alternatively, we can use Equation 8.16 to directly calculate the difference:

continued

[21] See McDonald (2003) for an alternative approach with formal proofs.

[22] The future losses are deductible as capital losses offsetting other capital gains or carried forward and deducted at $3,000 a year: Taxes are paid on ($P_e - X$) at t_p, while the subsequent losses are deducted at t_{cg}*. Further note that if the employee expects the stock price to decline, the best strategy is to exercise and sell the stock immediately before the price decline. See Neil Weinberg, "Out of Options" (*Forbes* April 29, 2002, pp. 50–54), for a discussion of losses suffered by employees exercising NQOs early and borrowing to buy additional shares.

continued from previous page

$$N_s P_s - X - (P_s - X)t_p + (P_s - P_e)t_{cg}(1 - N_s)$$

$$= .79(\$35) - \$10 - (\$35 - \$10).37 + (\$35 - \$15).20(1 - .79)$$

$$= \$9.24$$

As illustrated in **Table 8.6**, the tax advantage to the borrow-and-buy additional shares (or the tax disadvantage of the early exercise alternative) increases with the expected increase in stock prices.

Table 8.6 Analysis of the Early Exercise Decision: Exercise Early or Borrow and Buy Additional Stock[a]

	Early Exercise	Borrow and Buy Additional Stock	Difference
P_s	Equation 8.14	Equation 8.15	Equation 8.16
$15	$ (0.77)	$ (0.77)	$ 0.00
20	3.23	5.54	2.31
25	7.23	11.85	4.62
30	11.23	18.16	6.93
35	15.23	24.47	9.24
40	19.23	30.78	11.55
45	23.23	37.09	13.86
50	27.23	43.40	16.17
55	31.23	49.71	18.48
60	35.23	56.02	20.79

[a] Table values based on X = $10, P_e = $15, t_p = .37, t_{cg} = .20, n = 3 years, r = .10.

Tax Rates Are Expected to Increase Now consider the case where the employee's ordinary tax rates are expected to increase from t_{p1} in the current period to t_{p2} in the next period. Under what conditions should an NQO-holder exercise in the current period? The employee will favor exercise before the tax rate change when the after-tax gain from early exercise is greater than the after-tax gain on later exercise after the tax rate has increased. But what is the expected after-tax gain arising from later exercise? The present value of the expected pretax gain from later exercise is given simply by the current value of the option W, which we can estimate using an option valuation model such as the Black–Scholes model. The expected after-tax gain is then $W(1 - t_{p2})$. Thus early exercise is tax favored if

$$(P_e - X)(1 - t_{p1}) > W(1 - t_{p2})$$

or

$$\frac{(P_e - X)}{W} \qquad \frac{(1 - t_{p2})}{(1 - t_{p1})} \tag{8.17}$$

The left-hand side is the ratio of the gain to date on the option, or the option's intrinsic value, to the present value of the option. The right-hand side is the ratio of tax rates. Because the value of an option always exceeds its intrinsic value, except in the instant before maturity, the left-hand side is always less than unity. The ratio approaches unity when the option is deep in-the-money—the stock price is far greater than the exercise price—or when the option has only a short time to maturity. An out-of-the-money or at-the-money option ($P \le X$) or an option with a long maturity will have a low ratio. Let's interpret this relation: If tax rates are not expected to increase, the right-hand side equals unity. Because the left-hand side is always less than unity, the option will not be exercised early for tax reasons.[23] If tax rates are expected to increase $t_{p2} > t_{p1}$, the ratio $(1 - t_{p2})/(1 - t_{p1})$ is less than unity, and it is possible that the left-hand side will exceed this ratio. In particular, for deep in-the-money options with a short term to maturity, the ratio approaches unity, and early exercise before the tax rate increase captures a large fraction of the value of the option with the value taxed at the lower current rate.

EXAMPLE 8.8 Early Exercise of NQO When Employee Tax Rate Expected to Increase

Suppose an employee expects the top statutory tax rate to increase from 30% to 40% and holds two sets of options. The current stock price is \$50. The first set of options, with an exercise price of \$10 and an option value of \$41, is close to maturity. The second set of options, with an exercise price of \$30 and an option value of \$28, has 6 years to maturity. Should the employee exercise either series early, before the tax rate increase? The expected tax rate increase results in a ratio on the right-hand side of Equation 8.17 of (1 – .40)/(1 – .30) = .857. Thus if the ratio on the left-hand side of Equation 8.17 is greater than .857, the employee should exercise early.

For series 1: $\frac{(P_e - X)}{W} = \frac{(\$50 - \$10)}{\$41} = .9756 > .857$, so early exercise is tax favored.

For series 2: $\frac{(P_e - X)}{W} = \frac{(\$50 - \$30)}{\$28} = .7143 < .857$, so early exercise is not tax favored.

During the 1992 presidential elections, the widespread belief was that the top rates on ordinary income would increase. Proposals suggested an increase in the top rate from 31% for the tax year 1992 to 36% and 39.6% for tax years 1993 and thereafter. In fact, these rates became law. Thus during the last few months of 1992, high-tax-rate individuals faced the situation we covered in our example. The financial press highlighted Disney's CEO Michael Eisner as exercising options with pretax gains of approximately \$182 million to save approximately \$15.6 million in taxes, or \$182 (.396 – .31).[24] Huddart (1998) examines exercise behavior around this time period and reports evidence consistent with tax-motivated early exercise of deep in-the-money and shorter-term options.

Financial Accounting and Tax Comparison of Restricted Stock, Performance Share Awards, Stock Appreciation Rights, and Stock Options

For a variety of reasons we discussed in chapter 7, managers are not indifferent to the level of profits they report to shareholders and third parties for any given performance. Different methods of compensation have different tax and financial reporting implications. For example, a deferred cash compensation arrangement for work to be performed in one particular year typically gives rise to

[23] Recall that options can be exercised early for liquidity or diversification reasons. Further, this statement might seem to conflict with the earlier claim that an employee will favor early exercise for tax reasons so as to start the clock rolling on favorable capital gains treatment. Recall, however, that it was necessary to assume that the employee was very confident that the stock price would continue to increase. In the absence of this confidence, which might result from private knowledge from being an employee, the Black-Scholes value of the option is the best estimate of the present value of the eventual gain. If the employee were very confident of predicting the stock price at the future date, then we could substitute $(P_s - X)$ for W in the derivation of Equation 8.17. Finally, note that we have implicitly assumed the employer's tax rate is unchanged. Unless the employer also expects its tax rate to increase, the employer will prefer early exercise, because the employer company gets the tax deduction earlier, but at the cost of losing any incentives offered by the option to the employee.

[24] See, for example, "Disney Officials Get \$187 Million from Stock Sale," *Wall Street Journal* (December 2, 1992). See note 6 of Huddart (1998) for a list of other press articles.

compensation expense for financial reporting purposes in the period in which the services are rendered. For accounting purposes, restricted stock is accounted for as compensation expense, reducing reported earnings. The value of the restricted stock grant at the grant date is amortized over the vesting period (usually using a straight-line approach). A stock appreciation right, which may have the same cost to the employer at the date of grant as restricted stock or a deferred cash compensation arrangement, does not give rise to compensation expense until the stock appreciates in value in the future. Prior to December 2004, a stock option that was granted at an exercise price equal to the extant price of the underlying stock need not give rise to compensation expense at any time over the life of the option.[25] Statement of Financial Accounting Standard (SFAS) 123 encouraged but did not require firms to recognize the fair value of options granted as compensation expense in calculating net income reported in the income statement. Firms not recognizing compensation expense had to, however, provide footnote disclosures in the financial statements showing the effects on net income and earnings per share if the options were to be treated as compensation expense. Hence, firms that wished to avoid the recognition of compensation expense for financial reporting purposes, thereby increasing reported profits, had a natural preference for stock options over other forms of compensation. Until 2002–2003, close to 100% of firms elected footnote disclosure rather than recognition. However, in an apparent response to the corporate financial reporting scandals (e.g., Enron, Adelphia, Worldcom, Tyco, etc.), several hundred firms began recognizing compensation expense associated with ESOs. The accounting for ESOs was revised in SFAS 123R in December 2004 (now ASC 718). Firms must now recognize as compensation expense the fair value of ESOs. The fair value is to be amortized over the vesting period.

Suppose one share of restricted stock, a stock appreciation right, a performance share award, a nonqualified stock option, and an incentive stock option are issued with both option types having an exercise price equal to the current stock price of \$10 at the end of period 0. The estimated fair value of the NQO and ISO is \$4. The stock, which pays no dividends, increases in value by \$1 each year for the next 6 years. The restricted stock vests in 6 years, whereas the SAR, performance share award, and both types of ESO each vest in 4 years when the stock price is \$14, and the stock that is acquired from the performance share award and from exercising the option is sold 2 years later at a price of \$16. **Table 8.7** indicates the tax consequences to the employee and the employer for the three alternative stock-based compensation instruments.[26]

For the special case where the ordinary tax rate of the employee is equal to that of the employer, $t_p = t_c$, the total tax consequences to the two parties across the alternatives are shown in Panel B of **Table 8.7**. These results suggest that among the alternatives, stock appreciation rights are the most attractive from a tax standpoint, followed equally by restricted stock, nonqualified options, and performance share awards, with incentive stock options the least tax favored. If the employee's tax rate on ordinary income is below that of the employer, the preference ordering among the four compensation alternatives is the same, with the magnitude of the tax differences increased. Recall that if the employee's tax rate is well above the employer's rate (for example, if the employer faces current or future tax loss carryforwards), the preference ordering could be reversed. Also note in this example that the NQO is exercised earlier than the SAR. If the NQO is exercised at the same time as the SAR, the tax consequences would be the same for the two instruments.

[25] Prior to December 2004, Statement of Financial Accounting Standard 123 "Accounting for Stock-Based Compensation" (SFAS 123) issued by the Financial Accounting Standards Board in October 1995 and effective for fiscal years beginning after December 15, 1995, detailed the rules governing the accounting for employee stock options. SFAS 123 was superseded by SFAS 123R "Share Based Payment," issued in December 2004 and effective for the first interim or annual reporting period beginning after June 15, 2005. Weiner (2007, Table 8.2) provides a good chronology of the tax and accounting treatment of options dating back to the early 1970s.

[26] We ignore the cash flow differences between the different equity instruments. Note also that different assumptions will alter the comparisons. Note also that a performance award settled in cash is taxed similar to the SAR but with tax event occurring in year 4 when the award vests and is paid.

Table 8.7 Tax Consequences to Employees and Employers of Five Stock-Based Compensation Alternatives

Panel A General Case

Event	Options, RS, PSA Granted				RS Vests, Option Vests and Exercised, PSA Vests and Exercised				SAR Vests Stock Sold	
Time period	0		1, 2, 3		4		5		6	
Stock price	$10		$11, $12, $13		$14		$15		$16	
Tax consequences to	ee	er	ee	er	ee	er	ee	er	ee	er
RS	0	0	0	0	$-14t_p$	$14t_c$	0	0	$-2t_{cg}$	0
SAR	0	0	0	0	0	0	0	0	$-6t_p$	$+6t_c$
NQO	0	0	0	0	$-4t_p$	$+4t_c$	0	0	$-2t_{cg}$	0
ISO	0	0	0	0	0	0	0	0	$-6t_{cg}$	0
PSA	0	0	0	0	$-14t_p$	$14t_c$	0	0	$-2t_{cg}$	0

Panel B Total Tax Consequences of Five Stock-Based Compensation Alternatives When the Ordinary Tax Rates of Employees and Employers Coincide ($t_p = t_c$)

Time period	0	1	2	3	4	5	6
Instrument							
RS	0	0	0	0	0	0	$-2t_{cg}$
SAR	0	0	0	0	0	0	0
NQO	0	0	0	0	0	0	$-2t_{cg}$
ISO	0	0	0	0	0	0	$-6t_{cg}$
PSA	0	0	0	0	0	0	$-2t_{cg}$

RS = restricted stock, vests in 4 years; SAR = stock appreciation right, vests in 6 years.
NQO = nonqualified option, ISO = incentive stock option, vest and exercised in 4 years.
PSA = performance share award, vests in 4 years and is paid at that time.
Any stock obtained under any plan is sold at the end of year 6.
ee = employee, er = employer.
t_p = employee's tax rate on ordinary income, t_c = employer's tax rate on ordinary income. t_{cg} = employee's tax rate on capital gains.
Negative (positive) numbers indicate a tax payment (benefit).

What about financial reporting consequences? Financial reporting expense for each instrument is summarized in **Table 8.8**. The grant date fair value of the restricted stock, $10, is amortized over the 4-year vesting period resulting in $2.50 compensation expense each period. Stock appreciation rights yield compensation expense each period over its 6-year vesting period, with SAR compensation expense varying as the stock price changes each period. Prior to December 2004, under SFAS 123, nonqualified stock options and incentive stock options need not have given rise to compensation expense in the income statement for financial reporting purposes. Rightly or wrongly, such financial reporting considerations often appeared to swing the choice in favor of the more expensive compensation arrangements from a tax standpoint.[27] After December 2004, under the revised accounting for share-based payments in SFAS 123R, compensation expense for ESOs is recognized. The grant date fair value of the ESO is amortized over the vesting period. In this example, the estimated fair value of each option is $4, giving rise to a $1 per period compensation expense.[28] Finally, the previous

[27] Matsunaga (1995) provides evidence consistent with firms using employee stock options in lieu of cash compensation to avoid the reduction in reported financial accounting earnings.

[28] It is coincidental in this example that the compensation expense per period for the first 4 years is the same under the SAR and ESOs. If the grant date fair value of the ESOs is estimated to be $3, then the annual compensation expense is $3/4 = $0.75 per period. If the annual increase in stock price is greater (or less) than $1 per period, the SAR compensation expense will also be greater (less) than $1.

discussion ignores the financial statement accounting for the income tax benefits associated with these financial instruments. This discussion is included in Appendix 1.

Table 8.8 Financial Accounting Consequences of Five Stock-Based Compensation Alternatives

	Time	0	1	2	3	4	5	6
	RS	0	$2.50	$2.50	$2.50	$2.50	0	0
	SAR	0	$1	$1	$1	$1	$1	$1
SFAS 123								
	NQO	0	0	0	0	0	0	0
	ISO	0	0	0	0	0	0	0
SFAS 123R/ASC 718								
	NQO	0	$1	$1	$1	$1	0	0
	ISO	0	$1	$1	$1	$1	0	0

RS = restricted stock, vests in 4 years; SAR = stock appreciation right, vests in 6 years.
NQO = nonqualified option, ISO = incentive stock option, vest and exercised in 4 years. Estimated fair value at grant date is $4.
Any stock obtained under any plan is sold at the end of year 6.
ee = employee, er = employer.

The accounting for performance share/units/cash awards is a little more complex and is briefly summarized here (for more details, see ASC 718-10). The accounting depends on whether the performance goal or metric is accounting (for example, earnings) or stock price performance and whether the award is settled in cash or stock. But for all cases there is an expense reported for accounting purposes and the expense is recorded over the vesting period, with trueing up for the number of awards vesting/earned. If the award is settled in cash, fair value is estimated at each reporting date, similar to SARs, and if settled in stock, fair value is estimated on the grant date, similar to ESOs. Thus cash settlement leads to more volatility in reported earnings.

Other Differences between Restricted Stock and SARs, PSAs, and ESOs

In addition to differences in both taxation and financial accounting, compensation awards also differ in the incentives they offer to managers. The payoff to restricted stock is linear in stock price—a dollar increase/decrease in stock price increases/decreases the value of restricted stock by a dollar. On the other hand, the payoff function for a SAR, performance share award, and option is convex and the value of these awards is increasing in the variance of stock returns. Thus agency theorists argue that these latter awards are awarded not only to offer managers incentive to increase stock price (via increase in earnings and cash flows) but also to mitigate risk aversion in managers. Managers are assumed more risk averse (because more of their wealth and human capital is tied up in the firm) than diversified shareholders and thus managers might pass up positive net present value projects that they view as too risky. Because the value of a SAR/PSA/ESO is increasing in stock return variance, SARs/PSAs/ESOs help mitigate differences in risk aversion between managers and shareholders.[29]

Another difference between restricted stock and ESOs relates to dividends. Holders of restricted stock, even before vesting, are entitled to receipt of dividends on the stock. However, holders of ESOs do not receive any dividends and in fact the ESOs are not dividend protected. Paying a dividend reduces the stock price by the amount of the dividend reducing the value of the ESO. There is

[29] See Jensen and Meckling (1976); Smith and Watts (1992); Guay (1999); Hanlon, Rajgopal, and Shevlin (2003); Rajgopal and Shevlin (2002); and Ittner, Lambert, and Larcker (2003) for discussion and evidence on the relation between ESOs and managerial incentives. Note that ESOs have been linked by the financial press to the financial reporting scandals and earnings manipulations that occurred in the early 2000s. For academic evidence, see Cheng and Warfield (2005) and Erickson, Hanlon, and Maydew (2006). Rego and Wilson (2012) find that managers awarded employee stock options undertake riskier tax planning.

no adjustment to the exercise price reflecting the dividend payment. The lack of dividend protection incents manages to distribute excess cash flows via share repurchases rather than through dividends. Share repurchases are generally a tax preferred method of distributing cash to shareholders: the distribution as a share repurchase is taxed as a capital gain whereas distribution as a dividend is taxed as ordinary income to shareholders. In 2003, the tax rate on dividends to individuals was lowered from a top rate of 38% for individuals to 15% and the top capital gains tax rate was lowered from 20% to 15%. These rate changes altered the terms of trade between share repurchases and dividends for individual shareholders. However, most managers hold ESOs, which are not dividend protected, leading to a conflict between shareholders and managers over dividend policy given the changed terms of trade. Huston (2007) provides evidence that firms which increased their dividends increased cash payments to compensate managers for reduced ESO values. Aboody and Kasznik (2008) provide evidence that firms reduced ESO grants and increased restricted stock grants to CEOs leading to increased dividend payments. Thus shareholder-level taxes on dividends led to a change in compensation structure so as to align shareholder and manager incentives.

For performance share awards, where the target is stock price, similar to ESOs, when dividends are declared and paid, the stock price declines making it more difficult to meet the target. Because performance share awards are very flexible and firm specific, the firm can define the target to be inclusive of dividends (that is, cumulative dividends are added to the stock price to get total shareholder return over the target period, a very common approach); thus the employees are not disadvantaged by dividend payments. When the performance share award is based on accounting performance, there is little need to adjust for dividends. Because the employee does not hold the share settled awards, the employee does not receive the dividends during the vesting period.

Empirical Evidence on the Usage of the Different Long-Term Compensation Instruments

Compensation consulting firm FW Cook annually collects data from the largest 250 public companies in the US on their usage of the different compensation instruments awarded to the firms' top executives. Prior to 2011 stock options were the most prevalent type of long-term incentive instrument. However, Congress enacted a Say-on-Pay statute which mandated shareholders vote on the compensation packages of top executives—however, the vote was not binding on the firm. Proxy-advisory services recommended votes in support of performance-based plans and equity-based plans such as stock options which basically vest based on the passage of time are not viewed as performance-based.

In their 2017 analysis, FW Cook found that only 59% of the surveyed 250 firms use stock options and/or stock appreciation rights. They did not differentiate between nonqualified and incentive stock options. The use of restricted stock and performance award plans has increased through time: 95% of firms now use performance awards, while 65% use restricted stock. For the vast majority of firms, the contract term for stock options/SARs is 10 years. For all types of long-term awards, the vesting is most often 3 years, with 4 years being the next most common period. Some firms vest a portion of the award each year during the 3- or 4-year vesting period. Finally, among those firms using performance awards, 90% are settled in stock and the awards are earned (paid out) if certain targets are met, thus meeting the performance-based criteria. Many firms use multiple targets including total shareholder return (stock price appreciation and dividends), earnings, profitability (return on assets or return on equity), revenue, and cash flows.

Compensation in Venture-Capital-Backed Start-Ups

The ISO-NQO trade-off has a counterpart in start-up companies backed by venture capital firms. In many circumstances, management of the start-up ventures are awarded common stock and the venture capitalists are awarded convertible preferred stock. To provide incentives and rewards for managers, the price at which the preferred stock can be converted into common stock is often made contingent on the performance of the company: If the company does well, say, in terms of accounting measures of performance, the conversion price to the venture capitalists increases. The higher conversion price on the preferred stock is effectively a "bonus" to members of the management group who hold common shares. The higher the conversion price, the smaller the number of new shares issued to the venture capitalists and the more each remaining share is worth to management. This "bonus" is taxed to managers as deferred capital gains because they are taxed at a later date when they sell their shares. The "bonus" is not tax deductible to the company. Note that a cash bonus would result in immediate tax to managers at their personal tax rate. Even though this tax liability may appear worse than the stock-based bonus arrangement, the cash bonus would also yield an immediate corporate tax deduction assuming the company has taxable income to take advantage of the deduction. Therefore, the company could afford a larger tax-deductible cash bonus than a nondeductible stock-based bonus. As with NQOs compared to ISOs, the cash bonus arrangement is typically more efficient for tax reasons. However, the stock-based bonus as compared to the cash-based bonus reduces the start-up firm's cash outflows.

Limits on Deductibility of Executive Compensation

Congress has long been concerned with the magnitude of executive compensation especially relative to the median employee. The TCJA dramatically extended the prior limitation in Section 162(m) introduced in the Omnibus Budget Reconciliation Act of 1993. Section 162(m) limited corporate tax deductions for compensation to $1 million per individual. Firms can avoid the limitation by qualifying their compensation plan as performance based or by deferring the excess compensation to a time period in which it is deductible. To qualify for the performance-based exception, the following criteria had to be met:

1. The compensation was linked to the executives' attainment of objective performance goals such as stock price, market share, sales goals, and the like.
2. The performance goals were established by the firm's compensation committee of two or more independent directors.
3. The shareholders approved the compensation plan.
4. The compensation committee certified that the performance goals had been met before payment is made.

Note that employee stock options, restricted stock, and performance awards generally satisfied the performance-related exception. Any portion of salary in excess of $1 million was not deductible. Discretionary bonuses that might be used to shift income between periods in anticipation of tax rate changes, as we discussed earlier in the chapter, ran afoul of this limit to the extent the nonperformance-related total compensation exceeded $1 million. The first year after Section 162(m) went into effect, the value of ESO grants to top executives of the S&P 500 firms increased 45%. Balsam (2006) testified before Congress that in 1994 the average CEO received $1.6 million in total compensation including $682 thousand from the exercise of ESOs (representing 43% of total compensation). In 2004, total compensation had increased to $7.1 million, including $5.2 million from the exercise of ESOs (73%).

Empirical evidence suggests that although many firms did qualify their compensation plans so as to retain corporate tax deductions, many did not. In a sample of 297 publicly held U.S. firms, Johnson, Nabar, and Porter (1999) report that 46% of the firms did not preserve the deduction, 42% took actions to qualify their plans, and the remaining 12% deferred excess compensation. Balsam and Ryan (1996, note 1) provide the following information: Leucadia National Corporation stated in its proxy statement dated July 1, 1994, that it was forgoing the deduction because "the Committee agreed that the lack of flexibility in determining executive compensation under (preestablished performance criteria) would not be in the best interest of the company." Both Johnson et al. (1999) and Balsam and Ryan (1996) predict that those firms not qualifying their plans faced larger recontracting costs and higher levels of executive risk aversion. Tying compensation more closely to performance imposes risk on executives because firm performance (for example, stock price and market share) is also influenced by factors outside the managers' control. Risk-averse executives require a risk premium to compensate them for the increased risk. Both studies provide evidence consistent with their predictions.

Recall from earlier in the chapter, the TCJA limited the deduction a public corporation can take for compensation to qualified employees to $1 million per year. Thus, under the TCJA, both nonperformance, for example, salary, and performance-based, for example, all equity-based, compensation in excess of $1 million is no longer deductible. Covered employees include the CEO, CFO, and the three highest paid employees. If one assumes that covered employees earn a basic salary of $1 million or more, then all equity-based compensation is no longer deductible. Recall, all the analyses in this chapter that assume corporate tax deductibility of equity-based compensation no longer apply to covered employees. However, the analyses still apply to all other employees and to nonpublic corporations.

Concluding Remarks

We have now discussed all the compensation components listed in **Table 8.1** except for pensions, which are discussed in the next chapter. Furthermore, we have focused on the tax aspects of compensation. We do not want, however, to leave the impression that taxes are all that matter with respect to compensation. A number of nontax elements to compensation relate to motivating employees in order to mitigate hidden-information and hidden-action problems and the financial accounting differences between various compensation tools. These nontax elements are extremely important in compensation design.

Summary of Key Points

1. In determining the desirability of compensation alternatives, the tax consequences to both the employer *and* the employee must be considered.
2. Although employees prefer to receive taxable compensation at times and in ways that result in the income being taxed at lower rates, holding the compensation amounts fixed, employers prefer to pay tax-deductible compensation at times and in ways that result in the payments being deductible at high rates. By adjusting the level of compensation to reflect the tax costs and benefits of the compensation alternatives, the interests of employers and employees can be made to coincide.
3. In evaluating whether salary is tax preferred over deferred compensation, both the current and future tax rates of both parties (the employee and employer) must be considered as well as the after-tax earnings rate available to both parties. For example, while falling employee tax rates over time favor deferred compensation arrangements, such contracts may be undesirable when employer tax rates are also falling over time.
4. Nontax factors, such as incentive and risk-sharing considerations between employees and employers, might tip the choice in favor of current compensation even though deferred compensation is tax favored, or vice versa.
5. Even though certain fringe benefits yield tax deductions for employers and tax-exempt benefits for employees, such benefits are inferior to taxable cash compensation if employees place little personal value on the fringe benefits.
6. Discretionary cash bonus plans can be a very effective tax-planning tool because bonuses can be timed strategically to coincide with high tax rates for the employer and with low tax rates for the employee. However, such plans may run afoul of IRC §162(m) restrictions on the deductibility of total compensation to top executives—and they also require a great deal of mutual trust between the employer and the employee.
7. Restricted stock is similar to a deferred compensation arrangement—the employee recognizes taxable income at the vesting date at which time the employer obtains a tax deduction. Employees can make a Section 83(b) election recognizing taxable income at the grant date with future price appreciation (and depreciation) treated as capital gains (losses). A Section 83(b) election is generally not tax favored unless the employee expects his or her tax rate on ordinary income to increase in the future.
8. The popularity in the United States of incentive stock options (ISOs) in the early and mid-1980s may have resulted from unilateral tax planning. Nonqualified stock options (NQOs) impose more tax on employees but yield significantly higher tax benefits for employers.
9. Many ISOs that could have been disqualified or converted into NQOs following passage of the 1986 Tax Act at very significant tax savings were not disqualified or converted. One possible explanation is the adverse financial reporting consequences of this tax-saving transaction: It would have required the recognition of considerable sums of compensation expense in reports sent to shareholders and creditors.

10. In addition to liquidity or diversification motivations, employees might exercise employee stock options early for tax reasons—either to start the clock rolling to achieve capital gains treatment on subsequent stock price appreciation, or in advance of expected increases in tax rates. Similar to the analysis for restricted stock, the former is generally not tax favored, whereas the latter can be tax favored.
11. Managers in venture-capital-backed start-ups are often compensated in ways that yield deferred capital gains rather than immediate taxation at ordinary rates. Like ISOs, however, such compensation arrangements yield no tax deduction to the firm and therefore may be inferior to cash compensation alternatives. The more tax-efficient compensation arrangement often yields reduced income for financial reporting purposes. Some firms are apparently more interested in looking rich to investors than they are in looking poor to the tax collector.
12. In comparing compensation alternatives, such nontax factors as differences in administrative costs and in employee incentive effects may overwhelm the tax factors in importance.

Appendix 8.1

Accounting for the Tax Benefits of Employee Stock Options

As discussed in the chapter, the firm obtains a tax deduction equal to the amount of ordinary income recognized by the employee at the exercise date of a nonqualifed employee stock option. We discuss here the current accounting rules adopted in SFAS 123R 2004 (now ASC 718 and income tax accounting specifically ASC 740).

SFAS 123R requires firms to recognize as compensation expense the grant date fair value of ESOs. The fair value is amortized over the vesting period. Thus compensation expense is recognized prior to the tax deduction (which arises when the employee exercises the NQO), giving rise to a temporary difference. Recall, from Chapter 7, when an expense flows through the accounting statements before the tax books, the resulting temporary difference gives rise to a deferred tax asset. The easiest way to explain the accounting is via an example and journal entries. Suppose a firm issues 100 NQO ESOs with an exercise price of $20 and an estimated fair value of $6 each. The options vest in 3 years at which point the employees exercise the options. The total fair value of the option grant is $600 of which $200 is recognized as compensation expense each year of the vesting period. Assuming the firm's tax rate is 35%, the following journal entry is made in each of the 3 years of the vesting period:

Dr. Compensation Expense	$200	
Cr. Additional Paid-In Capital		$200
(To recognize ESO compensation expense)		
Dr. Deferred Tax Asset	$ 70	
Cr. Tax Expense		$ 70
(To recognize a deferred tax asset for the temporary difference arising from ESO compensation expense)		

The net effect each year in the income statements is to lower net income by $200 – $70 = $130, representing the after-tax ESO compensation expense. At the end of year 3, the balance in the deferred tax asset is $210 and $600 in the Additional Paid-In Capital account in Shareholders' Equity.

Suppose the stock price is $30 when the employee exercises the NQOs at the start of year 4. The journal entry on the exercise is:

Dr. Cash (100 ESOs x $20)	$2,000	
Dr. Additional Paid-In Capital	$ 600	
Cr. Common Stock		$2,600
(To record exercise of ESOs)		

The employee paid $2,000 in cash to exercise the ESOs and this amount together with the accumulated balance relating to these options in the Additional Paid-In Capital is credited to Common Stock.

The firm obtains a tax deduction of 100 ESOs times ($30 – $20) = $1,000, giving rise to a tax savings (or benefit) of $350. The tax savings exceed the deferred tax asset of $210. Prior to fiscal year end 2017, the firm accounts for the tax benefit as follows (assuming it has sufficient taxable income to take the tax deduction in the same year). The first entry closes out the deferred tax asset to deferred tax expense. The second entry reduces current income taxes payable by the full $350, with a corresponding reduction in current tax expense for the expected amount of the tax savings of $210 with the excess tax savings of $140 directly increasing Additional Paid-In Capital.

Dr. Deferred Tax Expense	$210	
Cr. Deferred Tax Asset		$210
(To close out the Deferred Tax Asset)		
Dr. Current Taxes Payable	$350	
Cr. Current Tax Expense		$210
Cr. Additional Paid-In Capital		$140
(To record the normal and excess tax savings)		

If the ESOs expire unexercised such that the firm receives no tax deduction, then the $210 deferred tax asset is closed out. If the firm has a balance in the Additional Paid-In Capital (APIC) account arising from ESOs, then the APIC account is debited with the $210. If there is no balance (or insufficient balance) in APIC, the debit is to Deferred Tax Expense (increasing the tax expense for that period).

What if the option is exercised but with a tax benefit of less than what was expected when granted (e.g., the $210 in our example)? For example, what if the stock price on the exercise date is $25? In such a case, when the deferred tax asset is closed out, the excess deferred tax asset [$210 – (actual tax savings of

$100 \times (\$25 - \$20) \times t_c)] = \$210 - \$175 = \$35$ (also referred to as shortfall in tax benefits) is treated as follows:

Dr. Deferred Tax Expense	$175	
Dr Additional Paid in Capital	$ 35	
Cr. Deferred Tax Asset		$210
(To close out the Deferred Tax Asset)		
Dr. Current Taxes Payable	$175	
Cr. Current Tax Expense		$175

If the firm issues incentive stock options (ISOs), the firm similarly amortizes the grant date fair value of the ISO over the vesting period. However, because ISOs do not give rise to a corporate tax deduction the firm does not record a deferred tax asset and tax expense during the vesting period. If the employee undertakes a disqualifying disposition of the ISO (for example by selling the acquired stock within 12 months of the exercise date), the firm receives a tax deduction in the amount of the ordinary income recognized by the employee as a result of the disqualifying disposition. Suppose the same facts as above except the 100 NQOs are now ISOs. Further the employee sells the acquired stock immediately on exercise when the stock price is $30. In this case, the firm receives a tax deduction of 100 × ($30 – $20) = $1,000 with a tax benefit of $350. The journal entry is as follows:

Dr. Current Taxes Payable	$350	
Cr. Current Tax Expense		$210
Cr. Additional Paid-In Capital		$140

Note the similarity in the accounting for the tax benefit between NQOs and ISOs under a disqualifying disposition. The tax savings reduce the Current Taxes Payable liability account. However, because there was no prior annual recognition of the tax benefit and accumulation of a deferred tax asset in the amount of .35 × recognized compensation expense, an equivalent tax benefit is recognized in the period of disqualification (.35 × $600) with any excess being credited to Additional Paid-In Capital (here $140).[30]

Disclosure in the Financial Statements: Under SFAS 123R, firms must use a "gross" approach to reporting excess tax benefits in the statement of cash flow. Each period, when calculating Cash Flow from Operations under the indirect method, which starts with net income, the increase in the deferred tax asset account (which includes the effects of the tax benefits recognized each period in the tax expense account) is subtracted from net income because deferred taxes are noncash items. When the tax deduction exceeds the estimated tax benefit as reflected in the deferred tax asset account, these excess tax benefits are treated as a cash inflow from financing and a cash outflow from operations (the latter is bound to confuse many financial statement readers). Thus in the previous example, the total tax savings is $350, with an excess of $140 over the $210 previously recognized as the tax benefit associated with the recognized compensation expense of $600. Thus, the net effect on the cash flow statement should be an addition to net income of $140 for excess tax benefits because this $140 is additional cash flow that does not show as a reduction in tax expense on the income statement (and the cash flow statement starts with net income and makes adjustments to get to cash flows). By section how it is shown is that in the year in which the tax savings arise, the operating section of the Statement of Cash Flows will show an outflow of $140 (because the $140 is included in the deferred tax adjustment in the operating section)—thus, the net effect on cash flow from operations is zero (there is an addition and a subtraction). The financing section of the cash flow statement includes an inflow of $140 to reflect that the excess tax benefits are treated as a financing cash flow (as determined by the FASB).

To illustrate the disclosures, the following are extracted from the Microsoft Corporation 2012 Annual Report. Note 20 reports that in 2012 Microsoft recognized $2,244 million in stock-based compensation expense with an associated expected tax benefit of $785 million (that is approximately 35% of the estimated fair value of the stock compensation recognized as an expense in that period). During 2012, the employees paid Microsoft $1,410 to exercise their options and the employees recognized a gain of $456, the intrinsic value of the options (the difference between the stock price at exercise date and the exercise price), which also equals Microsoft's tax deduction that saved corporate taxes of $160 (estimated as $456 × 35%). The Statement of Cash Flows shows that of the $160 million tax benefits realized, $93 million was in excess of the estimated amount, they are "excess tax benefits" that were credited to paid in capital. This excess amount is included in the deferred tax adjustment in the operating section and then separately subtracted in the operating section (i.e., the (93)) so that the net effect on cash flow from operations is zero. The amount is then reflected as a financing inflow so that these additional cash tax savings show as from financing activities. Finally, a listing of the firm's Deferred Tax Assets at the end of fiscal year 2012 shows an estimated future tax benefit of $882 million from stock compensation recognized as compensation expense in the financial books before the tax deduction is taken.

Extract from Microsoft Corporation Annual Report 2012

NOTE 20—EMPLOYEE STOCK AND SAVINGS PLANS (EXTRACT) Stock-based compensation expense and related income tax benefits were as follows:

(In millions)			
Year Ended June 30,	**2012**	**2011**	**2010**
Stock-based compensation expense	**$2,244**	$2,166	$1,891
Income tax benefits related to stock-based compensation	**$ 785**	$ 758	$ 662

During the periods reported, the following stock-option-exercise activity occurred:

[30] For further discussion of the accounting for ESO tax benefits under SFAS 123R, see Nichols and Betancourt (2006).

(In millions)	2012	2011	2010
Total intrinsic value of stock options exercised	**$ 456**	$ 222	$ 365
Cash received from stock option exercises	**$1,410**	$1,954	$1,839
Tax benefit realized from stock option exercises	**$ 160**	$ 77	$ 126

Statement of Cash Flows ($Millions, Fiscal year end June)

(In millions) Year Ended June 30,	2012	2011	2010
Operations			
Net income	**$16,978**	$23,150	$18,760
Adjustments to reconcile net income to net cash from operations:			
Goodwill impairment	**6,193**	0	0
Depreciation, amortization, and other	**2,967**	2,766	2 673
Stock-based compensation expense	**2,244**	2,166	1 891
Net recognized gains on investments and derivatives	**(200)**	(362)	(208)
Excess tax benefits from stock-based compensation	**(93)**	(17)	(45)
Deferred income taxes	**954**	2	(220)
Deferral of unearned revenue	**36,104**	31,227	29,374
Recognition of unearned revenue	**(33,347)**	(28,935)	(28,813)
Changes in operating assets and liabilities:			
Accounts receivable	**(1,156)**	(1,451)	(2,238)
Inventories	**184**	(561)	(44)
Other current assets	**493**	(1,259)	464
Other long-term assets	**(248)**	62	(223)
Accounts payable	**(31)**	58	844
Other current liabilities	**410**	(1,146)	451
Other long-term liabilities	**174**	1,294	1,407
Net cash from operations	**31,626**	26,994	24,073
Financing			
Short-term debt repayments, maturities of 90 days or less, net	**0**	(186)	(991)
Proceeds from issuance of debt, maturities longer than 90 days	**0**	6,960	4,167
Repayments of debt, maturities longer than 90 days	**0**	(814)	(2,986)
Common stock issued	**1,913**	2,422	2,311
Common stock repurchased	**(5,029)**	(11,555)	(11,269)
Common stock cash dividends paid	**(6,385)**	(5,180)	(4,578)
Excess tax benefits from stock-based compensation	**93**	17	45
Other	**0**	(40)	10
Net cash used in financing	**(9,408)**	(8,376)	(13,291)

continued

continued from previous page

Statement of Cash Flows ($Millions, Fiscal year end June)

(In millions)			
Year Ended June 30,	**2012**	**2011**	**2010**
Investing			
Additions to property and equipment	**(2,305)**	(2,355)	(1,977)
Acquisition of companies, net of cash acquired, and purchases of intangible and other assets (10,112)	**(71)**	(245)	
Purchases of investments	**(57,250)**	(35,993)	(30,168)
Maturities of investments	**15,575**	6,897	7,453
Sales of investments	**29,700**	15,880	15,125
Securities lending payable	**(394)**	1,026	(1,502)
Net cash used in investing	**(24,786)**	(14,616)	(11,314)
Effect of exchange rates on cash and cash equivalents	**(104)**	103	(39)
Net change in cash and cash equivalents	**(2,672)**	4,105	(571)
Cash and cash equivalents, beginning of period	**9,610**	5,505	6,076
Cash and cash equivalents, end of period	**$ 6,938**	$ 9,610	$ 5,505

NOTE 13—INCOME TAXES (EXTRACT) The components of the deferred income tax assets and liabilities were as follows:

(In millions)		
June 30,	**2012**	**2011**
Deferred Income Tax Assets		
Stock-based compensation expense	$ 882	$ 1,079
Other expense items	965	1,321
Unearned revenue	571	463
Impaired investments	152	424
Loss carryforwards	532	90
Other revenue items	79	69
Deferred income tax assets	$ 3,181	$ 3,446
Less valuation allowance	(453)	0
Deferred income tax assets, net of valuation allowance	$ 2,728	$ 3,446
Deferred Income Tax Liabilities		
International earnings	$ (1,072)	$(1,266)
Unrealized gain on investments	(830)	(904)
Depreciation and amortization	(670)	(265)
Other	(14)	0
Deferred income tax liabilities	(2,586)	(2,435)
Net deferred income tax assets	$ 142	$ 1,011
Reported As		
Current deferred income tax assets	$ 2,035	$ 2,467
Long-term deferred income tax liabilities	(1,893)	(1,456)
Net deferred income tax assets	$ 142	$ 1,011

In 2017, the FASB simplified the accounting for the income tax benefits of stock options, among other issues, in an Accounting Standards Update issued in March 2016 "Improvements to employee share-based payment accounting." When the amount of the tax deduction exceeds the recognized compensation cost on the financial statements, or equivalently, the realized tax benefit exceeds the accrued tax benefit giving rise to excess tax benefits, these excess tax benefits are no longer credited to Additional Paid in Capital, but rather are credited to tax expense, reducing the current period tax expense. Similarly, if the realized tax benefits are less than the accrued tax benefit, the shortfall is recognized as an increase in the tax expense account. The excess tax benefits are no longer broken out from the operating section to the financing section of the Statement of Cash Flows.

Using the numbers in our earlier example, the journal entries would now look like the following. For the case where the tax benefits exceed the accrued tax benefits by $130 in our example:

Dr. Deferred Tax Expense	$210	
Cr. Deferred Tax Asset		$210
(same as previously)		
Dr. Current Taxes Payable	$350	
Cr. Current Tax expense		$350

The above entries result in a reduction in the current period tax expense of $130 for the excess tax benefits.

For the case where the tax benefits are less than the accrued tax benefits by $35 in our example:

Dr. Deferred Tax Expense	$210	
Cr. Deferred Tax Asset		$210
(same as previously)		
Dr. Current Taxes Payable	$175	
Cr. Current Tax expense		$175

The above entries result in an increase in the current period tax expense of $35 for the shortfall in expected tax benefits.

Note that this accounting treatment will increase the volatility of the reported tax expense and hence net earnings. The accounting will also effect the GAAP effective tax rate (tax expense/pretax income)—increasing its volatility.

Questions

Q8-1. Why is the list of compensation alternatives in **Table 8.1** not necessarily ordered from most desirable to least desirable for an employee?

Q8-2. Why might salary be preferred to deferred compensation even if the employee's tax rate is falling over time? Illustrate your answer using the changes in tax rates introduced in the TRA 86. Was salary preferred for both higher- and lower-compensated employees?

Q8-3. In determining the tax advantage of a current salary contract versus a deferred compensation contract, why is it useful to set the contractual terms so as to hold one party indifferent to the choice of the contract? Does it matter whether the employee or employer is made indifferent between the two choices?

Q8-4. With the change in marginal tax rates in the TRA 86, would it have been tax disadvantageous for tax-exempt institutions such as Stanford University to establish deferred compensation arrangements in 1986 for their employees? Why might such institutions not have established these programs at that time?

Q8-5. What are the tax benefits of a fringe benefit such as employer-supplied life and health insurance? What are the nontax costs associated with such a program? Why would some employees prefer salary to the insurance program?

Q8-6. When are discretionary bonus plans attractive tax-planning vehicles? What incentives might induce the employer to renege on the bonus? What prevents the employer from reneging?

Q8-7. Is each statement true or false?

a. The expected return on stock appreciation rights always exceeds the expected return on the underlying stock.

b. The financial reporting differences for compensating employees with stock appreciation rights and stock options lead small start-up companies to prefer granting stock appreciation rights to their employees.

c. A nonqualified option is preferable to an incentive stock option for tax purposes.

d. The TRA 86 made incentive stock options less attractive.

e. The TCJA 2017 made incentive stock options more attractive.

Q8-8. In deriving Equation 8.12 comparing ISOs and NQOs, how were any stock price changes after exercise of an ISO treated?

Q8-9. If an employee exercises an NQO early in advance of an expected tax-rate increase, what costs or benefits might accrue to the employer?

Q8-10. Does an employee realize any benefits from exercising an ISO in advance of an expected tax-rate increase?

Q8-11. General Motors Corporation, in its 1994 Proxy Statement to shareholders, stated the following: "Compensation Deductibility Policy – . . . the Committee believes the regulation to be discriminatory toward the stockholders of publicly held corporations. . . ." Why might General Motors' compensation committee hold this belief?

Q8-12. General Motors Corporation, in its 1997 Proxy Statement to shareholders, stated the following: "To the extent it is practicable and consistent with the Corporation's executive compensation philosophy, the Committee intends to comply with Section 162(m) of the Internal Revenue Code (and any regulations promulgated thereunder) in order to preserve the deductibility of performance-based compensation in excess of $1 million per taxable year to each of the Named Executive Officers. . . . If compliance with the Section 162(m) rules conflicts with the compensation philosophy or is deemed not to be in the best interests of shareholders, the Committee will abide by the compensation philosophy, regardless of the tax impact of such actions." Why might noncompliance with Section 162(m) be in the best interests of shareholders (because by receiving a tax deduction for compensation, the firm saves taxes, which increases cash flows)?

Exercises

E8-13. Your employer is considering paying you deferred compensation in 5 years or a cash bonus of $1 million today. Here are the facts:

- Your tax rate today is 50%.
- Your tax rate in 5 years will be 35%.
- Your employer's tax rate today is 30%.
- Your employer's tax rate in 5 years will be 40%.
- Both you and your employer have an after-tax discount rate of 7%.

a. What is the highest deferred compensation payment (received 5 years from now) that your employer would be willing to pay?

b. What is the lowest deferred compensation payment (received 5 years from now) that you would settle for?

c. Can you and your employer get together and write a mutually beneficial deferred compensation contract? If so, describe the contract (amount).

E8-14. Suppose you will retire in 9 years. Throughout your life you will face a tax rate of 31% and earn an after-tax rate of return of 8% on your investments. Your company's pension plan earns a 12% return, and the company itself earns a 10% after-tax return on its own projects. The company faces a current tax rate of 34% and will face a 40% rate in year 9.

a. How much in deferred compensation (D^*) would the company have to pay you in year 9 to make you indifferent between future compensation and a $100 bonus now?

b. How much of a contribution to your pension plan (P^*) would the company have to make to make you indifferent between pension benefits in 9 years and a $100 bonus now?

c. What is the present value of the after-tax cost of each form of compensation (current bonus of $100, deferred compensation of D^*, and pension plan contribution of P^*) to the company, using a discount rate of 10%?

(Exercise written by Richard Sansing, Dartmouth College.)

E8-15. Under current law, employer-paid health insurance premiums are deductible by the employer and not taxable to the employee. Suppose instead only the first $1,000 of such premiums were nontaxable. If an employee was in the 12% tax bracket, how much would his employer have to pay him in cash to make him indifferent between the cash and $3,000 of health insurance premiums? Assume the employee cannot deduct any health insurance premiums he pays himself because his medical expenses are far below 7.5% of adjusted gross income. What if his tax bracket were 32%?

E8-16. Suppose you are an employee of Pactruck who just received 10,000 shares of restricted stock that vest in 4 years. Your current and expected tax rate on ordinary income is 37% and on capital gains is 20%. The stock is currently trading at $15 and you expect it to appreciate at 25% per annum over the next 4 years. You face an after-tax borrowing rate of 7%. You plan on selling the stock as soon as it vests. Should you simply hold the restricted stock through vesting and sell at that time or make a Section

83(b) election? As an alternative to the Section 83(b) election, you consider borrowing and purchasing additional stock using the money you would have used to pay the taxes on the Section 83(b) election. Evaluate this alternative.

Discuss any nontax costs associated with a Section 83(b) election and the alternative borrow-and-buy additional stock strategies. What is the ex post outcome if the stock price appreciates at 15% per annum? At 10% per annum? Fails to appreciate at all? Declines by 5% per annum?

E8-17. Assume the same facts as in Exercise 8-16. But now you expect your tax rate on ordinary income to decline to 30% in year 3. How do your answers in Exercise 8-16 change? Would you make the Section 83(b) election? Evaluate the borrow-and-purchase additional stock strategy.

E8-18. Same facts as Exercise 8-16. But now you expect your tax rate on ordinary income to increase to 50% in year 4. How do your answers in Exercise 8-16 change? Would you make the Section 83(b) election? Evaluate the borrow-and-purchase additional stock strategy.

E8-19. Suppose you are employed by MS Corporation. In year 1, you received nonqualified employee stock options (NQOs) to acquire 10,000 shares of MS's stock at an exercise price of $40 share. On that date, the stock traded at $35 per share. In year 2, you exercised your options when the stock price was $48 per share. In year 3, you sold the stock for $50 per share.

a. What is the amount and character (ordinary or capital gain) of your income in years 1, 2, and 3 because of these transactions?

b. How much is MS's tax deduction and when is it deductible?

c. How much will MS report as compensation expense each period?

d. How would your answers to questions (a), (b), and (c) change if the options were incentive stock options?

(Adapted from exercise written by Richard Sansing, Dartmouth College.)

E8-20. Wahoo, Inc., is a high-tech Internet company. It is trying to decide whether to issue NQOs or ISOs to its employees. Each employee will get 10 options. For purposes of this problem, assume that the options are exercised in 3 years and that the underlying stock is sold in 5 years. Here are the facts:

Corporate tax rate = 21%

Personal (employee) ordinary income tax rate = 37%

Personal (employee) capital gains tax rate = 20%

Personal (employee) after-tax discount rate = 5%

Exercise price of the options = $5

Market price of Wahoo stock at date of grant = $4

Market price of Wahoo stock at date of exercise = $30

Market price of Wahoo at date of sale = $40

a. Considering these facts, which type of option plan does Wahoo, Inc., prefer?

b. Which type of option plan do Wahoo's employees prefer?

c. Which type of plan should be used? Why?

E8-21. In December 1992, Michael Eisner and the late Frank Wells of Walt Disney exercised a large number of stock options. The facts are summarized here.

	Options Granted	Previously Exercised	Exercised 11/30/92***	Grant Date	Expiration Date	Exercise Price
Eisner	8.16 m	3.16 m	5.00 m*	1984	1994	$ 3.59
	6.00 m			1989	1999	$17.14
	2.00 m			1989	1999	$19.64
Wells	7.36 m	5.72 m	1.64 m**	1984	1994	$ 3.59
	2.25 m			1989	1999	$17.14
	0.75 m			1989	1999	$19.64

* Of the shares acquired, 3.45 million were sold immediately.

** All of the shares acquired were sold immediately.

*** Goldman Sachs executed these sales at $40 per share.

- In 1984, Michael Eisner became chairman of Walt Disney and Frank Wells became president. In late 1992, the options originally granted in 1984 were exercised when the stock price was $40 per share. Both Eisner and Wells were subject to the top marginal tax rate in 1992, which was 31%. Assume that both had salaries in excess of $1 million.

- In late 1992 there was a high probability that President Clinton's tax act would be passed, effective for 1993, and that the top tax rate for individuals would increase to 39.6%, the corporate rate would increase to 35%, and deductions for executive compensation in excess of $1 million would be disallowed.

a. Ignoring present-value considerations, how much did Eisner and Wells together personally save in taxes by exercising their options in 1992 instead of waiting until 1993 or 1994?

b. Michael Eisner exercised 5 million options and immediately sold 3,450,000 of the shares. What were the cash flow consequences to Eisner of these two transactions, including taxes?

c. Eisner told the *Wall Street Journal* he had to exercise the options in 1992 to avoid Disney incurring a substantial additional tax liability. Consider the claim that the early exercise saved Disney shareholders roughly $90 million in corporate income taxes. Assume that the corporation could not deduct any compensation paid in 1993 over $1 million.

d. Recompute your answer to (c) using the actual law as enacted, which has two provisions relevant for this problem. The first is that the $1 million disallowance did not take effect until 1994. The second is that transitional rules would have grandfathered these options and made the expenses fully deductible.

e. If early exercise was such a good deal for Disney, why didn't Eisner and Wells exercise all their options instead of just the options granted in 1984?

(Exercise written by Richard Sansing, Dartmouth College.)

Tax-Planning Problems

TP8-22. It is late 2018 and you are a successful oil executive currently working in Alaska for a major oil company. Tomorrow morning you will have the opportunity to negotiate with your employer to receive some amount of deferred salary in 5 years in exchange for $75,000 of your year-2018 compensation. If this compensation is not deferred, it will be paid to you on December 31, 2018, as a year-end bonus. Both you and your employer can earn a before-tax rate of return of 12%. Your employer's combined federal and state income tax rate is 25% and is expected to remain constant throughout the 5-year period.

Because Alaska does not have an individual income tax, you will pay only a federal tax of 37% on income earned in 2018. However, you are being transferred to New York at the beginning of next year, where you will be groomed for a top-level position in the firm. You expect your combined federal, state, and city income tax rate to be 45% in the year 2019 and to remain at this level throughout the 5-year period.

a. What is the highest deferred compensation payment that your employer would be willing to pay?

b. What is the lowest deferred compensation payment that you would settle for?

c. Can you and your employer get together and write a mutually beneficial deferred compensation contract? Now suppose you are married to a psychic. As you are making your computations in preparation for tomorrow's meeting, your spouse informs you that she is getting a clear image of you drinking beer at a bar on the Gulf Coast of Florida while reading a copy of *Deep Sea Fishing Weekly* dated 5 years from today and demanding that the bartender give you the AARP discount for retirees (which you will not get because you are not old enough).

d. Your spouse interprets this image as indicating that you will snap mentally from the stress 5 years from now (2023), quit your job, and move to Florida, where you will become the captain of a small charter boat and pay federal income taxes at a 31% rate when your deferred compensation is received in the year 2023. Note: Your spouse has never been wrong before. Under these conditions, what is the lowest deferred compensation payment that you would settle for?

e. Under these new conditions, can you and your employer get together and write a mutually beneficial deferred compensation contract?

TP8-23. Suppose Congress is expected to increase the corporate tax rate from 21% to 35% next year. RealNet.Com is scheduled to pay its CEO a salary of $1 million in the current period. The CEO's tax rate is 37%. The CEO is also entitled to a bonus that is up to the discretion of the compensation committee. As an adviser to the compensation committee, compare and contrast the following tax-planning strategies.

a. Do nothing.

b. Defer a large part of the salary ($300,000) from the current period to the next period.

c. Defer the bonus from the current period to the next period.

TP8-24. Suppose you are an employee of HP Corporation. You face a personal marginal tax rate on ordinary income of 50%, and on capital gains the tax rate is 20%. Your after-tax opportunity cost of capital is 7% per year. You hold 100 employee stock options that have an exercise price of $20 per option, and the current stock price is $35.

a. Assume the options you hold are incentive stock options (ISOs). What is the present value of any tax due given that you intend to hold the stock for 10 years after exercise? What is the present value of any tax deduction that HP might get, assuming HP's marginal tax rate is 10%?

b. Repeat part (a) but now assume the options are nonqualified stock options. Compare and summarize your results.

Now change the facts as follows. Suppose the tax law changed such that HP's marginal tax rate is 34% and your tax rate is 28% on both ordinary income and capital gains.

c. Repeat (a) assuming the 100 options are incentive stock options.

d. Repeat (c) assuming the 100 options are nonqualified stock options. Summarize and compare the results of (c) and (d). Do you notice any tax-planning opportunities available to the employee and HP?

TP8-25. Suppose you are a high-level employee of Drugstore.Com. You currently hold 50,000 NQOs, each with an exercise price of $20. The options vest—that is, you are no longer restricted from exercising them—in 1 month. Your current and expected future tax rate on ordinary income is 37% and on capital gains is 20%. The stock is currently trading at $35, and you expect the stock to appreciate at 20% per year over the remaining 7 years of the options' life. You have an after-tax discount rate of 10%. Should you exercise the NQOs immediately on vesting and hold the stock, or hold the options through to maturity before exercising? Would your answer change if you held ISOs instead of NQOs?

TP8-26. Suppose you hold two series of options, both NQOs. Because of a big promotion, you expect your tax rate to increase from a current 32% to 37%. The current stock price is $70. The first set of options, close to maturity, has an exercise price of $25 and an estimated Black–Scholes option value of $48. The second set of options, with 5 years to maturity, has an exercise price of $50 and an estimated option value of $30. Should you exercise either series of options in advance of your big promotion?

References and Additional Readings

Aboody, D., and R. Kasznik, 2008. "Executive Stock-Based Compensation and Firm's Cash Payout: The Role of Shareholders' Tax-Related Payout Preferences," *Review of Accounting Studies* (September), pp. 216–251.

Alexander, R., M. Hirschey, and S. Scholz, 2007. "Backdating Employee Stock Options: Tax Implications," *The CPA Journal*.

Austin, J., J. Gaver, and K. Gaver, 1998. "The Choice of Incentive Stock Options vs. Nonqualified Options: A Marginal Tax Rate Perspective," *Journal of the American Taxation Association* (Fall), pp. 1–21.

Balsam, S., R. Halperin, and H. Mozes, 1997. "Tax Costs and Nontax Benefits: The Case of Incentive Stock Options," *Journal of the American Taxation Association* (Fall), pp. 19–37.

Balsam, S., and D. Ryan, 1996. "Response to Tax Law Changes Involving the Deductibility of Executive Compensation: A Model Explaining Corporate Behavior," *Journal of the American Taxation Association* (Supplement), pp. 1–12.

Bernile, G., and G. Jarrell, 2009. "The Impact of the Options Backdating Scandal on Shareholders," Working Paper, *Journal of Accounting and Economics* (47, 1–2), pp. 2–26.

Cheng, Q., and T. Warfield, 2005. "Equity Incentives and Earnings Management," *The Accounting Review* (April), pp. 441–476.

Cicero, D., 2007. "Strategic Timing and Backdating of Executive Stock Option Exercises: Before and After the Sarbanes-Oxley Act," Working Paper, SEC and University of Georgia.

Coles J., N. Daniel, and L. Naveen, 2006. "Managerial Incentives and Risk Taking," *Journal of Financial Economics* (79), pp. 431–468.

Collins, D., G. Gong, and H. Li, 2009. "Corporate Governance and Backdating of Executive Stock Options," *Contemporary Accounting Research* (Summer), pp. 403–445.

Desai, M., 2002. "The Corporate Profit Base, Tax Sheltering Activity, and the Changing Nature of Employee Compensation," Working Paper 8866. Cambridge, MA: NBER.

Dhaliwal D., M. Erickson, and S. Heitzman, 2009. "Taxes and the Backdating of Stock Option Exercise Dates," *Journal of Accounting and Economics* (47), pp. 27–49.

Erickson, M., M. Hanlon, and E. Maydew, 2006. "Is There a Link between Executive Equity Holdings and Accounting Fraud?" *Journal of Accounting Research* (March), pp. 113–143.

Graham, J., M. Lang, and D. Shackelford, 2004. "Employee Stock Options, Corporate Taxes and Debt Policy," *Journal of Finance* (August), pp. 1585–1618.

Guay, W., 1999. "An Empirical Analysis of the Convexity between Stock Price and CEO's Wealth," *Journal of Financial Economics* (53), pp. 43–71.

Hanlon, M., S. Rajgopal, and T. Shevlin, 2003. "Are Executive Stock Options Associated with Future Earnings?" *Journal of Accounting and Economics* (36), pp. 3–43.

Hanlon, M., and T. Shevlin, 2002. "Accounting for Tax Benefits of Employee Stock Options and Implications for Research," *Accounting Horizons* (March), pp. 1–16.

Hemmer, T., S. Matsunaga, and T. Shevlin, 1996. "The Influence of Risk Diversification on the Early Exercise of Employee Stock Options by Executive Officers," *Journal of Accounting and Economics* (February), pp. 45–68.

Heron, R., and E. Lie, 2007. "Does Backdating Explain the Stock Price Pattern around Executive Stock Option Grants?" *Journal of Financial Economics* (83), pp. 271–295.

Heron, R., and E. Lie, 2009. "What Fraction of Stock Option Grants to Top Executives Have Been Backdated or Manipulated?" *Management Science* (55), pp. 513–525.

Hite, G., and M. Long, 1982. "Taxes and Executive Stock Options," *Journal of Accounting and Economics* (4), pp. 3–14.

Huddart, S., 1994. "Employee Stock Options," *Journal of Accounting and Economics* (September), pp. 207–231.

Huddart, S., 1998. "Tax Planning and the Exercise of Employee Stock Options," *Contemporary Accounting Research* (Summer), pp. 203–216.

Huddart, S., and M. Lang, 1996. "Employee Stock Option Exercises: An Empirical Analysis," *Journal of Accounting and Economics* (July), pp. 157–172.

Huston, G. R., 2007. "Can Compensation Policies and Director Independence Alleviate Agency Conflicts Associated with Shareholder Demands for Dividends?" Working Paper, Texas A&M University (February).

Ittner, C., R. Lambert, and D. Larcker, 2003. "The Structure and Performance Consequences of Equity Grants to Employees of New Economy Firms," *Journal of Accounting and Economics* (34), pp. 89–127.

Jaquette, S., M. Knittel, and M. Russo, 2003. "Recent Trends in Stock Options," U.S. Department of the Treasury, Office of Tax Analysts Working Paper 89 (March).

Jensen, M., and W. Meckling, 1976. "Theory of the Firm: Managerial Behavior, Agency Costs and Ownership Structure," *Journal of Financial Economics* (3), pp. 305–360.

Johnson, M., S. Nabar, and S. Porter, 1999. "Determinants of Corporate Response to Section 162(m)." Working Paper, Ann Arbor, MI: University of Michigan.

Lie, E., 2005. "On the Timing of CEO Stock Option Awards," *Management Science* (51), pp. 802–812.

Lipman, F., 2002. "Incentive Stock Options and the Alternative Minimum Tax: The Worst of Times," *Harvard Journal on Legislation* (39), pp. 337–373.

Madeo, S., and T. Omer, 1994. "The Effect of Taxes on Switching Stock Option Plans: Evidence from the Tax Reform Act of 1969," *Journal of the American Taxation Association* (Fall), pp. 24–42.

Manzon, G., and G. Plesko, 2002. "The Relation between Financial and Tax Reporting Measures of Income," *Tax Law Review* (55), pp. 175–214.

Matsunaga, S., 1995. "The Effects of Financial Reporting Costs on the Use of Employee Stock Options," *The Accounting Review* (January), pp. 1–26.

Matsunaga, S., T. Shevlin, and D. Shores, 1992. "Disqualifying Dispositions of Incentive Stock Options: Tax Benefits versus Financial Reporting Costs," *Journal of Accounting Research* (Supplement), pp. 37–76.

McDonald, R. 2003. "Is It Optimal to Accelerate the Payment of Income Tax on Share-Based Compensation?" Working Paper, Evanston, IL: Northwestern University.

McGill, G., and E. Outslay, 2002. "Did Enron Pay Taxes? Using Accounting Information to Decipher Tax Status," *Tax Notes* (August 19).

Narayanan, M., and N. Seyhun, 2008. "The Dating Game: Do Managers Designate Option Grant Dates to Increase Their Compensation?" *Review of Financial Studies* (21), pp. 1907–1945.

Nichols, N., and L. Betancourt, 2006. "Options and the Deferred Tax Bite," *Journal of Accountancy* (March).

Pippin, S., J. Wong, and R. Mason, 2007. "The Federal Tax Implications of Redating Stock Option Grant Dates and Exercise Dates," *Journal of Legal Tax Research* (December), pp. 79–98.

Rajgopal, S., and T. Shevlin, 2002. "Empirical Evidence on the Relation between Stock Option Compensation and Risk Taking," *Journal of Accounting and Economics* (33), pp. 145–171.

Rego, S., and R. Wilson, 2012. "Executive Compensation, Equity Risk Incentives, and Corporate Tax Aggressiveness," *Journal of Accounting Research*, Vol. 50(3), pp. 775–810.

Smith, C., and R. Watts, 1992. "The Investment Opportunity Set and Corporate Financing,

Dividend, and Compensation Policies," *Journal of Financial Economics* (7), pp. 117–161.

Stumpff, A., 2007. "Deferred Compensation and the Policy Limitations of the Nuclear Option," *Tax Notes* (November 5).

Wei, C., and D. Yermack, 2011. "Deferred Compensation, Risk, and Company Value: Investor Reactions to CEO Incentives," *Review of Financial Studies* (24), pp. 3813–3840.

Weiner, J., 2007. "Taxing Stock Options Is an Option," *Tax Notes* (April 2), pp. 53–71.

9

Pension and Retirement Planning

After completing this chapter, you should be able to

1. Explain the differences between a defined contribution pension plan and a defined benefit pension plan.
2. Analyze and compare the after-tax returns to current salary, pension plan, and deferred compensation.
3. Explain and illustrate the Black–Tepper tax arbitrage pension strategy.
4. Explain why it might pay for a firm to overfund a defined benefit pension plan.
5. Compare alternative strategies of funding retiree health care costs.
6. List the benefits of employee stock-ownership plans.

To encourage saving for retirement, many countries give favorable tax treatment to pension compensation, and pension plans have become extremely important components of the compensation package for both employers and employees. Consider the following points concerning alternative savings vehicles:

1. Contributions into the plan are tax deductible up to prescribed limits.
2. Earnings on pension investments are tax exempt.
3. Employees defer payment of tax until they receive payments from the plan.

These three conditions apply to all pension savings accounts except for a Roth individual retirement account (IRA) and a Roth 401(k), where contributions are not tax deductible; that is, after-tax dollars are contributed to the plan, and payments from the plan are tax free.

In this chapter, we discuss the tax advantages of corporate pension funds and highlight their nontax costs and benefits. We first discuss different types of pension plans and then compare them to salary and deferred compensation plans. We then discuss pension plan investment strategy (for example, stocks versus bonds) and funding strategy (how much to put into the plan). In the last two sections of the chapter, we discuss postretirement health care plans and employee stock-ownership plans.

9.1 TYPES OF PENSION PLANS

The two major categories of corporate pension plans are defined contribution plans and defined benefit plans. In a **defined contribution corporate pension plan** the employer and, in most cases, the employee make contributions into an account that will accumulate pension benefits on behalf of the employee. As its name implies, a defined contribution plan specifies contributions into the plan. Examples of corporate-defined contribution plans include profit-sharing plans, money-purchase plans, 401(k) plans, employee stock-ownership plans, and thrift plans. For example, a profit-sharing plan might require the employer to contribute a fixed fraction of the salary of the employee if profits exceed designated levels and a lesser fixed fraction if profits fall below these levels. Numerous formulas are used to determine company contributions. The average match made by the employer is 3.5% of the employees' contribution. Forty-nine percent of businesses with 401(k) plans do not match.

The employee's ultimate pension benefit depends on the amounts contributed into the plan and on investment performance. The employer does not guarantee the amount of its employees' pension benefit. In this regard, corporate-defined contribution plans are similar to IRAs, although contribution limits for corporate pension plans are far more generous than for IRAs. For example, for the year 2018, individuals could contribute up to $5,500 per year of pretax dollars into an IRA compared with a maximum contribution (by both employee and employer) of the lesser of (1) 100% of the employee's eligible pay or (2) $55,000 to a defined contribution plan. Defined benefit plans, discussed later in the chapter, face contribution limits if they are overfunded, that is, when plan assets exceed plan liabilities.

In a defined contribution pension plan, the employer deposits the contribution into an employee account. Because he or she bears the risk of investment performance, the employee is often given a choice among different investment alternatives in which to invest the money in his or her pension account, such as a bond fund, a stock fund, or a guaranteed annuity from an insurance company, which promises to pay the employee a specified annual amount in retirement.[1] The employer deducts its contribution in calculating corporate taxable income, and the employee contributions, if any, reduce salary that is subject to income taxation; that is, contributions are made from pretax salary (but the amount contributed is subject to withholding for Social Security and Medicare taxes). The earnings on the assets in the account are tax deferred until withdrawn by the employee. An employee's withdrawals from the account in retirement are taxed as ordinary income. Tax rules require that employees, if retired, begin withdrawing by April 1 following the year in which the employee reaches age 70.5. The withdrawal amount must be at least what would be available from a fixed life annuity at that time, although the withdrawal amount can be based on a joint annuity payable over the lives of the employee and a beneficiary. Except in the case of death or disability, the employee typically must pay a 10% excise tax in addition to the regular tax on withdrawals prior to age 59.5 (prior to age 55 for early retirees).

A **defined benefit corporate pension plan** promises the employee a stated benefit at retirement, often based on salary and/or years of service, usually in the form of an annuity. Defined benefit plans are either flat benefit plans or salary-related plans.[2] A flat benefit plan, usually provided to union employees, stipulates that the employee will receive a fixed dollar amount per year based on years of service—for example, $20 per month per year of service not to exceed 25 years. A salary-related plan typically provides a benefit that is a percentage of an employee's salary. For example, a salary-related plan might provide the employee with an annual annuity of 2% of her average salary over her last 5 years of employment for each year she worked for the firm. If the employee's salary averaged $120,000 in the last 5 years of her 15 years of employment before leaving the firm at age 50, she could receive a pension at age 65, the firm's normal retirement age, of $36,000 per year, or 15 × .02 × $120,000. To fund these promises, employers contribute to a pension trust. Unlike defined contribution plans, employees need not worry about the investment performance of the assets in the pension fund as long as the fund contains sufficient assets to support these promised benefits.

---

[1] Some companies contribute their own stock into 401(k) plans. This imposes risk on the employee because much of his or her wealth is then concentrated in the firm. If the firm fails, not only is the employee out of work, but his or her 401(k) investment in the company stock loses much of its value. See "When 401(k)s Are KO'd," (January 7, 2002), p. 104, discussing Enron employees' pension fund losses. More generally, readers interested in information on pension plan usage are referred to https://www.bls.gov/ncs/ebs/detailedprovisions/2017/ownership/private/retirement.htm.

[2] A third type of defined benefit plan is a cash balance plan. In a typical cash balance plan, the benefits are defined in terms of an account balance. However, the employer is responsible for ensuring that the account has the promised balance. A participant's account is credited each year with a "pay credit," such as 5% of compensation, and an "interest credit," which is either a fixed rate or a variable rate linked to some interest index. Fluctuations in the value of the plan's investments do not directly affect the benefit amounts promised to participants. Thus, the investment risk on plan assets is borne by the employer. For further discussion of these plans, see FAQs About Cash Balance Pension Plans at http://www.dol.gov/ebsa/ faqs/faq_consumer_cashbalanceplans.html. See also A. Arcady and F. Mellors, "Cash Balance Conversions: Assessing the Accounting and Business Implications," (February 2000), pp. 22–28, and E. McCarthy, "Staying Off the Cover of Time," (February 2000), pp. 31–34. McCarthy discusses IBM's conversion from a traditional defined benefit plan to a cash balance plan. See also "Not Your Father's Pension," (August 25, 2003), p. A10. The U.S. Department of Labor also has a frequently asked questions section on its website: http://www.dol.gov/ebsa/FAQs/faq_compliance_cashbalanceplans.html.

It is more difficult to value the promises to employees in a defined benefit plan than in a defined contribution plan. Each year, actuaries determine the required contributions to fund the target retirement annuity for defined benefit plans. They estimate the discount rate to value the retirement liability, the terminal salary to forecast the amount of the annuity, the life expectancy of employees and their survivors, the earnings rate on assets in the pension fund, the expected employee turnover rates, and the possibility of the employees' disability and death. All these assumptions make it difficult to define precisely the corporation's pension liability and its funding requirements. As a result, by changing the assumptions, actuaries have considerable latitude in determining the tax-deductible funding requirements of pension plan sponsors.

Some descriptive data on private-sector—that is, nongovernment—pension plans in the United States appear in **Table 9.1**. Panel A includes data for all private pension plans, and Panel B reports data on plans with 100 or more participants. Assets held by private pension plans totaled $8.15 trillion in 2015, the latest year for which data are available.[3] Defined contribution (DC) plans held $5.29 trillion of assets, with $2.86 trillion held in defined benefit (DB) plans. There are 648,000 DC plans covering 97.6 million active employees compared with 45,000 DB plans covering 37.3 million active employees. DC plans are smaller on average, covering 121 employees compared with 315 employees for DB plans. Not surprisingly, Panel B indicates that most of the assets and participants are in plans with 100 or more participants.

Table 9.1 Descriptive Data on Private U.S. Pension Plans for 2015

Panel A: All Plans

	Defined Contribution	Defined Benefit	Total
Assets ($ Trillions)	$5.292	$2.862	$8.154
Number of plans	648,252	45,672	693,925
Number of total participants			
(Active, retired, separated) (000s)	97,572	37,286	134,857
Number of active employees covered (000s)	78,130	14,405	92,535
Average number of active employees per plan	121	315	133

Panel B: Plans with 100 or more participants

	Defined Contribution	Defined Benefit	Total
Assets ($ Trillions)	$4.563	$2.813	$7.377
Number of plans	88,266	8,715	79,551
Number of total participants			
(Active, retired, separated) (000s)	85,904	36,823	122,727
Number of active employees covered (000s)	67,591	13,961	81,552
Average number of active employees per plan	766	1602	1025

In 2015 (latest year for which data are available), approximately 66% (35%) of employees at firms with more (less) than 100 employees were covered by pension plans. Interestingly and in contrast, 90% (87%) of full-time state and local government employees were covered by pension plans (DB plans). These numbers have been relatively stable over the past 20 years. Among the large firms, in 2015 30% of all employees are covered by DB plans with 54% covered by DC plans (many employees are

[3] The numbers are compiled by the federal government from Form 5500 reports filed with the Department of Labor by pension plan sponsors for 2015 plan years. The Department of Labor website, www.dol.gov, contains summary tables and other information on pension plans. See also "Retirement Prospects in a Defined Contribution World," edited by Dallas Salisbury, published by the Employee Benefit Research Institute (EBRI), 1997. The EBRI website, www.ebri.org, contains a wealth of information.

covered by both plans). These percentages mark a significant change from 25 years prior, when 80% of employees were covered by DB plans and 41% were in DC plans. The growth in DC plans has mostly occurred via 401(k) plans introduced in the Revenue Act of 1978. In 2015, 401(k) plans topped the 547,000 mark and made up 79% (84%) of all pension plans (of DC plans), cover 66% of all active participants, and hold 49.2% of all pension plan assets. A number of factors explain this change in coverage or increased popularity of DC plans. DC plans are easier to administer, the risk of investment is borne by the employee, which possibly requires a risk premium for the employee, and financial accounting is simpler.[4, 5] In addition, Congress has made it more difficult to extract excess assets from DB plans via pension terminations, and the sustained stock market increase over the last 30 years resulted in many DB plans being fully funded, reducing the tax advantages.

In terms of defined benefit pension plans, Willis Towers and Watson, a compensation consulting firm, conducted an analysis of the 389 Fortune 1000 corporations that sponsor a defined benefit plan. They found that in 2017, the aggregate pension plan funding was 83% of the projected liability. This number was slightly up from 2016 and down from the 100% funding observed in 2006 and 2007 before the financial crisis. Funding levels increased in 2017 due to a strong stock market and firms contributing extra cash before the low corporate tax rate of 21% under TCJA kicks in.

FIGURE 9.1 Plot of Number of Pension Plans by Type of Plan, 1975–2015

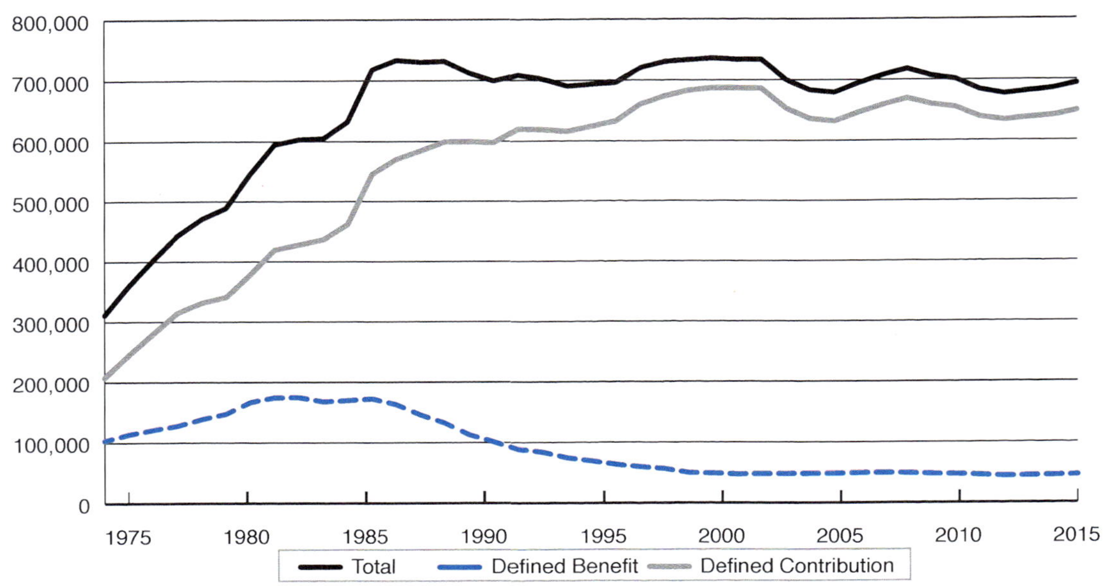

NOTE: The methods used to develop the statistics in this report have changed over time.
NOTE: Excludes "one-participant plans."
SOURCE: Form 5500 filings with the U.S. Department of Labor.

9.2 A COMPARISON OF SALARY AND PENSION COMPENSATION

Because of the tax exemption on the returns to the assets in the pension account, it might appear that a contribution to a pension dominates an equal dollar amount of salary. But even ignoring nontax factors, this is not so in all cases. Suppose an employer contemplates depositing \$100 into a defined contribution pension fund for its employee. If t_{co} is the corporate tax rate today, the after-tax cost to the corporation of the contribution would be \$100($1 - t_{co}$), the same as the after-tax cost of \$100 of

[4] The accounting for pension plans is laid out in Statement of Financial Accounting Standards (SFAS) 87 "Employers' Accounting for Pensions," Financial Accounting Standards Board (1985), now in Accounting Standards Codification (ASC) 960.

[5] As a follow-up to the TCJA 2017, Congress is considering allowing small businesses to join together to form 401(k) plans so as to reduce administration costs, simplifying the rules for participation, exempting smaller retirement accounts from mandatory payouts, and eliminating the age limit on IRA contributions. The intent is to increase employee participation in DC plans.

salary. As a result, the employer is indifferent between paying \$100 of salary and making a \$100 pension contribution in the current period.

For the employee, \$100 invested in the pension fund grows in value to $\$100(1 + R_{pen})^n$ in n periods, where R_{pen} is the before-tax rate of return on assets invested in the pension account.[6] Just what this before-tax return might be depends on the assets held in the pension account. The tax-favored treatment of the returns on stock to investors, compared with the tax treatment of corporate bonds, implies that the before-tax risk-adjusted returns on shares would be well below the before-tax returns on bonds.[7]

If employees compare the after-tax accumulation in a pension with that of taking a current salary and investing the after-tax amount on their own for n periods, their after-tax accumulations would be

$$\textbf{Pension: } \$100(1 + R_{pen})^n(1 - t_{pn}) \tag{9.1}$$

$$\textbf{Salary: } \$100(1 - t_{po})(1 + r_{pn})^n \tag{9.2}$$

where r_{pn} is the annualized after-tax rate of return per year available on personal nonpension investments, t_{po} is the current marginal tax rate of the employee, and t_{pn} is the marginal tax rate on ordinary income of the employee at time n. Pensions will be preferred to salary when Equation 9.1 > Equation 9.2:

$$\$100(1 + R_{pen})^n(1 - t_{pn}) > \$100(1 - t_{po})(1 + r_{pn})^n$$

which can be rearranged to

$$\frac{(1+R_{pen})^n}{(1+r_{pn})^n} \quad \frac{(1-t_{po})}{(1-t_{pn})} \tag{9.3}$$

When personal tax rates are constant over time ($t_{po} = t_{pn}$), the right-hand side of Equation 9.3 equals 1, and pensions provide higher after-tax accumulations than salary as long as the before-tax return on pension investments exceeds the after-tax return on nonpension investments ($R_{pen} > r_{pn}$). But suppose that the employee could earn after-tax at the same rate as the pension fund could earn before tax. A possible example here is the savings component of a "cash value" (whole life or universal life) insurance policy. In this case, ignoring nontax considerations, the only motivation for a pension plan would be declining marginal tax rates for the employee. Of course, cash-value life insurance policies do bear transaction-cost-related implicit taxes, so pension investments would normally be expected to provide an investment return advantage.

An important nontax cost of pension plans for some employees is that a pension investment is illiquid. Particularly for younger employees, pension investment may entail greater postponement of consumption than they desire. And although the opportunity to borrow to finance consumption can mitigate this disadvantage, the mitigation may be very slight, if at all, when significant transaction costs are associated with borrowing and where interest expense on personal borrowing is not fully tax deductible. In such circumstances, employees may require a rate of return far greater than R_{pen} per period after tax for them to prefer pension compensation over salary.

Because pension compensation yields future taxable income to the employee, whereas salary yields current taxable income, pensions become more desirable as future tax rates decline relative to current tax rates. In this regard, the 1981 and 1986 Tax Acts in the United States, both of which

[6] R_{pen} might be different for investments in the pension fund than outside the pension fund. For example, pension funds are not permitted to invest in certain kinds of assets. Pension funds also cannot invest as general partners in partnerships without attracting corporate taxation on their share of the income. Pension funds face some corporate taxation on the income they earn as limited partners in partnerships that engage in borrowing.

[7] The tax-favored treatment on stock includes a lower tax rate on dividends relative to the tax rate on interest income and favorable capital gains treatment provided the stock is held for longer than 12 months; the tax on gains can be deferred until the stock is sold; and the capital gains taxes can be avoided altogether by holding the stock until death or by donating appreciated stock to charity.

reduced tax rates, provided particularly strong incentives to undertake pension investments prior to the reduction in rates. These two earlier acts provided huge windfalls to older employees, many of whom had been expecting to face nearly twice as high of a marginal tax rate in retirement as they may have ended up facing. The 2017 TCJA by reducing the top rate from 39.6% to 37% did not provide a similar windfall to older employees.

Rates of Return on Investments in and out of Pension Accounts

We have assumed implicitly that investors earn a higher rate of return in the pension account than they could investing on their own. Although it may seem unlikely that the employee can earn a higher after-tax rate of return outside the pension account than inside the account, it is certainly possible. Let us consider the following examples:

1. Employees may be forced to invest in common stock in the pension plan, which is a common feature of employee stock ownership plans, and such assets may bear high implicit taxes, yielding low pretax rates of return.
2. Family tax-planning strategies may also permit investment deductions to be taken at high tax rates and income to be taxed at low rates (at the household level). That is, high-income parents might take tax deductions for part of the cost of investments early in the life of a tax-sheltered project and, later in its life, gift their interest in the shelter to lower-tax-bracket family members if the project starts producing income. As a result, the after-tax rates of return at the household level could exceed the before-tax rates of return in pension accounts.
3. Alternative savings vehicles such as investing in life insurance policies or single-premium deferred annuities may provide before-tax rates of return that are close to those available to employees in pension plans.

Antidiscrimination Rules

A major nontax disadvantage of both defined benefit as well as defined contribution pension plans is that highly compensated employees and a certain percentage of the firm's moderately compensated employees must be included in the firm's pension plan to qualify for tax-favored treatment. Highly compensated employees and, generally, older employees might want pension accounts. Moderately compensated employees, particularly the younger ones, typically prefer to consume now, to save later in their lives, and to fund their pension plans when their tax rates are higher in the future.

As a result, if lower-income employees prefer salary to pension, they will not be willing to give up $100 of before-tax salary for $100 of pension contribution. For example, they might value the $100 pension contribution at only $80 and thus, to be indifferent, they might require $125 of pension contribution for each $100 of salary, but the corporation only is indifferent between paying $100 of salary and depositing $100 into a defined contribution pension plan. In many cases, the more highly compensated employees must end up covering the $20 shortfall. They do so indirectly by trading off more than a dollar of salary reduction for each dollar they receive in pension contributions.[8]

Empirically, pension benefits, particularly in defined benefit plans, have been heavily skewed to older employees in the economy, which is efficient for tax-planning purposes for reasons we have already presented. The actuarial rules that determine whether the plan is "top heavy" with too many highly compensated employee dollars going into the plan make it easier to skew benefits to the older and more highly compensated employees than would be possible with a defined contribution plan. That is, the "rules" say that the plans cannot be top heavy, but it is relatively easier to get around them with a defined benefit plan than with a defined contribution plan.

[8] The Tax Reform Act of 1986 (TRA 86) tightened up the antidiscrimination requirements. To qualify for tax-favored treatment, the ratio of contributions of highly compensated employees to total contributions became more limited. Forcing more employees who prefer salary to pension into the plan reduces the benefit of maintaining corporate pension plans for those who want such plans.

9.3 DEFERRED COMPENSATION VERSUS PENSION

From the earlier discussion in Chapter 8, equation (8.1), we know an employer is indifferent, from a tax standpoint, between a dollar of current pension contribution or salary and

$$D_n \equiv (1+r_{cn})^n[(1-t_{co})/(1-t_{cn})]$$

dollars of deferred compensation in periods, where t_{co} and t_{cn} represent the employer's current and future tax rates and r_{cn} represents the annual after-tax rate the employer can earn on marginal investments. That is, the employer can afford to pay deferred compensation of \$1, plus its after-tax earnings on the dollar in salary or pension contribution postponed for n years, adjusted for changes in its tax rate over time.

For the employee, the deferred compensation payment provides an after-tax accumulation, for each dollar of salary or pension contribution sacrificed, of

$$D_n(1-t_{pn}) = \frac{(1-t_{co})(1+r_{cn})^n}{(1-t_{cn})}(1-t_{pn}) \tag{9.4}$$

In comparison, each dollar contributed to a pension plan would yield, in n periods,

$$(1+R_{pen})^n(1-t_{pn}) \tag{9.5}$$

Deferred compensation is preferred to pension if Equation 9.4 > Equation 9.5:

$$\frac{(1-t_{co})(1+r_{cn})^n}{(1-t_{cn})}(1-t_{pn}) > (1+R_{pen})^n(1-t_{pn}) \qquad **$$

which can be rearranged to

$$\frac{(1-t_{co})}{(1-t_{cn})} \quad \frac{(1+R_{pen})^n}{(1+r_{cn})^n} \tag{9.6}$$

Note that the employee's tax rates are irrelevant to this comparison, because both compensation arrangements give rise to taxation in the future. In other words $(1 - t_{pn})$ is on both sides of the ** equation so the term cancels out.[9] If the corporate tax rate is expected to be higher in the future, that is, $t_{cn} > t_{co}$, and $R_{pen} = r_{cn}$, then deferred compensation is preferred to pension. For example, if t_{co} is 21% and t_{cn} is 35%, then (1 − .21)/(1 − .35) is 1.215, which implies that deferred compensation is preferred to pension by 21.5%. If the employer has a defined benefit pension plan in place under such circumstances, it may pay a corporation to underfund, not overfund, the pension plan.

Conversely, suppose that r_{cn} = 7.5% and R_{pen} = 10% assuming t_{co} = 21% and t_{cn} = 35%. Then, deferred compensation is preferred to pension as long as

$$1.215 > (1.10)^n/(1.075)^n$$

which will occur if $n < 10$ years.

Suppose instead of the corporate tax rate increasing from a current 21% to 35%, that the corporate tax rate is expected to fall, say from 35% to 21%. Then t_{co} = 21% and t_{cn} = 35% and (1 − .35)/(1 − .21) = .822, which implies that pension is preferred to deferred compensation by 18%. If the employer has a defined benefit pension plan in place, under such circumstances it may pay a corporation to overfund the pension plan. In fact, this is exactly what many firms did in 2017 and 2018 when the TCJA decreased corporate tax rates from 35% to 21%.[10] Gaertner, Lynch, and Vernon (2018) find

[9] If the dates of future taxation differ, however, then employee tax rates become relevant to the comparison.

[10] Under the TCJA, firms can contribute to the pension plan in 2018 until they file their tax returns in September 2018.

that corporations increased their average pension contributions by about 24% in 2017. Note that such planning is an example of shifting income (in this case deductions) from one time period to another as discussed in chapter 2.

More tax rules restrict funding a defined benefit pension plan than restrict deferred compensation plans. With pension plans, (1) minimum funding requirements may force a corporation to take a tax deduction for funding earlier than would be necessary under a deferred compensation plan; (2) administration and legal costs are higher than for deferred compensation plans; and (3) many more antidiscrimination rules apply than for deferred compensation programs. However, nonqualified deferred compensation plans are subject to Section 409A, which places restrictions on the timing of distributions, restrictions against the acceleration of benefits, and restrictions on the timing of when the deferral election can be made. Violation of these restrictions are severe in that all amounts deferred in the plan become immediately taxable plus a 20% penalty tax under some conditions. Pension plans being qualified deferred compensation plans fall outside the scope of Section 409A.

The objective of the Congress in providing tax-favored treatment to pension plans was to encourage broad-based retirement savings; allowing such savings led to the introduction of contribution limits and nondiscrimination rules. Deferred compensation arrangements are free from these limits. They can also be used advantageously in special tax-planning situations. For example, an executive on assignment for 2 or 3 years in a Scandinavian branch office where local tax rates are high would prefer a deferred compensation program to salary (as long as the plan meets the requirements of Section 409A). Income could be received at substantially reduced home-country tax rates when returning to the home country. The employer cannot target such an individual with a pension plan.

The biggest nontax problem with deferred compensation programs is that, to avoid constructive receipt in which the employee is taxed as if he or she received the income in the current period, the employee must be an unsecured creditor of the firm.[11] A pension trust, by contrast, does provide security to the extent it is funded and/or insured. The beneficiary has a claim against the trust and the insurance agency, which for defined benefit plans, is the Pension Benefit Guarantee Corporation.

9.4 THE STOCKS-VERSUS-BONDS PUZZLE

Because the earnings on assets in pension funds are tax exempt, pension funds form a natural clientele to invest in fully taxable assets, such as corporate and government bonds, and tax disfavored assets. Recall that common stocks are tax-favored investments because they offer deferral and taxation at capital gains rates to the extent that current earnings are not distributed as dividends each period; thus we expect them to bear implicit taxes. High-tax-rate taxpayers form the natural clientele for corporate stocks, not tax-exempt pension plans. Thus it is somewhat surprising that in March 2012, across all defined benefit plans, approximately 55% of plan assets were invested in equities (with approximately 40% in U.S. equities and 15% in international equities), 30% in bonds (mostly U.S. bonds), and the remaining 15% in other assets. During the decade from 1985 to 1995, the percentage in equities fluctuated between 33% and 44% for DB plans.

Some have argued that corporate pension fund managers are willing to abandon investment in tax-disfavored assets for which pension funds are the natural clientele to garner the higher total rates of return available in stock. Until high-yield bonds came into vogue, it was not possible to earn risk premiums without investing in stock, but Fischer Black (1980) and Irwin Tepper (1981), in two separate articles, had a good counter to this line of attack. They argued that the corporation could secure the risk premiums without sacrificing the tax benefits of investing in bonds.

The **Black–Tepper tax arbitrage strategy** is to effect organizational-form arbitrage as outlined in **Table 9.2**. Suppose, as in plan A in **Table 9.2**, that a firm has \$1 in its pension fund invested in stock that earns a risky return of r^*_c.[12] Alternatively, consider plan B. Suppose the firm has \$1 in its pension plan invested in bonds earning R_b. If the corporation now borrows \$1 on corporate account

[11] This problem can be mitigated by setting aside funds in a trust on behalf of employees, a so-called "rabbi trust," but to avoid constructive receipt of income, secured creditors of the firm must have legal priority over the trust beneficiaries to the assets in the trust in the event of bankruptcy.

[12] Recall that r^*_c is the after-corporate-level-tax rate of return of the issuing firm but before the shareholder-level tax of the holder.

when its marginal tax rate is t_c and buys common stock with the proceeds of the loan, its net after-tax rate of return on corporate account is $r^*_c - R_b(1 - t_c)$ with this strategy. The total return on the pension fund investment in bonds and the corporate investment in stock, financed by issuing bonds, is $r^*_c + R_bt_c$, which exceeds the return from investing in stocks (plan A) by R_bt_c.

Note that the risk of the two strategies is exactly the same. The return from plan B exceeds that from plan A by a sure R_bt_c, irrespective of what happens to stock prices. The advantage of undertaking this organizational-form arbitrage arises from the corporation's ability to borrow on corporate account to secure the interest deduction and to invest the proceeds in the pension fund through the strategy illustrated in **Table 9.2**.

A few holes appear in the preceding argument, however. First, we have assumed that the corporation pays no tax on the return to investing in shares on corporate account. In fact, taxes must be paid, although the annualized corporate tax rate on shares, denoted t_{cs}, may be well below t_c. For a corporation, returns on stock investments are tax favored because of the dividend received deduction and deferral of taxation on share appreciation until the stock is sold. If the firm were to hold its own shares on corporate account, the return would be tax exempt.

If the effective annualized tax rate on shares held on corporate account is t_{cs}, then a slight change in arbitrage strategy displayed in **Table 9.2** is required. In particular, the corporation will now need to issue $1/(1 - t_{cs})$ dollars of bonds and invest the proceeds in stock to maintain the same level of risk in plan B and plan A. As **Table 9.3** shows, as long as the effective annualized corporate tax rate on shares held on corporate account, t_{cs}, is below the ordinary corporate tax rate, t_c, there remains an arbitrage opportunity, although it is not as large as when we assumed t_{cs} to be equal to zero as we did in **Table 9.2**.

Table 9.2 Stock Investment in the Pension Fund (Plan A) Compared with Bonds in the Pension Fund along with Debt-Financed Stock on Corporate Account (Plan B)

	Investment	Return	Example
Plan A:			
Pension:			
Purchase stock	$1	r^*_c	15%
Plan B:			
Pension:			
Purchase bonds	$1	R_b	10%
Corporation:			
Issue bonds	−$1	$-R_b(1 - t_c)$	−7.9%*
Purchase stock	$1	r^*_c	15%
Net position (pension plus corporation)	$1	$r^*_c + R_bt_c$	17.1%
Plan B − Plan A	$0	R_bt_c	2.1%

* For $t_c = 21\%$

Table 9.3 indicates that the annual tax advantage of investing the pension in bonds rather than stock is equal to the pretax interest rate on bonds times $(t_c - t_{cs})/(1 - t_{cs})$. The advantage increases as the corporate tax rate, t_c, increases and as the corporate tax rate on shares, t_{cs}, decreases.

The second hole in the argument is that the analysis in **Tables 9.2** and **9.3** ignores the nontax costs associated with implementing the arbitrage strategy. Bondholders cannot be sure that the corporation will maintain the position in bonds in the pension fund. After all, the pension fund has its own trustees, who could decide to revert to a strategy of investing in stocks in the pension fund after the loan was in place. This uncertainty increases the risk for bondholders. As a result, they might charge a higher rate of interest on the loan to cover their monitoring costs. Moreover, the firm could go bankrupt, and in bankruptcy it is not possible for the bondholders to claim the accumulated value of the $1 of bonds in the pension plan. Pension beneficiaries have first claim against the pension plan assets. As a result, the bondholders must look to the risky stock portfolio on corporate account as security for their loan, which most likely would cause the borrowing costs to increase further. For example, if the before-tax borrowing rate were 12.66% instead of 10%, the after-tax cost of the debt would be 10%, or .1266(1 – .21). At this rate, the arbitrage opportunity in **Table 9.2** would just disappear: The return to plan B would be 15%, composed of +10% in the pension account, plus 15% from stock less 10% after-tax cost of borrowing on corporate account. The return to plan B is the same as the return to plan A with no arbitrage.

Table 9.3 Stock Investment in the Pension Fund (Plan A) Compared with Bonds in the Pension Fund along with Debt-Financed Stock on Corporate Account (Plan B) with Positive Effective Annualized Tax Rate on Shares Held (versus Zero in **Table 9.2**)

	Investment	Return	Example
Plan A:			
Pension:			
Purchase stock	\$1	r^*_c	15%
Plan B:			
Pension:			
Purchase bonds	\$1	R_b	10%
Corporation:			
Issue bonds	$-\$1/(1 - t_{cs})$	$\frac{-R_b(1-t_c)}{(1-t_{cs})}$	−8.98%*
Purchase stock	$\$1/(1 - t_{cs})$	$\frac{-r^*_c(1-t_{cs})}{(1-t_{cs})}$	15%
Net position (pension plus corporation)	\$1	$r^*_c + \frac{R_b(t_c - t_{cs})}{(1-t_{cs})}$	16.02%
Plan B – Plan A	\$0	$\frac{R_b(t_c - t_{cs})}{(1-t_{cs})}$	1.02%

* For t_c = 21% and t_{cs} = 12%

It is worth noting that this arbitrage argument does not work as well for defined contribution plans. Whereas the assets in defined benefit plans can be viewed as being owned by the employers that promise beneficiaries a certain level of benefits and thus the employer captures the benefit of the tax arbitrage, the assets in defined contribution plans are owned by the beneficiaries. If beneficiaries in defined contribution plans wish to earn the risk premium on stock, they must effect the organizational-form arbitrage on personal account by borrowing to purchase stock. With limited interest deductibility for individuals, and with a large spread between the rate at which individuals borrow and the rate at which they can earn on bonds held in the pension plan, such organizational-form arbitrage strategies become too expensive to be profitable. Consequently, nontax factors, especially the desire to earn risk premiums on stock relative to bonds, may lead DC pension fund beneficiaries to prefer nontrivial amounts of stock to be invested in their pension funds, despite the implicit tax such tax-favored investments bear. This argument is consistent with the higher allocation of DC plan assets to equities as plotted in **Figure 9.2**. The figure graphs the percentage of pension plan assets held in equities.[13] Defined contribution plans hold close to 70% of their assets in equities compared to defined benefit plans of approximately 43% in equities.

[13] The figure ends in 2011 as this is the latest data available to the authors that compiled this plot (Munnell, et al. 2015).

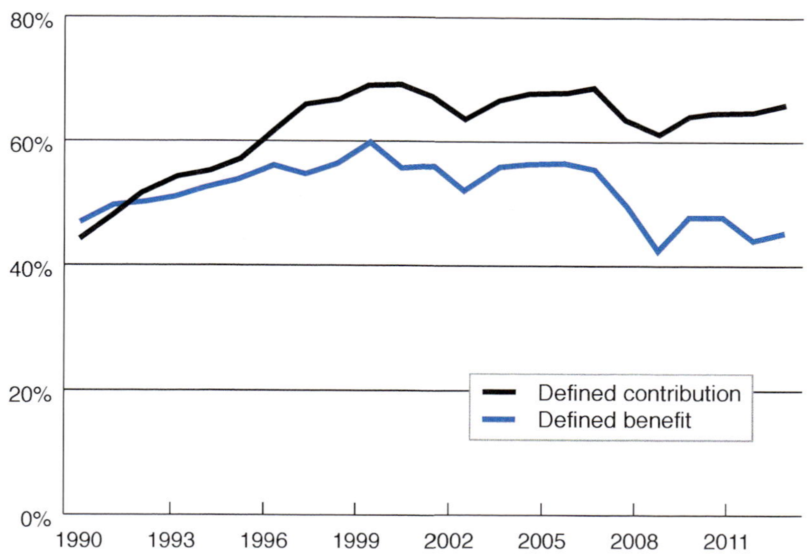

Source: From Munnell et al. (2015). Figure plots numbers based on Munnell et al.'s calculations based on Form 5500 data (1990–2012).

FIGURE 9.2 Percentage of Assets Held in Equities by Type of Pension Plan 1990–2011

Prior to Frank (2002), researchers had failed to find any association between a firm's tax benefits and the allocation of pension assets to bonds (see, for example, Bodie, Light, Morck, and Taggert, 1987; Petersen, 1996). Among other differences to prior studies, Frank uses an expanded sample over an extended time period to examine the issue. She estimates a regression of the percentage of defined benefit plan assets invested in bonds on the tax benefit from the arbitrage strategy.[14] She finds a significant positive relation between the two variables. And, as predicted, she finds no such association for defined contribution plans. These results are consistent with firms undertaking the Black–Tepper tax arbitrage strategy.

9.5 DOES IT PAY TO MAINTAIN AN OVERFUNDED PENSION PLAN?

An overfunded plan is one where the market value of the plan assets exceeds the present value of the firm's expected liability to its employees.

Advantages and Disadvantages

Several advantages and disadvantages accompany the overfunding of a pension plan, which we now discuss.

Expectations of Changing Tax Rates In 1986, U.S. corporations facing a marginal tax rate of 46% knew that in 1987 their marginal tax rate would fall to 40%, and they could anticipate that their marginal tax rates would fall further to 34% in 1988. This expectation encouraged overfunding in 1986. Moreover, each dollar invested in the pension plan in 1986 grows at the before-tax rate R_{pen} until it is withdrawn from the fund. By reducing its future funding, when its marginal tax rate is 34%, the corporation realizes a return bonus of 22%, or (1 – .34)/(1 – .46) – 1. This opportunity did not go unnoticed by General Motors Corp (GM). GM made a "special, unrequired contribution . . . of $1.04 billion (in 1986) . . . to its U.S. pension plans to take advantage of tax deductions."[15] As another example of strategic timing of pension plan contributions and **pension plan reversions**,

[14] Frank (2002) partitions the tax benefits from the tax arbitrage into two components: the benefit of issuing bonds on corporate account to finance equity investments and the benefit of investing the DB assets in bonds. Her results suggest that most of the tax benefit arises from the financing with corporate bonds.

[15] (September 16, 1987), p. 16.

Exxon terminated several of its overfunded pension plans in 1986, when it was experiencing "tax-free" status due to net operating losses for tax purposes. Recall the earlier numerical example for TCJA tax rate cut from 35% to 21% motivating firms to increase their contributions to defined benefit pension plans by 21% over prior years.

The Internal Revenue Service (IRS) is well aware of the benefits of generous levels of pension funding when tax rates are high. During 1990, the IRS announced its intention to conduct 18,000 audits of defined benefit pension plans for the 1986 tax year, expecting to raise hundreds of millions of dollars in additional tax revenues. In particular, it targeted plans that assumed unrealistically low interest rates on investments and unrealistically early retirement dates for plan participants.[16] Such assumptions imply larger current funding requirements to meet promised retirement benefits.

Investing in Stocks, Overfunding, and Flexibility Why have corporations invested so much of their pension assets in tax-favored assets, especially stock? As we have already noted, this was particularly mysterious prior to TRA 86 because one important reason the corporation has for overfunding its pension fund is that it can earn at a higher rate after tax in the pension account than on corporate account. Holding stocks reduces this advantage.

The answer to this question is also the answer to the following question: How can a firm overfund its pension plan? Actuaries, in setting pension contribution levels, are likely to assume conservative (low) earnings rates on pension assets to ensure that pension promises to beneficiaries can be fulfilled. The lower the assumed rate of return on investment, the greater is the current funding requirement if the pension fund is to have sufficient assets to meet promised payments. If the assets in the pension fund are invested only in riskless bonds, the actuary is forced to select a rate of return that is close to the rate earned on the bonds. If actuaries set the earning rate at this level, it would not be possible to overfund the pension plan.

But if the fund invests in stocks, the actuary might choose a lower earning rate on the assets to cushion the fund against adverse changes in the market value of its common stocks. For example, the actuary might wish to prevent the fund's market value from falling below a prescribed level more than 5% of the time. The greater the possible variation in the returns on the pension assets, the greater is the chance that the initial market value of the fund's assets will fall to this level at some future date. However, the greater the initial market value of the fund, the less likely it is to fall to this prescribed value given the variation in the returns on the underlying fund. By setting a low earning rate—or, equivalently, a low discount rate to be used in calculating the present value of the promised future pension payments—the actuaries can "authorize" an increase in funding to the desired level. The firm then can build up its excess assets by investing, in part, in common stock. At a later time, when it switches into bonds, the actuary will typically increase the assumed earnings rate on pension assets, thereby indicating an overfunded pension plan. Tax rules require that the excess assets in the pension fund be amortized over a number of years by reducing contributions each year. Thus, for this period of time, the firm can achieve the advantage of investing at the before-tax rate in bonds. It can also realize the tax rate advantage from advance funding if tax rates should fall in the future.

In summary, investing some of the pension assets in stocks allows flexibility in defining the funding level and thus in defining the tax-deductible annual contribution. This flexibility allows the firm to time contributions in periods when the firm faces high tax rates (increased contributions) and low tax rates (reduced contributions).[17]

Investment Alternatives with Overfunded Defined Benefit Pension Plans Being able to earn at the before-tax rate of return in the pension fund, as compared with the after-tax rate of return on corporate account, is one of the advantages of the corporation overfunding the plan. Generally, the

---

[16] (June 2, 1990), p. 22.

[17] Mushruwala (2007) discusses the effect the accounting for DB plans likely has on the equity allocation decision in DB plans. He examines changes in U.K. DB plan asset allocations as firms are required to adopt a fair value approach to accounting for the plan assets and liabilities. As in the United States, prior U.K. accounting rules allowed firms to smooth the reported pension expense for accounting purposes (to avoid volatility in reported earnings) with a reduction in the ability to smooth, Mushruwala predicts and finds evidence consistent with firms switching out of equities into bonds in their DB plans. Chuk (2013) documents that U.S. firms changed their defined benefit plan asset mix in response to increased disclosures about pension asset mix under SFAS 132R (now ASC 960). Both of these papers document the influence of financial accounting rules on tax planning.

risk-adjusted rate of return on assets in the pension fund will exceed the rate of return on marginal investments undertaken on corporate account. This generalization is true even if the firm can generate superior profits at the corporate level. After all, the Black–Tepper strategy suggests the firm can borrow to fund the pension plan while still undertaking the superior corporate investments. This approach dominates not funding the pension plan. Interest on the debt used to fund the pension contributions is tax deductible at the corporate level, while investment returns on assets in the pension account are tax exempt. Of course, we must not forget that nontax costs associated with convincing lenders that the firm has superior investments could increase borrowing costs to such an extent that the firm should forgo funding the pension plan.

Because the corporation "owns" the excess assets in the pension plan, its best investment strategy is to hold high-explicitly-taxed assets such as high-yielding risky bonds in the pension account.[18] If the firm commits to a policy of holding bonds in its pension plan, the borrowing rate on the bonds used to finance the contributions would be less than if the corporation undertook more risky investment strategies in the plan. As discussed earlier, however, it is difficult to commit to such an investment policy in advance. Once again, the deadweight costs associated with issuing risky debt would reduce the advantage of overfunding the plan.

Moreover, prior to TRA 86, corporations held 50% of their pension fund assets in stock and 50% in bonds. The rate of return advantage of investing the excess assets at the before-tax rate would be reduced by 50% of the implicit tax on shares. For example, if bonds returned 10% before tax and common stocks generated a risk-adjusted return of only 7% before shareholder-level tax, r_c, the combined pension fund portfolio would have returned 8.5%, or .5(10%) +.5(7%), for an implicit tax rate of 15%, or (10% − 8.5%)/10%. Moreover, the corporation could invest in other tax-advantaged assets, such as cash-value life insurance policies. So the tax advantages of overfunding the pension fund may have been small.

Following TRA 86, however, the tax disadvantage of investing pension plan assets in stocks became considerably less. The annualized effective explicit tax rate on shares, t_s, increased after 1986, implying that the implicit tax on shares should have become relatively low. As a result, U.S. and foreign pension funds became excellent candidates for increased investment in U.S. stocks. The 1987 Tax Act restricted the level of overfunding in a defined benefit pension plan by limiting deductions if the assets in the plan exceed 150% of the termination liability.

Possibility of an Excise Tax If the corporation were to surrender its pension plan and capture the excess pension assets, which is labeled a plan termination or asset reversion, it may face an excise tax in addition to the regular corporate tax on these assets. For example, TRA 86 imposed a 10% excise tax on excess assets withdrawn from a terminated pension plan in most circumstances, and the excise tax was raised to 15% in 1988 and 20% in 1989.[19] Did the imposition of excise taxes affect the number of terminations? Apparently so. Whereas $6.6 billion of pension plan assets reverted to their corporate sponsors upon termination of their pension plans in 1985, and another $4.3 billion in reversions took place in 1986, only $1.9 billion and $1.1 billion worth of reversions occurred in 1987 and 1988, respectively (Petersen, 1989). Also, a pension plan termination results in all unvested benefits vesting on termination. Additionally, many employees express displeasure when a defined benefit plan is replaced with a defined contribution plan. This displeasure arises because the risk of having sufficient assets on retirement is shifted from the firm to the employee and because often the expected total pension benefits are reduced for many employees who have been shifted to defined contribution plans.

The firm does not have to surrender its pension fund, however, to recapture its excess assets. It can (1) reduce future funding levels by changing plan assumptions, and (2) increase promised pension benefits for its employees in lieu of salary increases or bonuses. Reducing salary to employees or contributions to the plan will increase the corporation's current taxable income and reduce the level of overfunding in the plan.

[18] To the extent that ambiguity is involved regarding who owns the excess assets in a pension fund—the employer or employees—an additional nontax cost comes into play in overfunding the pension plan.

[19] The 1990 Tax Act raises the excise tax rate to 50% in certain circumstances.

Nontax considerations affect these choices. Employees might not give up a dollar of salary or bonus for an extra dollar of pension benefit. For them, the cost of borrowing to meet current consumption needs might exceed the returns that they can earn on this form of deferred compensation, as we discussed earlier. To compensate such employees, the employer might have to sweeten pension benefits so substantially that it might not be advantageous to take this path to reduce overfunding in the plan.

Incentive to Underfund because Pension Represents a Put Option Before the passage of the Employee Retirement Income Security Act (ERISA) in 1974, firms with defined benefit pension plans had a valuable put option because they could put the assets of the pension plan to the beneficiaries to satisfy the legal claims of the plan beneficiaries. After the passage of ERISA, firms now can put the pension plan assets plus 30% of the market value of the firm to the Pension Benefit Guarantee Corporation (PBGC) to satisfy the pension claims. This change reduced but did not eliminate the value of the pension put.

The pension put option offers incentives to underfund the pension, and the value of the put option is increasing in the variance of the returns on the pension assets, favoring stock investments in the pension plan, and variance of the firm's net assets, encouraging more risky investments by the firm if there is some chance of putting the option to the PBGC.

Empirical Evidence on Determinants of Defined Benefit Plan Pension Funding

Several researchers have empirically examined the determinants of pension funding. Francis and Reiter (1987) report the overfunding of defined benefit pension plans being positively associated with firms' estimated tax benefits. They also examine a number of other motivations for firms' funding levels. They find larger firms follow a funding strategy that both reduces reported income (contributions to the pension plan are reported as pension expense during their sample time period) and increases the reported funding ratio in order to reduce potential political costs. They also report evidence that the closer firms are to violating bond covenants, the greater the underfunding. Further, underfunding is more common among firms with unionized employees, which the researchers interpret to mean underfunding is a mechanism to bond these employees to the firm. Thus the research results indicate that not only tax motivations but also nontax motivations such as financial statement and employee incentive effects influence the level of funding.

Thomas (1988) finds that firms' tax status as proxied by the existence of a net operating loss (NOL) carryforward

- Is negatively associated with funding levels: NOL firms fund at a lower level.
- Influences the choice of actuarial variables: NOL firms choose less conservative assumptions, implying lower funding levels.
- Influences the use of defined benefit plans: NOL firms are less likely to choose defined benefit plans.

These results suggest that taxes are an important determinant of pension choices and funding.

Other researchers have examined the **pension plan termination** decision. Examples include Thomas (1989), Mittelstaedt (1989), and Clinch and Shibano (1996). Thomas concludes that terminations seem to be motivated by cash needs rather than tax, accounting, or transfer-of-wealth considerations. Mittelstaedt's results generally echo those of Thomas. Clinch and Shibano, however, using a different approach to estimating tax effects, find that tax considerations significantly influence whether and when a firm withdraws excess pension assets via a termination.

9.6 FUNDING POST-EMPLOYMENT HEALTH CARE BENEFITS

Retiree health benefits were first offered in the late 1940s, when the postwar economy was booming, businesses were profitable, and the number of retirees relative to the number of workers was small. Retiree health benefits arose as part of collective bargaining agreements, and employers were willing to provide the benefits because the cost was small relative to total compensation. With the enactment of Medicare in 1965, employer obligations and costs were lowered because employers were able to integrate their benefits with Medicare benefits. Both funding and accounting for these benefits were not of great concern and most employers were on a pay-as-you-go basis. However, over the last several decades, the workforce has aged, the ratio of retirees to active workers has increased, expected life spans have risen, and health care costs have increased dramatically. These changes have caused the cost of the benefits to increase.

Partially in response to the increase in the unfunded promises, the Financial Accounting Standards Board (FASB) in 1990 changed the accounting for retiree health care benefits.[20] Prior to this change, most firms did not recognize a liability for the unfunded promises and delayed recognition of an expense until the period in which the cost was paid. ASC 965 now requires firms to estimate the present value of the promised benefits and to accrue both a liability and recognize an expense each year of the employee's working life. Consequently, because many firms do not prefund retiree health care costs, large liabilities appeared on firms' balance sheets. This result led many firms to reevaluate their promises and many employers have attempted to modify or drop retiree health care benefits over the objections of both current workers and retirees. A Towers Watson 2010 Health Care Cost Survey indicated that only 45% of employers provide retiree coverage to future retirees and only 22% offer subsidized retiree coverage to new hires. This survey was before the passage of the Patient Protection and Affordable Care Act (aka ObamaCare) in 2010. Towers Watson reports from a 2010 Health Care Reform Survey that 77% of respondents indicate there is likely to be a moderate or significant decrease in the number of large employers offering retiree medical benefits, with 43% of respondents indicating they will eliminate or reduce retire medical programs as a result of health care reform.[21]

What is the best way for a firm to fund retiree medical benefits? In most cases, advance funding of such benefits cannot be done in as tax-advantaged a way as the advance funding of pension benefits. Except in 401(h) plans and collectively bargained Voluntary Employee Benefit Association programs (VEBAs), current tax deductions cannot be taken for advance funding. Deductions are available for advance funding through a 401(h) plan but such plans are expensive to administer. Moreover, the annual contribution to such plans cannot exceed 25% of the contributions made to the employer's pension plans. So when a firm's pension plan is overfunded, contributions to the pension and to a 401(h) plan are not permitted at all.

Firms have at least two alternative ways in which they might fund retiree medical benefits:

1. Inform employees that pension benefits will be sweetened and that employees will be made responsible for paying their own medical benefits.
2. Employ a pay-as-you-go plan, whereby the firm pays for employees' expenses as they are incurred in retirement.

The Sweetened Pension Benefit Approach

Suppose the firm wishes to cover the cost of a \$1 future medical benefit n years from today for its employee. If pension benefits are supplemented, the employee will receive taxable pension income at time n. After paying tax on this income at personal tax rate t_{pn}, the employee will require a full \$1 to pay for the medical benefits, because the expenditure will not be tax deductible.[22] So the amount of taxable pension benefits required at time n is

$$\$1/(1 - t_{pn})$$

The current cost to the employer of providing this benefit is the amount that must be deposited into the pension plan today less the value of the tax deduction, at a tax rate of t_{co}, that the employer obtains for the pension contribution. Because the pension fund is tax exempt, its assets grow at the before-tax rate, R_{pen}. So, to accumulate $1/(1 - t_{pn})$ dollars in n periods, when the funds in the

[20] See Statement of Financial Accounting Standard 106 "Employers' Accounting for Postretirement Benefits Other Than Pensions," Financial Accounting Standards Board (1990), now ASC 965 Health and Welfare Plans.

[21] More recent information could not be readily found.

[22] Medical costs are deductible in the United States as itemized deductions only to the extent they exceed 7.5% of the taxpayer's adjusted gross income and then only to the extent itemized deductions exceed the standard deduction that is available as an alternative.

retirement plan earn income at rate R_{pen} per period, the employer must deposit the following amount into the pension fund:

$$\frac{1}{(1-t_{pn})} \times \frac{1}{(1+R_{pen})^n}$$

Because of the tax deductibility of the contribution to the pension account, this calculation would result in an after-tax current cost, C, to the employer of [23]

$$\mathbf{C} \equiv \frac{1}{(1-t_{pn})} \times \frac{1}{(1+R_{pen})^n}(1-t_{co}) \tag{9.7}$$

EXAMPLE 9.1 Sweetened Pension Benefit

Suppose the employer wishes to provide the employee with \$1 to pay for medical benefits when the employee retires in 30 years. The retiree's expected tax rate in retirement is 22%, the employer's current tax rate is 21%, and the pension fund earns 10% per year on its investments. How much will the employer need to contribute to the pension plan today to provide the \$1 after-tax to the retiree in 30 years? Substituting the parameter values into Equation 9.7 gives an after-tax current period contribution of 5.80 cents. That is, 5.80 cents after-tax—7.34 cents pretax—contributed by the corporation will grow at 10% for 30 years to \$1.28 which is reduced to \$1 after the retiree pays tax at 22% on withdrawing the \$1.28.

The Pay-as-You-Go Approach

In the absence of advance funding of the benefits through a tax-qualified trust, the employer usually receives no current tax deduction. Instead, the employer secures a tax deduction in the future at time n when the benefit payment is made. If the benefit is provided to the employee as a fringe benefit through a group health benefit plan, as is typical, the employee is not taxed on the receipt of the benefit. Therefore, the employer need pay only \$1 at time n to satisfy the obligation. If the employer can invest funds on corporate account in the interim at an after-tax rate of r_c per year, then the current cost or present value to the employer is

$$\frac{(1-t_{cn})}{(1+r_c)^n} \tag{9.8}$$

Advance funding through the pension account is the superior choice if the current cost of the pension contribution is less than the current cost of the pay-as-you-go approach:

Equation 9.7 < Equation 9.8

$$1/(1-t_{pn}) \times 1/(1+R_{pen})^n(1-t_{co}) < (1-t_{cn})/(1+r_c)^n$$

which can be rearranged to

$$\frac{(1-t_{co})}{(1-t_{pn})(1-t_{cn})} \times \frac{(1+r_c)^n}{(1+R_{pen})^n} < 1 \tag{9.9}$$

[23] An alternate way to derive Equation 9.7 is to solve for the current cost, C, of providing \$1 to the employee in retirement in the following equation: $\frac{C}{(1-t_{co})}(1+R_{pen})^n(1-t_{pn}) = \$1$. A current contribution of C to the pension plan is tax deductible to the firm, the contribution grows at R_{pen} for n periods, and is then taxed to the employee on withdrawal. Rearranging, we get Equation 9.7.

Note that in the special case in which the employer's tax rates are constant over time, the pension funding route is cheaper if

$$\frac{(1+r_c)^n}{(1+R_{pen})^n} < (1-t_{pn}) \tag{9.10}$$

If r_c were equal to R_{pen}, the unfunded alternative would dominate, because it would allow employees to receive the benefits tax free, whereas the pension benefits would be taxable.

When might r_c be equal to R_{pen}? When the employer is tax exempt, such as a university or a not-for-profit hospital, or when the taxpaying employer invests idle funds in cash-value life insurance policies without incurring any implicit taxes. Another case in which r_c may be close to R_{pen} is where the corporation funds its health care program by investing in its own common stock. Because a U.S. corporation pays no tax on the dividend or capital gain income it earns from holding its own common stock, the risk-adjusted after-tax return on the stock will be below the pretax bond rate only to the extent the stock bears implicit tax.

However, suppose that r_c is less than R_{pen}. Then a trade-off must be made between earning at a higher after-tax rate by advance funding through a pension and providing a tax-exempt benefit to employees by not funding the plan. For example, suppose r_c is equal to 7%, R_b is 10%, and the employer's tax rate is constant over time. In **Table 9.4**, we show the employee's tax rates at time n, t_{pn}, below which pension funding beats the unfunded alternative. At higher values of t_{pn}, it is too costly to forgo the advantage of tax exemption for medical benefits at retirement available through the unfunded alternative. Note that longer horizons favor advance funding through the pension account because the advantage of tax-free investment becomes more important.

Table 9.4 Employee's Tax Rate, t_{pn}, below Which Pension Funding Dominates Corporate Pay-as-You-Go Funding of Retiree Health Benefits

n	$\frac{(1+r_c)^n}{(1+R_{pen})^n}$	t_{pn}
5	.8709	.13
10	.7585	.24
20	.5752	.42

n = time horizon in years
R_{pen} = 10% = Pension fund investment rate of return
r_c = 7% = After-tax rate of return on corporate investments, assuming employer's tax rates are constant through time ($t_{co} = t_{cn}$)

Other Factors Relevant to the Funding Decision

1. Future medical costs are uncertain. Employees must bear this risk if a supplemental pension plan is used, but not in an unfunded plan or a 401(h) plan.
2. In an unfunded plan, the employee bears the risk of default on the promise. For example, a leveraged buyout of the corporate employer can expose employees to a substantial risk of default on such unfunded obligations.
3. Increasing employer tax rates favor unfunded plans: Tax deductions are secured at higher tax rates.
4. Unfunded plans are more desirable for employees with high tax rates. So they may be more advantageous where the workforce is predominantly white collar rather than blue collar.
5. There are administrative costs associated with operating 401(h) plans. These costs can make unfunded plans more desirable than 401(h) plans even when the latter are available. For example, tax-exempt entities will typically find unfunded plans preferable to 401(h) plans.

9.7 EMPLOYEE STOCK-OWNERSHIP PROGRAMS

An employee stock-ownership plan (ESOP) is a special type of defined contribution plan, similar to an individual retirement account, a Keogh account, or a Code Section 401(k) plan. ESOPs were popular in the late 1980s, but their popularity has declined since that time due to some tax-rule changes. We discuss ESOPs here, although briefly, because ESOPs established in the late 1980s still exist today. As of 2018, the National Center for Employee Ownership estimates that there are almost 7,000 ESOP plans (largely unchanged from 2010), covering 14 million employees, holding over $1.3 trillion in assets (compared to $6.3 trillion in total in all private sector pension funds).

Just like other defined contribution plans, the corporation makes tax-deductible annual contributions to the ESOP, which are generally used to buy company stock or to pay down a loan that was used to acquire company stock when the program was initiated. Each year, employees are allocated, tax-free, company shares, and any investment income accumulates tax-free within the ESOP. Employees pay tax when they receive dividend distributions on ESOP shares during their working lives, when they receive other distributions from the ESOP during retirement, or when they otherwise leave the firm and "cash out" of the plan. However, when employees leave the firm, they can roll their ESOP shares into an individual retirement account to continue to defer payment of any tax. Unlike most defined contribution plans, the ESOP is required to invest primarily in the stock of the company establishing the plan, and this is commonly taken to mean that the ESOP must hold at least 50% of its assets in the sponsoring company's stock. Investment in the company stock concentrates the employee's wealth in the firm, increasing the risk borne by the employee—a nontax cost of ESOPs and 401(k) plans.

Also unlike other defined contribution plans, the ESOP can borrow to buy company stock to prefund the required number of shares that the firm expects to credit to its employees over the term of the loan. Such plans are called "leveraged ESOPs." As the firm contributes to the ESOP and debt is paid down, shares are credited to employees' accounts. Moreover, qualified lenders can exclude 50% of the interest that they receive on the ESOP loan.[24] If lending markets are competitive and if there are no special costs associated with ESOP loans, the risk-adjusted before-tax rate of return on the ESOP loan, R_{EL}, will be given by the following relation:

$$R_{EL}(1 - .5t_c) = R_b(1 - t_c)$$

or

$$\mathbf{R_{EL} = R_b(1 - t_c)/(1 - .5t_c)} \tag{9.11}$$

where R_b is the fully taxable rate on an equivalent loan. So if corporate marginal tax rates are 34%, it implies that the rate of interest on the loan will be 79.5% of the fully taxable rate. Shackelford (1991) compares the actual rates offered on ESOP loans, R_{ELA}, to the theoretical rate, R_{EL}, to calculate a discount ratio as follows:

$$\textbf{Discount ratio} = \mathbf{(R_b - R_{ELA})/(R_b - R_{EL})} \tag{9.12}$$

Shackelford estimates R_b as the interest rate stated in the ESOP loan agreement if for some reason the lender is not entitled to the 50% exclusion—that is, the rate on the ESOP loan if interest on it were fully taxable to the lender. The discount rate represents the percentage of the tax benefits enjoyed by the borrower. He finds that the discount rate averages between 67% to 79%. Alternatively stated, lenders retain between 33% and 21% of the tax benefits. Shackelford notes that the perception by Congress that lenders were retaining too much of the tax benefits of the loan subsidy led Congress, in the 1989 Tax Act, to restrict the 50% exclusion to loans in which the ESOP was the majority

[24] The Section 133 interest exclusion for qualified ESOP lenders was first restricted by the Revenue Reconciliation Act of 1989 (RRA). This act restricted loans to 15 years and generally required that for loans made after July 10, 1989, the ESOP own more than 50% of each class and of the total value of all of the corporation's outstanding stock. The exclusion was finally repealed by Section 1602(a) of the Small Business Job Protection Act of 1996. Loans in existence on August 10, 1996, were grandfathered, subject to certain binding commitment and refinancing rules found in Section 1602(c) of the act.

shareholder in the sponsoring company, which curtailed their popularity somewhat. Shackelford also presents evidence, consistent with the existence of tax clienteles, that the lenders are high-marginal-tax-rate firms.

A final tax benefit to ESOPs, introduced in the 1986 Tax Act, is that the corporation can deduct any dividends that are used to pay down the ESOP loan or are paid directly to employees on their ESOP shares. Under Code Section 404(k), the corporation can deduct dividends to an ESOP if (1) the dividends are paid in cash directly to ESOP participants, (2) the dividends are paid to the ESOP and it distributes them to participants within 90 days of the close of the plan year, or (3) the dividends on ESOP stock are used to make payments on an ESOP loan. Scholes and Wolfson (1990) provide a critical examination of the tax benefits claimed by proponents of ESOPs, including the dividend deduction, and make a good case that the tax benefits can be obtained via other organizational arrangements. They conclude that it is likely that nontax reasons contribute to the popularity of ESOPs.

One nontax reason why ESOPs became popular—and perhaps the most important one—is that they have been used effectively to thwart hostile takeover attempts, particularly in the state of Delaware.[25] In early 1989, Polaroid won an important decision in the Delaware Chancery Court, which upheld Polaroid's issuance of 14% of its stock to an ESOP prior to the initiation of a hostile tender offer by Shamrock Holdings. The ESOP helped Polaroid's management defeat Shamrocks' bid for its stock because employees voted their Polaroid shares with management. Delaware law requires that a firm wait 3 years after it acquires a 15% interest in a target before it can merge with the target, unless it can secure an 85% vote of the target shareholders. The waiting period can impose substantial costs on the acquiring firm if it had plans to use the target firm's assets as collateral for interim or longer-term loans. Firm managers might establish an ESOP because they believe that employee-shareholders are more likely to vote with them than outside shareholders. Polaroid's use of an ESOP as a successful takeover defense mechanism stimulated considerable interest in ESOPs.

ESOPs have been used by firms to sell company divisions to employees, to defer the capital gains tax incurred by owners of private companies on the sale of their shares to the ESOP, to allocate interest payments domestically to free up foreign tax credit limitations, to replace existing defined benefit pension plans, to replace other types of defined contribution plans, and to replace postretirement health care programs. In replacing postretirement health care programs with an ESOP plan, employees are required to fund their own postretirement health care costs from their accumulation in the ESOP—a form of prefunding by the employing firm but at the cost to the employee of increased risks associated with health care costs. As discussed in the earlier section, prefunding is not always tax advantageous.

Beatty (1995) examines the stock market reaction to corporate announcements of ESOP formations. She finds (1) stock returns were positively associated with the estimated tax benefits of ESOP debt; (2) negative stock returns for companies subject to a takeover attempt at the time of the ESOP announcement, suggesting that the corporate control effects of ESOPs are important; and (3) some evidence that ESOPs are related to increases in firm productivity.

In summary, an ESOP provides a pension savings alternative to more conventional tax-qualified retirement plans, one that provides employees with an ownership interest in the firm. Employee ownership might improve the firm's productivity as employee interests become better aligned with the firm's other shareholders. But such compensation arrangements may come at the expense of other more efficient forms (ignoring taxes), both for risk-sharing and incentive reasons. Moreover, severe nontax costs can be a factor if an ESOP must refinance to repurchase shares from departing employees. Shares that are initially contributed to the trust must eventually be cashed out, and high transaction costs might be incurred to accomplish this task, particularly in smaller businesses.

Summary of Key Points

1. To encourage saving for retirement, many countries give favorable tax treatment to pension compensation. In the United States, employers receive an immediate tax deduction for pension

[25] Approximately half the firms listed on the New York Stock Exchange are incorporated in Delaware.

contributions, while employees are taxed only when they receive payments in retirement. Moreover, qualified pension trusts are tax exempt, so earnings in the trust accumulate tax-free.

2. The two broad categories of pension plans are defined benefit plans and defined contribution plans. In defined benefit plans, the employees' retirement benefits are fixed by a contractually specified formula and may be subject to considerable uncertainty regarding how much and when the employer will fund the promised benefits. In defined contribution plans, the employer's pension plan contributions are fixed by a contractually specified formula and, depending on how well the pension fund investments perform, subject to considerable uncertainty regarding how much the employees will receive in retirement benefits.
3. Even when nontax factors are ignored, pensions do not always dominate salaries as a compensation alternative. In particular, if employees' tax rates are expected to increase over time, current compensation may be preferable.
4. When nontax factors are considered, current compensation is sometimes preferred to pensions because pension plans may force some employees to postpone consumption to a greater extent than they would like.
5. Nonqualified deferred compensation arrangements are typically less tax favored than qualified arrangements, such as pension plans. Not only must the employer defer the timing of the tax deduction in nonqualified arrangements, but the income earned on assets set aside to fund nonqualified deferred compensation is taxed to the employer. Nevertheless, deferred compensation plans face far fewer tax-rule restrictions than do pension plans, making them attractive in a broader set of circumstances. In particular, they are commonly used for highly paid employees who face binding constraints on contributions to qualified retirement plans.
6. Even though it is tax advantageous to invest pension plan contributions in assets that bear little implicit tax, such as bonds and other interest-bearing securities, a substantial fraction of plan contributions are invested in tax-favored assets, such as stocks and real estate because many of these tax-favored assets are also risky. Such an investment strategy is sensible only in the presence of substantial transaction costs of undertaking alternative strategies/investments and a desire to invest in risky assets in the hopes of earning risk premiums. In the absence of transaction costs, such risk premiums could typically be earned in a more tax-favored way by borrowing funds to invest in risky assets outside the pension plan and holding interest-bearing securities in the pension plan.
7. An advantage of defined benefit over defined contribution pension plans is a firm's ability to "overfund" the former. This advantage is greatest when employer tax rates are falling over time and when the difference between the after-tax rate of return on pension plan assets and the after-tax rate of return on marginal investments by the employer outside the pension plan is highest.
8. Retiree health benefits can be funded in several ways in the United States. The most tax advantaged are 401(h) plans or collectively bargained plans, but the availability of these arrangements is restricted. These plans allow a current tax deduction for advance funding, tax-free compounding of investment returns on plan assets, and tax exemption of benefits to employee recipients in retirement.
9. Alternative ways in which to fund retiree medical benefits include sweetening pension benefits in exchange for making retirees responsible for their own medical expenses and pay-as-you-go plans, where the employer pays for employees' expenses as they are incurred in retirement. The benefit of the pension plan alternative is that the employer receives an earlier tax deduction and funds accumulate free from tax in a pension trust. The benefit of an unfunded plan is that employees can receive retiree benefits free from tax because retiree health benefit payments can be structured as part of a tax-free medical benefit program. The unfunded alternative is more attractive the higher the employees' tax rates in retirement, the higher the employer's future tax rate relative to its current tax rate, and the lower the benefit of tax-free compounding of investment returns in a pension plan.
10. An employee stock-ownership plan (ESOP) is a defined contribution plan that invests primarily in employer securities on behalf of employees.

11. Special tax provisions apply to ESOPs. For example, dividends paid on employer stock held by the ESOP, and distributed to employees, are tax deductible to the corporation. In addition, half the interest on certain ESOP loans used to purchase employer stock is tax exempt to qualified lenders, although, following the 1989 Tax Act, this benefit is available only to new ESOP financings that own a majority of the employer stock. However, this interest exclusion was repealed on new loans starting in 1996.
12. ESOPs are often adopted by companies that are rumored to be takeover candidates. By locking up shares in presumably friendly hands, ESOPs add to management's arsenal of takeover defense weapons. In fact, given that ESOPs do not appear to offer unique tax or incentive benefits relative to alternative organizational arrangements, their popularity in the late 1980s may well have been driven by their antitakeover characteristics.

Questions

Q9-1. What are the major differences between a defined contribution pension plan and a defined benefit pension plan?

Q9-2. When is it tax advantageous for the firm to pay salary instead of an equivalent pension contribution?

Q9-3. What are the nontax costs associated with providing pension benefits for employees?

Q9-4. Under what conditions will the returns on investing outside the pension fund be greater than the returns on investing inside the pension fund?

Q9-5. How does the length of time that the pension contribution will remain in the pension account affect whether pension is preferred to salary? Under what conditions is the duration of the pension investment irrelevant?

Q9-6. How does the Black–Tepper stocks-versus-bonds puzzle pertain to pension planning? Is it still tax advantageous for corporations to hold bonds in their pension accounts subsequent to the 1986 Tax Act? Is it still tax advantageous for corporations to hold bonds in their pension accounts subsequent to the 2017 TCJA?

Q9-7. What is the meaning of the term *overfunded* in terms of a pension plan? What are the advantages and disadvantages to the corporation and its employees of an overfunded pension plan?

Q9-8. What role does the actuary play in deciding on whether the fund is overfunded or underfunded? How does this role affect dynamic tax-planning strategies for the pension fund?

Q9-9. What are the tax and nontax factors in choosing between compensating employees by way of a pension plan versus a deferred compensation program?

Q9-10. What factors are relevant to determining whether retiree medical benefits should be funded in advance?

Q9-11. What is an ESOP? Why has Congress encouraged their use over the years?

Q9-12. Three purported tax advantages of an ESOP are that the corporation can make tax-deductible contributions to fund the ESOP or pay down the principal on an ESOP loan, that qualified lenders can exclude from taxation 50% of the interest that they receive on the ESOP loan, and that the dividend paid on the shares held in the ESOP are tax deductible under certain circumstances. Do you agree with these claims?

Exercises

E9-13. Suppose a firm faces a current tax rate of 35% but expects this rate to fall to 21% in the future. Employees on average face a current marginal tax rate of 32% but expect this rate to fall to 22% when they retire in 15 years. The firm can earn 12% pretax on its pension investments and 10% after tax on corporate account. Employees on average can earn 10% after tax on their investments. Which among salary, pension, and deferred compensation is tax preferred? Explain your results.

E9-14. Suppose a firm has a defined benefit pension plan and faces a marginal tax rate on ordinary income of 35%. The firm can earn or issue fully taxable bonds that yield 12% and can purchase stock yielding 18%. Describe and illustrate the tax benefits to the Black–Tepper arbitrage strategy for this firm assuming the firm pays no tax on the stock investment yielding 18%. Repeat assuming $t_c = 21\%$. Explain your results.

E9-15. Suppose a firm has a defined benefit pension plan and faces a marginal tax rate on ordinary income of 35%. The firm can earn or issue fully taxable bonds that yield 12% and can purchase stock yielding

18%. The firm faces an annualized corporate tax rate, t_{cs}, of 25% on stock investments. Describe and illustrate the tax benefits to the Black–Tepper arbitrage strategy for this firm. Repeat assuming $t_c = 21\%$ and $t_{cs} = 15\%$.

E9-16. Suppose an employer wishes to provide an employee with $1,000 to pay for medical benefits when the employee retires in 25 years through a sweetened pension plan payment. The retiree's expected tax rate in retirement is 20%, the employer's current tax rate is 35%, and the pension fund earns 12% per year on its investments. How much will the employer need to contribute to the pension plan today to provide the $1,000 after tax to the retiree in 25 years? Repeat assuming $t_c = 21\%$.

E9-17. An employer wishes to provide health care benefits to its workers when they retire. The firm faces a current marginal tax rate of 21% and expects to face this rate in the future. On average, employees face a current tax rate of 31%, which is expected to fall to 20% in retirement. The firm earns 12% pretax in its pension account and 15% pretax from its own operations. The average years until retirement for employees is 20 years. The firm is considering funding the promised retiree health care costs through either a sweetened pension benefit or on a pay-as-you-go approach. Under the pay-as-you-go approach, the benefit to employees will be provided as part of a fringe benefit package that is tax deductible to the employer, and the employees are not taxed on the receipt of the benefit. Which alternative—the sweetened pension benefit or pay-as-you-go approach—is tax preferred?

Tax-Planning Problems

TP9-18. Suppose taxpayers were given a new option under the tax law for retirement funding. The new option requires that they forgo a current tax deduction for pension plan contributions. Any contribution would accumulate in the pension fund free of tax, and distributions from the plan to beneficiaries would also be tax free.

The usual rules provide for current tax deductibility of pension plan contributions and full taxation of pension plan distributions at ordinary tax rates. The tax rates at which contributions reduce taxes and the tax rates at which distributions increase taxes may differ because they occur at different points in time.

a. Who would prefer the new option?

b. What would likely happen to taxes collected by the government in the short run? In the long run?

c. What would likely happen to the aggregate amount of savings undertaken through pension accounts?

d. How would the new option compare to one in which pension plan contributions give rise to current tax deductions and pension plan distributions are taxed at the same rate at which deductions were taken?

e. How would the new option compare to a plan with the following?

- Pension plan contributions give rise to current tax deductions.
- Pension plan distributions are taxed at the ordinary tax rates that apply at the time the distributions are made.
- Distributions are taxed at a rate above (below) the rate at which contributions are deductible and taxpayers receive a tax credit or pay additional tax equal to the difference in tax rates multiplied by the pension plan contributions.

TP9-19. The chief financial officer of a profitable firm asks you to explain the advantages, if any, to his firm of overfunding the firm's defined benefit pension plan. Do these advantages accrue to a firm with a defined contribution pension plan?

TP9-20. A firm currently has an overfunded defined benefit pension plan and is short of cash. The chief financial officer (CFO) is considering terminating the defined benefit plan to recapture the "excess assets." The firm will replace the defined benefit plan with a defined contribution plan to continue to provide pension benefits to its employees. What are the tax and nontax costs and benefits of the CFO's planned action? What alternatives to the termination are available to the firm? Briefly compare these alternatives to a termination.

TP9-21. A newly established firm wants to establish a pension plan for its employees. The firm hires you to prepare a report comparing a defined benefit pension plan with a defined contribution pension plan. The firm also requires a recommendation from you as to which plan better suits them. On questioning management, you learn that the firm's future profitability is likely to be highly variable—sometimes large profits, at other times possible losses. You also learn that the firm is an aggressive tax planner. What type of pension plan would you recommend? Explain your reasoning.

TP9-22. The accompanying table can be used to make paired comparisons of the desirability of salary, deferred compensation, and pensions as a function of

$$a = (1 - t_{co})/(1 - t_{cn})$$

$$b = (1 - t_{po})/(1 - t_{pn})$$

$$c = (1 + r_1)/(1 + r_2)$$

where

- t_{co} and t_{cn} are employer current and future marginal tax rates; thus $a > 1$ ($a < 1$) implies that employer tax rates are expected to increase (decrease).
- t_{po} and t_{pn} are employee current and future marginal tax rates, respectively; thus $b > 1$ ($b < 1$) implies that employee tax rates are expected to increase (decrease).
- n denotes the number of time periods (i.e., length of the employment contract).
- r_1 is the employer's earnings rate and r_2 is the employee's earnings rate on investments; the precise definitions vary depending on the compensation comparison for which the table is used.

Use the table to answer the following questions and explain how the table enables you to determine the answers.

Salary vs. Deferred Compensation vs. Pensions

		a	0.80	0.80	0.80	1.00	1.00	1.00	1.20	1.20	1.20
		n	5	10	20	5	10	20	5	10	20
b	***c***		**Values for *a*/(*bc*ⁿ)**								
0.70	0.98		1.26	1.40	1.71	1.58	1.75	2.14	1.90	2.10	2.57
0.70	1.00		1.14	1.14	1.14	1.43	1.43	1.43	1.71	1.71	1.71
0.70	1.02		1.04	0.94	0.77	1.29	1.17	0.96	1.55	1.41	1.15
0.80	0.98		1.11	1.22	1.50	1.38	1.53	1.87	1.66	1.84	2.25
0.80	1.00		1.00	1.00	1.00	1.25	1.25	1.25	1.50	1.50	1.50
0.80	1.02		0.91	0.82	0.67	1.13	1.03	0.84	1.36	1.23	1.01
0.90	0.98		0.98	1.09	1.33	1.23	1.36	1.66	1.48	1.63	2.00
0.90	1.00		0.89	0.89	0.89	1.11	1.11	1.11	1.33	1.33	1.33
0.90	1.02		0.81	0.73	0.60	1.01	0.91	0.75	1.21	1.09	0.90
1.00	0.98		0.89	0.98	1.20	1.11	1.22	1.50	1.33	1.47	1.80
1.00	1.00		0.80	0.80	0.80	1.00	1.00	1.00	1.20	1.20	1.20
1.00	1.02		0.72	0.66	0.54	0.91	0.82	0.67	1.09	0.98	0.81
1.10	0.98		0.80	0.89	1.09	1.01	1.11	1.36	1.21	1.34	1.63
1.10	1.00		0.73	0.73	0.73	0.91	0.91	0.91	1.09	1.09	1.09
1.10	1.02		0.66	0.60	0.49	0.82	0.75	0.61	0.99	0.89	0.73
1.20	0.98		0.74	0.82	1.00	0.92	1.02	1.25	1.11	1.22	1.50
1.20	1.00		0.67	0.67	0.67	0.83	0.83	0.83	1.00	1.00	1.00
1.20	1.02		0.60	0.55	0.45	0.75	0.68	0.56	0.91	0.82	0.67
1.30	0.98		0.68	0.75	0.92	0.85	0.94	1.15	1.02	1.13	1.38
1.30	1.00		0.62	0.62	0.62	0.77	0.77	0.77	0.92	0.92	0.92
1.30	1.02		0.56	0.50	0.41	0.70	0.63	0.52	0.84	0.76	0.62

To get you started, note that salary will be preferred to deferred compensation if:

$$\frac{(1-t_{po})(1+r_{pn})^n}{(1-t_{pn})(1+r_{cn})^n} > \frac{(1-t_{co})}{(1-t_{cn})}$$

Given the definitions of a, b, and c, in the table, the above equation can be rewritten as

$$bc^n > a$$

$$= a/bc^n < 1$$

and, in defining c, $r_1 = r_{pn}$ and $r_2 = r_{cn}$.

a. If $r_1 = r_{pn}$ and $r_2 = r_{cn}$, what do table values greater than 1.00 tell you about the desirability of salary relative to deferred compensation?

b. What portion of the table—that is, which rows and columns—is relevant to a comparison of salary and pensions? What are the appropriate definitions of r_1 and r_2 in this case? And what do table values greater than 1.00 tell you?

c. What portion of the table is relevant to a comparison of pensions and deferred compensation? What are the appropriate definitions of r_1 and r_2 in this case? And what do table values greater than 1.00 tell you?

You have been asked to provide tax-planning assistance in formulating compensation policy for several of your corporate clients. You have three types of clients, each with seven types of employees:

Employer clients	t_{co}	t_{cn}
(1) Tax exempt	0%	0%
(2) Net operating loss carryforward firm	22%	35%
(3) Currently profitable corporation but expects future losses	35%	19%
Employees	t_{po}	t_{pn}
(1) Maintenance workers	15%	15%
(2) Young employees anticipating some career advancement	28%	40%
(3) Senior executive nearing retirement who has saved little for retirement	40%	15%
(4) Moderately-high-income employee near retirement	31%	15%
(5) Mid-career nonmanagement employee expecting moderate career advancement	34%	40%
(6) Highly compensated junior management employee expecting demotion	40%	33%
(7) MBA student working October to December in the first year of employment and 12 months per year in all future years of employment	20%	40%

d. For the case of $r_p = r_c = R_{pen}$, for which employee/employer/length-of-the-employment-contract (EEL) combinations would you recommend that marginal compensation dollars be allocated to each of the following?

1. Salary
2. Deferred compensation
3. Pension

e. Consider only employer client 3 and employees 1, 3, and 7. For the case of $r_p = r_c$ and R_{pen} exceeding r_c by approximately 2%, for which of the relevant EEL combinations would you recommend that marginal compensation dollars be allocated to each of the following?

1. Salary
2. Deferred compensation
3. Pension

References and Additional Readings

Beatty, A., 1995. "The Cash Flow and Informational Effects of Employee Stock Ownership Plans," *Journal of Financial Economics*, pp. 211–240.

Black, F., 1980. "The Tax Consequences of Long-Run Pension Policy," *Financial Analysts Journal* (July–August), pp. 1–28.

Bodie, Z., J. Light, R. Morck, and R. Taggert, 1987. "Funding and Asset Allocation in Corporate Pension Plans: An Empirical Investigation," edited by Z. Bodie, J. Shoven, and D. Wise. *Issues in Pension Economics.* Chicago IL: University of Chicago Press, pp. 15–44.

Chang, S., and D. Mayers, 1992. "Managerial Vote Ownership and Shareholder Wealth: Evidence from Employee Stock Ownership Plans," *Journal of Financial Economics*, pp. 103–131.

Chuk, E., 2013. "Economic Consequences of Mandated Accounting Disclosures: Evidence from Pension Accounting Standards," *The Accounting Review* (88, 2), pp. 395–427.

Clinch, G., and T. Shibano, 1996. "Differential Tax Benefits and the Pension Reversion Decision," *Journal of Accounting and Economics* (1), pp. 69–106.

Francis, J., and S. Reiter, 1987. "Determinants of Corporate Pension Funding Strategy," *Journal of Accounting and Research* (1), pp. 35–59.

Frank, M., 2002. "The Impact of Taxes on Corporate Defined Benefit Plan Asset Allocation," *Journal of Accounting Research* (4), pp. 1163–1190.

Gaertner, F., D. Lynch, and M. Vernon, 2018. "The Effects of the Tax Cuts & Jobs Act of 2017 on Defined Benefit Pension Contributions, Working paper, University of Wisconsin.

Gordon, L., and J. Pound, 1990. "ESOPs and Corporate Control," *Journal of Financial Economics*, pp. 525–556.

Mittelstaedt, F., 1989. "An Empirical Analysis of Factors Underlying the Decision to Remove Excess Assets from Overfunded Pension Plans," *Journal of Accounting and Economics* (4), pp. 369–418.

Munnell, A., J-P. Aubry, and C. Crawford, 2015. "Investment Returns: Defined Benefit vs. Defined Contribution Plans," Center for Retirement Research at Boston College, Number 15-21.

Mushruwala, S., 2007. "The Impact of Accounting Smoothing on Asset Allocation in Corporate Pension Plans: Evidence from the U.K.," Working Paper, New York: Baruch College.

Petersen, M., 1989. "Pension Terminations on Worker-Stockholder Wealth Transfers," Working Paper, Boston, MA: Department of Economics, MIT.

Petersen, M., 1996. "Allocating Assets and Discounting Cash Flows: Pension Plan Finance" in *Pension, Savings, and Capital Markets,* edited by P. Fernandez, J. Turner, and R. Hinz. Washington, DC: U.S. Department of Labor, Pension and Welfare Benefits Administration, pp. 1–26.

Scholes, M., and M. Wolfson, 1990. "Employee Stock Ownership Plans and Corporate Restructuring: Myths and Realities," *Financial Management Journal*, pp. 48–58.

Shackelford, D., 1991. "The Market for Tax Benefits: Evidence from Leveraged ESOPs," *Journal of Accounting and Economics* (2), pp. 117–145.

Tepper, I., 1981. "Taxation and Corporate Pension Policy," *Journal of Finance* (March), pp. 1–14.

Thomas, J., 1988. "Corporate Taxes and Defined Benefit Pension Plans," *Journal of Accounting and Economics* (3), pp. 199–237.

Thomas, J., 1989. "Why Do Firms Terminate Their Overfunded Pension Plans?" *Journal of Accounting and Economics* (11, 4), pp. 361–398.

10

Multinational Tax Planning

After studying this chapter, you should be able to

1. Appreciate the fundamental issues in international taxation.
2. Describe the pressures on tax systems posed by cross-border commerce.
3. Understand the differences between territorial and worldwide taxation.
4. Describe the U.S. participation exemption.
5. Perform basic foreign tax credit calculations.
6. Describe the efforts to prevent base erosion.
7. Analyze how taxes affect the location and structure of investments.
8. Describe the taxation of foreign investors.

How are firms taxed when they do business in more than one country? In this era of increasingly global markets, firms often earn income in multiple countries, and sometimes earn more income outside of their home country than inside it. Sometimes this is due to the firm being based in a country with a small domestic market. But even firms based in countries with large domestic markets, such as the United States or Japan, sometimes become so globally successful that they earn more abroad and pay more taxes abroad than they do in their home country. For example, the Coca-Cola Company reports that its beverages are sold in more than 200 countries. Consequently, it is not surprising that Coca-Cola's foreign earnings tend to be larger than its U.S. earnings. Similarly, Coca-Cola's income taxes were mostly from outside the United States. The same holds true for multinationals around the world. Honda Motor Co. is headquartered in Japan, but typically has more sales, more pretax income, and more current tax expense outside of Japan than inside Japan. Transocean, an offshore oil and gas drilling company, is incorporated in Switzerland (ironically a land-locked country), but its oil rigs are in oceans all around the world. As you think about the complex research and development (R&D), production, and sales processes of multinationals such as these, you can begin to appreciate the complexity of determining how much income should be taxable by the various countries involved. Unlike accounting, tax is highly jurisdictional. Each country has its own tax rules, which raises the possibility of multiple countries taxing the same income. This chapter introduces some of the key tax issues that arise when firms do business in multiple countries.

10.1 FUNDAMENTAL ISSUES IN INTERNATIONAL TAX

The fundamental issue in international taxation is that when firms invest abroad or engage in business abroad, they become subject to the tax laws of at least two countries. Although tax systems around the world have a great deal in common, they also differ from one another along a variety of dimensions. For example, marginal tax rates vary from 0% in certain tax-haven countries to more than 30% in certain high-tax countries, the definition of income varies from country to country, the use of taxes based on things other than income (e.g., the **value-added tax**, or VAT) varies considerably, and firms may be taxed on only domestic income or on worldwide income. The patchwork of tax laws applying to multinationals can lead to the same dollar of income being taxed by a single jurisdiction, taxed by more than one jurisdiction, or, in some cases, taxed by no jurisdiction.

But with variation in tax laws also comes opportunities. The variation in tax laws across countries provides fertile ground for creative tax strategies, many of which involve shifting income from high-tax jurisdictions to low-tax jurisdictions. In some cases shifting requires changing the physical structure of transactions, for example, where a factory is located; but in many cases the tax treatment can be improved by simply altering the financial structure of a transaction, for example, by routing transactions through subsidiaries located in tax-favorable countries.

Why is there so much variation in tax laws across countries? Much of it arises from differing policy objectives. Countries usually have several policy objectives with international taxation. The first is to relieve taxpayers from double (or more) taxation of the same income. The foreign tax credit (FTC) is an example of a provision designed to mitigate double taxation; excluding foreign income from taxation is another. A second objective is to enhance the competitiveness of the country as a place to invest and to do business. A third objective is to aid in the balance-of-payments position by encouraging exports. Whether the third objective is desirable is a matter of some debate among economists. Taxes often are used as a strategic tool by governments to attract certain kinds of business to their borders and to achieve certain economic goals.

10.2 INCREASING PRESSURES ON TAX SYSTEMS POSED BY CROSS-BORDER COMMERCE

Over time, cross-border commerce is putting increasing pressure on countries' tax systems. In this section, we describe some of the long-term trends that are leading to such pressure and how countries are adapting to these trends. The first trend is the increasing importance of cross-border commerce over time, which is sometimes referred to as globalization. For example, consider **Figure 10.1**, which plots trade (total imports or exports) as a percentage of world GDP.[1] While both trade and world GDP are increasing over time, trade is increasing at an even faster rate, accounting for a larger and larger fraction of world GDP. While increased trade is generally viewed by economists as increasing efficiency and production, it represents a challenge for countries' tax systems. For example, the complex, multi-country supply chains common in the manufacture of automobiles, airliners, medical equipment, cell phones, etc. can make it difficult to determine how much profit is attributable to a particular country.

The second major trend that poses a challenge for countries' tax systems is the increasing importance of intangible assets and intellectual property in firms' production functions. Consider, for example, a patent on a widely-used drug. The patent may be owned by a legal entity in one country, may have involved the work of scientists working in many other countries, and may be licensed to a firm that manufactures in yet another country and then sells the drug all over the world. How much of the income from the drug is attributable to the patent and where should the income from the patent be taxed? As intangible assets have increased in importance over time, so has their use for tax-planning purposes to shift income from high-tax countries to low-tax countries. From the perspective of the tax authorities in high-tax countries, such income shifting is referred to as base erosion, where base refers to the tax base.

[1] Trade is the sum of exports and imports of goods and services measured as a share of gross domestic product.

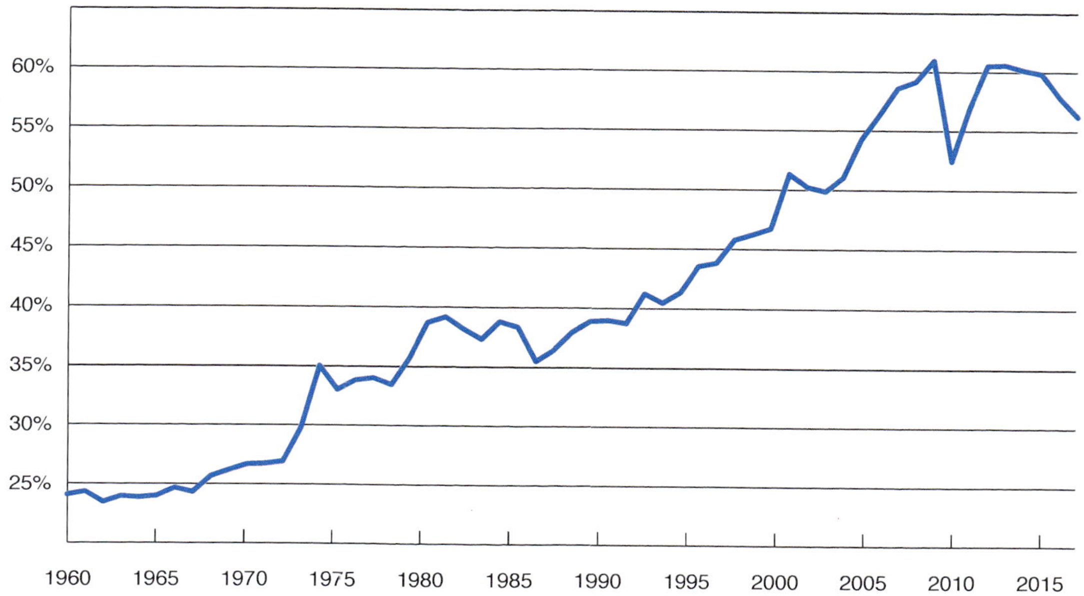

Source: https://data.worldbank.org/indicator/ne.trd.gnfs.zs
Note: Trade (% of GDP)

FIGURE 10.1 World trade as a share of world gross domestic product

The third major trend is the increase in capital mobility and the corresponding increase in tax competition among countries for mobile capital. As global trade has increased over time, so has the flow of capital across countries. Countries compete with one another for capital, and taxes are one aspect of this competition. Over the past several decades, many countries have decreased their corporate statutory income tax rates. In **Figure 10.2**, we show the trend in corporate tax rates over time for the U.S. and the average for members of the OECD (other developed countries). Note that the tax rates include both national and subnational (e.g., state) income taxes.

Top Corporate Income Tax Rate, United States vs. OECD, 1983–2018

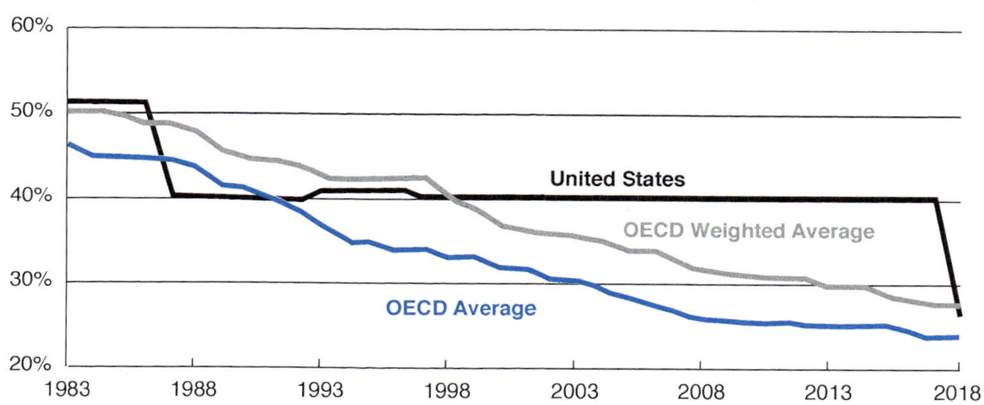

Source: https://taxfoundation.org/benefits-cutting-corporate-income-tax-rate/

FIGURE 10.2 Statutory corporate income tax rates over time, U.S. vs OECD

Additional aspects of tax competition include the rise over time in consumption-based taxation, such as value-added taxes (VAT), which have been adopted in various forms by most developed countries (the U.S. being a notable exception). By tilting the make-up of their tax systems towards taxing consumption rather than income, countries may make themselves more attractive places to locate income-producing capital investment. Additionally, over time countries have shifted their tax systems away from worldwide taxation in favor of territorial taxation. We describe the concepts of worldwide taxation and territorial taxation in detail in the sections that follow.

10.3 OVERVIEW OF INTERNATIONAL TAXATION

At the most fundamental level, countries choose between two main approaches to international taxation: the territorial tax system and the worldwide tax system. In a territorial tax system, the country taxes only income earned within its borders. Even though that statement sounds logical, determining where income was earned can be difficult in practice. Under a worldwide tax system, a country generally taxes the worldwide income of its permanent residents and domestic corporations and relies on foreign tax credits to mitigate double taxation of foreign income. It is best to think of territorial and worldwide as two ends of a spectrum. Most countries lie somewhere between the two extremes. For simplicity, it is common to refer to a given country as either territorial or worldwide depending on where it lies in the spectrum. Before 2018, the United States was generally considered to have a worldwide tax system. With the Tax Cuts and Jobs Act (TCJA), the U.S. adopted aspects of territorial taxation, but also retained and enacted provisions that are worldwide in nature. As with many countries' tax systems, the U.S. system can be thought of as a hybrid. For example, some countries nominally tax worldwide income but then provide for broad exemptions of foreign income. Some countries (including the U.S. as of 2018) exempt certain foreign income via a **participation exemption** in which certain dividends from foreign subsidiaries are exempt from taxation. Countries continue to experiment with their tax systems in the competitive struggle to attract and retain high-value operations. Over time, territorial taxation has become more popular around the world, with the U.S., the U.K., and Japan being prominent examples of countries that have adopted elements of territorial taxation.

We now focus on international taxation as employed by the United States. We begin with the taxation of corporations. There is a distinction between how the U.S. taxes domestic corporations and foreign corporations. Usually, the place of incorporation determines whether a corporation is domestic or foreign for U.S. tax purposes. Thus, any corporation incorporated under the laws of any state of the United States or the District of Columbia counts as a U.S. corporation. Corporations not incorporated in the U.S. generally are treated as foreign corporations.[2] For U.S. corporations, the U.S. applies a hybrid system in which the corporation's worldwide income is potentially subject to U.S. tax, but with important exemptions for certain foreign income (i.e., the participation exemption) and with foreign tax credits to mitigate the tax burden on foreign income that winds up being subject to U.S. tax. In contrast, foreign corporations are only taxed by the U.S. on income derived in the U.S. or income effectively connected with a U.S. trade or business. While most of this chapter focuses on international taxation of corporations, it is also important to consider international taxation of individuals.

For individuals, we must distinguish between those subject to worldwide taxation and those subject to taxation on U.S.-source income only. The United States taxes U.S. citizens on their worldwide income.[3] For U.S. citizens, it does not matter whether they actually live in the United States or not; they are all subject to taxation by the United States on their worldwide income. Like corporations, individuals are allowed credits against their U.S. tax to account for foreign taxes paid, subject to limitations. Resident aliens, including anyone with permanent resident status, are generally taxed in the same manner as U.S. citizens.[4] In contrast, nonresident aliens are taxed by the United States only on income derived within the United States or income deemed to be effectively connected with a U.S. trade or business. So although the United States has a worldwide tax system for U.S. citizens and resident aliens, nonresident aliens are essentially subject to territorial taxation. An element of practicality is at work here. Even if the United States foolishly tried to subject nonresident aliens to

---

[2] As in many areas of the tax law, there are exceptions. For example, there are exceptions for firms that have undertaken "inversions," which are discussed later in this chapter.

[3] An exception called the "foreign earned income exclusion" is that a limited amount of foreign earned income (e.g., wage income) of U.S. citizens or resident aliens living abroad can be exempt from U.S. tax.

[4] People can also be classified as resident aliens, and hence subject to worldwide taxation, by having a "substantial presence" in the United States. A substantial presence is based on a weighted average of the number of days in the U.S. during the current and prior 2 years. Special rules exempt many students and diplomats from the substantial presence test. Tax treaties can have an impact as well.

worldwide taxation, it would be impossible to enforce such a tax, and the diplomatic uproar would almost certainly lead to retaliatory taxes.

Operating as a Branch, Partnership, or a Foreign Subsidiary

Most of the foreign income of U.S. multinationals is earned in **foreign subsidiaries**. Generally, foreign subsidiary income is not subject to U.S. tax until it is repatriated to the U.S. parent (e.g., by paying a dividend to the parent). Even then, it might not attract U.S. tax by virtue of the participation exemption. There are important exceptions in which foreign subsidiary income is immediately taxable for U.S. purposes, which are discussed later in the chapter (e.g., Subpart F and GILTI income). Two alternatives to foreign subsidiaries, the **foreign branch** and the **foreign partnership**, can be useful in certain cases. For U.S. tax purposes, a foreign branch arises when the U.S. taxpayer has direct ownership of business operations located outside the United States. For example, a U.S. corporation may have direct ownership of a manufacturing facility, a warehouse, a sales office, or a laboratory located in another country. From a nontax perspective, foreign branches are simple to set up because they do not require the creation of a new legal entity. The major tax feature of a branch relative to a foreign subsidiary is that the profits and losses of a branch are reflected immediately on the tax return of the U.S. entity that owns the branch.

Foreign partnerships share some of the same attributes as a foreign branch under the U.S. tax law. A foreign partnership is a partnership organized under the laws of another country. Because partnerships are flow-through entities under U.S. tax law, U.S. partners in a foreign partnership are taxed currently on their share of the partnership income. Thus, losses from foreign operations are immediately deductible against U.S. domestic income, which is important for start-up operations that can reasonably be expected to generate losses. Moreover, it is possible to change the branch or partnership into a corporation when operations turn profitable. The cost of converting, however, is that the firm must recapture, as income, previously deducted losses. However, branch income is not eligible for the participation exemption and is placed in its own basket for FTC limitation purposes.

The U.S. tax rules for classifying entities, the so-called "check-the-box" regulations, give firms flexibility in selecting how their foreign entities will be treated for U.S. tax purposes. The election is made by checking a box on a special form filed with the Internal Revenue Service (IRS). A different election can be made for each foreign entity. Certain foreign entities, known as "per se corporations," are not eligible for this election and must be classified as corporations for U.S. purposes (i.e., subsidiaries). A foreign entity that is not a per se corporation generally can elect to be taxed by the United States as a subsidiary or, alternatively to be taxed by the United States as a branch (if it has a single owner it can elect to disregard the entity) or partnership (if it has two or more owners).

There is also variation in tax rules across countries, which affects these foreign entities. For example, the way loss carryforwards are treated in different foreign tax jurisdictions varies considerably. Although carryforwards are typically available to foreign subsidiaries, it is not the case in all countries. Moreover, some countries allow short carryforward periods, other countries allow some combination of carrybacks and carryforwards, and some countries allow carryforwards only. Some countries allow branches established in their country to carry losses forward, but this treatment is less common than for foreign subsidiaries.

Nontax considerations also play an important role in the choice of conducting foreign operations through a branch, partnership, or a subsidiary. For example, in contrast to foreign subsidiaries, the legal liability of the owner of a branch operation generally is not limited to the assets employed abroad. For this reason, entities that provide for limited liability are often used to set up foreign branches to limit the parent corporation's legal liability with respect to foreign operations.

Foreign Tax Credits and the Participation Exemption

To understand how the U.S. mitigates imposing too much tax on foreign income, it is necessary to understand how foreign tax credits and the participation exemption work. In this section we introduce the basics.

We begin with the participation exemption, an important tax relief provision that became effective in 2018. The participation exemption provides for a 100% dividends received deduction for the foreign source portion of dividends from foreign corporations that are at least 10% owned by a U.S. shareholder (such as a U.S. corporation). Effectively, the participation exemption results in territorial taxation for the foreign income to which it applies. For example, consider a U.S. corporation with a wholly owned foreign subsidiary that earns all of its income in a country with a 20% local tax. The foreign subsidiary will be subject to the 20% foreign income tax. Upon repatriation, the U.S. parent will offset the dividend income on its U.S. tax return with the 100% dividends received deduction, resulting in no incremental U.S. tax (assuming nothing else prevents the participation exemption from applying).

Prior to the participation exemption, the primary means of mitigating the U.S. tax on the foreign income was the foreign tax credit (the foreign tax credit can still be used when the participation exemption doesn't apply). The problem was that firms often faced net U.S. tax on their foreign income even after taking foreign tax credits. The reason is that, prior to 2018, the U.S. corporate tax rate was 35%, while most of the U.S.'s major trading partners had lower corporate tax rates. Thus, a firm with a foreign subsidiary in a country that had a 20% corporate tax rate could face an additional 15% U.S. tax (35% less a foreign tax credit for the 20% paid to the foreign country) upon repatriation of the foreign income to the U.S. parent. Many experts were concerned that the incremental U.S. tax on foreign income put U.S.-based multinationals at a competitive disadvantage to their foreign competitors, which did not face such a tax. The participation exemption and the corporate tax rate reduction to 21% were important moves to level the playing field for U.S.-based multinationals vis-à-vis their foreign competitors, and to move the U.S. tax system in line with the tax systems of its major trading partners.

As part of adopting the participation exemption, the U.S. imposed a one-time transition tax on the accumulated foreign earnings of foreign subsidiaries that had not previously been subject to U.S. tax. The rate was 15.5% if the foreign income was held in liquid form (e.g., cash) and 8% if held in non-liquid form. The transition tax could be paid in installments over an eight-year period. The transition tax was large for some firms; in 2018 Apple reported that it would pay $38 billion in transition taxes on its accumulated foreign earnings.[5]

If not eligible for the participation exemption (e.g., income from a foreign branch), U.S. taxpayers generally can elect to either receive a credit for foreign taxes paid or deduct the foreign taxes paid against their U.S. income. A dollar of tax credit is usually better than a dollar of deduction, as a dollar of tax credit reduces taxes by a dollar, but a dollar of deduction only reduces taxes by $\$1 \times \tau$, where τ is the taxpayer's marginal tax rate. However, with the benefits of the foreign tax credit also come limitations.

Not all foreign taxes are eligible for the foreign tax credit. In general, the United States allows foreign tax credits only for foreign taxes levied on income and withholding taxes on the repatriation of income. Thus foreign value-added taxes (VAT taxes), property taxes, and excise taxes are not eligible for the foreign tax credit unless an exception is made under a tax treaty. Foreign taxes not eligible for the foreign tax credit can be taken as a deduction for U.S. tax purposes, just like any other business expense. Credits are generally preferred to deductions, because a dollar of tax credit reduces the tax liability by $1, whereas a dollar of deduction reduces taxes by only $\$1 \times t_d$, where t_d is the domestic (U.S.) tax rate. The classification of a foreign tax as based on income for U.S. foreign tax credit purposes is sometimes a matter of disagreement between the taxpayer and the IRS. For example, the IRS and large oil companies have been involved in multibillion-dollar litigation over whether taxes levied on the extraction of oil, which are common taxes in Middle Eastern countries, qualify as taxes based on income for U.S. FTC purposes as opposed to a royalty or other payment for the use of these natural resources.[6] In another example, in 2013 the U.S. Supreme Court heard a case involving the creditability of a U.K. "windfall tax" and ruled that it was creditable under U.S. law.[7]

Even when a foreign tax is classified as an income tax for U.S. purposes, that does not automatically mean that the U.S. corporation receives an immediate foreign tax credit equal to the foreign tax. In some countries the income tax rate exceeds the U.S. tax rate, and in such cases the United States will not give credit for more in taxes than would have been paid had the income been earned in the

---

[5] Mickle, T., "Apple to Pay $38 Billion in Taxes on Cash Overseas, Build New U.S. Campus," *Wall Street Journal*, January 17, 2018.

[6] See, for example, *Exxon Corp. v. Commissioner*, 113 T.C. 338 (1999).

[7] *PPL Corp. et al. v. Commissioner of Internal Revenue*, 133 S. Ct. 1897, 2013-1 50335 (2013).

United States. The rules that prevent U.S. taxpayers from getting too much tax relief in the eyes of the tax authorities from foreign tax credits are known as the foreign tax credit limitation rules. Planning for foreign tax credits is among the most important tax considerations in the multinational arena.

We illustrate how the foreign tax credit mechanism works in Table 10.1. We assume that a U.S. multinational has established a branch in Australia and one in Ireland. Both branches earn $100. Assume for pedagogical purposes that the local tax rates on income earned in Australia and Ireland are 30% and 10%, respectively.[8]

First consider column A. The foreign branch earns $100 of taxable income in Australia. The Australian tax rate is 30%, resulting in $30 of Australian tax.

Table 10.1 Example of the Foreign Tax Credit

	A Australia Alone	B Ireland Alone	Together
Local taxable income	$100	$100	$200
Local tax (at 30% and 10%)	30	10	40
U.S. tax at 21%	21	21	42
Foreign tax credit	21	10	40
Net U.S. tax	0	11	2
Foreign tax credit carryforward	9	0	0

Notice that if only the Australian branch existed, only $21 of the $30 of Australian taxes paid can be used currently as a tax credit. The remaining $9 can be carried back up to 1 year and carried forward up to 10 years. To prevent a host of abuses, the United States imposes limitations on foreign tax credits. In general the foreign tax credit limitation is equal to the U.S. tax rate times the foreign source income. The FTC after limitation is equal to the minimum of the foreign taxes paid and the FTC limitation, or min($30, $21) = $21.

Now consider column B, the Irish branch, by itself. The Irish branch has $100 of income, which results in $10 of Irish tax. The U.S. tax on the Irish income is $21 before foreign tax credits. Because the Irish tax rate is below the U.S. tax rate, all $10 of the Irish tax is creditable against U.S. tax. The U.S. tax on the Irish income after foreign tax credits is thus $11 ($21 − $10).

In the last column of Table 10.1, we consider both branches together. The United States allows the foreign tax credit limitation to be calculated based on the combined income of the branches, rather than imposing a separate limitation on a country-by-country basis as some other countries do.[9] Given the ability to average the foreign tax rates paid on worldwide income, all of the $40 in foreign taxes paid can be used as a credit against the U.S. tax on foreign income. Why? Because the $42 foreign tax credit limitation is greater than the $40 foreign taxes paid. Essentially, the low-tax Irish operations provide $11 of excess foreign tax credit limitation that is used to soak up the $9 of excess foreign tax credits generated by the high-tax Australian operations.

Country-by-Country FTC Limitations

Most countries do not allow indiscriminate mixing of all types of income and/or high- and low-tax-rate foreign income in their FTC limitation calculations. The United States, for example, makes firms calculate a separate FTC limitation for four different "baskets" of income—a subject we examine in more detail in the next section. Some countries instead employ a country-by-country limitation.

Suppose that instead of being a U.S. corporation, the parent corporation in our example was resident in a country that imposed its FTC limitation on a country-by-country basis. In that case the FTC

[8] The given foreign tax rates are assumed for pedagogical purposes and not meant to reflect the actual current tax rates. The hypothetical tax rates in this example are set to illustrate how high-tax income and low-tax income interact in the foreign tax credit calculation.

[9] The United States does, however, require foreign tax credits to be computed separately on different "baskets" of income.

limitation for the Irish taxes would be $\$100 \times .21 = \$21$, and so all of the \$10 of Irish taxes paid would be creditable on the parent's tax return. The FTC limitation on the Australian taxes would also be $\$100 \times .21 = \$21$, so only \$21 of the \$30 of Australian taxes paid would be creditable on the parent's tax return. Making firms compute their FTC limits on a country-by-country basis reduces the ability to "cross credit," i.e., mix high- and low-tax-rate income together to maximize foreign tax credits.

Separate Basket Limitations

The United States requires its multinationals to compute the foreign tax credit limitation separately for four separate **baskets of income**: passive category income, foreign branch income, **global intangible low-taxed income (GILTI)**, and general category income. The motivation for the separate basket approach to FTC limitations is to prevent taxpayers from using cross-crediting strategies to maximize their foreign tax credits. For example, if a firm faced a severe FTC limitation as a result of the location of its operations and business, it would have an incentive to place income-earning assets in tax-haven countries where tax rates are low. This move would reduce the average tax rate on foreign-source income and give rise to larger credits for the foreign tax paid in high-tax countries. In other words, it would allow for additional cross-crediting. The U.S. tax law permits the averaging of high-tax and low-tax foreign income within baskets, but it does not permit the averaging of income and credits across baskets. Thus, a company that has general category income in high-tax jurisdictions cannot relax its FTC limitation by merely placing assets that produce passive income in a low-tax jurisdiction. In contrast, the company could relax its FTC limitation by generating general basket income in a low-tax jurisdiction. Like the country-by-country FTC limitations used by some countries, the U.S. baskets of income computations make it more difficult for companies to receive full credit for their foreign taxes paid.

10.4 BASE EROSION AND INCOME SHIFTING ACROSS COUNTRIES

Transfer Pricing

When income is taxed at different rates in different countries, it can matter a great deal how worldwide income is allocated to the various countries. In multinational corporations, many goods and services are routinely transferred among related entities in different tax jurisdictions. **Transfer prices**—the prices at which goods and services are transferred between related entities—can be critical in terms of their impact on worldwide taxes. The relationship of the entities would appear to provide great tax-planning opportunities by setting transfer prices judiciously. For example, if a U.S. manufacturer wanted to shift income from the U.S. to a foreign subsidiary, it could reduce the price it charges its foreign subsidiaries for parts. In contrast, in high-tax-rate foreign jurisdictions, transfer pricing represents not only a way to repatriate profits in a tax-deductible fashion, but also a way to avoid the imposition of withholding tax.

Tax authorities recognize these tax-planning opportunities, and **Section 482** of the U.S. Tax Code has been made available to the Internal Revenue Service (IRS) as an important weapon to deal with overzealous tax-planning. The regulations under Section 482 provide that transactions between related parties should be priced as if they involved unrelated parties: **Arm's-length pricing** is the principle. The arm's-length principle is widely applied by countries around the world. The basic problem, however, is that the circumstances under which the related parties find it desirable to integrate vertically are systematically different from those in which transactions take place at arm's length in the market. A second problem is that the good, service, or intangible being transferred frequently has no ready market outside the special relationship between the related parties. Transfer pricing for income from intangible assets such as patents and trademarks can be particularly contentious and difficult to price because there are so few third-party comparables.

The guidelines in transfer-pricing regulations can be unclear. To mitigate some of the uncertainty, the IRS allows firms to enter into **advance pricing agreements** (APAs). Under the APA program, the firm submits its proposed transfer pricing methodology to the IRS for review. If the IRS agrees, then the firm's transfer pricing should not be challenged as long as the firm adheres to the agreement. Transfer pricing uncertainty can also be reduced through bilateral APA agreements, which provide assurance under foreign law as well as U.S. law. In addition, disputes can be mediated by way of

Mutual Agreement Procedures in tax treaties, in which the Competent Authorities of the applicable governments (e.g., the Competent Authority for the United States is a Deputy Commissioner in the IRS) work to resolve the issue in a way that avoids double taxation.

Tax authorities around the world have become increasingly concerned about transfer pricing and, more generally, income shifting by firms and the resulting erosion of the tax base of their countries. Responding to these concerns, in 2013 the Organisation for Economic Co-operation and Development (OECD) announced a new initiative to address perceived abuses, the Action Plan on Base Erosion and Profit Shifting (BEPS). After years of work, the OECD finalized and published the action plan, which includes fifteen actions that countries can take to combat BEPS. One action, country-by-country reporting, requires firms to provide tax authorities with detailed financial information such as revenue, income, taxes paid, employment, tangible capital, etc. on a country-by-country basis. As of 2018, over 70 countries have adopted country-by-country reporting, including the U.S.

Subpart F Income and Controlled Foreign Corporations (CFCs)

Consider the following tax strategy. A highly profitable U.S. corporation sets up a wholly owned subsidiary in a tax haven through which it invests its excess funds in passive investments. Is it possible for the U.S. parent to essentially earn tax-free returns, indefinitely, by investing through subsidiaries domiciled in tax havens? Perhaps, but the tax authorities have known about such strategies for a long time and have built up formidable anti-abuse rules, namely the **Subpart F** and **controlled foreign corporation** (**CFC**) rules (and the GILTI rules, discussed later). The Subpart F and CFC provisions are designed to mitigate the tax benefits from forming paper foreign corporations in tax havens to record certain types of income. The rules are complex, but they tend to focus on easily movable income such as dividends, interest, rents, and royalties. In general, these rules work by subjecting Subpart F income to U.S. taxation as if the income was repatriated to the U.S. parent when the income is earned and without being eligible for the participation exemption.

Most foreign subsidiaries of U.S. corporations are classified as CFCs. A CFC is a foreign corporation owned more than 50% in terms of voting power or value by U.S. shareholders. A U.S. shareholder is any U.S. person or entity, including a U.S. corporation, owning at least 10% of the foreign corporation's voting stock.

Congress BEATs the (allegedly) GILTI

While the TCJA enacted significant tax relief with the statutory rate reduction (from 35% to 21%) and the participation exemption (which moved the U.S. closer to territorial taxation), all was not rosy for U.S. multinationals. The U.S. also enacted two important base erosion provisions as part of the TCJA. The first provision, known as global intangible low-tax income (GILTI), establishes a type of minimum tax on foreign income. GILTI creates a new category of income of CFCs, in a manner similar to Subpart F. Despite the word "intangible" in its name, GILTI applies broadly to income of CFCs, not just intangible income. The computation of GILTI is complex, but it applies when the income exceeds a "normal" rate of return equal to 10% of the qualified business asset investment. Generally, there is no U.S. tax on GILTI if it has been subject to foreign tax of 13.1% or more (before 2026). Otherwise, the U.S. tax on GILTI can grow to as much as 10.5% (if the foreign income was otherwise untaxed). The GILTI rules appear to be structured with severity in mind. Foreign tax credits are allowed with respect to GILTI but only up to 80% of the foreign taxes paid. Moreover, they are confined to a separate GILTI basket for FTC limitation purposes, making cross-crediting of high- and low-tax income difficult. Excess foreign tax credits on GILTI income cannot be carried back or carried forward to other years. The GILTI tax is significant, projected to generate approximately $112 billion in tax revenue over 10 years. It is important to note that while the participation exemption in the TCJA pushes the U.S. closer to territorial taxation, the GILTI rules push in the direction of worldwide taxation. For this and other reasons, experts use a variety of terms to describe the current U.S. system for taxing multinational corporations, including a hybrid system, a modified territorial system, or a territorial system with a worldwide minimum tax.

The second provision, the **base erosion and anti-abuse tax (BEAT)** acts a minimum tax on a broad set of payments (e.g., interest, rent, and royalties, but not cost of goods sold) to related foreign affiliates. The BEAT tax is 5% for 2018, 10% for 2019–2025, and 12.5% beyond. The BEAT applies to corporations with average annual gross receipts exceeding $500 million in the past 3 years. A significant tax, the BEAT is expected to generate approximately $150 billion in tax revenue over 10 years, but tax experts are actively working on strategies to mitigate the cost.[10]

Individuals Avoiding U.S. Taxation

A popular misconception is that a U.S. citizen, after making her millions on Wall Street or Silicon Valley, can set up residence in a Caribbean tax haven and live out the rest of her life on the beach, tax-free. Such dreams are as old as income taxation itself. As stated earlier, the United States subjects its citizens to taxation on their worldwide income, even those citizens who have permanently moved out of the country. Neither the foreign earned income exclusion, which exempts moderate amounts of foreign earned income from U.S. taxation, nor the foreign tax credit will help a U.S. citizen shelter passive income abroad. Other tax-reduction tactics include setting up offshore corporations or banks, but anti-abuse rules render most of those techniques ineffective.

Occasionally, wealthy U.S. citizens renounce their citizenship and move to tax havens.[11] Such a move comes with substantial tax and nontax costs, however. Even as a noncitizen, spending too much time in the United States risks triggering what is called the "substantial presence test" and being taxed by the United States on worldwide income. In some cases, persons renouncing their citizenship to avoid U.S. taxes can even be denied entry back into the United States. Moreover, if this person has a U.S. business, the income from the business is still subject to U.S. taxation. The main advantage of giving up U.S. citizenship is the possibility of avoiding U.S. income taxes at the personal level on future capital gains and dividends and U.S. estate taxes upon death. In response to public outrage from press accounts of such activity, every so often Congress strengthens what are known as the expatriation rules. For example, the laws were tightened again in 2008 such that renouncing one's U.S. citizenship can, under certain circumstances, subject the person to a special exit tax. The exit tax is essentially a mark-to-market tax in which the person is deemed to have sold all his or her property for fair market value the day before expatriating.

More common than renouncing one's citizenship is investing through entities organized in other countries, particularly tax havens. High-tax countries like the United States try to mitigate the flight of capital and income through a variety of provisions. Despite the numerous roadblocks put up by the United States, tax havens have attracted large amounts of capital from the United States and from around the world. It was reported that Cayman Islands banks hold $1.5 trillion of deposits and Switzerland banks manage some $4 trillion of assets on behalf of others. In the British Virgin Islands, corporations reportedly outnumber people by more than 30 to 1.[12] Research shows that the most successful tax havens are those that have strong legal systems, stable governments, and respect for property rights.[13]

However, in addition to attracting people and companies interested in legal tax avoidance, some tax havens also attract shady elements.[14] Many tax havens have strong bank secrecy laws and, historically, done little in the way of sharing tax information with other countries. Over time they have increased their information sharing due to pressure from the Organisation for Economic Co-operation and Development (OECD) and individual countries such as the United States. Currently, most tax havens have entered into bilateral Tax Information Exchange Agreements (TIEAs) with at least some other countries. TIEAs provide for sharing of information that can help in tax enforcement, but also have many limitations. One important limitation is that the information exchange usually takes place upon request. To facilitate automatic information exchange, the United States enacted the Foreign Account Tax Compliance Act (FATCA) in 2010, which imposes broader information collection,

---

[10] See R. Rubin, "Companies Hope to Beat a New Tax Called the BEAT," *Wall Street Journal*, June 26, 2018.

[11] See S. Prasso, S. Vallikapen, and J. Drucker, "Facebook's Saverin to Pay Hundreds of Millions in Tax," Bloomberg.com (May 18, 2012). For an older but colorful example, see E. Lesly, "The Darts: Fear, Loathing, and Foam Cups," *Business Week* (July 10, 1995).

[12] See M. Sullivan, "Tax Analysts Offshore Project," *Tax Notes Today* (October 10, 2007), p. 87.

[13] See Slemrod and Wilson (2006); Hines (2005); and Desai et al. (2006b).

[14] See Hanlon, Maydew, and Thornock (2015).

reporting, and withholding requirements on foreign financial institutions that have accounts from U.S. taxpayers. Individual countries have also been active in cracking down on tax evasion by their citizens via tax havens.

For example, the United States has pursued litigation against several large banks for allegedly facilitating tax evasion, obtaining the identities of some of the U.S. taxpayers. During the crackdown, the United States also collected over $11 billion of taxes, penalties, and interest from U.S. taxpayers and over $5 billion in settlements with various financial institutions.[15]

10.5 HOW TAXES AFFECT THE LOCATION AND STRUCTURE OF INVESTMENTS

You might be tempted to suppose that when a foreign country's tax rates are lower than domestic tax rates, the after-tax rates of return on investments should be higher in the foreign country. However, this assumption ignores the real possibility that pretax rates of return in the foreign country may be lower than those available domestically. In countries where the tax rate on income is relatively low, we would expect competition to bid up the price of investing in that country and force down pretax profitability. In other words, the foreign investments may bear *implicit taxes*. In addition, a number of nontax market imperfections may cause pretax returns to vary across countries, including restrictions on the free flow of capital across borders.[16]

For physical investments—factories and the like—firms must consider a variety of nontax costs in their location decisions. For example, despite having a favorable tax system, auto companies are not rushing to build large factories in the Cayman Islands. Possible reasons include a lack of large pools of skilled labor and a lack of infrastructure. Other nontax factors include legal differences across countries (for example, some countries may have lax property rights and inefficient bureaucracies), access to markets (for example, it may help to sell goods in China if you manufacture there), and proximity to customers or suppliers (for example, bottling facilities are typically located near population centers because of the costs of transporting bottled liquids across long distances). With physical investments, taxes often matter on the margin when two or more possible locations are roughly equal on nontax dimensions. Empirical research using large samples of firms has found evidence that cross-country variation in tax rates does affect the location of investment.[17]

To illustrate the role of implicit taxes in investment decisions, suppose that your U.S. corporation has $100 million to invest in one of two mutually exclusive projects, one at home and the other, of equal risk, located in a lower-tax-rate foreign country. Table 10.2 shows the tax rates and the rates of return available on the two projects.

Note from Table 10.2 the 20% − 16% = 4% implicit tax on investing abroad. Marginal dollars invested in the home country earn 20% pretax and 15.8% after a 21% tax. Marginal dollars invested in the foreign subsidiary earn 16% pretax and 13.6% after a 15% local tax. In this case the explicit tax advantage of foreign investment is not large enough to overcome its implicit tax disadvantage, and so domestic investment is favored.

Table 10.2 Tax Rates and Rates of Return to Investing at Home and Abroad

	Tax Rate	*Pretax Return*	*After-Local-Tax Return*
Home	21%	20%	15.8%, or 20%(1 − 21%)
Abroad	15%	16%	13.6%, or 16%(1 − 15%)

[15] See L. Saunders, "The IRS Is Still Coming for You: Offshore Tax Cheats," *Wall Street Journal*, September 14, 2018.

[16] In a nontax world with perfect, frictionless markets, we would expect capital to move freely across borders and prices bid up or down to the point where risk-adjusted expected returns were the same across all assets. Once market imperfections are allowed for, risk-adjusted expected returns could vary across assets and countries, even in the absence of taxation.

[17] See the Additional Readings at the end of the chapter.

Why might an implicit tax arise in investing abroad? As we have said, implicit taxes can arise because the foreign country encourages investment by offering generous tax benefits, and competition for the right to garner these benefits results in lower before-tax rates of return. Nontax factors can also account for some of the observed implicit tax. Low tax rates are typically offered to lure business that would not otherwise be undertaken in the low-tax jurisdiction.

A Tax Holiday for Repatriations

Prior to the reduction in U.S. tax rates and enactment of the participation exemption in 2018, U.S. multinationals accumulated large amounts of cash and other passive assets located in low-tax jurisdictions, consistent with their desire to defer their foreign earnings from being subject to U.S. tax.[18] Congress became concerned that the U.S. Tax Code might be discouraging U.S. firms from bringing cash back to the United States where that cash might improve U.S. capital investment and employment. Acting on these concerns, in 2004 Congress enacted a special tax holiday during which firms could repatriate their foreign earnings at a much lower tax rate than normal. Corporations could choose a onetime repatriation of their foreign earnings, during either 2004 or 2005, but not both, and have those earnings be taxed by the United States at a rate of 5.25%, provided the funds were reinvested in the United States (e.g., through spending on domestic research and development, worker training, capital investments, etc.). Corporations responded by repatriating at least $300 billion in aggregate, although some research suggests that a portion of the funds may have been used to fund stock repurchases, which was a prohibited use of the funds under the tax law.[19]

That holiday came and went, but with one holiday comes the hope of future holidays. In the years since, U.S. multinationals reportedly accumulated, in aggregate, over $1 trillion of earnings in their foreign subsidiaries. Periodically, there were calls for Congress to enact another holiday to free up this "trapped cash" or to enact territorial taxation as a more comprehensive solution. The TCJA was, in part, designed to address the trapped cash problem by moving the U.S. closer to territorial taxation via the participation exemption.

It is important to note that there were some common misconceptions about the trapped cash issue. Although the tax on repatriations may have led to increased cash holdings in the foreign subsidiaries, the earnings were not always held in the form of cash. To understand this, think back to your first financial accounting course, where you learned the difference between cash (an asset account) and retained earnings (an equity account). Despite this distinction, it is still true that foreign subsidiaries of U.S. multinationals did hold large amounts of cash and short-term investments.

Inversion Transactions

What is the optimal tax jurisdiction for the parent company? What happens if a parent company begins in one jurisdiction, say the United States, but later it becomes clear that for tax purposes there are better options out there? Prior to 2018, the United States had relatively high corporate tax rates and a worldwide tax system, so that a U.S.-based multinational would find its worldwide income, including that of its foreign subsidiaries, eventually subject to U.S. corporate taxation. In contrast, most other developed countries had moved toward territorial taxation. Under territorial taxation, the country taxes income earned within its borders, but does not attempt to tax active income that was earned in other countries. Another important trend is that most other developed nations reduced their corporate tax rates to below the U.S. corporate tax rate. Finally, there were and are tax-haven jurisdictions that impose little or no income tax. In these respects, many experts believed that U.S.-based multinationals were often disadvantaged for tax purposes compared with otherwise similar multinationals based in other countries.

This disparity caused the management of some U.S. multinationals to consider restructuring their corporate group so that the parent company would be incorporated in a more favorable tax jurisdiction. A common form of this restructuring, known as an inversion transaction, involves placing the former U.S. parent corporation under a newly created foreign parent corporation in a more favorable

[18] See C. F. Foley, J. Hartzell, S. Titman, and G. Twite, 2007, "Why Do Firms Hold So Much Cash? A Tax-Based Explanation," *Journal of Financial Economics* (86), pp. 579–607.

[19] See Blouin and Krull (2009).

tax jurisdiction. In certain respects, an inversion is the corporate equivalent of tax-motivated expatriations by individuals. While they were controversial, inversions could be thought of as do-it-yourself territorial taxation. There were two main tax benefits to an inversion. First, the foreign income of the multinational firm was no longer subject to taxation by the United States at the corporate level. The firm still paid U.S. tax on its U.S. income, however. Second, an inversion increased the tax incentive to engage in income shifting from high-tax to low-tax jurisdictions, such as by locating intercompany debt in a tax haven to achieve "interest stripping" of income into the tax haven. A similar principle held for royalties on intangible assets.[20]

An early transaction that serves as a useful example involved Helen of Troy, which makes personal care products. The public shareholders of Helen of Troy transferred their stock to a newly formed Bermuda corporation. The exchange qualified as a nontaxable exchange under Sections 351 and 368(a)(1)(B).[21] The transaction effectively moved a large portion of the corporation's income out of the U.S. tax base and into a country that has no corporate income tax (see **Figure 10.3**). The IRS and Treasury became concerned that the Helen of Troy transaction could be the first of many U.S. multinational departures. To prevent an exodus, the IRS ultimately issued a set of regulations under Section 367 known as the "anti-inversion regulations" that govern the application of what is sometimes referred to as the Section 367 "toll charge." These regulations generally prevent outbound mergers and stock transfers from qualifying for tax-free treatment unless the shareholders of the transferred U.S. corporation receive less than 50% of the shares of the foreign acquiring corporation in the transaction. In other words, an outbound merger may still be accomplished tax free if the foreign acquirer is larger than the U.S. target corporation. However, the transaction generally will be taxable (the Section 367 "toll charge") to the corporate shareholders if the foreign acquirer is the smaller corporation or is merely a new holding company.

FIGURE 10.3 Example of a Pre-2018 Inversion Transaction

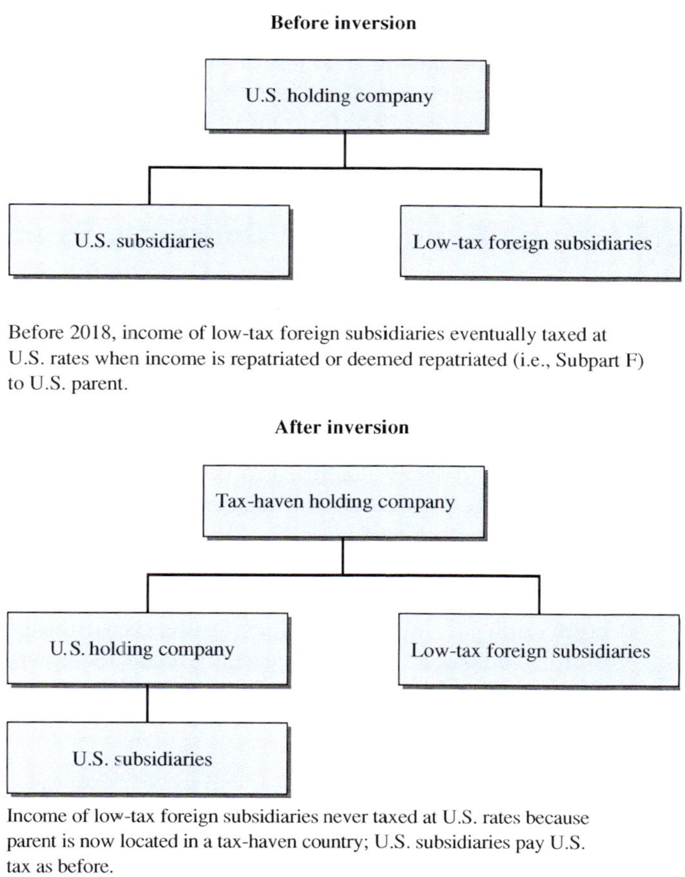

[20] See Cloyd, Mills, and Weaver (2003); Seida and Wempe (2002); and Desai and Hines (2002).

[21] Helen of Troy Limited, Prospectus/Proxy Statement, dated January 5, 1994.

In 2004, Congress tightened the anti-inversion rules further by enacting Sec. 7874. Under Sec. 7874, there are two ownership thresholds that can trigger adverse tax consequences. The ownership thresholds look at who winds up owning the foreign acquirer of the U.S. corporation. If shareholders of the U.S. corporation receive 80% or more of the vote or value of the foreign acquirer, then the United States will consider the foreign acquirer to be a U.S. corporation and thus subject to U.S. taxation on its worldwide income. If shareholders of the U.S. corporation receive at least 60% but less than 80% of the foreign corporation, then the consequences are less severe but still problematic. There is an exception, however, if the foreign corporation has substantial business activities in its country of incorporation. What constitutes a substantial business activity is not always clear, and the Treasury has issued different regulations since 2004. In 2012 the regulations established a bright-line where substantial business activity requires at least 25% of its employees, assets, and income to be in that foreign country.

The anti-inversion regulations did not completely stop corporations from migrating out of the United States. In some cases, prior to 2004, U.S. corporations simply moved to foreign jurisdictions in taxable transactions, creating a higher up-front tax cost to their shareholders that is presumably offset by lower corporate-level taxes for the indefinite future.[22] After 2004, inversions tended to be to developed countries where it was possible to have substantial business activity, such as the U.K., Switzerland, or the Netherlands. In some cases, companies have split off their non-U.S. operations into a separate company. Some experts argue that a consequence of the anti-inversion regulations is to complicate cross-border mergers of U.S. and foreign corporations, even when the acquirer is from another developed country and nontax motivations are the driving force behind the merger.[23]

Much of the motivation for inversions seems to have been mitigated by the 2018 reduction in corporate tax rates and move towards territorial taxation by the participation exemption, and Congress has included more provisions to discourage inversions. However, some experts believe there are still circumstances in which inversions could benefit the firm, particularly to avoid the GILTI rules, which acts as a minimum tax on foreign income of U.S. multinationals.[24]

It is important to note that even if the anti-inversion rules are successful at preventing existing U.S. firms from relocating their parent entities to countries with more favorable tax systems, they cannot prevent business activity (e.g., sales) from going to firms already located in countries with more favorable taxation.

Attempts to Encourage Exports and Domestic Production

The United States has a long history of enacting tax provisions designed to encourage exports and domestic production, dating back to (at least) the Domestic International Sales Corporation (DISC) rules, which were replaced in 1985 by foreign sales corporation (FSC) rules. The European Union (EU) asserted that under international trading agreements, the FSC rules were an illegal export subsidiary, and ultimately the World Trade Organization (WTO) agreed with the EU. In response, Congress replaced the FSC rules in 2000 with a provision that excluded from taxation certain extraterritorial income (ETI). The ETI provisions were also ruled to be illegal export subsidies by the WTO, so in 2004 Congress repealed the ETI provisions and enacted a deduction for qualified domestic production. The domestic production activities deduction (DPAD) provided taxpayers with a deduction equal to a percentage of a wide range of domestic production activities (e.g., manufacturing, construction, extraction of natural resources). Congress repealed the DPAD as of 2018 and replaced it with a new export and production incentive called **foreign-derived intangible income (FDII)**. While complicated, the FDII rules reduce the tax rate on certain export income from sales of property or services to below the 21% rate that would otherwise apply. The export income that is eligible for

[22] See, for example, ADT Ltd. Joint Proxy Statement/Prospectus, dated January 3, 1997, describing the Tyco International Ltd. Merger with Bermuda-based ADT; Fruit-of-the-Loom Ltd. Joint Proxy Statement/Prospectus, dated October 15, 1998, describing merger into new Cayman Islands holding company.

[23] In some cases firms have asked for and received private letter rulings from the IRS concluding that the anti-inversion regulations would not apply. See, for example, PLR 9849014 (Chrysler/Daimler-Benz) and PLR 199929039 (AirTouch/Vodafone).

[24] Indeed, in March 2018 the *Wall Street Journal* reported that Toledo-based auto parts supplier Dana Inc. was considering moving its corporate address to the U.K. for tax purposes. C. Dawson and T. Francis, "Despite U.S. Tax Overhaul, Ohio-Based Dana Considers a Move Abroad," *Wall Street Journal*, March 9, 2018.

the lower tax rate is the portion that exceeds a "normal" return on investment, defined as 10% of the tax basis of qualified business asset investment. Some experts believe that, as with preceding export incentives, FDII will be challenged as a violation of international trade agreements.

10.6 U.S. TAX TREATMENT OF FOREIGN INVESTORS

The market for capital is competitive, and it is common for countries to tax foreign investors favorably to attract foreign capital. For example, foreign investors who own U.S. government debt or securities of U.S. corporations are generally not subject to normal U.S. income tax. Instead, the United States subjects such investments to **withholding taxes** at rates varying from 0% to 30%. Withholding taxes are generally levied on payments of dividends, interest, rents, and royalties. To encourage foreigners to make deposits in U.S. banks and to invest in U.S. Treasury bills, notes, and bonds, most interest income from those investments received by foreign investors is subject to a 0% withholding tax. Capital gains on the sale or exchange of U.S. capital assets are typically not subject to U.S. taxation. An exception is gains on the sale of ownership interests in U.S. real property. When withholding rates do apply, they are often reduced through **bilateral tax treaties** with other nations. Most countries have withholding taxes. Companies and sophisticated investors sometimes attempt to route dividends and the like through countries that have favorable tax treaties, a practice known as **treaty shopping**.

U.S. subsidiaries of foreign corporations are subject to U.S. taxation like any other U.S. corporation. When a U.S. subsidiary repatriates its income to its foreign parent, however, it also faces a withholding tax on the dividend payment. Sometimes foreign corporations do business in the United States without setting up a U.S. corporation—that is, they conduct business through a branch operation. In that case, the foreign corporation is subject to U.S. taxation on its "income effectively connected with a U.S. trade or business." To tax U.S. subsidiaries and U.S. branches of foreign corporations on an equal basis, the United States also levies a **branch profits tax** of up to 30% on the "dividend equivalent amount" of U.S. branches of foreign corporations. Branch profits taxes are common in other countries as well and, as with withholding taxes, may be reduced through tax treaties.

The United States has income tax treaties with over 60 countries, including most major trading partners. However, that still leaves many countries without a U.S. tax treaty. There are some countries with wealthy foreign investors (such as Kuwait) that have no tax treaty with the United States. Consider a wealthy foreign investor from a nontreaty country who wants to invest in the U.S. equity markets but is not enamored with the prospects of a 30% withholding tax on dividends and does not want to restrict his investing to non-dividend-paying stocks. What can the investor do? The specific methods are beyond the scope of this text and continue to evolve over time as they are challenged by the tax authorities. In general, investors have used a variety of strategies involving derivative securities. For example, one strategy has been to invest in U.S. equities indirectly through the use of synthetic securities, such as buying U.S. Treasury bonds and entering into a cash-settlement forward contract to purchase the desired equity security from an investment bank. Others have entered into total return swaps with investors in the country in which the client wants to invest. Which method, if any, foreign investors use to avoid withholding taxes depends on the nontax costs of each strategy, in particular the transactions costs and the tax risks of the various strategies. However, as transactions costs continue to fall over time with decreasing costs of computing and communications, repackaging cash flows for tax purposes becomes more and more feasible. The proliferation of financial innovation continues to pose great challenges for the taxing authorities, particularly in taxes on income from financial assets, which can be easily repackaged using derivatives.

Summary of Key Points

1. Generally, countries choose between two different tax regimes to tax the income earned by multinational businesses. Worldwide taxation subjects the worldwide income of resident companies to tax, whereas territorial taxation subjects only domestic income to tax. Most countries have tax systems that are somewhere in between the two ends of the spectrum. The general trend over time has been for countries to move away from worldwide taxation towards territorial taxation.

2. Two provisions to mitigate or eliminate U.S. tax on foreign income are the participation exemption and the foreign tax credit. The participation exemption allows for a 100% dividends received deduction for certain dividends from foreign subsidiaries of U.S. corporations. The foreign tax credit allows for certain foreign taxes paid to be creditable against the U.S. tax liability. There are important limitations on both.
3. U.S. multinationals can structure their foreign operations as branches or subsidiaries. Income from foreign branches is taxable in the United States as it is earned. In contrast, income from foreign subsidiaries is generally deferred from U.S. taxation until it is repatriated, with important exceptions.
4. Countries around the world have struggled to contain what is called "base erosion." Base erosion strategies shift income from one country to another, usually from a high-tax country to a low-tax country. The U.S. has a number of provisions designed to mitigate base erosion, including regulations on transfer pricing, requiring country-by-country reporting, Subpart F rules, and special taxes called base erosion and anti-abuse tax (BEAT) and global intangible low-tax income (GILTI).
5. Companies sometimes restructure so that the parent company is incorporated in a more favorable tax jurisdiction. An inversion transaction involves placing the former U.S. parent corporation under a newly created foreign parent corporation in a more favorable tax jurisdiction. There are many rules designed to deter U.S. companies from inverting.
6. The U.S. has a long history of enacting tax provisions to encourage exports and domestic production. The most recent such provision is known as foreign-derived intangible income (FDII), and taxes certain export income at a reduced tax rate.
7. Foreign investors are subject to withholding taxes on income from passive investments such as dividends and interest. Withholding taxes are often reduced under tax treaties.

Questions

Q10-1. Why do countries with worldwide tax systems give foreign tax credits?

Q10-2. In principle, countries can band together to create uniform tax laws to ensure that each dollar of income is taxed once and only once. What are the costs and benefits of such uniformity from the perspective of lawmakers?

Q10-3. Can U.S. citizens avoid paying taxes to the United States by living and working abroad?

Q10-4. Consider a wealthy U.S. citizen who earns $1.3 million per year in dividends and capital gains from her portfolio of U.S. stocks. Can she legally avoid having this income subject to U.S. tax by forming an offshore holding company and having the holding company own the stock? She has her holding company reinvest the dividends and capital gains, so she personally receives no cash from her investments.

Q10-5. What are the tax differences between operating as a foreign branch and a foreign subsidiary of a U.S. corporation? What are the advantages and disadvantages of each form?

Q10-6. Why do U.S. multinationals generally like the "check-the-box" regulations?

Q10-7. What is the participation exemption?

Q10-8. What are the foreign tax credit limitations and why do they exist?

Q10-9. Under what conditions will foreign tax credits result in a U.S. corporation paying exactly the same tax on foreign income as it would if this income were earned directly in the United States?

Q10-10. What is Subpart F income?

Q10-11. Do low tax rates in a foreign country imply that expected after-tax rates of return on marginal investments should be higher than those on domestic investments? Explain.

Q10-12. What is "base erosion" and what provisions has the U.S. enacted to mitigate it?

Exercises

Unless otherwise stated, for all problems and exercises assume that the foreign entities are corporations and are treated as such for U.S. purposes under the check-the-box regulations. The foreign tax rates in these problems and exercises are assumed tax rates for pedagogical purposes, not the actual current tax rates.

E10-13. California Graphics is a U.S. corporation with $200 million of U.S.-source income and $10 million of foreign-source income. In addition, California Graphics has three-quarters ownership of a Canadian partnership that has total pretax income of $30 million, all of which are Canadian-source income and subject to a 40% Canadian tax rate. The Canadian partnership repatriates $5 million back to California Graphics in the current year. For U.S. purposes, California Graphics treats the Canadian partnership as a partnership under the check-the-box regulations.

a. How much taxable income will California Graphics report on its U.S. tax return?

b. Suppose that, instead of treating the Canadian partnership as a partnership, California Graphics elects to treat it as a corporation for U.S. purposes. How much taxable income will California Graphics report on its U.S. tax return?

E10-14. Michigan Motors is a U.S. corporation with $1 billion of U.S.-source income. In addition, Michigan Motors owns 60% of Detroit Parts, a U.S. corporation with a total of $200 million of U.S.-source income, and 100% of Air Paris, a French corporation that has $500 million of French-source income. Neither Detroit Parts nor Air Paris repatriated any earnings in the current year. Assume no book tax differences except those caused by differences in consolidation requirements.

a. How much GAAP income will Michigan Motors report on its consolidated income statement?

b. How much taxable income will Michigan Motors report on its U.S. tax return?

E10-15. Hawkeye Networks is a U.S. corporation with $20 million of U.S. source income and no foreign-source income of its own. Hawkeye Networks has wholly owned subsidiaries in Korea and Singapore. The Korean subsidiary has $43 million of pretax Korean-source income, faces a 40% Korean tax rate, and pays a $10 million dividend to Hawkeye Networks. The Singapore subsidiary has $7 million of pretax Singapore-source income, faces a 25% Singapore tax rate, and pays a $2 million dividend to Hawkeye.

a. How much taxable income will Hawkeye Networks report on its U.S. tax return? Assume repatriation of income from the foreign subsidiaries will qualify for the participation exemption for U.S. purposes.

b. Now suppose the Singapore subsidiary's income is Subpart F income. How much taxable income will Hawkeye Networks report on its U.S. tax return? Assume Hawkeye will take foreign tax credits for foreign taxes paid rather than deducting foreign taxes.

E10-16. Intrepid Industries is a U.S. corporation with $30 million of U.S.-source pretax income and an Argentinian branch that has $10 million of pretax income, which is subject to an Argentinian tax rate of 30%. The U.S. corporate tax rate is 21%.

a. How much taxable income will Intrepid Industries report on its U.S. tax return?

b. How much U.S. tax, after taking into account foreign tax credits, will Intrepid have to pay? What will its effective tax rate be (worldwide taxes divided by worldwide pretax income)?

c. Now assume that in addition to the Argentinian branch, Intrepid also has a Canadian branch with $20 million of pretax income, subject to a 15% Canadian tax. How much U.S. tax, after taking into account foreign tax credits, will Intrepid have to pay? What will its effective tax rate be?

E10-17. Bloomington Pharmaceuticals is a U.S. corporation considering where to locate a new manufacturing facility. It is choosing between a location in the U.S., Ireland, or Mexico. If Ireland or Mexico, the facility will be owned and operated by a wholly owned foreign subsidiary of Bloomington Pharmaceuticals incorporated in the country where the facility is located. Assume subsequent repatriation of income from the foreign subsidiaries will qualify for the participation exemption for U.S. purposes. The pretax returns and local tax rates are as follows:

	Tax rate	Pretax return
U.S.	21%	20%
Ireland	10%	18%
Mexico	15%	18%

What would Bloomington's after-tax return be in each of the three locations, after considering both U.S. and foreign taxes?

E10-18. Illinois Steel is a specialty steel manufacturer that does business in the United States, Canada, and Brazil. Illinois Steel is organized as follows. The parent, Illinois Steel, is incorporated in Illinois and had pretax income from its U.S. operations of $5 million. Illinois Steel has a Brazilian branch, which reported pretax income of $3 million. Illinois Steel also has a Canadian branch, which recorded pretax income of $10 million. Assume the tax rates in the countries are United States, 21%; Canada, 15%; Brazil, 34%. What is Illinois Steel's U.S. tax liability after foreign tax credits?

References and Additional Readings

Albring, S., L. Mills, and K. Newberry, 2011. "Do Debt Constraints Influence Firms' Sensitivity to a Temporary Tax Holiday on Repatriations?" *Journal of the American Taxation Association* (33), pp. 1–27.

Altshuler, R., and H. Grubert, 2008. "Corporate Taxes in the World Economy: Reforming the Taxation of Cross-Border Income," *Fundamental Tax Reform: Issues, Choices, and Implications*, edited by J. Diamon and G. Zodrow. Cambridge, MA: MIT Press, pp. 319–355.

Bird, A., A. Edwards, and T. Shevlin, 2017. "Does U.S. Foreign Earnings Lockout Advantage Foreign Acquirers?" *Journal of Accounting and Economics* 64(1): pp. 150–166.

Blouin, J., 2011. "Taxation of Multinational Corporations," *Foundations and Trends in Accounting* (6), pp. 1–64.

Blouin, J., L. Hail, and M. Yetman, 2009. "Capital Gains Taxes, Pricing Spreads and Arbitrage: Evidence from Cross-Listed Firms in the U.S.," *The Accounting Review* (84), pp. 1321–1361.

Blouin, J., and L. Krull, 2009. "Bringing It Home: A Study of the Incentives Surrounding the Repatriation of Foreign Earnings Under the American Jobs Creation Act of 2004," *Journal of Accounting Research* (47), pp. 1027–1057.

Blouin, J., L. Krull, and L. Robinson, 2012. "Is U.S. Multinational Intra-Firm Dividend Policy Influence by Reporting Incentives?" *The Accounting Review* (87), pp. 1463–1491.

Clausing, K., 2005. "Tax Holidays (and Other Escapes) in the American Jobs Creation Act," *National Tax Journal* (58), pp. 331–346.

Clausing, K., 2009. "Multinational Firm Tax Avoidance and Tax Policy." *National Tax Journal* (62), pp. 703–725.

Cloyd, C., L. Mills, and C. Weaver, 2003. "Firm Valuation Effects of the Expatriation of U.S. Corporations to Tax Haven Countries," *Journal of the American Taxation Association* (25), pp. 87–105.

Collins, J., D. Kemsley, and M. Lang, 1997. "Cross-Jurisdictional Income Shifting and Earnings Valuation," *Journal of Accounting Research* (36), pp. 209–229.

Collins, J., D. Kemsley, and D. Shackelford, 1997. "Transfer Pricing and the Persistent Zero Taxable Income of Foreign-Controlled U.S. Corporations," *Journal of the American Taxation Association* (Supplement), pp. 68–83.

Collins, J., and D. Shackelford, 1992. "Foreign Tax Credit Limitations and Preferred Stock Issuances," *Journal of Accounting Research* (Supplement), pp. 103–124.

Collins, J., and D. Shackelford, 2003. "Do U.S. Multinationals Face Different Tax Burdens Than Other Companies?" *Tax Policy and the Economy,* Vol. 17, edited by J. Poterba, Cambridge, MA: MIT Press, pp. 141–168.

Desai, M., C. F. Foley, and J. Hines, 2006a. "The Demand for Tax Haven Operations," *Journal of Public Economics* (90), pp. 513–531.

Desai, M., C. F. Foley, and J. Hines, 2006b. "Do Tax Havens Divert Economic Activity?" *Economics Letters* (90) pp. 219–224.

Desai, M., and J. Hines, 2002. "Expectations and Expatriations: Tracing the Causes and Consequences of Corporate Inversions," *National Tax Journal* (55), pp. 409–441.

De Simone, L., 2016. "Does a Common Set of Accounting Standards Affect Tax-Motivated Income Shifting for Multinational Firms?" *Journal of Accounting and Economics* (61): pp. 145–165.

De Simone, L., K. Klassen, and J. K. Seidman, 2017. "Unprofitable Affiliates and Income Shifting Behavior." *The Accounting Review,* (92): pp. 113–136.

Devereux, M., and H. Freeman, 1995. "The Impact of Tax on Foreign Direct Investment: Empirical Evidence and the Implication for Tax Integration Schemes," *International Tax and Public Finance* (2), pp. 85–106.

Dharmapala, D., C. Foley, and K. Forbes, 2011. "Watch What I Do, Not What I Say: The Unintended Consequences of the Homeland Investment Act," *Journal of Finance* (66), 753–788.

Dharmapala, D., and J. Hines, 2009. "Which Countries Become Tax Havens?" *Journal of Public Economics* (93), pp. 1058–1068.

Dyreng, S., M. Hanlon, E. Maydew, and J. Thornock, 2017. "Changes in Corporate Effective Tax Rates over the Past Twenty-Five Years," *Journal of Financial Economics* (124), pp. 441–463.

Dyreng, S., J. Hoopes, and J. Wilde, 2016. "Public Pressure and Corporate Tax Behavior," *Journal of Accounting Research* 54(1): pp. 147–186.

Dyreng, S., and B. Lindsey, 2009. "Using Financial Statement Accounting Data to Examine the Effect of Foreign Operations Locating in Tax Havens and Other Countries on U.S. Multinational Firms' Tax Rates." *Journal of Accounting Research* (47), pp. 1283–1316.

Dyreng, S. D., and K. S. Markle, 2016. "The Effect of Financial Constraints on Income Shifting by U.S. Multinationals," *The Accounting Review*, 91(6), pp. 1601–1627.

Edwards, A., T. Kravet, and R. Wilson, 2016. "Trapped Cash and the Profitability of Foreign Acquisitions," *Contemporary Accounting Research* (33), pp. 44–77.

Foley, C. F., J. Hartzell, S. Titman, and G. Twite, 2007. "Why Do Firms Hold So Much Cash? A

Tax-Based Explanation," *Journal of Financial Economics* (86), pp. 597–607.

Graham, J., M. Hanlon, and T. Shevlin, 2011. "Real Effects of Accounting Rules: Evidence from Multinational Firms' Investment Location and Profit Repatriation Decisions." *Journal of Accounting Research* (49), pp. 137–185.

Grubert, H., T. Goodspeed, and D. Swenson, 1993. "Explaining the Low Taxable Income of Foreign-Controlled Companies in the U.S.," in *Studies in International Taxation,* edited by A. Giovannini, R. G. Hubbard, and J. Slemrod. Chicago: University of Chicago Press.

Hanlon, M., R. Lester and R. Verdi. 2015. "The Effect of Repatriation Tax Costs on U.S. Multinational Investment," *Journal of Financial Economics* 116(1): pp. 179–196.

Hanlon, M., and E. Maydew, 2009. "Book-Tax Conformity: Implications for Multinational Firms," *National Tax Journal* (62), pp. 127–153.

Hanlon, M., E. Maydew, and J. Thornock, 2015. "Taking the Long Way Home: U.S. Tax Evasion and Offshore Investments in U.S. Equity and Debt Markets," *Journal of Finance,* (70), 257–287.

Harris, D., 1993. "The Impact of U.S. Tax Law Revision on Multinational Corporations' Capital Location and Income Shifting Decisions," *Journal of Accounting Research* (Supplement), pp. 111–140.

Harris, D., R. Morck, J. Slemrod, and B. Yeung, 1993. "Income Shifting in U.S. Multinational Corporations," in *Studies in International Taxation,* edited by A. Giovannini, R. G. Hubbard, and J. Slemrod. Chicago: University of Chicago Press.

Hartman, D., 1985. "Tax Policy and Foreign Direct Investment," *Journal of Public Economics* (26), pp. 475–487.

Hasegawa, M., J. Hoopes, R. Ishida, and J. Slemrod, 2013. "The Effect of Public Disclosure on Reported Taxable Income: Evidence from Individuals and Corporations in Japan," *National Tax Journal* 66(3): pp. 571–608.

Hines, J., 1996. "Dividends and Profits: Some Unsubtle Foreign Influences," *Journal of Finance* (51), pp. 661–689.

Hines, J., 1997. "Tax Policy and the Activities of Multinational Corporations," in *Fiscal Policy: Lessons from Economic Research,* edited by A. Auerbach. Cambridge, MA: MIT Press, pp. 401–445.

Hines, J., 2005. "Do Tax Havens Flourish?" in *Tax Policy and the Economy*, Vol. 19, edited by J. Poterba. Cambridge, MA: MIT Press.

Hines, J., and E. Rice, 1994. "Fiscal Paradise: Foreign Tax Havens and American Business," *Quarterly Journal of Economics* (109). pp. 149–182.

Hoopes, J., L. Robinson, and J. Slemrod, 2018. "Public Tax-Return Disclosure," Forthcoming. *Journal of Accounting and Economics* 66(1).

Huizinga, H., and L. Laeven, 2008. "International Profit Shifting within Multinationals: A Multi-Country Perspective," *Journal of Public Economics* (92), pp. 1164–1182.

Jacob, J., 1996. "Taxes and Transfer Pricing: Income Shifting and the Volume of Intra-Firm Transfers," *Journal of Accounting Research* (34), pp. 301–312.

Klassen, K., M. Lang, and M. Wolfson, 1993. "Geographic Income Shifting by Multinational Corporations in Response to Tax Rate Changes," *Journal of Accounting Research* (Supplement), pp. 141–173.

Klassen, K., and S. Laplante, 2012. "The Effect of Foreign Reinvestment and Financial Reporting Incentives on Cross-Jurisdictional Income Shifting," *Contemporary Accounting Research,* (29), pp. 928–955.

Klassen, K., Lisowsky, P., and Mescall, D., 2017. "Transfer Pricing: Strategies, Practices, and Tax Minimization," *Contemporary Accounting Research* 34 (1): pp. 455–493.

Kleinbard, E., 2011a. "Stateless Income," *Florida Tax Review* (699), pp. 699–704.

Kleinbard, E., 2011b. "The Lessons of Stateless Income," *Tax Law Review* (65), pp. 99–171.

Markle, K. S., 2015. "A Comparison of the Tax-Motivated Income Shifting of Multinationals in Territorial and Worldwide Countries," *Contemporary Accounting Research*, doi: 10.1111/1911-3846.12148.

Markle, K., and D. Shackelford, 2012. "Cross-Country Comparisons of Corporate Income Taxes," *National Tax Journal* (65), pp. 493–527.

Markle, K. S., and D. A. Shackleford, 2014. "The Impact of Headquarter and Subsidiary Locations on Multinationals' Effective Tax Rates," *Tax Policy and the Economy/National Bureau of Economic Research*, (28), pp. 33–62.

Markle, K. S., D. A. Shackelford, S. D. Dyreng, and B. P. Lindsey, 2015. "The Effect of Tax and Nontax Country Characteristics on the Global Equity Supply Chains of U.S. Multinationals," *Journal of Accounting and Economics*, 59(2-3), pp. 182–202.

Mills, L., and K. Newberry, 2004. "Do Foreign Multinationals' Tax Incentives Influence Their U.S. Income Reporting and Debt Policy?" *National Tax Journal* (57), pp. 89–107.

Nessa, M., 2017. "Repatriation Tax Costs and U.S. Multinational Companies' Shareholder Payouts," *The Accounting Review*, 92(4): pp. 217–241.

Newberry, K., 1998. "Foreign Tax Credit Limitations and Capital Structure Decisions," *Journal of Accounting Research* (36), pp. 157–166.

Rego, S., 2003. "Tax-Avoidance Activities of U.S. Multinational Corporations." *Contemporary Accounting Research* (20), pp. 805–833.

Seida, J., and W. Wempe, 2002. "Market Reaction to Corporate Inversion Transactions," *Tax Notes* (97), pp. 1098–1102.

Seida, J., and R. Yetman, 2003. "Business Purpose/Profit Motive: Compaq's Purchase and Sale of Shell Common Stock," in *Cases in Tax Strategy,* 3rd ed., edited by M. Erickson. Boston: Pearson Custom Publishing.

Slemrod, J., 2010. "Location, (Real) Location, and Tax (Location): An Essay on the Place of Mobility in Optimal Taxation," *National Tax Journal* (63), pp. 843–864.

Slemrod, J., and J. Wilson, 2009. "Tax Competition with Parasitic Tax Havens," *Journal of Public Economics* (39), pp. 1261–1270.

11

Introduction to Mergers, Acquisitions, and Divestitures

After completing this chapter, you should be able to

1. Understand the basic types of taxable acquisitions of freestanding C corporations.
2. Understand the basic types of tax-free acquisitions of freestanding C corporations.
3. Describe the basic options available to divest a portion of a corporation.
4. Explain the major tax implications of various acquisition and divestiture methods.
5. Describe major nontax issues associated with acquisition and divestiture methods.
6. Realize when goodwill is tax deductible and when it is not tax deductible.

This chapter[1] is the first in a series on mergers, acquisitions, and divestitures. This chapter provides an overview of the economics of corporate reorganizations from the tax planner's vantage point. The next chapter concentrates on taxable acquisitions, where a freestanding C corporation's stock or assets are purchased by another corporation. Included in Chapter 13 is an analysis of taxable acquisitions of S corporations, a conduit-type entity. The fourth chapter in the series concentrates on tax-free acquisitions of freestanding C corporations. Such mergers and acquisitions may be effected without either a change in the basis of assets inside the corporation *or* an immediate tax on target shareholders. Chapter 14 also considers the effects of an acquisition on a corporation's tax attributes, such as net operating loss carryforwards (NOLs). Chapter 15 analyzes various divestiture techniques, including spin-offs, equity carve-outs, and subsidiary sales.[2] Throughout the latter three chapters in this series, we focus on the tax and nontax costs and benefits of various acquisition and divestiture structures. We also provide a rigorous introduction to the most salient tax rules and regulations associated with mergers, acquisitions, and divestitures in each chapter. We do so because, in our opinion, without such knowledge you will be unable to take full advantage of the tax-planning framework we have used to build this text.

---

[1] Chapters 11 to 15 are based in large part on three research papers: M. Erickson, "The Effect of Taxes on the Structure of Corporate Acquisitions," *Journal of Accounting Research* (Autumn 1998); M. Erickson and S. Wang, "The Effect of Transaction Structure on Price: Evidence from Subsidiary Sales," *Journal of Accounting and Economics* (August 2000); and "Tax Benefits as a Source of merger premiums in Acquisitions of Privately Held Corporations," *The Accounting Review* (March 2007). The writings of Martin Ginsburg and Jack Levin, notably their *Mergers, Acquisitions and Buyouts* texts (Aspen Publishers, 1999, 2001, 2007), also had a significant impact on these chapters.

[2] In a Spin-Off, the divesting firm is separated into two entities in a tax-free transaction. An equity carve-out is the sale of the stock of a subsidiary by a parent corporation. Equity carve-outs are also referred to as subsidiary initial public offerings (IPOs). In a subsidiary sale, the divesting firm sells the stock or assets of a subsidiary to an acquirer, typically for cash.

11.1 OVERVIEW OF ISSUES

What drives mergers, acquisitions, and divestitures? What are the major types of mergers, acquisitions, and divestitures? In this section, we provide answers to both questions.

Reasons for Mergers, Acquisitions, and Divestitures

At least three broad reasons can be given for acquisitions: (1) to improve economic efficiency, (2) to extend the power base of management, and (3) to effect transfers of wealth from one class of stakeholders to another. In the camp that stresses the improvement of economic efficiency, the arguments typically refer to the advantages of integration to achieve economies of scale and/or scope and gains that result from removing inefficient management.

The second camp stresses that many acquisitions stem from managerial demand for power, larger salaries, and job security, or more broadly, management self-interest triumphs over the interest of society. This argument arises particularly often in explaining conglomerate mergers, which proliferated in the second half of the 1960s. Because of this alleged self-interest, management wastes corporate resources acquiring other firms.

The third camp emphasizes how a change in corporate control can cause a transfer of some of the wealth of target corporation bondholders, employees, and other stakeholders to target shareholders. One way to accomplish such a wealth transfer is to increase leverage, thereby increasing the risk of default to creditors, such as bondholders, bank lenders, and employees who have been promised certain unfunded benefits, such as postretirement health care, without increasing the level of promised payments. The wealth transfer may be also accomplished by canceling unwritten promises to employees, suppliers, customers, or the community to provide certain future benefits for which the firm has already received economic consideration.[3]

In a variation on this theme, some in the academic research community and in the financial press have argued that mergers and acquisitions are motivated by a desire to transfer wealth from stockholders, creditors, and employees to the investment banking community. Investment banking fees in a large deal can easily run into the tens of millions of dollars. These fees, however, remain a small fraction of the value of the assets restructured, and are small relative to the typical merger premium that target shareholders enjoy when a purchaser buys them out.

Firms are motivated to divest for several reasons. The financial press typically argues that divestitures allow management to focus on core competencies. For this reason, the market typically views such divestitures as wealth-increasing for divesting parent shareholders. Others in academia and the financial press argue that a divestiture, particularly a spin-off, frees managers of the divested business to focus on the divested firm. Divesting parent managers occasionally motivate these divestitures with claims of market mispricing. Specifically, management or investment bankers claim that a particular segment of a firm's business is adversely affecting the pricing of the entire concern. Some financial analysts believe that divestitures solve this mispricing. Finally, management and financial analysts argue that greater access to capital markets motivates some corporate restructuring transactions.

Types of Mergers, Acquisitions, and Divestitures[4]

Acquisitions of freestanding companies can be structured to be taxable or tax free. The status of a transaction (taxable or tax free) defines the tax treatment of the transaction for the target's shareholders. Generally, the tax status of an acquisition is determined by whether the acquirer uses cash or

[3] For example, canceling a labor contract favorable to employees results in a wealth transfer to the owners of the company. Selling a factory that received special tax benefits at the time it was built transfers those benefits to the seller (target shareholders). These topics are covered in detail in many corporate finance textbooks.

[4] The terms *merger* and *acquisition* are used synonymously. Some types of divestitures are also accurately referred to as acquisitions by the acquiring firm. For example, the sale of a subsidiary is a divestiture to the divesting parent firm at the same time that it is an acquisition by the acquiring firm. We do not distinguish between mergers and acquisitions in this text. We do distinguish between the tax treatments used in various types of transactions, however. You should focus on the tax structures we discuss and not the common names applied to the transactions.

stock to acquire the target. When the acquirer uses mostly stock, the transaction is usually tax free. "Tax free" is a misnomer; these transactions merely provide tax deferral until the stock received is sold for cash. Conversely, when cash is used to acquire the target firm, the deal is taxable.

A freestanding company can acquire other freestanding companies, such as happened in the Disney/LucasFilm merger, or it can acquire a subsidiary of another company, for example, when Lockheed acquired Sikorsky Aircraft. The tax status of an acquisition of another company's subsidiary can also be either taxable or tax free. Unlike acquisitions of freestanding companies where the seller could be an individual or a tax-exempt entity, the selling shareholder in a subsidiary sale is a corporation. Several other significant factors differentiate the tax treatment of subsidiary sales and sales of freestanding corporations, which we discuss in Chapters 12 and 15. Recognizing the tax differences in acquisitions of subsidiaries and freestanding corporations is critical.

A corporation that wishes to divest a subsidiary but does not wish to sell the subsidiary to another company has several options. Most commonly the corporation can divest the subsidiary in a tax-free spin-off. A spin-off results in the division of the parent corporation into two or more distinct corporations, tax free. Shareholders of the combined entity receive new shares in the spun-off subsidiary and after the transaction is completed, they own the stock of the newly spun-off business and the former combined entity, less the divested subsidiary. Another type of divestiture involves the sale of a portion of the equity of a subsidiary. In this type of divestiture, known as an equity carve-out, a divesting parent typically sells a noncontrolling equity stake of the subsidiary for cash to investors.

11.2 MAJOR TAX ISSUES ASSOCIATED WITH MERGERS, ACQUISITIONS, AND DIVESTITURES

Five major tax issues are associated with a merger, acquisition, or divestiture:

1. Will the restructuring transaction result in a tax on the selling firm's shareholders? In the case of a divestiture, will the transaction result in an immediate tax on the shareholders of the divesting corporation?
2. How will the acquisition or divestiture affect the tax attributes (for example, NOLs, tax credits) of the target firm or the divested business?
3. Will the restructuring transaction result in a taxable gain or loss at the level of the selling or divesting corporation?
4. Will the restructuring transaction result in a change in the tax basis of the assets of the target or the divested subsidiary?
5. Will the use of leverage in an acquisition generate tax savings?

Shareholder Tax Liabilities

In any type of acquisition or divestiture, selling-shareholder tax consequences often influence the structure of the transaction and perhaps the pretax value of the deal. We briefly discuss the tax implications for selling shareholders in various types of mergers, acquisitions, and divestitures here.

Mergers and Acquisitions A merger or acquisition can be taxable or tax free. In a taxable transaction, target shareholders receive cash from the acquirer in exchange for the stock of the target firm.[5] Target shareholders recognize a taxable gain on the transaction equal to the difference between the

[5] It is unusual for an acquirer to purchase the assets of a freestanding target firm rather than its stock in anything other than a small transaction, or unless there are unusual factual circumstances. See, for example, Martin D. Ginsburg and Jack S. Levin, *Mergers, Acquisitions and Buyouts: A Transactional Analysis of the Governing Tax, Legal and Accounting Considerations* (Aspen Publishers, Inc., June 2001), who state "In general, post-1986 acquisitions have been structured to avoid a purchase of assets, and Code §338 elections have not been made when stock is purchased. The normal structure has been a purchase of stock with no Code §338 election. . . . " See also Louis S. Freeman, *Tax Strategies for Corporate Acquisitions, Dispositions, Spin-Offs, Joint Ventures, Financings, Reorganizations & Restructurings* (New York, NY: Practising Law Institute, 2002), which states: "These changes [General Utilities repeal] make it quite disadvantageous to structure acquisitions of corporations as asset sales designed to provide the buyer with a step-up in the basis of T's assets. In other words, asset acquisitions or stock acquisitions followed by a Section 338 election will generally be avoided; rather, stock purchases with no Section 338 election will be encouraged. . . . "

purchase price and their basis in the stock of the target. If shareholders are individuals—not corporations or tax-exempt entities—and they have owned the stock for more than 12 months, the gain on the sale is a long-term capital gain and is taxed at 20% under current law.[6]

For an acquisition to be tax free, it must meet several statutory requirements. Most notably, target shareholders must maintain a continuity of interest in the combined entity. For practical purposes, the continuity of interest test is met if 40% of the total consideration paid for the target company's equity is acquiring firm stock. If the transaction qualifies as tax free, target shareholders do not recognize a gain or loss on the exchange of target shares for acquirer shares. However, if target shareholders receive cash from the acquirer, that cash triggers a taxable gain. Note that transactions that are tax free overall can nonetheless result in a taxable gain for target shareholders to the extent they receive cash.

Divestitures If the divesting parent sells a division or subsidiary to another corporation for cash, the transaction will be taxable to the divesting corporation. But unless the divesting corporation distributes the proceeds of the subsidiary sale to its shareholders, no taxable gain or loss is recognized by the divesting corporation's shareholders.[7] If the divesting corporation separates into two or more entities and distributes stock in the new entities to its shareholders in a spinoff, no gain or loss is recognized by shareholders receiving the distribution.[8] If the divesting corporation sells some of the stock of a subsidiary in an initial public offering—a so-called equity carve-out—usually no taxable gain is recognized by the divesting corporation and no taxable gain or loss is recognized by shareholders of the divesting corporation.

Effect on Tax Attributes

Corporations have a large array of tax attributes—net operating losses, various types of tax credits, bases in the stock, and assets of subsidiaries, to name a few. In a merger or acquisition these attributes may either be eliminated or survive. Whether the attributes survive is determined by the **tax structure** of an acquisition. In a divestiture, the tax attributes of the divested corporation always survive. These surviving tax attributes may remain in the hands of the seller or they may be transferred to the acquirer, and where these attributes reside posttransaction is again defined by the tax structure of the deal.

In most taxable acquisitions of freestanding C corporations, the tax attributes of the target survive, as does the target corporation itself, and are transferred to the acquirer.[9] However, use of the target's net operating losses and credits is limited post-acquisition.[10] Nonetheless, in some acquisitions, the target's NOLs provide significant value to the acquirer. In a tax-free merger, the tax attributes of the target always survive and carry over to the acquirer. The post-acquisition use of net operating losses by acquirers is also limited in tax-free acquisitions.

In a subsidiary sale, the tax attributes of the sold subsidiary always survive. Whether the divesting firm retains the tax attributes or the acquirer obtains them is determined by the structure of the subsidiary sale. In a spin-off or equity carve-out, the tax attributes of the divested subsidiary survive but may be limited.

---

[6] For ease of exposition, we assume the marginal capital gains tax rate is the current top capital gains tax rate (20%). In many computations, we use a 20% capital gains rate to reflect federal, state, and local capital gains taxes although the combined tax rate likely exceeds 20%. From 1997 to 2003, the top capital gains rate was 20%. Between 1987 and 1997, the top capital gains tax rate for individual shareholders was 28%. Before 1987, the top capital gains tax rate was 20%.

[7] If the divesting corporation distributes the after-tax proceeds of the subsidiary sale to its shareholders in return for some of their stock, the distribution will be taxed as a sale and not a dividend under Section 302(B)(4).

[8] Although Taxable spin-Offs were rare prior to the Tax and Jobs Act of 2017, they do occur. In such a case, the distribution is taxable to shareholders.

[9] In some types of taxable acquisitions of freestanding corporations, the tax attributes of the target firm are eliminated. These transaction structures are rare.

[10] The total value of the target's NOLs survives; however, their use post-acquisition is limited. As discussed at length in Chapter 14, the limitation that applies to a target's NOLs constrains the annual use of the NOLs to a specified amount.

Target Corporate-Level Tax Effect of the Merger, Acquisition, or Divestiture

In a merger or acquisition, the acquirer can purchase the stock or assets of the target. If the acquirer purchases the target's assets in a taxable transaction, a taxable gain or loss will be recognized by the target corporation. If the acquirer purchases the stock of the target from the target's shareholders in either a taxable or tax-free transaction, no taxable gain or loss accrues at the target *corporation level*. As noted previously, there is a taxable gain or loss at the target shareholder level if the transaction is taxable.

In a subsidiary sale, the divesting corporation recognizes a taxable gain or loss if the transaction is taxable, and subsidiary sales are usually taxable transactions. Subsidiary sales can be structured as **stock sales** or as **asset sales**. The gain or loss recognized by the seller is computed as the difference between the purchase price and the seller's basis in the stock or assets of the subsidiary, whichever was sold.

In a spin-off, the divesting corporation does not recognize a taxable gain if the spin-off qualifies for tax-free treatment, and most spin-offs are tax-free. Equity carve-outs generally do not result in a taxable gain or loss for the divesting corporation.

Change in the Tax Basis of the Target or Divested Subsidiary Assets

The tax basis of the assets of an acquired business can be stepped up to the purchase price in certain taxable transactions. An increase in the tax basis of the assets, or a step-up in basis, of the target company creates increased future depreciation deductions, which provide valuable tax savings. But a change in the tax basis of the assets of a freestanding C corporation rarely occurred under pre-2018 U.S. tax law. As illustrated in Chapter 12, under current law, the tax costs of obtaining this step-up typically are greater than the tax benefits from future additional depreciation deductions in acquisitions of freestanding C corporations. Conversely, acquisitions of S corporations and other conduit entities frequently result in a step-up in the tax basis of the target's assets. The incremental tax cost of a step-up structure when the target is an S corporation is much lower than the incremental tax cost of a step-up structure when the target is a C corporation.

Even though it is unusual for the sale of a freestanding C corporation to result in a step-up in the tax basis of the target's assets, a step-up is common in subsidiary sales. When a divesting corporation sells a subsidiary in a taxable transaction, the transaction is often structured so that a step-up in the tax basis of the assets of the sold subsidiary occurs.[11] Consequently, the acquiring firm may obtain substantial tax benefits in certain subsidiary sales. Because a step-up is common in the acquisition of a subsidiary, but not in the acquisition of a freestanding corporation, the structuring and pricing of each type of transaction is different. In Chapter 15 we discuss the types of subsidiary sales that are likely to result in a step-up in the tax basis of the divested subsidiary.

Effect of Leverage on Mergers and Acquisitions

Debt-financed acquisitions are taxable transactions in which the acquirer purchases the target, whether a freestanding corporation or a subsidiary of another corporation, for cash. Various special interest groups and politicians claim that the tax deductibility of interest payments encourages debt-financed acquisitions. If managers of the target maintain low debt-to-equity ratios, and thereby fail to exploit the tax advantages of debt financing, the interest deduction on new debt financing allows purchasers to acquire such targets at bargain prices. If debt financing has become increasingly tax advantageous since the early 1980s, however, it begs the question of why the target corporation cannot borrow or recapitalize *without* resorting to a debt-financed acquisition. The answer to such a question is that other nontax costs make one method of recapitalization more efficient than another tax-equivalent method.

[11] These transactions either are structured as asset sales or are stock sales followed by a **Section 338(H)(10) election**.

11.3 NONTAX ISSUES IN MERGERS, ACQUISITIONS, AND DIVESTITURES

The tax effects of a merger, acquisition, or divestiture are important, but often the nontax effects of a restructuring are at least as, if not more, important. Sometimes nontax factors will have a greater influence on whether a transaction is completed than tax factors do. Also, nontax factors may determine the structure for an acquisition or divestiture despite significant forgone tax benefits or increased tax costs. Several types of nontax costs frequently influence corporate restructuring transactions:

1. Transactions costs
2. Contingent or unrecorded liabilities
3. Managerial and/or control issues

Under current U.S. generally accepted accounting principles (GAAP) standards, the acquisition method of accounting must be used for all acquisitions. However, any goodwill recorded in the acquisition is not amortized. Rather, goodwill values are written down if and when the acquirer determines the recorded goodwill has been impaired. As we discuss at length later, just because an acquirer records goodwill for financial accounting purposes does not necessarily mean that goodwill is also recorded and recognized for tax purposes.

Transactions costs can include fees paid to professionals, information costs, and financing costs, among others. In some cases, these costs become large enough to render an acquisition or divestiture too expensive to pursue. Contingent liabilities may influence the structure selected for an acquisition or divestiture or may hinder the completion of a transaction that would otherwise generate wealth for both the acquirer and the target. For example, an acquirer may forgo the acquisition of a conglomerate with numerous valuable nontobacco subsidiaries because of potential litigation costs associated with a tobacco company subsidiary. Similarly, costs associated with managerial control may affect the completion of a transaction or the form in which the transaction is ultimately executed. For example, acquiring firms with a significant amount of managerial ownership may cancel the acquisition of a target company that demands acquiring firm stock as the primary consideration in the acquisition. Managers of the acquirer in such a situation would dilute their ownership through the exchange of acquirer stock for the target corporation.

11.4 FIVE BASIC METHODS TO ACQUIRE A FREESTANDING C CORPORATION

These are the five main methods for an acquirer (A) to purchase a freestanding target C corporation (T):

1. A's taxable purchase of T's assets
2. A's taxable purchase of T's stock followed by a Section 338 election, which results in a step-up/down in the tax basis of the target's assets
3. A's taxable purchase of T's stock *not* followed by a Section 338 election
4. A's acquisition of T's stock in a tax-free exchange
5. A's acquisition of T's assets in a tax-free exchange

To understand the tax implications of an acquisition, it is crucial to keep in mind which of the five methods is being used to effect the transaction. We refer to them repeatedly over the next several chapters.

In a taxable purchase of T's assets, the target corporation receives cash and/or notes for its assets, and it must pay taxes on the recognized asset sale gain. The gain can be ordinary or capital in nature depending on the assets sold. For example, the sale of inventory gives rise to ordinary income. The acquirer takes a basis in T's assets equal to the price paid, typically a stepped-up basis. If T's shareholders retain their shares, they do not realize capital gains or losses until T liquidates or they otherwise dispose of their shares.

In a taxable purchase of T's stock, T's shareholders receive cash or notes for their shares. A's basis in T's stock is generally the purchase price. Under Section 338, A can elect to treat the purchase of T's stock as if it purchased T's assets. As a result of the **Section 338 election**, the tax basis of T's assets are stepped up to fair market value, which is the purchase price plus tax liabilities associated with the step-up. Then, T's tax attributes, other than an ability to use T's NOL carryforwards to reduce T's recapture and capital gains taxes on the asset sale, are eliminated. If A does not elect to treat its purchase of T's stock as an asset purchase under Section 338, however, the tax basis in T's assets carries over instead of being stepped up, and T's tax attributes are preserved. Tax restrictions hinder A's ability to use these surviving tax attributes in both taxable and tax-free acquisitions.

If A acquires T's stock in a tax-free exchange under **Section 368**, T's shareholders will not, in general, recognize gains on the exchange of their T stock for A stock. In this case, A is not permitted to step up the tax basis of T's assets. Moreover, A generally retains T's tax attributes. But as in a taxable purchase of T's stock when A does not elect under Section 338 to treat the transaction as an asset purchase, A has limited use of T's net operating losses, capital losses, and tax-credit carryforwards.

If A acquires T's assets in a tax-free exchange under Section 368 in exchange for A stock, and T's stockholders exchange their T stock for A stock, the T shareholders do not pay tax on the exchange. A takes a **carryover basis** in T's assets; that is, the tax basis to A is the same as it was in the hands of T, and A will generally acquire T's tax attributes. But, once again, the use of these attributes is limited. **Table 11.1** summarizes the basic tax effects of the structures discussed in this section.

Table 11.1 Basic Structures Employed in the Acquisition of Freestanding C Corporations and Major Tax Implications of Each Structure

	Taxable Acquisitions			Tax-Free Acquisitions	
Structural and Tax Factors	Asset Acquisition	Stock Acquisition with a §338 Election[1]	Stock Acquisition without a §338 Election	Asset Acquisition	Stock Acquisition
Typical form of consideration	Cash	Cash	Cash	Stock	Stock
Taxable to target shareholders[2]	Yes[3]	Yes	Yes	No	No
Target *corporation*-level taxable gain	Yes	Yes	No	No	No
Step-up in the *tax basis* of the target's assets	Yes	Yes	No	No	No
Target's tax attributes survive[4]	No[3]	No	Yes	Yes	Yes

[1] The §338 election results in the transaction being taxed like an asset sale.
[2] Tax-free acquisitions provide gain deferral and are not really tax free, but rather tax deferred.
[3] Only if the target corporation liquidates after the asset sale.
[4] Target tax attributes include net operating loss carryforwards (NOLs), capital loss carryforwards, and various types of tax credits.

11.5 FOUR METHODS TO DIVEST A SUBSIDIARY OR LINE OF BUSINESS

Four basic methods can be used in divesting a line of business:

1. A subsidiary stock sale
2. A subsidiary asset sale
3. A spin-off
4. An equity carve-out

A subsidiary sale occurs when the divesting corporation sells the stock or assets of a subsidiary to another company. If the acquirer purchases the stock of the subsidiary, the acquirer and seller can jointly elect under **Section 338(h)(10)** to treat the stock sale as an asset sale. If the subsidiary sale is structured as an asset sale or as a stock sale accompanied by a Section 338(h)(10) election, the acquirer will obtain a stepped-up basis in the sold subsidiary's assets. If the subsidiary sale is structured as a stock sale *without* a Section 338(h)(10) election, then the acquirer will take a carryover basis in the assets of the acquired subsidiary.

In a nontaxable spin-off, the divesting firm distributes the stock in a subsidiary in which it owns at least 80% of the stock. The stock of the subsidiary is distributed to shareholders of the divesting parent pro rata. After the spin-off, shareholders own the stock of two independent companies. Spin-offs are almost always tax free to the distributing corporation and its shareholders, and the tax basis of the assets of the divested (spun-off) firm carry over, meaning that no step-up is involved.[12]

When a divesting firm sells the stock of a subsidiary to the public for cash in a so-called equity carve-out, the selling corporation is not taxed on the sale if the shares sold are held by the subsidiary. The tax basis of the subsidiary's assets is not changed in an equity carve-out. **Table 11.2** presents an overview of the tax implications of various divestiture methods.

Table 11.2 Divestiture Methods and Major Tax Implications of Each Method

Tax Issue or Structural Factor	Subsidiary Stock Sale	Subsidiary Asset Sale[1]	Spin-Off	Equity Carve-Out
Cash received by divesting parent?	Yes	Yes	No	Yes
Taxable gain to divesting parent	Yes	Yes	No	Not usually
Taxable gain to divesting parent's shareholders	Not usually[2]	Not usually[2]	Not usually[3]	Not usually[2]
Step-up in the *tax basis* of the divested subsidiary's assets	No	Yes	No	No[4]

[1] A divesting parent can either sell the assets of the subsidiary or it can sell the stock of the subsidiary and make a §338(h)(10) election, which will result in the transaction being taxed as an asset sale.

[2] There is no tax at the divesting parent shareholder level unless the divesting parent distributes the after-tax proceeds of the stock or asset sale to shareholders.

[4] In certain circumstances, an equity carve-out can be structured so the tax basis of the carved-out subsidiary's assets are stepped up. The step-up is facillitated through a §338(h)(10) election.

11.6 TAX DEDUCTIBILITY OF GOODWILL AND OTHER INTANGIBLE ASSETS UNDER SECTION 197

A tax issue associated with mergers, acquisitions, and divestitures often mentioned in the financial press is the tax deductibility of goodwill. In 1993, as part of the Omnibus Budget Reconciliation Act of 1993 (OBRA 1993), Congress enacted **Section 197**, which makes goodwill and nearly all other purchased intangible assets tax deductible. Prior to 1993, goodwill and many other types of intangible assets acquired in an acquisition were not amortizable or depreciable for tax purposes. Since 1993, most tax-based intangible assets are amortizable over a 15-year period.

However, a great deal of confusion surrounds the tax deductibility of goodwill. The financial press and even financial analysts often assume goodwill that is recorded on a firm's financial statements is deductible for tax purposes, but in many cases, it is not. Tax-deductible goodwill arises only in acquisitions in which the tax basis of the target's assets are stepped up. As we noted earlier in this chapter, it is rare for the target's assets to be stepped up for tax purposes in acquisitions of freestanding C corporations; in other words, tax-deductible goodwill is rare when the target is/was a freestanding C corporation. In contrast, with the acquisition method of accounting under U.S. GAAP,

[12] I.R.C. Section 336(e) provides for a potential step up in basis in certain spin-off transactions.

large amounts of financial accounting goodwill typically arise. This accounting goodwill does not necessarily appear on the tax-basis balance sheets; that is, it is not tax-deductible goodwill.

When then is goodwill tax deductible? Goodwill is tax deductible when the tax basis of the acquired firm's assets are stepped up. A step-up in the acquired firm's assets occurs frequently in acquisitions of conduits, such as S corporations or partnerships, and in subsidiary sales, but not in acquisitions of freestanding C corporations.

It is often useful to know whether the goodwill on a firm's balance sheet is tax deductible. Under the current GAAP accounting rules, firms are required to report the amount of tax-deductible goodwill recorded in an acquisition.

Summary of Key Points

1. The tax motivations for mergers include a desire to enhance depreciation deductions, to transfer valuable tax attributes such as net operating loss carryforwards to a company that values them more highly, and to create debt to secure interest deductions and thereby reduce corporate taxes.
2. None of the motivations listed in point 1 are unique to mergers and acquisitions. Indeed, some transactional alternatives can achieve the same gross tax benefits at a lower cost.
3. The five basic methods for a purchaser to acquire a freestanding target (T) are a taxable purchase of T's stock without a Section 338 election; a taxable purchase of T's stock with a Section 338 election; a taxable purchase of T's assets; a tax-free purchase of T's stock; and a tax-free purchase of T's assets. The term *tax free* refers to the tax consequences of the transaction to the seller. The methods have different effects on the tax basis of the target's assets (Is it stepped up or stepped down to market value, or does the basis carry over?) and the target's tax attributes (for example, NOLs and tax-credit carryforwards).
4. The four basic methods to divest a subsidiary or a line of business are a spin-off, a subsidiary stock sale, a subsidiary asset sale, and an equity carve-out.
5. Section 197 made goodwill tax deductible. Tax-deductible goodwill is created only in transactions in which the tax basis of the acquired business's assets is stepped up. A step-up occurs almost exclusively in subsidiary sales and acquisitions of conduits (e.g., S corporations), and not in acquisitions of freestanding C corporations.

Questions

Q11-1. What factors motivate acquisition transactions? Which do you think are most important? **LO4**

Q11-2. What key tax factors are most influential in mergers and acquisitions? Are mergers and acquisitions unique in their tax consequences? **LO4**

Q11-3. What are the tax benefits and costs of a transaction that changes the depreciable basis of an asset? **LO1**

Q11-4. What are the tax advantages of transferring T's tax attributes to A? **LO2**

Q11-5. What are the five basic acquisition methods used to acquire freestanding companies? **LO1, 2**

Q11-6. What are four common divestiture techniques? **LO5**

Q11-7. What is a step-up in the tax basis of a firm's assets? How does a step-up generate cash flow for an acquirer? **LO1**

Q11-8. How often do step-up acquisition structures occur when the target is a freestanding C corporation? **LO1, 2**

Q11-9. With what organizational form or entity type are step-up acquisition structures common? **LO1**

Q11-10. What are some of a firm's tax attributes? Why is an acquirer concerned with the effect of an acquisition on a target firm's tax attributes? **LO4**

Q11-11. What does a carryover basis transaction imply about the basis of the assets of the target firm? Does a carryover basis transaction generate incremental cash flow for the acquirer? **LO1, 2**

References and Additional Readings

Ginsburg, M., and J. Levin, 1995. *Mergers, Acquisitions, and Buyouts: A Transactional Analysis of the Governing Tax, Legal, and Accounting Considerations*. Boston: Little, Brown.

Ginsburg, M., and J. Levin, 2001. *Mergers, Acquisitions, and Buyouts*. Frederick, MD: Aspen.

Ginsburg, M., and J. Levin, 2007. *Mergers, Acquisitions, and Buyouts*. Frederick, MD: Aspen

Other *academic research on the taxation of mergers, acquisitions, and divestitures:*

Ayers, B., C. Lefanowicz, and J. Robinson, 2000. "The Effects of Goodwill Tax Deductions on the Market for Corporation Acquisitions," *Journal of the American Taxation Association* (Supplement).

Dhaliwal, D., and M. Erickson, 1998. "Wealth Effects of Tax-Related Court Rulings," *Journal of the American Taxation Association,* pp. 21–48.

Erickson, M., 1998. "The Effect of Taxes on the Structure of Corporate Acquisitions," *Journal of Accounting Research,* pp. 279–298.

Erickson, M., 2013a. "Analyzing Quaker Oats' Sale of Snapple to Triarc," in *Cases in Tax Strategy 6th edition,* edited by M. Erickson.

Erickson, M., 2013b. "Tax Benefits in Triarc's Sale of Snapple to Cadbury Schwepps," in *Cases in Tax Strategy 6th edition,* edited by M. Erickson.

Erickson, M., and S. Wang, 2013. "The Value of AirTran's NOLs in the Southwest/AirTran Merger," in *Cases in Tax Strategy 6th edition,* edited by M. Erickson.

Erickson, M., and S. Wang, 1999. "Exploiting and Sharing Tax Benefits: Seagram and DuPont," *Journal of the American Taxation Association* (Fall).

Erickson, M., and S. Wang, 2000. "The Effect of Transaction Structure on Price: Evidence from Subsidiary Sales," *Journal of Accounting and Economics.*

Erickson, M., and S. Wang, 2007. "Tax Benefits as a Source of Merger Premiums in Acquisitions of Privately Held Corporations," *The Accounting Review* (March).

Kaplan, S., 1989. "Management Buyouts: Evidence on Taxes as a Source of Value," *Journal of Finance* (July), pp. 611–632.

Martin, K., 1996. "The Method of Payment in Corporate Acquisitions, Investment Opportunities, and Management Ownership," *Journal of Finance* (September), pp. 1227–1246.

Maydew, E., K. Schipper, and L. Vincent, 1999. "The Effect of Taxes on Divestiture Method," *Journal of Accounting and Economics,* pp. 117–150.

12

Taxable Acquisitions of Freestanding C Corporations

Under U.S. generally accepted accounting principles (GAAP) as well as other accounting standard regimes, acquirers recognize goodwill as a result of purchasing a target for a price in excess of the value of its tangible and monetary assets. For example, when Google purchased YouTube in 2006 for about $1.2 billion, Google recorded about $1.13 billion of goodwill on its audited U.S. GAAP financial statements. However, none of that $1.13 billion of goodwill would produce tax deductions on Google's tax return. That is, the GAAP goodwill recorded by Google in the YouTube acquisition would not produce tax deductions—either currently for goodwill amortization deductions, or at the time of any write-off of the goodwill. As a result, there would be no tax savings arising from the more than $1 billion of goodwill recorded by Google in the YouTube acquisition. In this chapter, you will learn about the types of acquisitions of freestanding C corporations (e.g., corporations like Microsoft, Cisco, YouTube) that create goodwill that produces tax deductions and therefore tax benefits for an acquirer as well as the type of acquisitions that do not create goodwill that yields such tax benefits.

After completing this chapter, you should be able to

1. Understand the types of acquisitions that result in a step-up in the tax basis of the target's assets and those types that do not.
2. Compute the prices at which a seller (target shareholders) and an acquirer are indifferent between various taxable acquisition structures.
3. Understand the effect of acquisition structure on the target firm's tax attributes.

In Chapter 11 we introduced the major tax issues associated with corporate combinations and divestitures. In this chapter we focus on taxable acquisitions of freestanding C corporations. We consider the taxable acquisitions of an S corporation in the following chapter and the taxable acquisition of a division or a subsidiary of a corporation in Chapter 15. Chapter 14 covers tax-free acquisitions of freestanding C corporations.

In a **taxable acquisition**, the purchaser may buy either the assets or the stock of a target company. In the latter case, it is possible via election to treat a stock purchase, for tax purposes, as if the acquirer had purchased the target's assets. If the assets are purchased or if a step-up election is made in a taxable stock acquisition, a stepped-up (or stepped-down) tax basis in the target's assets is achieved. As a result, the acquired fixed assets will be depreciated from a base equal to their fair market value at the time of acquisition. Tax-deductible goodwill amortization expense will often result from the step-up in the tax basis of the target's assets in acquisitions of freestanding C corporations.

The step-up in basis is not obtained without a cost, however. A tax must be paid on the ordinary income resulting from the sale of inventory and on any depreciation and other ordinary income recapture, as well as on any taxable capital gains. Under current U.S. law, the corporate tax rate (21%) is the same as the corporate capital gains tax rate

(21%).[1] Therefore, the distinction between ordinary income and capital gains is generally not of first-order importance.

In an acquisition, the overriding considerations are the following:

1. What are the tax consequences of the transaction for target shareholders?[2]
2. What are the incremental tax costs and tax benefits if the buyer changes the basis in the target's assets?
3. What happens to the target company's tax attributes, including its NOLs?

We begin the chapter with an overview of four cases that cover the broad spectrum of taxable acquisitions of freestanding C corporations, along with the major tax consequences associated with each structure. We defer discussion of tax-free acquisitions until Chapter 14. As part of our analyses, we discuss the structures that are most common and the reasons for the observed empirical regularities. We also discuss nontax aspects of each of these acquisition structures.

12.1 TAX CONSEQUENCES OF ALTERNATIVE FORMS OF CORPORATE ACQUISITIONS

Table 12.1 lays out the major tax consequences—for the **target company**, **acquiring company**, and shareholders of the target company—of the various taxable corporate acquisition structures. We consider four basic acquisition methods:

1. A taxable asset acquisition without liquidating the target corporation
2. A taxable asset acquisition followed by a complete liquidation of the target
3. A taxable stock acquisition followed by a Section 338 election
4. A taxable stock acquisition that is not followed by a Section 338 election

As indicated in **Table 12.1**, the target company recognizes a gain or loss on the sale if it sells assets, regardless of whether the asset sale is followed by a liquidation *or* if it sells its stock and the acquirer elects under Section 338 to treat the transaction for tax purposes as a sale of assets. By contrast, neither a sale of stock that is *not* accompanied by a Section 338 election nor a tax-free reorganization generates a taxable gain for the target corporation.

Table 12.1 also shows that the target corporation's recognition of a taxable gain is linked to a change in the tax basis of the assets acquired (to market value) for the purchaser. Moreover, with the exception of a sale of assets by a target company that is not liquidated (Case 1), a change in the tax basis of acquired assets by the purchaser leads to a loss of the **target firm's tax attributes**, such as net operating loss and tax credit carryforwards.

As for tax consequences to the shareholders of the target company, the general rule is that when shareholders exchange their stock for consideration other than stock of the acquirer, they are taxed on the excess of the value received over their tax basis in the shares. Alternatively, target shareholders recognize a loss equal to the excess of their basis above the purchase price.

Having outlined the basic tax consequences of taxable acquisitions, we next analyze the factors relevant to choosing among the transactional alternatives. After briefly discussing the tax and nontax implications of the four tax structures in **Table 12.1**, we quantify the differences between them.

Case 1: Taxable Asset Acquisition Without a Complete Liquidation of the Target

This is our benchmark case. In this transaction, the identity of the target's shareholders does not change, and they retain control of the target firm.

The target's shareholders do not pay a direct tax on the asset sale unless they receive a dividend or sell their shares. This is true because they retain their shares in the target company and do not receive any cash in the transaction.

---

[1] Prior to the Tax and Jobs Act of 2017, the top U.S. corporate tax rate was 35%.

[2] In general, there are no tax consequences for the shareholders of the acquiring firm.

Table 12.1 Significant Tax Consequences of Various Taxable Acquisition Structures: Acquisitions of Freestanding C Corporations

	Asset Acquisition		Stock Acquisition	
Structural or Tax Issue	**Without Liquidation[1]**	**With Liquidation[2]**	**With a §338 Election[3]**	**Without a §338 Election[4]**
Consideration/method of payment	Cash	Cash	Cash	Cash
Taxable gain at target *corporation* level.	Yes	Yes	Yes	No
Taxable gain recognized by target shareholders	No	Yes	Yes	Yes
Step-up in the *tax basis* of the target's assets	Yes	Yes	Yes	No
Target's tax attributes survive	Yes	No	No	Yes
Tax deductible goodwill[5] . . .	Yes	Yes	Yes	No

[1] Transaction in which the target corporation sells its assets to the acquirer for cash. The target corporation pays any resulting tax (or receives a tax refund) on the gain (loss) recognized but the target corporation does not distribute the proceeds of the asset sale to its shareholders.

[2] Same as 1, but in this case, the target corporation distributes the after-tax proceeds of the asset sale to its shareholders in redemption of all of their target stock. The target's stock is then cancelled and the target corporation vanishes.

[3] Target corporation shareholders receive cash from the acquiring firm in return for their target corporation shares. The acquiring corporation then makes a §338 election, post-stock acquisition, which results in a deemed sale of the target's assets. This deemed sale results in a step-up in the tax basis in the target's assets.

[4] Target corporation shareholders sell their stock to the acquirer, but the acquirer does not make the step-up election (§338 election). There is no step-up in the tax basis of the target's assets; the acquirer takes a carryover basis in the target's assets.

[5] Financial accounting goodwill is recorded with the acquisition method of accounting (formerly the purchase method of accounting) under U.S. GAAP. Tax-based goodwill is only created if the tax basis of the target's assets is stepped-up.

Tax Consequences If a firm sells its assets for a price that exceeds the tax basis in the assets—usually the original acquisition price less accumulated depreciation or amortization since acquisition—it realizes a gain. The way the gain is taxed depends on the nature of the assets sold. For example, gains from the sale of inventories and accounts and notes receivable acquired in the normal course of business for services rendered or inventory sold generally give rise to ordinary income. Gains from the sale of depreciable property used in a trade or business (so-called Section 1231 property) yield capital gains, except to the extent that past depreciation must be **recaptured** as ordinary income. Sales of **Section 1231 property** at a loss give rise to an **ordinary loss**. Other assets that might be sold, such as stock held for investment, are capital assets, and their sale triggers capital gains or losses. If a corporation suffers a capital loss, the loss can be used only to offset other current or future realized corporate capital gains. Ordinary losses can offset ordinary income or net capital gains.

For a comparison of taxable acquisitions of freestanding C corporations, assume the following facts:

- The target corporation (T) has assets with a basis of $100. **Historical cost** and current basis equals $100, accumulated depreciation is $0.
- T's shareholders have a basis in the stock of T of $100, and they have held the stock for more than 1 year.[3]
- T's shareholders are individual investors, not corporations or tax-exempt entities.

[3] It is extremely unusual for a C corporation's shareholders to have the same basis in their stock as the corporation has in its net assets because shareholder stock basis does not change with the profits and losses of the company, whereas the corporation's net asset basis does. Similarly, when shareholders buy and sell shares, the basis of the new shareholders changes independent of changes in the basis in the corporation's net assets. For most publicly traded corporations, shareholder stock basis exceeds the corporation's net asset basis by a substantial margin. Consider, for example, an Internet company with a market capitalization of $10 billion and net assets of less than $100 million.

- The acquirer (A) wants to purchase the assets of T for $1,000.
- T does not have any net operating loss carryforwards (NOLs), tax-credit carryforwards, or loss carryforwards.
- T does not have any liabilities.

Figure 12.1 illustrates the structure of the transaction. In a taxable asset sale without a liquidation of T corporation, T would recognize a gain on the sale of its assets of $900 ($1,000 less $100). This gain would be capital in nature because the historical cost of T's assets is the same as its current basis. That is, no accumulated depreciation is recaptured and, for this reason, no ordinary income results from the sale. If T's asset basis was less than the historical cost due to depreciation, then the **recaptured depreciation** would be ordinary income.[4] For ease of illustration, we assume that no depreciation has been taken on T's assets. The $900 capital gain would be taxed, under current law, at T's top marginal tax rate. Ignoring state and local taxes and assuming T's marginal federal tax rate is the top statutory U.S. tax rate (21%), we find that T would face a capital gains tax of $189 on the asset sale.[5] Because T corporation does not liquidate under this scenario, it would retain all of its tax attributes (e.g., NOLs). After taxes, T corporation therefore would have $811 ($1,000 less $189 of taxes) from the asset sale. T's shareholders do not face any tax on the asset sale as long as T does not liquidate.

In this first of our four cases, the acquirer, A, directly obtains the assets of T. Assuming that T's only asset was a building, A would take a basis in that building equal to the purchase price paid—in this case, a basis of $1,000. When T corporation is a business comprising many assets—tangible and intangible—the purchase price of the assets is allocated to the tangible and intangible assets based on an appraisal. Specifically, the **residual valuation approach** under **Section 1060** specifies the manner in which the purchase price is allocated to the assets of T. Any portion of the purchase price allocated to goodwill will be amortizable over 15 years under **Section 197**. Returning to our simple numerical example, the acquirer corporation would obtain a step-up of $900 in the tax basis of T's assets ($1,000 new basis of T's assets in A's hands less $100 basis preacquisition). This $900 step-up gives rise to valuable increased depreciation deductions in future periods. We quantify the value of these additional tax deductions later in this chapter.

Nontax Consequences With a taxable asset sale and no liquidation, the acquiring firm purchases the tangible assets of the target and may not acquire certain of its liabilities. Acquirers cannot, however, fully avoid the liabilities of the target by acquiring its assets instead of its stock. Ginsburg and Levin (1995, p. 1528), note in regard to this issue that:

> [C]ourts have increasingly held P (the acquirer) responsible for some or all of T's (the target) debts and contingent liabilities (especially tort liabilities for defective products) under the common law doctrines of '*de facto* merger' and 'successor liability.' This can occur when T's business has been transferred to P as a going concern and T goes out of existence (especially, but not exclusively, when T's shareholders receive an equity interest in P).

FIGURE 12.1
Taxable Asset Acquisition without a Subsequent Liquidation

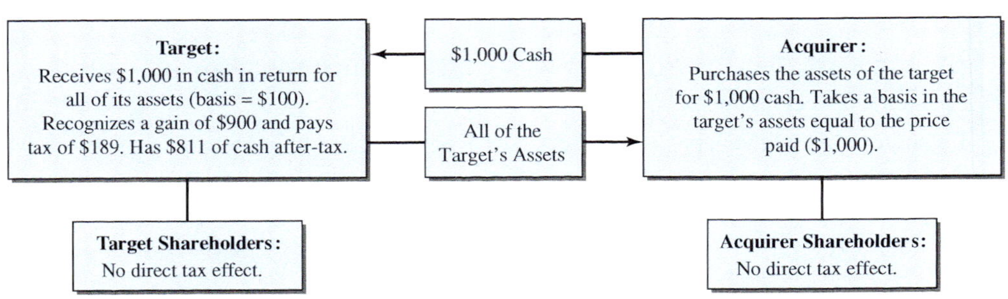

[4] Much of the depreciation recapture may cover various classes of Section 1231 property, and therefore the nature of the gain may be capital rather than ordinary income.

[5] Including state income taxes might increase T's total tax rate to 25% or more.

Thus acquirers may be unable to walk away from the liabilities of the target in an asset purchase. This is a complex issue and practitioners are encouraged to seek the assistance of counsel when dealing with this non-tax issue.

When a target sells its assets, the costs of transferring title in each of those assets may be high. Title transfer is required with this structure because the acquirer is actually acquiring not the stock, but the assets of the target. When stock is purchased, the acquirer obtains title to the target's assets indirectly through its ownership of the target's stock. Some types of assets are difficult to transfer. For example, certain contracts such as licenses and government permits are unassignable, or unassignable without a third party's consent.

Case 2: Sale of the Target Firm's Assets Followed by a Liquidation

Figure 12.2 illustrates the sale of a target's assets followed by liquidation. This transaction is similar to the transaction described in Case 1, but here the target distributes the after-tax proceeds of the asset sale to its shareholders in return for their T corporation shares in liquidation.

Tax Consequences Unlike the situation in Case 1, T corporation's tax attributes vanish when it liquidates. However, if T has NOLs, it can offset both capital gain and ordinary income on the asset sale with its NOLs. We analyze the use of a target's NOLs to offset the gain on a step-up relative to preserving the target's NOLs in Chapter 14.

Returning to our facts from Case 1, we see the tax consequences of the liquidation to the target corporation would be the same as in that case. The target would recognize a capital gain of $900 and pay a capital gains tax of $189. After corporate taxes, the target corporation, T, would have $811, which it would distribute to its shareholders in return for all their T stock. T's shareholders would therefore recognize a gain on the stock repurchase of $711 ($811 less their basis of $100).[6] Because we are assuming that T's shareholders have held the T stock for more than 12 months, their capital gain on the stock redemption is long term. Assume that investors' combined federal and state capital gains income tax rate is 20%, so T's shareholders would face a tax liability of $142.20, or 20% of $711. After tax, they would therefore have $668.80, or the $811 distribution minus $142.20 of capital gains taxes. The acquiring corporation would once again have a basis in T corporation's assets of $1,000—a $900 step-up.

Nontax Consequences Because the basis structure of the acquisition remains an asset purchase, the nontax consequences are essentially the same as in Case 1.

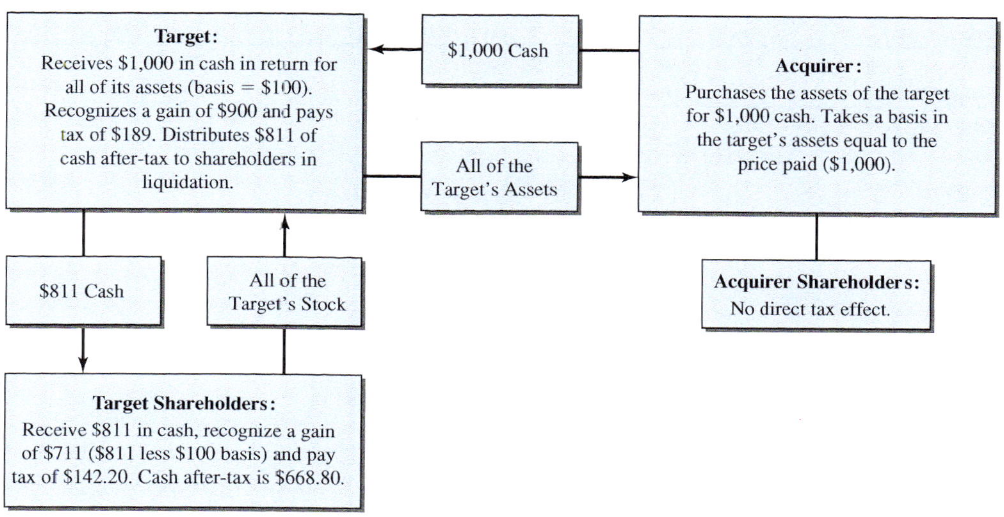

FIGURE 12.2 Taxable Asset Acquisition with Subsequent Liquidation of the Target

[6] Note that if shareholders had purchased T stock at different prices, some may have gains on the liquidation while others would have losses.

Case 3: Purchase of the Target's Stock Followed by a Section 338 Election

As we suggested in Case 1, the nontax costs of acquiring the assets of a target firm with far-flung operations and numerous tangible and intangible assets such as contracts and licenses may make a taxable asset sale structure prohibitive. Most taxable acquisitions of freestanding C corporations are structured as stock acquisitions, in part due to the nontax costs of an asset acquisition. Acquirers may, however, prefer to obtain the step-up in the tax basis of the target's assets associated with a taxable asset acquisition. The U.S. Tax Code provides an acquirer with the ability to obtain taxable asset sale treatment in a taxable stock acquisition, thereby avoiding the potentially onerous nontax costs associated with title transfers and nontransferable assets.

Under U.S. Tax Code Section 338, an acquirer can elect to treat a stock purchase of a freestanding C corporation as a taxable asset purchase.[7] The acquirer is eligible to make the Section 338 election if it acquires at least 80% of the stock of the target firm within a 12-month period in a taxable manner, a so-called **qualified stock purchase**. The Section 338 election is made by the acquirer and does not require the consent of the target's shareholders.[8] **Figure 12.3** illustrates a taxable stock acquisition of a freestanding target followed by a Section 338 election.

FIGURE 12.3
Taxable Stock Acquisition of the Target with a §338 Election

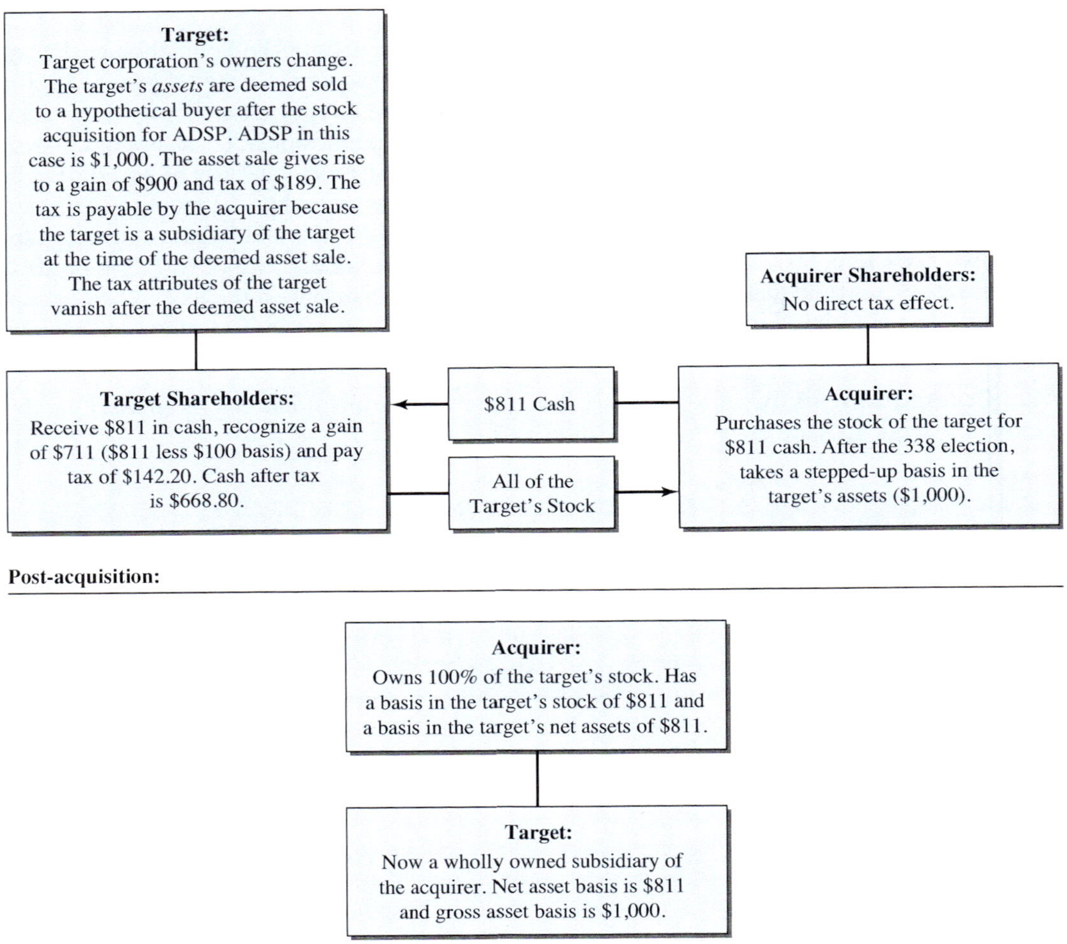

[7] We refer to the 338 election when the target is a freestanding C corporation as a "regular 338 election." Some refer to this as a 338(g) election, which is the provision of the tax code that denotes the making of the election. In Chapters 13 and 15, we discuss Section 338(h)(10) elections which can be made in the acquisition of an S corporation or the subsidiary of a C corporation.

[8] The election must be made within 8.5 months of the acquisition.

Tax Consequences In a taxable stock acquisition followed by a Section 338 election, the target corporation is treated, for tax purposes, as if it sold its **gross assets**[9] to the new target for what is known as the **aggregate deemed sale price (ADSP)**. *ADSP* is computed as:[10]

$$ADSP = P + L + t(ADSP - \text{Basis})$$

where

P = the price paid for the stock of the target
L = the liabilities of the target (now assumed by the acquirer)
t = the corporate tax rate
Basis = the adjusted tax basis of the target's gross assets

ADSP is the gross tax basis of the assets of the target in the hands of the acquirer after the Section 338 election. Notice that the *ADSP* formula is self-referential; that is, *ADSP* is on both sides of the equation. The reason will become clear as we solve for *ADSP* using the numerical facts established in our example.

One fact is different: Here the acquirer is willing to pay $811 for the stock of the target corporation. We also assume that the acquirer makes a Section 338 election after acquiring the stock of the target. T's shareholders would therefore recognize a gain on the sale of their T stock of $711 ($811 less $100 basis). As before, this gain is capital in nature and, under our assumptions, target shareholders would be subject to a capital gains tax of $142.20, leaving them with $668.80 after tax. Because the transaction is structured as a stock acquisition, there is no taxable gain at the T corporation level. After the stock sale, T corporation becomes a subsidiary of the acquirer.

The acquiring firm, after obtaining 80% of the stock of the target, makes the Section 338 election. As a result of this election, T corporation (now a subsidiary of A) is deemed to have sold its assets to a hypothetical new target for *ADSP*. *ADSP* equals $1,000 under our scenario, computed as follows:

$$\begin{aligned} ADSP &= \$811 + \$0 + 21\%(ADSP - \$100) \\ ADSP &= \$811 + .21\ ADSP - \$21 \\ 0.79\ ADSP &= \$790 \\ ADSP &= \$1{,}000 \end{aligned}$$

The deemed sale of the target's assets for $1,000 results in a taxable gain of $900 ($1,000 *ADSP* less basis of $100) at the target corporation level. Assuming the top marginal federal tax rate applies, a tax liability of $189 results. This tax liability is payable by the target corporation, which is a subsidiary of the acquirer after the stock purchase. In total, the acquirer has paid $1,000 for the target corporation: $811 for the target's stock and $189 for the tax liability associated with the Section 338 election. The *ADSP* computation is self-referential because the acquirer, through the target, contractually pays the tax associated with the Section 338 election. Hence the deemed price paid for the target's assets (*ADSP*) includes the price paid for the stock *plus* the tax on the deemed asset sale, or $t(ADSP - \text{Basis})$. As a result of the election, the acquirer obtains a step-up in the target's assets of $900 ($1,000 *ADSP* less $100 preacquisition basis) and has a gross basis in these assets of $1,000. Any portion of the purchase price allocated to goodwill will be amortizable over 15 years under Section 197.

Unlike the case in a taxable asset acquisition, in a taxable stock acquisition, the acquirer has a tax basis in the stock and the assets of the target. Under the current scenario, the acquirer would have a basis in T's stock of $811 and a basis in T's gross assets of $1,000. The **net asset basis** of the target's assets would be $811, or $1,000 gross basis less $189 tax liability arising from the Section 338 election. As a result of the Section 338 election, T corporation's tax attributes vanish, but its NOLs can be used to shield the gain associated with the step-up in its asset basis. The *acquirer's* NOLs cannot be used to offset the gain on the step-up, however.

Nontax Consequences Several nontax benefits are associated with a taxable stock acquisition. First, the transaction costs of obtaining the stock of a freestanding target are likely to be much smaller

[9] Gross assets are total assets, whereas net assets are gross assets less liabilities. Net assets are typically synonymous with owner's equity.

[10] When the target has NOLs, the general form of the *ADSP* computation becomes $ADSP = P + L + t\,(ADSP - \text{Basis} - \text{NOL})$.

than the title transfer costs associated with an asset sale. Second, the problem of nontransferable assets is largely avoided with a stock acquisition, thereby providing the potential for significant nontax benefits in certain circumstances.

Several significant nontax costs are also associated with this structure. Unlike the case in an asset sale, the target corporation in a stock acquisition survives as a legal entity, including its contingent liabilities. However, because the target becomes a *corporate* subsidiary of the acquirer, it enjoys some protection from legal liabilities through the properties of corporate ownership.

Case 4: Purchase of the Target's Stock Without a Section 338 Election

Case 4 is the same as Case 3 except that the acquirer does not make the Section 338 election. The numerical facts remain the same, and the structure employed is nearly the same, as **Figure 12.4** illustrates.

Tax Consequences With a taxable stock acquisition, the target's shareholders recognize a taxable gain equal to the purchase price less their basis in T's stock. Given the numbers in this case, target shareholders recognize a capital gain of $711 ($811 less $100 basis) on the stock sale to the acquirer and have $668.80 after tax. The target corporation's tax attributes survive but are limited by Section 382.

The acquiring firm obtains the stock of the target firm and takes a basis in this stock equal to the purchase price paid, which is $811. The target becomes a subsidiary of the acquirer and because the acquirer did not make the Section 338 election, the asset basis of the target is not stepped-up for tax purposes. Therefore, the target's asset basis carries over and is $100 postacquisition. Notice that the acquirer's tax basis in the stock and assets of the target are $811 and $100, respectively.

Nontax Consequences The nontax consequences of this transaction structure are essentially the same as those described for Case 3. One notable difference between Cases 3 and 4 occurs in the tax and financial accounting basis of the assets of the target. In Case 3, the gross financial accounting

FIGURE 12.4
Taxable Stock Acquisition of the Target without a §338 Election

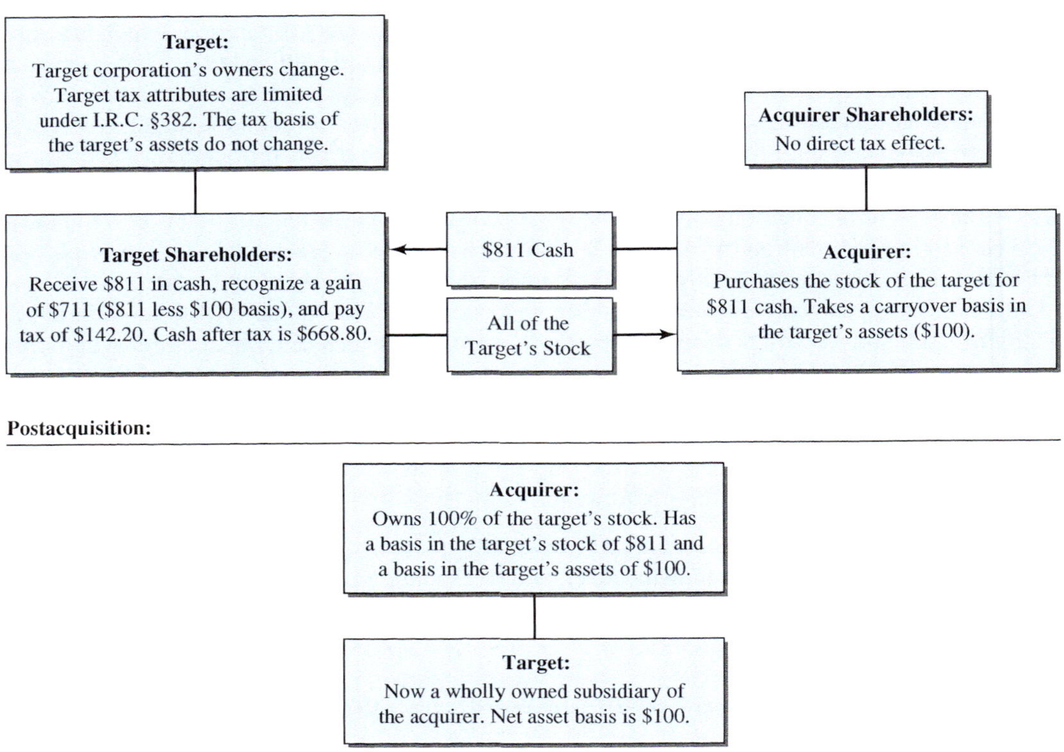

basis in the assets of the target would be approximately \$1,000,[11] as would the gross tax basis of the target's assets.

However, in Case 4, the acquirer's gross financial accounting basis in the target would be \$811, whereas the gross tax basis of the target's assets post-acquisition is \$100. This difference in financial accounting and tax basis is often manifested to a large degree in the goodwill account on the acquirer's financial statements. That is, the acquirer will have a large amount of recorded GAAP goodwill that is *not* tax deductible under Case 4. Under Case 3, any goodwill recorded for GAAP purposes in the acquisition will be tax based and tax deductible.

12.2 COMPARISON OF TAXABLE ACQUISITION STRUCTURES

The four preceding examples present the tax implications of the various taxable acquisition structures used when purchasing a freestanding C corporation. Even though that information is valuable, our objective is applying that knowledge to a tax-planning problem. Which of these structures is best given the specific fact pattern presented? When does each of these structures become preferential?

Based on the preceding facts, which structure is optimal, from a tax perspective only? As demonstrated in prior chapters, we can solve for the optimal contract by setting one party indifferent and determining which contract the other prefers. **Table 12.2** lays out the tax implications of the four structures discussed in Section 12.1. Essentially what we have done is set the seller (target shareholders) indifferent between the structures. That is, we computed the acquisition price required under each of the four structures to leave the target's shareholders with the same amount of cash after tax. Notice that the target's shareholders receive \$668.80 after tax in the three right-hand scenarios in **Table 12.2**; and were the target to liquidate in Case 1, target shareholders would have \$668.80 after tax in that scenario also.

To answer the question of which structure is optimal (ignoring nontax costs), next we develop algebraic expressions that allow us to determine acquirer and seller indifference prices across various acquisition structures.[12] We use algebra only as a tool.[13]

Target shareholders' after-tax cash under Case 2 (asset sale followed by a liquidation) can be represented by Equation 12.1. We first define the target shareholders' after-tax wealth as the liquidation proceeds, which is cash distributed by the target corporation after paying the corporate-level tax, less the shareholder tax liability associated with the liquidation. We then specify the amount of cash distributed to shareholders in the liquidation algebraically, as a function of purchase price, in Equation 12.2.

$$\begin{aligned}\mathbf{ATAX_{asset}} &= \textbf{Liquidation} - \textbf{Tax on liquidation}\\ &= \textbf{Liquidation} - (\textbf{Liquidation} - \textbf{Stock})t_{cg}\\ &= \textbf{Liquidation}(1 - t_{cg}) + \textbf{Stock} \times t_{cg}\end{aligned} \tag{12.1}$$

where

$$\begin{aligned}\textbf{Liquidation} &= \textbf{Price}_{asset} - \textbf{Tax on asset sale}\\ &= \textbf{Price}_{asset} - (\textbf{Price}_{asset} - \textbf{Asset})t_c\\ &= \textbf{Price}_{asset}(1 - t_c) + \textbf{Asset} \times t_c\end{aligned} \tag{12.2}$$

[14]

[11] This estimate ignores the effects of merger costs, such as investment banking fees, as well as other such items. The net asset tax basis is \$811 as is the net financial accounting basis.

[12] Note that the analysis used ignores target shareholder tax attributes such as capital loss carryforwards, as well as target corporation tax attributes such as NOLs and capital loss carryforwards, and that we assume all involved parties face the maximum individual or corporate tax rate. After working through the logic, you should be convinced that such complications could be added quite easily. We omit them here for ease of illustration.

[13] Those of you who prefer electronic spreadsheet models for such tasks may want to compare the algorithm used in such models to those presented here. The algebraic equations presented here should be logically identical to those in the spreadsheet models.

[14] We ignore the effect of target net operating losses on liquidation proceeds here for ease of illustration. As noted previously, target NOLs can be used to offset the gain associated with stepping up the target's assets.

Table 12.2 Comparison of the Tax Effects of Various Taxable Acquisition Structures: Acquisitions of Freestanding C Corporations

Fact Pattern:

Asset purchase price	$1,000.00
Stock purchase price	$811.00
ADSP[1] =	$1,000.00
Target's net asset basis	$100.00
Target shareholders' stock basis	$100.00
t_c =	21%
t_{cg} =	20%
r =	7%
Amortization/depreciation period (n)=	10

	Transaction Structure			
	Asset Acquisition		Stock Acquisition	
	No Liquidation	Liquidation	With a §338 Election	Without a §338 Election
Purchase Price	$1,000.00	$1,000.00	$ 811.00	$ 811.00
Tax Costs:				
Tax paid by T corporation[2]	(189.00)	(189.00)	0.00	0.00
Tax paid by A from the §338 election[3]	0.00	0.00	(189.00)	0.00
Tax paid by T's shareholders[4]	0.00	(142.20)	(142.20)	(142.20)
Total Tax Paid	$ (189.00)	$ (331.20)	$ (331.20)	$(142.20)
Target Shareholder Consequences:				
Gross cash received	n/a	811.00	811.00	811.00
Less: shareholder taxes[4]	n/a	(142.20)	(142.20)	(142.20)
After-tax cash to target's shareholders	n/a	$ 668.80	$ 668.80	$ 668.80
Acquirer Net After-Tax Cost:				
Gross cost	$1,000.00	$1,000.00	$1,000.00	$ 811.00
Less: present value of tax benefits[5]	(132.75)	(132.75)	(132.75)	0.00
Net after-tax cost of the acquisition	$ 867.25	$ 867.25	$ 867.25	$ 811.00
Acquirer's Tax Basis in the Target's:				
Stock	n/a	n/a	$ 811.00	$ 811.00
Assets	$1,000.00	$1,000.00	$1,000.00	$ 100.00

[1] *ADSP* is the aggregated deemed sale price of the target's assets in a taxable stock transaction in which a §338 election is made. *ADSP* is computed as: $ADSP = G + L + t_c(ADSP - \text{Basis})$; where G is the price paid for the target's stock, L are the target's liabilities, t_c is the corporate tax rate, and Basis is the gross tax basis of the target's assets pre-acquisition.

[2] Tax liability at the target corporation level from the sale of the target's assets pre-acquisition.

[3] Tax liability at the target corporation level on the deemed sale of its assets after the stock acquisition. The liability is ultimately the contractual responsibility, indirectly, of the acquiring firm because when the liability is triggered, the target is a subsidiary of the acquirer.

[4] Capital gains taxes resulting from the redemption of target shares by the target corporation in the liquidation following an asset sale and from the direct sale of the shares to the acquirer in the stock acquisitions.

[5] The present value of the tax savings resulting from stepping-up the target's assets assuming that the step-up is amortized/depreciated straight line over a 10-year period, the applicable tax rate is 21% and the after-tax discount rate is 7%.

$ATAX_{asset}$ = target shareholders' after-tax cash in a taxable asset sale
Liquidation = after-corporate-tax liquidation proceeds paid to target shareholders
Stock = target shareholders' stock basis
t_{cg} = the individual investor capital gains tax rate[15]
t_c = the corporate tax rate (ordinary and capital gain)
$Price_{asset}$ = the price paid to the target corporation for its net assets
Asset = the net tax basis of the target's assets

Substituting the definition of Liquidation in Equation 12.2 into Equation 12.1 and simplifying, we obtain:

$$\mathbf{ATAX_{asset} = [Price_{asset}(1 - t_c) + Asset \times t_c](1 - t_{cg}) + Stock \times t_{cg}} \quad (12.3)$$

We can represent target shareholders' after-tax cash under Case 3 and Case 4 by the following expression

$$\begin{aligned} \mathbf{ATAX_{stock}} &= \mathbf{Price_{stock} - TAX} \\ &= \mathbf{Price_{stock} - (Price_{stock} - Stock)t_{cg}} \\ &= \mathbf{Price_{stock}(1 - t_{cg}) + Stock \times t_{cg}} \end{aligned} \quad (12.4)$$

where

$ATAX_{stock}$ = target shareholders' after-tax cash in a taxable stock sale
$Price_{stock}$ = the pretax price paid to target shareholders in a taxable stock acquisition (other variables are as previously defined)

If we set Equation 12.3 and 12.4 equal to each other, we find the price demanded by target shareholders in a taxable asset acquisition ($Price_{asset}$) given the price demanded in a taxable stock acquisition ($Price_{stock}$).

$$\begin{aligned} &\mathbf{Price_{stock}(1 - t_{cg}) + Stock \times t_{cg}} \\ &= \mathbf{[Price_{asset}(1 - t_c) + Asset \times t_c](1 - t_{cg}) + Stock \times t_{cg}} \end{aligned} \quad (12.5)$$

Substituting, rearranging, and simplifying yields the following expression:

$$\mathbf{Price_{asset} = (Price_{stock} - Asset \times t_c)/(1 - t_c)} \quad (12.6)$$

With the facts in Case 4 and given $Price_{stock}$ = \$811, $Price_{asset}$ is equal to \$1,000, which is computed as (\$811 – \$100 × 21%)/(1 – 21%) using Equation 12.6. **Table 12.2** indicates that the numerical solution provided by Equation 12.6 does in fact leave target shareholders indifferent between a taxable stock sale at a price of \$811 and a taxable asset sale at \$1,000. That is, target shareholders' after-tax wealth is \$668.80 in both cases.

Given target shareholder indifference, we then need to determine which of the transaction structures is the least costly to the acquirer after tax. To estimate the after-tax cost of each structure, we need an estimate of the value of the tax benefits associated with stepping up the tax basis of the target's assets. For ease of computation, we assume that the average depreciable/ amortizable life of the target's assets is 10 years.[16] Further we assume **straight-line depreciation/amortization**, an after-tax discount rate of 7%, and an appropriate corporate tax rate of 21%.[17] Under those assumptions, the step-up in the target's assets generates \$90 per year (\$900/10-year life) in additional depreciation

[15] This rate includes both federal and state income taxes.

[16] Under the Tax Cut and Jobs Act of 2017, qualifiying assets are immediately deductible. We assume an average useful life for all assets acquired of 10 years here for ease of illustration.

[17] These assumptions are overly general and do not represent the true complexity and economic effects associated with allocating the purchase price to the target's assets. We make these simplifying assumptions here for ease of illustration. Note, however, that the allocation of the purchase price to various target asset classes (e.g., land vs. goodwill) can have a dramatic impact on the cash flows of the combined firm post-acquisition.

deductions and $18.90 in tax savings each year for 10 years, or $90 multiplied by 21%. At a discount rate of 7%, the present value of the additional tax savings from the depreciation deductions is $132.75. **Table 12.3** presents these computations.

Table 12.3 Estimation of Tax Benefits from Stepping Up the Tax Basis of a Target's Assets

Fact Pattern:

Purchase price	$1,000.00
Target's net asset basis	100.00
Step-up[1]	900.00
Amortization/depreciation period	10
Depreciation method	straight-line
Annual incremental amortization/depreciation[2]	$90.00
t_c =	21%
r =	7%

Period	Incremental Depreciation[2]	Tax Savings[3]	Present Value of Tax Savings[4]
1	$ 90.00	$ 18.90	$ 17.66
2	90.00	18.90	16.51
3	90.00	18.90	15.43
4	90.00	18.90	14.42
5	90.00	18.90	13.48
6	90.00	18.90	12.59
7	90.00	18.90	11.77
8	90.00	18.90	11.00
9	90.00	18.90	10.28
10	90.00	18.90	9.61
Total	$900.00	$189.00	$132.75

[1] Step-up is the increase in the tax basis of the target's assets computed as the purchase price less the net asset basis preacquisition.
[2] Incremental amortization/depreciation deductions is the step-up divided by the amortization period.
[3] Tax savings are incremental amortization/depreciation deductions multiplied by the corporate tax rate (t_c).
[4] Present value of tax savings discounted at the after-tax rate discount rate (r).

From the acquirer's perspective, in Case 1, the net after-tax cost of acquiring the target is $867.25, or $1,000 acquisition cost less $132.75 in *incremental* tax savings from the step-up. The after-tax cost of acquiring the target under Case 2 is also $867.25 for the same reason. Under Case 3, the after-tax cost of acquiring the target is the sum of the $811 paid for the target's stock plus the $189 tax associated with the Section 338 election less the present value of tax savings from the step-up ($132.75), which is again $867.25. Under Case 4, the pretax cost of acquiring the target is $811, but no incremental tax benefits come from stepping up the tax basis of the target's assets. So after any tax benefits, the acquirer's net cost in Case 4 is $811.[18] Therefore, the acquirer prefers Case 4 to the other three options. Why? The acquirer's net after-tax cost is lowest under Case 4.

Does this conclusion seem reasonable? The optimal structure in our example is the one in which the tax basis of the target's assets is not stepped up. For each of the first three cases, we can see that the incremental tax cost of stepping up the target's assets is $189. Under Cases 1 and 2, the target

[18] Each of these four computations ignores the tax benefits attributable to the existing tax basis of the target's assets. The computations do so because those tax benefits are constant across transaction structure. Thus those tax benefits have no incremental affect on the determination of the optimal tax structure.

corporation pays this incremental tax, whereas in Case 3 the acquiring firm pays it. In Case 4, no incremental tax cost is associated with stepping up the tax basis of the target's assets.

We also know that the present value of the tax benefits from stepping up the tax basis of the target's assets in Cases 1, 2, and 3 is $132.75. Therefore, the net *cost* of a step-up is $56.25, or $189 less $132.75. This answer is quite reasonable when we realize that the taxable gain associated with a step-up ($900) is equivalent to the amount of the step-up. Furthermore, the immediate associated tax liability is equal to the gross amount of tax savings derived from additional depreciation deductions; $900 step-up multiplied by 21% = $189 of additional deductions (see **Table 12.3**) that will be realized in future periods, assuming constant tax rates. With any discount rate greater than 0%, the present value of the tax savings from the step-up will be less than the tax liability due today from the step-up.

As we noted in Chapter 11, acquisitions of freestanding C corporations are rarely structured to result in a step-up in the tax basis of the target's assets. The reason is that it does not make sense to pay $1 in taxes today to generate $1 of tax savings over the next 10 or *n* years. In our numerical example in **Table 12.2**, it doesn't make sense to pay $189 in tax today to generate $132.75 in present-value tax savings.

Analysis of Acquiring Firm Indifference Price

In Equation 12.1 through 12.6 we expressed target shareholders' indifference between taxable acquisition structures algebraically. We can do the same for acquiring firms. Doing so will provide a relatively complete framework for you to analyze the tax consequences of a taxable acquisition of a freestanding C corporation. An acquiring firm's net after-tax cost in a taxable stock acquisition in which a Section 338 election is not made (Case 4) can be expressed as:

$$\begin{aligned} ATAXCOST_{stock} &= \text{Acqprice}_{stock} - \text{Incremental tax benefits} \\ &= \text{Acqprice}_{stock} - \$0 \\ &= \text{Acqprice}_{stock} \end{aligned} \tag{12.7}$$

where

$ATAXCOST_{stock}$ = the acquirer's net after-tax cost of the acquisition in a taxable stock transaction in which the target's assets are not stepped up

Acqprice_{stock} = the price the acquirer pays for the target's stock in a taxable stock acquisition in which the target's assets are not stepped up

An acquirer's net after-tax cost in a step-up transaction can be expressed as follows. We use a taxable asset acquisition because, algebraically, it is less complex than a Section 338 transaction. The results are identical if we use a taxable stock acquisition followed by a Section 338 election.

$$\begin{aligned} ATAXCOST_{asset} &= \text{Acqprice}_{asset} - \text{Incremental tax benefits} \\ ATAXCOST_{asset} &= \text{Acqprice}_{asset} - [(\text{Acqprice}_{asset} - \text{Asset})/n] \times PVANN \times t_c \end{aligned} \tag{12.8}$$

where

$ATAXCOST_{asset}$ = the acquirer's net after-tax cost of the acquisition in a taxable asset acquisition

Acqprice_{asset} = the pretax price paid by the acquirer for the target's net assets in a taxable asset acquisition

Asset = the target's net tax asset basis preacquisition

$PVANN$ = the present value of an annuity for n periods

t_c = the corporate tax rate

n = the period over which the step-up will be depreciated/amortized on a straight-line basis[19]

[19] A formula that reflects the complexities of accelerated depreciation methods and various asset classes (e.g., buildings and equipment) would be more realistic but unwieldy for our purposes. You can use the intuition derived from these equations to develop financial models that capture reality more precisely.

If we set Equation 12.7 and 12.8 equal to each other, we can solve for the maximum price the acquirer will pay in a taxable asset sale, given the price in a taxable stock sale. Also, assume the price an acquirer will pay in a taxable stock sale ($Acqprice_{stock}$) is the same as the price the target will demand ($Price_{stock}$) in Equation 12.4 through 12.6.

$$\mathbf{Price_{stock} = Acqprice_{asset} - [(Acqprice_{asset} - Asset)/\mathit{n}] \times \mathit{PVANN} \times \mathit{t_c}} \quad (12.9)$$

After rearranging, we can express Equation 12.9 as

$$Acqprice_{asset} = (Price_{stock} - Asset \times Factor \times t_c)/(1 - Factor \times t_c)$$

where Factor is equal to *PVANN*/*n*.

Using the facts in **Table 12.2**, we find that $Acqprice_{asset}$ is equal to

$$\begin{aligned} Acqprice_{asset} &= (\$811 - \$100 \times 0.70235 \times 21\%)/(1 - 0.70235 \times 21\%) \\ &= \$934.01 \end{aligned}$$

That is, the acquirer is indifferent between paying $685 in a taxable stock acquisition without a step-up election and paying $934.01 in a taxable asset sale. If we insert the maximum price the acquirer will pay in a taxable asset sale into Equation 12.3, we find that target shareholders' after-tax wealth is $627.10,[20] which is less than the shareholder receives in a taxable stock sale at a price of $811. Hence the taxable stock sale is the optimal structure.[21]

When, then, would a tax planner want to structure an acquisition of a freestanding company to result in a step-up in the tax basis of the target's assets? As a general rule, this structure makes sense only when the target has large NOLs that can be used to offset the gain on the step-up. Some assert that taxable asset acquisitions are desirable because such a structure allows the acquirer to avoid the contingent liabilities of the target. As noted in Chapter 11, it is not necessarily true that purchasing the assets of the target provides this nontax benefit.[22] Furthermore, it is well known in the investment banking and tax practitioner community that taxable asset sale structures are atypical in the purchase of a freestanding C corporation.[23] Due to limitations on the transfer of target NOLs in acquisitions, which we discuss in Chapter 14, offsetting the gain on a step-up can be an efficient

[20]

$$ATAX_{asset} = [Price_{asset}(1 + t_c) + Asset \times t_c](1 - t_{cg}) + Stock \times t_{cg}$$

$$ATAX_{asset} = [\$934.01(1 - 0.21) + \$100 \times 0.21] \times (1 - 0.20) + \$100 \times 0.20$$

$$ATAX_{asset} = \$627.10$$

[21] That is, we reach the same conclusion regarding the structuring of the deal regardless of which party's (acquirer or target shareholders) after-tax wealth is held constant.

[22] Martin D. Ginsburg and Jack S. Levin, in *Mergers, Acquisitions and Buyouts: A Transactional Analysis of the Governing Tax, Legal and Accounting Considerations* (Aspen Publishers, Inc., June 2001), state: "In addition, even if the parties have complied with the notice and other requirements of the bulk sales law (so that UCC Article 6 does not make P liable for T's debts), courts have increasingly held P responsible for some or all of T's debts and contingent liabilities (especially tort liabilities and defective products) under the common law doctrine of 'de facto merger' and 'successor liability.' This can occur when T's business has been transferred to P as a going concern and T goes out of existence (especially, but not exclusively, when T's shareholders receive an equity interest in P)."

[23] See for example, Martin D. Ginsburg and Jack S. Levin, *Mergers, Acquisitions and Buyouts: A Transactional Analysis of the Governing Tax, Legal and Accounting Considerations* (Aspen Publishers, Inc., June 2001), who state: "In general, post1986 acquisitions have been structured to avoid a purchase of assets, and Code §338 elections have not been made when stock is purchased. The normal structure has been a purchase of stock with no Code §338 election. . . ." See also Louis S. Freeman, *Tax Strategies for Corporate Acquisitions, Dispositions, Spin-Offs, Joint Ventures, Financings, Reorganizations and Restructurings* (New York, NY: Practising Law Institute, 2002), which states: "These changes [General Utilities repeal] make it quite disadvantageous to structure acquisitions of corporations as asset sales designed to provide the buyer with a step-up in the basis of T's assets. In other words, asset acquisitions or stock acquisitions followed by a Section 338 election will generally be avoided; rather, stock purchases with no Section 338 election will be encouraged. . . ." Finally, see Robert Willens, "Acquiring an S Corporation," *Lehman Brothers Tax and Accounting*, (May 19, 1998), which states: "Unfortunately, corporate buyers *rarely* get to purchase a target's assets. Since the 1986 repeal of the General Utilities doctrine, a sale of corporate assets is a fully taxable transaction and a second level of tax is imposed (on the seller's shareholders) . . . ."

use of the target's NOLs. However, even when the target has NOLs, a step-up structure is still typically not desirable.[24]

Summary of Key Points

1. Mergers and acquisitions occur across a number of transactional forms. These alternative forms yield varying tax consequences to the target company, to the purchasing company, and to the shareholders of the target company.
2. Mergers and acquisitions that allow the buyer to step up the basis of assets acquired typically result in a loss of the target's tax-loss and tax-credit carryforwards, as well as other tax attributes of the target company. An example of such a transaction is a sale of the target's assets followed by a liquidation of the target company.
3. When the stock of a freestanding C corporation is acquired, the buyer may elect under Section 338 to treat the transaction *as if* the target's assets had been acquired, followed by a liquidation of the target company.
4. In the sale of a freestanding C corporation, a structure that results in a step-up in the target's assets is usually suboptimal from a tax perspective because the incremental tax cost associated with the step-up usually exceeds the incremental tax benefits.
5. Although a step-up in a target's assets doesn't occur frequently in sales of entire freestanding C corporations, in two types of transactions a step-up structure is common. In sales of subsidiaries of companies, transactions are often structured in a manner that results in a step-up in the tax basis of the target's assets. It is also common to structure the sale of a conduit entity such as an S corporation in a similar manner.
6. Substantial differences in terms of nontax implications separate selling a target's assets from selling a target's stock. In the former case, title transfer costs may be excessive. In the latter case, acquisition transaction costs are likely lower, and with this structure the acquirer may be able to obtain certain assets such as licenses that will not transfer in an asset sale. With a stock acquisition, the acquirer obtains all of the target's assets and liabilities.

Questions

Q12-1. What are the main tax considerations in the sale of a target's stock to a purchaser?

Q12-2. What are the disadvantages of effecting a change in the basis of all of the firm's assets either by their sale, followed by a complete liquidation, or by a stock purchase, along with an election to treat the stock purchase as a purchase of all the firm's assets followed by a liquidation?

Q12-3. Because a purchaser can use a target's NOL carryforwards to offset the ordinary and capital gain and recapture tax on the sale of the target's assets, it has been argued that this reduces the cost of achieving a stepped-up basis in assets and makes it advantageous for the purchaser to acquire the target. Do you agree with this argument?

Q12-4. What types of transactions generate tax-deductible goodwill? How many acquisitions of freestanding C corporations, as a general rule, give rise to tax-deductible goodwill?

Q12-5. What are the nontax benefits, if any, of an asset acquisition? What are the nontax costs, if any, of an asset acquisition?

Q12-6. What are the nontax benefits, if any, of a stock acquisition? What are the nontax costs, if any, of a stock acquisition?

---

[24] Some asset sales of freestanding C corporations have occurred when sellers engaged in what some refer to as a "midco" transaction or "intermediary tax shelter." In such transactions, the business owner sells shares to an intermediary who then sells the assets of the business to the ultimate buyer. The intermediary engages in some transactions so as to avoid paying the corporate level tax on the asset sale. One commentator stated in regard to the intermediary's behavior that "The scoundrel (intermediary), however, makes the cash from the sale of corporate assets vanish into a rabbit warren of foreign accounts and disappears without paying corporate tax on the sale of assets." See C. Johnson, "Profits from Tax Evasion under the Midco Transaction," *Tax Notes*, March 25, 2013.

Tax-Planning Problems

TP12-7. Consider the following facts to quantify the tax costs of various taxable acquisition structures when the target is a freestanding C corporation. Wolverine, Inc., wants to purchase Reel Deal, Inc., in a taxable acquisition. Reel Deal is a freestanding C corporation with a net asset tax basis of $250. Reel Deal has no NOLs and is currently owned by five shareholders that have a basis in their Reel Deal stock of $5. Wolverine is planning to offer $10,000 for all of the assets of Reel Deal. The corporate tax rate is 40%, the after-tax discount rate is 15%, and the shareholder-level capital gains tax rate is 20%.

a. How much cash after tax will the shareholders of Reel Deal have in a taxable asset sale at a price of $10,000?

b. What is Wolverine's net after-tax cost of this transaction, assuming that any step-up in Reel Deal's assets are amortized/depreciated over 15 years straight line, the appropriate corporate tax rate is 40%, and the after-tax discount rate is 15%?

c. What price could Wolverine pay for Reel Deal in a taxable stock acquisition without a Section 338 election? What would Wolverine's net after-tax cost of this structure be?

d. Given the price computed in part (c), what would *ADSP* be if Wolverine decided to make the Section 338 election? What would Wolverine's net after-tax cost be with this structure of a taxable stock sale with a Section 338 election?

e. Which structure should be used in this acquisition? Why?

TP12-8. Abaco is planning to acquire Cozumel Airlines, a freestanding C corporation, in expectation that new management can be brought in to achieve substantial operating efficiencies. You have been retained to advise Abaco on how to structure the acquisition.

Two graduate school friends, Monique and Denise, own Cozumel Airlines. Together, they have a $1 million basis in their Cozumel Airlines stock. Both Monique and Denise have held their Cozumel Airlines stock for several years but must sell their stock for nontax reasons. Cozumel Airlines' tax-basis balance sheet contains $14 million of assets, no liabilities, and no net operating loss carryovers. All parties agree that Cozumel Airlines would be worth $20 million to Abaco with no step-up in Cozumel's inside (asset) basis, but $21.25 million if its inside (asset) basis was stepped up to fair market value. Monique and Denise each face a 40% tax rate on ordinary income and a 20% tax rate on capital gains. The corporate tax rate is 21%.

Option 1: Abaco buys outright all Cozumel Airlines' assets for $18 million—a taxable asset acquisition. Cozumel Airlines pays resulting taxes on the sale, if any, and distributes the proceeds to Monique and Denise in a complete liquidation.

Option 2: Abaco pays Monique and Denise $ _____ million in cash for their stock in Cozumel and *does not* make a Section 338 election.

a. How much after-tax cash will Monique and Denise get in aggregate if Option 1 is chosen?

b. In Option 2, how much cash would Abaco have to pay to make Monique and Denise indifferent between Option 1 and Option 2?

c. What is Abaco's net present value if Option 1 is chosen?

d. What is Abaco's net present value if Option 2 is chosen—based on your answer to part (b)?

TP12-9. Walkers is planning to acquire Cayman Bank, a freestanding C corporation, in expectation that new management can be brought in to achieve substantial operating efficiencies. You have been retained to advise Walkers on how to structure the acquisition.

Two grad school friends, Joe and Jim, own Cayman Bank. Together, Joe and Jim have a $6 million basis in their Cayman Bank stock. Both Joe and Jim have held their Cayman Bank stock long enough to get long-term capital gain treatment but must sell their stock for nontax reasons. Cayman Bank's tax-basis balance sheet contains $3.5 million of assets, no liabilities, and $2.5 million of net operating loss carryovers. All parties agree that Cayman Bank would be worth $8 million to Walkers with no step-up in Cayman's inside (asset) basis, but would be worth $8.75 million if its inside (asset) basis was stepped up to fair market value. Joe and Jim each face a 40% tax rate on ordinary income and a 20% tax rate on capital gains. The corporate tax rate is 21%.

Option 1: Walkers buys outright all of Cayman Bank's assets for $7 million in a taxable asset acquisition. Cayman Bank pays resulting taxes on the sale, if any, and distributes the proceeds to Joe and Jim in a complete liquidation.

Option 2: Walkers pays Joe and Jim $ _____ million in cash for their stock in Cayman and *does not* make a Section 338 election.

a. How much after-tax cash will Joe and Jim get in aggregate if Option 1 is chosen?

b. In Option 2, how much cash would Walkers have to pay to make Joe and Jim indifferent between Option 1 and Option 2?
c. What is Walkers' net present value if Option 1 is chosen?
d. What is Walkers' net present value if Option 2 is chosen, based on your answer to part (b)?
e. Which structure is optimal? Why?

References and Additional Readings

See the list at the end of Chapter 11.

Teaching Cases:

See the list at end of Chapter 11.

13

Taxable Acquisitions of S Corporations

When Blackstone and KKR went public (in 2007 and 2010, respectively) and sold shares of these previously private entities, the selling partners of both firms reaped hundreds of millions in tax benefits. It was reported that the total tax benefits generated as a result of the tax structure of the Blackstone initial public offering (IPO) were in excess of $1 billion. Of the total tax benefits created through the tax structure of these IPO transactions, the partners of Blackstone and KKR reportedly kept 85% of the tax benefits.[1] Blackstone's partners were reported to capture about $750 million of tax benefits.[2] Such tax benefits are not generated in most IPOs (e.g., Google, Facebook). In this chapter, you will learn what tax issues generate the tax benefits realized in the Blackstone and KKR deals. Moreover, you will learn that these tax benefits are prevalent in sales of certain types of privately held businesses. For example, in 2016, when Dr. Pepper purchased Bai Brands LLC (makers of Bai Water) for $1.7 billion, it was reported that the purchase price included $400 million in tax benefits. Similarly, in 2017, when Kellogg purchased Chicago Bar Company LLC (maker of RX Bars) for $600 million, it was reported that the acquisition created $200 million in tax benefits.

After completing this chapter, you should be able to

1. Explain the tax implications of various taxable acquisition structures of S corporations.
2. Understand when a structure that steps up the tax basis of the acquired S corporation is optimal and when it is not.
3. Compute the prices at which a seller (target shareholders) and an acquirer are indifferent between various taxable acquisition structures.
4. Understand the major tax differences between the taxable sale of an S corporation and the taxable sale of a C corporation.

As illustrated in Chapter 10, the various organizational forms exhibit a number of tax and nontax differences. In this chapter, we analyze the tax treatment of taxable acquisitions of S corporations, which are conduit entities. We concentrate on S corporations, but the same basic principles and economic conclusions apply to acquisitions of other types of pass-through or conduit entities (e.g., partnerships and limited liability companies [LLCs]). As you will see, taxable acquisitions of S corporations and of conduits in general are quite different from taxable acquisitions of C corporations, which we discussed in Chapter 12. We do not discuss tax-free acquisitions of S corporations, although those structures are an option, because tax-free acquisitions of S Corporations are similar to tax-free acquisitions of C corporations (see Chapter 14).

Because acquisitions of S corporations, partnerships, and other conduits such as LLCs are quite common, it is important to understand the basic tax issues associated with buying and selling a conduit. In fact, there are more S

[1] See for example, Allan Sloan, "KKR Leaders Get a Tax Deal Most of Us Can Only Dream Of," *Washington Post*, July 28, 2010.

[2] David Cay Johnston, "Tax Loopholes Sweeten a Deal for Blackstone," *New York Times*, July 13, 2007.

corporations than C corporations in the United States.[3] Thus acquisitions of conduit entities are prevalent. As you will see, significant tax benefits are available in acquisitions of conduit entities that are not typically available in the purchase of a C corporation. In our analysis of acquisitions of S corporations, we do not discuss the nontax implications of various acquisition structures because they are similar to or the same as the nontax implications associated with acquisitions of C corporations.

Recall that S corporations are conduits whose earnings at the corporate level pass through to shareholders where they are taxed. Generally, no tax is due at the S corporation level. We analyze the tax implications of acquiring the assets of an S corporation in a taxable transaction and the tax implications of a taxable stock acquisition of an S corporation. A taxable stock acquisition of an S corporation can be taxed as if the assets of the S corporation were sold if both the buyer and seller make a **Section 338(h)(10) election**.

In the taxable acquisition of an S corporation, the overriding considerations are (1) What are the tax consequences of the transaction for target shareholders?[4] and (2) What are the incremental tax costs and tax benefits if the buyer changes the basis in the target's assets?

13.1 TAX CONSEQUENCES OF TAXABLE S CORPORATION ACQUISITION STRUCTURES[5]

Table 13.1 lays out the major tax consequences—for the target company, the acquiring company, and the shareholders of the target company—of these three basic taxable methods used to acquire S corporations:

1. A taxable asset acquisition followed by a complete liquidation of the target
2. A taxable stock acquisition followed by a Section 338(h)(10) election
3. A taxable stock acquisition that is not followed by a Section 338(h)(10) election

As indicated in **Table 13.1**, the target company recognizes a gain or loss on the sale if it sells assets *or* if it sells its stock and the acquirer and seller elect under Section 338(h)(10) to treat the transaction for tax purposes as a sale of assets. By contrast, a sale of stock that is *not* accompanied by a Section 338(h)(10) election does not generate a taxable gain at the target level. Rather, a tax is assessed at only the shareholder level on the stock sale. **Table 13.1** also shows that the target corporation's recognition of a taxable gain is linked to a change in the tax basis of the assets acquired (to market value) for the purchaser.

Shareholders of the target company recognize a taxable gain in each of the three scenarios. In the first two scenarios, the taxable gain at the target corporation level flows directly through to shareholders.[6] No tax is levied at the S corporation level because the S corporation is a pass-through or conduit entity. The nature of the gain, whether ordinary or capital, at the S corporation level also passes through to shareholders. In the third scenario, the transaction is taxed as a stock sale, so no direct tax effect occurs at the S corporation level. Shareholders recognize taxable gain or loss on the sale of the S corporation stock.

Having outlined the basic tax consequences of the three basic types of taxable acquisitions of S corporations, we next analyze the factors relevant to choosing among the transactional alternatives. After briefly discussing the tax implications of the three tax structures, we quantify the differences between them.

[3] For example, most joint ventures are conduit-type entities, and these enterprises are frequently sold to one of the partners or a third party. The issues covered in this section are therefore likely relevant in joint-venture transactions, among others. Many profitable businesses are organized as pass-through entities. For example, it was reported that about 60% of businesses generating $1 million or more of annual income were pass-through entities. Source: 'More Firms Enjoy Tax Free Status,' J. Mckinnon, *Wall Street Journal*, January 10, 2012.

[4] In general, the shareholders of the acquiring firm experience no tax consequences.

[5] The remainder of the chapter is based in large part on M. Erickson and S. Wang, "Tax Benefits as a Source of Merger Premiums in Acquisitions of Privately Held Corporations," *The Accounting Review* (March 2007). David Goldberg of Endeavour Capital (Portland, Oregon) pointed out some of the anecdotal examples later in the chapter, and we are grateful for his assistance.

[6] We ignore the pass through deduction for qualifying business income in the analyses in this chapter for simplicity.

Table 13.1 Significant Tax Consequences of Various Taxable Acquisition Structures: Acquisitions of S Corporations

Structural or Tax Issue	Asset Acquisition[1]	Stock Acquisition with a §338(h)(10) Election[2]	Stock Acquisition without a §338(h)(10) Election[3]
Consideration/method of payment	Cash	Cash	Cash
Taxable gain at target *corporation* level	Yes	Yes	No
Taxable gain recognized by target shareholders	Yes	Yes	Yes
Nature of target shareholder gain	Ordinary income and capital gain	Ordinary income and capital gain	Capital gain
Step-up in the tax basis of the target's assets	Yes	Yes	No
Tax-based goodwill[4]	Yes	Yes	No

[1] Transaction in which the target corporation sells its assets to the acquirer for cash. The target corporation does not pay any resulting tax (or receive a tax refund) on the gain (loss) recognized. Any gain or loss recognized passes through to target shareholders.

[2] Target corporation shareholders receive cash from the acquiring firm in return for their target corporation shares. The acquiring corporation and the target's shareholders then make a §338(h)(10) election, which results in a deemed sale of the target's assets. The acquirer takes a stepped-up tax basis in the target's assets.

[3] Target corporation shareholders sell their stock to the acquirer, and the §338(h)(10) election is not made. There is no step-up in the tax basis of the target's assets; the acquirer takes a carryover basis in the target's assets.

[4] Financial accounting (i.e., GAAP) goodwill is generally recorded in these transactions. Tax-basis goodwill is only created if the tax basis of the target's assets are stepped up.

Case 1: Taxable Asset Acquisition

The mechanics of a taxable acquisition of an S corporation's assets are essentially identical to those associated with a taxable asset acquisition of a C corporation. **Figure 13.1** provides a diagram of the structure of an asset acquisition followed by a liquidation when the target is an S corporation. As in any taxable asset acquisition, the seller recognizes a gain and the acquirer obtains a basis in the assets equal to the purchase price, plus various adjustments in certain circumstances. A major difference in this case, however, is that the S corporation does not pay a tax on the asset sale gain.[7] Rather, that gain passes through to shareholders of the S corporation, who are responsible for any tax associated with the gain.

For illustrative purposes, we use the same set of facts used in Chapter 12 to compare and contrast the tax implications of various acquisition structures. **Table 13.2** provides an overview of the computations that follow. We make the following assumptions about the hypothetical S corporation sale:

- The target (T) S corporation has assets with a historical cost of $100 and accumulated depreciation of $0.
- T corporation shareholders have a tax basis in their T stock of $100, which they have held for more than 12 months.
- T corporation has no liabilities.
- The acquirer (A) pays T corporation $1,000 for the assets of T.[8]

The asset sale will give rise to a gain of $900 ($1,000 price less $100 basis in the assets) at the T corporation level. This gain is capital in nature because no accumulated depreciation was associated with T's assets and we assume the types of assets sold give rise to only capital gains. Any recaptured

[7] If the S corporation target was converted to S corporation status from C corporation status, additional taxes may be levied on the sale of the S corporation's assets under US Tax Code Section 1374.

[8] We assume throughout that the acquirer is a C corporation.

Figure 13.1 Taxable Asset Acquisition with Subsequent Liquidation of the Target: Target Is an S Corporation

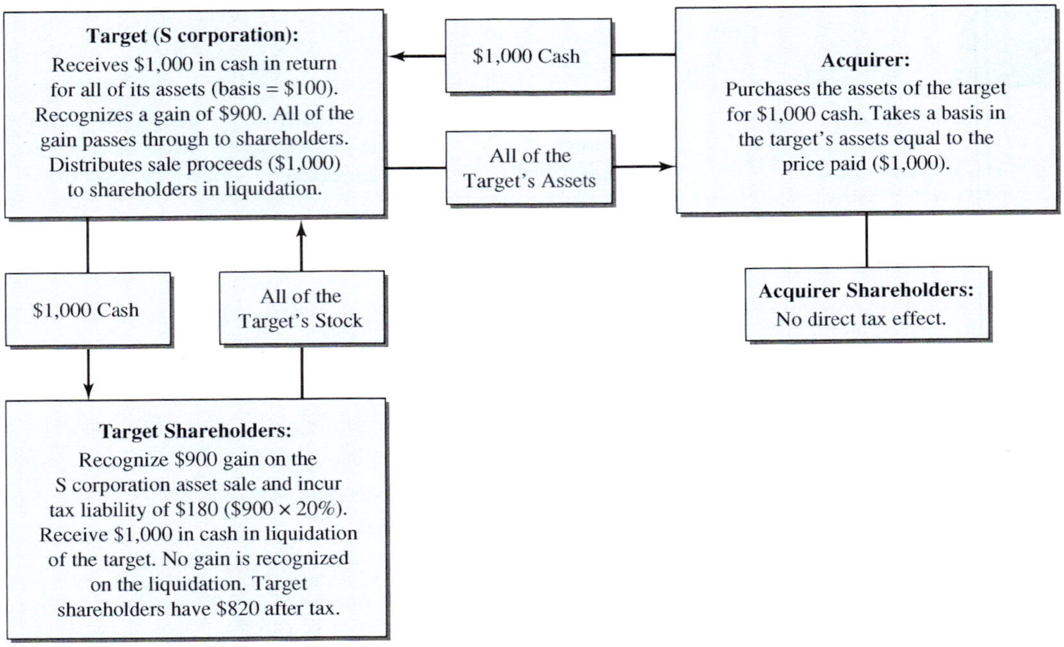

depreciation on the sale would be ordinary income.[9] No tax will be due on the $900 capital gain at the T corporation level. The acquirer (A) will take a basis in the assets of T equal to the purchase price ($1,000). Therefore, A corporation obtains a step-up in tax basis of $900, as shown in **Table 13.3**. The purchase price will be allocated to the tangible and intangible assets of T in accordance with the residual method described in Chapter 12. Any portion of the purchase price allocated to goodwill will be amortizable over 15 years under Section 197. Amounts allocated to qualifying property will be immediately deductible under the Tax and Jobs Act of 2017, while amounts allocated to other (non-qualifying) tangible assets will be depreciated.

The shareholders of T corporation will recognize a capital gain of $900 on the sale of T's assets. The nature of the gain (ordinary or capital) at the S corporation level passes through to the shareholders of T; hence the gain at the shareholder level is capital given our facts. Assuming the shareholders of T are individual investors—corporations cannot hold stock of S corporations—who are subject to federal capital gains taxes at 20%, the shareholder tax on the asset sale is $180, or $900 multiplied by a 20% capital gains tax rate.[10] Notice that T's shareholders must pay this tax whether or not they receive any cash from T corporation.

We are assuming here that T corporation liquidates after the asset sale. What is the tax on its shareholders on the liquidation? When T corporation recognizes the $900 gain on the asset sale, the gain is passed through to shareholders. Consequently, shareholders increase their basis in the stock of T corporation by the amount of the gain. The increase in shareholder basis occurs when the S corporation recognizes gains, and provides the mechanism to ensure that only a single level of tax is levied on S corporation shareholders. Therefore, prior to the liquidation of T, the shareholders of T have a basis in their T stock of $1,000 ($100 original basis plus the $900 gain on the asset sale). Consequently, when T liquidates and distributes the proceeds of the asset sale ($1,000) to its shareholders in return for their T stock, no gain is recorded on the liquidation because the shareholders of T have

[9] The type of property sold determines the tax treatment of recaptured depreciation. For purposes of this text, we assume that all recaptured depreciation is taxed as ordinary income. It is important for you to be aware here, as elsewhere, that numerous additional technical complications must be considered.

[10] Although the top federal tax rate for individual investors is 37% under the Tax and Jobs Act of 2017, we assume a 40% ordinary income tax rate for S corporation shareholders to simplify the computations and analyses.

Table 13.2 Comparison of the Tax Consequences of Various Taxable Acquisition Structures: Acquisitions of S Corporations

Fact Pattern:

Stock purchase price	$1,000.00	t_c =	21%
Asset purchase price	$1,000.00	t_{oi} =	40%
Net tax basis in assets	100.00	t_{cg} =	20%
Historical cost	100.00	r =	7%
Accumulated depreciation	0.00	Amortization/depreciation period (N) =	10
Shareholders' tax basis in target's stock	100.00		
Liabilities of target	0.00		

	S Corporation Acquisition Structure			
	Taxable Asset Acquisition	**Taxable Stock Acquisition with a §338(h)(10) Election[1]**	**Taxable Stock Acquisition without a §338(h)(10) Election**	**Taxable Stock Acquisition with a §338(h)(10) Election[1]**
Purchase price	$1,000.00	$1,000.00	$1,000.00	
Acquirer indifference price[2]				$1,155.71
Target Corporation:				
Taxable gain[3]	$ 900.00	$ 900.00	$ 900.00	$1,055.71
Taxable liability[4]	0.00	0.00	0.00	0.00
Shareholder Effect:				
Taxable gain[5]	$ 900.00	$ 900.00	$ 900.00	$1,055.71
Cash to shareholders	$1,000.00	$1,000.00	$1,000.00	$1,155.71
Tax liability[6]	180.00	180.00	180.00	211.14
After-tax cash	$ 820.00	$ 820.00	$ 820.00	$ 944.57
Acquirer Cost:				
Gross cost	$1,000.00	$1,000.00	$1,000.00	$1,155.71
Less: Tax benefits[7]	132.75	132.75	0.00	155.71
Net after-tax cost	$ 867.25	$ 867.25	$1,000.00	$1,000.00
Acquirer Basis in:				
Target's stock	n/a	$1,000.00	$1,000.00	$1 155.71
Target's net assets	$1,000.00	$1,000.00	$100.00	$1 155.71

[1] A §338(h)(10) election causes the stock sale to be taxed as if the target's shareholders sold the assets of the target corporation instead of the target's stock.

[2] The purchase price at which the acquirer is indifferent between a transaction that is taxed as an asset sale (stock sale with a §338[h][10] election) relative to a transaction that is taxed like a stock sale at a purchase price of $1,000 (column 3).

[3] Taxable gain at the target corporation level from the sale of the target's assets or the deemed sale of the target's assets under a §338(h)(10).

[4] Tax liability at the target corporation level on the taxable gain from the asset sale, stock sale, or the deemed asset sale under §338(h)(10) election.

[5] Taxable gain at the target shareholder level. This gain is equivalent to the gain at the target corporation level as the gain passes through to target shareholders. The gain retains its character (ordinary or capital) as it passes through to target shareholders.

[6] Target shareholder tax liability is the taxable gain from the asset sale at the target corporation level multiplied by the appropriate tax rate [(4; multiplied by the shareholder tax rate on ordinary income or capital gains] or the taxable gain on a stock sale multiplied by the capital gains tax rate.

[7] The present value of the tax savings resulting from stepping up the tax basis of the target's assets assuming that the step-up is amortized/depreciated straight line over a 10-year period, the applicable tax rate is 21%, and the after-tax discount rate is 7%.

Table 13.3 Estimation of Tax Benefits from Stepping Up the Tax Basis of a Target's Assets

Fact Pattern:

Purchase price	$1,000.00
Target's net asset basis	100.00
Step-up[1]	900.00
Amortization/depreciation period	10
Depreciation method	straight line
Annual incremental amortization/depreciation[2]	$90.00
t_c =	21%
r =	7%

Period	Incremental Depreciation[2]	Tax Savings[3]	Present Value of Tax Savings[4]
1	$ 90.00	$ 18.90	$ 17.66
2	90.00	18.90	16.51
3	90.00	18.90	15.43
4	90.00	18.90	14.42
5	90.00	18.90	13.48
6	90.00	18.90	12.59
7	90.00	18.90	11.77
8	90.00	18.90	11.00
9	90.00	18.90	10.28
10	90.00	18.90	9.61
Total	$900.00	$189.00	$132.75

[1] Step-up is the increase in the tax basis of the target's assets computed as the purchase price less the net asset basis preacquisition.
[2] Incremental amortization/depreciation deductions are the step-up divided by the amortization period.
[3] Tax savings are incremental amortization/depreciation deductions multiplied by the corporate tax rate (t_c).
[4] Present value of tax savings discounted at the after-tax rate discount rate (r).

a basis in their T stock of $1,000.[11] After the liquidation, then, T's shareholders have $820 after tax ($1,000 received in the liquidation less $180 tax on the capital gain).

Case 2: Taxable Stock Acquisition with a Section 338(h)(10) Election

Rather than acquire the assets of the S corporation, an acquirer can purchase the stock of the corporation. The transaction costs of acquiring the stock of an S corporation might be much lower than the

[11] The taxation of conduit entities causes the entity owner to increase its basis in the stock of the entity for any gain recognized. In our example, the shareholders of the target would increase their basis in the stock of the target by the amount of the gain recognized on the asset sale ($900). Shareholder basis after the asset sale but before the liquidating distribution would therefore be $1,000 or the $100 presale basis plus the $900 corporate-level gain on the asset sale. Consequently, the target shareholders' basis in the stock of the S corporation is $1,000 before the corporate liquidation. This required basis adjustment prevents double taxation of the S corporation's income. Notice here that there is no gain or loss because the shareholders' stock basis is equivalent to the amount of the distribution. If shareholders' stock basis was not equivalent to the corporation's net asset basis, there would be a gain or loss on the liquidating distribution. Differences in S corporation stock and asset basis can occur in a variety of situations, including (i) the shareholder purchased the S corporation's stock (rather than obtaining the stock at the time the corporation was founded), (ii) the shareholder inherited the stock of the S corporation, or (iii) the S corporation was previously a C corporation that converted to S corporation status.

costs of acquiring its assets because S corporations are by definition closely held, and an acquirer is likely dealing with a small group of shareholders. Therefore, the transaction costs associated with acquiring their shares are often relatively small.

However, a stock acquisition does not produce a step-up in the tax basis of the target's assets. An acquirer may prefer the tax consequences of a taxable asset purchase while seeking to avoid the associated transaction costs. Under Section 338(h)(10), a taxable stock acquisition of an S corporation can be taxed as if the acquirer purchased the target's assets instead of its stock. A Section 338(h)(10) election is made jointly by the buyer and the seller.[12] To qualify for a Section 338(h)(10) election, the acquirer must obtain at least 80% of the target's stock during a 12-month period. In addition, the acquirer must obtain the explicit cooperation of the target's shareholders in the making of the election. Without the seller's consent, the acquirer cannot make a valid Section 338(h)(10) election. In fact, target shareholders must make the 338(h)(10) election by filing a form with the Internal Revenue Service (IRS).

Note that when a Section 338(h)(10) election is made, no tax is due on the stock sale, only a tax on the asset sale. Using the facts outlined in Case 1 and assuming a taxable stock acquisition followed by the Section 338(h)(10) election, we find that the shareholders of T would have $820 after tax ($1,000 purchase price less $180 tax liability), and the acquirer would obtain a $1,000 tax basis in the stock and assets of T. **Table 13.2** illustrates the tax consequences of a taxable stock acquisition with a Section 338(h)(10) election, and **Figure 13.2** illustrates the structure of the transaction. One difference between a taxable asset acquisition and a taxable stock acquisition is that T corporation would survive as a subsidiary of the acquirer in a taxable stock acquisition. T would lose its S corporation status, however, because one of its shareholders (A) would now be a C corporation.

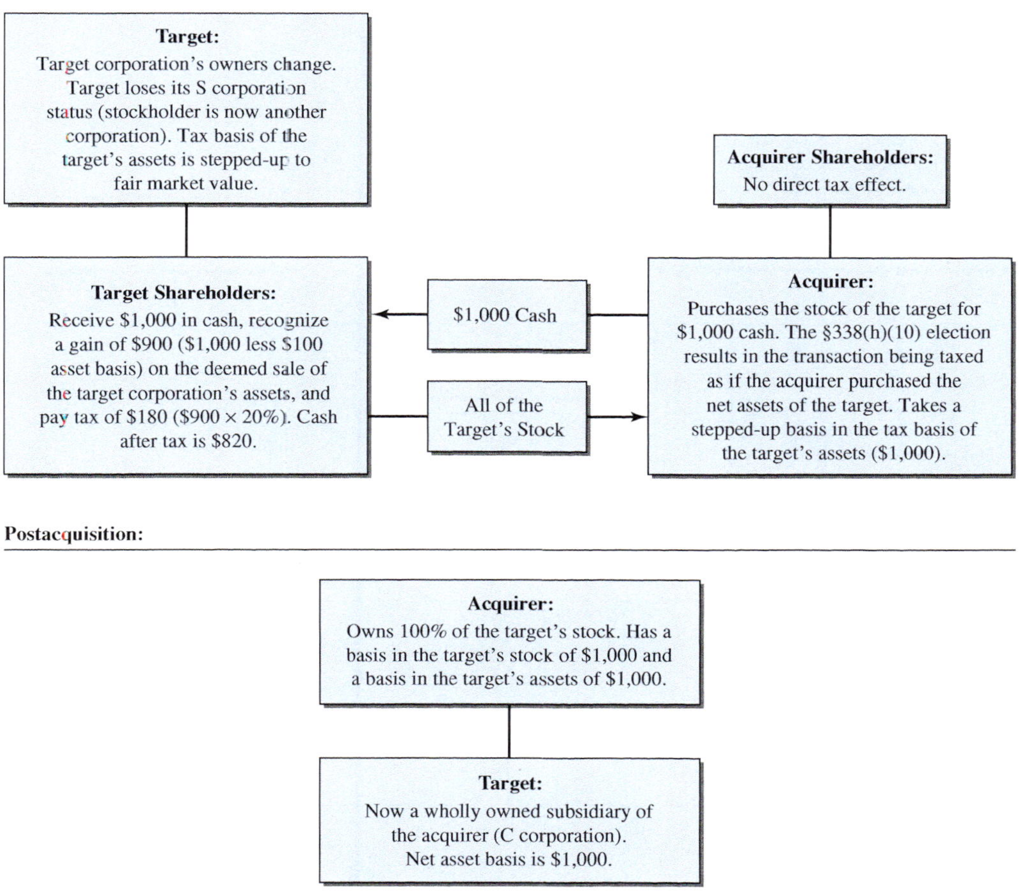

Figure 13.2 Taxable Stock Acquisition of the Target with an IRC §338(h)(10) Election: Target Is an S Corporation

[12] Recall that a regular Section 338 election is made unilaterally by the acquirer.

Case 3: Taxable Stock Acquistion without a Section 338(h)(10) Election

An acquirer can also purchase an S corporation in a taxable stock acquisition in which a Section 338(h)(10) election is not made. If the election is not made, the transaction is taxed as a stock sale, and the tax basis of the target corporation's assets carries over, meaning that there is no step-up in the tax basis of the target's assets. **Figure 13.3** illustrates the structure of a taxable stock sale of an S corporation without a Section 338(h)(10) election.

Returning to our facts from Case 1, assume the acquirer is willing to pay $1,000 for the stock of T and that no Section 338(h)(10) election will be made. Under this structure, T corporation would become a subsidiary of the acquirer, and T corporation would lose its S corporation status because it would be owned by a corporation. A will take a basis in the *stock* of T corporation equal to the price paid, or $1,000. The tax basis of T's assets will carry over and be $100. Hence, A does not obtain a step-up in the tax basis of T's assets and the corresponding tax benefits associated with the step-up. The shareholders of T corporation will recognize a capital gain of $900 on the sale of their *shares* to A for $1,000. Stock is a capital asset, and therefore the sale of stock gives rise to a capital gain. Assuming the appropriate capital gains tax rate is 20%, T's shareholders will face a capital gains tax liability of $180 and have $820 after tax.

Which Structure Is Optimal in the Sale of an S Corporation?

Which of the three taxable acquisition structures discussed is optimal in the sale of an S corporation, and what are the pivotal issues influencing the structure of an S corporation acquisition? Because the tax consequences of Cases 1 and 2 are identical, we compare Case 2 and Case 3, which also avoid nontax cost differences between stock and asset sales because Case 2 and Case 3 are both stock sales.

Figure 13.3 Taxable Stock Acquisition of the Target without an IRC §338(h)(10) Election: Target Is an S Corporation

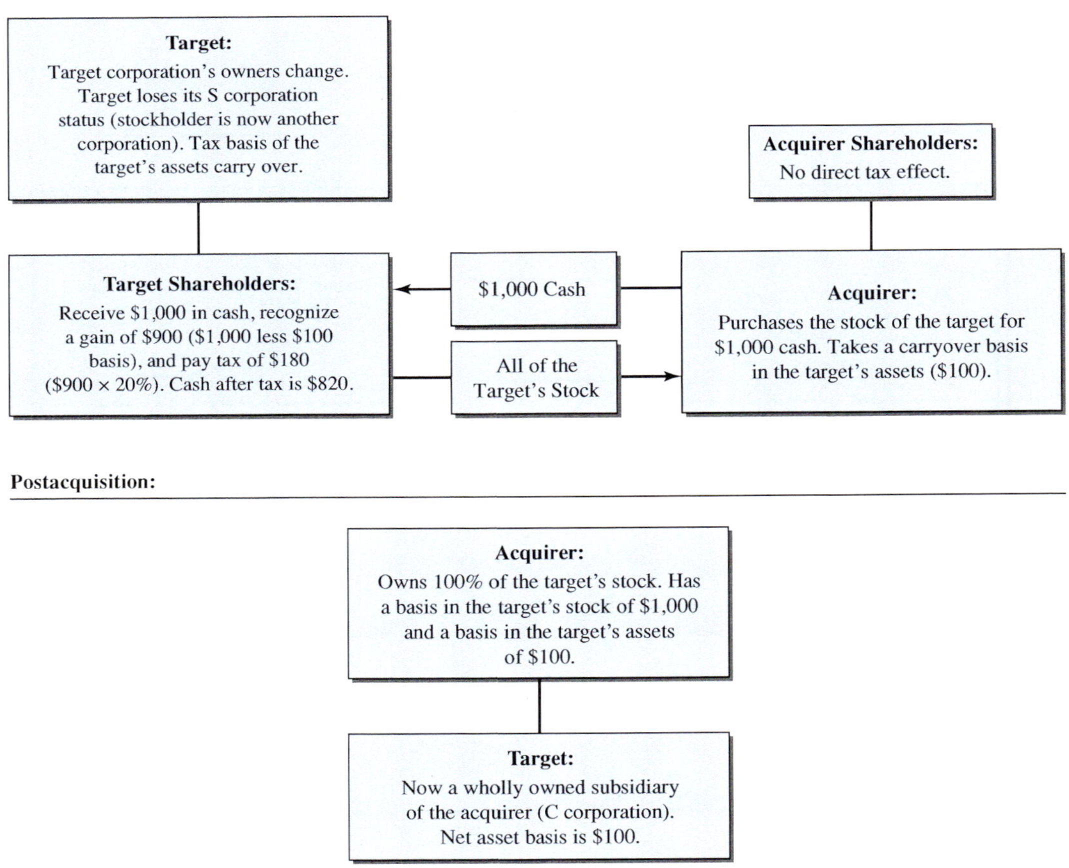

Which structure, then, is optimal between Case 2 and Case 3? We can algebraically express the relationship between the two structures in terms of target shareholder after-tax *wealth* and acquiring firm after-tax *cost*. In Case 2, a Section 338(h)(10) transaction, target shareholders' after-tax wealth can be expressed as

$$\begin{aligned} ATAX_{338h10} &= \text{Price}_{338h10} - \text{Tax} \\ &= \text{Price}_{338h10} - (\text{Price}_{338h10} - \text{Basis})t \\ &= \text{Price}_{338h10} - [(\text{Price}_{338h10} - \text{HC}_{\text{asset}})t_{cg} + (\text{Accum} \times t_{oi})] \\ &= \text{Price}_{338h10}(1 - t_{cg}) + \text{HC}_{\text{asset}} \times t_{cg} - \text{Accum} \times t_{oi} \end{aligned} \quad (13.1)$$

where

Price_{338h10} = the purchase price in a section 338(h)(10) transaction[13]

Basis = the net asset basis of the target's assets, which is equal to the historical cost basis of the target's assets (HC_{asset}) less the accumulated depreciation and amortization associated with the target's assets (Accum)[14]

t = the tax rate

t_{cg} = the appropriate capital gains tax rate for individual shareholders

t_{oi} = the ordinary income rate for individual shareholders

In Case 3, target shareholders' after-tax wealth can be expressed as

$$\begin{aligned} ATAX_{no338h10} &= \text{Price}_{no338h10} - \text{Tax} \\ &= \text{Price}_{no338h10} - (\text{Price}_{no338h10} - \text{Stock})t_{cg} \\ &= \text{Price}_{no338h10}(1 - t_{cg}) + \text{Stock} \times t_{cg} \end{aligned} \quad (13.2)$$

where

$\text{Price}_{no338h10}$ = the purchase price if the Section 338(h)(10) is not made

Stock = the target shareholders' basis in the stock of the target firm

The other variables are as defined previously.

We can find the purchase price with the election (Case 2) that leaves target shareholders indifferent between Case 2 and Case 3 at a given purchase price in Case 3, the no Section 338(h)(10) election scenario. We can do so by setting Equations 13.1 and 13.2 equal to each other and then simplifying:

$$\text{Price}_{338h10} = \text{Price}_{no338h10} + [\text{Stock} \times t_{cg} - \text{HC}_{\text{asset}} \times t_{cg} + \text{Accum} \times t_{oi}]/(1 - t_{cg}) \quad (13.3)$$

Using Equation 13.3, we see that target shareholders are indifferent between receiving $1,000 in Case 3 or $1,000 in Case 2 where the Section 338(h)(10) election is made.[15] Under Case 2 or Case 3, T's shareholders ultimately have $820 after tax when they receive $1,000 pretax. They are therefore indifferent between Case 2 and Case 3 at any price, given our simple fact pattern.

[13] We assume that Price_{338h10} exceeds HC_{asset}. The algebraic relationship is slightly different if Price_{338h10} is less than HC_{asset}. As you grasp the logic presented in Equations 13.1 through 13.6, you can develop financial models that deal with various fact patterns and contingencies.

[14] Recall that recaptured depreciation can be taxed as ordinary income. Under the assumption that all recaptured depreciation gives rise to ordinary income, Equation 13.1 estimates tax liabilities on recaptured depreciation at ordinary rates. The excess of the purchase price over the historical cost of the assets (HC_{asset}) is capital gain. As a practical matter, in many circumstances, some or all of what we are defining as recaptured depreciation will be taxed at capital gains rates. The algebraic expressions here, and the corresponding financial models, can be modified to reflect these additional complexities. Alternatively, we could alter the fact pattern such that a portion of the target's assets are inventory. The deemed sale of inventory at a price in excess of cost would typically generate ordinary income.

[15] The second term on the right-hand side of Equation 13.3 is equal to zero because (stock) basis equals asset basis (HC_{asset} − Accum) and there is no accumulated depreciation on the assets of the target.

The acquiring firm's pretax cost of acquiring T corporation is $1,000 in each case. Under Case 2, A takes a tax basis in T's assets of $1,000, whereas under Case 3, A takes a basis in T's assets of $100. The $900 step-up in tax basis under Case 2 generates gross undiscounted tax savings of $189 ($900 multiplied by a 21% tax rate) for A. Assuming that these incremental depreciation deductions occur evenly over 10 years and an appropriate after-tax discount rate is 7%,[16] the present value of the tax benefits from the step-up is $132.75 (see **Table 13.3**). The acquirer's *net* after-tax cost under Case 2 is therefore $867.25 ($1,000 less $132.75), whereas net after-tax cost is $1,000 under Case 3. Therefore Case 2 dominates Case 3.

It is apparent that, given our example numbers, the acquirer is willing to pay a higher pretax price in order to obtain the target shareholders' consent in making the Section 338(h) (10) election, because the acquirer's after-tax cost is lower, other things equal, when the Section 338(h)(10) election is made. How much more, then, is the acquirer willing to pay the seller to induce the seller to make the Section 338(h)(10) election, assuming that the acquirer believes $1,000 is a reasonable price to pay to acquire the target if the basis of the target's assets does not change (Case 3)? With Case 2, the net after-tax cost of the acquisition to the acquirer can be expressed as

$$\begin{aligned} \boldsymbol{ATAXCOST}_{\mathbf{338h10}} &= \mathbf{Acqprice}_{\mathbf{338h10}} - \mathbf{Incremental\ tax\ benefits} \\ &= \mathbf{Acqprice}_{\mathbf{338h10}} - \boldsymbol{t_c(PVANN)}[(\mathbf{Acqprice}_{\mathbf{338h10}} - \mathbf{Asset})/\boldsymbol{n}] \end{aligned} \tag{13.4}$$

where

Acqprice$_{338h10}$ = the price that the acquirer will pay in a Section 338(h)(10) transaction
PVANN = the present value of an annuity
t_c = the corporate tax rate
Asset = the net tax basis of the target's assets
n = the useful life of the target's assets postacquisition

Under Case 3, the acquirer's net after-tax cost can be expressed as

$$\begin{aligned} \boldsymbol{ATAXCOST}_{\mathbf{no338h10}} &= \mathbf{Acqprice}_{\mathbf{no338h10}} - \mathbf{Incremental\ tax\ benefits} \\ &= \mathbf{Acqprice}_{\mathbf{no338h10}} - \mathbf{\$0} \end{aligned} \tag{13.5}$$

where

Acqprice$_{no338h10}$ = the price the acquirer will pay if the Section 338(h)(10) election is not made

The acquirer gains no incremental tax benefits in Case 3 because the tax basis of the target's assets is not stepped-up. The acquirer is indifferent between Case 2 and Case 3 when Equation 13.4 equals Equation 13.5. We assume for ease of exposition that Acqprice$_{no338h10}$ and Price$_{no338h10}$ are equivalent. That is, we assume the acquirer and the target agree on the value of the target corporation if the Section 338(h)(10) election is not made and the tax basis of the target's assets does not change. Simplifying, we find

$$\mathbf{Acqprice}_{\mathbf{338h10}} = (\mathbf{Price}_{\mathbf{no338h10}} - \boldsymbol{t_c} \times \mathbf{Factor} \times \mathbf{Asset})/(\mathbf{1} - \boldsymbol{t_c} \times \mathbf{Factor}) \tag{13.6}$$

where Factor is equal to *PVANN*/*n* and all other variables are as defined previously.

Given Price$_{no338h10}$ equals $1,000, the acquirer is indifferent between Case 3 at $1,000 and Case 2 at a price of $1,155.71, computed as[17]

$$\text{Acqprice}_{338h10} = (\$1{,}000 - .14749 \times \$100)/(1 - .14749)$$

[16] As noted in Chapter 12, these assumptions are oversimplified and the computation of the tax benefits of a step-up in asset basis would be more complex than demonstrated here. We make these simplifying assumptions to expedite analysis of the economic benefits under consideration.

[17] Factor equals 0.70235 when $n = 10$ and $r = 7\%$, so Factor × $t_c = 0.14749$.

At that price, the acquirer would take a basis in the assets of T of $1,155.71. Stated another way, the acquirer would obtain a step-up in basis of $1,055.71. Under the same assumptions (10-year straight-line amortization, $t_c = 21\%$, $r = 7\%$), the present value of the $1,055.71 step-up is $155.71. Therefore, A's net after-tax cost under Case 2 at a price of $1,155.71 is $1,000.

Note that, even at a 15% pretax *premium*, or ($1,155.71 – $1,000)/$1,000, in Case 2, A is equally well off after tax under Case 2 as it is in Case 3. At a purchase price of $1,155.71, T's shareholders would recognize a capital gain on the sale of T's assets of $1,055.71 ($1,155.71 less $100 basis in T's stock), pay capital gains taxes of $211.14 ($1,055.71 × 20%), and have $944.57 after tax. It amounts to $124.57 ($944.57 minus $820) more after tax than under the original Case 3. The last column of **Table 13.2** illustrates these computations.

Advanced Analysis: S Corporation Acquisition

In Section 12.2 of Chapter 12, we illustrated why sales of freestanding C corporations are rarely structured in a manner that results in a step-up in the tax basis of the target's assets. In this section, we illustrated that, in S corporation acquisitions, structuring the transaction to achieve a step-up in the tax basis of the target's assets can leave both the acquirer and the target's shareholders better off after tax.

How do we explain why different acquisition structures are preferred with different target organizational forms? As with any tax-planning strategy, the fundamental issue is a comparison of incremental tax costs with incremental tax benefits, holding nontax factors constant. In the case of an acquisition of a C corporation, the incremental cost of obtaining a step-up is usually the tax rate multiplied by the amount of the step-up (in Section 12.2 of Chapter 12, this amount was $189). The incremental tax savings from the step-up is the present value of the tax savings from the step-up (in Section 12.2, we estimated this amount as $132.75), which is always less than the incremental tax cost if tax rates are constant and discount rates are greater than 0%.

In the case of an S corporation acquisition, the incremental cost of the step-up is not the tax rate multiplied by the step-up amount. It is usually something less.[18] This is true because there is only one level of tax on an "asset sale" in an S corporation, whereas there are two levels of tax on an "asset sale" of a C corporation.[19] The example that we used for an S corporation acquisition is oversimplified, but it illustrates these fundamental principles. We next work through a more realistic example in which the incremental cost of asset sale tax treatment for the S corporation's shareholders is not $0.

The facts for our more realistic example are the following:

- T corporation, the target, is an S corporation that has assets with a net tax basis of $200. The historical cost of these assets is $400, and the assets have accumulated depreciation of $200.
- T corporation has no liabilities, and it is owned by individual shareholders that have held their shares for more than 12 months and are subject to federal income taxes at the top statutory rates (20% for capital gains and 40% for ordinary income). T's shareholders have a basis in their T stock of $200.
- All recaptured depreciation is taxable at the ordinary income rate.
- The acquiring firm is willing to pay $1,000 to acquire the stock of T corporation when a Section 338(h)(10) election will not be made.

Should the acquirer and seller make the Section 338(h)(10) election? **Table 13.4** illustrates the following computations. Starting with our base facts (column 1 of **Table 13.4**), T shareholders would have $840 after tax in a taxable stock sale without the election. The acquiring firm's net after-tax cost of this acquisition structure would be $1,000, with no incremental tax benefits from a step-up. To determine what structure is optimal, we must set one party to the transaction indifferent and find which structure is preferable to the other party, under the terms defined by the first party's indifference. At what pretax price, assuming that a Section 338(h)(10) election is made, would the target's

[18] In our simple example, the incremental cost of the step-up was $0 because, under either Case 2 or Case 3, target shareholders faced a tax liability of $180.

[19] These two levels are the oft-repeated "double tax" on C corporations.

Table 15.4 Comparison of the Tax Consequences of Various S Corporation Acquisition Structures: Advanced Example

Fact Pattern:

Stock purchase price	$1,000.00	t_c =	21%
Net tax basis in assets	200.00	t_o =	40%
Historical cost	400.00	t_{cg} =	20%
Accumulated depreciation	200.00	r =	7%
Shareholders' tax basis in target's stock	200.00	Amortization/depreciation period (N) =	10
Liabilities of target	0.00		

	S Corporation Acquisition Structure			Tax Benefit Split[1]	
	Taxable Stock Acquisition without a §338(h)(10) Election	Taxable Stock Acquisition with a §338(h)(10) Election[2]	Taxable Stock Acquisition with a §338(h)(10) Election[2]	Taxable Stock Acquisition with a §338(h)(10) Election[2]	Estimated Incremental After-Tax Benefit
Purchase price—base case	$1,000.00				
Seller's indifference price[3]		$1,050.00			
Acquirer's indifference price[4]			$1,138.41		
Tax benefit split[1]				$1,094.21	
Target Corporation:					
Taxable gain[5]	$ 0.00	$ 850.00	$ 938.41	$ 894.21	
Taxable liability[6]	0.00	0.00	0.00	0.00	
Shareholder Effect:					
Taxable gain[7]	$ 800.00	$ 850.00	$938.41	$894.21	
Cash to shareholders	$1,000.00	$1,050.00	$1,138.41	$1,094.21	
Tax liability[8]	160.00	210.00	227.68	218.84	
After-Tax cash	$840.00	$840.00	$910.73	$875.36	$35.36
Acquirer After-Tax Cost:					
Gross cost	$1,000.00	$1,050.00	$1,138.41	$1,094.21	
Less: Tax benefits[9]	0.00	125.37	138.41	131.89	
Net after-tax cost	$1,000.00	$924.63	$1,000.00	$962.31	$37.69
Acquirer Basis in:					
Target's stock	$1,000.00	$1,050.00	$1,138.41	$1,094.21	
Target's net assets	$200.00	$1,050.00	$1,138.41	$1,094.21	

[1] Purchase price that splits, approximately evenly, the net tax benefits from stepping up the tax basis of the target's assets.

[2] A §338(h)(10) election causes the stock sale to be taxed as if the target's shareholders sold the assets of the target instead of the target's stock.

[3] The purchase price at which the seller is indifferent between making the §338(h)(10) election and not making the election when the purchase price is $1,000 (column 1).

[4] The purchase price at which the acquirer is indifferent between making the §338(h)(10) election and not making the election when the purchase price is $1,000 (column 1).

[5] Taxable gain at the target corporation level from the sale of the target's assets or the deemed asset sale associated with the §338(h)(10) election.

[6] Tax liability at the target corporation level on the taxable gain from the sale of the target's assets or the deemed sale of its assets with the §338(h)(10) election.

[7] Taxable gain at the target shareholder level. This gain is equivalent to the gain at the target corporation level in an asset sale or a stock sale with the §338(h)(10) election as the gain passes through to target shareholders. The gain retains its character (ordinary or capital) as it passes through to target shareholders. In a stock sale without the §338(h)(10) election, the gain is computed as the difference between the purchase price and target shareholders' stock basis. In the latter case, the gain is capital in nature.

[8] Target shareholder tax liability is the taxable gain from the stock or asset sale multiplied by the appropriate tax rate [(7) multiplied by the shareholder tax rate on ordinary income or capital gains].

[9] The present value of the tax savings resulting from stepping-up the tax basis of the target's assets assuming that the step-up is amortized/depreciated straight line over a 10-year period, the applicable tax rate is 21%, and the after-tax discount rate is 7%.

shareholders be indifferent relative to the $1,000 purchase price and no election? We can solve for the pretax price by finding the price that leaves target shareholders with $840 after tax from Equation 13.3.

$$\begin{aligned} Price_{338h10} &= Price_{no338h10} + (Stock \times t_{cg} - HC_{asset} \times t_{cg} + Accum \times t_{oi})(1 - t_{cg}) \\ &= \$1,000 + [\$200(t_{cg}) - \$400(t_{cg}) + \$200(t_{oi})]/(1 - t_{cg}) \\ &= \$1,050 \end{aligned}$$

At a purchase price of $1,050, the stock sale accompanied by a Section 338(h)(10) election would give rise to a $850 taxable gain at the T corporation level. Of this gain, $200 would be ordinary income (recaptured depreciation) and $650 would be capital gain ($1,050 less historical cost of $400). The $850 gain and the character of the gain passes through to T's shareholders. T's shareholders would therefore have a tax liability of $210 computed as 40% multiplied by $200 of ordinary income and 20% multiplied by $650 of capital gain. They would have $840 after tax ($1,050 price less $210 of taxes) and would be indifferent between receiving $1,000 pretax in a stock sale with no election and $1,050 in a stock sale with a Section 338(h)(10) election (see column 2 of **Table 13.4**).

Which structure, then, does A prefer: no election at a price of $1,000 or a deal priced at $1,050 with the election? The net after-tax cost of a taxable stock acquisition without a Section 338(h)(10) election is $1,000 ($1,000 purchase price and zero incremental tax benefits). If the election is made, and the purchase price is $1,050, A's net after-tax cost is $924.63.[20] The size of the step-up, if the election is made, is $850 ($1,050 purchase price less $200 net basis in T's assets), and the present value of the tax savings from the step-up is $125.37, using the same assumptions about depreciable lives, tax, and discount rates as previously. Clearly then, A prefers to pay the higher pretax price to get the step-up in T's assets.

From A's perspective, the incremental cost of obtaining a step-up is $50 ($1,050 purchase price less $1,000 price without the election), and the incremental tax benefit is $125.37. Thus, A is better off by $75.37 after tax when the transaction is structured in a manner that results in a step-up in T's assets.[21] The $75.37 can be thought of as the net tax benefits from stepping up the tax basis of the target's assets. These tax benefits can be split between the acquirer and the target, as we will illustrate in a moment.

Under our new facts, we see the purchase price at which the acquirer is indifferent or the maximum price the acquirer will pay when T's assets are stepped up is given by Equation 13.6:

$$\begin{aligned} \mathbf{Acqprice_{338h10}} &= \mathbf{(\$1,000 - .14749 \times \$200)/(1 - .14749)} \\ &= \mathbf{\$1,138.41} \end{aligned} \tag{13.6}$$

The acquirer will therefore be indifferent between a stock acquisition without the Section 338(h) (10) election at a price of $1,000 and a stock acquisition with the election at a price of $1,138.41, because the acquirer's net after-tax cost under either scenario is $1,000, as illustrated in the first and third columns of **Table 13.4**.

For an advisor to target shareholders, the ability to estimate this price is obviously quite useful because the shareholders benefit from knowing the maximum price the acquirer will pay under varying acquisition tax structures. Notice that, at a price of $1,138.41, with the election, target shareholders have $910.73 after tax, which is about 8.4% more than if the election is not made and the purchase price is $1,000.

At any price between $1,050 and $1,138.41, with the Section 338(h)(10) election, both the acquirer and target shareholders are better off after tax than if the deal is priced at $1,000 and the election is not made jointly by the buyer and seller. As the purchase price approaches $1,050 ($1,138.41), the acquirer (target shareholders) is (are) relatively better off. Essentially, the difference between $1,050 and $1,138.41 is the incremental tax benefit from stepping up the tax basis of the target's assets that can be shared between the buyer and seller. For example, consider a price exactly halfway between these amounts ($1,094.21). At this price, target shareholders' after-tax wealth is $875.36, which is $35.36 more after tax than they receive if the transaction is priced at $1,000 and the *joint* election is

[20] Notice that the acquirer's net after-tax cost is about 7.5% lower than when the election was not made.

[21] The difference in A's net after-tax cost is $75.37, as illustrated in the first two columns of **Table 13.4**.

not made. Similarly, the acquirer's net after tax cost is $37.69 less than if the deal is priced at $1,000 and the election is not made. The last two columns of **Table 13.4** contain these computations. Notice that, even at a pretax *premium* of 9.4% [($1,094.21 – $1,000)/$1,000], the acquirer is better off after tax by about 3.7% if the tax basis of the target's assets is stepped up.

Is this conclusion reasonable, or is it an ivory tower fantasy? What is the source of this value that increases both the buyer's and the seller's wealth?

The preceding equations formally explain this phenomenon but, stated simply, in an S corporation acquisition, a step-up in the tax basis of the target's assets incrementally costs much less than the incremental benefits of such a step-up. That is, in the absence of a step-up election, S corporation shareholders face almost the same amount of tax they do if the step-up election is made. Therefore, the incremental cost of the election is often relatively low. The incremental tax benefit of the election, however, can be large. The same is generally true in acquisitions of other types of conduits. The net benefit is the source of wealth gains that can be shared between the buyer and seller. Of course, informed parties should make the most of these net benefits when structuring and pricing an acquisition.

13.2 COMPARISON OF THE SALE OF SIMILAR S AND C CORPORATIONS

Important differences mark the way in which acquisitions of conduits (e.g., S corporations) and C corporations are taxed. Notably, two levels of tax characterize the acquisition of a C corporation and only one in the acquisition of an S corporation. Here, via numerical illustration, we want to highlight these differences. The computations discussed in this section are illustrated in **Table 13.5**. The facts for this example include the following:

- The two identical corporations are T1 and T2: T1 is a freestanding C corporation and T2 is an S corporation.
- The net tax basis of each firm's assets is $200 ($400 historical cost, $200 accumulated depreciation).
- Neither firm has any liabilities.
- Shareholders of both T1 and T2 are individuals facing the maximum ordinary and capital gains tax rates (assumed to be 40% and 20%) and have a tax basis in the stock of each corporation of $200.
- All parties agree that the present value of the after-tax future cash flows of T1 and T2 is $900 each, ignoring any value created by tax structuring.
- T1's ordinary income tax rate is 21%, as is its capital gains tax rate.
- All recaptured depreciation is taxed at the ordinary income rate.
- An acquirer wishes to purchase both T1 and T2 and is willing to pay $900 for each company in a *taxable stock acquisition* in which the tax basis of the target's assets carries over.

What price will an acquirer (A) pay to purchase the *assets* of T1 and T2 in a taxable acquisition? Will shareholders accept this price? Will the S corporation and C corporation sell for the same price, or will they sell at different prices due to the divergent tax treatment of S corporations and C corporations? We first consider the tax consequences of a taxable stock sale.

Tax Consequences for T1 and T2 Shareholders in a Taxable Stock Sale

In each case, shareholders will have a capital gain of $700 ($900 purchase price less $200 stock basis) and will pay tax of $140 ($700 × 20%). After tax, the shareholders of both T1 and T2 will have $760.

Tax Consequences for the Acquirer ("A") Corporation A will take a basis in the stock of T1 equal to $900. T1 will become a subsidiary of the acquirer and the net tax basis of T1's assets will

Table 13.5 Comparison of Acquisition Prices of S Corporations and C Corporations with Identical Tax Attributes and Cash Flows

Fact Pattern:

Stock purchase price	$900.00	t_c =	21%
Net tax basis in assets	200.00	t_o =	40%
Historical cost	400.00	t_{cg} =	20%
Accumulated depreciation	200.00	r =	7%
Shareholder's tax basis in target's stock	200.00	N =	10
Liabilities of target	0.00		

	S Corporation Acquisition Structure			C Corporation Acquisition Structure		
	Taxable Stock Acquisition without a §338(h)(10) Election	Taxable Stock Acquisition with a §338(h)(10) Election	Taxable Stock Acquisition with a §338(h)(10) Election	Taxable Stock Acquisition without a §338 Election	Taxable Asset Acquisition	Taxable Asset Acquisition
Purchase price	$900.00			$900.00		
Seller's indifference price[1]		$950.00			$1,086.08	
Acquirer's indifference price[2]			$1,021.11			$1,021.11
Target Corporation:						
Taxable gain[3]	$700.00	$750.00	$821.11	$0.00	$886.08	$821.11
Tax liability[4]	0.00	0.00	0.00	0.00	186.08	172.43
Shareholder Effects:						
Taxable gain[5]	$700.00	$750.00	$821.11	700.00	700.00	648.68
Cash received	$900.00	$950.00	$1,021.11	$900.00	$900.00	$848.68
Tax liability[6]	140.00	190.00	204.22	140.00	140.00	129.74
After-tax cash	$760.00	$760.00	$816.89	$760.00	$760.00	$718.94
Acquirer After-tax Cost:						
Gross cost	$900.00	$950.00	$1,021.11	$900.00	$1,086.08	$1,021.11
Less: Tax benefits[7]	0.00	110.62	121.11	0.00	130.69	121.11
Net after-tax cost	$900.00	$839.38	$900.00	$900.00	$955.38	$900.00
Acquirer Tax Basis in the:						
Target's stock	$900.00	$950.00	$1,021.11	$900.00	n/a	n/a
Target's net assets	$200.00	$950.00	$1,021.11	$200.00	$1,086.08	$1,021.11

Notes:

[1] The purchase price at which the seller is indifferent between making the §338(h)(10) election and not making the election when the purchase price is $900 (column 1) when the target is an S corporation. When the target is a C corporation, the purchase price at which the seller is indifferent between an asset sale and a taxable stock sale without a §338 election at a price of $900 (column 4).

[2] The purchase price at which the acquirer is indifferent between making the §338(h)(10) election and not making the election when the purchase price is $900 (column 1) when the target is an S corporation. When the target is a C corporation, the purchase price at which the acquirer is indifferent between an asset sale and a taxable stock sale without a §338 election at a price of $900 (column 4).

[3] Taxable gain at the target corporation level from the stock sale or the deemed sale of the target's assets (S corporation) or the sale of the target's assets (C corporation).

[4] Tax liability at the target corporation level on the taxable gain from the stock sale, the deemed asset sale (S corporation), or the asset sale (C corporation).

[5] Taxable gain at the target shareholder level. This gain is equivalent to the gain at the target corporation level if the target is an S corporation as the gain passes through to target shareholders. The gain retains its character as it passes through to target shareholders. If the target was a C corporation, this is the gain on the liquidation (redemption of target shares by the target) of the C corporation after the asset sale.

[6] Target shareholder tax liabilities are computed based on (5) and the nature of the gain to the target's shareholders if the target was an S corporation. If the target was a C corporation, the tax liability is the gain (5) multiplied by the capital gains tax rate.

[7] The present value of the tax savings resulting from stepping up the tax basis of the target's assets assuming that the step-up is amortized/depreciated straight line over a

be $200. The acquirer will have the same basis in the stock and assets of T2. T2 will also become a subsidiary of A.

Indifference Point for T1's Shareholders (C Corporation) with an Asset Sale Structure T1's shareholders will be indifferent between a stock sale at $900 and an asset sale when they have $760 after tax from the asset sale. We can compute the purchase price they will demand as follows using Equation 12.6 from Chapter 12.

$$\begin{aligned} \textbf{Price}_{\textbf{asset}} &= (\textbf{Price}_{\textbf{stock}} - \textbf{Asset} \times t_c)/(1 - t_c) \\ &= (\$900 - \$200 \times t_c)/(1 - t_c) \qquad (12.6) \\ &= \$1{,}086.08 \end{aligned}$$

Indifference Price for T2's Shareholders (S Corporation) with an Asset Sale Structure T2's shareholders will be indifferent between a stock sale at $900 and an asset sale (stock sale with a Section 338[h][10] election) when they have $760 after tax under the asset sale structure. We can compute the purchase price they will demand as follows using Equation 13.3. The second column of **Table 13.5** presents this computation.

$$\begin{aligned} \text{Price}_{338h10} &= \text{Price}_{no338h10} + [\text{Stock}(t_{cg}) - \text{HC}_{asset}(t_{cg}) + \text{Accum}(t_{oi})]/\ (1 - t_{cg}) \\ &= \$900 + [\ 200(t_{cg}) - 400(t_{cg}) + 200(t_{oi})]/\ (1 - t_{cg}) \\ &= \$950 \end{aligned}$$

Will the Acquirer Pay T1's (C Corporation) Indifference Price in a Taxable Asset Sale? In a taxable asset sale, A will obtain a step-up in the basis of the target's assets. We already computed that T1's shareholders will not agree to a taxable asset sale structure unless A pays them at least $1,086.08. Is A willing to pay that price to obtain a step-up in T1's assets?

If A pays $1,086.08 in a taxable asset acquisition, it will take a basis in T1's assets of $1,086.08. This step-up in basis is equal to $886.08 ($1,086.08 less $200 net tax basis in T1's assets preacquisition). Assuming the step-up in basis is amortized straight line over 10 years, the appropriate tax rate is 21%, and the after-tax discount rate is 7%, the present value of tax savings from the step-up is $130.69. A's net after-tax cost is therefore $955.38, which is more than A's net after-tax cost in a taxable stock acquisition ($900).

Alternatively, as the sixth column of **Table 13.5** indicates, the maximum price that the acquirer will pay in a taxable asset sale is $1,021.11, which is computed using Equation 12.9 from Chapter 12. At that price, T1's shareholders receive $718.94 after tax, which is less than they receive in the taxable stock acquisition case at a price of $900. T1's shareholders would obviously not accept a taxable asset sale at $1,021.11. Therefore, a step-up in T1's assets is not optimal. This result is the same as obtained in Section 12.2 of Chapter 12 (i.e., a step-up structure does not make sense in the acquisition of a freestanding C corporation). Notice here that the incremental cost of the step-up to A is $186.08 ($1,086.08 less $900 price with no step-up) and the incremental tax benefits from the step-up are $130.69.

Will the Acquirer Pay T2's (S Corporation) Indifference Price in a Taxable Asset Sale (Stock Sale with a Section 338[h][10] Election)? We already computed that T2's shareholders will not agree to a taxable asset sale structure—a stock sale with a Section 338(h)(10) election—unless A pays them at least $950. Is A willing to pay that price to obtain a step-up in T2's assets?

If A pays $950 in a taxable asset acquisition, it will take a basis in T2's assets of $950. This step-up in basis is equal to $750 ($950 less $200 net tax basis in T2's assets preacquisition). Assuming that the step-up in basis is amortized straight line over 10 years, that the appropriate tax rate is 21%, and that the after-tax discount rate is 7%, the present value of tax savings from the step-up is $110.62. A's net after-tax cost is therefore $839.38 (see the second column of **Table 13.5**), which is less than A's net after-tax cost in a taxable stock acquisition ($900). So A will (gladly) pay $950 in a taxable stock acquisition followed by a Section 338(h)(10) election.

Continuing with the example, A will pay T2 more than $950 in a taxable asset acquisition. A will pay a pretax price that leaves its after-tax cost equal to $900. Specifically, as illustrated in the third column of **Table 13.5**, A will pay *up* to $1,021.11 pretax in a transaction that is taxed as an asset acquisition and still be as well off as when it pays $900 in a taxable stock sale.[22] At a price of $1,021.11, and a taxable asset sale structure, T2's shareholders would have $816.89 after tax, which is $56.89 more after tax than in a taxable stock sale at $900. It is important to notice that S corporation shareholders are able to obtain $56.89 (about 7.5%) more after tax than their counterparts who sold the C corporation (T1).[23] Again, any price between $950 and $1,021.11 with a taxable asset sale type structure in an S corporation acquisition leaves both the acquirer and seller better off, and any price within that range provides a split of the tax benefits from the asset sale structure.

The point of these numerical exercises is simple but important. An S corporation can often be sold for a higher price pretax than a similar C corporation because the sale of the former can be

[22] We can compute this amount using Equation 13.5.

[23] Compare the third and fourth columns of **Table 13.5**.

structured in a way that results in a step-up in the tax basis of the target's assets in a cost-effective manner. That is, acquirers are willing to pay S corporation target shareholders for the tax benefits associated with the step-up.[24] The same is not true of sales of C corporations.[25] Acquirers of C corporations are not willing to incur the incremental costs of stepping-up the tax basis of the target's assets. There are a number of examples that illustrate this basic phenomenon, and we present some of those next.

In its 2000 acquisition of Leeson Electric, Regal Beloit made the following disclosure:[26]

> Leeson Electric was acquired for approximately $260 million in cash. The definitive agreement provides for treating the acquisition as a purchase of assets for tax purposes, utilizing a 338(h)(10) election under the Internal Revenue Code. This election will provide Regal-Beloit with a net present value of future tax benefits of an estimated $47 million. When this tax benefit is deducted from the $260 million purchase price, the result is a 7.6 times purchase multiple on Leeson's adjusted EBITDA of approximately $28 million for the 12 months ended June 30, 2000. The purchase multiple paid for the Company's acquisition of Marathon Electric in March 1997 was 7.5 times trailing 12-month EBITDA.

Leeson Electric was an S corporation, and Marathon Electric was a C corporation. This disclosure indicates that Regal Beloit obtained tax benefits from a 338(h)(10) election in the acquisition of Leeson, and those benefits were equivalent to about 18% of the transaction's value ($47 million/$260 million = ~18%). Furthermore, the disclosure indicates that Regal Beloit paid a higher purchase multiple for the S corporation than the C corporation. The price-to-EBITDA multiple paid for Leeson Electric was about 9.3 ($260 million price/$28 million EBITDA), whereas the price-to-EBITDA multiple paid for Marathon was 7.5. However, after adjusting for the tax benefits in the Leeson deal ($47 million), the adjusted after-tax benefits-price-to-EBITDA multiples were similar[($260M – $47M)/$28M = ~7.6 price-to-EBITDA multiple].

When Coca Cola Enterprises (CCE) acquired HerbCo in 2001 for more than $1 billion, the *Wall Street Journal* reported that "CCE said it also plans to pay $100 million in incremental tax benefits associated with the transaction."[27] HerbCo was an S corporation and the transaction was structured to include a 338(h)(10) election. CCE paid $100 million to the shareholders of HerbCo to make the 338(h)(10) election. Moreover, we learned that CCE valued the incremental tax benefits of the 338(h)(10) election at about $145 million. Therefore, CCE paid the selling shareholders of HerbCo almost 70% of the tax benefits created by the 338(h)(10) election. We also confirmed with executives at CCE that CCE would not have paid the $100 million tax-driven premium if HerbCo had been a C

[24] As a result of this institutional feature of S corporations, owners of privately held C corporations that are contemplating a sale of the business at some date in the future may want to consider switching from C corporation status to S corporation status. Such switches are not uncommon. However, when switching to S corporation status, if the business is sold within 5 years after the switch, the business sale is in general terms taxed as if it were a C corporation during that 5-year post-switch window. The tax during this 5-year window is the "built in gains tax" under Section 1374.

[25] See Jeffrey Wagner, "Obtaining Maximum Value on the Sale of an S Corporation," (Washington, DC: McDermott, Will & Emery), Mondaq Business Briefing, August 13, 2012, which makes a similar point and states:

> As a general rule, businesses that are organized as state law corporations are subject to a double level of tax—that is, earnings and realized appreciation are taxed once at the corporate level and a second time when the earnings or appreciation are distributed to the stockholders. This double level of tax generally precludes the stockholders from structuring a sale of the business as an asset sale—which happens to be the purchaser's preferred acquisition structure. Importantly for the selling stockholders, it prevents them from obtaining the premium (as described below) that a purchaser is generally willing to pay for assets as compared to a stock purchase. Fortunately, many family enterprises that are organized as state law corporations qualify (and, importantly, have elected to be taxed for income tax purposes) as S corporations. There are 4.5 million S corporations in the United States, according to the S Corporation Association, and many of them are large, mature businesses that are prime acquisition targets. A simple tax election [338(h)(10) election] that is made in connection with the sale of the stock of an S corporation significantly enhances the value of an S corporation target, and such value should be captured by the selling stockholders.

[26] Source: October 13, 2000, 8-K of Regal Beloit.

[27] Betsy McKay, "Coca-Cola Enterprises Is Set to Acquire Bottlers Hondo, Herbco for $1.07 Billion," *Wall Street Journal*, May 1, 2001.

corporation.[28] *Crain's Chicago Business* noted the tax benefits associated with the sale of an S corporation and pass-through entities and to HerbCo in particular, "A spokesman at Coca-Cola Enterprises' Atlanta headquarters confirmed that it bumped the price paid to Mr. Herb and other shareholders by $100 million, strictly because of the tax benefits of purchasing a pass-through company."[29]

In 2010, GP Strategies acquired PerformTech Inc. (an S corporation) for about $15.9 million of cash plus an earnout with an estimated value of about $4.3 million for a total deal value of about $20.2 million. The PerformTech acquisition was structured to include a 338(h)(10) election.[30] In that transaction, GP strategies estimated that the tax benefits of the 338(h)(10) election were equivalent to "roughly $4 million."[31] Thus, the tax benefits of the election are equivalent to about 20% of the reported deal value ($4 million/$20.2 million = ~20%). The stock purchase agreement specifies "Lost 338(h)(10) Benefits" as an amount equivalent to $2.2 million (plus other adjustments) that the seller must pay the acquirer in the event that a valid 338(h)(10) election is not completed in the acquisition.[32] Thus, if the transaction is completed without a 338(h)(10) election, the price paid for the target declines by $2.2 million. This contractual language is consistent with the selling firm shareholders capturing about 50% of the tax benefits created in the transaction ($2.2 million "lost 338[h][10] benefits" divided by "roughly" $4 million of total tax benefits from the 338[h][10] election).

The tax benefits of acquiring a pass-through entity are not exclusive to S corporations. When Blackstone went public in 2007, it structured its IPO in a manner that resulted in a step-up in basis in its assets. Blackstone was a partnership pre-IPO and it executed what is known as a Section 754 election as part of the IPO. The Section 754 election is in simplified terms the partnership analog to the S corporation 338(h)(10) election. As a result of the tax structure of the IPO, Blackstone's partners were set to receive about $751 million of tax benefits in the IPO.[33] Similarly, when KKR went public in 2010, it structured its IPO to include a Section 754 election, thereby creating the same kind of tax benefits generated in the Blackstone IPO.[34]

As noted at the beginning of this chapter, when Bai Brands LLC was acquired by Dr. Pepper in 2016 for $1.7 billion, it was reported that the acquisition generated $400 million of tax benefits.[35] Similarly, Kellogg's $600 million purchase of Chicago Bar Company, LLC, generated $200 million of tax benefits.[36] These tax benefits are the result of a step-up in the basis of the target LLCs' assets.

The tax benefits of a 338(h)(10) election are well known in the investment banking community. It is also widely accepted that the tax benefits of a 338(h)(10) election significantly reduce the cost of an acquisition for the buyer and that these tax benefits are typically shared with the seller in the form of a higher purchase price.

> However, it is an investment banking rule of thumb that the ability to secure a cost basis in acquired assets—and in the process, gain access to the benefits of Section 197(a)—reduces the "effective cost" of the deal by approximately 20 percent. Of course, here, as in most Section 338(h)(10) situations, a portion of the benefit will be "shared" with the seller in the form of a higher purchase price for the properties.[37]

---

[28] This example is drawn from Erickson and Wang (2007). Similarly, Erickson and Wang (2007) report that Stoneridge paid a premium in the range of $30 to $35 million for the 338(h)(10) election in its $362 million acquisition of Hi-Stat, Inc (an S corporation).

[29] M. Hendricks, "The S-Corp Windfall," *Crain's Chicago Business*, May 9, 2005.

[30] Source: GP Strategies 8-K dated January 5, 2010.

[31] Source: July 11, 2011, GP Strategies conference call transcript available through CQ FD Disclosure.

[32] Source: Stock purchase agreement dated December 30, 2009, between General Physics Corporation and PerformTech (attached to January 5, 2010, GP Strategies 8-K).

[33] David Cay Johnson, "Tax Loopholes Sweeten a Deal for Blackstone," *New York Times*, July 13, 2007.

[34] See Allan Sloan, "KKR Leaders Get a Tax Deal Most of Us Can Only Dream Of," *Washington Post*, July 28, 2010.

[35] Source: Jennifer Kaplan, "Dr. Pepper Buys Bai Brands for $1.7B, Ups Low-Calorie Game," *Chicago Tribune*, November 22, 2016.

[36] Source: "Kellogg Adds RXBAR, Fastest Growing US Nutrition Bar Brand, to Wholesome Snacks Portfolio," *PR Newswire*, October 6, 2017.

[37] Source: Robert Willens, "ESRX Will Enjoy a Basis 'Step-Up,'" *Willens Report*, April 14, 2009.

For tax planners selecting an organizational form for a new or reorganized business entity, conduits such as S corporations, limited liability corporations, and partnerships provide significant tax benefits relative to C corporations if and when the entire entity is sold, as illustrated in this section and in **Table 13.5**.[38] Thus, when forming a new business, we encourage entrepreneurs to think about the acquisition related tax benefits of pass-through organizational forms. Similarly, owners of C corporations that intend to sell those entities in the future may wish to consider switching to a pass-through entity structure to reap the benefits of those structures denoted in this chapter.

Valuation Consequences and Issues

As we have seen in Section 13.1, the price at which a conduit entity (S corporation) is sold is a function of the tax structure of the transaction (e.g., taxable stock sale with and without a Section 338[h][10] election). In Section 13.2, we demonstrated that comparable S and C corporations could sell for different prices due to tax differences that spring from organizational form. Specifically, the sale of an S corporation often includes a premium that is associated with incremental tax benefits from stepping up the S corporation's assets.

When evaluating a potential target corporation, or when contemplating the sale of a business, we often derive an estimate of the value of the subject company from comparable acquisitions. Similarly, the reasonableness of a purchase or sale price is often evaluated relative to comparable transactions. It is common to use various valuation benchmarks including multiples such as acquisition price to earnings or cash flows. Those of you performing a so-called comparables analysis should be aware of the effect of organizational form and acquisition tax structure on acquisition prices as illustrated in Sections 13.1 and 13.2.

Summary of Key Points

1. Acquisitions occur across a number of transactional forms. These alternative forms yield varying tax consequences to the target company, to the purchasing company, and to the shareholders of the target company.
2. In the sale of a freestanding C corporation, a structure that results in a step-up in the target's assets is usually suboptimal from a tax perspective because the incremental tax cost associated with the step-up usually exceeds the incremental tax benefits.
3. In the sale of a conduit entity, such as an S corporation, it often makes sense to structure the acquisition in a manner that steps up the tax basis of the target's assets because the incremental cost of stepping up the basis of the target S corporation's assets is usually less than the tax savings associated with the step-up. Sales of conduits (S corporations) are quite different from acquisitions of C corporations in this respect.
4. A taxable stock sale of an S corporation can be taxed as an asset sale if the buyer and seller (target corporation shareholders) agree to make a Section 338(h)(10) election.
5. Tax planners who are considering organizational forms for a new entity should consider the differences in the taxation of acquisitions of conduits relative to the taxation of C corporations. Specifically, if planners anticipate a sale of the entire entity rather than an IPO, for example, a conduit can be sold for a higher pretax price than a C corporation, everything else being equal. As a result, the conduit entity may be the wealth-maximizing organizational form, holding other factors constant.

Questions

Q13-1. What are the main tax considerations to a purchaser in the sale of a target's stock when the target is an S corporation?

[38] The same basic principles apply to the sale of other types of conduit entities, such as partnerships, REITs, and LLCs with, of course, additional complicating factors in some circumstances.

Q13-2. Why does the taxable acquisition of an S corporation give rise to incremental tax benefits from stepping up the target's assets while the acquisition of a freestanding C corporation does not?

Q13-3. If you were advising the founders of a new internet-based business, what would you tell them about the benefits of using a conduit organizational form to operate their business?

Tax-Planning Problems

TP13-4. Hurricane, Inc., is an S corporation. Orleans, Inc., wants to acquire Hurricane for cash. Hurricane's shareholders have a tax basis in their stock of $3,000, and Hurricane has assets with a net tax basis of $3,000 (cost = $4,500, accumulated depreciation = $1,500). Hurricane has no liabilities. Assume the transaction can be structured one of two ways:

Option 1: As a taxable stock acquisition without a Section 338(h)(10) election
Option 2: As a taxable stock acquisition with a Section 338(h)(10) election

Further assume that Orleans is willing to pay $5,000 to acquire Hurricane under either structure and that all depreciation claimed to date must be recaptured to the extent of the purchase price. Assume that all recaptured depreciation is taxed at the highest ordinary income rate and that no additional taxes will apply in an asset sale due to US Tax Code restrictions relating to S corporations.

a. How much cash after tax will Hurricane's shareholders have under Option 1? Assume the tax rate appropriate for capital gains is 20% and for ordinary income is 40%.

b. How much cash after tax will Hurricane's shareholders have under Option 2? Assume the tax rate appropriate for capital gains is 20% and for ordinary income is 40%.

c. Assume that Orleans is willing to pay $5,000 using Option 1. At what purchase price when employing Option 2 are Hurricane's shareholders indifferent between the two transaction structures?

d. What is the maximum price that Orleans will pay under Option 2 assuming that Orleans will pay $5,000 under Option 1? Assume that any step-up amount is depreciated/amortized over 10 years using the straight-line method, that the marginal tax rate for Orleans is 21%, and that the after-tax discount rate is 10%.

e. Should the Section 338(h)(10) election be made? Why or why not?

f. If the answer to part (e) was yes, how much better off are Orleans and Hurricane at the midpoint price between the amounts you computed in parts (c) and (d), if the election is made, relative to no election at a price of $5,000?

TP13-5. Cambridge, Inc., is an S corporation. Courtesan, Inc., wants to acquire Cambridge for cash. Cambridge's shareholders have a tax basis in their stock of $5,000 (they have held the stock for 5 years), and Cambridge has assets with a net tax basis of $5,000 (cost = $7,500, accumulated depreciation = $2,500). Cambridge has no liabilities. Assume that the transaction can be structured one of two ways:

Option 1: As a taxable stock acquisition without a Section 338(h)(10) election
Option 2: As a taxable stock acquisition with a Section 338(h)(10) election (*Recall that this election results in the transaction being taxed as an asset sale.*)

Further assume that Courtesan is willing to pay $12,500 to acquire Cambridge under either structure and that all depreciation claimed to date must be recaptured to the extent of the purchase price. Assume that no additional taxes will apply in an asset sale due to US Tax Code restrictions relating to S corporations.

a. How much cash after tax will Cambridge's shareholders have under Option 1? Assume the tax rate appropriate for capital gains is 20% and for ordinary income is 40%.

b. How much cash after tax will Cambridge's shareholders have under Option 2? Assume the tax rate appropriate for capital gains is 20% and for ordinary income is 40%.

c. Assume that Courtesan is willing to pay $12,500 using Option 1. At what purchase price *P* when employing Option 2 are Cambridge's shareholders indifferent between the two transaction options?

d. Given the purchase price you computed in part (c), which structure is optimal from Courtesan's perspective (Option 1 at a purchase price of $12,500 or Option 2 at a price *P* computed in part [c])? Assume any step-up amount is depreciated/amortized over 10 years using the straight-line method, the marginal tax rate for Courtesan is 21%, and the after-tax discount rate is 12%.

e. What is the maximum price that Courtesan will pay under Option 2 assuming that Courtesan will pay $12,500 under Option 1? Assume that any step-up amount is depreciated/amortized over 10 years using the straight-line method, the marginal tax rate for Orleans is 21%, and the after-tax discount rate is 12%.

f. Should the Section 338(h)(10) election be made? Why or why not?

g. Assume you are an advisor to Cambridge's shareholders and they agreed to pay you 30% of any after-tax increase in their wealth associated with your advice on this transaction. Could you increase their after-tax wealth beyond what they receive under Option 1? If yes, explain briefly how (20 words will do). If yes, how much could you increase their wealth after tax approximately (before your 30% fee) if Cambridge persuaded Courtesan to pay the maximum price computed in part (e)? How much would you stand to make if they listened to you? Use the assumptions in part (e) if necessary.

TP13-6. The following facts relate to the purchase of an S corporation and a C corporation. These two corporations have identical tax bases and are similar in every respect except for their organizational form. The acquirer is willing to pay $10,000 to purchase the stock of each corporation.

Fact Pattern:	
Stock purchase price	$10,000.00
Net tax basis in assets	500.00
Historical cost of assets	2,000.00
Accumulated depreciation	1,500.00
Shareholders' tax basis in target's stock	500.00
Liabilities of target	0.00
t_c =	21%
t_o =	40%
t_{cg} =	20%
r =	7%
n =	10

a. What is the maximum price that an acquirer will pay to acquire the target C corporation in taxable asset sale given that it will pay $10,000 in a taxable stock acquisition?

b. What is the maximum price that an acquirer will pay to acquire the target S corporation in taxable stock sale followed by a Section 338(h)(10) election given that it will pay $10,000 in a taxable stock acquisition without the election?

c. What is the minimum price that the target's shareholders will accept under part (a)?

d. What is the minimum price that the target's shareholders will accept under part (b)?

e. Given your answer to parts (a) and (c), should a taxable asset sale structure be employed in the sale of the C corporation?

f. Given your answers to parts (b) and (d), should the Section 338(h)(10) election be made in the sale of the S corporation?

g. How much more cash after tax can shareholders of the S corporations get relative to shareholders of the C corporation, assuming the acquirer pays the maximum price that it will pay in a Section 338(h)(10) transaction? Note that the C corporation is sold in a taxable stock sale at $10,000 and the S corporation is sold for the price you computed in part (b).

TP13-7. Assume you are performing a comparable company analysis for a pending acquisition. You are advising the target company and the target company is a privately held S corporation. The comparable company acquisitions, for which you have data, are exclusively taxable acquisitions of freestanding C corporations.

Your assistant has computed the following common valuation benchmarks for the comparable company acquisitions:

	Mean	Median
Price to revenues	.82	.76
Price to book value	2.21	2.07
Price to earnings	23.4	18.6
Price to EBITDA	9.58	7.13

Further assume that the target company is considered similar to the comparable companies in terms of revenue and profitability prospects—that is, the target company is about the same as the comparables in terms of operations.

Would you recommend any adjustments to the comparable company analyses, or would you tell your client to accept an acquirer's offer that is equal to the average price to EBITDA of the comparable company acquisitions?

References and Additional Readings

See the list at the end of Chapter 11.

14

Tax-Free Acquisitions of Freestanding C Corporations

Facebook acquired Instagram in 2012 for around $1 billion. It was reported that Facebook paid about $300 million in cash and about $700 million of Facebook stock in the deal. In this chapter, you will learn the tax consequences to Facebook and Instagram of the tax structure selected in that transaction. Similarly, in 2012, Disney agreed to acquire LucasFilm for Disney stock and cash. This chapter discusses the tax implications of the Disney/LucasFilm transaction to the acquirer, target, and target shareholders. In 2010, Airtran had about $477 million of net operating loss carryforwards (NOLs) when it was acquired by Southwest Airlines for about $1.4 billion. Post-acquisition, Southwest was able to use Airtran's NOLs to reduce its tax liabilities, subject to certain limitations in the tax law. As a result, Airtran's NOLs generated positive cash flow for Southwest. In this chapter, you will learn how to estimate the positive post-closing cash flow effects resulting from using a target's NOLs.

After completing this chapter, you should be able to:

1. Describe the four basic types of tax-free acquisitions of freestanding C corporations and the requirements for tax-free treatment.
2. Identify the tax consequences for the acquirer, the target, and the target's shareholders of various tax-free acquisition structures.
3. Compare the tax and nontax costs and benefits of taxable and tax-free acquisitions of freestanding C corporations.
4. Quantify the differential tax effects of taxable and tax-free acquisitions of freestanding C corporations.

In the last two chapters, we concentrated on taxable acquisitions of freestanding C corporations and taxable acquisitions of S corporations, respectively. Under all taxable structuring alternatives, the target's shareholders face an immediate tax liability. If the parties can agree to combine in a tax-free transaction under U.S. Tax Code Section 368 or Section 351, the target's shareholders avoid recognizing a current capital gain on the transaction. The buyer also has access to the target's tax attributes (e.g., NOLs, tax credits, etc.), with some limitations, in a tax-free reorganization. However, in a tax-free acquisition, it is not possible to step up the tax basis of the target's assets.

In this chapter, we discuss various types of tax-free reorganizations under Section 368 and Section 351. We focus exclusively on tax-free acquisitions of freestanding C corporations in this chapter. The term *tax free* is actually a misnomer because these transactions provide target shareholders with tax deferral of the gain on the acquisition, not tax-free treatment. In this chapter, we discuss and analyze tax-free acquisitions using several numerical examples similar to those in the prior two chapters. We also analyze the limitations imposed on a target's tax attributes by Section 382 in carryover-basis transactions. We defer our discussion of tax-free acquisitions of corporate subsidiaries until Chapter 15.

14.1 BASIC TYPES OF TAX-FREE REORGANIZATIONS

Of the four basic tax-free methods to acquire a freestanding C corporation, three are defined under **Section 368(a)(1)**. These three types are commonly known as **"A," "B," and "C" reorganizations**. The major differences between these reorganization structures relate to whether assets or stocks are acquired and to the quantity and type of consideration required for tax-free treatment, such as at least 40% acquirer stock. Two variants of the Section 368 reorganization, known generally as **triangular mergers**, use a subsidiary of the acquiring firm to facilitate the acquisition. The fourth type of acquisition is defined by Section 351, which specifies the conditions under which a **corporate formation** qualifies for tax-free treatment.[1] Under any of these tax-free reorganization structures, target shareholders must recognize a taxable gain to the extent they receive cash or other forms of boot. *Boot* is broadly defined as cash and debt-type securities.

As we describe and contrast the various tax-free reorganization structures in this chapter, we focus on the tax consequences of the structure to the acquirer, the target firm, and the target's shareholders. We pay particular attention to the resulting tax basis in the property transferred and received among these three parties.

First, we describe the general requirements for tax-free treatment in a merger. We then provide a detailed explanation of various types of tax-free reorganizations. **Table 14.1** provides an overview of the tax consequences of the tax-free acquisition structures discussed in those sections.

General Requirements for Tax-Free Treatment under Section 368

To qualify as tax free under **Section 368**, an acquisition has to meet several general requirements. First, target shareholders must maintain a continuity of interest in the assets of the target. For practical purposes, continuity of interest simply means that target shareholders must receive stock of the acquirer in return for their target shares.[2] It is generally agreed that 40% acquiring firm stock is the minimum amount of acquirer stock necessary to qualify for tax-free treatment. As we discuss later, certain types of transactions under Section 368 impose additional restrictions on the form and percentage of total consideration required for tax-free treatment.

Second, an acquirer cannot purchase a target company in a tax-free transaction and then immediately liquidate the target's assets. This principle of **continuity of business interest** means that the acquirer must continue to use the assets of the target in a productive capacity post-acquisition. The acquirer can, however, dispose of some of the target's assets after the transaction is completed. In fact, in some cases, for regulatory reasons, acquirers must sell off portions of the target's business. Also note that the acquirer need not use the target's assets in the same business in which the target operated. The acquirer must simply use those assets in a productive capacity. Finally, the acquisition must have a valid business purpose and cannot be motivated purely as a mechanism to avoid tax. We next discuss specific types of tax-free acquisitions, requirements for tax-free treatment under each structure, and the tax implications of each structure.

14.2 SECTION 368 "A" REORGANIZATION: STATUTORY MERGER

Under a **Section 368 "A" reorganization**, depicted in **Figure 14.1**, the acquirer exchanges its stock and possibly some boot (e.g., cash) for the assets and liabilities of the target. The target corporation must distribute the consideration received from the acquirer to its shareholders in return for their target stock in liquidation. The **liquidating distribution** is tax free as long as target shareholders receive stock of the acquirer. If they receive cash, the cash is taxable even if the transaction is tax free. Specifically, target shareholders recognize a taxable gain that is the lesser of the gain realized or the boot received. Gain realized is computed as the difference between the purchase price (value of consideration received) and the selling shareholders' tax basis in the target's stock. Losses realized are not recognized, however. After the transaction, shareholders of the target become shareholders of the acquirer, which post-merger owns the assets of the target.

[1] A merger can be structured as a corporate formation transaction.

[2] By obtaining acquiring firm stock, target shareholders maintain an interest in the target's assets—a so-called continuity of interest.

Table 14.1 Overview of Tax-Free Acquisition Structures of Freestanding C Corporations

	IRC §368 "A"[1]	Triangular IRC §368 "A"[2]	IRC §368 "B"[3]	IRC §368 "C"[4]	IRC §351[5]
Consideration/method of payment required for tax-free treatment	At least 40% acquiring firm stock; stock can be voting, nonvoting, preferred, or common	At least 40% acquiring firm stock	100% acquiring firm voting stock; stock can be preferred or common	At least 80% acquiring firm voting stock	Mixed consideration, including stock, debt, and cash. Transferors must receive stock of newly formed company and control newly formed company to qualify for tax-free treatment
What is acquired?	Assets	Assets	Stock	Assets	Stock or Assets
Primary benefits	(1) Flexibility of consideration (2) Tax-free treatment for some target shareholders while providing cash to up to 60% of shareholders	(1) Some liability shield provided by subsidiary (2) Assets of target that would not transfer can be acquired (reverse triangular merger)	(1) Simplicity and low transaction costs (2) Target becomes a subsidiary of the acquirer, providing some liability protection from target's liabilities (3) All assets of the target are acquired (e.g., licenses)	(1) Less restrictive consideration requirements (relative to some structures, such as the "B" structure)	(1) Very flexible in terms of providing target shareholders with desired form of consideration (e.g., cash or stock)
Primary costs	(1) Assumption of all of the target's liabilities (2) Some assets may not transfer (3) Must qualify as a merger under state law	(1) Restriction on type and quantity of stock consideration (2) Must qualify as a merger under state law	(1) Very restrictive rules with respect to consideration (2) All of the target's liabilities survive (3) Dilution of the acquiring firm's shareholder control	(1) If boot used, all of target's liabilities count toward 20% nonstock limitation (2) Some assets may not transfer	(1) Can be complex structure that generates numerous tax and nontax issues that are not present in other structures

[1] Statutory merger in which the acquirer exchanges stock and boot with the target corporation in return for the target's assets and liabilities. The target liquidates and distributes the acquirer stock and boot to its shareholders in return for their target stock.

[2] In a forward triangular merger, the acquirer establishes a wholly owned subsidiary that exchanges acquirer stock and possibly some boot for the target's assets and liabilities. In this manner, the assets and liabilities of the target are held in a corporate subsidiary of the acquirer. In a reverse triangular merger, the target is the surviving subsidiary of the acquirer. Under the reverse triangular merger structure, the acquirer must purchase the target with at least 80% target firm voting stock. There are other technical restrictions with the reverse triangular merger that are beyond the scope of this text.

[3] A stock-for-stock merger in which the acquirer directly exchanges its stock with target shareholders in return for their target stock.

[4] A stock-for-asset merger that is similar to a statutory merger in form.

[5] A corporate formation transaction in which the target corporation contributes stock or assets to a newly formed entity in return for stock and boot. Simultaneously, the acquirer contributes stock or assets to the new company in exchange for stock of the new company. The transaction is tax free to contributors (i.e., target firm shareholders), to the extent of stock received, if it qualifies under §351.

FIGURE 14.1
Tax-Free 368 "A" Merger

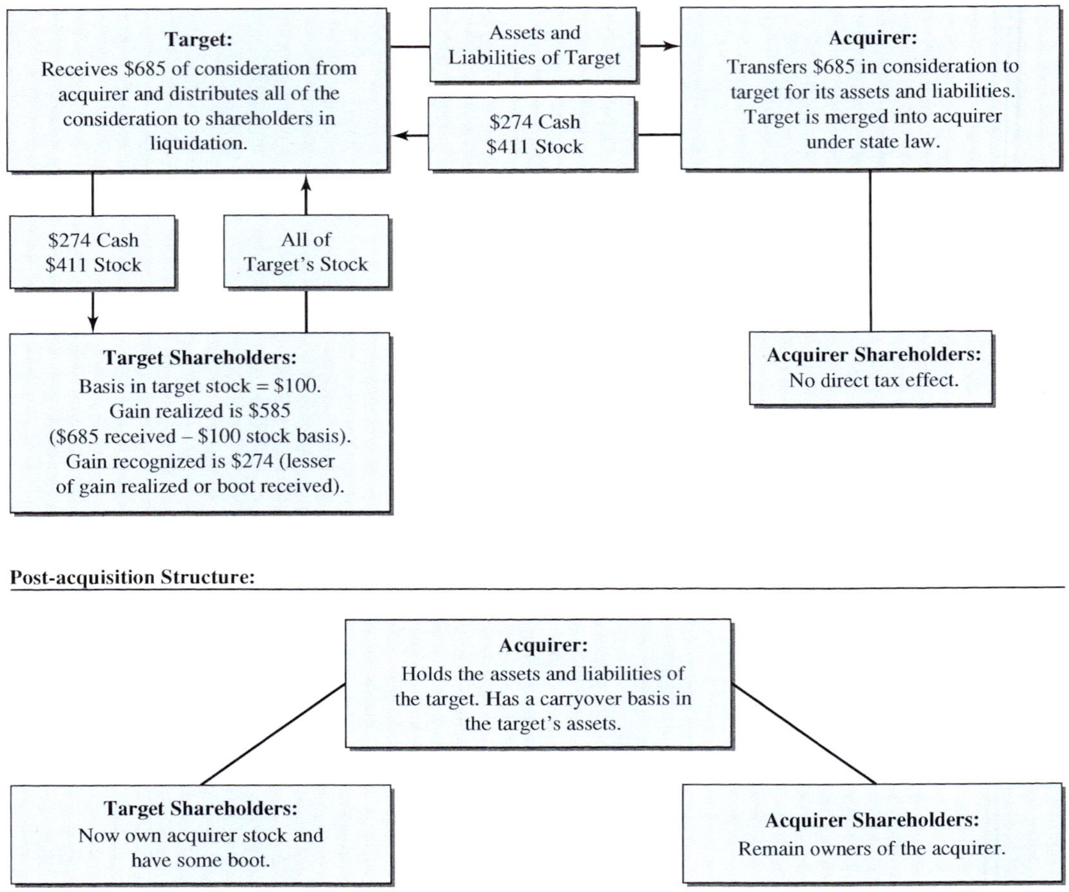

Requirements to Qualify for Tax-Free Treatment under Section 368(a)(1)(A)

"A" reorganizations must qualify as **statutory mergers** under applicable state law. As a result, the merger must be approved by both the acquirer's and the target's shareholders. For tax purposes, an "A" reorganization generally requires that at least 40% of the total consideration received by target shareholders in the acquisition is acquirer stock. Acquirers can use either voting or nonvoting stock to meet the continuity-of-interest test, and they may also use either common or preferred stock.

Of course, target shareholders price the attributes of the type of security they receive from the acquirer. For example, target shareholders may demand additional compensation if they receive nonvoting stock of the acquirer. A benefit of this structure is that the acquirer can purchase the target partially for cash while at the same time providing tax-deferred consideration (acquirer stock) to those target shareholders seeking to avoid an immediate taxable gain.

Tax Consequences of a Section 368 "A"

To illustrate the tax consequences of the various tax-free acquisition structures, we again use a common set of facts. **Table 14.2** contains the quantitative tax effects of various tax-free acquisition structures when applying these facts. **Table 14.2** also includes, for reference, the tax effects of a taxable stock acquisition without a Section 338 election using the same input factors.

The facts in our hypothetical Section 368 "A" transaction are as follows:

- The target, T, has assets with a net tax basis of $100 (historical cost equals $100 and no accumulated depreciation).
- T's shareholders have a basis in the stock of T corporation equal to $100, and they are individuals facing a capital gains tax rate (t_{cg}) equal to 20% (federal and state combined).

Table 14.2 Comparison of Tax Implications of Tax-Free Acquisitions of Freestanding C Corporations

Fact Pattern:

Purchase price	$685.00
Target shareholder stock basis	100.00
Net tax basis of target's assets	100.00
t_c =	21%
t_{cg} =	20%
r =	7%

	Tax-Free Acquisitions				Taxable Acquisitions
	§368 "A"[1]	§368 "B"[2]	§368 "C"[3]	§351[4]	Stock Sale without a §338 Election
Purchase Price:	$685.00	$685.00	$685.00	$685.00	$685.00
Cash	274.00	0.00	137.00	411.00	685.00
Stock	411.00	685.00	548.00	274.00	0.00
Target corporation tax liability[5]	0.00	0.00	0.00	0.00	0.00
Target shareholder gain recognized[6]	274.00	0.00	137.00	411.00	585.00
Target shareholder tax liability[7]	54.80	0.00	27.40	82.20	117.00
Target Shareholder After-Tax Wealth:					
Cash[8]	$219.20	$ 0.00	$109.60	$328.80	$568.00
Stock	411.00	685.00	548.00	274.00	0.00
Total	$630.20	$685.00	$657.60	$602.80	$568.00
Acquirer Net After-Tax Cost:					
Pretax cost	$685.00	$685.00	$685.00	$685.00	$685.00
Less: Incremental tax savings[9]	0.00	0.00	0.00	0.00	0.00
Net after-tax cost	$685.00	$685.00	$685.00	$685.00	$685.00

[1] Assumes the mix of consideration is 60% stock and 40% cash.
[2] The acquirer purchases the target for 100% stock as required by this structure.
[3] Assumes the mix of consideration is 80% stock and 20% cash.
[4] Assumes the mix of consideration is 40% stock and 60% cash.
[5] Tax liability at the target corporation level.
[6] Gain recognized by target shareholders is equal to the lesser of boot received or gain realized.
[7] Tax liability at the target shareholder level. Computed as the lesser of the gain realized or boot received multiplied by the capital gains tax rate.
[8] Cash received in the transaction less tax liability associated with any recognized gains (footnote 6).
[9] There are no incremental tax savings because there is no step-up in the tax basis of the target's assets.

- Any acquirer stock received by T's shareholders in the transaction is held until death.[3]
- The acquirer, A, is willing to purchase the target for $685. The acquirer will use $274 in cash (40% of the total) and $411 of acquirer stock (60% of the total).

The shareholders of T will *realize* a gain of $585 on the acquisition. The realized gain is the difference between the value of consideration received ($685) and T's shareholders' basis in their T stock ($100). T's shareholders will recognize a gain of $274, which is computed as the lesser of

[3] Throughout these examples, we implicitly assume all shareholders receive an equal proportion of stock and boot. As a practical matter, target shareholders often have a choice as to whether they want stock or cash in an acquisition but only if the tax structure permits the use of cash. The taxable gain from the acquisition is determined by each shareholder as a function of the consideration received and their basis in the target shares surrendered.

the gain realized ($585) or boot received ($274). A recognized gain is the taxable gain, whereas a realized gain is not subject to tax until it is subsequently recognized. As a result of the taxable gain of $274, T's shareholders incur a tax liability of $54.80 ($274 × 20%) and have $219.20 in cash after tax and stock worth $411.

T's shareholders will take a **substituted basis** in the acquiring firm stock received in the transaction. A substituted basis means that the shareholders have the same basis in the A stock as they had in the T stock, plus any gain recognized and minus boot received. In this case, T's shareholders will take a basis in the A stock equal to $100 plus the gain recognized of $274 less the boot received of $274 for a basis of $100. If T shareholders were to sell this A stock for its fair market value ($411), they would recognize a capital gain of $311.[4] This gain brings the total gain eventually *recognized* on the transaction up to $585 ($274 + $311), which is equal to the gain *realized* on the transaction. The substituted basis computation we demonstrated previously ensures that the realized gain is ultimately recognized in total.

The acquirer will take a carryover basis in the assets of the target. In this case, A will also have a tax basis in the net assets of the target of $100. The acquirer will not have a basis in the stock of the target because the target was liquidated; that is, the stock of the target was cancelled. The tax attributes of the target will carry over to the acquirer, but they will be limited by **Section 382**. (We present the mechanics of the Section 382 limitations in Section 14.6.) The first column of **Table 14.2** presents the particulars of the computations in this section.

Nontax Issues Associated with the Section 368 "A" Structure

Under this structure, the acquirer obtains all the liabilities of the target. This structure therefore subjects the acquirer to potentially significant nontax costs. In addition, because it is an asset acquisition, some of the target's assets (e.g., licenses, royalty agreements, and governmental permits) may not transfer to the target. These assets may be nontransferable based on the law or based on the contractual arrangement that created the asset.

An important consideration, from the target shareholders' perspective, relates to the consideration received. When target shareholders receive acquiring firm stock, they are subject to more risk than if they had received cash and used it to purchase a diversified basket of assets. This factor is true of all tax-free structures to the extent target shareholders receive stock of the acquiring firm. In the 1990s and early 2000s, a number of acquiring firms purchased numerous companies with their stock, only to see a subsequent collapse in the price of that stock.[5]

Triangular Mergers

Figure 14.2 illustrates a **forward triangular merger**. Here, the acquirer establishes a subsidiary through which it acquires the target. In a forward triangular "A" merger, the acquirer's subsidiary acquires the assets and liabilities of the target in exchange for stock of the acquiring firm. The surviving entity in the merger is the subsidiary of A. As you can see, this structure is similar to the basic A structure, except that A uses a subsidiary to facilitate the acquisition. Another notable difference is that A must acquire substantially all of T's assets, which are defined as 90% of the net fair market value of T's assets and 70% of the gross fair market value of those assets.

This type of structure provides a significant nontax benefit to the acquirer because the target's assets and liabilities, including contingent liabilities, are held in a subsidiary of A. As a result, the acquirer has some protection against contingent and unrecorded liabilities of T through the limited liability accorded to corporate ownership because T's assets and liabilities are held in a subsidiary of A. In addition, because the acquirer uses a subsidiary to complete the merger, acquiring firm shareholders do not have to approve a triangular merger formally. However, if the merger involves the exchange of a substantial amount of acquirer stock, the corporate charter of the acquiring firm may require formal shareholder approval of the deal.

[4] T shareholders' holding period for the A stock is the same as it was for the T stock. That is, the holding period is also substituted.

[5] There were more than $100 billion of stock-financed acquisitions completed by firms accused of accounting fraud during this time period. Cendant, Enron, and Worldcom are some notable acquiring firms that purchased target firms with their stock during periods of alleged accounting fraud. See, for example, "Shares of Former High-Flier Cendant Plunge on Accounting Troubles," *Dow Jones Online News* (April 16, 1998).

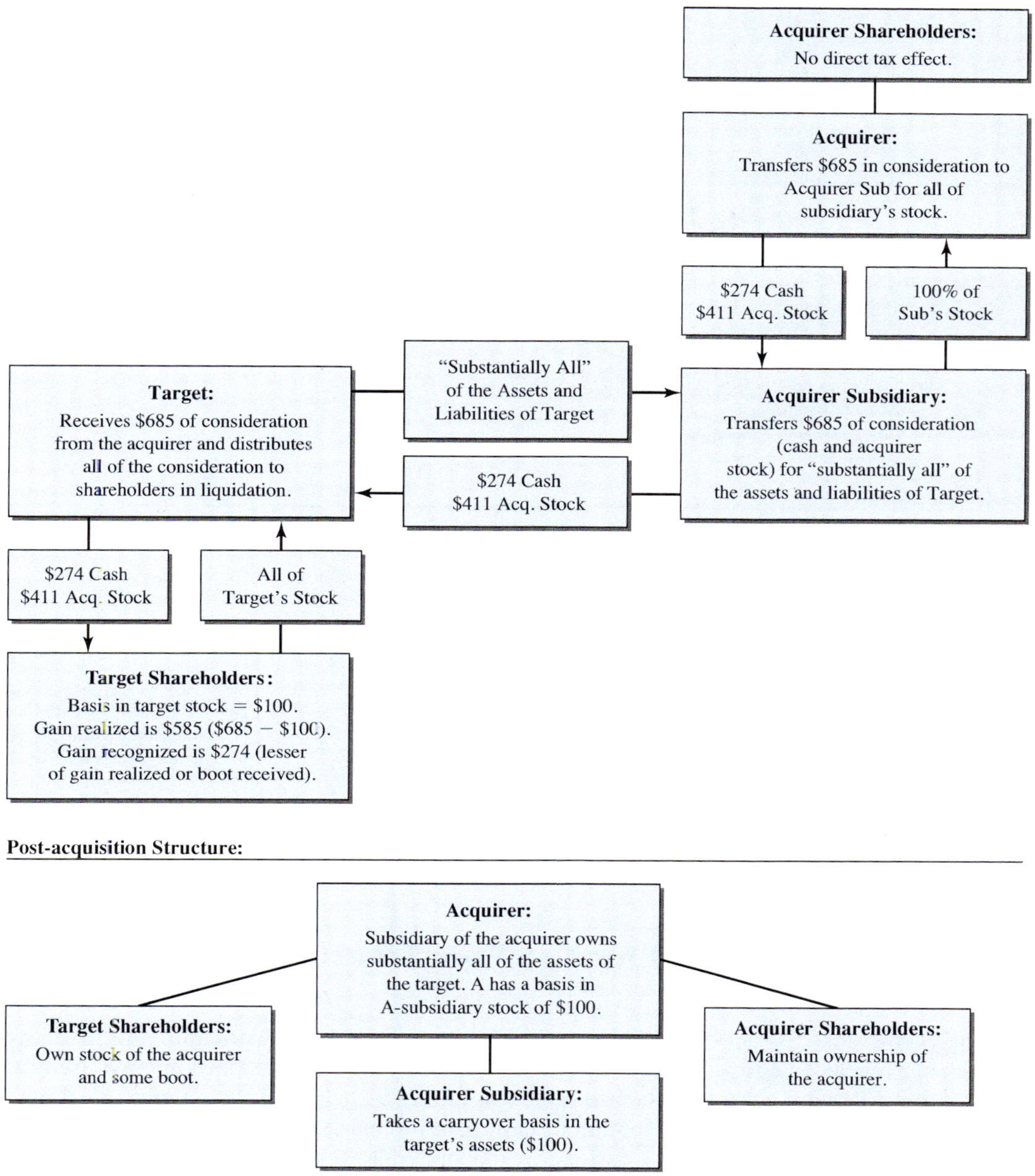

FIGURE 14.2 Tax-Free Forward Triangular 368 "A"

In a **reverse triangular merger**, the surviving entity is the target corporation instead of the acquirer's subsidiary, which is a subsidiary of A after the transaction. This structure is particularly beneficial relative to a forward merger or a basic "A" merger if the target has assets that are difficult to transfer. Additional qualifiers restrict tax-free treatment in reverse triangular mergers, which are beyond the scope of this text. Note, however, that reverse triangular mergers are fairly common.

14.3 SECTION 368 "B" REORGANIZATION: STOCK-FOR-STOCK ACQUISITION

The "B" reorganization is a stock acquisition rather than an asset acquisition. The acquirer exchanges its stock directly with that of target shareholders, thereby obtaining ownership of the target's assets through ownership of its stock. **Figure 14.3** illustrates a **Section 368 "B" reorganization**. Notice that the target becomes a subsidiary of the acquirer with this structure and therefore maintains its legal identity while the owners of the target's stock change. After the acquisition, this structure looks like a reverse triangular merger under Section 368 "A."

FIGURE 14.3
Tax-Free 368 "B" Merger

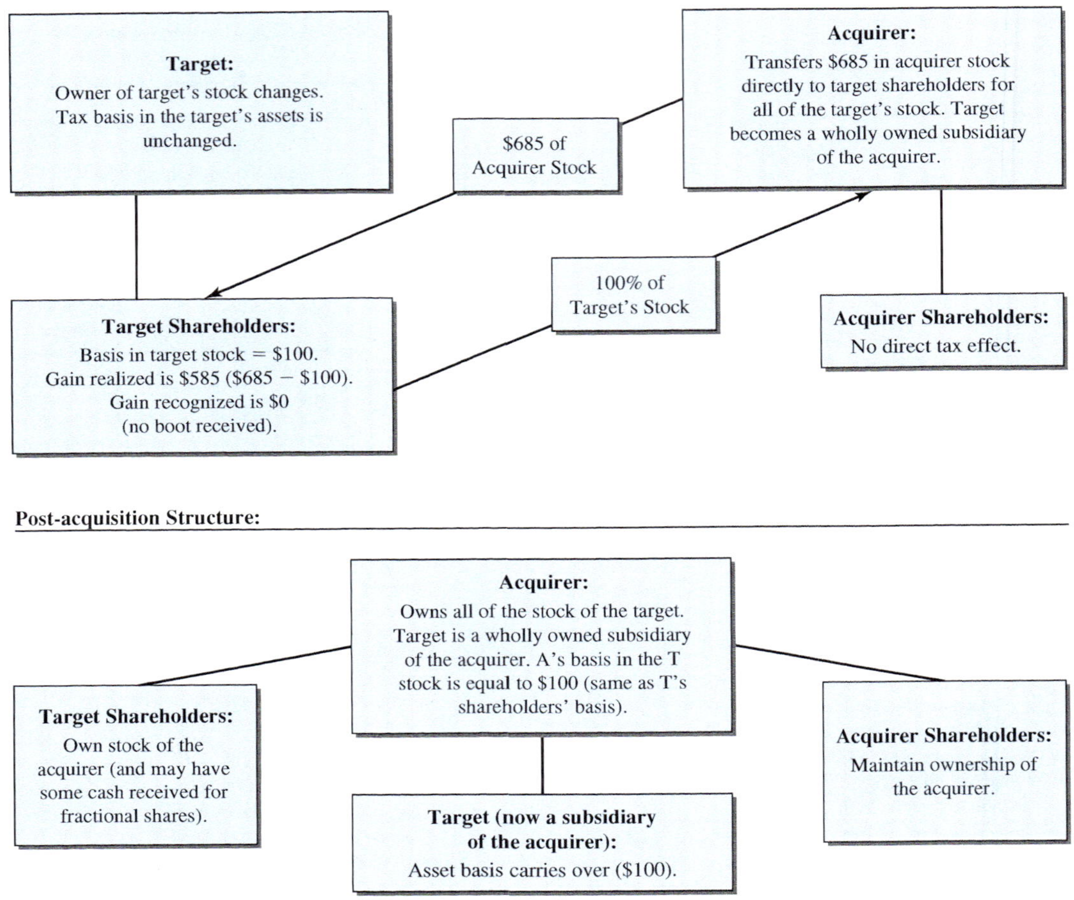

Requirements to Qualify for Tax-Free Treatment under Section 368(a)(1)(B)

As a general rule, this "B" structure is more restrictive than the 368 "A" structure. For the transaction to qualify for tax-free treatment under Section 368 "B," 100% of the consideration used in the acquisition must be voting stock of the acquirer. Use of any cash in the transaction disqualifies the deal's tax-free treatment, with the exception of cash paid in lieu of fractional shares. Acquirers can use either common or preferred stock as long as the stock has voting rights. Finally, the acquirer must obtain 80% control of the target for the transaction to qualify as tax free. As a result of this last requirement, transactions of this type are typically unwound prior to formal completion of the deal if the acquirer doesn't obtain 80% of the target corporation's stock.

Tax Consequences of a Section 368 "B"

We again use the facts presented in Section 14.2 to illustrate the tax consequences of this structure, with one slight modification related to the percentage of stock received by target shareholders. Under this structure, the acquirer is willing to purchase the target for $685 (100% of the consideration) of its voting common stock.

The shareholders of T will realize a gain of $585 on the acquisition. The realized gain is the difference between the value of the consideration received ($685) and T shareholders' basis in the T stock ($100). T's shareholders will recognize a gain of $0, which is computed as the lesser of the gain realized ($585) or boot received ($0). As a result, T's shareholders will have stock worth $685 after tax, and they will take a substituted basis in the acquiring firm stock received in the transaction. Thus, they will have a basis in the A stock equal to $100, plus the gain recognized of $0 less the boot received of $0 for a basis of $100. If T shareholders were to sell this A stock for its fair market value ($685), they would recognize a capital gain of $585.

The acquirer will again take a carryover basis in the assets of the target. In this case, the acquirer will have a tax basis in the net assets of the target of $100. Unlike the case in the 368 "A" structure, the acquirer will have a basis in the stock of the target as well. The acquirer takes a carryover basis in the stock of the target equal to the target's shareholders' basis in the target's stock preacquisition, in this case, $100. The second column of **Table 14.2** illustrates the computations in this section.

The target corporation becomes a subsidiary of the acquirer and we again encounter a situation in which the acquiring firm could have a different basis in the stock and assets of the target, now a subsidiary of the acquirer.[6] For example, if the target shareholders' basis in the stock of the target had been $200 instead of $100, then the acquirer would have had basis in the target's stock and assets of $200 and $100, respectively. The tax attributes of the target will carry over to the acquirer, but they will be limited by Section 382.

Nontax Issues Associated with the Section 368 "B" Structure

Because the acquirer obtains the stock of the target with this structure, it also is liable for all the target's liabilities, recorded and unrecorded. This structure therefore subjects the acquirer to potentially significant nontax costs. However, the acquirer's liability is limited to its investment in the target because the target is a subsidiary of the acquirer. Unlike the case in a Section 368 "A" merger, the target corporation now becomes a subsidiary of the acquirer. Therefore, the acquirer indirectly obtains all the assets of the target. Title to the target's assets does not change because the target retains its corporate identity. For this reason, the Section 368 "B" structure can be beneficial if the target has assets that are difficult to transfer. Target shareholders receive stock of the acquirer and are subjected to the same potential costs as mentioned with respect to an "A" structure.

Triangular type structures under 368 "B" are also options, and similar restrictions apply to these structures as noted previously, although the basic restrictions under 368 "B," such as 100% stock, are typically more onerous than those governing triangular "A" mergers, such as 40% stock minimum.

14.4 SECTION 368 "C" REORGANIZATION: STOCK-FOR-ASSETS ACQUISITION

The "C" reorganization, like the "A," is an asset acquisition rather than a stock acquisition. The acquirer exchanges its voting stock, and perhaps some boot, with the target firm in return for substantially all of the target's assets. The target then distributes the acquirer's stock and other consideration received in the acquisition to its shareholders in liquidation. **Figure 14.4** illustrates a **Section 368 "C" reorganization**. This structure is similar to the "A" reorganization, with a few notable differences.

Requirements to Qualify for Tax-Free Treatment Under Section 368(a)(1)(C)

This structure is more restrictive on some dimensions than the 368 "A" structure but less restrictive in other respects. Unlike an "A," a "C" structure does not have to be a statutory merger. However, the acquirer must purchase substantially all the assets of the target for the transaction to qualify as tax free. The term "substantially all of the target's assets" is defined as 70% of their gross fair market value and 90% of their net fair market value.

In a "C" reorganization, at least 80% of the total consideration used must be voting stock of the acquiring firm. If the acquirer uses any boot in the transaction, the liabilities of the target assumed by the acquirer count as boot in the 80% test. For example, if an acquirer used 5% cash in a transaction designed to qualify as a "C," all the target's liabilities assumed by the acquirer would be treated as if

[6] Recall from Chapter 12 that taxable stock acquisitions of freestanding C corporations typically result in the acquirer having a basis in the stock of the target that exceeds the net asset basis of the target. See **Table 12.2**.

FIGURE 14.4
Tax-Free 368 "C" Merger

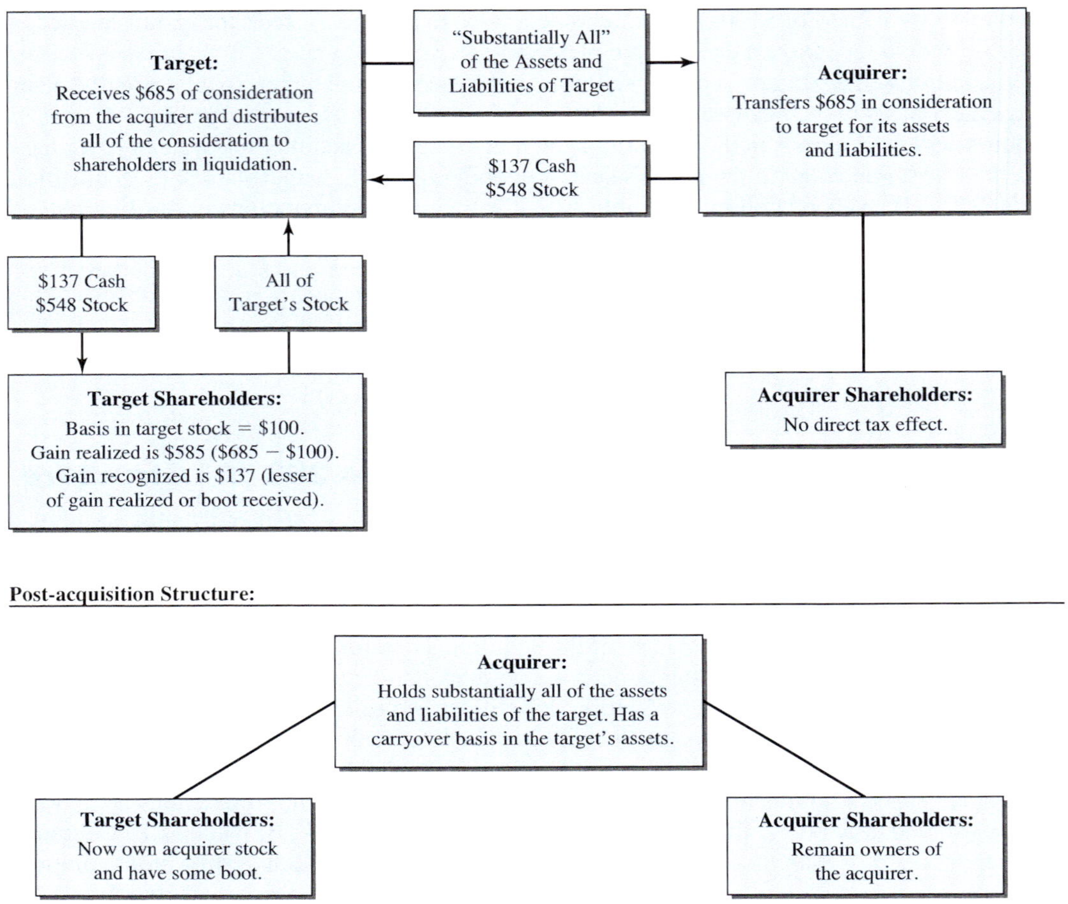

the acquirer had paid cash to satisfy those liabilities in the merger. As a result, all the target's liabilities are counted as boot in determining whether 80% or more of the consideration received by the target is stock. As a practical matter, this requirement results in "C"-type mergers frequently using 100% stock of the acquirer as consideration.

Tax Consequences of a Section 368 "C"

We use the same facts familiar from the "B" structure now, but we assume target shareholders receive 20% cash ($137) and 80% acquiring firm voting stock ($548 worth). We also assume that the target has no liabilities. Target shareholders still receive $685 of total consideration in the merger.

The shareholders of T will realize a gain of $585 on the acquisition. The realized gain is the difference between the value of consideration received ($685) and T's shareholders' basis in the T stock ($100). T's shareholders will recognize a gain of $137, which is computed as the lesser of the gain realized ($585) or boot received ($137). As a result, T's shareholders will have $109.60 (the tax liability equals $137 × 20%, or $27.40) of cash after tax and acquirer stock worth $548. T's shareholders will take a substituted basis in the acquiring firm stock received in the transaction. With this structure, T's shareholders will take a basis in the A stock equal to $100 ($100 substituted basis plus the gain recognized of $137 less the boot received of $137). If T's shareholders were to sell the A stock for its fair market value ($548), they would recognize a capital gain of $448. **Table 14.2** illustrates these computations.

The acquirer will again take a carryover basis in the assets of the target and have a tax basis in the net assets of the target of $100. The stock of the target is not acquired, and therefore the acquirer does not have a basis in the target's stock. The tax attributes of the target will carry over to the acquirer, but they will be limited by Section 382.

Triangular Section 368 "C" mergers must meet similar requirements as Section 368 "A" triangular mergers. The tax and nontax effects of these triangular Section 368 "C" mergers are nearly identical to those described with respect to triangular Section 368 "A" triangular mergers. The nontax consequences of "C" reorganizations are similar to those described for "A" reorganizations, with the exception of issues relating to statutory mergers.

14.5 TAX-FREE REORGANIZATIONS UNDER SECTION 351

For a variety of reasons, it is sometimes impractical to structure a transaction to qualify as tax free under the various provision of Section 368. For example, target shareholders may demand more than 60% of the purchase price in cash, making it essentially impossible to qualify an acquisition as tax free under the continuity of interest principle. It may be the case that the other shareholders of the target demand tax-free treatment and will not participate in a merger that does not provide tax-free treatment.

For those deals that cannot qualify as tax free under Section 368, Section 351 provides a vehicle to achieve tax-free status.[7] For those of you who are unfamiliar with Section 351, it governs corporate formation transactions. We provide a brief overview of it here to assist with the discussion of Section 351 mergers. Before doing so, it is worth noting that Section 351 has been used in some significant transactions (e.g., the Sears/Kmart merger).

Requirements for Tax-Free Treatment under Section 351

When a new corporation is formed, the founding shareholders generally contribute property, including cash, to the new entity in return for ownership interests (stock). To the extent that shareholders contribute appreciated property, they could be forced to recognize a gain on the exchange of stock for property. Such gain recognition would have undesirable economic consequences because many viable endeavors would be forgone due to the initial start-up-related tax cost. Section 351 allows the contribution of property to a corporation, tax free, if certain conditions are met. Specifically, after the contribution, all the contributors must have control of the newly formed entity, which we call NEWCO. **Control** is defined as ownership of 80% of NEWCO. The contributors can receive NEWCO common or preferred stock and transferors may receive different classes and types of stock.

Contributors who receive stock in NEWCO do so tax free, whereas those who transfer property to NEWCO in exchange for debt or cash must recognize a taxable gain equal to the lesser of the gain realized on the transfer or the boot received. Contributors who receive stock in NEWCO take a substituted basis in the stock of NEWCO, that is, a basis equal to the basis in the property transferred, which is adjusted for gains recognized and boot received. NEWCO takes a carryover basis in the property transferred increased by any gains recognized by transferring shareholders.

Tax Consequences of a Section 351 Merger

Figure 14.5 provides an illustration of a merger under Section 351. Under this structure, NEWCO is formed by the acquirer. The shareholders of the acquirer (A) contribute their stock in A to NEWCO in return for NEWCO voting stock. A's shareholders have a basis in their A stock of $500 (fair market value of $10,000) and A's net asset tax basis is $200. A's shareholders will receive NEWCO stock worth $10,000 in exchange for their A stock. The target (T) corporation's shareholders contribute their T stock to NEWCO in return for NEWCO voting stock.

After the contribution of A and T stock for NEWCO stock, the shareholders of A and T control more than 80% of NEWCO. Therefore, the exchange of property (stock) for NEWCO stock is tax free under Section 351. Under the structure in **Figure 14.5**, T and A become wholly owned subsidiaries of NEWCO. As a practical matter, after the Section 351 transaction, NEWCO will likely be

[7] Section 351 may also be used in the creation of a joint-venture enterprise.

FIGURE 14.5
IRC §351 Tax-Free Acquisition

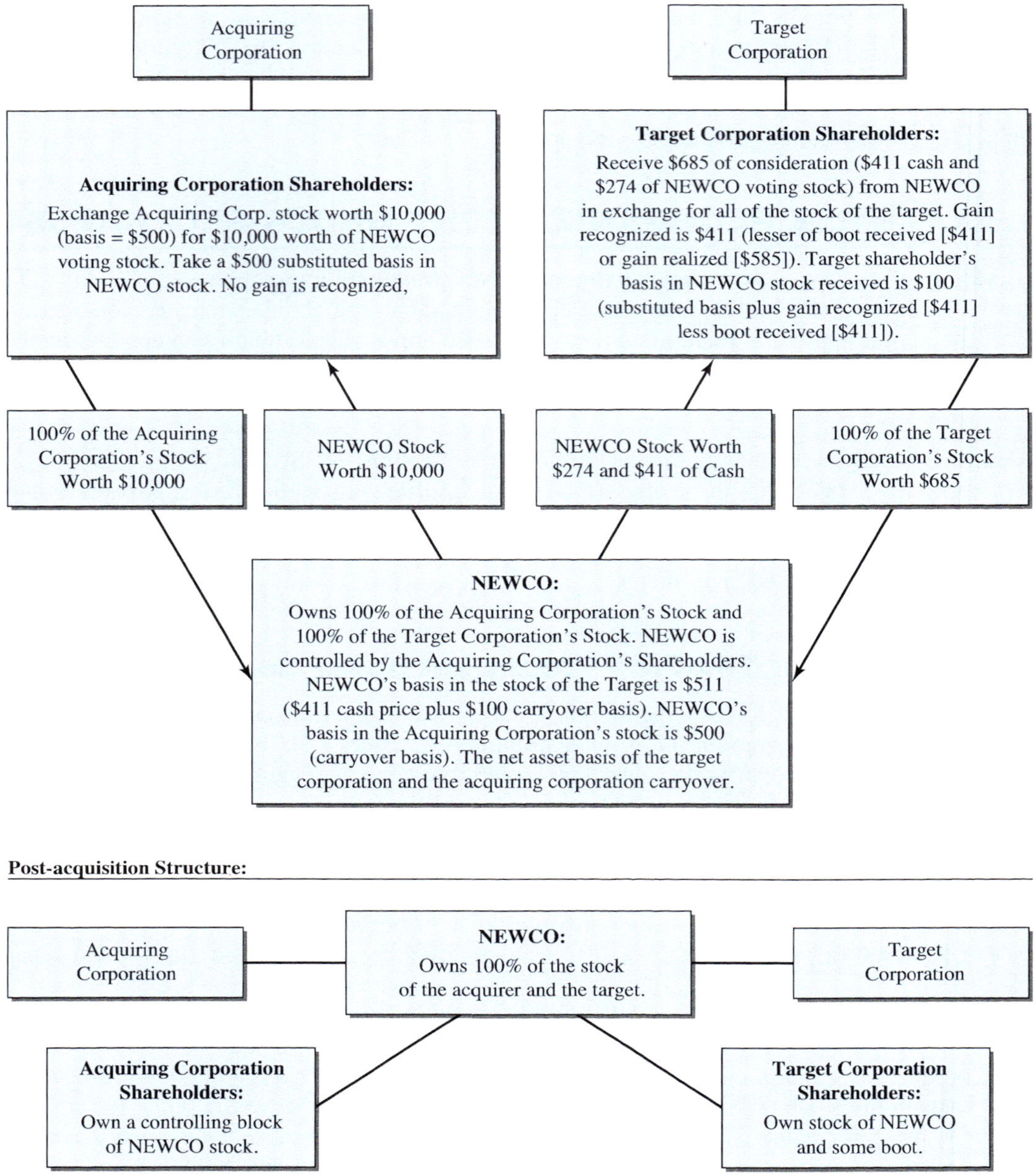

restructured using **Section 332**.[8] NEWCO will also be renamed, perhaps with a name similar to that of the acquirer.

To illustrate the tax consequences of the Section 351 structure, let us once again return to our facts (see **Table 14.2**). NEWCO is willing to purchase the stock of T for $685 in total consideration, in other words, $411 of cash and $274 of NEWCO voting common stock. (Assume that NEWCO borrows the $411.) Notice that T's shareholders will receive 60% cash and 40% stock of NEWCO.

The shareholders of T will realize a gain of $585 on the merger. The realized gain is the difference between the value of consideration received ($685) and T's shareholders' basis in the T stock ($100). T's shareholders will recognize a gain of $411, which is computed as the lesser of the gain realized ($585) or boot received ($411). They will have a tax liability of $82.20 ($411 × 20%). After tax, they will have stock worth $274 and cash of $328.80 ($411 less tax of $82.20), and they will take a substituted basis in the NEWCO stock received in the transaction. In this case, T's shareholders

[8] Section 332 allows a corporation to liquidate wholly owned subsidiaries in a tax-free manner. Such corporate liquidations are common in various types of acquisitions.

take a substituted basis in the NEWCO stock equal to $100, plus the gain recognized of $411 less the boot received of $411 for a basis of $100.

A's shareholders will realize a gain on the Section 351 transaction equal to $9,500, but they will not recognize a gain for tax purposes. They will have a substituted basis in the NEWCO stock received equal to $500.

NEWCO will take a cost basis in the stock of T acquired for cash and a carryover basis in the stock of T acquired for stock. In this case, NEWCO's basis in the T stock acquired will be $411 (cost basis) plus $100 (carryover basis) for a total of $511.[9] T becomes a subsidiary of NEWCO and the net asset basis of T carries over and is therefore $100. The tax attributes of T will likely be limited by Section 382. NEWCO will take a carryover basis in the stock of A ($500) and a carryover basis in A's net assets ($200), and A will become a wholly owned subsidiary of NEWCO as a result of the Section 351 exchange.

Comparison of Tax-Free Acquisition Structures

In the previous sections, we presented the salient features of basic tax-free acquisition structures. Here, we compare and contrast tax and nontax differences across types of **tax-free acquisition structures**.

Nontax Dimensions **Table 14.1** compares and contrasts differences in the tax and nontax implications of various tax-free acquisition structures discussed in this chapter. Understanding these differences is paramount to being an effective tax planner. In particular, it is important to understand the requirements of the different tax-free transactions in order to anticipate opportunities and constraints associated with a sale or acquisition. When then is each of these structures most beneficial, ignoring pricing issues? You can use **Table 14.1** to identify which acquisition tax structure is functional given the nontax constraints present in the transaction.

The Section 368 "A" structure provides a great degree of flexibility in terms of the types of consideration that can be offered while maintaining tax-free treatment. This structure may be particularly preferable when the acquirer is sensitive to dilution of voting control because target shareholders can be given nonvoting stock without disqualifying the transaction's tax-free status.

A primary benefit of the Section 368 "B" structure is that it avoids the complexities associated with qualifying the transaction as a statutory merger. It also provides a degree of liability protection because the target becomes a subsidiary of the acquirer. One of the most significant benefits of a "B" reorganization is that it allows the acquirer to obtain all the target's assets, even those that are not transferable to another entity.

The Section 368 "C" structure can be used when the transaction cannot meet the requirements of a "B" reorganization and is similarly unable to qualify as a statutory merger as required for a valid "A" reorganization. A Section 351 structure allows target shareholders to receive tax-free consideration when Section 368 transactions would not.

Tax Dimensions As **Table 14.2** illustrated, the tax-free acquisition structures discussed in Sections 14.2 through 14.5 have differing wealth effects for target shareholders.[10] Notice that the net after-tax cost of the acquisition to the acquirer is $685 in each of our examples. Putting aside nontax differences, target shareholders should prefer the Section 368 "B" transaction because their after-tax wealth is highest with this alternative when considering only tax consequences.

However, target shareholders may be indifferent between the Section 368 "B" and "A" structures if they are sufficiently averse to holding acquirer stock. That is, target shareholders may demand a premium for receiving relatively more acquirer stock because acquirer stock is riskier than cash. In particular, cash can be invested in a diversified portfolio of assets, but acquirer stock cannot, absent significant transaction costs.[11]

---

[9] Notice again that the acquirer's (NEWCO's) tax basis of the stock and net assets of the target are different ($511 and $100, respectively) with this structure.

[10] The differential wealth effects are a function of the portion of consideration received by target shareholders that is acquirer stock. If target shareholders received 100% acquirer stock across transaction tax structure, their wealth would be identical.

[11] For example, target shareholders could borrow against acquirer shares and use the loan proceeds to purchase a diversified basket of securities. The transactions cost of such a strategy may be relatively high.

14.6 LIMITATIONS ON TARGET FIRM TAX ATTRIBUTES

Any transaction that results in a 50% change in ownership of a corporation triggers a limitation on the firm's net operating losses under Section 382.[12] Other limitations apply to the use of other target firm tax attributes, such as capital loss carryforwards and excess tax credits, as specified in Sections 381, 383, and 384. We focus on the limitations on a target's net operating losses as defined under Section 382.[13] The Section 382 limitation is computed as a function of the market value of the subject firm's stock at the time of the ownership change and the **long-term tax-exempt rate**. Specifically, an annual limitation on the amount of the subject firm's tax attributes, such as NOLs, that can be used is computed as the market value of the subject firm's equity at the date of the ownership change multiplied by the long-term tax-exempt rate of return.[14] The long-term tax-exempt rate of return is defined and reported periodically by the U.S. government.

Consider a target firm with NOLs of $100 that is purchased for $200 in a taxable stock acquisition without a Section 338 election, when the long-term tax-exempt rate is 5%. Each year post-acquisition, the acquiring firm can use $10 (5% multiplied by $200 equity value at the time of the ownership change) of T's NOLs to offset taxable income. If the combined entity had $20 of income in the year following the acquisition, only $10 of the income could be offset by the NOL. If the combined entity has $5 of taxable income in a particular year post-acquisition, the $5 of unused NOL for that year can be carried forward to the following year. The same general limitations apply to capital losses, tax credits, and so-called built-in losses.[15] To the extent that a target firm—a subsidiary of the acquirer post-acquisition—generates losses *post-acquisition*, however, these losses can be offset by profits of the acquirer without limitation.

As noted in Chapter 12, in taxable transactions in which the tax basis of the target's assets are stepped up, the target firm's NOLs can be used to offset the corporate-level gain on the actual or deemed asset sale. For this reason, some acquisitions are structured to result in a step-up of a freestanding C corporation's assets when the target has large NOLs, although, even then, a step-up structure is still uncommon. However, any of the target's NOLs and other valuable tax attributes that are not used to offset the gain on the step-up are lost. Therefore, the decision to step-up the tax basis of the target's assets, which results in the loss of the target's NOLs, is optimal only if the loss of tax savings from the target's tax attributes does not exceed the net tax benefits of the step-up.

How does the acquirer determine whether to structure the acquisition to preserve the target's NOLs? **Table 14.3** presents an analysis of the tax costs and benefits of preserving a target's NOLs in a carryover basis transaction relative to using the NOLs to offset the gain on a step-up in the target's assets. In this table, we compare a taxable stock acquisition of a freestanding C corporation in which no Section 338 election is made to a taxable stock acquisition in which the Section 338 election is made. We choose to compare two taxable acquisition structures rather than a taxable and tax-free acquisition to avoid the differences in shareholder tax effects.[16]

Given the facts in **Table 14.3**, the target corporation has NOLs of $450, the net basis in the target's assets is $100, and the price an acquirer is willing to pay for the stock of the target is $685. The corporate tax rate is 21%, the shareholder capital gains tax rate is 20%, and the after-tax discount rate is 7%. We assume any step-up in the tax basis of the target's assets is amortized over 10 years on a straight-line basis. We also assume the appropriate long-term tax-exempt rate applicable to target

[12] The definition of a qualifying ownership change is quite complex. It is sufficient for you to understand that in essentially any acquisition, taxable or tax free, an ownership change as defined under Section 382 occurs.

[13] Section 381 provides the general rules regarding the post-acquisition use of target tax attributes in carryover basis transactions. Section 382 deals primarily with limitations on acquirer use of target preacquisition NOLs. Section 383 controls limitations on capital loss carryforwards and target preacquisition tax credits. Section 384 provides restrictions on the use of the acquirer's losses to offset built-in gains of the target.

[14] Prior to the Tax Reform Act of 1986, the limitation on a target's NOLs differed across carryover basis taxable and tax-free transactions. Since 1986, the limitations on a target's tax attributes are essentially identical in taxable and tax-free transactions.

[15] A built-in loss occurs when the target corporation has assets with a tax basis greater than fair market value at the time of the acquisition. If the acquirer sells these assets post-acquisition, it is realizing tax losses that were derived from the preacquisition target. Hence, these losses are also limited.

[16] A similar analysis could be performed comparing a tax-free carryover basis transaction with a taxable acquisition that resulted in a step-up in the target's assets. We leave such an analysis as an exercise for you.

Table 14.3 Comparison of Tax Effects on Target Tax Attributes of Various Acquisition Structures

Fact Pattern:

Purchase price	$685.00
Target shareholders' stock basis	500.00
Net tax basis in the target's assets	100.00
ADSP[1]	720.89
Preacquisition target NOLs	450.00
t_c =	21%
t_{cg} =	20%
r =	7%
Long-term tax-exempt rate =	5%
Amortization period (n) =	10

	Taxable Stock Acquisition with a §338 Election	Taxable Stock Acquisition without a §338 Election
Target Shareholder Effects:		
Cash received	$685.00	$685.00
Tax on stock sale[2]	37.00	37.00
After-tax cash[3]	$648.00	$648.00
Target Corporation Tax Effects:		
Gain on step-up[4]	$620.89	$ 0.00
Less: NOLs	450.00	n/a
Taxable gain on step-up[5]	$170.89	n/a
Tax on gain[6]	$ 35.89	n/a
Tax Benefits:		
From Carryover of NOLs:		
Gross NOL carryovers	$ 0.00	$450.00
Annual limitation[7]	0.00	34.25
Annual tax savings[8]	0.00	7.19
Present value of tax savings[9]	0.00	60.50
From a Step-up in Target's Assets:		
Gross step-up[10]	$620.89	n/a
Annual deduction[11]	62.09	n/a
Annual tax savings[12]	13.04	n/a
Present value of tax savings[13]	91.58	n/a
Computation of Net Tax Benefits:		
Gross tax benefits[9, 12]	$ 91.58	$ 60.50
Incremental tax cost[6]	35.89	0.00
Net tax benefits[14]	$ 55.69	$ 60.50

[1] ADSP is computed as $G + L + t_c(ADSP - \text{Basis} - \text{NOL})$. In this case, G = $685, L = $0, Basis = $100, NOL = $450, and t_c = 21%.
[2] Tax on stock sale is equal to the gain ($685 less $500 stock basis) multiplied by the capital gains tax rate.
[3] Purchase price less tax. Notice that target shareholders are indifferent between these two structures because their after-tax cash is identical. The structure decision therefore turns on the incremental corporate tax effects on the target corporation.
[4] Gain on the step-up is computed as *ADSP* less the net tax basis in the target's assets. This amount is zero when the §338 election is not made.
[5] Taxable gain on step-up is the gain on step-up less the NOL. NOLs reduce the gain dollar for dollar.
[6] Tax on the gain is the corporate tax rate multiplied by the taxable gain (footnote 5).
[7] The annual amount of the target's NOLs available to offset taxable income of the target as defined by IRC §382. Computed as the total value of the target's stock at the date of acquisition ($685) multiplied by the long-term tax-exempt rate of return (5%).
[8] The annual limitation (footnote 7) multiplied by the corporate tax rate.
[9] The present value of reducing the combined firm's tax liability by $7.19 for 13.1 years discounted at the after-tax discount rate (7%).
[10] The gross step-up is equal to the difference between *ADSP* and the net tax basis of the target's assets preacquisition.
[11] The gross step-up ($620.89) divided by the estimated amortization period (10 years) for the step-up.
[12] Footnote 11 multiplied by the corporate tax rate.
[13] The present value of depreciation deductions from the step-up discounted at the after-tax discount rate of 7%.
[14] Net tax benefits are the gross tax benefits resulting from stepping up the target's assets less the incremental cost of doing so and tax benefits from preserving the target's NOLs, respectively.

NOLs under Section 382 is 5% and the target's NOLs expire in exactly 20 years.[17] Notice that under these facts, target shareholders are indifferent between the two structures because they have $648 after tax with either structure. Therefore, the structuring choice is determined by target corporation NOL-related tax effects.

Under these assumptions, the aggregate deemed sale price (*ADSP*) in a Section 338 transaction is $720.89, and the target corporate-level gain is $620.89 ($720.89 *ADSP* less $100 target asset basis).[18] The target's NOLs can be used to offset $450 of the $620.89 gain on the step-up. The target corporation (now a subsidiary of the acquirer) will therefore face a tax liability of $35.89 on the gain on step-up. The step-up in the target's assets is $620.89 and, under our assumptions, the step-up will generate $62.09 ($620.09/10 years) of additional depreciation deductions each year. The present value of the tax deductions from the step-up under the preceding assumptions is $91.58. The tax cost of obtaining the step-up is $35.89 ($170.89 taxable gain after NOL utilization multiplied by 21%), so the net tax benefit from the step-up is $55.69 ($91.58 incremental tax benefit less $35.89 incremental tax cost).

If the Section 338 election is not made, the NOLs of the target carry over. The annual limitation on the target's NOLs under our scenario is $34.25 and is computed as the long-term tax-exempt rate (5%) multiplied by the purchase price of the target's equity ($685).[19] The target's NOLs then will generate $7.19 ($34.25 multiplied by the tax rate of 21%) worth of tax savings a year for approximately 13.1 years ($450 of NOLs divided by $34.25 per year).[20] The present value of the tax savings from these NOLs is $60.50 (discounted again at a 7% after-tax rate).

In the example presented here, it would be optimal not to make the Section 338 election because the net benefit under the Section 338 structure is $55.69, whereas the net tax benefit of preserving the target's NOLs is $60.50. However, it is a close call. The estimates in **Table 14.3** are sensitive to the useful life applied to any step-up in the target's assets and the number of years remaining before the target's NOLs expire.[21] As the useful life of the target's assets increases, the present value of additional depreciation-related tax deductions declines. Similarly, as the remaining carryforward years for the target's NOLs decline, the present value of preserving those tax attributes also declines because some of the NOLs will expire unused. NOLs generated post 2017 have unlimited useful lives under the Tax and Jobs Act of 2017.

In any event, the computations in **Table 14.3** provide a basic financial model to compare the tax implications for a target's tax attributes of various acquisition structures. Additional complexity can obviously be added.

How Much Are the Target Firm's NOLs Worth?

In many acquisitions, the target firm's NOLs can provide substantial cash flow to the acquirer in post-closing periods. Estimating the value that the target's NOLs create for the acquirer is not difficult given some simplifying assumptions. Based on the Section 382 limitations just discussed, one can compute the amount of target NOLs available to shield acquirer post-closing profits from taxation. Future projections of such tax savings can then be discounted to derive an estimate of the present value of future tax benefits from use of the target's NOLs. As may be expected, the present value of the tax benefits from using the target's NOLs can be a notable portion of an acquisition's value.

[17] The computation assumes that all target NOLs were generated prior to the Tax and Jobs Act of 2017. Under post-2017 law, NOLs do not expire.

[18] The *ADSP* computation (previously discussed in Chapter 12) when the target had NOLs can be represented in general as

$$ADSP = P + L + t_c\,(ADSP - \text{BASIS} - \text{NOL})$$

The NOL variable in the equation cannot be larger than *P* less Basis, however.

[19] There are additional complications associated with the amount of the target's NOLs that can be used post-merger that are beyond the scope of this text, but those complications often increase the amount of the target's NOLs that can be used in post-closing years. For simplicity, this example also ignores the limit on use of NOLs to 80% of a firm's taxable income (included in the Tax and Jobs Act of 2017).

[20] It is possible that the target's NOLs may expire in less than 13 years. In such a scenario, the estimation must be modified accordingly.

[21] Under the Tax and Jobs Act of 2017, amounts assigned to qualifying assets are immediately tax deductible. As a result, as the proportion of the target's assets that qualify for such immediate deduction increases, so does the relative desirability of the Section 338 structure in this example.

When Bank of America acquired Countrywide Financial for about $6 billion in 2008, Countrywide had a significant amount of NOLs and built-in losses that Bank of America gained access to in the acquisition. Under the Section 382 limitations and related provisions, it was reported that Bank of America could use about $270 million of Countrywide's tax losses per year post-closing.[22] Using some simple discounting conventions, the tax losses of Countrywide were potentially worth more than 5% of the $6 billion purchase price.[23]

General Limitations on a Firm's NOLs and NOL Poison Pills

The change of ownership rules of Section 382 can also affect the tax attributes of an acquirer in a stock-financed acquisition. A large stock issue by the acquirer has the potential to trigger the 50% ownership change rule under Section 382 and therefore an acquirer needs likewise to consider the impact of the structure of an acquisition on its tax attributes. More generally, the Section 382 rules can adversely affect any firm with NOLs.

Prior to and following the recent financial crisis, many firms have experienced net operating losses. Because such losses are valuable and can provide significant tax savings in the future, firms take action to protect their NOLs.[24] In response to concerns about inadvertent triggering of Section 382, many firms have adopted so-called NOL poison pills. NOL poison pills typically are designed to limit the acquisition of blocks of a firm's stock in excess of 5% because there is a 5% threshold specified in the Section 382 rules.[25]

14.7 COMPARISON OF TAXABLE AND TAX-FREE ACQUISITIONS OF FREESTANDING C CORPORATIONS

You should now be armed with a solid understanding of the tax and nontax issues associated with various types of acquisitions. But how do we use this knowledge when planning for the acquisition of a freestanding company? In this section, we briefly synthesize the differences in taxable and tax-free acquisitions.

Table 14.4 compares various tax and nontax factors associated with seven tax structures commonly used to acquire freestanding C corporations. Three of the structures are taxable and four are tax free. Of these seven structures, the methods presented in the last five columns are the most common. These five structures are actually quite similar in many respects. Notice that in each of these transactions, the target's assets are not stepped up, the tax attributes of the target survive, and tax-based goodwill is not created. The structures do differ in terms of what is acquired (stock or assets), the status of the target's liabilities, the acquirer's source of deal financing, and whether an immediate gain is recognized by target shareholders on the transaction.

As **Table 14.4** illustrates, a major difference between acquisition methods relates to the tax treatment at the target shareholder level. When target shareholders hold highly appreciated stock, they are going to prefer to receive a tax-free consideration. Stated another way, these types of shareholders will demand a higher pretax price in a taxable deal relative to a tax-free deal.

From the acquirer's perspective, the tax structure of the deal influences the manner in which the transaction is financed. For example, if the transaction is a taxable cash deal, the acquirer will most

---

[22] See Allan Sloan, "B of A's Awesome Countrywide Tax Break," *CNN*, January 14, 2008.

[23] See also Wells Fargo's acquisition of Wachovia.

[24] For example, in 2002, prior to United Airlines filing for bankruptcy protection, United filed legal action against the Trustee of the United Airlines ESOP plan to prevent sales of United Airlines stock that would have triggered a Section 382 limitation on United NOLs. United was successful in its efforts to protect its NOLs and reported on the outcome of this legal action in its 2003 Annual Report as follows:

> On December 9, 2002, we filed a motion with the Bankruptcy Court to prevent the sale of UAL common stock by substantial holders of equity or claims in order to protect our net operating loss ("NOL") credits. The Bankruptcy Court issued a temporary injunction but permitted us to allow State Street to sell a certain number of shares in January of 2003.

[25] For further discussion of NOL poison pills, see M. Erickson and S. Heitzman, "NOL Poison Pills: Selectica v. Versata," *Tax Notes*, June 23, 2010.

Table 14.4 Overview of Tax and Nontax Features of Various Taxable and Tax-Free Acquisition Structures: Freestanding C Corporations

	Taxable Structures			Tax-Free Structures			
	Asset Acquisition Followed by a Liquidation	Stock Acquisition					
Tax or Structural Factor		**With a §338 Election**	**Without a §338 Election**	**IRC §368 "A"**	**IRC §368 "B"**	**IRC §368 "C"**	**IRC §351**
Consideration/method of payment	Cash	Cash	Cash	Stock/cash	Stock	Stock	Mixed but some stock
Consideration required to be tax free	n/a	n/a	n/a	40% stock	100% stock	80% stock	Varied
Taxable gain recognized by target shareholders?	Yes	Yes	Yes	Partially	No	No	Partially
Step-up in the target's assets	Yes	Yes	No	No	No	No	No
Target's tax attributes survive[1]	No	No	Yes	Yes	Yes	Yes	Yes
What is acquired (stock or assets)?	Assets	Stock	Stock	Assets	Stock	Assets	Stock or assets
Acquirer obtains all of the target's liabilities?	No	Yes	Yes	Yes	Yes	No	No
Tax-based goodwill?[2]	Yes	Yes	No	No	No	No	No
Acquirer's finance the acquisition with:[3]	Debt	Debt	Debt	Stock/debt	Stock	Stock	Stock/debt
Target shareholders ultimately have?	Cash	Cash	Cash	Stock/cash	Stock	Stock	Stock/boot
Primary benefit of the structure	Target shareholders get cash, which provides diversification[4]	Target shareholders get cash, which provides diversification[4]	Target shareholders get cash, which provides diversification[4]	Tax deferral of target shareholder gains[5]	Tax deferral of target shareholder gains[5]	Tax deferral of target shareholder gains[5]	Tax deferral of target shareholder gains[5]

[1] Target tax attributes include net operating loss carryforwards and various types of tax credits, among others.

[2] This row indicates whether any goodwill recorded in the acquisition, for financial accounting purposes, would also be recorded on the tax-basis balance sheet. Tax-based goodwill only occurs when the tax basis of the target's assets are stepped up.

[3] In taxable transactions, acquirers almost always pay cash for the target. In tax-free acquisitions, the acquirer, by definition, must use its stock as payment for the target. These deals are therefore, by definition, stock financed.

[4] When shareholders receive cash in an acquisition, they have the ability to invest the after-tax proceeds from the transaction in a diversified basket of securities. In a tax-free acquisition in which target shareholders receive stock of the acquiring firm instead of cash, they do not have this option. Subsequent transaction planning may provide avenues for diversification, but at a cost.

[5] Target shareholders defer gains on their exchange of target stock for acquirer stock until they sell the acquirer stock. When acquirer stock is sold, target shareholders recognize the taxable gain associated with the acquisition (assuming acquirer stock has at least retained its value post-acquisition).

likely obtain the cash from debt-type borrowings. But if the transaction is tax free, the acquirer must purchase the target with its stock and therefore the deal will be primarily or totally stock financed. The acquirer's tax status and relative stock price influences the acquirer's after-tax financing costs associated with each of the tax structures presented in **Table 14.4**. The acquirer's relative resistance to diluting its ownership will also influence the viability of a tax-free structure. Conversely, target shareholders may prefer to receive cash instead of acquiring firm stock if they are averse to holding acquirer stock post-acquisition.[26]

Summary of Key Points

1. The most common of tax-free reorganization structures are so-called Section 368 A, B, and C reorganizations. "A" reorganizations are statutory mergers, "B" reorganizations involve an acquisition of at least 80% of the target company's stock solely in exchange for the purchaser's stock, and "C" reorganizations involve an acquisition of substantially all the target company's assets primarily in exchange for the purchaser's stock.
2. Conditions that must be met to qualify as a tax-free reorganization include a business purpose, continuity of shareholder interest, and continuity of the business.
3. Financial accounting consequences (balance sheet and income statement) of reorganizations can differ significantly from their tax consequences.
4. Corporate reorganization is an area in which nontax factors often dominate tax factors. But the legal form that many transactions take could simply not be explained were it not for tax considerations.
5. Tax-free structures provide tax benefits but are also associated with substantial nontax costs. Specifically, the stock issue associated with a tax-free deal may dilute the control of acquirer shareholders. Target shareholders may resist receiving payment in the form of acquirer stock due to real or perceived risks associated with holding the acquirer's stock.
6. Essentially, any type of acquisition that results in a carryover basis in the target's assets, taxable or tax free, triggers limitations on the target's tax attributes. These limitations can substantially reduce the value of the target's tax attributes post-acquisition.
7. The tax costs and benefits that are traded off in the acquisition of a freestanding company include target shareholder capital gains taxes, target corporation capital gains and ordinary income taxes, target corporation tax attributes, and incremental benefits from stepping up the tax basis of the target's assets.

Questions

Q14-1. Why might two corporations wish to combine tax free? How could tax costs inhibit an otherwise efficient combination?

Q14-2. Why might an acquirer want to maintain a target company as a separate legal entity and not merge the target into one of its own subsidiaries or buy the target's assets?

Q14-3. What are the tax benefits of using a Section 351 transfer of property to a controlled corporation? In what ways is it superior to a Section 368 reorganization?

Q14-4. Why might you expect a cash merger to fetch a higher price for the target's shares than one in which the purchaser's stock is exchanged for the target's stock?

Q14-5. What are the primary tax and nontax benefits of a

a. Section 368 A tax-free reorganization

b. Section 368 B tax-free reorganization

c. Section 368 C tax-free reorganization

d. Section 351 tax-free acquisition

[26] See A. Rappaport and M. Sirower, "Stock or Cash? The Trade-offs for Buyers and Sellers in Mergers and Acquisitions," *Harvard Business Review* (November–December 1999), pp. 147–158, for additional discussion of these issues.

Q14-6. What are the primary tax and nontax costs of a

a. Section 368 A tax-free reorganization

b. Section 368 B tax-free reorganization

c. Section 368 C tax-free reorganization

d. Section 351 tax-free acquisition

Tax-Planning Problems

TP14-7. Assume the following factors in assessing the value of preserving NOLs in the acquisition of a target:

- The target corporation has NOLs of $675.
- The net basis in the target's assets is $200.
- The cash price an acquirer is willing to pay for the stock of the target is $900.
- Target shareholders have a basis in the stock of the target of $400.
- The corporate tax rate is 21%.
- The shareholder capital gains tax rate is 20%.
- The after-tax discount rate is 7%.
- Any step-up in the tax basis of the target's assets is amortized over 10 years on a straight-line basis.
- The appropriate long-term tax-exempt rate applicable to target NOLs under Section 382 is 4%. The target's NOLs will expire in 20 years.

  a. Should the acquirer make a Section 338 election and use the target's NOLs to offset any gain on the step-up, or should it forgo the election and preserve the target's NOLs?

  b. What if the step-up in the tax basis of the target's assets is amortized straight line over a 15-year period and the long-term tax-exempt rate applicable to target NOLs under Section 382 is 4.75%? Should the acquirer make a Section 338 election and use the target's NOLs to offset any gain on the step-up, or should it forgo the election and preserve the target's NOLs?

TP14-8. Here is a set of facts about the pending acquisition of Baja Inc. (the target) by Calstar Inc. (the acquirer).

- Baja, Inc. is owned by Smith and Calegari. Smith owns 30% of Baja's common stock and has a basis in his Baja stock of $10. Calegari owns the remaining 70% of Baja stock and has a basis in his stock of $1,000.
- Calstar, Inc. wants to acquire Baja and is willing to pay $100,000.
- Calstar's outstanding common stock is currently worth $50,000. Calstar's management owns approximately 45% of the currently outstanding common stock.
- Baja possesses valuable patents, licenses, and other intangible assets that cannot be sold and has assets with titles that are nontransferable.
- Baja does not have substantial contingent liabilities.
- Calegari will not sell unless he receives only cash for his Baja stock.
- Smith will not sell unless he receives consideration that is tax free.
- Calstar's management will not purchase Baja with its common stock, which would significantly reduce its voting control.

What acquisition structure would you recommend for this transaction (please mention the Internal Revenue Code section)? Diagram the structure and provide details and description as necessary. Be concise.

TP14-9. It was announced today that Matrix Inc. will acquire Cajun Systems. Cajun Systems has assets with a tax basis of $5 billion and has $1 billion of liabilities. Prior to being acquired, Cajun Systems had no goodwill on its tax books, although it had approximately $2 billion of goodwill on its financial statements. Cajun's identifiable assets, which include intangible assets other than goodwill, are estimated by Matrix to have a fair market value of $9 billion and its liabilities have a fair market value of $1 billion.

Cajun has two primary classes of shareholders. The first consists of taxable investors, who own 15 million of Cajun Systems outstanding shares with an aggregate basis of $2 billion. For simplicity, assume these stockholders have all held Cajun stock more than 18 months and all purchased the stock at the same price. The second consists of various nontaxable entities, including pension funds and certain foreign investors, who own the remaining 5 million of Cajun's outstanding shares and have an aggregate basis of $1 billion.

Neither Matrix nor Cajun Systems has any net operating loss carryovers, and both face a 35% tax rate. Assume any boot is taxable at capital gains rates of 20%.

Matrix gives voting stock in itself in exchange for all of the outstanding stock of Cajun Systems (a Section 368 "B" structure). Cajun becomes a wholly owned subsidiary of Matrix. At the time of the exchange, the Matrix stock given has a market value of $10 billion.

a. What tax basis will Matrix take in the stock of Cajun Systems acquired?

b. What tax basis will Cajun (and Matrix through its ownership of Cajun) have in its net assets, or assets less liabilities, following the acquisition?

Instead, assume Matrix gives voting stock in itself of $7.5 billion and cash of $2.5 billion, and Cajun is merged under state law into a newly created, wholly owned acquisition subsidiary of Matrix called Newco, a Section 368 "A" structure.

c. Assuming the cash portion of the purchase price all goes to the nontaxable investors, and the entire stock portion of the purchase price goes to the taxable investors. How much tax will the Cajun shareholders pay in aggregate at the time of the sale?

d. Now, assume instead that the cash and stock portions of the purchase price are prorated, so each Cajun shareholder gets a package of cash and Matrix stock. That is, every share of Cajun stock is exchanged for $125 cash and $375 of Matrix stock. How much tax will Cajun shareholders pay in aggregate at the time of the sale?

e. Assuming the structure outlined in part b, what tax basis will Newco have in the net assets of Cajun?

f. Assuming the structure outlined in part b, how much tax-deductible goodwill will Matrix/Cajun have post-acquisition?

TP14-10. It was announced today that Florida, Inc., will acquire Menlo Park, Inc. Menlo Park has assets with a gross tax basis of $6 million and has $1.5 million of liabilities. Prior to being acquired, Menlo Park had no goodwill on its tax books, although it had approximately $2 million of goodwill on its financial statements. Menlo Park's identifiable assets, which include intangible assets other than goodwill, are estimated by Florida to have a fair market value of $22 million, and its liabilities have a fair market value of $1.5 million.

Menlo Park has two primary classes of shareholders. The first consists of taxable investors, who own 1,200 of Menlo Park's outstanding shares with an aggregate basis of $10 million. For simplicity, assume these stockholders have all held Menlo Park stock more than 12 months and all purchased the stock at the same price. The second consists of various nontaxable entities, such as pension funds and certain foreign investors that own the remaining 800 outstanding Menlo Park shares. These stockholders have an aggregate basis of $1 million.

Neither Florida nor Menlo Park has any net operating loss carryovers, and both face a 35% tax rate. Assume any boot is taxable at capital gains rates of 20%.

Florida gives voting common stock in itself in exchange for all of the outstanding stock of Menlo Park, a Section 368 "B" structure. Menlo Park becomes a wholly owned subsidiary of Florida. At the time of the exchange, the Florida stock given has a market value of $20 million.

a. What tax basis will Florida take in the stock of Menlo Park acquired?

b. What tax basis will Menlo Park and Florida through its ownership of Menlo Park have in its net assets following the acquisition?

Instead, assume Florida gives voting stock in itself of $16 million and $5 million in cash, and Menlo Park is merged under state law into a newly created, wholly owned acquisition subsidiary of Florida called Biscayne, Inc., which is a triangular 368 "A" structure.

c. Assume the cash and stock portions of the purchase price are prorated so that each Menlo Park shareholder gets a package of cash and Florida stock. That is, every share of Menlo Park stock is exchanged for $2,500 cash and $8,000 of Florida stock ($10,500 of consideration per share of stock multiplied by 2,000 shares outstanding is $21 million). How much tax will Menlo Park's shareholders pay in aggregate at the time of the sale?

d. What tax basis will Florida's Biscayne subsidiary have in the net assets of Menlo Park?

e. How much tax-deductible goodwill will Florida/Menlo Park have post-acquisition?

TP14-11. Assume the following factors in assessing the sensitivity of the optimal acquisition structure when the target has NOLs:

- The target corporation (a freestanding C corporation) has NOLs of $16,500.
- The net basis in the target's assets is $1,800.
- The cash price an acquirer is willing to pay for the stock of the target is $19,275.

- Target shareholders have a basis in the stock of the target of $4,000.
- The corporate tax rate is 21%.
- The shareholders capital gains tax rate is 20%.
- The after-tax discount rate is 7%.
- Any step-up in the tax basis of the target's assets is amortized over 5 years on a straight-line basis.
- The appropriate long-term tax-exempt rate applicable to target NOLs under Section 382 is 5%. The target's NOLs will expire in 12 years.
  a. Should the acquirer make a Section 338 election and use the target's NOLs to offset any gain on the step-up, or should it forgo the election and preserve the target's NOLs?
  b. Now, assume instead the after-tax discount rate is 9%. What structure—to make or forgo the Section 338 election—do you recommend?

References and Additional Readings

See the list at the end of Chapter 11.

Teaching Cases

See the list at the end of Chapter 11.

15

Tax Planning for Divestitures

In 2009, Express Scripts acquired two subsidiaries of Wellpoint for about $4.7 billion. Express Scripts reported that both parties agreed to make a Section 338(h)(10) election, which is a tax election that creates tax benefits for the acquiring entity. Furthermore, Express Scripts reported that it valued the tax benefits of the tax structure of the deal at between $800 million and $1.2 billion, or about 20% of the deal's value.[1] It was reported that Wellpoint was likely to receive some of the tax benefits, potentially half of the $1+ billion of benefits, through a higher purchase price. Similarly, in 2015, Lockheed Martin agreed to acquire Sikorsky Aircraft from United Techonologies for $9 billion. The transaction included a 338(h)(10) election, and the tax benefits of the tax structure were reported to be about $1.7 billion.[2] In this chapter, you will learn about how these tax benefits are generated, how they affect purchase prices, and what types of divestitures are likely to feature such tax benefits.

After completing this chapter, you should be able to

1. Understand the various types of taxable and tax-free divestiture methods.
2. Explain when a Section 338(h)(10) election should be made in the sale of a subsidiary.
3. Compute the price at which a divesting parent and an acquirer are indifferent between different subsidiary sale tax structures.
4. Explain the requirements under which a divestiture qualifies for tax-free treatment.
5. Understand the tax implications of tax-free divestitures for the distributing corporation and its shareholders.

Corporations seek to restructure through divestiture for a variety of reasons. Some conglomerates are unable to manage far-flung unrelated businesses effectively and efficiently. For this reason, they may choose to divest unrelated businesses or separate the conglomerate into distinct portions. Alternatively, firms sometimes conclude that the market doesn't appropriately price the various divergent portions of the company. They therefore believe that separating it into several stand-alone businesses will result in appropriate, and presumably higher, prices for the separate underpriced businesses.

From a tax perspective, several structural divestiture alternatives are available. Several methods are tax free; others are taxable. Tax-free divestiture methods include spin-offs, **tax-free subsidiary sales** (under Section 368), and equity carve-outs. Taxable divestiture methods include taxable asset sales and taxable stock sales.

In general, a tax-free divestiture method does not result in a taxable gain or loss at the divesting parent corporation level. It also does not usually result in the recognition of a financial accounting gain or loss, although certain balance sheet accounts are affected. Under certain tax-free divestiture structures, the historical shareholders of the parent retain ownership of the divested subsidiary.

---

[1] Express Scripts April 29, 2009 10-Q.

[2] Source: Lockheed Martin, July 20, 2015, press release.

In a taxable divestiture, the divesting parent recognizes a taxable gain or loss and also typically recognizes a financial accounting gain or loss. Generally, a taxable divestiture results in a change in ownership of the divested business—that is, historical shareholders of the divesting parent do not retain control of the divested business. In this chapter, we introduce and analyze the tax and nontax implications of various divestiture methods. [3]

15.1 SUBSIDIARY SALES[3]

In Chapters 12 and 14, we analyzed several ways to acquire freestanding C corporations using either taxable or tax-free structures. Some of the same options are available in acquisitions of subsidiaries of freestanding companies, although several differences are notable. In particular, the seller of a subsidiary is a corporation and not an individual shareholder or a group of various types of shareholders. We focus on taxable subsidiary sales because they are most common, but we begin with a brief analysis of tax-free subsidiary sales. **Table 15.1** provides a summary of the tax consequences of various subsidiary sale structures.

Table 15.1 Tax Implications of Various Subsidiary Sale Tax Structures

	Tax Structure			
Factors Influenced by Structure	**Tax-Free Stock Sale**	**Taxable Asset Sale**	**Taxable Stock Sale without an IRC §338(h)(10) Election**	**Taxable Stock Sale with an IRC §338(h)(10) Election[1]**
What is acquired?	Stock	Assets	Stock	Stock
Consideration used:	Acquirer stock	Usually cash[1]	Usually cash[1]	Usually cash[1]
Effect on the Divesting Parent:				
Gain or loss recognized:	No	Yes	Yes	Yes
Gain computed as:	No gain recognized	Price less basis in subsidiary's *net assets*	Price less basis in subsidiary's *stock*	Price less basis in subsidiary's *net assets*
Character of gain:	n/a	Ordinary income and capital gain[2]	Capital gain	Ordinary income and capital gain[2]
Sold subsidiary's NOLs	Remain with subsidiary, but limited by §382	Remain with divesting parent, and can offset gain on sale; not limited by §382	Remain with subsidiary, but limited by §382	Remain with divesting parent, and can offset gain on sale; not limited by §382
Effect on the Acquirer:				
Basis in subsidiary's assets:	Carryover	Step-up to purchase price paid	Carryover	Step-up to purchase price paid
Basis in subsidiary's stock:	Carryover	n/a[3]	Purchase price	Purchase price
Tax benefits from additional depreciation and amortization deductions:	No	Yes	No	Yes

[1] Consideration can be cash, debt securities, acquiring-firm stock, or some combination. Most often, however, the acquirer uses primarily cash in these transactions.
[2] Ordinary income arises from recaptured depreciation, whereas capital gain is the difference between the purchase price and the historical cost of the assets. The top corporate statutory federal tax rate on ordinary income and capital gain income is currently 21%.
[3] The stock of the subsidiary is not acquired and therefore the acquirer does not have a basis in the acquired subsidiary's stock.

---

[3] This section is based on M. Erickson and S. Wang, "The Effect of Transaction Structure on Price: Evidence from Subsidiary Sales," *Journal of Accounting and Economics* (2000), v. 30. David Goldberg of Endeavour Capital (Portland Oregon) pointed out some of the anecdotal examples later in the chapter, and we are grateful for his assistance.

Tax-Free Subsidiary Sales

In a tax-free subsidiary sale, the divesting parent exchanges the stock or assets of the subsidiary for the stock of the acquiring firm. The same principles that applied in tax-free reorganizations of free-standing companies generally apply in nontaxable subsidiary sales as well. For ease of exposition, we illustrate with an example of a tax-free subsidiary stock sale. In this case, the divesting parent sells the stock of the subsidiary to an acquirer in exchange for the acquirer's stock.

Figure 15.1 illustrates this transaction. Assuming the transaction is structured to qualify as a Section 368 "B" reorganization, the divesting parent will not recognize a taxable gain or loss on the exchange. The selling parent will take a substituted basis in the acquiring-firm stock received equal to its basis in the sold subsidiary's stock. The sold subsidiary becomes a wholly owned subsidiary of the acquirer, and the net asset basis of the sold subsidiary carries over. The sold subsidiary's tax attributes survive and remain with the sold subsidiary, but they are limited under Section 382. The acquirer takes a basis in the sold subsidiary's stock equal to the divesting parent's basis in the sold subsidiary's stock, a so-called carryover basis.

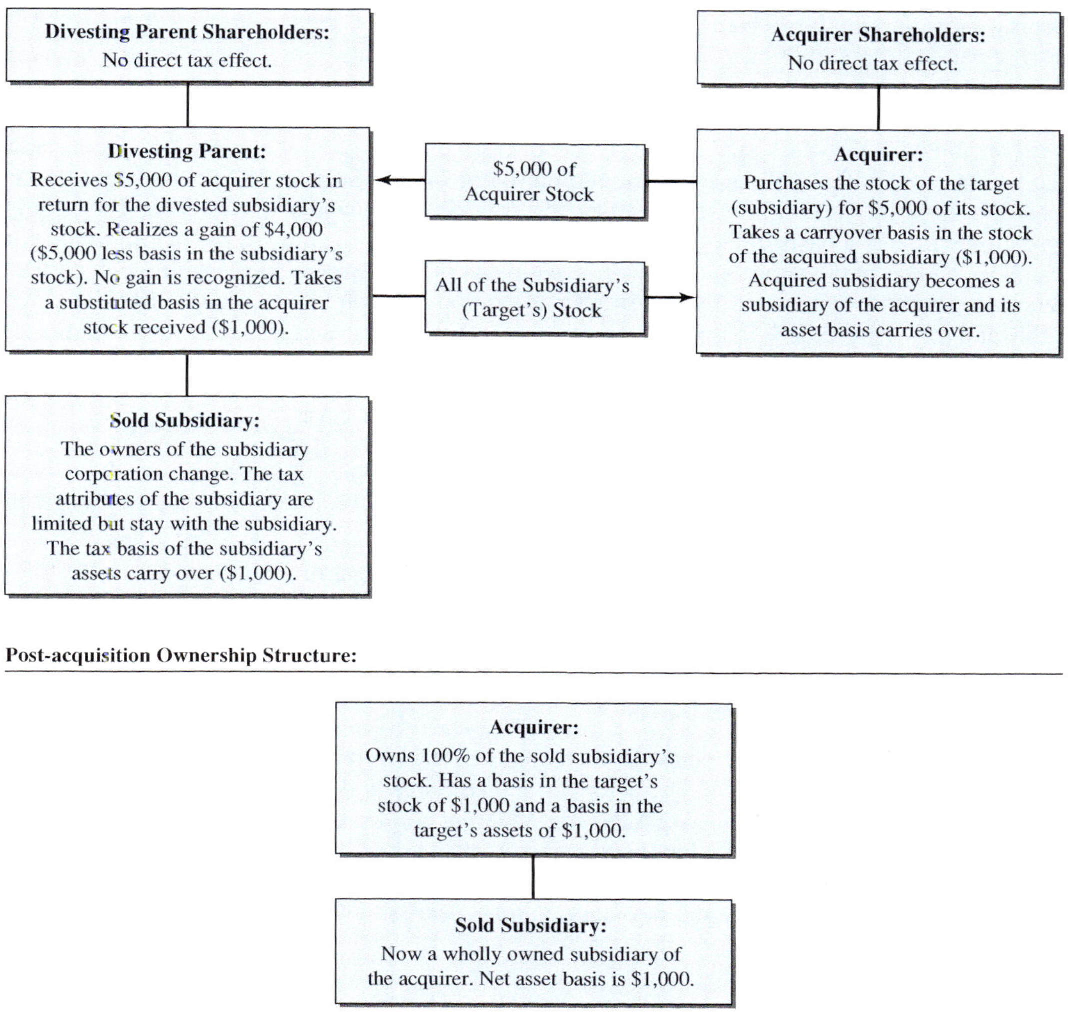

FIGURE 15.1
Tax-Free 368 "B" Subsidiary Stock Sale

This structure is generally undesirable for several reasons. First, the seller holds a large block of acquirer stock after the transaction and therefore the seller has not truly divested its holding in the sold subsidiary. Furthermore, the seller will hold a relatively illiquid block of the acquirer. Finally, if the fair market value of the subsidiary is greater than the seller's tax basis in the subsidiary's stock, the acquirer and the seller will both hold financial positions with a built-in gain after consummation of the transaction.[4] For these reasons, tax-free subsidiary sales are somewhat unusual.

Taxable Subsidiary Sales

The three basic taxable structures in which a corporation can sell a subsidiary are (1) a taxable asset sale, (2) a taxable stock sale, and (3) a taxable stock sale accompanied by a Section 338(h)(10) election.[5] The latter results in the stock sale being taxed as if the divesting parent sold the assets of the subsidiary instead of the subsidiary's stock. As in the analyses presented in Chapter 12, we work through the mechanics of these structures with the help of a simple numerical example.

Taxable Asset Sale In a taxable subsidiary asset sale, the acquirer—we will assume that the acquirer is a corporation—purchases the assets of the target subsidiary corporation, usually for cash, from the divesting parent. The target corporation recognizes a gain or loss equal to the difference between the purchase price and the net tax basis of the assets. To the extent the gain is recaptured depreciation (or arises from the sale of inventory), the gain will be ordinary. The difference between the purchase price of the target's assets and their historical cost will be a capital gain. Because the target is a subsidiary of the divesting parent, the taxable gain or loss passes through to the parent. The divesting parent corporation may or may not liquidate the sold subsidiary, but generally, liquidation of the sold subsidiary occurs.

If the parent liquidates the target corporation, no gain or loss is recognized under Section 332.[6] The tax attributes of the subsidiary, such as its net operating losses or NOLs, survive and are available to the parent corporation without incurring the limitations under Section 382. If the target or parent has NOLs, these NOLs can be used to offset the gain on the subsidiary asset sale. The acquiring corporation will take a basis in the assets of the acquired subsidiary equal to the purchase price, and the step-up in basis of the target's assets will be equivalent to the amount of the gain—purchase price less net asset basis—recognized by the target corporation. The purchase price will be allocated to tangible and intangible assets, including goodwill, as prescribed by the residual method, as discussed in Chapter 12.[7]

Figure 15.2 presents the structure of a taxable subsidiary asset acquisition followed by a liquidation of the target subsidiary. For purposes of illustration, assume the following basic facts for our taxable subsidiary asset sale:

- The target corporation has assets with a net basis of $1,000 (historical cost equals $1,000 with $0 of accumulated depreciation) and no liabilities.
- The parent corporation has a basis in the stock of the target of $1,000, and the subsidiary is 100% owned by the parent.
- The subsidiary has no NOLs, nor has the divesting parent.
- The acquirer pays the parent $5,000 for all the target's assets, and the sold subsidiary is liquidated by the parent after the sale.

Given these facts, the target corporation recognizes a gain on the sale of its assets of $4,000 ($5,000 less $1,000 basis), and the character of the gain is capital in nature. A $4,000 capital gain taxed at 21% results in a tax liability of $840 for the target corporation. After tax, the target corporation has $4,160, which is distributed to the parent in exchange for all the target's stock in liquidation. **Table 15.2** provides the details of these computations and those that follow. The parent corporation does not recognize a gain on the liquidation under Section 332. The shareholders of the parent

[4] Essentially, the parent's built-in gain presale is duplicated in the acquirer's hands while being preserved in the divesting parent's hands, thereby leaving both parties facing a tax liability when they sell the acquirer or divested subsidiary's stock.

[5] IRC Section 336(e) and a Section 336(e) election provide similar tax treatment to a 338(h)(10) election structure in cases in which the purchaser is not a corporation.

[6] Section 332 allows a corporation to liquidate wholly owned subsidiaries in a tax-free manner. Such corporate liquidations are common in various types of acquisitions.

[7] The amortization associated with these intangible assets is tax deductible under Section 197.

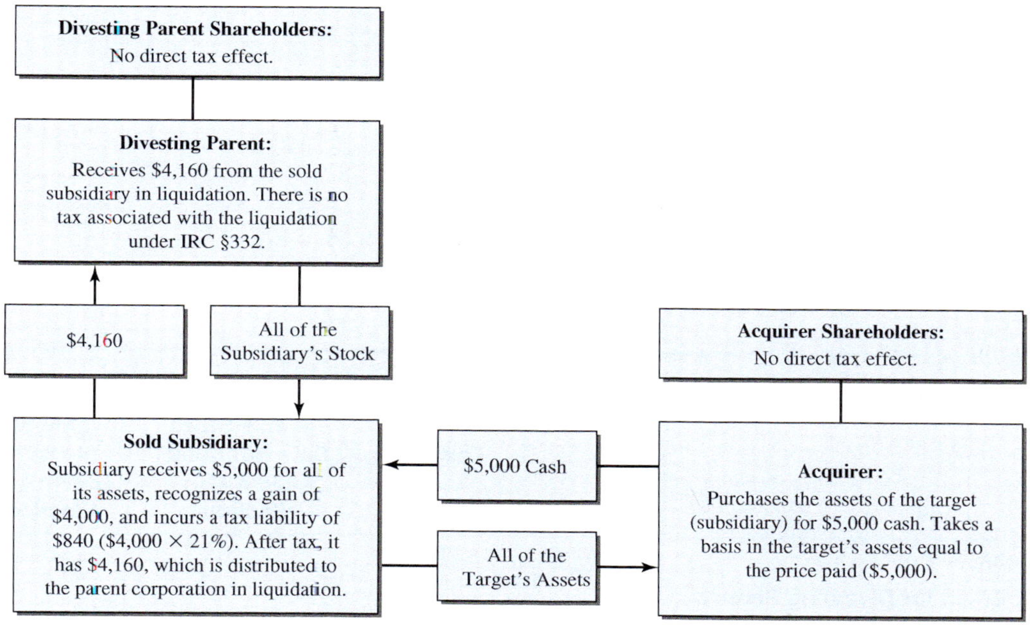

FIGURE 15.2 Taxable Subsidiary Asset Sale

corporation do not recognize a gain or loss unless the parent corporation distributes the proceeds of the asset sale, which is unusual.

The acquiring corporation takes a basis in the assets of the target equal to the purchase price ($5,000), so the step-up in the tax basis of the target's assets is $4,000. A portion of the $4,000 step-up may be allocated to goodwill and other intangibles. As we noted in Chapter 12, asset acquisitions are potentially costly in terms of transaction costs, such as title transfer, and some assets may not be transferable. However, this structure may be particularly useful when selling pieces of a business or selected assets rather than an entire incorporated subsidiary.

Taxable Stock Sale without a Section 338(H)(10) Election The divesting parent may sell the stock of the subsidiary rather than the assets. Under this structure, the acquirer purchases the stock of the target corporation from the parent for cash. The parent corporation recognizes a gain or loss on the sale of the subsidiary's stock equal to the difference between the purchase price and its basis in the subsidiary's stock. The gain or loss will be capital in nature because stock is a capital asset.

The acquiring firm will take a basis in the target subsidiary's stock equal to the purchase price, and it will take a carryover basis in the assets of the target. The acquirer obtains all the assets and liabilities of the target, and the target becomes a subsidiary of the acquirer post-acquisition. **Figure 15.3** illustrates the mechanics of a taxable subsidiary stock sale without a Section 338(h)(10) election.

Returning to our numerical example, we make the same assumptions here. The acquirer is willing to pay $5,000 for the stock of the target. The selling parent will recognize a capital gain on the stock sale equal to $4,000, which is the $5,000 purchase price less stock basis of $1,000, and faces a tax liability of $840. After tax, the divesting parent will have $4,160. The acquirer will take a basis in the target's stock of $5,000 and will have a basis in the target's assets of $1,000 (carryover).

Notice that, with this structure, the acquirer does not obtain a step-up in the tax basis of the target's assets. To the extent the acquirer records financial accounting goodwill on this transaction, it will be goodwill that is not tax deductible because the tax basis of the target's assets is not stepped up. The tax attributes of the target survive with this structure and remain with the target subsidiary corporation. However, the target's tax attributes will be limited by Section 382.

From a nontax perspective, a stock sale is often cheaper than an asset sale in terms of transaction costs. In most cases, the divesting parent will hold a minimal number of shares (e.g., 100) that possess 100% of the voting control of the divested subsidiary. As a result, the cost of transferring these shares is typically much lower than the cost of transferring title in the subsidiary's numerous assets. A stock sale preserves the identity of the target with all its liabilities—recorded and unrecorded.

Table 15.2 Tax Implications of Various Taxable Subsidiary Sale Structures

Fact Pattern:

Purchase price	5,000.00
Target's tax net asset basis	1,000.00
Divesting parent's tax basis in target's stock	1,000.00
t_c =	21%
r =	7%
Amortization Period (n) =	10

	Subsidiary Sale Structure		
	Taxable Asset Sale	Taxable Stock Sale without a §338(h)(10) Election	Taxable Stock Sale with a §338(h)(10) Election
Purchase Price	$5,000.00	$5,000.00	$5,000.00
Tax Effect for Divesting Parent:			
Gain on sale[1]	$4,000.00	$4,000.00	$4,000.00
Cash received	$5,000.00	$5,000.00	$5,000.00
Tax on gain[2]	840.00	840.00	840.00
After-tax cash	$4,160.00	$4,160.00	$4,160.00
Acquirer Cost:			
Purchase price	$5,000.00	$5,000.00	$5,000.00
Less: Incremental tax savings[3]	589.98	0.00	589.98
Net after-tax cost	$4,410.02	$5,000.00	$4,410.02
Acquirer's Tax Basis in Target's:			
Stock	n/a	5,000.00	5,000.00
Net assets	$5,000.00	$1,000.00	$5,000.00
Step-up in the tax basis of the target's assets	4,000.00	0.00	4,000.00

Notes:

[1] Computed as the purchase price less the divesting parent's basis in the sold subsidiary's stock or net assets, depending on the transaction's structure.

[2] Corporate tax liability on the subsidiary sale. The tax is computed based on the nature of the gain (capital or ordinary) and the appropriate tax rate. We assume here that ordinary and capital gains rates are identical for divesting parents.

[3] The present value of the tax savings resulting from stepping up the tax basis of the target's assets, assuming that the step-up is amortized/depreciated straight line over a 10-year period, the applicable tax rate is 21%, and the after-tax discount rate is 7%.

However, the acquirer does obtain some degree of liability protection because the target corporation becomes a wholly owned subsidiary of the acquirer. If the target has assets that are difficult to transfer, however, a stock sale facilitates ownership transfer of these assets to the acquirer.

Taxable Stock Sale with a Section 338(H)(10) Election An acquirer and divesting parent can structure the divestiture to be completed as a stock sale while being taxed like an asset sale. The acquirer may prefer to obtain a stepped-up basis in the target's assets, but the nontax costs of an asset sale may be prohibitive. In Section 338(h)(10), the tax law provides a vehicle to facilitate the potentially favorable tax treatment of an asset sale without incurring the nontax costs of an asset sale.

Under Section 338(h)(10), a subsidiary stock sale can be taxed as an asset sale if both the buyer and seller agree to such tax treatment. In a qualifying stock purchase with at least 80% of the target's stock obtained during a 12-month period, the acquirer and divesting parent can jointly agree to make a Section 338(h)(10) election. This election will cause a taxable subsidiary stock sale to be taxed

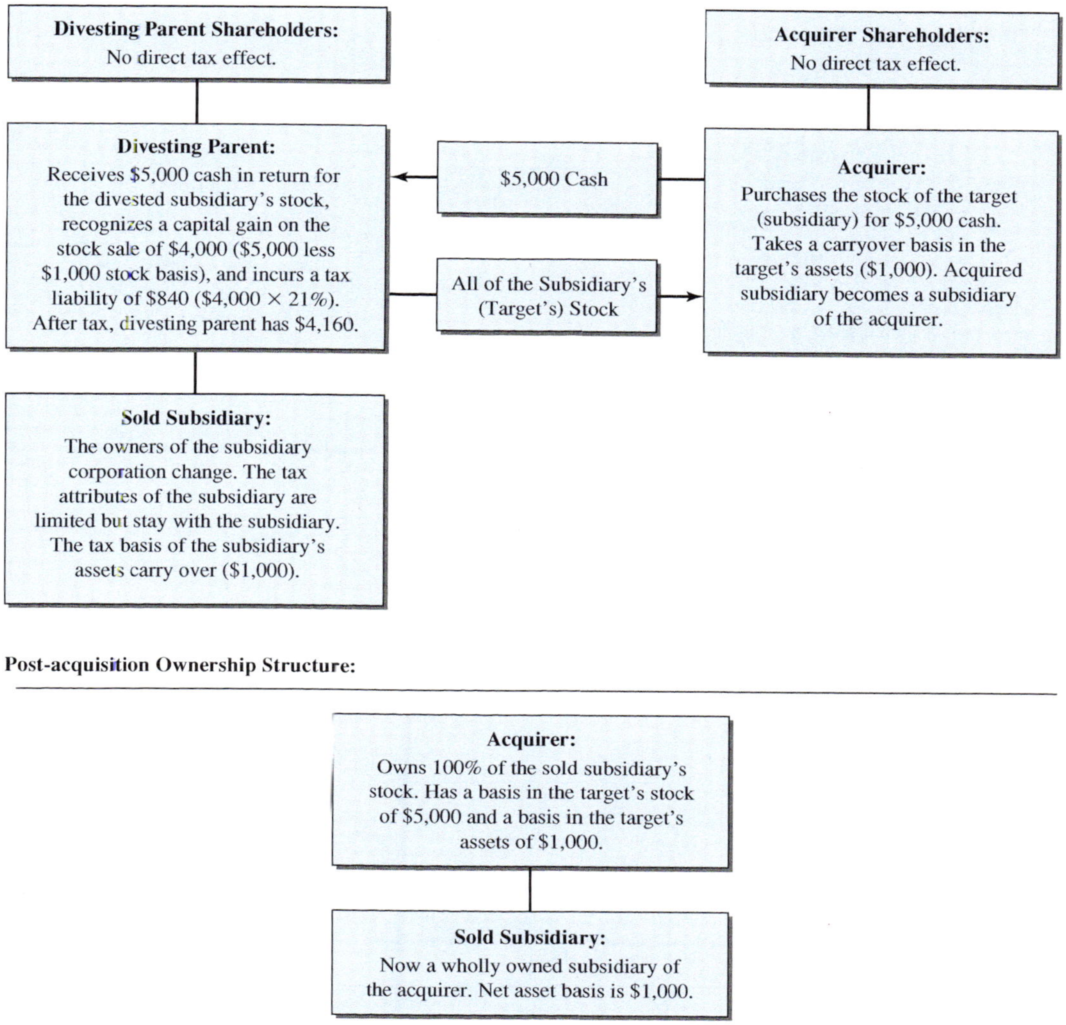

FIGURE 15.3 Taxable Subsidiary Stock Sale without a §338(h)(10) Election

as if the divesting parent had sold the subsidiary's assets to the acquirer rather than the subsidiary's stock. The taxable gain or loss on the transaction is computed as the purchase price less the divesting parent's basis in the *net assets* of the target. No tax is assessed on the stock sale.

Returning to our hypothetical numbers, we illustrate the case in **Figure 15.4**. With this structure, the stock sale is taxed as if the target sold its assets for $5,000. Hence, the parent corporation recognizes a gain on the sale of $4,000 equal to the difference between the purchase price ($5,000) and its basis in the target's *net assets* ($1,000). The gain is capital in nature because the target has no accumulated depreciation. The divesting parent faces a tax liability of $840 on the sale and has $4,160 after tax. If the divesting parent or the target subsidiary had NOLs, they could serve to offset the gain on the deemed asset sale. The divesting parent retains the tax attributes of the target.

The acquiring firm takes a basis in the stock of the target equal to the purchase price paid ($5,000) and takes a basis in the net assets of the target also equal to $5,000. The acquirer obtains a stepped-up basis in the target's assets because the transaction was taxed like an asset sale (a gain at the target *corporation* level was triggered). The step-up in the target's assets is $4,000, and purchase price will be allocated to the sold subsidiary's assets under U.S. Tax Code Section 1060 (residual method).

Note that a valid Section 338(h)(10) election can occur only when both the acquirer and the divesting parent jointly make the election. Without the seller's explicit cooperation, the acquirer cannot obtain a step-up in the tax basis of the target's assets in a stock sale. Recall that in a taxable stock acquisition of a freestanding company, the acquirer unilaterally makes a so-called regular Section 338 election.

FIGURE 15.4 Taxable Subsidiary Stock Sale with a §338(h)(10) Election

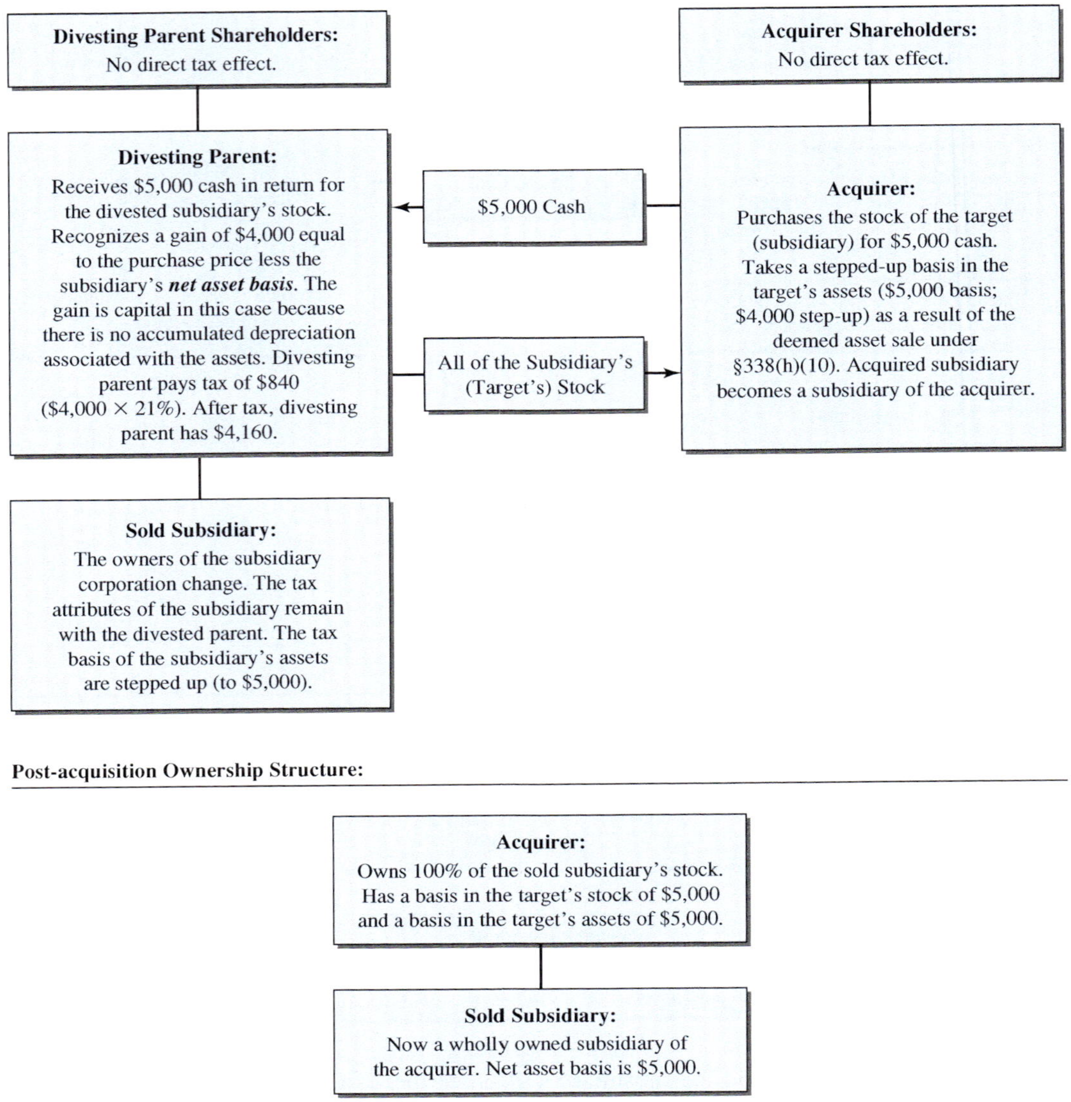

Comparison of Taxable Acquisition Structures

Table 15.2 compares the tax implications of the three taxable acquisition structures using the numerical examples we just described. Notice that, in each case, the divesting parent's after-tax wealth is $4,160. In the first and third columns of the table, the acquirer obtains a step-up in the tax basis of the divested subsidiary's assets; in the middle column, the tax basis of the target's assets carry over.

It is important to note that in step-up-basis transactions under a fact pattern like this one *only,* the incremental cost of the step-up in the tax basis of the target's assets is $0. The reason is that the tax basis of the target's net assets is exactly equal to the divesting parent's tax basis in the target's stock. Therefore, whether the parent sells the stock or assets of the target, the gain on the sale will be the same because the basis in the property sold is identical whether the property is assets or stock. Recall that the incremental cost of obtaining a step-up in the assets of a freestanding C corporation was not $0. This point is a major difference between subsidiary sales and sales of free standing C corporations.

Returning to the numerical example illustrated in **Table 15.2**, we see that the optimal structure is either a taxable asset sale or a taxable stock sale with a Section 338(h)(10) election. Those structures result in the lowest after-tax cost to the acquirer ($4,410.02); the seller is indifferent between structures. From the acquirer's perspective, making the Section 338(h)(10) election is worth $589.98.[8] That is, the acquirer is better off after taxes by $589.98 when the election is made. Because the election cannot be made without the seller's cooperation, the acquirer should be willing to pay the seller up to $589.98 more than $5,000 to get the seller to join in making the Section 338(h)(10) election. Actually, the acquirer is willing to pay up to $5,692.06, as illustrated in **Table 15.3**.

Table 15.3 Tax Implications of Various Taxable Subsidiary Sale Structures

Fact Pattern:

Purchase price—without the §338(h)(10) election	$5,000.00
Purchase price—with the §338(h)(10)election	$5,692.06
Target's tax net asset basis	1,000
Divesting parent's tax basis in target's stock	1,000
t_c =	21%
r =	7%
Amortization Period (n) =	10

	Subsidiary Sale Structure		Tax Benefit Split[1]	
	Taxable Stock Sale without a §338(h)(10) Election	Taxable Stock Sale with a §338(h)(10) Election	Midpoint Price with a §338(h)(10) Election	Incremental Difference
Purchase price—Base case	$5,000.00			
Acquirer indifference price[2]		$5,692.06		
Purchase price—Tax benefit split[1]			$5,346.03	
Tax Effect for Divesting Parent:				
Gain on sale[3]	$4,000.00	$4,692.06	$4,346.03	
Cash received	$5,000.00	$5,692.06	$5,346.03	
Tax on gain[4]	840.00	985.33	912.67	
After-tax cash	$4,160.00	$4,706.72	$4,433.36	$273.36
Acquirer Cost:				
Purchase price	$5,000.00	$5,692.06	$5,346.03	
Less: Incremental tax savings[5]	0.00	692.06	641.02	
Net after-tax cost	$5,000.00	$5,000.00	$4,705.01	$294.99
Acquirer's Tax Basis in Target's:				
Stock	$5,692.06	$5,692.06	$5,346.03	
Net assets	$1,000.00	$5,692.06	$5,346.03	
Step-up in the tax basis of the target's assets	$ 0.00	$4,692.06	$4,346.03	

Notes:

[1] This column presents the split in the net tax benefits from the step-up election assuming a price that is between the divesting parent's and acquirer's indifference price in a step-up transaction (relative to a taxable stock sale without a §338[h][10] election at a price of $5,000).

[2] Price at which the acquirer is indifferent between making the §338(h)(10) election and a purchase without the election at a price of $5,000.

[3] Computed as the purchase price less the divesting parent's basis in the sold subsidiary's stock or net assets, depending on the transaction's tax structure.

[4] Corporate tax liability on the subsidiary sale. The tax is computed based on the nature of the gain (capital or ordinary) and the appropriate tax rate. We assume here that ordinary and capital gains rates are identical for divesting parents.

[5] The present value of the tax savings resulting from stepping up the tax basis of the target's assets assuming that the step-up is amortized/depreciated straight line over a 10-year period, the applicable tax rate is 21%, and the after-tax discount rate is 7%.

[8] The same is true of the taxable asset sale structure, but we focus on the stock sale with the election here for ease of exposition and because the nontax costs of the stock sale with the election are the same as those without the election.

The acquirer is willing to pay more than \$589.98 because as the purchase price rises, so does the tax benefit from a step-up in the tax basis of the target's assets. Any price between \$5,000 and \$5,692.06 when the election is made leaves both the buyer and the seller better off after tax than a taxable stock acquisition at \$5,000 with no election. That is, the step-up election generates a net tax benefit that increases the wealth of both the divesting parent and the acquirer.

As the price of the sale approaches \$5,000 (\$5,692.06), the acquirer (divesting parent) captures relatively more of the tax benefits. For example, at a purchase price of \$5,346.03 (midpoint between \$5,000 and \$5,692.06), the acquirer's net after-tax cost is \$294.99 lower than it is if the election is not made and the deal is priced at \$5,000. Similarly, the divesting parent's after-tax wealth is \$273.36 higher if the election is made and the deal is priced at \$5,346.03. **Table 15.3** contains these computations. You should now see a pattern developing. Note once again how important it is to consider the tax implications of a transaction to both parties.

When Should the Section 338(H)(10) Election Be Made? Assuming a divesting parent has decided to sell a subsidiary in a taxable transaction, what structure should be employed? We restrict our analysis to taxable subsidiary stock sales for ease of illustration.

Because the seller and the buyer jointly make a Section 338(h)(10) election, the buyer cannot unilaterally determine the structure of the transaction but requires the seller's cooperation in defining the transaction's tax structure. Consequently, the differential tax effects of the Section 338(h)(10) election on the seller influence the election decision. The seller's tax cost in the absence of a Section 338(h)(10) election is computed as the difference between the sale price and the seller's basis in the sold subsidiary's stock multiplied by the tax rate. The seller's tax cost when a Section 338(h)(10) election is made, in contrast, is the difference between the purchase price and the seller's basis in the net assets of the sold subsidiary multiplied by the corporate tax rate. The seller will be indifferent between a Section 338(h)(10) election and no election when both choices leave it equally well off. More formally, the seller is indifferent if the price with an election meets the following condition:

$$\mathbf{Price_{338h10} - \mathit{t_c}(Price_{338h10} - Asset) = Price_{NO338h10} - \mathit{t_c}(Price_{NO338h10} - Stock)} \quad (15.1)$$

where

$Price_{338h10}$ = the price when a Section 338(h)(10) election is made
$Price_{NO338h10}$ = the purchase price if the election is not made
t_c = the corporate tax rate
Stock = seller's basis is the sold subsidiary's stock
Asset = seller's basis in the sold subsidiary's net assets

Assume $Price_{NO338h10}$ is the price of the subsidiary, ignoring any change in its asset basis, and the seller and the acquirer agree on this price. The *minimum* price demanded by the seller to make the Section 338(h)(10) election can be expressed by simplifying Equation 15.1 as

$$\mathbf{Price_{338h10} = Price_{NO338h10} + [\mathit{t_c}/(1 - \mathit{t_c})]\ (Stock - Asset)} \quad (15.2)$$

As Equation 15.2 indicates, the minimum price demanded by the seller in a Section 338(h)(10) transaction can be greater or less than the price without the election. The relationship between the price under the differing structures is a function of the seller's basis in the subsidiary's stock and net assets. If the seller has an equivalent basis in the stock and the assets of the subsidiary, then it will be equally well off after tax, at any price, whether or not the election is made.[9] If the seller's basis in the subsidiary's stock is greater than its basis in the subsidiary's net assets, as is often the case, then the seller will have the same wealth after tax only when $Price_{338h10}$ exceeds $Price_{NO338h10}$.[10]

[9] This point was illustrated numerically in **Table 15.2**.

[10] Net asset basis exceeds stock basis relatively infrequently.

If the parties make the Section 338(h)(10) election and the purchase price exceeds the subsidiary's net asset basis, the acquirer will obtain tax benefits from a step-up in the tax basis of the acquired subsidiary's assets. Like a seller, an acquirer is indifferent between tax structures when it is equally well off after tax, that is, when the after-tax *cost* of the acquisition is the same. Because the acquirer obtains incremental tax benefits with the Section 338(h)(10) election, it is equally well or better off after tax with the election even if the *pretax* purchase price of the subsidiary is higher.

As a result of the tax benefits from the basis step-up, the acquirer should be willing to pay a higher purchase price if the Section 338(h)(10) election is made. Assuming the acquirer uses straight-line depreciation and amortization after purchasing the subsidiary, we can express the maximum price that the acquiring firm will pay in a Section 338(h)(10) transaction as

$$\textbf{Acqprice}_{\textbf{338h10}} = \textbf{Price}_{\textbf{NO338h10}} + t_c \times \textbf{\textit{PVANN}}[(\textbf{Acqprice}_{\textbf{338h10}} - \textbf{Asset})/\textbf{\textit{n}}] \qquad (15.3)$$

where

Acqprice_{338h10} = the maximum purchase price the acquiring company is willing to pay in a Section 338(h)(10) transaction

PVANN = the present value of an annuity

n = the average useful life of the acquired subsidiary's assets

$\text{Price}_{NO338h10}$, Asset, and t_c are defined earlier.

The second term on the right-hand side of Equation 15.3 is the present value of the tax benefits from stepping up the tax basis of the acquired subsidiary's assets. Rearranging, substituting, and simplifying Equation 15.3 yields

$$\textbf{Acqprice}_{\textbf{338h10}} = (\textbf{Price}_{\textbf{NO338h10}} - t_c\textbf{Factor} \times \textbf{Asset})/(1 - t_c\textbf{Factor}) \qquad (15.4)$$

where Factor is *PVANN*/*n* and all other terms are as previously defined. In general, Equation 15.3 shows that the acquirer is willing to pay a higher price to persuade the seller to make the Section 338(h)(10) election if the subsidiary's net asset basis is less than the purchase price without the election ($\text{Price}_{NO338h10}$).[11] If the purchase price is less than the net tax basis of the subsidiary's assets, Equation 15.4 indicates that the price paid by the acquirer in a Section 338(h)(10) election would be lower than if the election were not made. The election would therefore result in a step-down in the asset basis of the subsidiary.

A Section 338(h)(10) election will be made in a subsidiary sale when the maximum price that the acquirer is willing to pay in a Section 338(h)(10) transaction (Acqprice_{338h10}) is greater than or equal to the minimum price the seller is willing to accept (Price_{338h10}) in a transaction with the election, or when $\text{Acqprice}_{338h10} - \text{Price}_{338h10} > 0$. The difference between Acqprice_{338h10} and Price_{338h10} is the difference between Equations 15.2 and 15.4. After rearrangement and substitution,

$$\begin{aligned}\textbf{Acqprice}_{\textbf{338h10}} - \textbf{Price}_{\textbf{338h10}} &= \left[t_c \Big/ \left(\frac{\mathbf{1}}{\textbf{Factor}} - t_c\right)\right](\textbf{Price}_{\textbf{NO338h10}} - \textbf{Asset}) \\ &\quad [t_c/(1 - t_c)]\ (\textbf{Stock} - \textbf{Asset})\end{aligned} \qquad (15.5)$$

If the right-hand side of Equation 15.5 is greater (less) than zero, a Section 338(h)(10) election will (will not) be made. Therefore, the Section 338(h)(10) election decision depends in large part on the difference between the seller's basis in the subsidiary's stock (Stock) and the seller's basis in the subsidiary's net assets (Asset). Specifically, a Section 338(h)(10) election becomes less likely as the difference between the tax basis of the subsidiary's net assets and stock increases.[12]

[11] This point was illustrated numerically in **Table 15.3**.

[12] This conclusion ignores a divesting parent's tax status. For example, if the divesting parent had large capital loss carryforwards, its relative preference for a stock sale without the election would be much greater.

Additional Complexities: Subsidiary Sale

Let's consider a more complex subsidiary sale example that illustrates the concepts laid out in Equations 15.1 through 15.5. Our objective is to determine whether the hypothetical subsidiary stock sale should be accompanied by a Section 338(h)(10) election. Assume the following facts relating to the pending sale of Richard Stevens Inc.;

- Richard Stevens, Inc., an investment bank, is a subsidiary of York Securities, and the net tax basis of Richard Stevens's assets is $1,000 (historical cost equals basis).
- York Securities tax basis in the stock of Richard Stevens is $4,000.[13]
- Chicago Bank wants to purchase Richard Stevens and believes that the value of Richard Stevens is $5,000 if the tax basis of Richard Steven's assets carryover.
- Chicago Bank wants to pay cash to acquire Richard Stevens.
- The corporate tax rate is 21%, any step-up in the tax basis of Richard Stevens's assets will be amortized straight line over a 10-year period, and the appropriate after-tax discount rate is 7%.

Table 15.4 provides the particulars of the following computations. In a taxable stock sale without the election, York Securities would have $4,790 after tax, which is $5,000 price less $210 tax, or $5,000 minus $4,000 times 21%. Therefore, York Securities would need to receive a pretax price in a Section 338(h)(10) transaction that left it with $4,790 after tax.

Equation 15.2 provides the minimum price demanded by York Securities to make the election ($PRICE_{338h10}$):

$$\begin{aligned} \textbf{Price}_{338h10} &= \textbf{Price}_{NO338h10} + [t_c/(1 - t_c)]\ (\textbf{Stock} - \textbf{Asset}) \\ &= \$5{,}000 + (.21/.79)(\$4{,}000 - \$1{,}000) \\ &= 5{,}797.47 \end{aligned} \tag{15.2}$$

Would Chicago Bank be willing to pay $5,797.47 in a transaction that results in a Section 338(h)(10) election if it will pay $5,000 (and York Securities will accept) in a non—Section 338(h)(10) transaction? The acquirer's net after-tax cost in a transaction in which the election is not made, at a price of $5,000, is $5,000. At a pretax price of $5,797.47 in a Section 338(h)(10) transaction, the present value of tax benefits from stepping up the target's assets is $707.60.[14] The acquirer's net after-tax cost is therefore $5,089.86 if the election is made, which is greater than the acquirer's net after-tax cost if the election is not made. Equation 15.4 provides the maximum price that Chicago Bank will pay ($Acqprice_{338h10}$) to purchase Richard Stevens if the election is made:

$$\textbf{Acqprice}_{338h10} = (\textbf{Price}_{NO338h10} - t_c\textbf{Factor} \times \textbf{Asset})/(1 - t_c\textbf{Factor})$$

Factor is equal to .7024(n = 10, r = 7%).

$$\begin{aligned} \textbf{Aprice}_{338h10} &= [\$5{,}000 - .21(.7024) \times 1{,}000]/[1 - ..21(.7024)] \\ &= \$5{,}692.06 \end{aligned} \tag{15.4}$$

Given these numbers, the election should not be made because $Acqprice_{338h10}$ is less than $Price_{338h10}$. That is, the *maximum* price the acquirer will pay if the election is made is less than the *minimum* price the seller will accept if the election is made. The incremental cost of making the election is more than the incremental tax benefits associated with the election. Stated another way, the acquirer's net after-tax cost in a Section 338(h)(10) transaction is higher than its net after-tax cost if the election is not made and the deal is priced at $5,000.

[13] York Securities acquired Richard Stevens in a taxable stock acquisition 3 years ago.

[14] Assuming the step-up is amortized straight line over a 10-year period, the tax rate is 21%, and the appropriate after-tax discount rate is 7%.

Table 15.4 Tax Implications of Various Taxable Subsidiary Sale Structures

Fact Pattern:

Purchase price—without a §338(h)(10) election	$5,000.00
Target's tax net asset basis	1,000
Divesting parent's tax basis in target's stock	4,000
t_c =	21%
r =	7%
Amortization Period (n) =	10

	Subsidiary Sale Structure		
	Taxable Stock Sale without a §338(h)(10) Election	Taxable Stock Sale with a §338(h)(10) Election	Taxable Stock Sale with a §338(h)(10) Election
Purchase price	$5,000.00		
Divesting parent indifference price[1]		$5,797.47	
Acquirer indifference price[2]			$5,692.06
Tax Effect for Divesting Parent:			
Gain on sale[3]	$1,000.00	$4,797.47	$4,692.06
Cash received	$5,000.00	$5,797.47	$5,692.06
Tax on gain[4]	210.00	1,007.47	985.33
After-tax cash	$4,790.00	$4,790.00	$4,706.72
Acquirer Cost:			
Purchase price	$5,000.00	$5,797.47	$5,692.06
Less: Incremental tax savings[5]	0.00	707.60	692.06
Net after-tax cost	$5,000.00	$5,089.86	$5,000.00
Acquirer's Basis in Target's:			
Stock	$5,000.00	$5,797.47	$5,692.06
Net assets	$1,000.00	$5,797.47	$5,692.06
Step-up in the target's assets	$ 0.00	$ 4,797.47	$ 4,692.06

Notes:

[1] Price at which the divesting parent is indifferent between making the §338(h)(10) election and a purchase without the election at a price of $5,000.

[2] Price at which the acquirer is indifferent between making the §338(h)(10) election and a purchase without the election at a price of $5,000.

[3] Computed as the purchase price less the divesting parent's basis in the sold subsidiary's stock or net assets, depending on the transaction's structure.

[4] Corporate tax liability on the subsidiary sale. The tax is computed based on the nature of the gain (capital or ordinary) and the appropriate tax rate. We assume here that ordinary and capital gains rates are identical for divesting parents.

[5] The present value of the tax savings resulting from stepping up the target's assets, assuming that the step-up is amortized/depreciated straight line over a 10-year period, the applicable tax rate is 21%, and the after-tax discount rate is 7%.

Difference between Subsidiary Sales and Sales of Freestanding C Corporations

Subsidiary sales are often structured to result in a step-up in the tax basis of the target subsidiary's assets, whereas in acquisitions of freestanding C corporations, the target's assets almost always carry over. Why the disparity between the two transaction types? In the sale of a subsidiary, the incremental cost of the step-up is a function of the difference between the divesting parent's basis in the stock and assets of the sold subsidiary. In many but not all cases, the incremental cost of the step-up in a subsidiary sale is less than the incremental tax benefits from the step-up.

But in an acquisition of a freestanding company, the incremental tax cost of obtaining $.21 of tax benefits in the future is $.21. With a nonzero discount rate, the incremental cost of the step-up is therefore always greater than the incremental tax benefits from the step-up. The only exception occurs when the freestanding target has large NOLs. As we illustrated in Chapter 14 (see **Table 14.3**), even when the target has NOLs, a carryover basis transaction is still often optimal.

When Is a Section 338(H)(10) Election Optimal? Assuming tax rates are constant, a Section 338(h)(10) election is wealth maximizing when the stock and asset basis of the target subsidiary are identical and the purchase price exceeds the net asset basis. In such a case, the incremental cost of the step-up election is $0, as we discussed and illustrated in **Table 15.2**. The election also makes sense when the tax basis of the target's assets exceeds the tax basis of the target's stock. Although such a circumstance is unusual, in this situation, the tax costs associated with the election are actually less than the tax costs if the election is not made. Finally, if the tax basis of the subsidiary's stock exceeds the asset basis of the subsidiary by a relatively small amount, the election is optimal. Equation 15.5 indicates when the 338(h)(10) election is optimal under such a set of facts. With changing tax rates, these generalizations can change. Equation 15.5 presented formally the case in which the step-up decision is optimal from a tax perspective.

When Is a Section 338(H)(10) Election Suboptimal? Again, assuming tax rates are constant, the step-up election doesn't make sense when the divesting parent's tax basis in the sold subsidiary's stock substantially exceeds the net tax basis of the subsidiary's assets. Again, see Equation 15.5 to determine when the election does and does not make sense for the given fact pattern. You may wonder when such a circumstance is likely to arise. Recall the analyses in Chapters 12 and 14. If the divested subsidiary was previously acquired in a taxable stock acquisition, the divesting parent's basis in the stock of the sold subsidiary is likely to exceed the tax basis of the sold subsidiary's net assets. Because carryover basis transactions are the most common structure used to acquire freestanding companies, in a significant number of situations, the Section 338(h)(10) election will not be viable.

Valuation Effects

The computations and illustrations in the preceding section and in **Tables 15.2**, **15.3**, and **15.4** indicate that the value created by a 338(h)(10) election can be substantial and a subsidiary's *pretax* selling price can vary based on the subsidiary sale's tax structure.[15] We present some notable examples of this phenomenon next.

In 2001, Bristol Myers sold Clairol to Proctor and Gamble for $4.95 billion. At the time of the sale, Clairol was a subsidiary of Bristol Myers, and the deal included a 338(h)(10) election. The value of the tax benefits from the 338(h)(10) election were reportedly valued at around $1 billion, or about 20% of the deal's value.[16]

UIL's $1.296 billion acquisition of three gas utilities (subsidiaries) from Iberdola USA, Inc. in 2010 was structured to include a 338(h)(10) election.[17] The CEO of UIL disclosed that the tax benefits of the deal's tax structure were estimated to be worth about $135 million, which is equivalent to about 10% of the deal's value.[18] The CFO explained more completely the effect of the 338(h)(10) election as follows: "Just to emphasize a little more detail on the financial impacts of this transaction.

[15] M. Erickson and S. Wang, "The Effect of Transaction Structure on Price: Evidence from Subsidiary Sales," *Journal of Accounting and Economics* (2000), provide evidence that pretax prices are higher in subsidiary sales that include a Section 338(h)(10) election.

[16] See Craig Schneider, "P&G's Clairol Purchase Gets a Double Dose of Savings," *CFO.com*, May 24, 2001.

[17] See Purchase Agreement dated May 25, 2010, between Iberdola USA, Inc. and UIL Holdings (attached to UIL Holdings May 25, 2010 8-K).

[18] Source: May 25, 2010, UIL Holdings conference call transcript available from CQ FD Disclosure

As Jim mentioned, a $1.296 billion purchase price. But as part of that we are also expecting to realize about $135 million of net present value on a tax adjustment to use what is known as affectionately the 338(h)(10) adjustment which steps up the assets, the tax bases in the assets, and will provide significant additional cash flow for the combined entities."[19] Similarly, UIL Holdings' 2011 10-K explained the tax effects of the acquisition's tax structure.[20]

In March of 2011, Catalyst Health Solutions purchased a subsidiary of Walgreen's, Walgreen's Health Initiatives, for about $525 million. The CFO of Catalyst Health disclosed that the subsidiary sale would include a 338(h)(10) election and the election would create tax benefits worth between $90 and $110 million.[21] Thus, the tax benefits of this subsidiary sale's tax structure were expected to be worth about 19% of the deal's value ($100 million/$525 million = ˜19%).

Express Scripts, $4.675 billion acquisition of NextRx from Wellpoint in 2009 included a 338(h)(10) election, and the deal's structure generated significant tax savings for Express Scripts. In its April 29, 2009, 10-Q, Express Scripts reported: "We estimate the value of such election to us to be between $800 million and $1.2 billion dependent upon the discount factor and tax rate assumed." In reference to the Express Scripts/NextRx transaction, CFO.com articulated a general rule about the value and impact of 338(h)(10) elections:

> However, ***it is an investment banking rule of thumb*** that the ability to secure a cost basis in acquired assets—and in the process, gain access to the benefits of Section 197(a)—reduces the "effective cost" of the deal by approximately 20 percent. Of course, here, as in most Section 338(h)(10) situations, a portion of the benefit will be "shared" with the seller in the form of a higher purchase price for the properties. Accordingly, it is probable that the 20 percent benefit will be equitably shared by Wellpoint and Express Scripts with each enjoying roughly 50 percent of the overall benefit.[22]

Although this text does not focus on valuation, our analyses in Chapters 12 through 15 have some potentially important consequences for valuation. We have discussed various tax-related factors (use of target NOLs, tax benefits from a 338[h][10] election, etc.) that can impact the value of a target. A standard preacquisition analysis employed by investment bankers compares the terms and price of a proposed acquisition to the terms and price of historical acquisitions that are deemed similar to the pending transaction. Such procedures are broadly called **comparables analysis**.

Figure 15.5 presents an example of a fairness opinion from an investment bank. A fairness opinion is prepared in many acquisition transactions. The purpose of the opinion is to provide assurance to shareholders of the acquirer and/or the target that the pending acquisition is priced fairly. Point 11 of the investment bankers' letter refers to a comparables analysis. A comparable company analysis typically compares the acquisition price and the acquisition premium associated with the acquisition of companies similar to the target company. Executives, advisors, and tax planners, as part of their overall planning for a merger or acquisition, should consider how tax factors such as target firm NOLs, transaction tax structure (e.g., 338[h][10] structure), and acquiring firm tax rates affected acquisition prices and premiums in comparable company transactions and how those same factors might affect the transaction under consideration.

---

[19] Source: May 25, 2010, UIL Holdings conference call transcript available from CQ FD Disclosure

[20] Footnote N of the December 31, 2010, UIL 10-K states,

> As a component of the acquisition of CEC and CTG, UIL Holdings and Iberdrola USA have agreed to effect a tax election pursuant to Section 338(h)(10) of the Internal Revenue Code (338 Election) with respect to the purchase of the stock of CEC and CTG. The 338 Election allows UIL Holdings to treat the transaction for tax purposes as if UIL Holdings was purchasing the assets of CEC and CTG rather than the stock of each corporation. As a result of the 338 Election, the assets of SCG and CNG have newly-established higher tax bases for tax depreciation purposes, resulting in incremental federal income tax deductions of approximately $639 million as those assets are depreciated for tax purposes. The acquisition will also generate approximately $175 million of tax goodwill which will be deductible by UIL Holdings over a 15 year period.

[21] Source: March 9, 2011, Catalyst Health Solutions conference call transcript available from CQ FD Disclosure.

[22] Source: Robert Willens, "ESRX Will Enjoy a Basis 'Step Up,'" *Willens Report*, April 14, 2009.

FIGURE 15.5 Fairness Opinion of Fama, Miller, Thaler & Co. Inc.

Appendix C
Fama, Miller, Thaler & Co. Inc.
295 Park Avenue New York, NY 10107
(212) 494-9000
November 13, 1995
The Merrimac Company
900 South Buena Vista Street
Burbank, CA 91521

Dear Sirs:

We understand that The Merrimac Company ("Merrimac") and North Drop Inc. ("North Drop") have entered into an Amended and Restated Agreement and Plan of Reorganization, dated as of July 31, 1995 (the "Reorganization Agreement"), pursuant to which (i) a new holding company will be formed, which will be renamed "The Merrimac Company" ("New Merrimac"), (ii) newly formed subsidiaries of New Merrimac will be merged with and into each of Merrimac and North Drop, (iii) each share of Merrimac common stock will be converted into one share of New Merrimac common stock and (iv) each share of North Drop common stock will be converted into either New Merrimac common stock or cash, or a combination thereof, based on each stockholder's election and subject to certain proration provisions, such that in the aggregate North Drop stockholders will receive the value equivalent of one share of Merrimac common stock plus $65 in cash per share of North Drop (the "Transaction"). You have provided us with the joint Proxy Statement/Prospectus, which includes the Reorganization Agreement, in substantially the form to be sent to the shareholders of Merrimac and North Drop, respectively (the "Proxy Statement").

You have asked us to render our opinion as to whether the Transaction is fair, from a financial point of view, to the stockholders of Merrimac.

In the course of our analysis for rendering this opinion, we have:

1. reviewed the Proxy Statement;
2. reviewed North Drop's Annual Reports to Shareholders and Annual Reports on Form 10-K for the fiscal years ended December 31, 1992 through 1994, and its Quarterly Reports on Form 10-Q for the periods ended April 2, July 2 and October 1, 1995:
3. reviewed certain historical financial statements and certain budget financial statements by business segments of North Drop provided to us by North Drop management:
4. reviewed Merrimac's Annual Reports to Stockholders and Annual Reports on Form 10-K for the fiscal years ended September 30, 1992 through 1994 and its Quarterly Reports on Form 10-Q for the periods ended December 31, 1994 and March 31 and June 30, 1995:
5. reviewed certain operating and financial information provided to us by Merrimac management relating to Merrimac's and North Drop's businesses and prospects, including financial forecasts of Merrimac and North Drop, respectively, prepared by Merrimac management:
6. met with North Drop's Chief Financial Officer to discuss North Drop's historical and certain budget financial statements by business segment:
7. met with certain members of Merrimac's senior management to discuss its operations, historical financial statements and future prospects:
8. reviewed the pro forma financial impact of the Transaction on the stockholders of Merrimac:
9. reviewed the historical prices and trading volumes of the common stock of North Drop and Merrimac:
10. reviewed certain publicly available financial data and stock market performance data of companies which we deemed generally comparable to North Drop and/or Merrimac:
11. reviewed the terms of certain other recent acquisitions of companies and businesses which we deemed generally comparable to North Drop and its component businesses and
12. conducted such other studies, analyses, inquiries and investigations as we deemed appropriate.

In the course of our review, we have relied upon and assumed without independent verification the accuracy and completeness of the financial and other information provided to us by North Drop and Merrimac as well as the completeness of the financial and other information provided to us by SEC filings of North Drop and Merrimac, respectively. With respect to the financial forecasts provided to us by North Drop and Merrimac we have assumed that they have been reasonably prepared on bases reflecting the best currently available estimates and judgments of the managements of North Drop and Merrimac as to the expected future performance of North Drop and Merrimac, respectively. We have not assumed any responsibility for the information or financial forecasts provided to us and we have further relied upon the assurances of the managements for North Drop and Merrimac that they are unaware of any facts that would make the information or financial forecasts provided to us incomplete or misleading. In arriving at our opinion, we have not performed or obtained any appraisals of the assets of North Drop or Merrimac and except as described in paragraphs 3, 5 and 6 above, we have not had discussions with

(continued)

continued from previous page

FIGURE 15.5 (*Continued*)

management or employees of North Drop regarding North Drop's operations, historical financial statements and future prospects or had access to financial forecasts of North Drop prepared by North Drop. Our opinion is necessarily based on economic, market and other conditions, and the information made available to us as of the date hereof.

Based on the foregoing, it is our opinion that as of this date, the Transaction is fair, from a financial point of view to the stockholders of Merrimac.

We have acted as financial advisor to Merrimac in connection with the Transaction and will receive a fee for such services.

Very truly yours,
Fama, Miller, Thaler & Co. Inc.
By /s/Elizabeth Erickson, Katie Erickson, Jack Erickson
Managing Directors

15.2 TAX-FREE DIVESTITURE METHODS

Although taxable subsidiary sales are the most common form of divestiture, in many cases, a taxfree divestiture method may be preferable. We focus on two tax-free divestiture methods: equity carve-outs and spin-offs. An **equity carve-out** is essentially a subsidiary initial public offering (IPO) that is tax free to the divesting parent and its shareholders. The divesting parent gets cash from its sale of the subsidiary's shares. A spin-off, on the other hand, is much like a large stock dividend. Shareholders of the divesting parent receive stock of the spun-off subsidiary, tax free, in proportion to their ownership of the divesting parent. In a spin-off, the divesting parent does not obtain cash as part of the transaction, although the spun-off division may in some cases pay a debt-financed dividend to the divesting parent prior to the spin-off.

Equity Carve-Outs

Figure 15.6 illustrates an equity carve-out. The divesting parent firm issues shares in the subsidiary to investors for cash. If the shares are held by the subsidiary, no gain or loss is recognized on the stock issue. This tax treatment is associated with any stock issue by a corporation.

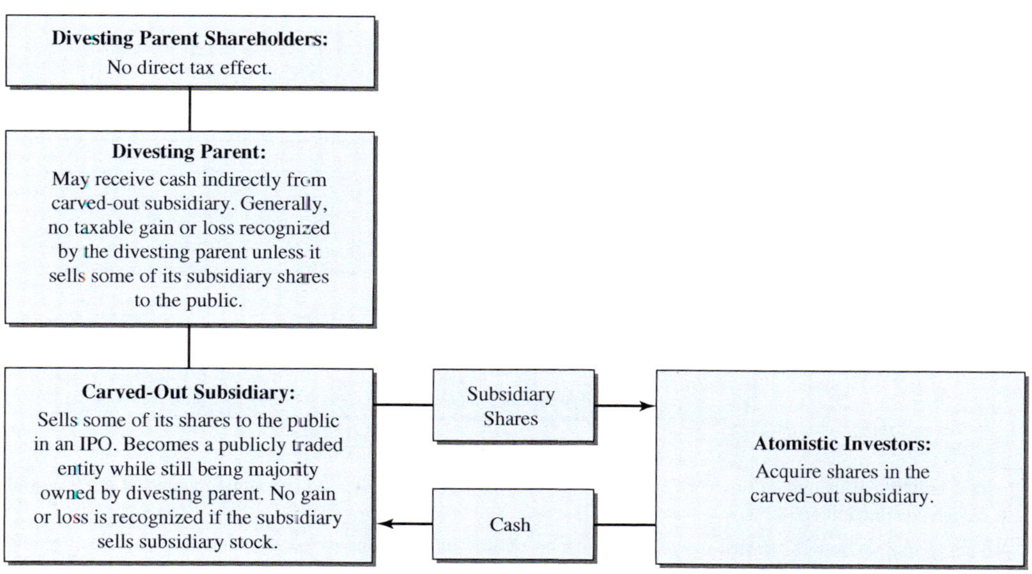

FIGURE 15.6 Equity Carve-Out

If the shares sold to the public are the parent's shares of the subsidiary, however, then the sale gives rise to a taxable gain or loss because the parent's stock ownership of the subsidiary constitutes a capital asset in the parent's hands. When this asset is sold, a gain or loss on the sale of the capital asset occurs. If the parent firm wants or needs cash, the subsidiary can pay cash to the divesting parent in the form of a tax-free dividend prior to the stock issue.[23]

For this reason, an equity carve-out can be a tax-free source of cash for the divesting parent. As an empirical fact, equity carve-outs typically involve the issue of a small portion, or less than 20%, of the stock of the subsidiary. Divesting parents are believed to complete these relatively small stock issues because it allows them to ascertain the fair market value of the subsidiary with a complete divestiture likely subsequent to the carve-out. By issuing less than 20% of the subsidiary's stock, the parent retains the ability to either complete a tax-free spin-off or sell the entire subsidiary in a qualifying taxable stock acquisition that can be followed by a Section 338(h)(10) election.[24] For accounting purposes, the divesting parent does not recognize any gain or loss on the equity carve-out.[25]

Tax-Free Spin-Offs

In a spin-off, the divesting parent divides its operations into two (or more) distinct corporate entities. If the parent's business is operated as two subsidiaries, restructuring prior to the spin-off is unnecessary. In either case, the parent firm distributes the stock of the divested subsidiary to its shareholders pro rata. **Figure 15.7** illustrates the structure of a spin-off. Essentially, the parent pays a large stock

FIGURE 15.7
Illustration of a Tax-Free Spin-Off

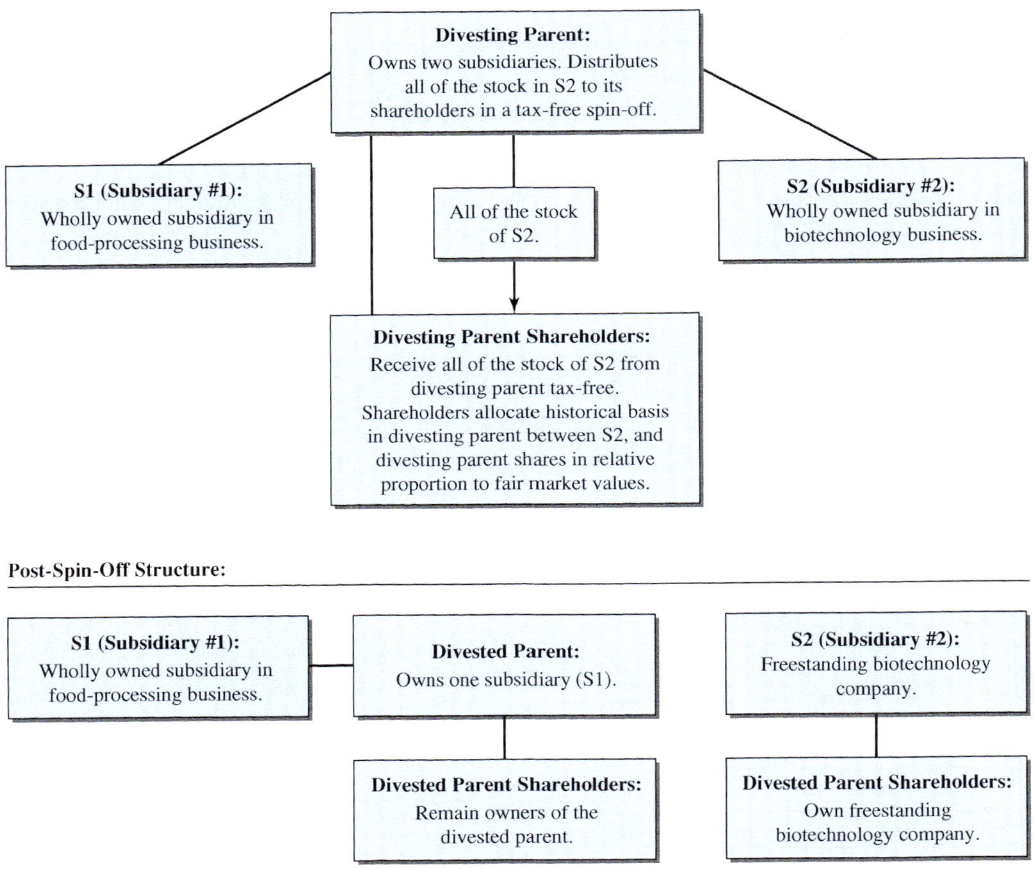

[23] This point is only true if the parent's ownership of the subsidiary is greater than 80%. Ownership of greater than 80% results in a dividends received deduction of 100%.

[24] A qualifying stock purchase is one that results in acquisition of 80% of the voting power of the target. A tax-free spin-off must involve the distribution of at least 80% of the divested subsidiary's stock.

[25] If the divesting parent sells some of its subsidiary stock, an accounting gain or loss is recognized. In addition, a divesting parent can elect to recognize a gain on an equity carve-out under the Securities and Exchange Commission's *Staff Accounting Bulletin* (SAB) 51. See J. Hand and T. Skantz, "The Economic Determinants of Accounting Choices: The Unique Case of Equity Carve-Outs under SAB 51," *Journal of Accounting and Economics* (December 1997), pp. 175–204, for additional details.

dividend but uses stock of a *subsidiary* for the dividend. After the distribution, shareholders hold interest in two separate businesses: the old parent less the spun-off subsidiary and the spun-off subsidiary. If the transaction qualifies as tax free under Section 355, the distribution is tax free to the parent's shareholders and to the divesting parent firm.

In order for such a distribution to qualify for tax-free treatment under Section 355, several general requirements must be met:

- The distributing corporation must have control of the divested subsidiary prior to the distribution. Control is defined as 80% ownership of the subsidiary.
- The divesting parent must distribute a controlling block of subsidiary's stock to shareholders. Control is defined as 80% of the divested subsidiary's stock.
- After the distribution, both the parent and the divested subsidiary must be involved in an active trade or business.
- The transaction cannot be designed as a device for distributing the earnings and profits to the shareholders of the parent.
- The historical shareholders of the divesting parent must maintain a continuity of interest in the parent and spun-off subsidiary.
- The divesting parent cannot have acquired the divested subsidiary during the previous 5 years in a taxable transaction.
- The divestiture must have a valid business purpose and the shareholders of the divesting parent must maintain control of the parent and the divested subsidiary post-spin-off.
- The divesting parent or the spun-off entity cannot be acquired within 2 years of or 2 years after the spin-off.

In a spin-off, the divesting parent's shareholders allocate their basis in the stock of the parent to the stock of the divested subsidiary and to the "new" parent in proportion to the fair market values of the two separate businesses at the date of the spin-off. For example, consider a shareholder that had a tax basis in a divesting parent's stock of $100 per share prior to the spin-off. At the date of the spin-off, assume the fair market value of the spun-off business was $200 per share and the value of the remaining parent business (old parent less the divested subsidiary) was $50. The shareholder would have a basis in the stock of the spun-off subsidiary of $80 [(200/($200 + $50))] × $100 basis and a basis in the stock of the parent of $20. The tax basis of the net assets of the remaining parent and the divested subsidiary carry over; that is, they are the same as they were for the combined business.

Factors That Influence Divestiture Method Choice

In this chapter, we have provided a mathematical framework from which to quantify the tax and cash flow effects of various divestiture methods. To structure a divestiture effectively, however, we need to consider a number of other factors. **Table 15.5** provides an overview of the major tax and nontax consequences of the divestiture methods described and analyzed in this chapter. How does a tax planner determine which of these methods is optimal given a pending divestiture?

Of course, the choice of method will be a function of the tax and nontax preferences of the divesting parent and the tax and nontax attributes of the subsidiary to be divested. If the parent is in need of cash, it could select one of the methods that generates cash, such as a stock sale or equity carve-out. If the subsidiary to be divested has a market value that greatly exceeds the tax basis of the subsidiary's net assets, the divesting parent may want to consider a spin-off rather than a subsidiary sale structure.

Conversely, if the subsidiary to be divested has a basis that exceeds its fair market value, the divesting parent may want to consider a sale to capture the taxable loss on the sale. Similarly, if the divesting parent has capital loss or operating loss carryforwards, the sale of an appreciated subsidiary may allow the use of the divesting parent's tax attributes in a relatively tax-efficient manner. If the divesting parent is interested in generating accounting gains in order to "smooth" its earnings, a taxable subsidiary sale—or in some cases, an equity carve-out—could provide the needed accounting gains.

Table 15.5 Overview of Tax and Nontax Implications of Various Divestiture Methods

Tax or Structural Factor	Tax-Free Subsidiary Sale	Taxable Subsidiary Asset Sale	Taxable Subsidiary Stock Sale without a §338(h)(10) Election	Taxable Subsidiary Stock Sale with a §338(h)(10) Election[1]	Tax-Free Spin-off	Equity Carve-Out
Divesting parent receives cash	No	Yes	Yes	Yes	No[2]	Yes
Divesting parent maintains control of divested subsidiary	No	No	No	No	No	Yes[3]
Taxable gain or loss at the divesting parent level	No	Yes	Yes	Yes	No	No[4]
Taxable gain for divesting parent shareholders	No	No	No	No	No	No
Step-up in the tax basis of the divested subsidiary's assets	No	Yes	No	Yes	No	No
Accounting gain or loss recognized by divesting parent	Possibly	Yes	Yes	Yes	No	Possibly

[1] Subsidiary stock sale that is taxed as if the divesting parent sold the assets of the subsidiary rather than subsidiary stock.

[2] In some cases, the spun-off subsidiary pays a debt-financed dividend to the divesting parent pre-spin-off.

[3] A carve-out can involve less than or more than enough equity to constitute control of the divested subsidiary.

[4] If the subsidiary sells the shares in the IPO, there is no taxable gain. If the shares sold are shares owned by the divesting parent, a taxable gain or loss results.

To a large extent, the divestiture method chosen is a function of the relative demand for the divested subsidiary. That is, does the subsidiary have willing buyers? Conversely, the spin-off of a poorly performing subsidiary may not be well received by the parent's shareholders, making it a wealth-reducing divestiture mechanism.

Summary of Key Points

1. A corporation can divest a subsidiary or division in several ways. The most common divestiture methods are subsidiary sales, spin-offs, and equity carve-outs.
2. A sale of the entire subsidiary is typically structured in a manner that gives rise to a taxable gain or loss. An equity carve-out or a spin-off is typically tax free; the former generates cash flow for the divesting parent firm, whereas the latter does not.
3. A subsidiary sale can be taxed as a stock sale or an asset sale. Asset sale tax treatment results in a step-up in the tax basis of the sold subsidiary's assets. A stock sale may be preferable due to the costs of title transfer associated with an asset sale. Certain types of stock sales can be taxed under Section 338(h)(10) as if the subsidiary had sold its assets.
4. If an acquirer purchases 80% or more of a subsidiary's stock within a 12-month period, the acquirer and seller can jointly elect to have the stock sale taxed as an asset sale under Section 338(h)(10).
5. Subsidiary sales are often structured in a manner that results in a step-up in the tax basis of the sold subsidiary's assets. As we noted in Chapter 12, sales of freestanding C corporations rarely result in a step-up in the tax basis of the target's assets.
6. In a subsidiary sale, the tax attributes of the sold subsidiary always survive. The tax attributes of the subsidiary stay with the divesting parent in a taxable asset sale or in a taxable stock sale

followed by a Section 338(h)(10) election and remain with the subsidiary in a taxable stock sale without a Section 338(h)(10) election.

Questions

Q15-1. If a corporation wishes to divest a subsidiary and needs cash, what possible alternative methods can it consider?

Q15-2. If a corporation wishes to divest a subsidiary in a tax-free manner and wants its historical shareholders to maintain a direct ownership in the divested subsidiary, what technique should it employ?

Q15-3. In general, when should a Section 338(h)(10) election be made in a subsidiary sale? Consider the relationship between purchase price, subsidiary stock basis, and subsidiary net asset basis.

Q15-4. In general, when should a Section 338(h)(10) election not be made in a subsidiary sale? Consider the relationship between purchase price, subsidiary stock basis, and subsidiary net asset basis.

Q15-5. Name four requirements for a spin-off to qualify as tax-free.

Q15-6. In a taxable subsidiary stock sale without a Section 338(h)(10) election, do the sold subsidiary's tax attributes such as NOLs survive? If so, who obtains/maintains these attributes?

Tax-Planning Problems

TP15-7. You are a summer associate at a large Wall Street investment bank and your direct supervisor has informed you that the Sunglass Hut (the acquirer) has engaged your firm to analyze the prospect of acquiring RK, Inc., a wholly owned subsidiary of Consumer Devices, Inc. Consider the following relevant facts:

- RK has assets with a net tax basis of $800 million and a fair market value of $1.9 billion. RK has no liabilities.
- RK is 100% owned by Consumer Devices.
- Consumer Devices has a tax basis in RK stock of $1 billion. Consumer Devices acquired this stock 5 years ago.
- Sunglass Hut wants to acquire the stock of RK from Consumer Devices for $1.9 billion in cash.
- RK, Consumer Devices, and Sunglass Hut are all C corporations.
- Assume the transaction is structured as a taxable stock sale without a Section 338(h)(10) election.

a. What tax basis in the assets of RK will Sunglass Hut have post-acquisition?

b. How much cash after tax will Consumer Devices have from the transaction? Assume Consumer Devices' marginal tax rate is 21%.

Now, assume the transaction is structured as a taxable stock sale with a Section 338(h)(10) election.

c. What tax basis in the assets of RK will Sunglass Hut have post-acquisition?

d. How much cash after tax will Consumer Devices have? Assume that Consumer Devices' marginal tax rate is 21%.

e. At what price is Consumer Devices indifferent between a stock sale with a Section 338(h)(10) and a stock sale without a Section 338(h)(10) election at a $1.9 billion purchase price?

f. At what price is Sunglass Hut indifferent between a stock sale with a Section 338(h)(10) and a stock sale without a Section 338(h)(10) election at a $1.9 billion purchase price? Assume any basis step-up in RK's assets in a Section 338(h)(10) transaction is depreciated/amortized over 10 years and that the appropriate discount rate for any tax savings from these additional deductions is 7%. Assume Sunglass Hut's tax rate is 21%.

g. Should the Section 338(h)(10) election be made? Why or why not?

h. If Sunglass Hut captured all the net tax benefits associated with the Section 338(h)(10) election (assuming your answer to part [g] is yes), how much *lower* would its net *after-tax* cost be relative to a sale without a Section 338(h)(10) election at a $1.9 billion purchase price?

i. If Consumer Devices captured all the net tax benefits associated with the Section 338(h)(10) election (assuming your answer to part [g] is yes), how much higher would its after-tax wealth be relative to a sale without a Section 338(h)(10) election at a $1.9 billion purchase price?

TP15-8. Consider only circumstances involving the sale of a subsidiary of a C corporation.

a. Under what circumstances does a Section 338(h)(10) election make sense?

b. When is a Section 338(h)(10) election suboptimal in the sale of a subsidiary of a C corporation? Be concise.

TP15-9. You are a newly hired analyst at a large Wall Street investment bank and your direct supervisor has informed you that Parker (the acquirer) has engaged your firm to analyze the prospect of acquiring JM, Inc., a wholly owned subsidiary of Ontario. Consider the following relevant facts:

- JM has assets with a net tax basis of $300 million and a fair market value of $900 million. JM has no liabilities.
- JM is 100% owned by Ontario.
- Ontario has a tax basis in JM stock of $600 million. Ontario acquired this stock 5 years ago.
- Parker wants to acquire the stock of JM from Ontario for $900 million in cash.
- JM, Ontario, and Parker are all C corporations.
- Assume the transaction is structured as a taxable stock sale without a Section 338(h)(10) election.

a. What tax basis in the assets of JM will Parker have post-acquisition?

b. How much cash after tax will Ontario have from the transaction? Assume that Ontario's marginal tax rate is 21%.

Assume that the transaction is structured as a taxable stock sale with a Section 338(h)(10) election.

c. What tax basis in the assets of JM will Parker have post-acquisition?

d. How much cash after tax will Ontario have? Assume that Ontario's marginal tax rate is 40%.

e. At what price (*P*) is Ontario indifferent between a stock sale with a Section 338(h)(10) and a stock sale without a Section 338(h)(10) election at a $900 million purchase price?

f. Given the price (*P*) that you computed in part (e), which structure does Parker prefer: a taxable stock sale without a Section 338(h)(10) election for a price of $900 million or a taxable stock sale with a Section 338(h)(10) election at price (*P*)? Assume any basis step-up in JM's assets in a Section 338(h)(10) transaction is depreciated/amortized over 7 years and that the appropriate discount rate for any tax savings from these additional deductions is 7%. Assume that Parker's tax rate is 21%.

g. Should the Section 338(h)(10) election be made? Why or why not?

h. If Parker captured all the net tax benefits associated with the Section 338(h)(10) election (assuming that your answer to part [g] is yes), how much *lower* would its net *after-tax* cost be relative to a sale without a Section 338(h)(10) election at a $900 million purchase price?

i. If Ontario captured all the net tax benefits associated with the Section 338(h)(10) election (assuming your answer to part [g] is yes), how much higher would its after-tax wealth be relative to a sale without a Section 338(h)(10) election at a $900 million purchase price?

References and Additional Readings

See the list at the end of Chapter 11.

Teaching Cases

See the list at the end of Chapter 11.

16

Estate and Gift Tax Planning

After studying this chapter, you should be able to

1. Use the vocabulary of estate and gift taxation.
2. Explain the fundamentals of estate and gift taxation.
3. Describe some common estate-planning techniques.
4. Understand how to monetize appreciated property without triggering taxation.
5. Analyze the tax advantages of charitable giving.
6. Quantify the trade-off between gifts and bequests.

Suppose you, a relative, or a client has accumulated a substantial amount of wealth. You would like to ensure that family members, friends, and favorite causes are the beneficiaries of your good fortune. In most cases, you would not consider the taxing authority to be a desired beneficiary. Once you decide to transfer wealth, however, whether by gift or bequest, several forms of taxation can arise: gift taxes on the value of the assets given away, income taxes on the earnings generated by the transferred assets, and estate taxes on your death. Moreover, generation-skipping transfer taxes might await you if you make transfers, whether through gift or bequest, that skip over one or more successive generations of beneficiaries.

Family tax planning for estate and gifts is linked with family income tax planning. A reduction in estate and gift taxes for one family member could lead to higher income taxes for the family as a whole. For example, the transfer of assets from an elderly parent to a child in his or her prime earning years who faces a higher income tax rate might reduce the estate tax but increase income taxes for the family.

Like other tax-planning problems, estate and gift tax planning involves a repackaging of assets among tax-payers. Efficient tax planning trades off tax and nontax considerations among transferors and transferees of accumulated wealth. Nontax considerations loom large when parents give away assets to children: Parents do not always have complete trust that their children will employ the assets in the desired way, which can make certain tax-planning strategies costly. Tax-payers have long tried to "give away" assets to relatives and to charity to reduce the size of their estate while at the same time retaining control over the use of these assets.

For the most part in this chapter, we take a tax planner's point of view, leaving aside the broader question of whether the current estate tax is fair, efficient, or in need of reform. Note, however, that the estate tax is one of the most controversial taxes in existence and one over which people's views tend to be highly polarized. On one side of the debate, the estate tax—or "death tax" as it is sometimes called—is perceived as the purest form of the "grabbing hand" of government: The government taxes income as it is earned and then effectively taxes it again by taxing accumulated wealth bequeathed to the next generation. This is seen by some to be punitive, unfair, and driven by jealousy more than anything else. Opponents of the estate tax emphasize it as a disruptive penalty on those individuals who build successful businesses and create jobs, and argue that it discourages savings and encourages excessive consumption. On the other side, some people view the estate tax as an essential tool to combat inequality. Large concentrations of wealth that can be passed on ad infinitum, the argument goes, create the potential for a ruling aristocracy that in the long run can undermine democratic society.[1]

Adding to the charged emotions surrounding estate taxation, surveys have shown that most individuals believe their estates will wind up paying estate taxes. It appears, however, that most individuals are either misinformed about the tax law, overly optimistic about their prospects for future wealth accumulation, or both. The vast majority of people die with estates far too small to be subject to estate taxation. The estate tax effectively exempts estates smaller than $11.18 million from taxation (for 2018, indexed for inflation, although the exemption is scheduled to decrease in 2025). The exemption level has increased greatly since 2001, when it was $675,000. The increased exemption has resulted in a decrease in the number of estate tax returns. In 2001, Internal Revenue Service (IRS) data show there were more than 108,000 estate tax returns. By 2016, only about 12,400 deaths resulted in estate tax returns being filed. Aggregate estate taxes were approximately $18.3 billion in 2016. Although this is quite a bit of tax per estate, it is fairly minor in terms of the federal budget, accounting for less than 1% of all federal tax collections.[2] Moreover, 12,400 estate tax returns filed is not the same as 12,400 taxable estates. Because of deductions for bequests to spouses, charities, and so forth (which we discuss in detail in this chapter), a large fraction of these estates wind up not owing estate tax. The Centers for Disease Control (CDC) estimates that there were approximately 2.7 million deaths in the United States in 2015. If we assume roughly the same number for 2016, that implies that only about 0.5% of deaths result in an estate tax return being filed.[3]

However, wealth is highly concentrated, so even though the estate tax applies to only a small fraction of all people, those people hold a large fraction of the wealth in the United States. Estimates are that the top 1% of households in the United States (about 1.6 million households) account for approximately 41.8% of the total wealth of all U.S. households.[4] In recent years the ranks of the well-off have been growing at a faster rate than the overall population and faster than gross domestic product (GDP). The same phenomenon of the rising ranks of the wealthy is occurring worldwide.

Researchers estimate that 18 million people worldwide (less than 0.3% of the world's population) have at least $1 million of investable assets (excluding things like primary residences).[5] Together, the world's millionaires by this definition hold approximately $70 trillion of wealth. Roughly 31% of the these millionaires reside in North America, another 34% in Asia, about 27% in Europe, and the rest in Latin America, the Middle East, and Africa. The United States has the largest number of people with $1 million or more of investable assets, with approximately 5.3 million, followed by Japan with 3.2 million, Germany with 1.4 million, and China with about 1.3 million. Each of these countries has some form of estate or inheritance tax with the exception of China, which has reportedly considered one.[6] Not all countries levy estate or inheritance taxes (e.g., Australia does not), but enough do that it is a common issue for wealthy families to face. We will focus on U.S. estate and gift taxation. At present in the United States, estate taxation is something that only a small fraction of the population deals with, but it can involve large sums to those people who must pay the tax, and they hold a significant fraction of the aggregate wealth. You, as a reader of this text, are much more likely than the average person to face potential estate taxation.

Since 2001, estate tax planning has been in a state of uncertainty. Under the 2001 Tax Act, the estate tax was to be gradually phased out over the years 2002 to 2009. In 2010, the estate tax was

---

[1] These debates have raged for years. See, for example, I. Fisher, "Some Impending National Problems," *Journal of Political Economy* (1916). Numerous articles have been written on both sides of the debate, for example: E. McCaffery, "The Uneasy Case for Wealth Transfer Taxation," *Yale Law Journal* (1994); and *Rethinking Estate and Gift Taxation*, edited by J. Slemrod, W. Gale, and J. Hines (Washington, DC: Brookings Institution Press, 2001).

[2] *Internal Revenue Service Data Book, 2017*. Note that this is for fiscal year 2017, which runs from October 1, 2016, to September 30, 2017.

[3] Centers for Disease Control and Prevention, "Deaths: Final Data for 2015," *National Vital Statistics Reports* (November 27, 2017).

[4] Estimates for 2012. Emmanuel Saez and Gabriel Zucman, "Wealth Inequality in the United States since 1913: Evidence from Capitalized Income Tax Data," *Quarterly Journal of Economics*, Vol. 131, No. 2, May 2016. Other research suggests that correcting for data issues reduces the magnitude and trend in inequality; see Gerald Auten and David Splinter, "Income Inequality in the United States: Using Tax Data to Measure Long-Term Trends," working paper, August 23, 2018.

[5] Estimates in this paragraph are as of 2017 and come from the *World Wealth Report* (2018), by Capgemini and RBC Wealth Management.

[6] Ernst & Young, *International Estate and Inheritance Tax Guide* (2017).

to be repealed. However, for budgetary reasons, the 2001 Tax Act contained a sunset provision causing the law to expire after 2010. Thus, as the law was written in 2001, the estate tax was to be repealed for a single year, 2010, after which it was to return in full force with rates up to 55%. Most observers thought that Congress would change the law well before 2010. However, the years went by and Congress could not reach consensus. Finally, in December of 2010, Congress temporarily reinstated the estate tax for 2010–2012, with a $5 million exemption and maximum rate of 35% (there were special rules for 2010). That gave Congress more time to reach a permanent solution (or at least as permanent as tax can be). At the end of 2012, Congress again could not reach consensus. As the temporary provisions expired on New Year's Day 2013, Congress passed the American Taxpayer Relief Act of 2012 (signed into law on January 2, 2013), which set a maximum estate tax rate of 40% and a $5 million exemption. In 2017, Congress increased the exemption as part of the Tax Cuts and Jobs Act (TCJA). As of 2018, the exemption stood at $11.18 million. It is indexed so it will increase with inflation.

This chapter begins with a description of the general structure of estate and gift tax rules, including the lifetime exclusion (also known as the unified credit), the annual gift exclusion, treatment of life insurance, the marital deduction, the charitable deduction, and the Generation-Skipping Transfer Tax. We then discuss some common estate-planning techniques, beginning with those that can be used to eliminate estate taxes on small and moderate-sized estates and progressing to techniques used to reduce estate taxes on large estates. We describe a set of techniques we broadly refer to as monetization techniques, which have been used for both income and estate tax planning purposes.

We then discuss the substantial incentives provided by the tax law to engage in charitable giving. We show that such incentives are even larger than is commonly believed, and that for the wealthy it generally pays to transfer wealth while alive rather than through the estate at death. We then demonstrate that taxpayers have similar incentives to make noncharitable gifts early, to freeze the accumulation of wealth taxed in the estate. We present a model that considers both tax and nontax factors, which often conflict, to assess the trade-offs between gifting now and making a bequest.

16.1 FUNDAMENTALS OF ESTATE AND GIFT TAXATION

Individuals can transfer their assets to others through bequests at death or through gifts while they are alive. Consequently, estate and gift taxes are integrated. As we will see in detail, lifetime taxable gifts increase the marginal tax rate on the estate. The purpose behind the gift tax is to prevent taxpayers from easily circumventing the estate tax by gifting property before their death (although gifting can still be useful, as we will learn).

Who pays gift taxes? Two common misconceptions among the general public are that the recipient of the gift (the donee) pays the gift tax and/or that the recipient pays income tax upon receipt of a gift. Neither is true. First, gifts are by definition not income and therefore not subject to income tax. Second, it is the giver (the donor) who pays any gift taxes due (although if the donor is unable to pay the tax the IRS can take part of the gift from the donee).

So the next question is: What gifts are taxable? Surely the government will not tax a $10 gift to a friend. There are important exclusions from gift tax. There is an annual exclusion of $15,000 (as of 2018, indexed for inflation) of gifts per year, per donee. Thus, a married couple could *each* gift *each* of their children $15,000 per year free of any gift tax. If they had three children, they could gift $90,000 in total to them free of gift tax, every year (2 × 3 × $15,000). Gifts to charities are generally not subject to gift tax and neither are gifts to spouses.

Estate and gift taxes are levied on the *fair market value* of the assets transferred, not their tax bases. Normally the fair market value for tax purposes is the value on the date of transfer, although special rules, such as the "alternate valuation date" six months after death, provide some relief if bequeathed assets decline in value after death. More important, fair market values are often not knowable with exact precision, especially in the case of real estate and closely held businesses. A significant strategy of estate and gift planning is to reduce the fair market values of gifted and bequeathed assets for estate and gift purposes. Family limited partnerships, discussed later in the chapter, are a prime example of such strategies.

Although a gift tax is paid as gifts are made, the estate and gift taxes are integrated in that the value of any taxable gifts above the $15,000 annual exclusion is added back into the taxable estate at death, and any gift tax paid during the decedent's lifetime is credited against the estate tax liability. What is the effect of adding lifetime taxable gifts to the taxable estate and then giving a credit for gift taxes paid? The effect is to increase the marginal tax rate on the estate and to prevent taxpayers from getting more than one "trip" through the lower tax estate and gift tax brackets. The estate and gift tax schedule that is in effect at the date of death is used to compute the tax credit for previously taxed gifts.

Specifics of the Gift Tax

As already mentioned, a donor can give a donee $15,000 of gifts per year exempt from gift tax. Note that the $15,000 exclusion is per donee. Although many gifts are to family members, there is no requirement that the donor and donee be related. A billionaire, for example, could give $15,000 to each of 100,000 people in a given year completely free of gift taxes. Gifts to one's spouse are completely exempt from gift tax, as are gifts to qualified charities. Gifts to charity have the added benefit of generally being deductible for income tax purposes. Some of the estate- and gift-planning techniques described later in the chapter make use of lifetime giving to charities. Contributions to political organizations are also not subject to gift tax. Transfers of property under legal obligation of support, such as providing for the upbringing of minor children, are not gifts. In addition, tuition payments made on behalf of another person, even if unrelated, are excluded from gift tax provided they are made directly to the educational institution. A similar rule excludes payments of medical expenses for another person provided they are made directly to the provider.

Some things we would not normally think of as gifts are, in fact, gifts for tax purposes. Below-market loans are the prime example. Suppose a mother lends $150,000 to a child, interest free, to start a business or make a down payment on a house. The mother has in effect made a gift to the extent she does not charge a market rate of interest on the loan. Each year that the child retains the money, the mother is deemed to have made a gift to the child to the extent the interest charged is below market. Further, the mother will have taxable imputed interest income, as if she had collected interest from her child and then made a gift of the same amount to the child.[7]

Not all gifts qualify for the $15,000 annual exclusion. The exclusion is available for gifts of present interests; gifts of future interests generally do not qualify. For example, a gift of a remainder interest in a piece of land, where the donor retained the life interest, would not generally qualify for the annual exclusion. The gift would be valued at the present value of the future interest, but the annual exclusion would generally not shelter the gift because the donee does not have an unrestricted immediate right to possession of the property.

The rule that gifts of future interests do not qualify for the annual exclusion would seem to present a problem for parents gifting to their young children. Accordingly, Congress allows an exception for gifts made under the Uniform Trusts for Minors Act (UTMA). Even though the minor doesn't have an unrestricted right to the assets until he or she reaches a certain age (usually 18 or 21, depending on the state), the gift can qualify for the annual exclusion. UTMA accounts (and related Uniform Gifts to Minors Act [UGMA] accounts) were at one time quite useful for income tax purposes as a way to shift the income from investments to a child's tax return, where it was often taxed at a rate lower than what the parent faced. However, the usefulness of UTMA accounts has decreased over time with the expansion of the so-called kiddie tax, which can cause unearned income (e.g., income from investments) of a child to be taxed at the rate for trusts and estates.

The attractiveness of UTMA accounts has also decreased over time with the spread of 529 plans (named for Section 529).[8] Section 529 plans are a tax-efficient means of saving for college education. For income tax purposes, contributions to 529 plans are not tax deductible (although some states allow tax deductions for 529 plan contributions), but income earned from investments in the plan is nontaxable if used to pay qualified educational expenses. For gift tax purposes, contributions to 529

[7] There are special *de minimus* rules for small loans.

[8] Section 529 plans are covered in more detail in chapter 3.

plans are eligible for the $15,000 annual exclusion. Lump-sum contributions to a 529 plan can be spread over 5 years for gift tax purposes (e.g., in 2018 a parent could contribute $75,000 toward a 529 plan for her child free of gift tax by electing to use 5 years' worth of $15,000 annual exclusions). Section 529 plans are also attractive for estate tax purposes because they generally are not included in the estate of the giver.

Note that although it is common for states to have inheritance taxes, most states do not impose gift taxes. For residents of states that do not have gift taxes but do have inheritance taxes, there is an incentive to gift property rather than bequeath it. Gifting property also has advantages at the federal level, as we discuss later in the chapter.

Specifics of the Estate Tax

The estate tax is levied on the fair market value of property transferred at death. The starting point of the estate tax is the computation of the gross estate, which includes the fair market value of property that the decedent owned at the time of death, but also includes other things. To better understand the gross estate it is helpful to first define the probate estate. The probate estate consists of the assets administered by the executor or administrator of the estate. When someone dies with a will, they are said to die "testate," and the will ordinarily has an executor named to carry out the will. When someone dies without a valid will, they are said to die "intestate," and then the court appoints an administrator. The majority of decedents whose estates are subject to estate tax die testate. Generally, you can think of the gross estate as including more assets than the probate estate.

What assets does the gross estate commonly include? The starting point for the gross estate is all property owned by the decedent at death. This is fairly broad, including cash, bank accounts, investments, real estate, personal effects such as cars, jewelry and household items, interests in a business, and retirement accounts. Both tangible and intangible property count. For U.S. citizens and residents, it does not matter where the property is located. Even foreign assets of a U.S. citizen or resident are subject to U.S. estate tax. In addition, the gross estate includes:

1. The proceeds from life insurance policies owned by the decedent
2. The value of certain annuities

What are common deductions from the gross estate to arrive at the taxable estate? They include:

1. Indebtedness of the decedent (e.g., mortgages, other loans) and claims against the estate, such as unpaid property taxes
2. Funeral expenses and expenses of administering the estate (e.g., attorney's fees)
3. Bequests to the spouse
4. Charitable bequests
5. State death taxes

We next discuss in more detail some of the important inclusions in the gross estate and deductions from the gross estate.

Life Insurance The tax treatment of life insurance is commonly misunderstood. It is true that proceeds on life insurance policies are generally exempt from *income* tax. However, life insurance proceeds can be subject to *estate* tax unless careful planning is done. Specifically, the proceeds from a life insurance policy on the decedent are included in the decedent's gross estate if *either* of the following conditions holds: (1) the decedent's estate is the beneficiary on the policy or (2) the decedent possessed any of the "incidents of ownership" in the policy. Beyond outright ownership, incidents of ownership include the power to change a beneficiary, the power to cancel the policy, and the like.

To avoid life insurance on the decedent being included in the gross estate of the decedent, it is common to have someone other than the decedent own the life insurance policy. For example, a life insurance trust can be set up to hold the life insurance. We have more to say about this subject when we discuss life insurance trusts in Section 16.2.

Marital Deduction and Deduction for Charitable Bequests The estate tax generally grants deductions for unlimited amounts bequeathed to the spouse and amounts bequeathed to qualified charities. The marital deduction and charitable deduction are the two most significant estate tax deductions. The total gross estate of estates filing returns for 2016 was $192 billion. Estates reported $73 billion of marital deductions and $18 billion of charitable deductions. Estates with gross estates over $50 million accounted for the majority of charitable deductions.[9]

Unlimited amounts may be bequeathed to one's spouse. The marital deduction requires that the property is transferred to the decedent's spouse at death. The decedent and surviving spouse must be married at the time of death (i.e., bequests to former spouses do not qualify) and the spouse must survive the decedent. In addition, the marital deduction requires that the surviving spouse be a U.S. citizen.[10] The marital deduction is allowed for bequests to a U.S. citizen from a nonresident alien (someone who is neither a U.S. citizen nor a U.S. resident). Estate tax cases involving the marital deduction sometimes make national news. In 2013, the Supreme Court ruled that a same-sex couple lawfully married in their home state was eligible for the marital deduction. The broader significance was that the case hinged on whether the Defense of Marriage Act (DOMA) was constitutional, and the Court ruled that it violated the due process and equal protection provisions of the Constitution.[11]

Unlimited amounts may be bequeathed to qualified charities and deducted from the gross estate. In most cases, a charity that qualifies for income tax deductions for donations will also qualify for the charitable deduction for estate purposes. Care should be taken to make the charitable bequests explicit in the will, as giving too much discretion to the executor has, in certain cases, caused the charitable deductions to be disallowed.

Portability of the Estate and Gift Exclusion An important benefit that was made permanent in 2013 is referred to as the "portability" of the estate and gift exclusion. For example, suppose Jay and Gloria are married to each other and they are both U.S. citizens. In 2018, Jay passes away, bequeathing his entire $15 million estate to Gloria. Because of the marital deduction, there is no estate tax due on Jay's death. But what happens to Jay's unused $11.18 million lifetime exclusion? If Jay had died before 2011, it would have been wasted. Now, however, Jay's estate can make an election to allow Gloria to essentially inherit his unused exclusion (in this example, all $11.18 million). That raises Gloria's lifetime estate and gift exclusion to include both her $11.18 million exclusion plus the $11.18 million exclusion transferred from Jay's estate, for a total of $22.36 million. Thus, portability makes it easier for spouses to receive the benefit of their combined $22.36 million exclusion. Suppose Gloria later passes away, leaving a $30 million estate (it grew from her savvy investing) to be divided equally among her son, Manny, her stepson, Mitchell, and her stepdaughter, Clair. Assuming the exclusion amount was still $11.18 million in her year of passing, Gloria's estate would have $22.36 million of exclusion, leaving $7.64 million of her estate subject to tax. There is a trap for the unwary, however. If Gloria later remarries and also outlives her new spouse, her estate will no longer receive the benefit of Jay's unused estate tax exclusion, although she could receive unused estate tax exclusion from her new husband's estate.

Income Tax Consequences of Gifts and Bequests

Even though gifts generally do not create taxable income for the donee, they do have income tax consequences. Specifically, the tax basis of property received by gift carries over, so the donee's basis is generally equal to the donor's basis in the property.[12] The donor's holding period also carries over to the donee. Special rules for gifted property later sold at a loss are designed to prevent shifting of deductions from low-tax donors to high-tax donees.

In contrast to gifted assets, the heirs to bequeathed assets get a basis equal to the fair market value at death. If the assets had appreciated while owned by the decedent, this represents a free step-up in basis at death (at least free from income tax). Note that assets worth less than the decedent's basis are stepped down in basis. The decedent's unrealized gains (the excess of fair market value over

[9] Table 1. Estate Tax Returns Filed in 2016, https://www.irs.gov/pub/irs-soi/16es01fy.xls.

[10] There is an exception to the disallowance for property passing to the surviving spouse via a Qualified Domestic Trust (QDOT).

[11] *United States v. Windsor, Executor of the Estate of Spyer, et al.*, Supreme Court (2013).

[12] The donee can also add to basis any gift tax that was paid by the donor attributable to the unrealized gain in the property at the time of the gift, where the unrealized gain is the fair market value less the donor's tax basis in the property.

the decedent's tax basis) go untaxed for income tax purposes.[13] Consider an elderly mother who is deciding between giving each of her children $10,000 in cash or giving them stock that has a fair market value of $10,000 but a tax basis of only $500. Assume that whatever is not gifted will be bequeathed; the children eventually get everything and will sell the stock upon receiving it. Giving the stock would cause the children to pay income tax on $9,500 of gain in the stock. Bequeathing the stock eliminates the income tax on the $9,500 unrealized gain by virtue of the tax-free step-up at death. The children would inherit the stock with a tax basis equal to fair value, so that it could be sold immediately with no taxable gain or loss.

Generation-Skipping Transfer Tax

Suppose you give or bequeath a portion of your assets to your grandchildren or to your great-grandchildren. You pay gift or estate tax on the transfer, but your sons and daughters pay no transfer taxes on their death. The idea is that by skipping one or more generations, you also avoid one or more layers of estate and gift tax. That effectively defeats the estate tax system, and Congress does not like that. To curb such activities, Congress imposed the Generation-Skipping Transfer (GST) Tax. The GST is an additional tax levied on such transfers at the maximum estate tax rate.

Although the details are beyond the scope of our discussion, in brief, the GST rules include an exclusion for generation-skipping transfers aggregating up to $11.18 million (2018 amount). A married couple can transfer $22.36 million without being subject to the GST. Once the GST exclusion has been exhausted, the transfer is subject to a 40% GST rate in addition to any normal estate and gift tax that might apply. Because of the generous exclusion, however, one strategy is for a married couple to make generation-skipping transfers to grandchildren up to the exclusion amount, assuming, of course, that leaves enough in the estate to provide for the spouse and children.

16.2 ESTATE- AND GIFT-PLANNING STRATEGIES

Now we discuss some common estate and gift tax strategies. We order the strategies according to the frequency of their use by most planners. That is, we put the simplest and lowest-cost strategies first and move to progressively more complicated and costly strategies. For most estates a few relatively simple strategies should be able to eliminate all gift and estate taxes even without any charitable bequests. For larger estates, the exercise often becomes one of reducing gift and estate taxes using strategies that maximize the deduction for charitable giving and strategies that reduce the fair market value of the gifted or bequeathed property for tax purposes.

Making Full Use of the Annual Gift Tax Exclusion

For most families the practice of regular, sustained giving can be an effective estate tax planning strategy. Recall that a husband and wife each have a $15,000 (as of 2018, indexed for inflation) annual gift tax exclusion, so by using what is called gift-splitting, they could give $30,000 per year to each donee, free of gift tax. For example, a couple with three children could gift $90,000 per year to their kids free of estate and gift tax. It has been estimated, however, that even among high-net-worth elderly households, only 45% engage in tax-free giving. Moreover, researchers have estimated that roughly a fourth of all estate taxes could be avoided by sustained maximum giving to descendants, but that actual use of the gift exclusion reduced estate taxes by less than 4% of the amount that could be saved.[14]

Why don't people avoid estate and gift taxes by making more extensive use of the annual exclusion? Probably several nontax costs explain the reluctance to give while one is alive. By giving, the

[13] There are exceptions for inherited retirement accounts, such as traditional individual retirement accounts (IRAs) and 401(k)s, so that distributions from those accounts to heirs are still subject to income tax. Other assets representing income that was not taxed to the decedent at death (called income with respect of a decedent) are also not stepped up to fair market value at death, but instead the basis to the decedent (often a zero basis) carries over to the heirs.

[14] See Poterba (2000, 2001).

donor loses control of the assets. Parents may not trust their children with the money, particularly if the children are young. A parent may be worried about adverse effects on the children's incentive to work and study. Finally, parents may be concerned at outliving their remaining assets and having to ask for the money back from their children, which could be humiliating or even fruitless if the children have spent the money.

Paying for the Kids' and Grandkids' Educational and Medical Expenses

Recall that tuition payments for others are exempt from gift tax, provided they are made directly to the educational institution. This is most frequently done for family members, such as one's children or grandchildren, although it does not have to be for a family member. It could be for college tuition but it also could be for private school tuition. For example, a grandparent could pay the tuition for her granddaughter to attend a private elementary school. This strategy also works for medical expenses paid directly to the provider.

Section 529 plans can also be used for estate tax planning. Recall that 529 plans are used to save for college on a tax-advantaged basis. Contributions to 529 plans are not tax deductible for federal income tax purposes (although some states allow deductions). The main benefit of a 529 plan is that income earned in the plan is not subject to income tax as long as it is used to pay for qualified education expenses. The expenses that qualify are somewhat different than with the gift tax exclusion discussed earlier. Section 529 plans can be used to pay for not only tuition but also room, board, books, and fees. In addition, the TCJA extended the benefits of 529 plans to include up to $10,000 of tuition, per student, paid to elementary or secondary schools. Section 529 plans also have estate tax benefits because plan assets are not included in the estate at death. For example, a married couple could contribute, using gift-splitting, $30,000 per year to a 529 plan with their 2-year-old son as the beneficiary. The assets would grow inside the 529 plan free of income tax as well as gift and estate tax. The boy's grandparents could do the same. These plans can be tax-advantaged ways to pay for post-secondary educational expenses that are in the future.

Gifting in Excess of the Annual Exclusion

In some cases, gifting above the annual exclusion is preferred over bequeathing. The trade-offs are many and formally modeled in Section 16.5, but we briefly discuss some trade-offs here. Gifting is one way to freeze the value of the estate, in that the gift tax is levied based on the value of the gifted property at the time of the gift. Consequently, if the donor expects the property to appreciate in the future, gifting avoids paying transfer tax on appreciation. For example, suppose the value at the time of the gift is $30,000, so that is the value for gift tax purposes. If the property increases in value to $100,000 by the time of death, gifting saves transfer taxes on $70,000 of appreciation.

An additional benefit of gifting is that the gift taxes themselves are not included in the taxable gift. For example, assume the estate and gift tax rate was 25% and a taxpayer had $1,000,000 to either gift or bequeath before paying estate and gift taxes. One option is to make an $800,000 gift and pay $200,000 in gift tax, or 25% of $800,000. Another option would be to bequeath the $1,000,000, but that would result in $250,000 of estate tax (25% of $1,000,000) and an after-tax bequest of $750,000. Thus, from the perspective of a pre-estate and gift tax transfer of $1,000,000, gift taxes are, in effect, deductible for gift and estate tax purposes whereas estate taxes are not.

An income tax consequence of gifting, however, is that the donor's basis transfers over to the donee. In contrast, heirs receive a basis stepped up to fair market value for bequeathed property. If the donor is deciding between gifting cash and gifting appreciated property, he or she may be better off gifting the cash and holding the appreciated property until death, at which time the unrealized tax gain is essentially forgiven by virtue of the step-up in basis at death.

However, if the donor knows the property is going to be sold shortly, he or she may be better off gifting it to a relative who has a lower marginal tax rate. But caution must be exercised with gifts to young children because unearned income of children is often taxed at trust tax rates under the so-called kiddie tax.

Keeping Life Insurance Out of the Gross Estate

Recall that life insurance is included in the gross estate if the decedent had any of the incidents of ownership such as the ability to change beneficiaries. For young professionals with families and high earnings prospects, it is common to have several million dollars of life insurance. If one has other assets that use up the lifetime exclusion, allowing the life insurance to enter the gross estate can trigger estate taxes. For older people, it is common to have whole life or universal life policies with substantial cash buildups in the policies.

Several strategies can be used to keep life insurance out of the gross estate. The first is to continue to own the policy but have one's spouse as the sole beneficiary. Although the life insurance would still be included in the gross estate, it would also be deductible under the unlimited marital deduction and thus would avoid estate tax for the time being. When the spouse passes away, of course, any remaining proceeds from the life insurance would be included in the spouse's gross estate.

Another strategy is to have one's spouse or children be the owner of the policy. As long as the decedent had no incidents of ownership and the beneficiary is not the decedent's estate, then the life insurance will not be included in the gross estate. The decedent can even make annual gifts to the holder of the policy to cover the premiums. Unless the policy is quite large, the annual gift exclusion should be sufficient to make such gifts nontaxable. If the policies are whole or universal life policies with a large buildup, a disadvantage of having one's spouse own them is the risk that the spouse dies first; in that case the buildup value of the policy (but not the face value) is included in the spouse's gross estate.

A parent may not want his or her children to have ownership of a whole or universal life policy. A rebellious child might cash out the policy and squander the money. An irrevocable life insurance trust can be used to avoid such problems. The life insurance trust is the owner of the policy, and the insured makes annual contributions to the trust to fund the premiums.[15]

Using Each Spouse's Lifetime Exclusion: Credit-Shelter or Bypass Trusts

This strategy has lost some, but not all, of its appeal now that the tax code allows portability of unused lifetime exclusions (discussed earlier in this chapter). Suppose John and Jane are married and each is worth $10 million. John dies leaving his entire $10 million estate to Jane. No estate tax is assessed because of the unlimited marital deduction. Jane dies a few years later and bequeaths $25 million to her son, Chip. The $25 million is Jane's original $10 million, plus the $10 million she inherited from John, and 25% of appreciation, or $5 million, which we assume was earned equally across all the assets. Assume that when John died the lifetime exclusion was $6 million and that by the time Jane dies the lifetime exclusion has increased to $8 million. The first $14 million of Jane's estate is offset by her exclusion equivalent (John's unused $6 million exclusion and Jane's $8 million exclusion), and $11 million of Jane's estate will be taxable.

Some of the estate taxes could have been avoided. One option would be for John to bequeath $6 million directly to Chip, using up John's exclusion. That leaves $4 million of John's estate going to Jane. When the assets bequeathed to Chip subsequently appreciate by $1.5 million (25% of $6 million), they do so in the hands of Chip, not in the hands of Jane, where they would eventually pass through her estate and be subject to tax. When Jane dies she bequeaths her entire estate to Chip, but it is only her original $10 million, plus $4 million from John's estate and $3.5 million of appreciation for a total estate of $17.5 million. After applying her $8 million exclusion, $9.5 million of her estate is subject to estate tax. Essentially, this strategy removes $1.5 million from being subject to estate tax, which is equal to the appreciation the assets bequeathed to Chip following John's death (this is called "freezing" the estate).

But some people do not want to give their children immediate access to the money and would prefer leaving the money to their spouse. A credit shelter trust, also called a bypass trust, can help. John can have his estate leave his $10 million to a bypass trust with his son Chip or other nonspouse

[15] To have the contributions count as gifts of a "present interest" and therefore be eligible for the annual gift exclusion, one can structure the trust to qualify as a Crummey Trust, which is beyond the scope of this chapter.

heirs as the beneficiary. The "bypass" comes from the fact that the bequest bypasses the spouse's estate. If John is worried that Jane will not have enough income to live on, he can set up the trust with Jane as the income beneficiary of the trust during her life, with Chip having the remainder interest. Because Jane's interest in the trust terminates at her death, the remainder passes to Chip without being included in Jane's gross estate.

Portability has reduced the attractiveness of credit shelter trusts. However, they help protect against the loss of the decedent's unused exclusion in the event the surviving spouse remarries. In addition, some states do not provide for portability of estate or inheritance tax exclusions. The trusts can also provide nontax benefits in terms of keeping the assets from passing to the new spouse in the event of remarriage, as well as asset protection from creditors of the surviving spouse.

Using the Marriage Deduction to Defer Estate Taxation: QTIPs

Another type of trust is the qualified terminable interest property (QTIP) trust, which is useful when a person is married but also has children from a prior marriage. The QTIP is often used once the exclusion equivalent has been fully utilized by direct bequest or through a bypass trust. The tax strategy with a QTIP is to defer the estate tax until the death of the second spouse. Actually, the taxpayer does not need a QTIP per se to take advantage of this strategy. Continuing with our example, suppose John is worth $10 million and has already provided for the first $6 million to pass to the children from his prior marriage. John could simply bequeath the remaining $4 million to his new spouse. John's estate would pay no estate tax. When Jane died, the $4 million would be taxable to Jane's estate, assuming she still had the money and in addition to her other assets.

John's real intent, however, may be to provide Jane with income during her life but guarantee that his children will inherit the bulk of his estate upon her death. He may be particularly concerned about a direct bequest to Jane if she also has children from a prior marriage, or if she might remarry after he dies. A direct bequest to Jane runs the risk that Jane will not include John's other children in her will.

With a QTIP trust, the $4 million is bequeathed to a trust where Jane has a life interest in the trust's income with the remainder going to John's children, including perhaps his children from the prior marriage. Assuming John's executor makes the proper election, the entire $4 million will qualify for the marital deduction on John's estate, even though some of the value winds up accruing to his children. The cost, however, is that Jane's estate will include the entire trust assets at whatever value they have at her death. To qualify for a QTIP, the spouse must be entitled to a life interest in all or a portion of the trust's income, paid at annual or more frequent intervals.

Family Limited Partnerships

A strategy to reduce the estate tax is to give away a minority interest in the family business to several children. The courts allow the shares to be valued at a discount relative to a majority interest in the company due to the lack of control. Because estate and gift taxes are levied based on the fair market value of property transferred, valuation discounts can reduce the taxes due.

A popular planning technique that results in discounts for estate and gift tax purposes is the family limited partnership (FLP). In an FLP the donor contributes his or her property (often a business or real estate) to a limited partnership while retaining the general partnership interest. The donor then gifts the limited partnership interests away, usually to his or her children, valuing them at a discount. The discounts arise because the limited partnership interests are minority interests in the firm and lack marketability. The donor can split an entity into parts and gift the parts over a period of time, obtaining discounts for each part.

The gifts are potentially subject to gift tax, but the donor can string the gifts out over several years to make maximum use of the annual gift tax exclusion. By retaining the general interest, the donor retains control over the business, which may have significant nontax advantages. However, the IRS has contested and won a number of court cases involving FLPs in which the donor retained what was considered too much control. Gifting the limited partnership interest can also have the income tax advantage of shifting some or all of the income from the business from the parents to the children, who may have lower marginal tax rates. In 2016, the Treasury proposed some controversial regulations that would have curtailed discounts available to FLPs, but withdrew the proposed regulations in 2017.[16]

Disputes with the IRS about the valuation of estates can be quite large. In a Tax Court case, the estate of the founder of Hallmark Cards was able to save more than $200 million in estate taxes due to valuation discounts. Valuation discounts also helped Samuel Newhouse, Sr., who at one time had the largest privately held newspaper fortune in the United States. His plan saved more than half a billion dollars in estate taxes.

Transfers of Knowledge, Information, and Services

One way to avoid the gift tax is to transfer information or knowledge to children. For example, the parent might inform the child, free of charge, of a good venture capital investment opportunity. In effect, it is a nontaxed gift. The IRS cannot tax this activity effectively. It is difficult to tax the advice that parents give to children as a gift, even though it could be extremely valuable advice. It is hard to assess a gift tax on the value of babysitting services provided by grandparents to their children. Parents cosign notes for mortgages and business ventures; they provide information and services, all of which transfer wealth to their children.

Charitable Remainder Trusts and Grantor Retained Trusts

In charitable remainder trusts, the donor takes a lead annuity (an income interest) from a charitable trust, and the charity receives a remainder interest in the assets at a specified future date or upon the death of the donor. This allows the donor to get a charitable deduction for the difference between the fair market value of the property donated and the present value of the annuity the donor retains.

Other strategies are the grantor retained annuity trust (GRAT) and its cousins, the grantor retained income trust (GRIT) and grantor retained unit trust (GRUT). With the GRAT the grantor transfers assets to the trust, but retains a fixed stream of income from the trust for a period of time, while the grantor's beneficiaries (usually children or grandchildren) receive the remainder interest in the property. When the assets are transferred to the trust, there is a gift for tax purposes of the value of the remainder interest. The value of the remainder interest is the value of the assets transferred to the trust, less the present value of the annuity retained by the grantor. GRATs can be useful when the assets in the trust generate a higher return than the statutory rate used in the present-value calculations. In a low-interest-rate environment, some advisors view GRATs as particularly useful. A drawback of GRATs is that if the grantor dies during the term of the trust, the appreciation in value of the trust assets must be included in the grantor's estate.

16.3 MONETIZING APPRECIATED ASSETS WITHOUT TRIGGERING TAXATION: A CASE STUDY

A problem faced by many today that involves both income and estate tax planning is the "low basis problem." It is a good problem to have. Entrepreneurial individuals have founded companies with small amounts of capital, built the companies up, and often taken them public. If the stock is held until death, the unrealized gains escape income taxation, although the value of the stock will be subject to estate taxation. The problem is that it is not always desirable to have the bulk of one's wealth tied up in the stock of a single firm. Individuals may wish to diversify their investment or otherwise hedge their risk. Further, they may want to convert a portion of their stock holdings into cash to fund consumption such as buying large houses, travel, and the like.

The problem faced by these successful individuals is not new. Consider, for example, the clever tax planning of the Lauder family. This case study illustrates the fundamental principles of

[16] S. Schreiber, "Treasury to Pull Regulations after Review of Burdensome Tax Rules," *Journal of Accountancy*, October 4, 2017.

monetization strategies, and it was so high profile that it led to important changes in the tax law—changes that shape the way people monetize their assets today.

Estee Lauder ("Estee") founded the cosmetics company known as Estee Lauder in 1946. The company grew to become a cosmetics giant and remained privately held until late 1995. Estee held a large portion of the outstanding stock, and her sons and daughters held the rest. For nontax reasons, Estee wanted to liquidate part of her holdings in Estee Lauder and also wanted to take the company public. Specifically, she wanted to sell 13.8 million of her 23.8 million shares of Estee Lauder as part of the initial public offering (IPO).[17] At this time Estee Lauder was estimated to be at least 87 years old.

The problem was that Estee had a large unrealized gain in her Estee Lauder stock, so selling the stock would trigger a massive capital gains tax. Estee's tax basis in her Estee Lauder stock was equal to what she originally paid for the stock. Because the company was founded more than 50 years ago, we can safely assume her basis was quite low, and for simplicity we assume it was zero. With a stock price of about $24 per share, selling the 13.8 million shares outright would have generated about $330 million of taxable gain and about $120 million of federal and state taxes.

Taxation of Short Sales

To understand what Estee did, we need to know what short sales are and how they are taxed. Briefly, in a short sale you borrow stock and sell the borrowed stock in the open market. Sometime in the future, you close out the short position by replacing the borrowed stock. A short sale will produce a gain when the stock price declines before you replace it through a "sell high, buy low" strategy. For example, you might sell GE short at $100. Later, GE stock might fall to $75, allowing you to close out the short sale with a $25 gain. Shorting a stock that you do not own is called a "naked" short sale, and it is quite risky. Shorting a stock that you already own, by borrowing additional stock and selling it, is called a short-sale-against-the-box.

To understand how short sales are taxed, first recall how normal sales are taxed. Suppose you buy (go long in) a share of IBM stock for $15 and later sell the stock for $20. You have a $5 gain based on the difference between the proceeds of $20 and your basis in the stock of $15. Gains on short sales are taxed the same way, but the timing is reversed. Suppose you sell (borrowed) GE stock for $100, the price later falls to $75, and you purchase GE stock to close out the short sale, for a $25 gain.[18] In the case of Estee Lauder, the proceeds from the short sale were fixed at $330 million when Estee initiated the short sale. The gain or loss on the short sale depends on the basis of the stock her estate would use to close out the short sale, which could be well higher than $330 million with future appreciation in the stock and the step-up in basis at her death.

The Strategy

The solution was for Estee to borrow 13.8 million shares of Estee Lauder stock from her sons and daughters (who are also her heirs) and to sell this borrowed stock in the November 1995 IPO. The transaction is illustrated in **Figure 16.1**. Essentially, it was a very large short-sale-against-the-box. Assume that at her death Estee has three and only three items in her estate: (1) the cash from the short sale, (2) her original "long" position of 23.8 million shares in Estee Lauder, and (3) her obligation to her sons and daughters to replace 13.8 million shares of borrowed Estee Lauder stock. Upon her eventual death, Estee's estate would close out the 13.8 million shares short position with 13.8 million shares from her long position. After estate taxes had been paid, the remaining 10 million Estee Lauder shares and any cash in the estate would then be distributed among her sons and daughters in accordance with her will.

The outcome of the strategy was that Estee Lauder effectively sold her stock without triggering tax on the gain. She received the $330 million from the short sale. She had no potential for gain or risk of loss on 13.8 million of her 23.8 million shares because she was short by 13.8 million shares.

---

[17] Actually, the 13.8 million shares represented sales by both Estee and her son Ronald and the 23.8 million shares figure is assumed. See A. Sloan, "Lauder Family's Stock Maneuvers Could Make a Tax Accountant Blush," *Washington Post* (November 28, 1995).

[18] Special tax rules are designed to prevent investors from using short-sales-against-the-box to convert short-term capital gains to long-term capital gains. Be aware that such rules exist, although they do not come into play in this case.

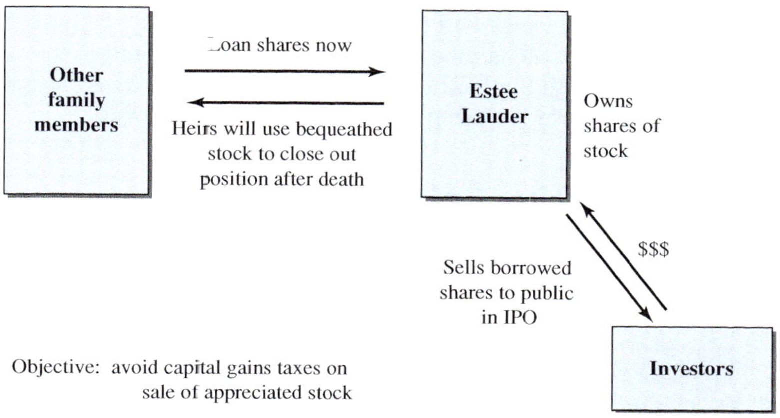

FIGURE 16.1
Estee Lauder's Tax Arbitrage

Because all the 23.8 million shares would receive the step-up in tax basis at her death, the $330 million gain would go untaxed, permanently wiping out the potential $120 million tax liability.

But the Estee Lauder strategy went even further, turning the potential tax liability into a potential tax *refund*. How so? If the Estee Lauder stock traded above $24 at her death, as it likely would with normal returns, when Estee's estate closed out the short position with the newly stepped-up stock from her long position, her estate would generate an artificial but perfectly legal tax *loss*. It turns out her heirs would be able to inherit the tax loss and use it to offset other capital gains they might have in their own stockholdings. Essentially, the Estee Lauder strategy was designed to turn a tax liability into a tax refund.

What about estate tax consequences? The 13.8 million short shares effectively cancel out 13.8 million of the long shares for estate tax purposes, leaving only the 10 million net long shares and whatever proceeds from the short sale that remain at death as the gross estate. Actually, the strategy increases Estee's estate taxes relative to an outright sale of the stock because, by avoiding capital gains taxes, Estee dies with more wealth. But it turns out that the income tax savings are about twice as big as the increased estate taxes, even without factoring in the tax benefit from any artificial tax losses inherited by Estee's heirs.

Congress Takes Action

Unfortunately for the Lauder family, this transaction attracted a great deal of public scrutiny and Congress took action against such deferral techniques, although it took a few years. As part of the so-called Taxpayer Relief Act of 1997, Congress created the "constructive sale" rules of Section 1259. The constructive sale rules require taxpayers to recognize gain (but not loss) upon entering into a "constructive sale" of an "appreciated financial position" as if the taxpayer had sold the security for fair market value on the date of the constructive sale and then immediately repurchased the security.

An appreciated financial position is defined as any "position" with respect to a stock, debt instrument, or partnership interest that would generate gain if sold for fair market value. "Position" includes long positions, short sales, futures, forwards, and options.

A *constructive sale* is said to exist if the taxpayer enters into any of the following with respect to the appreciated financial position that eliminates all or substantially all of the appreciated position's potential for gain and risk of loss:

- A short sale of substantially identical property
- An offsetting notional principal contract with respect to substantially identical property, such as an equity swap
- A futures or forward contract to deliver substantially identical property
- Other transactions having substantially the same effect as the preceding

Section 1259 applies to any constructive sale taking place after June 8, 1997, which is *after* the date Estee Lauder executed her short sale. However, Section 1259 also contains a provision stating that any grandfathered constructive sales will not be eligible for the tax-free basis step-up at death. It appears that the latter provision was aimed directly at the Lauder family. Shortly after the constructive sale rules were enacted, the Lauder family executed a series of transactions to unwind their former positions and engage in new tax strategies. But that is another story.

Avoiding the Constructive Sale Rules

Tax planners quickly devised several strategies designed to avoid the constructive sale rules. One technique is to borrow money and buy a collar around the stock (sell a call and buy a put) with a spread around the stock price. By maintaining enough risk of loss, investors avoid the constructive sale provisions. In another technique, investors simply short a different but highly correlated stock. This strategy does involve some risk of loss and potential for gain, to be sure, but if the stocks are highly correlated, the investor likely has less risk with the strategy than by simply holding a long position. Other strategies for monetizing appreciated positions without triggering gain recognition have included exchange funds and variable prepaid forward contracts. These strategies sometimes fail. In 2010, the Tax Court ruled against billionaire Philip Anschutz in a case involving the use of prepaid forward contracts.[19] However, strategies using prepaid forward contracts have been used by many others, reportedly even by Ronald Lauder in 2011.[20]

16.4 THE TAX SUBSIDY TO CHARITABLE GIVING

The tax law encourages charitable giving, and the subsidy is generally greater the earlier the gift. Gifts to qualified charities are exempt from estate and gift taxes, whether made while living or at death. Beyond this exclusion, however, two important tax advantages characterize charitable giving during the donor's lifetime: (1) unlike bequests, gifts made to qualified charities while alive yield income tax deductions; and (2) charities, because they are tax exempt, can, in principle, invest funds at a higher after-tax rate of return than the donor can.

To illustrate how the tax rules encourage charitable giving, suppose you are considering whether to make a bequest to your daughter or a gift to a charity. If you are in a 30% marginal tax bracket, or $t_p = 30\%$, each \$1 gift to charity costs you only \$.70. Ignoring interest for the moment, you must decide then between making a \$1 gift to charity and increasing the size of your taxable estate by \$.70. Suppose the estate tax, t_e, is 60%, \$.70 added to your estate will give rise to \$.42 of estate tax, leaving only \$.28 to be passed on to your daughter. So each \$1 of gift to charity reduces your daughter's bequest by $\$1(1 - t_p)(1 - t_e)$ or only \$.28. This difference is impressive. You must value leaving an extra dollar to your daughter more than 3.5 times as much as a dollar to charity. The income and estate tax rules create a significant incentive to make charitable gifts.

If the charity is going to use the gift in n years, charitable giving has further tax advantages because charities are tax exempt and in theory can earn interest at a higher rate than can the benefactor. Moreover, giving early yields an income tax deduction, whereas bequests do not. The benefit of making a \$1 after-tax gift now versus setting aside \$1 to leave as a bequest in n years, depends on whether

$$[1/(1 - t_{p0})](1 + R_{ch})^n > [1 + R_p(1 - t_{pn})]^n$$

where t_{p0} and t_{pn} are the donor's marginal tax rates now and in the future over the n years, respectively, R_{ch} is the before-tax return earned by the charity, and R_p is the before-tax return earned on personal account by the donor.

Suppose current (t_{p0}) and future (t_{pn}) income tax rates are 30%, that both the charity (R_{ch}) and the taxpayer (R_p) can earn 10% before tax, and that the future bequest will be made in $n = 15$ years when the estate tax rate is 60%. One dollar set aside now for a bequest in 15 years grows to \$2.76 given an *after-tax* rate of return of 7% and, after the estate tax, leaves \$1.10 for your daughter.

---

[19] *Anschutz v. Commissioner*, 135 T.C. No 5 (July 22, 2010). The Tenth Circuit later affirmed the ruling.

[20] See D. Kocieniewski, "A Family's Billions, Artfully Sheltered," *New York Times* (November 26, 2011). See also J. Drucker, "Buffett-Ducking Billionaires Avoid Reporting Cash Gains to IRS," *Bloomberg* (November 21, 2011).

A tax-deductible gift of \$1.4286 today to a charity has an after-tax cost of \$1, that is, \$1.4286 (1 − .3) = \$1. It accumulates to \$5.97, or \$1.4286 $(1.1)^{15}$ in 15 years, or 5.4 times the value of a gift to your daughter. Giving to charity now yields 216% of a bequest to charity (\$5.97 versus \$2.76). The reason is that, if you give at death, you lose the income tax deduction and the opportunity to accumulate at the before-tax rate.

Future tax rates would have to increase dramatically to justify deferral of the charitable gift. Moreover, with increases in tax rates, the investment return advantage of the tax-exempt charity over the donor would likely increase.

Of course, nontax factors must be considered as well. Perhaps you will want to change your mind between now and the date of your death as to which charity should be your beneficiary. Alternatively, your tastes or economic circumstances could change over the coming years, such that you decide you would prefer to have the resources for your own consumption.

Donors of securities held more than 12 months can take a tax deduction equal to the fair market value of securities contributed to charities. Moreover, donors do not pay a capital gains tax on the appreciation in the value of assets contributed. However, this tax advantage does not apply if the securities have been held 12 months or less. In that event, the deduction effectively is limited to the cost basis of the securities. Donating toward year-end allows taxpayers to determine whether their tax rates are high, giving them an option to contribute, and to select stocks that have appreciated in value.

16.5 A MODEL OF THE TRADE-OFFS BETWEEN GIFTING NOW VERSUS BY BEQUEST

Giving away assets during one's lifetime, even to noncharitable entities, can be tax advantageous. How? First, each dollar of the annual \$15,000 gift exclusion per donee (2018 amounts, indexed for inflation; \$30,000 for married couples) given this way removes more than a dollar, tax-free, from the estate. It essentially removes the future appreciation from the estate or "freezes" the estate. That is, the estate is reduced by $(1 + r)^n$, where r is the after-tax rate of return that would have been earned on the assets and n is the number of years until bequest. The same logic applies to gifts up to the equivalent of the unified estate and gift tax exclusion.

For gifts above the annual plus overall exclusion equivalent, the benefactor pays a gift tax now and will receive a tax credit later (without interest), for the tax paid. The advantage of the gift is that the benefactor keeps the appreciation on the gifted assets out of the estate. In special cases, this turns out to be equivalent to obtaining an estate tax deduction for the gift tax paid plus interest on the gift tax. As a result, in a wide variety of circumstances, giving early offers tax advantages. Let us take a closer look.

Suppose a \$1 current gift triggers a gift tax today of t_{e0}. The marginal estate tax rate, in n years, at death is t_{en}. Let R_k and R_p denote the before-tax rates of return on investments for the children and their parents, respectively. Let t_k and t_p denote the income tax rates of the children and their parents, respectively.

Notice that a \$1 gift requires a present outlay of $1 + t_{e0}$ dollars and triggers a gift tax of t_{e0}. So a comparison of the after-tax accumulations of a current gift and a future bequest requires that, for bequests, $1 + t_{e0}$ dollars be set aside currently, for each dollar of current gift.

$$\textbf{Gift: } [1 + R_k(1 - t_k)]^n\text{-}(t_{en} - t'_{e0}) \qquad (16.1)$$

$$\textbf{Bequest: } (1 + t_{e0})[1+R_p(1 - t_p)]^n(1 - t_{en}) \qquad (16.2)$$

Because the gift tax credit is based on the schedule in place at death, t'_{e0} might differ from t_{e0}. The term $(t_{en} - t'_{e0})$ represents the difference between the estate tax at time n on \$1 of additional taxable gifts that were added back to the estate and the gift tax that can be used as a credit against this tax. If the tax rate schedule is the same at time n as it was at the time of the gift, then t'_{e0} is equal to the actual tax that was paid on the gift initially, t_{e0}. To simplify the analysis, we assume in what follows that the tax rate schedule remains unchanged.

To illustrate how the integration of the estate and gift tax could increase the benefits of early gifting, assume that the parent and child invest in assets that earn the same after-tax rate, r, and that the gift and estate tax rates are constant across time $t_e = t_{e0} = t_{en}$. In this case,

$$\textbf{Gift now: } (1 + r)^n \tag{16.3}$$

$$\textbf{Bequest: } (1 + t_e)(1 + r)^n(1 - t_e) = (1 - t_e^2)(1 + r)^n \tag{16.4}$$

So the family is better off with a current gift by. $t_e^2(1+ r)^n$. Alternatively stated,

$$\frac{\text{Gift now}}{\text{Bequest}} = \frac{1}{1-t_e^2}$$

If, for example, $t_e = 50\%$, then

$$\frac{\text{Gift now}}{\text{Bequest}} = 1.333$$

that is, the family is 33% better off with a current gift than a bequest. What is going on here? The family effectively achieves not only a tax credit for the gift tax paid earlier but also an estate tax deduction for the gift tax paid earlier with interest. That is, the size of the taxable estate is reduced by the gift taxes paid, plus any income that would have been earned from investing the additional funds.

Suppose a benefactor gave a $1 million gift to a relative and paid the $.5 million tax due on the gift the day before she died. Although the estate includes the value of the gift, $1 million, absent any special rule it would not include the $.5 million gift tax. At a 50% tax rate, this gift saves $250,000 in tax by removing $500,000 from the taxable estate. Recognizing the tax planning incentive to make deathbed gifts, the tax law requires that the gift tax paid be added back to the estate if the gift is made within 3 years of death.

The Trade-Offs between Gifting and Losing the Step-Up in Basis on Bequests

We next expand the model to account for the fact that many assets transferred from a donor to a donee may have a built-in capital gain or may produce one in the future. This feature favors bequests because of the tax-free step-up in the basis of the assets transferred by bequest. Beneficiaries retain their benefactor's original basis in assets that are gifted prior to death. The trade-off, then, comes between obtaining a step-up in the basis of assets on a bequest (an *income* tax benefit) versus the *estate* tax benefits of early gifts.

Assume that a parent has owned an unincorporated business for m years. The initial basis in the business was b dollars, the initial value of the business was V dollars, and the business has been increasing in value at after-tax rate r_p per year. The parent is now contemplating a gift of the business to his children. He has n years left until his death. Each year, the business pays out distribution, d. For simplicity, assume the distribution paid is that amount that leaves the income tax basis unchanged at amount b. The excess of r_p over d, then, represents the appreciation rate on the value of the business that is not *currently* subject to taxation.

A sale of the business, however, would trigger a capital gains tax. If control of the business is transferred to the children, we assume the parent receives the same compensation and "dividends" that would have been received had control *not* been transferred. Similarly, the children's compensation is assumed to be the same as if control had *not* been transferred. To make the model simple, we assume a constant rate of return through time, but we allow for the possibility that the parent and children do not operate the business with equal efficiency. In other words, we allow r_p to differ from r_k. We also assume a constant dividend yield, d, each year. At the date of the potential gift, the value of the business is

$$A = V(1 + r_p - d)^m$$

which would attract a gift tax of At_{em}. If a gift is made, we assume the business is sold when the parent dies. The children must then pay income tax at a rate of t_{im+n} on the total appreciation of the business in excess of its basis of b. The children retain

$$\mathbf{A(1 + r_k - d)^n - t_{im+n}[A(1 + r_k - d)^n - b]} \quad (16.5)$$

Comparing gifting with the parent's decision to retain the business until death, a bequest would yield

$$\mathbf{A(1 + t_{em})(1 + r_p - d)^n(1 - t_{em+n})} \quad (16.6)$$

If we assume $r_k - d = r_p - d = r$; $t_{em} = t_{em+n} = t_e$; and $b = 0$ and $d = 0$ (which most favors a bequest), we find

$$\text{Gift: } A(1 + r)^n(1 - t_{im+n})$$

$$\text{Bequest: } A(1 + r)^n(1 - t_e^2)$$

For example, if $t_{im+n} = 30\%$ and $t_e = 50\%$, then a bequest is superior to a gift by 75/70 or 7.1%. If, however, the appreciated asset will be retained by the donee beyond the death of the donor, so the effective capital gains tax rate is lower (say, 20%), then the *gift* is better by 80/75 = 6.1%. The higher b, the more favorable is the gift. The intuition is that as b becomes smaller, the greater becomes the benefit of the free step-up in tax basis from bequeathing the property.

Beyond these tax considerations, nontax costs to gifting early must be considered. A benefactor might not be willing to relinquish control of the assets for personal reasons. Children have been known to squander their newfound wealth, or they might turn against their benefactors (the King Lear syndrome). Gifting entails transferring assets to children who may be less skillful in managing them, which also exacts a cost. This is particularly important if the assets represent an operating business. Moreover, it is not uncommon for donors to claim that their donees are doing a poor job in managing the transferred assets. Such tensions can be painful for both parties. Finally, many parents resist transferring wealth to their children out of fear of removing incentives for them to succeed on their own.

Summary of Key Points

1. Efficient tax planning trades off tax and nontax considerations among transferors and transferees of accumulated wealth.
2. Estate taxes are rare. Only about 0.5% of deaths will result in an estate tax return being filed. However, wealth is highly concentrated, so even though the estate tax applies to only a small fraction of all people, those people hold a large fraction of the wealth in the United States.
3. Estate and gift taxes are levied on the fair market value of the assets transferred, not their tax bases.
4. A donor can give a donee $15,000 (2018, indexed for inflation) of gifts per year exempt from gift tax. The $15,000 exclusion is per donee. For example, a donor could give away $150,000 in a year free of gift tax if it was spread equally over 10 people. Although many gifts are to family members, there is no requirement that the donor and donee be related.
5. The American Taxpayer Relief Act of 2012 set a maximum estate tax rate of 40% and a $5 million exclusion. In 2017, the Tax Cuts and Jobs Act increased the exclusion to $11.18 million (2018, indexed for inflation).
6. The estate tax generally grants deductions for unlimited amounts bequeathed to the spouse and amounts bequeathed to qualified charities.
7. Tax planning strategies for income taxes sometimes conflict with those for estate and gift taxes. Most estate plans have important income tax consequences. Substantial conflicts may also arise between the tax and the nontax aspects of estate and gift tax planning.

8. Giving away assets during one's lifetime freezes an estate. Under U.S. tax laws, gifts can be made tax-free in the amount of $15,000 per donee per year. Each dollar of exclusion used removes more than a dollar, tax-free, from the estate. It also removes the income that can be earned on these assets. A nontax cost of early giving, however, is the donor's loss of control over the assets.
9. Life insurance owned by the decedent is included in his or her taxable estate. Life insurance trusts are used to keep life insurance out of the gross estate of the decedent.
10. Family limited partnerships are used to reduce the value for gift and estate tax purposes of limited partnership interests transferred to heirs.
11. The constructive sale rules of Section 1259 are designed to prevent taxpayers from monetizing appreciated financial positions by, say, executing a short-sale-against-the-box transaction. Planners have devised strategies in an attempt to avoid the constructive sale rules, such as borrowing and executing a collar around the appreciated security, and variable prepaid forward contracts.
12. Making charitable gifts during one's lifetime has two important tax advantages: (1) unlike bequests, gifts to charity over one's lifetime provide income tax deductions; and (2) the earnings on the assets given to the charity are tax exempt.
13. Many factors are involved in the decision between a bequest and a current gift of assets that have appreciated in value. On death, the beneficiary receives the assets with a tax-free step-up in basis to fair market value. If received as a gift, however, the beneficiary retains the original basis of the donor. Gifting early removes the assets from the estate and reduces the estate tax. The greater the basis in the assets and the more liberal the dividend policy and therefore the lower the future appreciation, the more likely it is that gifting the asset dominates bequeathing the asset.

Questions

Q16-1. In what sense are the estate and gift taxes "unified"?

Q16-2. What is the Generation-Skipping Transfer (GST) Tax, and why does it exist?

Q16-3. What are constructive sales, and why is Congress worried about them?

Q16-4. How is life insurance treated for income tax and estate tax purposes? Can estate taxation on life insurance proceeds be avoided? If so, how?

Q16-5. What are family limited partnerships (FLPs), and how are they used as a tax-planning strategy?

Q16-6. Under what circumstances is it more tax advantageous to give to charity during your lifetime rather than on bequest? What nontax factors might influence your decision?

Q16-7. What are the advantages of gifting rather than bequeathing assets? What are the nontax costs of doing so?

Q16-8. If the basis in an asset is low relative to its current market value, why might bequeathing the asset be more efficient than giving it as a gift? Under what conditions will the gift route be preferred?

Q16-9. Apart from the exclusion equivalent, should tax planners recommend that all estate assets be transferred to the surviving spouse, if the goal is to transfer resources to successive generations? What nontax issues arise in the planning problem?

Exercises

E16-10. Carlos passes away in 2018, bequeathing $10 million of his property to his wife, Sandra. Carlos also owned a $2 million life insurance policy on himself, with his kids, Juan and Roberto, as equal beneficiaries. Will Carlos's estate owe estate tax?

E16-11. Paula makes the following gifts in the current year: $20,000 to the United Way; $15,000 to her brother Skip, who is a compulsive gambler; $45,000 to her husband Larry, to fund a new boat; and $32,000 to a UTMA account for her son Philip. To what extent will these be taxable gifts? That is, to what extent do they exceed the annual exclusion and begin to offset the unified credit?

Tax-Planning Problems

TP16-12. Suppose your parents founded a wildly successful business in which they still own 90% of the outstanding stock, which is the source of most of their wealth. The basis in their stock is close to zero. Your parents are nearing retirement age and are considering their options. They would like to buy a condo in Vail and a winter home in Vero Beach. They also would like to have sufficient money to travel extensively each year. They want to contribute half their wealth to charity, although they have not decided which charities they want to support, with the remainder of their wealth being divided equally between you and your sister. You have recently graduated with your MBA and your sister is about to enter college. Prepare a plan for your parents' consideration and carefully explain each part of the plan.

TP16-13. A 70-year-old recently retired engineer is discussing with you, over coffee, whether to gift $500,000 today to his only daughter or invest the $500,000 and bequeath the $500,000 plus earnings to his daughter in his will. The engineer expects to live another 10 years. What would you advise the engineer to do? Carefully explain your reasoning and make explicit any assumptions you make, such as taxes, earnings rates, spending patterns, and so on.

TP16-14. Following graduation, you meet Mr. Big at a country club. Mr. Big is a venture capitalist who has a sizable stock portfolio concentrated in a single firm, Blue Hat. After several weeks of golfing together, Mr. Big confides in you regarding his financial situation. He owns $30 million of Blue Hat stock ($100 per share, 300,000 shares) with a basis of $20 per share. Mr. Big has one child, Big Jr. Mr. Big, who is 75 years old and in poor health, tells you that he just put in an order to sell half his Blue Hat stock and that he will invest the after-tax proceeds in T-bills because he thinks the market is overvalued. Assume the gains from the sale are taxed at a 15% long-term capital gains rate.

One year later, Mr. Big passes away, leaving his entire estate to Big Jr. Because of changes in short-term interest rates, the T-bill portfolio he had purchased with the stock sold has produced no after-tax return. At the date of death, Blue Hat is trading at $150 per share. Mr. Big's estate pays for any estate taxes by first liquidating a portion of the T-bill portfolio and then, if necessary, a portion of the Blue Hat stock. Consider these two reminders about estate taxation: First, estates pay an estate tax on the fair market value of the net estate (assets less liabilities). Assume the estate tax rate is 45% for the year in question. Second, it often takes some time for an estate to pay off the debts of the decedent and distribute the net assets to the heirs. In the meantime the assets of the estate may generate income. To prevent this income from going untaxed, estates are required to pay income tax on their earnings. Assume that the income tax rate faced by the estate is 40%. Sometimes estates have negative taxable income. If an estate reports net losses on its final tax return, assume those losses pass through to the heirs; otherwise they would be lost.

a. How much will Big Jr. inherit after all estate taxes have been paid?

b. Later in the year after Mr. Big's death, Big Jr. recognizes $5 million in long-term capital gains from the sale of other stock from his personal portfolio. How much tax will Big Jr. pay on the sale, net of any capital losses he may have inherited from Mr. Big?

c. With the same facts as part (a), and instead of selling his Blue Hat stock, Mr. Big sells short $15 million of Green Hat stock, which Mr. Big figures is somewhat correlated with Blue Hat stock. Assume Federal Reserve rules on short sales prevent Mr. Big from selling short more than 50% of the value of his long position. The proceeds from the short sale are invested in T-bills. The short sale is held open until Mr. Big's death. Mr. Big's estate liquidates enough T-bill and Blue Hat stock (T-bills first) to close out the short sale of Green Hat and any estate taxes. Any remaining Blue Hat stock is distributed to Big Jr. At the date of death, Blue Hat stock has increased in price to $150 per share. Green Hat stock has also increased in value and the short position requires $22.5 million to close out. What will be the current market value of the Blue Hat stock that Big Jr. gets from the estate?

d. Later in the year after Mr. Big's death and given the circumstances in part (c), Big Jr. recognizes $5 million in long-term capital gains from the sale of other stock from his personal portfolio. How much tax will Big Jr. pay on the sale, net of any capital losses he may have inherited from Mr. Big?

References and Additional Readings

A sampling of research on the economics of estate and gift taxation:

Fisher, I., 1916. "Some Impending National Problems," *Journal of Political Economy* (24), pp. 694–712.

Gale W., and M. Perozek, 2001. "Do Estate Taxes Reduce Saving?" in *Rethinking Estate and Gift Taxation*. Washington, DC: Brookings Institution Press, pp. 216–247.

Joulfaian, D., 2000. "Estate Taxes and Charitable Giving," *National Tax Journal* (Part 2, Sept.), pp. 743–763.

Kopczuk, W., 2009. "Economics of Estate Taxation: Review of Theory and Evidence," *Tax Law Review* (63), pp. 139–157.

Kopczuk, W., and E. Saez, 2004. "Top Wealth Shares in the United States, 1916–2000: Evidence from Estate Tax Returns," *National Tax Journal* (57), pp. 445–487.

Kopczuk, W., and J. Slemrod, 2001. "The Impact of the Estate Tax on the Wealth Accumulation and Avoidance Behavior of Donors," in *Rethinking Estate and Gift Taxation*. Washington, DC: Brookings Institution Press, pp. 299–343.

McCaffery, E., 1994. "The Uneasy Case for Wealth Transfer Taxation," *Yale Law Journal* (104), pp. 283–365.

Mitchell, O., J. Poterba, M. Warshawsky, and J. Brown, 1999. "New Evidence on the Money's Worth of Individual Annuities," *American Economic Review* (December).

Piketty, T., and E. Saez, 2013. "A Theory of Optimal Inheritance Taxation," *Econometrica* (81), pp. 1851–1886.

Poterba, J., 2000. "The Estate Tax and After-Tax Returns," in *Does Atlas Shrug: The Economic Consequences of Taxing the Rich,* edited by J. Slemrod. Boston: Harvard University Press.

Poterba, J., 2001. "Estate and Gift Taxes and Incentives for Inter Vivos Giving in the United States," *Journal of Public Economics* (January), pp. 237–264.

Poterba J., and S. Weisbenner, 2001. "The Distributional Burdens of Taxing Estates and Unrealized Capital Gains at the Time of Death," in *Rethinking Estate and Gift Taxation*. Washington, DC: Brookings Institution Press, pp. 422–449.

Repetti, J. 2000. "The Case for the Estate Tax," *Tax Notes* (March 13). Slemrod, J., W. Gale, and J. Hines, editors, 2001. *Rethinking Estate and Gift Taxation*. Washington, DC: Brookings Institution Press.

Saez, E., and G. Zucman, "Wealth Inequality in the United States since 1913: Evidence from Capitalized Income Tax Data," *Quarterly Journal of Economics*, Vol. 131, No. 2, May 2016.

Slemrod, J., W. Gale, and J. Hines, editors, 2001. *Rethinking Estate and Gift Taxation*. Washington, DC: Brookings Institution Press.

Glossary

A

Accrual accounting—the method of accounting used to report the results of business operations. A system of accounting that recognizes revenues when net assets (not just cash) increase and expenses when net assets (not just cash) decrease as a result of the firm's operating activities. Net assets are defined as total assets less total liabilities.

Accumulated earnings and profits—see "earning and profits."

Acquiring company—entity that purchases the target in an acquisition.

Acquisition method of accounting—financial accounting method used in mergers and acquisitions. Requires the acquirer to record the target on its books at the purchase price.

Acquisition structure—method of payment (cash or stock) and tax treatment (taxable or tax free) used in an acquisition. May also apply to method used to acquire a subsidiary of another corporation, in which case other tax issues are also relevant.

Adaptive tax planning—type of tax planning designed to offset the cost of being in the wrong clientele following unexpected changes in tax status where reversibility is impossible or impractical. See also "reversibility of tax plans."

Adjusted tax basis—the tax version of "adjusted book value." Adjusted basis is generally equal to historical cost less accumulated tax depreciation. See also "tax basis."

Advance pricing agreements—occur when a firm submits a transfer pricing methodology to the IRS for approval. If the IRS approves, then, in principle, the firm's transfer pricing should not be challenged as long as the firm adheres to the agreement. See also "Section 482," "arm's-length pricing," and "transfer prices."

Adverse selection—see "hidden-information problem."

Aggregate deemed sale price (ADSP)—the price at which the target's assets are deemed sold to the acquirer in a Section 338 election transaction.

Appreciated financial position—financial position in which the asset's value is in excess of its tax basis.

Arbitrage techniques—an activity that generates positive after-tax returns by buying one asset while simultaneously seeking another asset such that the taxpayer has a zero net investment position and bears zero risk.

A reorganization—see "Section 368 A reorganization."

Arm's-length pricing—transfer prices used by related parties are required under the U.S. Tax Code to approximate the prices that would have been used between unrelated parties, that is, parties at "arm's length." See also "transfer prices," "Section 482," and "advance pricing agreements."

Asset sale—transaction in which the acquirer purchases the assets of the target or the assets of the sold subsidiary from the seller.

Assignment of income—the taxpayer instructs one party to pay income on the taxpayer's behalf to a third party, transferring the tax liability to the third party as well (the third party is presumably in a lower tax bracket). The assignment of income doctrine requires that the taxpayer must give away the income-generating asset to be successful in shifting taxable income.

At-risk limitations—a limit on the deductibility of losses. The at-risk rules can apply to individuals (partners and S corporation shareholders), estates, trusts, and certain closely held C corporations. Losses are limited to the amount "at-risk" (i.e., the investment and certain amounts borrowed).

Average tax rate—broadly, is some measure of taxes paid, divided by some measure of income. Importantly, an average rate will likely not be the rate that is paid on the taxpayer's next transaction (the marginal transaction) but instead is the average rate that is paid on all transactions combined.

B

Base erosion and anti-abuse tax (BEAT)—a type of minimum tax imposed by the U.S. on certain payments to related foreign affiliates.

Basis—gains (and losses) on the sale of an asset are computed as the difference between the sale price and the basis of the asset (usually the purchase price less accumulated depreciation, if any). See also "adjusted tax basis."

Baskets of income—where the foreign tax credit limitation must be computed separately for different types, or "baskets," of income. The United States uses this approach. See also "foreign tax credit limitation" and "country-by-country limitation."

Before-tax rates of return—the rate of return earned from investing in an asset before any taxes are paid to domestic and foreign federal, state, and local taxing authorities.

Benchmark asset—the calculation of implicit taxes for any given asset requires a benchmark asset against which to compare pretax returns. Unless otherwise noted, we use a fully taxable corporate bond as the benchmark asset because the income is taxed at ordinary tax rates each period and the investment uses after-tax dollars. See also "tax-favored treatment."

Bilateral tax treaties—tax treaties between a pair of countries, e.g., a treaty between the United States and Japan.

Black–Tepper tax arbitrage strategy—corporate pension funds have traditionally held 50% of their assets in common stocks that bear high implicit taxes even though pension funds, because tax exempt, form a natural tax clientele for taxable bonds. One explanation is that fund managers want to invest in riskier projects that have risk premiums and, thus, higher expected returns. Black and Tepper argue that firms would be better off holding bonds in their pension funds and purchasing risky stocks outside the fund with corporate debt.

Book-tax differences—where the financial accounting treatment and tax treatment of the same transaction result in different effects on income. Some book-tax differences are permanent differences, such as municipal bond interest; others are temporary differences, such as depreciation.

Boot—property (e.g., cash) that, when received, can trigger gain recognition in an otherwise nontaxable transaction, such as corporate formation or nontaxable acquisitions.

Branch profits tax—a special tax levied on U.S. branches of foreign corporations to put them on equal footing with U.S. subsidiaries of foreign corporations, which are subject to withholding taxes. Like withholding taxes, taxes on branch profits are often reduced by tax treaties. See "withholding taxes."

B reorganization—see "Section 368 B reorganization."

Built-in gain—arises when an asset is acquired in a carryover basis transaction and the fair market value of the asset is in excess of the acquired asset's tax basis. See also "carryover basis," "carryover basis transaction," and "adjusted tax basis."

Business-purpose doctrine—see "valid business purpose."

Bypass trust—same as a credit shelter trust. See also "credit shelter trust."

C

Capital asset—assets whose sale gives rise to capital gains and losses. Examples of capital assets generally include stocks, bonds, puts, and calls. See also "Section 1231 assets."

Capital asset pricing model (CAPM)—model used to estimate expected security returns for individual stocks.

Capital gains—income or gains from the sale of capital assets such as securities. Gains may be taxed at capital gains rates.

Carried interest—typically, the general partner in a private equity or hedge fund is compensated with a fee based on the gross assets under management (for example, 2% of the gross assets) and a profits interest of generally 20% of the fund's return. This latter profits interest is referred to as "carried interest" and is taxed as favorable capital gains tax rates.

Carryover basis—a basis in the property received that is derived from the basis that the transferor had in the property that was transferred. See also "substituted basis."

C corporation—an organizational form in which the entity's taxable income is taxed at the corporate level. Owners (shareholders) do not face taxation until dividends are paid or the stock is sold. Shareholders enjoy limited liability. C corporations can be subsidiaries of other corporations or freestanding.

Centralized management—organizational arrangement in which the top management makes most of the decisions for the organization. See also "decentralized management."

Charitable deduction—gifts and bequests to qualified charities are not subject to gift and estate tax by virtue of the unlimited charitable deduction. Gifts to charities may also yield income tax deductions.

Charitable remainder trust—a trust that allows for tax-efficient bequests to charities while retaining an income interest in the trust assets.

Check-the-box regulations—a set of Treasury Regulations allowing an eligible entity not automatically treated as a corporation to elect (check-the-box) to be treated as a corporation for federal tax purposes; basically an election that applies to unincorporated businesses. Those not electing corporate tax treatment are treated as flow-through entities (see "conduits"). Allows firms to elect, in some cases, to have their foreign operations taxed as either foreign branches or foreign subsidiaries for U.S. purposes. See also "foreign branch" and "foreign subsidiary."

Clientele-based arbitrage—type of arbitrage. The nature of clientele-based arbitrage depends on whether the taxpayer starts out with a relatively high or a relatively low marginal tax rate. For the high-tax-rate taxpayer, clientele-based arbitrage is taking a long position in a relatively tax-favored asset (one that bears a relatively high degree of implicit tax) and a short position in a tax disfavored asset (one that bears relatively more explicit tax). For the low-tax-rate taxpayer, clientele-based arbitrage is taking a long position in a tax-disfavored asset and a short position in a tax-favored asset.

Closely held corporations—corporations owned by just a few shareholders, which is common in family or small business concerns. Relative to widely held firms, considerable trust tends to exist among the owners and employees of closely held firms. In fact, closely held firms are typically managed by their owners. By paying themselves generous salaries and bonuses, owner-managers can avoid part of the corporate-level tax. Thus the Treasury keeps close watch on these firms for non-arm's-length transactions structured with a primary motivation to avoid tax.

Collar—the sale of a call option and the purchase of a put option on the same underlying asset, which limits the risk of loss and potential for gain. See also "constructive sale rules."

Comparable analysis—valuation technique, commonly used in acquisitions, in which similar companies' valuation is compared with the valuation of the subject firm, typically in terms of some accounting benchmark (e.g., price to earnings).

Conduits—earnings for these organizations, also known as pass-through entities, are not taxed at the entity level but rather are passed through to the entity's owners and taxed at the owner level. Examples of pass-through entities are partnerships, proprietorships, S corporations, REITs, LLCs, and LLPs. For example, partners record their share of partnership profits and losses on their own returns, whether the profits are distributed or not.

Constructive dividends—occur when shareholders receive some benefit from the corporation without the corporation formally declaring a dividend. Constructive dividends are taxed the same as other dividends.

Constructive receipt—even though the taxpayer has not received the income, she is treated as having received it if she has already earned and easily could collect it. Examples include (1) interest credited on bank accounts where funds are available for withdrawal at any time and (2) yearend paychecks that can be picked up at the payroll department.

Constructive sale rules—a set of rules in Section 1259 that causes investors to be taxable on unrealized gains in securities that they have effectively sold, for example, in a short-sale-against-the-box transaction. See also "short-sale-against-the-box."

Continuity of business interest—requirements for tax-free treatment in a Section 368 reorganization. The acquirer must use the assets of the target in a productive capacity post-acquisition.

Contractual perspective—contracts specify the rights of various parties to make decisions and to receive cash flows in differing circumstances. The tax-related cash flows specified by contracts affect the prices at which assets are traded and the ways in which production is organized by business units.

Control—definition used in various tax-law-related tests. Control relates to the proportion of the entity that is owned by a particular party. In many cases, control is defined as 80% ownership, although it is a definition subject to exceptions.

Controlled foreign corporation (CFC)—most foreign corporations more than 50% owned by U.S. corporations or individuals are CFCs. Subpart F income of CFCs is deemed to be repatriated as earned. See also "Subpart F income."

Convex tax function—see "progressive income tax system."

Corporate formation—transaction that creates a corporation, generally governed by Section 351.

Cost basis—basis in an asset that is equal to cost or purchase price. See "adjusted tax basis," "carryover basis," and "substituted basis."

Country-by-country limitation—where the foreign tax credit limitation must be computed separately on income from each country in which the firm does business. The United States does not use this system. See also "foreign tax credit limitation" and "basket of income."

Credit shelter trust—a trust that bypasses the spouse's estate but provides income for the spouse if necessary. Same as a bypass trust. It has lost some of its appeal due to portability of the lifetime exclusion.

C reorganization—see "Section 368 C reorganization."

Current earnings and profits—see "earnings and profits."

D

Decentralized management—organizational arrangement in which lower-level management makes many of the decisions for the organization. See also "centralized management."

Deemed asset sale—transaction that is structured contractually as a stock sale but that is taxed as an asset sale. The target's assets are "deemed" to have been sold even though the target's stock was actually sold.

Deferred compensation contract—a contract between an employer and an employee. An employee can arrange to save for future consumption by agreeing to defer the receipt of current compensation until a future date. The employer deducts the compensation when paid in the later period and the employee includes it in taxable income in the later period when received.

Defined benefit corporate pension plan—type of corporate pension plan that promises the employee a stated benefit at retirement, often based on salary and/or years of service, usually in the form of an annuity.

Defined contribution corporate pension plan—type of corporate pension plan in which the employer and, in some cases, the employee make contributions into an account that will accumulate pension benefits on behalf of the employee. As its name implies, a defined contribution plan specifies contributions into the plan. For example, employees might be required to contribute a certain percentage of their compensation to receive a matching contribution by their employers. The employee's ultimate pension benefit depends on the amounts contributed into the plan and on investment performance.

Discount—when a bond is issued at less than its face (par) value. The discount represents deferred interest and is amortized over the life of the bond, creating interest income for the holder and interest expense for the issuer. See also "premium," "original issue discount," and "market discount."

Disqualifying disposition—terms used to describe the situation when the incentive stock option holder disposes of the stock within 12 months of exercise of the incentive stock option. The disqualification means that the incentive stock option is then taxed as a nonqualified stock option. See also "employee stock options," "incentive stock options," and "nonqualified stock options."

Distribution—occurs when a corporation pays cash or property to its shareholders. Distributions are normally taxed as dividends, but, in some cases, they can be taxed as a return of capital or capital gains.

Divestiture methods—modes that can be used to sell or separate a component of a company from the remainder of the company. The most common types include subsidiary sales, spin-offs, and equity carve-outs.

Dividend—occurs when a distribution is treated as having been paid from the corporation's "earnings and profits" and is taxable as ordinary income to the recipient but often at reduced rates after 2002. See also "earnings and profits" and "distribution."

Dividends received deduction (DRD)—allows a corporation receiving a dividend from another corporation to a deduction so that the dividend is only partially taxable. The DRD exists to mitigate the potential for triple taxation of corporate profits. See also "double taxation."

Dividend tax imputation—a system where the shareholders receiving a corporate dividend also receive a credit for corporate taxes already paid on the corporate earnings from which the dividend is declared. The intent is to mitigate the double taxation of corporate dividends (once at the corporate level and again at the shareholder level). Also known as a corporate-tax or dividend-tax integrated system.

Double taxation—a phrase used to describe the situation where an entity's earnings (for example, corporate profits) are taxed first at the entity level and then again at the owner level (either when distributed as dividends or when the owner sells his ownership share). In contrast, partners and sole proprietors are subject to only one level of taxation, at their own personal rates.

E

Earnings and profits (E&P)—a tax attribute that determines whether a distribution is taxable as a dividend or as a return of capital and capital gain. Accumulated earnings and profits are the tax analogue to retained earnings; current earnings and profits are the tax analogue to net income.

Effective annualized tax rate on shares (denoted *ts*)—if shareholders paid tax at rate *ts* each year on their total stock returns (dividends plus capital gains), they would end up with the same after-tax accumulation as they actually achieve.

Effective tax planning—involves considering not only the role of explicit taxes when implementing the decision rule of maximizing after-tax returns, but also consideration of other costs that arise in a world of costly contracting where implementation of tax-minimizing strategies may introduce significant costs along nontax dimensions.

Effective tax rates—(1) for financial reporting purposes (known as the GAAP effective tax rate) it is the sum of current tax expense and deferred tax expense (that is, total tax expense) divided by income before taxes. (2) A second definition is cash taxes paid divided by income before taxes (the cash effective tax rate).

Employee stock options (ESOs)—type of equity-based compensation. A stock option is a right to acquire stock at a specified price (exercise price) for a specified period of time (until the expiration date of the contract). ESOs are typically granted with an expiration date of 5 to 10 years and at an exercise price equal to the price of the underlying stock at the date of the grant.

Employee stock ownership plan (ESOP)—a special type of defined contribution corporate pension plan. Unlike most defined contribution plans, the ESOP is required to invest primarily in the stock of the company establishing the plan, which is commonly taken to mean the ESOP must hold at least 50% of its assets in the sponsoring company's stock. Just like other defined contribution plans, the corporation makes tax-deductible annual contributions to the ESOP, which are generally used to buy company stock or to pay down a loan that was used to acquire company stock when the program was initiated. Do not confuse with "employee stock options (ESOs)" See also "defined contribution corporate pension plan."

Entity-level tax—tax levied on the income of the entity at the entity level and before any distributions to the owners of the entity. For example, regular U.S. corporations (see "C corporations") must pay an entity-level tax on their taxable income. They file tax returns and pay tax on corporate taxable income in ways very similar to individuals.

Equity carve-out—transaction in which a corporation sells stock in a subsidiary to the public; also known as a subsidiary initial public offering (IPO).

Exchange fund—partnership-type arrangement in which the owner of assets or securities contributes those assets to the fund in return for a share of the returns derived from all the assets in the fund. Contribution to the fund provides owners of appreciated assets with diversification.

Explicit taxes—tax dollars paid directly to taxing authorities (federal, foreign, state, and local).

F

Family limited partnership (FLP)—occurs when property is placed in a limited partnership and the donor gifts minority limited partnership interests in the business, usually to his or her children. The limited partnership interests are discounted for estate and gift tax purposes because of their lack of marketability and their lack of control.

FASB (Financial Accounting Standards Board)—the independent, private-sector organization that establishes financial accounting and reporting standards for public and private companies and not-for-profit organizations that follow Generally Accepted Accounting Principles. The rules often differ from the tax rules due to differences in objectives between the FASB and the U.S. government in establishing a measure of income.

Financial accounting basis—value assigned to the assets and liabilities of a firm for financial accounting purposes. Often varies from tax basis due to differences in accounting procedures used for financial reporting and tax purposes.

Financial reporting costs—those costs to the organization arising from reporting lower book income or a higher debt-to-equity ratio. Such costs arise from explicit contracts with, for example, lenders and employees and from implicit contracts with other stakeholders.

Financing policies—how the firm structures the funding (debt and equity) side of its economic balance sheet. A firm is said to make a "capital structure decision" when it decides how it will finance its activities.

529 plan—a tax-favored means of saving for college named after Section 529.

Foreign Account Tax Compliance Act (FATCA)—a U.S. law that imposes broad information collection, reporting, and withholding requirements on financial institutions that have accounts from U.S. taxpayers.

Foreign branch—where a firm has direct ownership of a foreign business and not through a foreign subsidiary or other entity. See also "foreign subsidiary," "foreign partnership," and "check-the-box regulations."

Foreign-derived intangible income (FDII)—an export and production incentive used by the U.S. that results in a decreased tax rate on certain export income from the sale of property or services.

Foreign partnership—a partnership that is organized under the laws of another country.

Foreign subsidiary—a separate, legal business entity (corporation) operating under the tax and legal rules of a foreign jurisdiction that is owned by a domestic firm. See also "foreign branch," "foreign partnership," and "check-the-box regulations."

Foreign tax credit (FTC)—a credit to mitigate double taxation of foreign earnings. See also "worldwide tax system."

Forward triangular merger—merger in which the acquirer forms a subsidiary and merges the target corporation into the acquiring firm subsidiary.

401(k) plan—type of defined contribution pension plan set up by employers for their employees. The employer often matches the employee's pretax contributions, at least in part. Contributions are tax deductible, and earnings are tax deferred until withdrawn.

Frictions—transactions costs incurred by taxpayers in the marketplace that make implementation of certain tax-planning strategies costly. It is these frictions and tax-rule restrictions that make the potential returns to tax planning so high. See also "tax-rule restrictions."

Fringe benefits—benefits provided by the employer such as employer-provided term life insurance or business meals that are tax deductible to the employer but not taxable to the employee.

FTC limitations—see "foreign tax credit limitation."

G

General partners—type of partner in a partnership who manages the business and faces unlimited liability, making the partner personally liable for all the debts of the partnership.

Generation-Skipping Transfer Tax (GST)—a special additional tax levied on gifts and bequests that skip one generation, such as a bequest to a grandchild.

Global intangible low-tax income (GILTI)—a provision enacted by the U.S. that can be thought of as a minimum tax on certain foreign income. Despite the name, it is not limited to income from intangible assets.

Grantor retained trusts—a trust in which the grantor retains the income from the property, loses control over the assets, and the remainder interest goes to someone other than the grantor.

Gross assets—total asset basis, equal to the sum of liabilities and shareholders' equity.

Gross estate—usually includes assets in the probate estate plus other bequests of the decedent such as life insurance owned by the decedent. See also "probate estate."

H

Health savings account—a tax-advantaged savings vehicle where contributions are tax deductible and earnings are tax exempt, and no tax is due if the funds are used for qualified medical expenses. The funds can be withdrawn tax-free as long as they are used to pay for qualified medical expenses. To contribute to an HSA, the taxpayer must have a high-deductible health plan. Funds in HSAs can be carried over from year-to-year.

Hedge fund—a private investment fund open to wealthy investors that is similar in many ways to a private equity fund except that hedge funds generally invest in stocks, bonds, and other financial instruments undertaking arbitrage activities or risky positions.

Hedging—an activity that reduces the volatility (or spread) in expected cash flow outcomes. For corporations facing progressive tax schedules, the reduction in volatility in cash flows and taxable income can lower expected tax liabilities. Hedging can be undertaken via financial instruments such as options, swaps, and other derivatives.

Hidden-action problem—a type of strategic uncertainty. Arises when one contracting party has control over an action choice that affects future cash flows and where the action choice is *unobservable* to other contracting parties; also known as moral hazard. See also "strategic uncertainty."

Hidden-information problem—a type of strategic uncertainty. Arises when one contracting party has observed a characteristic of the production function he or she cannot control that affects future cash flows and that characteristic is only imperfectly observable by the other contracting parties; also known as adverse selection. See also "strategic uncertainty."

Historical cost—original cost of acquired property.

I

Identification problem—when a contractual relationship is consistent with more than one economic explanation and observers cannot tell which economic force is responsible for it.

Implicit tax rate (tIa)—the difference in pretax returns on a given asset, a, and the benchmark asset, b; algebraically, $tIa = (Rb - Ra)/Rb$.

Implicit taxes—arise because the before-tax investment returns available on tax-favored assets are less than those available on tax-disfavored assets. Taxpayers wishing to obtain the tax-favored treatment offered by the investment bid up the price of the investment, thus lowering the pretax rate of return.

Incentive stock options (ISOs)—type of employee stock option with no tax to employee at exercise date. Employee is taxed at capital gains tax rate at stock sale date on the difference between the stock sale price and option exercise price. No deduction to corporation at either date.

Information asymmetry—see "strategic uncertainty."

Inframarginal investors—investors who prefer to invest in one asset over another asset because the after-tax rate of the first asset is higher. See also "tax clienteles" and "marginal investors."

Installment sale—sale in which the buyer pays the seller in periodic payments (installments) that include a principal and interest component.

Intangible assets—assets that are not tangible. Examples of intangible assets include customer lists, trained workforce, and goodwill.

Investment strategies—how the firm structures the asset side of its economic balance sheet, which includes not only the actively managed assets the firm uses to run its business, but also passive assets such as bonds, stocks, and direct investments in other entities.

Irrevocable life insurance trust—a trust set up to hold one's life insurance to make sure it stays out of one's gross estate.

K

Keogh plans—type of pension plan available to individuals with self-employment income; contributions are tax deductible; earnings are tax deferred until withdrawn. Self-employment income includes income earned as a sole proprietorship or from a partnership, income earned as an independent contractor or as a consultant, and book royalties.

L

Last-in-first-out (LIFO)—an inventory cost system in which the cost of items sold are considered to have come from the newest (last-in) inventory. Contrast with first-in, first-out (FIFO), the inventory cost system in which the cost of items sold are considered to have come from the oldest (first-in) inventory.

Limited liability—the investor is at risk for only the amount he or she has invested in the business. Corporate shareholders and limited partners have limited liability.

Limited liability companies (LLCs)—hybrid entities that, under state law, are neither partnerships nor corporations. Under state law, they offer shareholders limited liability, whereas under current federal tax law, these entities can elect to be taxed as a partnership.

Limited liability partnerships (LLPs)—modified general partnerships designed specifically for professional service organizations, such as the Big 4 accounting firms, to operate as a partnership with some personal liability protection. The partners are not protected for breaches of professional responsibility. Many but not all states recognize LLPs, which offer advantages similar to the LLC—namely limited liability with a single level of taxation.

Limited partners—type of partner in a partnership. The liability of limited partners for the partnership's debts is limited to the amount the partner has invested in the business. They face no personal liability for the debts of the partnership. As with most shareholders in widely held corporations, a limited partner typically does not participate actively in the operations of the business.

Liquidating distribution—transaction in which the corporation distributes all of its assets to shareholders in return for all of the stock (ownership interests) in the corporation.

Long-term performance awards—a type of compensation plan where payout (shares or cash) is earned based on performance over a predefined performance period.

Long-term tax-exempt rate—interest rate used to compute the limitation on a target's tax attributes post-acquisition under U.S. Tax Code Section 382. The U.S. government publishes this rate periodically.

M

Marginal investors—investors who are indifferent between two or more assets because the (risk-adjusted) after-tax return is the same across the assets. The marginal investors determine the price at which the asset trades because the prices are set such that the after-tax rates of return are the same across the assets. See also "tax clienteles" and "inframarginal investors."

Marginal tax rate—the effect on the present value of explicit taxes of earning another dollar of taxable income in the current period. This calculation includes the effect of a current dollar of taxable income on future period tax liabilities.

Marital deduction—gifts and bequests to spouses are not subject to estate and gift tax by virtue of the unlimited marital deduction.

Market discount—occurs if the price of the bond falls after issuance. Market discounts are amortized over the life of the bond and reclassify what would otherwise be capital gains into ordinary income. See also "original issue discount."

Market frictions—see "frictions."

Master limited partnerships (MLPs)—basically partnerships with two types of partner: general partners and limited partners. Provided the limited partners do not actively participate in the management of the partnership, their liability for partnership debts is limited to their invested capital. General partners manage the partnership and have unlimited liability for the partnership's debts.

Monetization techniques—methods by which an asset is converted into cash without actually selling the asset itself and often without triggering taxation of the unrealized gain on the asset. Monetization strategies often involve some sort of borrowing against the asset or the income from the asset.

Money market savings accounts—an investment funded with after-tax dollars, the income (interest) from which is taxed each period as ordinary income.

Moral hazard—see "hidden-action problems."

N

"Naked" short sale—occurs when the short seller does not have a long position in the security sold short. The downside risk from a naked short sale is unlimited. Contrast with a "short-sale-against-the-box."

Net asset basis—gross asset basis less liabilities; also generally equivalent to shareholders' equity.

Net operating losses (NOLs)—when a firm's taxable income is negative (or deductions exceed gross income). Under the tax law prior to 2017, a U.S. NOL could be carried back 2 years to claim a refund of prior taxes paid or carried forward for up to 20 years to be claimed as a deduction against future taxable income. After 2017, tax losses incurred starting in 2018 must be carried forward, with an indefinite carryforward period. Tax loss deduction is limited to 80% of taxable income before the deduction. Losses created before 2018 are subject to the prior rules—no 80% limit and a 20 year carryforward period.

Nondeductible IRAs—if the taxpayer does not or cannot make (because of the income limitations) a deductible contribution to an IRA or a contribution to a Roth IRA, the taxpayer may make nondeductible contributions to a traditional IRA. The earnings in the pension account are tax deferred until the taxpayer makes withdrawals in retirement. It receives tax treatment similar to a "single-premium deferred annuity."

Nonqualified stock options (NQOs)—type of employee stock option. Employee pays tax on gain at the exercise date at ordinary income rates and the employer/corporation is allowed a corporate deduction for the amount of gain. Any subsequent stock price appreciation between exercise date and stock sale date is taxed as capital gains to the employee.

Not-for-profit corporation—a tax-exempt entity that can produce certain goods and services and avoid the corporate tax on the earnings. Prominent examples include not-for-profit hospitals, universities, and religious organizations.

O

Ordinary income—income derived in the normal course of business from, for example, the sale of goods and/or services. Wages and salaries are classified as ordinary income. See also "capital gains."

Ordinary loss—loss on the sale of good or services in the ordinary course of business. The loss may offset ordinary income.

Organizational-form arbitrage—the taking of a long position in an asset or a productive activity through a *favorably* taxed organizational form and a short position in an asset or a productive activity through an *unfavorably* taxed organizational form.

Original issue discount (OID)—the tax term for when a bond is issued at less than its face (par) value. OID is amortized over the life of the bond, creating taxable interest income for the holder and interest deductions for the issuer. See also "premium" and "market discount."

Overfunded—term used to describe the funding status of a defined benefit corporate pension plan. Defined benefit pension plans are funded according to actuarial formulas, and an overfunded plan is funded by an amount that exceeds the present value of the firm's expected liability to its employees. See also "defined benefit corporate pension plan."

P

Participation exemption—a system that exempts certain dividends and capital gains received by a shareholder from taxation. A participation exemption with respect to dividends foreign subsidiaries is a common method that countries use to adopt territorial taxation. The U.S. has a participation exemption for foreign-source portion of dividends received from certain foreign subsidiaries.

Partnership—legal organizational form that serves as a tax conduit between the business and its partners. The partnership files its own information tax return, including an income statement, a balance sheet, and a schedule of specific allocations to each of the partners. The partnership entity does not pay any income tax.

Passive activity losses—losses arising from activities in which the taxpayer does not play an active role. Passive activity losses can only be deducted against other passive income and cannot be deducted against other types of (nonpassive) income until the underlying investments are sold.

Pass-through entities—see "conduits."

Pension plan reversions—when a corporation terminates its defined pension plan and reclaims the excess assets; that is, the excess of the value of the plan assets over the present value of the firm's expected liability to its employees. Also known as a "pension plan termination." See also "defined benefit corporate pension plan."

Pension plan termination—see "pension plan reversions."

Perfect capital market—a hypothetical market in which there are no transaction costs, no taxes, no information asymmetry, and no frictions and restrictions.

Permanent difference—difference in financial accounting and tax accounting treatment that is permanent. An example is goodwill that might be recorded for financial accounting purposes but not for tax purposes. Another example is tax-exempt municipal bonds interest—excluded from taxable income but included in financial accounting income.

Premium—when a bond is issued at more than its face (par) value. Amortization of premiums reduces the issuer's interest expense and reduces the holder's interest income. See also "discount."

Primary authority—highest level of authoritative support for the proper tax treatment of a particular transaction. The U.S. Tax Code provides *statutory* authority. Other primary authorities include Treasury Regulations, judicial decisions, IRS administrative pronouncements, and Congressional Committee Reports.

Private equity fund—a fund that invests in other companies or businesses with the objective of obtaining a controlling interest so that the fund can then restructure the business.

Private letter rulings—similar to Revenue Rulings but not considered to be of sufficient general interest to publish as Revenue Rulings. Private rulings are available to the public under the Freedom of Information Act, but they cannot be cited as precedent in a court of law. Still, they may be valuable as an indication of IRS policy.

Probate estate—that part of the estate administered by an executor (if the decedent had a will) or by the administrator (if the decedent died without a will). Some bequests, such as life insurance, are not part of the probate estate. See also "gross estate."

Progressive income tax system—a schedule of marginal tax rates that increases as taxable income increases. Contrast with a flat tax system where the same tax rate is applied to all levels of income. Progressiveness can also arise if tax losses have to be carried forward. Also known as a convex tax schedule.

Property distributions—occur when the firm distributes property to shareholders instead of cash. Property distributions are taxed like cash distributions with a special rule so that corporations cannot recognize a loss on a property distribution.

Publicly traded partnerships (PTPs)—in the early 1980s, some partnerships, especially oil and gas entities, listed their partnership interests on organized stock exchanges, which made it easier for partners to sell or expand their partnership holdings. However, with the 1987 Tax Act, easy transferability of partnership interests (for example, interests traded on an organized exchange such as the New York Stock Exchange) results, with some exceptions, in the partnership being taxed as a corporation.

Q

Qualified business income (Section 199A)—certain types of business income that qualify for the 20% deduction for pass-through entities as provided by the TCJA. The income is only for certain types of business activities and the deduction is limited based on the taxpayer's income and other factors.

Qualified small business stock—business where shareholders can exclude 50% of the realized gain. Shareholder must own the stock for at least five years and meet other conditions specified in IRC Section 1202.

Qualified stock purchase—stock purchase in which the acquirer purchases at least 80% of the target's stock during a 12-month period.

Qualified terminable interest property (QTIP) trust—a trust that makes use of the unlimited marital deduction to defer estate tax until the death of the spouse while ensuring that the remainder interest in the trust goes to someone other than the spouse, usually the children.

R

Real estate investment trust (REIT)—a business entity organized as a trust or corporation that receives most of its earnings from real estate activities. If 90% or more of the earnings are distributed each year to beneficiaries or shareholders, the REIT avoids an entity-level tax. To qualify for pass-through treatment, the REIT must satisfy such constraints as having a minimum of 100 shareholders, no significant concentration of ownership, and at least 75% of its assets and income in qualified real estate.

Real Estate Mortgage Investment Conduit (REMIC)—another pass-through entity. Substantially all of the REMIC assets must consist of qualified mortgages and mortgage-related assets. REMICs have two classes of owners: owners of "regular" interests and owners of "residual" interests. The former are like bondholders and the latter are like stockholders (except that REMICs do not pay an entity-level tax).

Realization principle—basis on which revenues and gains are recognized and included in taxable income. Revenues and gains are not typically taxed until certain types of exchanges take place. For example, gains from the appreciation of most assets is not taxed until the assets are sold.

Recaptured depreciation—depreciation taken previously that is now recognized as ordinary income because the associated asset has been sold for a price in excess of adjusted basis (historical cost less accumulated depreciation).

Redemption—occurs when a corporation pays cash or property to its shareholders in exchange for a portion of their stock in the firm. Redemptions can be taxed as sales or as dividends.

Related parties—parties that are not economically independent (such as families, affiliated companies, and businesses). The IRS worries much less about substance-over-form problems in contracts between parties with opposing interests (arm's-length transactions) than it does between related parties because parties with opposing interests cannot always afford to write a contract in which the legal form differs much from the economic substance.

Residual method—see "residual valuation approach."

Residual valuation approach—method used to assign value to the various assets, tangible and intangible, of a target after an acquisition. Value is first assigned to tangible assets based on an appraisal, and the remainder or residual is assigned to intangible assets, including goodwill.

Restricted stock—stock that is contractually restricted in some way. Typically recipients of restricted stock cannot sell the stock for a specified period of time from the date of grant.

Return of capital—a distribution that is nontaxable but does reduce the shareholder's basis in the corporation's stock by the amount of the distribution.

Revenue Rulings—result from a request for rules clarification from a taxpayer with a particular set of actual or proposed transactions and published as Revenue Rulings provided the IRS believes it is of sufficient general interest. Revenue Rulings represent official IRS policy. See also "private letter rulings."

Reverse triangular merger—merger in which the acquirer forms a subsidiary and merges the acquiring firm subsidiary into the target corporation with the target corporation surviving as a subsidiary of the acquirer.

Reversibility of tax plans—situation in which, if tax rates or tax rules change in ways that make existing agreements inefficient, the contracts can be voided. If the contract can be voided when specified tax-related contingencies occur, then the contract allows for the reversibility of tax plans.

Risk adjusted—term used to indicate we are comparing the returns on alternative investments after adjusting for risk differences. Holding taxes constant, the required rate of return on a risky bond exceeds that of a less risky bond because, for the same amount of promised coupons and principal repayment, the prices of bonds with a high risk of default are lower than the prices of bonds with a low risk of default. Thus, to isolate the effects of differential tax treatments on required before-tax rates of return, we must adjust the before-tax rates of return on bonds and other assets for differences in risk.

Roth 401(k)—pension plan where the employee contributes after-tax dollars to the plan and earnings are exempt from future taxation. Compare and contrast with 401(k).

Roth IRA—taxpayers (meeting certain income requirements) may contribute up to $5,500 (2018 limit) after tax per year. Contributions are not tax deductible but withdrawals are tax free. That is, earnings in a Roth IRA are not tax deferred but tax exempt, provided the withdrawals meet certain conditions.

S

Savings incentive match plan for employees (SIMPLE)—an employee benefit plan for small employers wishing to avoid the complexities of other pension plans. Can be adopted by firms with fewer than 100 employees and can be set up as an IRA for each employee. Employees are allowed to make elective contributions of up to $12,500 per year (pretax; 2018 limit; contribution limits increase over time), which the employer must then match.

S corporations—limited liability corporations that are taxed as pass-through entities. Stockholders report their pro rata share of income (loss) on their own income tax return just as if they were taxed as partners. See also "limited liability companies."

Secondary authorities—second level of authority, after primary authority, for proper tax treatment of a particular transaction: consist primarily of tax professionals (for example, accountants and lawyers), commercial tax services, and tax journals. See also "primary authority."

Section 83(b) election—allows the recipient (a corporate employee) of restricted stock to elect to be taxed at the grant date on the value of the stock as opposed to waiting until the future period in which the restriction lapses. In either case, the value of the stock is taxed as ordinary income. Subsequent gains or losses are taxed as capital gains (with the rate depending on the holding period).

Section 162(m)—regulation that limits corporate tax deductions for compensation to $1 million per individual top executive. Prior to 2017, firms could avoid the limitation by qualifying their compensation plan as performance based or by deferring the excess compensation to a time period in which it is deductible.

Section 197—provides for the tax deductibility of amortization associated with intangible assets such as goodwill; prior to 1993, when this code section was enacted, goodwill amortization was not tax deductible.

Section 199A—see "qualified business income"

Section 332—provides for the tax-free liquidation of corporate subsidiaries; allows a corporation to liquidate a subsidiary in a tax-free manner.

Section 338—U.S. Tax Code section giving acquirers and sellers the ability to have a stock sale taxed as if the target's assets were sold. See also "Section 338 election" and "Section 338(h)(10) election."

Section 338 election—election made after the acquisition of the stock of a freestanding C corporation that results in the transaction being taxed as if the acquirer purchased the target's assets instead of its stock (sometimes referred to as a Section 338(g) election).

Section 338(h)(10) election—election made after the acquisition of the stock of a subsidiary of a C corporation or the stock of an S corporation; the election results in the transaction being taxed as if the acquirer purchased the target's assets instead of its stock.

Section 351—specifies the rules required for a corporate formation transaction to qualify for tax-free treatment; also applies to certain types of tax-free acquisition structures. Allows most corporate formations to be nontaxable events to the extent that shareholders do not receive cash (boot) from the corporation. See also "boot."

Section 355—stipulates the conditions under which a spin-off transaction will qualify as tax free to the divesting parent and its shareholder. See also "spin-offs."

Section 368—U.S. Tax Code section that governs tax-free reorganizations.

Section 368 A reorganization—a tax-free reorganization under Section 368—a statutory stock-for-asset merger.

Section 368 B reorganization—a tax-free reorganization under Section 368—a stock-for-stock merger.

Section 368 C reorganization—a tax-free reorganization under Section 368—a stock-for-asset merger.

Section 382—limits the usage of a target firm's net operating loss carryforwards post-acquisition.

Section 409A—governs deferred compensation arrangements, including stock option plans. This rule provides that unless certain requirements are met, the amount of income that is deferred under a nonqualified deferred compensation plan is subject to a 20% penalty tax plus interest equal to the IRS underpayment penalty rate plus 1%. Issuing ESOs with an exercise price below the grant date stock price (in-the-money or discount ESOs), as happens with backdated options, subjects the options to 409A treatment.

Section 482—gives the IRS authority to combat abusive transfer pricing schemes. See also "transfer prices," "arm's-length pricing," and "advance pricing agreements."

Section 1060—governs the allocation of the purchase price to a target's assets.

Section 1231 assets—noninventory assets used in a trade or business that have been held for more than 1 year. Gains from sales of 1231 assets are treated as long-term capital gains, whereas losses are treated as ordinary losses. See also "capital asset."

Section 1231 property—noninventory assets used in a trade or business that have been held for more than 1 year. Gains from sales of 1231 assets are treated as long-term capital gains, whereas losses are treated as ordinary losses. See also "capital assets."

Short sale—occurs when an investor sells a borrowed security and promises to replace the borrowed security in the future. The short seller hopes the price of the security will decline so she can replace the borrowed security at a lower price than for which she sold it.

Short-sale-against-the-box—occurs when an investor shorts a security that he already owns, so he is long and short in the same security at the same time.

Simplified employee pension plan (SEP)—for small employers wishing to avoid the complexities of other pension plans, a SEP is a program in which the employer opens IRAs for its employees (limited to 25 or fewer employees) and can contribute, similar to regular corporate pension plans, up to the maximum of the lesser of $55,000 a year or 25% of the employee's compensation.

Single-premium deferred annuity (SPDA)—an investment that is funded using after-tax dollars with the income on the account taxed as ordinary income when the funds are withdrawn (as an annuity). That is, the earning in the account are not taxed each period but tax is deferred until the earnings are withdrawn. See also "nondeductible IRAs."

Small Business Corporations (Section 1244)—original stockholders that collectively contribute up to $1 million of equity in such an entity are permitted to deduct realized capital losses against their other income without regard to the usual annual limitation that applies to the sale of regular stock (currently $3,000). The annual Section 1244 deduction limit is $50,000 per taxpayer ($100,000 for a joint return). To qualify, the corporation must be an operating company rather than engaging primarily in passive investment.

Socially undesirable economic activity—an activity, undertaken in response to the tax laws by taxpayers, that was unanticipated or not intended by legislators. Such activities are undertaken with the major (or sole) purpose of reducing the taxpayers' tax bills without any real positive nontax benefits to society.

Sole proprietorship—the taxable income or loss of the business is included with the owner's personal tax return (Schedule C of Form 1040).

Spin-offs—transaction in which a corporation splits into two or more separate companies, typically in a tax-free manner. Shareholders of the divesting corporation own two complete separate corporations after the spin-off.

Split-off—variation on a spin-off but may involve a non-pro-rata distribution of the stock of the divested firm to parent shareholders. See also "spin-offs."

Split-up—variation on a spin-off but involves breaking the parent into two corporations and the subsequent distribution, possibly non-pro-rata, of stock in the two new companies to parent shareholders.

Statutory merger—a valid merger under state law.

Step-up—an increase in basis of acquired assets to fair market value or to the purchase price.

Step-up election—in certain types of stock acquisitions, an election (the step-up election) can be made to step up the tax basis of the target's assets. See also "step-up."

Step-up in the tax basis—a step-up in tax basis occurs when the tax (depreciable) basis of assets acquired is increased to the price paid.

Step-up transaction—transaction in which the tax basis of the target's assets are stepped up. See also "step-up."

Stock appreciation rights (SARs)—type of equity-based compensation that provides employees with cash payments equal to the change in market value of the firm's stock over some specified period of time. Taxation occurs when the employee has the right to receive the appreciation on the stock that has occurred since the date of grant, i.e., at the vesting date.

Stock dividends—corporate distribution of additional stock to its existing shareholders. Stock dividends are generally nontaxable events.

Stock rights (warrants)—options in the corporation that the corporation distributes to its shareholders. Distributions of stock rights are generally nontaxable.

Stock sale—transaction in which the acquirer purchases the stock of the target or the sold subsidiary from the seller.

Straight-line depreciation/amortization—depreciation method under which the asset basis is depreciated in an equal amount each period over the estimated useful life of the asset.

Strategic uncertainty—a situation also known as information asymmetry in which the contracting parties are not equally well informed about what the future investment cash flows might be.

Strategy dependent—situations in which the taxpayer's marginal tax rate is affected by the very decisions that the taxpayer undertakes to alter its investment and financing activities. For example, if clientele-based arbitrage activities alter a firm's marginal tax rate, it cannot rely on its initial calculation to make an optimal decision. Strategy dependence increases the complexity of tax planning. Also referred to as the marginal tax rate being endogenous to the decision. See also "clientele-based arbitrage."

Subpart F income—generally passive income from a foreign subsidiary that is deemed for tax purposes to be repatriated to the domestic parent as it is earned. See also "controlled foreign corporation."

Substance-over-form doctrine—allows the IRS to look through the legal form of transactions to their economic substance and to reclassify the transaction to reflect its economic substance.

Substituted basis—where the basis of property *received* in a nontaxable transaction is determined by the basis of the property *exchanged* in the transaction. See also "carryover basis."

Symmetric uncertainty—a situation where all contracting parties are equally well informed, but still uncertain, about what the future cash flows from an investment might be.

T

Tangible assets—assets that are tangible in nature such as buildings, equipment, vehicles, and so on.

Target company—entity that is acquired in an acquisition.

Target firm's tax attributes—see "tax attributes."

Taxable acquisitions—transactions in which the seller recognizes a taxable gain or loss.

Taxable asset sale—transaction in which the target's assets are sold for cash or other taxable consideration.

Taxable stock sale—transaction in which the target's stock is sold for cash or other taxable consideration.

Tax arbitrage—the purchase of one asset (a "long" position) and the sale of another (a "short" position) to create a sure profit despite a zero level of net investment. See also "organizational-form arbitrage" and "client-based arbitrage."

Tax attributes—tax-related characteristics of an entity such as net operating loss carryforwards, tax credits, and asset tax basis.

Tax basis—the value assigned to property or assets for *tax* purposes. A factor in the determination of the gain/loss on a sale. Generally the tax basis of an asset equals its cost. The tax basis of assets acquired in nontaxable transactions and by gift or bequest are subject to special rules. See also "adjusted tax basis."

Tax clienteles—taxpayers facing similar marginal tax rates are attracted to the same investments because they offer the highest after-tax rate of return to these taxpayers. Thus certain taxpayers are more likely than others to own various kinds of assets or to organize production in particular ways. See also "marginal investors" and "inframarginal investors."

Tax exemption—when the returns to an activity escape explicit taxation. Tax exemption means that the after-tax rate of return equals the before-tax rate of return.

Tax-exempt organization—entities that are not taxed. Examples of such entities include pension funds, universities, hospitals, charities, and religious organizations.

Tax-favored treatment—when an activity receives favorable tax treatment defined relative to immediate full taxation on current income at ordinary tax rates. Tax-favored treatment occurs for example, if the investment is immediately deductible, if taxation on income is deferred until future periods, or if income is taxed at lower capital gains rates. See also "implicit taxes."

Tax-free acquisition structure—method or technique used to acquire a target that is tax free. Sellers who receive cash nonetheless recognize taxable gains.

Tax-free acquisitions—acquisition in which the transaction qualifies as tax free. Sellers receiving tax-free consideration (e.g., stock) experience tax deferral, whereas sellers receiving cash must recognize a taxable gain.

Tax-free subsidiary sale—sale of a subsidiary in a manner that results in tax deferral of any gain or loss on the sale.

Tax indemnity—where the other party to the transaction (for example, the issuer of a security) indemnifies (insures) the taxpayer against less favorable tax treatment than that promised.

Tax law ambiguity—where tax rules are too general to indicate clearly how particular transactions are to be taxed, leaving the tax treatment of the transaction open to more than one interpretation. Aggressive exploitation of tax law ambiguity can lead to socially undesirable economic activities. See also "Treasury Regulations," "Revenue Rulings," and "private letter rulings."

Tax minimization—involves simply minimizing taxes without consideration of other dimensions of the transaction or business problem. The simplest way to minimize taxes is to earn zero income, which is not considered an effective tax plan.

Tax-rule restrictions—restraints imposed by the taxing authority that prevent taxpayers from using certain tax arbitrage techniques to reduce taxes in socially undesirable ways. See also "frictions."

Tax structure—manner in which a transaction is structured for tax purposes.

Technical advice memoranda—a published form of "letter ruling" issued by the IRS national office in response to a request for technical advice from an IRS district or appeals office that is auditing a complex tax matter.

Temporary differences—difference between financial accounting and tax accounting treatment that is temporary. The difference will ultimately reverse itself. An example of a temporary difference is different depreciation methods for financial accounting and tax purposes.

Territorial tax system—a tax system whereby a country taxes only income that was earned within its borders. See also "worldwide tax system," "base erosion and anti-abuse tax," "global intangible low-tax income," and "foreign-derived intangible income."

Total tax rate—the sum of the implicit tax rate and the explicit tax rate. See also "explicit tax rate" and "implicit tax rate."

Traditional deductible IRA—eligible taxpayers may contribute up to $5,500 pretax (or 100% of compensation if less than $5,500) per year (2018 amount). Contributions are tax deductible and, as with most other pension plans, deferred until the taxpayer makes withdrawals in retirement. Withdrawals are taxed as ordinary income.

Transfer prices—prices at which goods and services are transferred between related parties such as a parent and its subsidiary. Transfer prices can be used to shift income from high tax jurisdictions to low tax jurisdictions. Tax authorities try to prevent abuse of transfer prices. See also "Section 482," "arm's-length pricing," and "advance pricing agreements."

Treasury Regulations—issued by the Treasury Department to provide general interpretations of newly passed tax bills. Interested parties (such as tax lawyers, tax accountants, and other affected taxpayers) can request hearings of proposed regulations.

Treaty shopping—the practice of routing transactions (e.g., dividends) through countries that have favorable tax treaties.

Triangular merger—transaction in which a subsidiary of the acquirer merges with the target corporation.

Trust preferred stock—stock treated by the issuer as debt for tax purposes that during some periods received quasi-equity treatment on the balance sheet, reported between the equity and debt sections. Trust preferred stock was popular with banks due to its regulatory capital advantages.

U

Uniform Trusts for Minors Act (UTMA)—gifts made to minors under this act qualify for the annual gift exclusion even though the minors do not have unrestricted access to the gifts until they reach age 21.

V

Valid business purpose—transaction must be motivated by some reason other than tax avoidance. Some valid business purpose must characterize the structure of the transaction; otherwise the IRS can recharacterize the transaction, leading to a less favorable tax treatment. A requirement for tax-free treatment in a Section 368 reorganization.

Value-added tax (VAT)—a type of consumption tax levied on the increase in value of goods and services at each stage of production or distribution. Some form of VAT is used by over 160 countries but not the U.S.

W

Withholding taxes—taxes levied on payments of dividends, interest, rents, and royalties to foreign entities. Withholding taxes are often reduced by tax treaties. See also "treaty shopping" and "branch profits tax."

Worldwide tax system—a tax system whereby a country taxes its citizens, permanent residents, and resident corporations on their worldwide income, providing foreign tax credits to mitigate double taxation. See also "territorial tax system" and "foreign tax credit."

Index

A

B

C

D

E

T